W9-AXY-370

THE GOSPEL OF MATTHEW

Sacra Pagina Series

Volume 1

The Gospel of Matthew

Daniel J. Harrington, S.J.

Daniel J. Harrington, S.J.
Editor

A Michael Glazier Book
THE LITURGICAL PRESS
Collegeville, Minnesota

Cover design by Don Bruno.

A Michael Glazier Book published by The Liturgical Press.

8 9

Library of Congress Cataloging-in-Publication Data

Harrington, Daniel J.
The gospel of Matthew / Daniel J. Harrington.
p. cm. — (Sacra pagina series : 1)
"A Michael Glazier book."
Includes bibliographical references and index.
ISBN 0-8146-5803-2
1. Bible. N.T. Matthew—Commentaries. I. Title. II. Series.
BS2575.3.H37 1991
226.2'077—dc20 91-12955
CIP

CONTENTS

Editor's Preface ix
Abbreviations xi

Introduction

1. A "Jewish" Commentary 1
2. Text and Language 3
3. Composition and Sources 4
4. Origin and Authorship 8
5. Setting 10
6. Theological Perspectives 17
7. Matthew and Anti-Semitism 20
8. General Bibliography 22

Translation, Notes, Interpretation

1. The Birth-Record of Jesus (1:1-17) 27
2. The Birth of Jesus (1:18-25) 34
3. The Visit of the Magi and the Flight to Egypt (2:1-23) 40
4. John the Baptist (3:1-6) 50
5. John's Preaching (3:7-10) 55
6. The Baptisms of John and Jesus (3:11-12) 58
7. Jesus Made Manifest (3:13-17) 61
8. The Testing of God's Son (4:1-11) 65
9. Jesus Begins in Galilee (4:12-25) 70
10. Introduction to the Sermon on the Mount (5:1-20) 77
11. Six "Antitheses" (5:21-48) 85
12. Three Acts of Piety (6:1-18) 93

13. Other Teachings (6:19–7:12) 100
14. Warnings about Judgment (7:13-29) 107
15. Jesus the Healer (8:1-17) 112
16. More Acts of Power (8:18–9:8) 118
17. Interlude (9:9-17) 125
18. More Healings (9:18-34) 130
19. Setting (9:35–10:4) 135
20. Mission to Israel (10:5-15) 139
21. Future Sufferings (10:16-25) 144
22. Other Instructions (10:26-42) 149
23. John and Jesus (11:1-19) 154
24. Threats against Unrepentant Cities (11:20-24) 163
25. Revelation and Its Recipients (11:25-30) 166
26. Two Sabbath Controversies (12:1-14) 171
27. Jesus As God's Servant (12:15-21) 179
28. The Source of Jesus' Power (12:22-37) 182
29. The Sign of Jonah (12:38-42) 187
30. This Evil Generation; The Family of Jesus (12:43-50) 190
31. The Parable of the Sower (13:1-23) 193
32. Other Parables (13:24-52) 203
33. Rejection of His Own (13:53-58) 210
34. The Death of John the Baptist (14:1-12) 214
35. The Feeding of the Five Thousand (14:13-21) 218
36. Walking on the Water (14:22-36) 223
37. Debate about Tradition (15:1-20) 228
38. The Canaanite Woman (15:21-28) 234
39. Healings (15:29-31) 239
40. Feeding of the Four Thousand (15:32-39) 240
41. A Controversy and a Conversation (16:1-12) 243
42. Promise to Peter; First Passion Prediction (16:13-28) 246
43. The Transfiguration and Elijah (17:1-13) 253
44. The Disciples' Little Faith (17:14-20) 257
45. Second Passion Prediction; Temple Tax (17:22-27) 260
46. Care for the "Little Ones" (18:1-14) 263
47. The Brother Who Sins (18:15-35) 268
48. Marriage and Divorce, Celibacy, Children (19:1-15) 272
49. The Dangers of Wealth (19:16-30) 277

50. The Parable of the Good Employer (20:1-16) 282
51. The Cup of Suffering (20:17-28) 286
52. The Healing Son of David (20:29-34) 289
53. Jesus' Entrance into Jerusalem and Its Temple (21:1-17) 292
54. The Fig Tree (21:18-22) 296
55. Jesus and John (21:23-32) 298
56. The Parable of the Vineyard (21:33-46) 301
57. The Parable of the Wedding Feast (22:1-14) 305
58. Taxes to Caesar (22:15-22) 309
59. Resurrection (22:23-33) 312
60. The Great Commandment (22:34-40) 314
61. David's Son or Lord? (22:41-46) 317
62. Good Deeds and Prestige (23:1-12) 319
63. The Woes against the Scribes and Pharisees (23:13-31) 324
64. Final Warning (23:32-39) 328
65. The Beginning of the Birthpangs (24:1-14) 331
66. The Coming of the Son of Man (24:15-31) 336
67. Parables of Watchfulness (24:32-51) 341
68. The Parable of the Ten Maidens (25:1-13) 347
69. The Parable of the Talents (25:14-30) 351
70. The Judgment (25:31-46) 355
71. The Plot to Kill Jesus (26:1-16) 361
72. Jesus' Last Passover (26:17-35) 365
73. The Arrest of Jesus (26:36-56) 372
74. The Jewish "Trial" and Peter's Denial (26:57-75) 378
75. The Condemnation of Jesus and Judas' Death (27:1-10) 384
76. The Condemnation of Jesus (27:11-26) 387
77. The Crucifixion of Jesus (27:27-44) 393
78. The Death of Jesus (27:45-56) 399
79. The Burial of Jesus (27:57-66) 404
80. The Empty Tomb (28:1-15) 408
81. The Great Commission (28:16-20) 414

Indexes

1. Principal Ancient Parallels 419
2. Subjects 424
3. Authors 426

EDITOR'S PREFACE

Sacra Pagina is a multi-volume commentary on the books of the New Testament. The expression *Sacra Pagina* (''Sacred Page'') originally referred to the text of Scripture. In the Middle Ages it also described the study of Scripture to which the interpreter brought the tools of grammar, rhetoric, dialectic, and philosophy. Thus *Sacra Pagina* encompasses both the text to be studied and the activity of interpretation.

This series presents fresh translations and modern expositions of all the books of the New Testament. Written by an international team of Catholic biblical scholars, it is intended for biblical professionals, graduate students, theologians, clergy, and religious educators. The volumes present basic introductory information and close exposition. They self-consciously adopt specific methodological perspectives, but maintain a focus on the issues raised by the New Testament compositions themselves. The goal of *Sacra Pagina* is to provide sound critical analysis without any loss of sensitivity to religious meaning. This series is therefore catholic in two senses of the word: inclusive in its methods and perspectives, and shaped by the context of the Catholic tradition.

The Second Vatican Council described the study of the ''sacred page'' as the ''very soul of sacred theology'' (*Dei Verbum* 24). The volumes in this series illustrate how Catholic scholars contribute to the council's call to provide access to Sacred Scripture for all the Christian faithful. Rather than pretending to say the final word on any text, these volumes seek to open up the riches of the New Testament and to invite as many people as possible to study seriously the ''sacred page.''

DANIEL J. HARRINGTON, S.J.

ABBREVIATIONS

Biblical Books and Apocrypha

Gen	Nah	1-2-3-4 Kgdms	John
Exod	Hab	Add Esth	Acts
Lev	Zeph	Bar	Rom
Num	Hag	Bel	1-2 Cor
Deut	Zech	1-2 Esdr	Gal
Josh	Mal	4 Ezra	Eph
Judg	Ps (*pl.*: Pss)	Jdt	Phil
1-2 Sam	Job	Ep Jer	Col
1-2 Kgs	Prov	1-2-3-4 Macc	1-2 Thess
Isa	Ruth	Pr Azar	1-2 Tim
Jer	Cant	Pr Man	Titus
Ezek	Eccl (*or* Qoh)	Sir	Phlm
Hos	Lam	Sus	Heb
Joel	Esth	Tob	Jas
Amos	Dan	Wis	1-2 Pet
Obad	Ezra	Matt	1-2-3 John
Jonah	Neh	Mark	Jude
Mic	1-2 Chr	Luke	Rev

Qumran Texts

CD	*Damascus Document*
1QH	*Thanksgiving Hymns*
1QM	*War Scroll*
1QS	*Manual of Discipline*
$1QS^a$	Appendix to 1QS
$4QpPs^a$	Pesher on Psalms
$11QPs\ Ap^a$	Apocryphal Psalms

Rabbinic Texts

Arak.	*Arakin*
Bab. B.	*Baba Batra*
Bab. M.	*Baba Mezia*
Ber.	*Berakot*
Eduy.	*Eduyyot*
Gitt.	*Gittin*
Hag.	*Hagiga*
Ketub.	*Ketubot*
Ned.	*Nedarim*
Pesah.	*Pesahim*
Qidd.	*Qiddushin*
Šabb.	*Šabbat*
Sot.	*Sotah*
Yad.	*Yadayim*
Yebam.	*Yebamot*

Other Texts

Ant.	Josephus' *Antiquities*
ARN	*Abot deRabbi Nathan*
Bar	Baruch
Bib. Ant.	ps.-Philo's *Biblical Antiquities*
Hist. eccl.	Eusebius' *Ecclesiastical History*
Jub	Jubilees
LXX	Septuagint

Periodicals, Reference Works, and Serials

AB	Analecta Biblica
ASTI	*Annual of the Swedish Theological Institute*
ATR	*Anglican Theological Review*
AUSS	*Andrews University Seminary Studies*
BAR	*Biblical Archaeology Review*
BETL	Bibliotheca Ephemeridum Theologicarum Lovaniensium
BGBE	Beiträge zur Geschichte der biblischen Exegese
Bib	*Biblica*
BJRULM	*Bulletin of the John Rylands University Library of Manchester*
BLE	*Bulletin de Littérature Ecclésiastique*
BR	*Biblical Research*
BT	*Bible Translator*
BTB	*Biblical Theology Bulletin*
BZ	*Biblische Zeitschrift*
CBQ	*Catholic Biblical Quarterly*

ETL	*Ephemerides Theologicae Lovanienses*
ExpTim	*Expository Times*
HTR	*Harvard Theological Review*
HUCA	*Hebrew Union College Annual*
IEJ	*Israel Exploration Journal*
Int	*Interpretation*
JAAR	*Journal of the American Academy of Religion*
JBL	*Journal of Biblical Literature*
JJS	*Journal of Jewish Studies*
JQR	*Jewish Quarterly Review*
JSNT	*Journal for the Study of the New Testament*
JSOT	*Journal for the Study of the Old Testament*
JTS	*Journal of Theological Studies*
LavThPh	*Laval Théologique et Philosophique*
LCL	Loeb Classical Library
LD	Lectio Divina
MScRel	*Mélanges de Science Religieuse*
NovT	*Novum Testamentum*
NTAb	Neutestamentliche Abhandlungen
NTS	*New Testament Studies*
OTP	*Old Testament Pseudepigrapha*
RB	*Revue Biblique*
RQ	*Revue de Qumran*
RTL	*Revue Théologique de Louvain*
RTP	*Revue de Théologie et Philosophie*
SBFLA	*Studium Biblicum Franciscanum Liber Annus*
SBLDS	Society of Biblical Literature Dissertation Series
SBS	Stuttgarter Bibelstudien
ScEs	*Science et Esprit*
SJT	*Scottish Journal of Theology*
SNTSMS	Society of New Testament Studies Monograph Series
SNTU	*Studien zum Neuen Testament und Umwelt*
TCGNT	B. M. Metzger, *A Textual Commentary on the Greek New Testament*
TQ	*Theologische Quartalschaft*
TS	*Theological Studies*
TTZ	*Trierer Theologische Zeitschrift*
TZ	*Theologische Zeitschrift*
ZDPV	*Zeitschrift des Deutschen Palästina-Vereins*
ZNW	*Zeitschrift für die neutestamentlichen Wissenschaft*
ZTK	*Zeitschrift für Theologie und Kirche*

INTRODUCTION

1. *A "Jewish" Commentary*

This commentary on Matthew's Gospel has been written from a "Jewish" perspective—one that I believe is demanded from the text itself. The author is a Roman Catholic who has long been interested in the Hebrew Bible and later Jewish writings, especially as these provide the context for understanding the New Testament and early Christianity. Besides my academic concern with Judaism in antiquity, I have also experienced the vitality of modern Judaism, continue to admire it, and seek to be sensitive and sympathetic toward it as I interpret early Christian writings.

The genre of biblical commentary has determined some of the tasks undertaken in this book. After an introduction, it provides a new (literal) translation of each section in Matthew's Gospel. It explains the textual problems, philological difficulties, and other matters in the notes. It presents a literary analysis of each text: context, form, use of sources, structure, etc. The bibliographies direct the reader to important modern studies and sometimes to other interpretations.

The "Jewish" dimension is the distinctive feature of this commentary. It is developed on three levels. The first and most obvious level is the effort to inform the reader about the Old Testament and other Jewish texts that seem to have influenced or at least run parallel to Matthew's Gospel. I argue that the community for which Matthew wrote was largely (though not exclusively) Jewish Christian. For such an audience Matthew could use Jewish rhetoric and themes without explanation. This is not the case for the twentieth-century Americans and others who read the Gospel today. And so both in the notes and in the interpretative essay for each passage I try to supply the Jewish background that Matthew could presume on the part of his original readers. Thus I try to put today's readers of Matthew in a place analogous to that of the first readers.

The second level of "Jewishness" concerns the situation in which Matthew wrote: the conflict among the Jews after the destruction of the Jerusalem Temple in A.D. 70 about the continuation and nature of Judaism. During the late first century A.D., somewhere in Palestine or Syria, a Jewish-Christian evangelist used Mark's Gospel, a collection of sayings designated by modern scholars as Q, and some special material (M) to write what is known as the "Gospel according to Matthew" for a largely Jewish-Christian community that existed still within the framework of Judaism but in tension with other Jewish groups. In the interpretations I indicate what each text might have meant in that situation as the Matthean community sought to define its own identity and to situate itself within the Jewish tradition.

The third level of "Jewishness" comes toward the end of each interpretation. While the basic concern of the work is to explain Matthew as a first-century text, I know that religious educators and preachers want help in teaching the significance of Matthew for people today. And so using the term "actualization" I offer brief suggestions about how each text might be presented in a classroom or a liturgical situation. I do not accuse Matthew of anti-Semitism, as some interpreters do. But I am aware of the anti-Semitic potential that some Matthean texts have, when taken out of their historical setting, and want to warn teachers and preachers about this. At the same time I try to provide theological comments appropriate to the new relationship that exists between Jews and Christians since the Second Vatican Council, and thus help teachers and preachers to contribute to this positive but also fragile development.

The focus of the work is on Matthew as a Jewish text—Jewish in its conceptual and rhetorical assumptions, in its sociological setting, and in its theological message. The approach is literary, historical, and theological. There are, however, important matters that get little attention: the concerns of the new literary methods (reader response criticism, structuralism, semiotics), the history of the Gospel tradition (especially the parallels in *Gospel of Thomas*), and determining the historical events behind the texts. The explosion of information about the ancient world and the emergence of new methods of interpretation make impossible the production of a truly comprehensive commentary (one that tries to do it all).

Even the effort at demonstrating the Jewish background of Matthew is not complete. Rather than amassing lists of parallels that few readers will ever check out, I prefer to bring to the fore the most illuminating Jewish sources and parallels, and treat them with sufficient context so that the readers may grasp the significance for understanding Matthew's Gospel. The truly distinctive feature of this work is its attempt to state what each text might have meant in the late first-century conflict between Matthew's community and his Jewish rivals.

2. *Text and Language*

The text of Matthew's Gospel that is translated and interpreted in this commentary is the Greek text printed in *Novum Testamentum Graece* (26th ed.), edited by K. Aland and B. Aland (Stuttgart: Deutsche Bibelgesellschaft, 1981). It is based on the fourth- and fifth-century manuscripts (Sinaiticus, Alexandrinus, Vaticanus, etc.) and other ancient evidence in Greek manuscripts and in early translations. The earliest fragmentary evidence for the Greek text of Matthew appears in several papyri (1,45,64[67]) from the late second or third century A.D.

The Greek language of Matthew's Gospel is usually described as "good."[1] It seems to have been a deliberate improvement over the Greek language of its sources (Mark and Q). It is "biblical" Greek in line with that of the Greek version of the Old Testament (Septuagint). It is "Semitic" Greek in the sense that Hebrew idioms and expressions show through their Greek form. The style is generally simple and straightforward, without many complicated periodic sentences. Instead it favors the biblical style of short units connected by "and," after the model of the historical books in the Hebrew Bible. The vocabulary presents few problems in comparison with some other NT writings (Romans, Hebrews, Revelation).

The tradition that the Greek text of Matthew was translated from a Hebrew (or Aramaic) original goes back to an early second-century bishop of Hierapolis named Papias, as quoted by Eusebius (*Hist. eccl.* 3.39.16). The usual translation of the Greek text is the following: "Matthew compiled the sayings in the Hebrew language, and everyone translated them as well as he could." Papias' statement was taken by Irenaeus, Origen, and Eusebius to mean that Matthew composed his Gospel in Hebrew or Aramaic. But Papias' statement involves more problems than it resolves. What were the *logia* ("sayings")—words of Jesus, OT quotations, or the whole story? Why does Papias say "Hebrew" when it appears certain that Jesus spoke Aramaic? Were there multiple translations of the Semitic Matthew? Did Papias have any special reasons for making Matthew's Gospel prior to and independent of Mark's Gospel? Moreover, every important element in Papias' statement is ambiguous, leaving open the possibilities of variant

1. J. Gnilka, *Das Matthäusevangelium* (Freiburg–Basel–Vienna: Herder, 1988) 2.525.

translations. Furthermore, there is no firm evidence in the Greek text that it was translated from a Semitic original. At any rate, the canonical text of Matthew is and always has been the Greek version. Our commentary proceeds on the assumption that the Gospel was composed in Greek.

A complete Hebrew text of Matthew's Gospel appears in the body of a fourteenth-century Jewish polemical treatise entitled *Even Bohan* ("The Touchstone") and written by Shem-Tob ben Isaac ben Shaprut (sometimes called Ibn Shaprut). At some points (Matt 5:32, 34) it reflects less disparity between Judaism and Christianity than the Greek text does. It also contains a higher estimation of John the Baptist (see Matt 11:11, 13; 17:11; 21:28-32). Since it is unlikely that Ibn Shaprut made such changes on his own, it is entirely possible that he used an existing version of the Hebrew Matthew. How far back did the version go? Was it a translation of the Greek text? Or was it an independent version of the same traditional material, as its editor George Howard contends?[2] Study of this and other versions of the Hebrew Gospels is still at an early stage; much work remains to be done before any certain results can be determined. But no responsible scholar claims that we now have access to the original Hebrew of Matthew's Gospel.

3. *Composition and Sources*

Rather than defend one outline for the structure of Matthew's Gospel, I prefer to call attention to the various structural principles within the Gospel text. The most obvious structural feature is the presence of five large blocks of speech material (chs. 5–7, 10, 13, 18, 24–25), each ending with a similar formula ("when Jesus finished these words"). There is some debate whether Matthew 23 (the woes against the Pharisees and scribes) should be taken as a separate (sixth) speech, or as a preface to the fifth and final speech (with the woes functioning as the equivalent of the Beatitudes in Matt 5:3-12), or simply as discourse material interspersed in the narrative but separate from chapters 24–25.

Another obvious structural feature of Matthew in comparison with Mark is the presence of the infancy narrative (chs. 1–2) that takes the story of Jesus back to his origins. The infancy narrative is balanced by the accounts of Jesus' passion and resurrection (chs. 26–28), with attention given to his appearance in Galilee. These gross elements of structure are supplemented by intervening narrative blocks, so that an alternating pattern of narrative and

2. *The Gospel of Matthew according to a Primitive Hebrew Text* (Macon, Ga.: Mercer, 1987).

discourse emerges. An outline based on the most obvious structural features looks something like this:

- The "who" and "where" of Jesus (1:1–2:23)
- The beginning of Jesus' activity (3:1–4:25)
- The Sermon on the Mount (5:1–7:29)
- Jesus' powerful deeds (8:1–9:38)
- The missionary discourse (10:1-42)
- The rejection of Jesus (11:1–12:50)
- Parables of the kingdom (13:1-53)
- Miracles, controversies, and the Cross (13:54–17:27)
- Advice to a divided community (18:1-35)
- Opposition to Jesus (19:1–23:39)
- The coming of the kingdom (24:1–25:46)
- Jesus' death and resurrection (26:1–28:20)

Besides making an outline on the basis of broad literary features (narrative v. discourse) it is possible also to construct a geographical outline according to Jesus' movements in the land of Israel: preparation involving various movements (1:1–4:11); in Galilee (4:12–13:58); around Galilee and toward Jerusalem (14:1–20:34); and in Jerusalem (21:1–28:20).

The Gospel begins and ends with a promise regarding God's presence in Jesus—first with the naming of Jesus as "Emmanuel" ("God with us") in Matt 1:23, and finally with Jesus' promise to be with his disciples always, "until the end of the age" (28:20). Still another structural feature is the formula "from then on Jesus began . . ." (4:17; 16:21), which marks first Jesus' public activity and then his journey toward Jerusalem as the place of his passion, death, and resurrection. Another formula ("he went about . . .") is used to frame the Sermon on the Mount and the miracles (4:23; 9:35), making the point that Jesus is powerful both in word and in deed. Moreover, certain key words and themes ("righteousness," "little faith," "pay homage," etc.) serve to move the narrative forward and give it a sense of unity.

Matthew's Gospel is generally considered to be a revision or second edition of Mark's Gospel. Most of the material in the sixteen chapters of Mark is included in Matthew. Yet Matthew did not merely copy his source. Rather he edited Mark freely and joined it with material from a collection of Jesus' sayings (Q) and material peculiar to Matthew (M).

Matthew's revision of Mark was guided by literary and theological factors. On the literary level Matthew compressed the accounts in Mark to include only what he considered essential and frequently turned narration into dialogue. In the first part of the Gospel (chs. 1–12) Matthew did not follow the Markan sequence very closely. But from Matthew 13 onward he observed Mark's outline more carefully. On the theological level Matthew supplemented the Markan narratives with large blocks of teaching, thus giving more content to the message of Jesus. He also seems to have adapted Mark for a Jewish-Christian audience, omitting unnecessary explanations (as in Matt 15:2; cf. Mark 7:3-4) and giving even more attention to the opponents of Jesus (as in Matthew 23). The Law and its observance were lively issues still for the Matthean community, whereas they mattered less to Mark (see Mark 7:19; Matt 15:17). It was much more important for Matthew to root Jesus in the Old Testament than it was for Mark. Some even refer to Matthew's project as an attempt at "rejudaizing" Christianity. I prefer to describe it as Matthew's attempt at addressing the new situation and new problems that had emerged for Jewish Christians in the late first century A.D. He did so by emphasizing Jesus' place in the Jewish tradition.

One obvious reason why Matthew determined to produce a revision of Mark's Gospel was to include additional material. A major source for this additional material was the sayings-source used by both Matthew and Luke independently. The source is designated by the letter "Q," a symbol developed in the late nineteenth century from the German word for "source" (*Quelle*). Q was a collection of Jesus' sayings (and some other material) already in Greek form by the fifties of the first century A.D. In literary form it was something like the canonical Book of Proverbs, the rabbinic tractate *Abot*, and *Gospel of Thomas*. It apparently had no passion narrative.

According to the Two-Document hypothesis assumed in this commentary, Matthew and Luke used the Gospel of Mark, Q, and their own special material. The relationship can be diagrammed as follows:

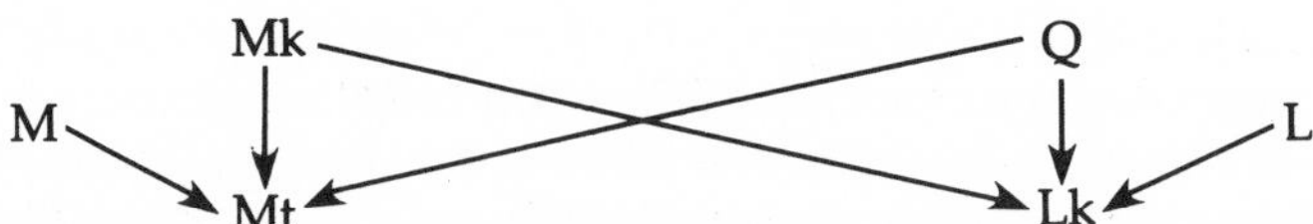

The Two-Document hypothesis is only a hypothesis. No copy of Q is available today. Its texts must and can be reconstructed by careful analysis of the parallels in Matthew and Luke. Some scholars (following patristic tradition) argue that Mark was not the earliest Gospel. They claim that Matthew and Luke were used independently by Mark to form a synthesis. This modern version of the Griesbach hypothesis can be diagrammed as follows:

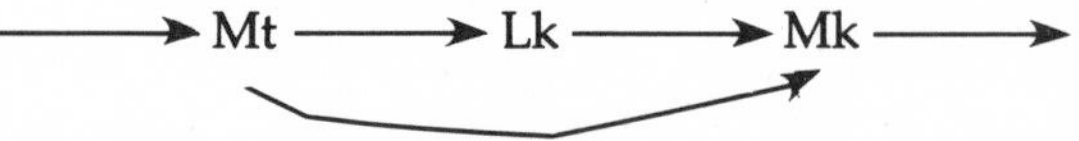

But the Two-Document hypothesis seems to me (and to most biblical scholars) to be the better, or at least most economical explanation for the development of the Synoptic Gospels.

By definition Q refers to material found in both Matthew and Luke but not in Mark. It is generally admitted that Matthew was freer than Luke in dealing with the wording and the order of Q. Matthew used Q especially in constructing the speeches of Jesus. Since Q consisted mainly of discourse material presented with little or no context, Matthew had to construct a setting for the Q sayings if he was to use them in his narrative about Jesus. And he did so by weaving the sayings into discourses like the Sermon on the Mount (chs. 5–7), the mission discourse (ch. 10), etc. How Matthew dealt in detail with Q will be treated in the literary analysis contained in the commentaries on individual texts. The use of a Gospel synopsis is essential for understanding Matthew's achievement.[3]

The traditional material peculiar to Matthew is designated by the letter M. It too features prominently in the discourses but also includes the infancy narrative (chs. 1–2) and the appearances (ch. 28). There are some serious methodological problems involved in talking about M as a source. How can one distinguish M traditions from material composed by the evangelist? Was M a single document or many? Did all the M material originate at the same time and in the same place?

A recent analysis of M by S. H. Brooks[4] shows how one scholar has dealt with these matters. His criteria for isolating M material are the following: the absence of parallel material in Mark and/or Q, the occurrence of non-Matthean stylistic features and vocabulary, and content that is at odds with the immediate context or the Gospel as a whole. Using these criteria, Brooks argues that M is found in Matt 5:19, 21-22, 23-24, 27-28, 33-35, 36, 37; 6:1-6, 7-8, 16-18; 7:6; 10:5-6, 23; 12:36-37; 18:18, 19-20; 19:12; 23:2-3, 5, 8-10, 15, 16-22, 24, 33.

Brooks also claims that these sayings were not taken from a single source and that they were not necessarily in written form. Rather they distribute themselves into three distinct life-settings: a Christian-Jewish group before A.D. 70 that was relatively at peace within the synagogue (Matt 6:1-6, 16-18; 23:2-3, 5; 10:5-6, 23b); an interim period of tension with the synagogue authorities (Matt 23:15, 16-22, 24, 33; 5:23-24; 6:7-8; 7:6); and a Jewish Christian community apart from and in ideological opposition to the synagogue (Matt 5:19, 21-22, 27-28, 33-35, 37; 23:8-10; 12:36-37; 18:18, 19-20; 19:12). Whatever the merits of this analysis may be, it at least illustrates the problems and possibilities involved in talking about M as a source in Matthew's Gospel.

3. For example, K. Aland, ed., *Synopsis of the Four Gospels.* English ed. (New York: United Bible Societies, 1982).

4. *Matthew's Community: The Evidence of His Special Sayings Material* (Sheffield: JSOT, 1987).

4. *Origin and Authorship*

On the basis of possible allusions to Matthew's Gospel in late NT (see 1 Pet 2:12; 3:14) and patristic writings (*Didache* 8; Letters of Ignatius) it has become customary to set the latest possible date of the Gospel's composition around A.D. 100. On the other hand, there seem to be within the Gospel itself a few references to the destruction of Jerusalem in A.D. 70: "The king was angry, and he sent his troops and destroyed those murderers and burned their city" (22:7; see also 21:41; 27:25). These references along with Matthew's use of Mark (composed around A.D. 70) as a source suggest a date of composition for Matthew around A.D. 85 or 90.

Nothing in the text names the author; the title "according to Matthew" was not part of the first edition. The author nowhere claims to have been an eyewitness to the events that he describes. The traditional ascription of the Gospel to Matthew the tax collector (see 9:9) who became an apostle (10:3) raises many questions. Why is the same tax collector named Levi, son of Alphaeus, in Mark 2:14? Where did a tax collector on the margin of Jewish religious life get such an extensive education to produce this very "Jewish" Gospel? Why did an apostle and companion of Jesus not put forward any claim to have been personally involved in the events of Jesus' life? Why did he rely on Mark and Q as his written sources rather than personal memory? Yet if the traditional ascription is rejected, then we are still hard pressed to explain why the Gospel was assigned to Matthew. Was "Matthew" a missionary to the area in which the Gospel was composed? Was he considered the "patron" of that community? Was he responsible for some early stage of the special Matthean tradition (M)? At any rate, the anonymous Gospel of Matthew seems to have been composed around A.D. 85.

Calling the Gospel anonymous does not mean we know nothing about its author. The evangelist (and his community) seems to have been Jewish in background and in interests. He shows a special interest in the Hebrew Scriptures as a witness to the person and activity of Jesus, most dramatically so in the so-called fulfillment quotations (1:22-23; 2:15, 17-18, 23; etc.). Much of Matthew's "ethical" teaching in the Sermon on the Mount and in the debates is analogous to Jewish halakah, which is advice on how people are to behave. The Matthean community assumes that the Jewish Sabbath is still to be observed (see 12:1-14; 24:20) by Christians. The evangelist stands in opposition to Jews who have control of "their synagogues" (4:23; 9:35; 10:17; 12:9; 13:54), which are synagogues of the hypocrites (6:2, 5; 23:6, 34) according to Matthew. He is particularly concerned with determining the proper relationship between Jesus the Messiah and the Torah (see 5:17-20) and with opposing the authority of the "scribes and Pharisees" as the interpreters of the Torah.

The Matthean ideal is expressed in 13:52: "Every scribe who has become a disciple for the kingdom of heaven is like a householder who brings out of his treasury new things and old things.'' Not only does Matthew take an interest in the fulfillment of Scripture, but he also seems familiar with Jewish traditions of interpretation (see 5:34-35; 23:16-22; 27:51-53). His principal themes (kingdom of heaven, righteousness, perfection) and Christological titles (Son of David, Son of Man, Son of God, etc.) have rich Jewish backgrounds. He places Jesus' views on divorce in the context of the Jewish debate about the grounds on which a man may divorce his wife (5:32; 19:9). He sees no need to explain Jewish practices of ritual purity (15:2; cf. Mark 7:3-4) or the Jewish customs of wearing phylacteries and prayer shawls (23:5). His version of the Lord's Prayer expands the more primitive text in Luke 11:2-4 with the help of phrases and conventions typical of Jewish prayer. The sophisticated use of Scripture and the signs of a developing body of halakah have led some scholars to speak of a ''School of St. Matthew,'' with Matt 13:52 as its motto or slogan.

The primary mission field for the community of the Matthean Jesus was Israel: ''Do not go among the Gentiles, nor enter into the city of the Samaritans. Rather, go to the lost sheep of the house of Israel'' (10:5-6). The Matthean Jesus states: ''I have been sent only to the lost sheep of the house of Israel'' (15:24). He acknowledges the authority of the Torah (5:17-19) and of the scribes and Pharisees as its interpreters (23:2). Yet the Matthean Jesus warns his disciples of only partial success among Jews and of persecution for their trouble (5:10-12; 10:17, 23; 23:34). And the climax of the appearances of the risen Jesus is his command to ''make disciples of all the Gentiles'' (28:19). Though largely Jewish, the Matthean community seems to have been open to non-Jews and probably took the ''great commission'' of Matt 28:19 as a stimulus to even greater effort in carrying out the Gentile mission.

Almost all interpreters locate the composition of Matthew's Gospel in Syria or Palestine. Two factors go into these efforts at determining where this Gospel was composed: The place must have had a large Jewish population to accommodate both the Matthean community and their Jewish opponents. Since the Gospel was composed in Greek for a Greek-speaking community, it must be a place in which Greek was known and used. The passing comments about Gentiles (see Matt 5:47; 6:7; 18:17) indicate that there was also a significant non-Jewish population in the area.

The two criteria of large Jewish population and Greek language are met by several cities in Syria (Antioch, Damascus, Edessa). That there was a large Jewish population in Syria is affirmed by Josephus in *War* 7:43: ''Men of Jewish blood in great numbers are diffused among the native populations all over the world, especially in Syria, where the two nations are neighbors. The biggest Jewish colony was at Antioch owing to the size of the city, and still more because the kings who followed Antiochus had made it safe for them to settle there." In these major Hellenistic cities Greek was spoken and written by both Jews and non-Jews.

While it is plausible and now customary to place the composition of Matthew in Syria, a good case can also be made for Palestine as the place of origin. What stands in the way of this location is the old and poorly founded distinction between Palestinian Judaism and Hellenistic Judaism. This distinction assumed that Palestine was a cultural backwater separated from the Hellenistic world, one in which the Greek language was seldom used. But recent discoveries and reflection on the literary sources indicate that Palestine was integrated into the economic, administrative, military, and cultural life of the Hellenistic world. And the population of Palestine was not entirely Jewish. So there is no objection to some place in Palestine such as Caesarea Maritima or one of the cities of Galilee as the place for Matthew's composition. The chief argument for a Palestinian origin is the presence there of the opposing Jewish movement portrayed under the banner of "scribes and Pharisees" (though that movement may also have penetrated into Syria). Other candidates are Phoenicia (Tyre and/or Sidon) and Transjordan (Pella or one of the other cities of the Decapolis).

5. *Setting*

If (as seems likely) Matthew wrote his Gospel after A.D. 70 and in or near Palestine, his work must be viewed as an attempt to respond to the crisis posed by the Jerusalem Temple's destruction. This central and unifying institution of Judaism was suddenly no more, and there was little expectation that it would be rebuilt. What about the future of Judaism—deprived of its Temple and political control over the land? That question faced all Jews in the late first century A.D.

How the Temple came to be destroyed is well described in Josephus' *Jewish War.* In A.D. 44 with the death of Agrippa I Judea became a Roman province administered by a procurator responsible to the legate of Syria. Most of these procurators were insensitive and incompetent, and thus a cycle of popular resistance and governmental repression played itself out over the next twenty years. War broke out in Caesarea Maritima in A.D. 66 with an incident involving Jews and Gentiles in dispute over building rights and the desecration of a synagogue. The emperor Nero appointed Vespasian to oversee the Roman conduct of the war, and he quickly subdued Galilee and probably would have made fast work of Judea and Jerusalem except for Nero's assassination and a succession of short-term emperors. When Vespasian himself set out for Rome in A.D. 69 to become emperor, he entrusted the completion of the war to his son Titus. All that remained to be conquered were Jerusalem and three fortresses (Herodium, Machaerus, Masada).

The siege of Jerusalem lasted about six months, until September A.D. 70. The Jewish defense of the city was hardly systematic, since various parts were in the hands of the several factions that had developed there. John of Gischala held the temple and the surrounding area. Simon bar Giora held the Upper City. What lay between them was reduced to a battleground between the Jewish factions. Meanwhile the Romans gradually penetrated the defenses of the city, destroyed the Jerusalem Temple, and defeated the Jewish factions. The siege came to an end on 8 September A.D. 70, with the defeat of the factions and the utter destruction of the city.

Josephus was no unbiased chronicler of these events. He himself had been the Jewish commander of Galilee and (as he describes himself) a serious foe of the Roman army. But on suffering defeat he went over to the Roman side and wrote his account under the patronage of the Flavian emperors, the line begun by Vespasian and Titus. In his account he presents Vespasian and Titus as courageous and unwilling conquerors. The blame for the Jewish defeat is placed upon the leaders of the various Jewish factions. These former rivals of Josephus are presented as ruthless and immoral bandits. According to Josephus, Jerusalem and Judea were destroyed by internal dissensions, which forced the Romans to come in and set fire to the Temple (*War* 1:10). He writes in order to contrast the brutality of the party chiefs toward their countrymen with the clemency of the Romans toward aliens (*War* 1:12). He ascribes the misery of Jerusalem's destruction to the Jews and justice to the Romans, for "internal divisions destroyed the city, and the Romans destroyed the internal divisions" (*War* 6:256-257). If the Romans had not destroyed the city, either the ground would have opened and swallowed up the city, or a flood would have overwhelmed it, or lightning would have destroyed it like Sodom (*War* 5:566). Josephus insists that the sanctuary was set on fire in defiance of Titus' wishes (*War* 6:266).

Josephus' interpretation of the Jewish War between A.D. 66 and A.D. 70 is clear: The responsibility for the destruction of the Jerusalem Temple lay with the leaders of the Jewish factions, not the Romans. But we only know what Josephus tells us about those factions. Whatever speeches are attributed to them were composed by Josephus himself, following the conventions of historiography in antiquity. It is possible that the leaders of the factions were the despicable bandits portrayed by Josephus. Yet they may also have been political revolutionaries or even religious zealots driven on by apocalyptic speculations.

What were early Christians doing during the Jewish War? All we know comes from the early Church historian Eusebius, who claims that an oracle directed the members of the Jerusalem Church to leave the city before the war began and to settle in Pella, a city east of the Jordan in the Decapolis

(*Hist. eccl.* 3.5.3). We do not know how reliable this report is. We do not know what other Christians outside of Jerusalem may have done or how they reacted to events during the war.

The Temple was destroyed. Jerusalem was in Roman hands. Judaism would have to adjust to these new realities or die out. We know a few responses to the new situation: the apocalyptic, the early rabbinic, and the Jewish Christian (represented by Matthew's Gospel). The three responses had many points in common and some distinct differences. Examining their relationships with Matthew will highlight the particularity of each response. It will also provide insight into the early stages of the parting of the ways between Judaism and Christianity.

The apocalyptic response to Jerusalem's destruction in A.D. 70 is expressed in 4 Ezra and 2 Baruch, two apocalypses written in Palestine in the late first or early second century A.D.[5] Though the literary setting for both apocalypses is the sixth-century B.C. destruction of Jerusalem by the Babylonians, there is little doubt that they are really talking about the Roman conquest of Jerusalem in A.D. 70. The question facing both writers is: How could God have allowed this to happen to his chosen people Israel?

The Ezra Apocalypse (4 Ezra 3–14; chs. 1–2, 15–16 are later additions) takes as its point of departure the events of A.D. 70: "our sanctuary has been laid waste, our altar thrown down, our temple destroyed" (10:21); "Zion, the mother of us all, is in deep grief and great humiliation" (10:7). These events pose the problem of theodicy: "You have destroyed your people, and have preserved your enemies . . . . Are the deeds of Babylon better than those of Zion?" (3:30-32); "Why has Israel been given over to the Gentiles as a reproach?" (4:23); "These nations, which are reputed as nothing, domineer over us and devour us. . . . If the world has indeed been created for us, why do we not possess our world as an inheritance?" (6:57-59).

The solution to the problem of theodicy is basically that "the Most High has made not one world but two" (7:50)—this present world/age and the world/age to come. This age "is hastening swiftly to its end" (4:26). The arrival of the world/age to come will be signalled by various signs (4:52–5:13; 6:11-29; 7:26-44; 8:63–9:12). Following the resurrection of the dead and the judgment, the wicked will be punished and the righteous rewarded (7:31-36). Between the preliminary signs and the establishment of the new world/age "my son the Messiah shall be revealed" (7:28) to form a temporary kingdom for four hundred years. But this Messiah shall die before the fullness of the new age. The Messiah appears in other contexts later in 4 Ezra, first as the victor over the Roman "eagle" (12:31-34) and then as the "man from the sea" who will reprove the Gentiles for their ungodliness (13:21-45).

5. For intro. and trans., see J. H. Charlesworth, ed., *The Old Testament Pseudepigrapha* (Garden City, N.Y.: Doubleday, 1983) 1.517-59 (B. M. Metzger on 4 Ezra); 1.615-52 (A.F.J. Klijn on 2 Baruch).

How are faithful Jews to act in the meantime? The advice they receive in the Ezra Apocalypse is more an exhortation to patience than a rational explanation of the evils that have befallen Israel. They are told that the time left for the present evil age is short (5:50-55; 14:10-18), that the way to the world to come is narrow (7:10-14; see Matt 7:13-14) and reserved only for a few (8:3; see Matt 22:14), and that the Law (=Torah) is the only sure guide for the present (14:22).

The Apocalypse of Baruch (2 Baruch) uses the same literary setting (sixth century B.C.) and appears to have been composed at the same time (late first or early second century A.D.) as 4 Ezra. It refers to the destruction of the Second Temple in A.D. 70: "That building will not remain; but it will again be uprooted after sometime and will remain desolate for a time" (32:3). Again the events of A.D. 70 bring into question the election of Israel and God's fidelity. How can it be that Babylon is happy and Zion has been destroyed (11:2)? This work hints at certain providential dimensions to the catastrophe—so that the dispersed of Israel may do good to the nations (1:4), and the time of the divine visitation may be advanced (20:2). Nevertheless, the fundamental problem to be explained is how God could permit such destruction to happen to his chosen people.

The answer in 2 Baruch is like the one in 4 Ezra. There are two worlds/ages (74:2). Salvation from this evil world and for the world to come is near (23:7); indeed God is hastening the times (83:1; 85:10). The coming of the new world/age will be accompanied by signs (25:1-4; 70:1-10). The Messiah will play a major role in its coming, either as a military conqueror or judge (39:7–40:2; 70–72).

In the meantime Israel should live according to the Torah, the lamp given to Israel through Moses (17:4). Thus the readers are urged not to withdraw from the way of the Law (44:2) or to forget God's Law (44:7), for "that Law that is among us will help us, and that excellent wisdom which is in us will support us" (48:24) whereas "those who do not love your Law are justly perishing" (54:14). The basic stance recommended in 2 Baruch is summed up in 85:3, "Zion has been taken away from us, and we have nothing now apart from the Mighty One and his Law."

The two apocalypses deal with theological questions raised as a result of the destruction of the Jerusalem Temple in A.D. 70: Is the God of Israel still powerful and faithful to his promises? Is there any benefit in keeping the Torah? The answers to both questions are "yes." What makes possible these affirmative responses is the apocalyptic scheme of the two worlds/ages and the confidence that Israel and Israel's God will soon be vindicated for all to see.

The same questions concerned Matthew. On approaching Jerusalem, Matthew's Jesus says: "Behold your house is forsaken to you and desolate" (23:38). Matthew's additions to parables in 21:43 and 22:7-8 suggest that the rejection of Jesus by part of Israel had led to the destruction of Jerusalem and its temple in A.D. 70. Matthew (and other early Christians) shared the broad outline of apocalyptic theology found in 4 Ezra and 2 Baruch. This theology, of course, appears in earlier Jewish documents (the Enoch material, Dead Sea Scrolls, etc.) and seems to have been part of Jesus' own theology. Its major features include the idea of two worlds/ages, the imminent end of this world/age to be preceded by certain signs, the coming of the Messiah to mark the turn of the ages, the resurrection of the dead, judgment with rewards and punishments, and the new and better world/age in its fullness. The proper dispositions for the faithful who await these happenings are hope, fidelity, and constant watchfulness.

There is no firm evidence of direct dependence by Matthew on the two apocalypses or of the two apocalypses on Matthew, though they may have been composed at roughly in the same time and in roughly the same place. But there are two points at which they clash: the identity of the coming figure and the source of guidance in the present. For the Jewish apocalyptists the coming figure is "the Messiah" or "my son the Messiah," whereas Matthew prefers the title "Son of Man" and identifies this figure with Jesus of Nazareth. According to the apocalyptists the one sure guide in the present is the Torah; for Matthew it was Jesus' teaching and example—whether understood as an interpretation of the Torah or as a supplement to it.

Still another response to the destruction of Jerusalem in A.D. 70 was the early rabbinic movement. The major documents of the rabbinic movement are the Mishnah, Tosefta, Palestinian and Babylonian Talmuds, Targums, and Midrashim. The earliest of these documents—the Mishnah—was put more or less into its present form only around A.D. 200. It is methodologically dangerous to assume (as many scholars do) that these documents reflect Jewish life in the first century A.D. and so can be used directly to illumine the Gospels. Nevertheless, there is some relation between the mature rabbinic movement and the scribes and Pharisees of the Gospels.

The rabbinic movement in its origins is best seen as a response to the events of A.D. 70. Before A.D. 70 the Temple, the land, and the Torah were the unifying factors in Palestinian Judaism that allowed a multiplicity of sects and movements to exist together. After A.D. 70 the Temple lay in ruins and the land was even more clearly under Roman control. Only the Torah remained unscathed. The challenge facing the founders of the rabbinic movement was to shape a form of Judaism that remained faithful to the tradition while dealing with the changed political realities for Jews in Palestine. Their rivals in this task seem to have included the Jewish Christians of the Matthean community.

After A.D. 70 a group of scholars devoted to the Jewish way of life emerged. They were addressed by the honorific title "rabbi" and referred to themselves as "sages." Their chief center was Yavneh (also called Jamnia) near the Mediterranean coast, though there may also have been other centers throughout Judea. They were led first by Yohanan ben Zakkai and then by Gamaliel II, perhaps the grandson of the Gamaliel mentioned in Acts 5:34; 22:3. Although later rabbinic documents portray them as immediately taking over the leadership of Judaism, it is more likely historically that they only gradually developed their program, propagated it within the Jewish community, and gained authority in Jewish life several centuries later.

The early rabbinic movement was a coalition of sects and movements in Judaism before A.D. 70.[6] Without Temple and political power, the early rabbis emphasized careful study of the Torah and developed interpretations to guide Jewish life. The presence of priests among them and their concentration on ritual purity and matters pertaining to the Temple indicate that priestly traditions were incorporated into the early rabbinic movement. But the most distinctive elements came from the groups that Matthew refers to as the "scribes and Pharisees."

Scribes were originally those who wrote legal documents, a task that demanded not only literacy but also knowledge of the laws. Since in Israel the law was the Torah, the scribes were also the keepers and interpreters of the religious tradition. By the time of Ben Sira (ca. 200 B.C.) the scribes seem to have constituted a guild of religious intellectuals. The scribal contribution to early rabbinism allowed the Temple cult and sacrifice to be replaced by study of Torah, and the priests to be succeeded by the rabbis.

Before A.D. 70 the Pharisees were a religious sect distinct from the scribes.[7] The scribes made up a profession (like lawyers), whereas the Pharisees were a religious movement (like Jesuits or Opus Dei). The chief interests of the Pharisees before A.D. 70 were eating food in a state of ritual purity, tithing and giving agricultural offerings to the priests, obeying biblical rules and taboos about raising crops, keeping the Sabbaths and festivals, and observing marriage laws and rules about when sexual relations may or may not take place. This list derives from analysis of the Mishnah, especially the passages about the "houses" of Hillel and Shammai. Attention to Josephus and the Gospels adds to the picture of the Pharisees as a religious movement: the importance of meals in common, proselytism, seeking popular respect and influence, insistence on prayer and the search for perfection through careful observance of the Torah, and a stress on tradition. In contrast to the Sadducees, the Pharisees insisted on free will, resurrection of the dead, and judgment issuing in rewards and punishments. Underlying the Pharisaic program was a cult-centered piety that imposed the Temple's purity laws on the table of the ordinary Jews, thus replicating the Temple

6. J. Neusner, *Judaism: The Evidence of the Mishnah*, 2nd ed. (Atlanta: Scholars Press, 1988).

7. A. J. Saldarini, *Pharisees, Scribes and Sadducees in Palestinian Society. A Sociological Approach* (Wilmington: Glazier, 1988).

cult in the home and turning Israel into a "kingdom of priests and a holy nation."

The combination of these currents in pre-A.D. 70 Judaism—legal, priestly, scribal, and Pharisaic—allowed the early rabbis to begin fashioning a form of Judaism without Temple or political control of the land of Israel. Rather than mourning over the loss of the Jerusalem Temple as the apocalyptists represented in 4 Ezra and 2 Baruch did, the early rabbis assumed that matters were to go forward as if the Temple still stood and the land retained its holiness. In this age of transition the rabbis were lay people and priests who aspired to act like priests. They managed to move the beginnings of Mishnaic law out of a narrow, sectarian framework, though still far from attaining the full rabbinic vision for Jewish life as a whole.

The Matthean texts about the "scribes and Pharisees" (especially ch. 23) represent an outsider's perspective on the early rabbinic movement. While set on the literary level in Jesus' lifetime and perhaps reflecting his own tensions with those groups, these sayings have even more significance in their Matthean setting ca. A.D. 90 when the Jewish Christians and the "scribes and Pharisees" (=the early rabbis) were laying out rival programs for reconstituting Judaism without Temple and land.

Thus the scribes and Pharisees are criticized for cultivating the honorific titles of rabbi, father, and master (see 23:7-10), for seeking to attract new adherents to their movement (23:15), for their complicated practice of oaths (23:16-22) on the assumption that the temple still exists, and for their excessive attention to tithing agricultural products (23:23-24) and to ritual purity at meals (23:25-26) and to the sources of uncleanness (23:27-28). These teachers are granted some authority ("everything that they might tell you, do it and observe it; but do not act according to their works," 23:3). The biting references to "their synagogues" (4:23; 9:35; 10:17; 12:9; 13:54) and the "synagogues of the hypocrites" (6:2, 5; 23:6, 34) suggest that part of the early rabbinic program was the encouragement of local centers of Jewish life and piety—at which Jews taking another path were not welcome. Indeed the Christian missionaries seem to have been flogged at such synagogues (10:17) and run out of town by their leaders (10:23; 23:34).

After A.D. 70 Judaism was very much in transition. Several movements arose that claimed to provide the authentic means of continuing the Jewish tradition. Among such movements were the early rabbis ("scribes and Pharisees") and the early Christians (such as Matthew's community). The stakes were high (the survival of Judaism), the transition was at a very early stage (late first century A.D.), and tensions were severe (as Matthew 23 and other texts show). It is against this background that we need to understand Matthew's theological program, for it was intended as a way of preserving and continuing the Jewish tradition.

6. *Theological Perspectives*

Matthew's Gospel should be read as one of several Jewish responses to the destruction of the Jerusalem Temple in A.D. 70. The Matthean community still existed within the framework of Judaism but in tension with other Jewish groups—especially the early rabbinic movement. Matthew's theological program should be viewed as an attempt to show how the Jewish tradition is best preserved in a Jewish-Christian context. This preliminary sketch of Matthew's theology seeks only to indicate how Matthew dealt with the crisis posed by the events of A.D. 70 and rooted Jesus and his teaching in Jewish tradition.

Whereas the early rabbis appealed to pre-A.D. 70 teachers like Hillel and Shammai for precedents, Matthew went back to the Scriptures to show a continuity between the ancient Jewish tradition and the Christian movement. The most obvious element in this program is the use of "fulfillment" or "formula" quotations in which an OT quotation is introduced by a phrase such as "all this took place to fulfill what the Lord had spoken through the prophet." In the infancy narrative the fulfillment quotations confirm the extraordinary nature of Jesus' birth (1:23) and his itinerary as a child (2:15, 18, 23). They also appear in connection with Jesus' ministry in Galilee (4:15-16), his healing activities (8:17), his role as God's Servant (12:18-21), use of parables (13:35), entrance into Jerusalem on Palm Sunday (21:5), arrest (26:56), and betrayal by Judas (27:9-10). The point is that Jesus' life from start to finish was in perfect harmony with the Scriptures. Or to put it more in keeping with Matthew's outlook—the Scriptures are in perfect harmony with Jesus' life.

A similar dynamic pertains to Matthew's approach to the Torah. With the destruction of the Temple and the loss of political control over the land the Torah gained even more prominence in Jewish life. Every post-A.D. 70 Jewish movement had to take a position vis-à-vis the Torah. The apocalyptists found in the Torah sure guidance in the present time as they awaited the coming of the new age/world. The early rabbis discovered in the Torah the rudiments of a Judaism without Temple or land, one that could exist in any place or time. Matthew presents Jesus as the authoritative interpreter of the Torah: "I did not come to destroy but to fulfill" (5:17). In the six antitheses ("you have heard . . . but I say to you") Jesus either extends the commandment's scope by going to the root of the abuse (avoiding anger and lust to forestall murder and adultery) or going beyond a biblical commandment (as in the case of divorce and oaths). The Matthean Jesus not only expresses opinions about the early rabbinic traditions designed to protect against infringement of the Torah (23:1-39), but he also emerges as the interpreter of the Torah itself, able to play one part off against another as in the cases of the disputes about Sabbath observance (12:1-8) and divorce

(19:3-9). The point is that if you want a sure guide to understanding and practicing the Torah, look to the teaching of Jesus.

The titles that Matthew used to describe Jesus serve to root him in the Jewish tradition while showing that in Jesus the meaning of these titles reaches a certain fullness. In using the term "Messiah" ("anointed one" in English, *Christos* in Greek) Matthew shows less hesitation and embarrassment than Mark does in applying it to Jesus. Whereas Mark labors to show that Jesus was a "different" kind of Messiah from what people expected (see Psalms of Solomon 17), Matthew assumes that his readers know what Messiah meant and still could apply it to Jesus. Likewise he shows no hesitation about characterizing Jesus as the Son of David—the royal Messiah sent to Israel, especially to heal those who in the eyes of society count for nothing.

The most important Christological title for Matthew was Son of God. It extends through all phases of Jesus' life and is the natural complement to the Matthean idiom of "my Father" as Jesus' way of talking about God. Yet the Father-Son relationship may not be the only background for this title as applied to Jesus, for it is related to the king/Son of David in Jewish tradition (see Ps 2:7) and at several points in Matthew (2:15; 3:17; 4:1-11) there seems to be an equation between Son of God and Israel on the basis of OT texts.

Other titles applied by Matthew to Jesus have rich Jewish backgrounds: Servant of God (12:18-21 = Isa 42:1-4), Shepherd (9:36; 10:6; 12:9-14; etc.), and Son of Man (Dan 7:11-14). At several points the prophet Jeremiah serves as a model for Jesus, especially as a context for portraying Jesus as a prophet who suffers for speaking hard truths. Thus all the major Christological titles in Matthew's Gospel have deep roots in Jewish tradition and contribute to the picture of Jesus as thoroughly Jewish.

Some other strands of Matthean Christology seem to go beyond the Jewish framework by attributing to Jesus what in the biblical tradition is reserved for God. Thus in Matt 24:42 the title "Lord" (*Kyrios*) is applied to Jesus: "you do not know on what day your Lord is coming." Moreover, Jesus abides with his people much as the God of Israel abided with them in earlier times (see 1:23; 8:23-27; 10:40; 14:22-33; 18:5, 20; 25:31-46; 28:18-20). These "flashes of divinity" taken along with other NT texts (especially in John's Gospel) led ultimately to the Church's recognition of Jesus' divinity. The point here is that without the biblical theme of God's abiding presence to Israel the claims for Jesus' divinity have no context or root. By identifying God and Jesus so closely such themes probably go beyond the limits of strict Jewish monotheism. Nevertheless, without the Jewish tradition of speaking about God these claims would have been unintelligible.

Central to the preaching of the Matthean Jesus was the kingdom of God—God's future display of power and judgment and eventual establishment of his rule over all creation. In response to the apocalyptists Matthew stresses the importance of Jesus the Son of Man in the events of the future and of his teaching as the authoritative guide for life in the present. In response to the early rabbis Matthew retains a lively sense of history moving toward a goal and of halakah as shaped by Jesus' teaching and example.

For Matthew the followers of Jesus constitute the people of God. The inclusion of non-Jews in God's people had been made possible through Jesus the Jew and in response to his command (28:19-20). The parable of the vineyard (Matt 21:33-46) is crucial for understanding Matthew's approach to this matter. The vineyard is clearly Israel (see Isa 5:1-7), the tenants are Israel's leaders, the servants are the prophets, and the murdered Son is Jesus. The owner (God) "will put those wretches (the leaders) to a miserable death and let out the vineyard (Israel) to other tenants (Christians) who will give him the fruits in their seasons" (21:41). By way of conclusion the Matthean Jesus warns: "the kingdom of God will be taken away from them (Jewish leaders) and given to a nation bearing fruit" (21:43). The image of people bearing fruit establishes the recipients of God's kingdom as followers of Jesus (see 3:8, 10; 7:16-20; 12:33; 13:8; etc.). Those from whom the kingdom is taken are the Jewish leaders and their allies. Matthew and his community probably saw the events of A.D. 70 as vindication of the claims made by Jesus' followers and the appropriate punishment for their opponents. Pre-A.D. 70 Israel was no more. The challenge facing all Jews was to discover how Israel's tradition might continue.

The disciples not only represent the companions of the earthly Jesus but also serve as models for the Matthean Christians. Whereas the disciples in Mark frequently misunderstand Jesus, those in Matthew do understand him (see Matt 13:52; 16:12). Though not "perfect," they do exhibit a "little faith" (see Matt 6:30; 8:26; 14:31; 16:8; 17:20), which, even though it fails, is real nonetheless. By calling the disciples "brothers" and "little ones" Matthew fosters the identification of the disciples with the members of his own community. He forbids the honorific titles of his Jewish rivals—rabbi, father, and master (see Matt 23:8-10). He prefers *mathētēs* (disciple), and the command of the risen Jesus to the Eleven is to make disciples (*mathēteusate*) of others (Matt 28:19). Through Peter the "rock" (Matt 16:17-19), who really understands who Jesus is, the powers to bind and loose sins are given to the disciples. Throughout the Gospel Matthew tries to combine two perspectives: The disciples share in the power of the risen Lord and faithfully transmit the teaching of the earthly Jesus.

7. *Matthew and Anti-Semitism*

Matthew is often described as the most "Jewish" of the four Gospels. More than any other Gospel, Matthew is unintelligible without reference to the Hebrew Bible and other Jewish writings. The major theological themes depend upon the Jewish tradition for their vocabulary and content. The occasion for its composition was the crisis posed for all Jews by the destruction of the Jerusalem temple in A.D. 70. It was written for a largely Jewish-Christian community in order to help them see that their Christian faith was consistent with their Jewish heritage and the continuation of it.

At the same time Matthew is sometimes called anti-Jewish or anti-Semitic. His emphasis on Jesus as the fulfillment of the Old Testament seems to leave that tradition exhausted and therefore without value. The idea of Jesus as the authoritative interpreter of the Torah is taken so far as to make Jesus' teaching the criterion by which the Torah is judged, and not the other way around. The scribes and Pharisees—the religious and intellectual leaders whom many modern Jews view as the founders of post-biblical Judaism—are caricatured and criticized. Their synagogues are called "synagogues of the hypocrites." They represent an unbending and heartless legalism, in opposition to the free and compassionate Jesus. This negative attitude toward the opponents reaches a climax in chapter 23 with the "woes" against the scribes and Pharisees on account of their religious pride, their shutting the kingdom of heaven, their casuistry, and their hypocrisy. In the passion narrative Matthew deliberately heightens the involvement and responsibility of the Jewish leaders, and brands their explanation of the empty tomb (Jesus' disciples stole his body) as fraudulent (see 27:62-66; 28:11-15).

A Jewish authority on the New Testament, Samuel Sandmel, put it this way: "One senses in reading Matthew that his anger and hatred of Jews increases as he writes, especially against the Pharisees, until in chapter 23 it boils over into a unique, unparalleled specimen of invective."[8] Some Jewish scholars argue that there is so much anti-Jewish material in Matthew's Gospel that its author could not have been Jewish. Even the alleged "pro-Jewish" statements—"neither one yodh nor one hook will pass away from the Law" (5:18); "go to the lost sheep of the house of Israel" (10:6); "I have been sent only to the lost sheep of the house of Israel" (15:24); "everything that they might tell you, do it and observe it" (23:3)—are said to serve merely as preparation for the anti-Jewish offensives in the Gospel, and so are constitutive of Matthew's anti-Jewish stance and not genuinely pro-Jewish at all.[9]

No inventory of alleged anti-Semitism in Matthew would be complete without the response of the Jewish crowd to Pilate during the Roman trial

8. S. Sandmel, *Anti-Semitism in the New Testament?* (Philadelphia: Fortress, 1978) 68.
9. M. J. Cook, "Interpreting 'Pro-Jewish' Passages in Matthew," *HUCA* 54 (1983) 135-46.

of Jesus: "His blood be upon us and upon our children" (27:25).[10] This "self-curse" has often been imputed to the entire Jewish people in Jesus' time. Moreover, it has been taken as applying to all Jews throughout the centuries. Joined with the Christian claim about the divinity of Jesus, this text became the basis for the charge of deicide, i.e., the Jews killed God (= Jesus), and served as the slogan for anti-Semites through the years to persecute and destroy Jews and their communities.

Calling Matthew anti-Jewish or anti-Semitic is a harsh verdict. Yet this conclusion has been drawn by Jewish and Christian scholars who have studied the matter seriously. There are, of course, some obvious terminological problems. The term "anti-Semitic" arose in the late nineteenth century as a result of the prevailing racial theories and is so imprecise as to be unhelpful. "Anti-Semitic" is used today to mean "anti-Jewish," which in fact is a far more precise and useful term.

Was Matthew anti-Jewish? Another question must be answered first: Was Matthew Jewish? Some Christian and Jewish scholars maintain that Matthew was not Jewish. They are, however, by far the minority. For us who stand with the majority, Matthew's knowledge of and interest in Judaism are so great as to establish as beyond doubt his Jewishness.

How then explain the alleged "anti-Jewishness" in Matthew's Gospel? Some have recourse to the socio-psychological figure of the self-hating Jew. But that is too abstract and imposes an identity upon Matthew from without. Sandmel (unwittingly it seems) provided a clue toward a better explanation when he said: "Christianity is conceived of as its own entity, different from Judaism. . . . For Matthew, as for later Christians, humanity was divisible into three distinct entities: Jews, Christians, and Gentiles."[11]

In my opinion this way of looking at Matthew is wrong and leads to the judgment that Matthew was anti-Semitic or anti-Jewish. Instead of reading Matthew in the context of the late first-century crisis facing all Jews it imposes on the Gospel the categories of a later time when Judaism and Christianity had become separate religions. In Matthew we are only at the beginning of the transition from Christianity understood as a movement within Judaism to its being conceived as distinct from and over against Judaism. Matthew and his fellow Jewish Christians still considered themselves Jews and sought to show that their identity as followers of Jesus was compatible with their Jewish heritage. Matthew and his church still lived within the framework of Judaism.

It makes little sense to call Matthew anti-Semitic or anti-Jewish. Yet it must be admitted that the text of Matthew's Gospel has anti-Semitic or anti-Jewish potential and that it has been used by anti-Semites through the ages

10. V. Mora, *L'Refus d'Israël: Matthieu 27, 25* (Paris: Cerf, 1986).
11. Sandmel, 58.

(especially Matt 27:25) as the "theological" justification for their evil deeds. When taken out of its late first-century context within Judaism and read by Christians unaware of that context, Matthew can be interpreted as anti-Jewish. But that approach misses the very point of Matthew's Gospel.

For those concerned with Christian-Jewish relations today the serious study of Matthew's Gospel is necessary. Matthew reminds us of the need for *historical* study in order to appreciate the message of a NT writing. Without attention to its historical setting Matthew becomes a dangerous text, capable of giving encouragement to anti-Semites. Historical study of Matthew enables us to see the thrust of his historical project of rooting Jesus in the Jewish tradition. It also gives a context for the admittedly polemical and harsh judgments raised against his Jewish opponents. For Matthew, Jesus' fulfillment of the Scriptures did not mean that those Scriptures had lost their significance and therefore could be disregarded. Rather, for Matthew the Hebrew Scriptures gained significance through Jesus and continue to be part of the "treasure" of the scribe trained for the kingdom of heaven (see Matt 13:52).

Historical study of Matthew can give Jews and Christians today important insight into the context of and reasons for the eventual parting of the ways between them and their long history over against one another. The aim of such study is not to try to erase the distinctiveness of either Judaism or Christianity. The aim, instead, is for both Jews and Christians to look at a turning point in the history of both movements and to ask themselves whether theological differences necessarily demand conflict and eventual separation. They did in the past. But do they have to in the future? Can Christians and Jews perceive themselves as partners along the way rather than as opponents? Can we be *with* one another rather than *over against* one another? Can we Christians work out a positive position vis-à-vis Jews for a time and place different from those of Matthew and his apocalyptic and early rabbinic rivals?

8. *General Bibliography*

Commentaries:

Allen, W. C. *A Critical and Exegetical Commentary on the Gospel according to St. Matthew*. Edinburgh: Clark, 1912.

Beare, F. W. *The Gospel according to Matthew*. San Francisco: Harper & Row, 1981.

Bonnard, P. *L'Evangile selon Saint Matthieu*. 2nd rev. ed. Neuchâtel: Delachaux & Niestlé, 1970.

Davies, W. D. and Allison, D. C., *A Critical and Exegetical Commentary on Matthew.* Vol. 1. Edinburgh: T. & T. Clark, 1988.
Fenton, J. C. *St. Matthew.* Philadelphia: Westminster, 1978.
Filson, F. V. , *The Gospel according to St. Matthew.* London: A. & C. Black, 1960.
France, R. T. *The Gospel according to Matthew. An Introduction and Commentary.* Grand Rapids: Eerdmans, 1985.
Gnilka, J. *Das Matthäusevangelium.* Freiburg-Basel-Vienna: Herder, 1986, 1988.
Gundry, R. H. *Matthew: A Commentary on His Literary and Theological Art.* Grand Rapids: Eerdmans, 1982.
Hill, D. *The Gospel of Matthew.* London: Oliphants, 1972.
Lagrange, M.-J. *Évangile selon Saint Matthieu.* Paris: Gabalda, 1948.
Limbeck, M. *Matthäus-Evangelium.* Stuttgart: Katholisches Bibelwerk, 1986.
Lohmeyer, E. *Das Evangelium des Matthäus.* 4th ed. Göttingen: Vandenhoeck & Ruprecht, 1956.
Luz, U. *Matthew 1-7. A Commentary.* Minneapolis: Augsburg, 1989.
McNeile, A. H. *The Gospel according to St. Matthew. The Greek Text with Introduction and Notes.* Grand Rapids: Baker, 1980.
Meier, J. P. *Matthew.* Wilmington, Del.: Glazier, 1980.
Patte, D. *The Gospel according to Matthew: A Structural Commentary on Matthew's Faith.* Philadelphia: Fortress, 1987.
Plummer, A. *An Exegetical Commentary on the Gospel according to Matthew.* London: Scott, 1909.
Sabourin, L. *The Gospel According to St. Matthew.* 2 vols. Bombay: St. Paul Publications, 1982.
Sand, A. *Das Evangelium nach Matthäus.* Regensburg: Pustet, 1986.
Schweizer, E. *The Good News according to Matthew.* Atlanta: John Knox, 1975.
Smith, R. H. *Matthew.* Minneapolis: Augsburg, 1989.

Studies:

Bacon, B. W. *Studies in Matthew.* New York: Holt, 1930.
Bauer, D. R. *The Structure of Matthew's Gospel. A Study in Literary Design.* Sheffield, U.K.: Almond, 1988.
Bornkamm, G., Barth, G. and Held, H. J. *Tradition and Interpretation in Matthew.* 2nd rev. ed. London: SCM, 1982.
Brooks, S. H. *Matthew's Community: The Evidence of His Special Sayings Material.* JSNT Sup 16. Sheffield: JSOT, 1987.
Cope, O. L. *Matthew: A Scribe Trained for the Kingdom of Heaven.* Washington, D.C.: Catholic Biblical Association, 1976.
Davies, W. D. *The Setting of the Sermon on the Mount.* New York-London: Cambridge University Press, 1964.
Didier, M., ed. *L'Evangile selon Matthieu. Rédaction et théologie.* Gembloux: Duculot, 1972.
Frankemölle, H. *Jahwebund und Kirche Christi.* 2nd ed. Münster: Aschendorff, 1984.
Gerhardsson, B. *The Mighty Acts of Jesus according to Matthew.* Lund: Gleerup, 1979.
Gundry, R. H. *The Use of the Old Testament in Matthew's Gospel.* Leiden: Brill, 1967.

Hare, D. R. *The Theme of Jewish Persecution of Christians in the Gospel of Matthew.* New York–London: Cambridge University Press, 1967.

Howard, G. *The Gospel of Matthew according to a Primitive Hebrew Text.* Macon, Ga.: Mercer, 1987.

Howell, D. B. *Matthew's Inclusive Story.* Sheffield, U.K.: JSOT, 1990.

Hummel, R. *Die Auseinandersetzung zwischen Kirche und Judentum im Matthäusevangelium.* Munich: Kaiser, 1966.

Kilpatrick, G. D. *The Origins of the Gospel according to St. Matthew.* Oxford: Clarendon Press, 1946.

Kingsbury, J. D. *Matthew.* 2nd ed. Philadelphia: Fortress, 1986.

__________. *Matthew: Structure, Christology, Kingdom.* rev. ed. Minneapolis: Fortress, 1989.

__________. *Matthew As Story.* 2nd ed. Philadelphia: Fortress, 1988.

Lachs, S. T. *A Rabbinic Commentary on the New Testament. The Gospels of Matthew, Mark, and Luke.* Hoboken, N.J.: Ktav, 1987.

Lange, J., ed. *Das Matthäus-Evangelium.* Darmstadt: Wissenschaftliche Buchgesellschaft, 1980.

Levine, A.-J. *The Social and Ethnic Dimensions of Matthean Social History. "Go nowhere among the Gentiles . . ." (Matt. 10:5b).* Lewiston, N.Y.: Mellen, 1988.

McConnell, R. S. *Law and Prophecy in Matthew's Gospel: The Authority and Use of the Old Testament in the Gospel of St. Matthew.* Basel: Reinhardt, 1969.

Meier, J. P. *Law and History in Matthew's Gospel. A Redactional Study of Mt. 5:17-48.* Rome: Biblical Institute Press, 1976.

__________. *The Vision of Matthew: Christ, Church and Morality in the First Gospel.* New York: Paulist, 1979.

Neusner, J. *Judaism: The Evidence of the Mishnah.* 2nd. ed. Atlanta: Scholars Press, 1988.

Orton, D. E. *The Understanding Scribe. Matthew and the Apocalyptic Ideal.* Sheffield, U.K.: JSOT, 1989.

Overman, J. A. *Matthew's Gospel and Formative Judaism. The Social World of the Matthean Community.* Minneapolis: Fortress, 1990.

Perlewitz, M. *The Gospel of Matthew.* Wilmington: Glazier, 1988.

Przybylski, B. *Righteousness in Matthew and His World of Thought.* New York–Cambridge, U.K.–London: Cambridge University Press, 1980.

Sand, A. *Das Gesetz und die Propheten.* Regensburg: Pustet, 1974.

Schenk, W. *Die Sprache des Matthäus.* Göttingen: Vandenhoeck & Ruprecht, 1987.

Senior, D. *What Are They Saying about Matthew?* New York–Ramsey, N.J.: Paulist, 1983.

Shuler, P. L. *A Genre for the Gospels. The Biographical Character of Matthew.* Philadelphia: Fortress, 1982.

Sigal, P. *The Halakah of Jesus of Nazareth according to the Gospel of Matthew.* Lanham, Md.: University Press of America, 1986.

Stanton, G., ed. *The Interpretation of Matthew.* Philadelphia: Fortress, 1983.

__________. "The Origin and Purpose of Matthew's Gospel: Matthean Scholarship from 1945 to 1980." *Aufstieg und Niedergang der römischen Welt.* 25/3, ed. W. Haase. Berlin–New York: de Gruyter, 1985. Pp. 1889–1951.

Stendahl, K. *The School of St. Matthew and Its Use of the Old Testament.* 2nd ed. Philadelphia: Fortress, 1968.

Strecker, G. *Der Weg der Gerechtigkeit. Untersuchung zur Theologie des Matthäus.* Göttingen: Vandenhoeck & Ruprecht, 1962.

Suggs, M. J. *Wisdom, Christology, and Law in Matthew's Gospel.* Cambridge, Mass.: Harvard University Press, 1970.

Thysman, R. *Communauté et directives ethiques: La Catechese de Matthieu.* Gembloux: Duculot, 1974.

Trilling, W. *Das Wahre Israel.* 3rd ed. Munich: Kösel, 1964.

van Tilborg, S. *The Jewish Leaders in Matthew.* Leiden: Brill, 1972.

Wagner, G., ed. *An Exegetical Bibliography of the New Testament. Matthew and Mark.* Macon, Ga.: Mercer University Press, 1983.

Walker, R. *Die Heilsgeschichte im ersten Evangelium.* Göttingen: Vandenhoeck & Ruprecht, 1967.

Wilkins, M. J. *The Concept of Disciple in Matthew's Gospel.* Leiden–New York: Brill, 1988.

Zumstein, J. *La condition du croyant dans l'évangile selon Matthieu.* Fribourg: Editions Universitaires, 1977; Göttingen: Vandenhoeck & Ruprecht.

TRANSLATION, NOTES, INTERPRETATION

1. *The Birth-Record of Jesus* (1:1-17)

1. The birth-record of Jesus Christ, son of David, son of Abraham. 2. Abraham was the father of Isaac; Isaac was the father of Jacob; Jacob was the father of Judah and his brothers; 3. Judah was the father of Perez and Zerah by Tamar; Perez was the father of Hezron; Hezron was the father of Aram; 4. Aram was the father of Amminadab; Amminadab was the father of Nahshon; Nahshon was the father of Salmon; 5. Salmon was the father of Boaz by Rahab; Boaz was the father of Obed by Ruth; Obed was the father of Jesse; 6. Jesse was the father of David the king. David was the father of Solomon by the wife of Uriah; 7. Solomon was the father of Rehoboam; Rehoboam was the father of Abijah; Abijah was the father of Asaph; 8. Asaph was the father of Jehoshaphat; Jehoshaphat was the father of Joram; Joram was the father of Uzziah; 9. Uzziah was the father of Jotham; Jotham was the father of Ahaz; Ahaz was the father of Hezekiah; 10. Hezekiah was the father of Manasseh; Manasseh was the father of Amos; Amos was the father of Josiah; 11. Josiah was the father of Jechoniah and his brothers at the Babylonian exile. 12. After the Babylonian exile Jechoniah was the father of Shealtiel; Shealtiel was the father of Zerubbabel; 13. Zerubbabel was the father of Abiud; Abiud was the father of Eliakim; Eliakim was the father of Azor; 14. Azor was the father of Zadok; Zadok was the father of Achim; Achim was the father of Eliud; 15. Eliud was the father of Eleazar; Eleazar was the father of Matthan; Matthan was the father of Jacob; 16. Jacob was the father of Joseph, the husband of Mary, from whom Jesus called "Messiah" was born. 17. So all the generations from Abraham to David were fourteen generations, and from David to the Babylonian exile fourteen generations, and from the Babylonian exile to the Christ fourteen generations.

Notes

1. *birth-record*: The phrase is usually translated "book of the genealogy (or, generation)." But the use of the term "birth" (*genesis*) in Matt 1:18 demands a less technical translation, one that brings out a relation between the two verses. The expression in 1:1 probably echoes the introduction to the genealogy in Gen 5:1.

   Jesus Christ . . . David . . . Abraham: The nomenclature brings out the characters stressed in the genealogy, though in reverse order: Abraham (1:2), David (1:6b), the exile (1:11-12), and Jesus Christ (1:16). The point of this schema is to root Jesus in the royal line of Israel (David) and to trace his ancestry back to Israel's ancestor (Abraham).

2. *was the father of*: The Greek term *egennēsen* carries a more active connotation, perhaps better captured by the now archaic "begat." The entire genealogy follows the formal pattern set in Ruth 4:18-22. It is classified as a linear genealogy in that it traces the direct line from Abraham to Jesus. A segmented genealogy might treat several branches within the same generation.

   Judah and his brothers: This allusion to the twelve-tribe structure of Israel relates Jesus to "all Israel" while maintaining the linear pattern of the genealogy. The reference to Israel's three great ancestors—Abraham, Isaac, and Jacob—is culled from the stories in Genesis and (perhaps more directly) from 1 Chronicles 1–2.

3. *Perez and Zerah by Tamar*: The names from 1:2 to 1:6a appear in 1 Chr 2:1-15 and Ruth 4:12, 18-22. The story of Tamar's dressing up as a harlot to get children by Judah is told in Genesis 38. The result of her deception was the birth of the twins Perez and Zerah (Gen 38:29-30). Jesus' lineage from Abraham to David is carried on through Perez.

   Aram: Ram is the name given to Hezron's son in Ruth 4:19 and 1 Chr 2:9 according to the Hebrew text. But the Septuagint of Ruth reads "Arran" and of 1 Chronicles reads "Ram and Aram"; see H. Heater, *JSNT* 28 (1986) 25-29.

4. *Nahshon*: According to Num 2:3; 7:12 Nahshon the son of Amminadab was the leader of Judah during the wandering in the wilderness. According to Exod 6:23 his sister Elisheba was married to Aaron the priest and brother of Moses. Thus the genealogy allots only a short time (from Aram to Nahshon) to the period of Israel's stay in Egypt (see Gen 15:16).

5. *Boaz by Rahab*: Rahab is most likely the harlot of Jericho described in Joshua 2; see the debate between J. D. Quinn and R. E. Brown in *Bib* 62 (1981) 225-28 and 63 (1982) 79-80. The idea that Rahab the harlot was the mother of Boaz is unattested in the OT. For rabbinic traditions connecting Rahab with Ruth and Tamar, see Y. Zakowitch, *NovT* 17 (1975) 1-5.

   Ruth: The story of how the Moabite Ruth became part of the people of Israel is told in the OT book that bears her name. The genealogy of David that concludes the book seems to have provided the model for the Matthean genealogy of Jesus. But note that the OT list (Ruth 4:18-22) does not mention Ruth.

6. *David the king*: The addition of "the king" breaks the pattern set up for the previously mentioned males. It serves to underline David's royal dignity, to mark

a break in Israel's history, and to point forward to "Jesus who is called Christ (=Messiah)."

David: The material for the second part of the genealogy—from David to the Babylonian exile—is found in 1 Chr 3:5, 10-17. The story about David's shameful action in having Uriah the Hittite killed in battle so he could take Bathsheba for himself is told in 2 Samuel 11–12. Uriah was a Gentile; it is not clear that his wife was Jewish or Gentile.

7. *Asaph*: According to 1 Chr 3:10 (see 1 Kgs 15:9) this king's name was Asa. Asaph is mentioned in connection with psalms (see Pss 50, 73-83; 1 Chr 16:5-37; 2 Chr 29:30). The scribes responsible for later NT manuscripts have restored the name Asa in place of Asaph. A similar problem appears in 1:10 (Amos/Amon).

8. *Joram was the father of Uzziah*: In fact there were three kings between Joram and Uzziah (also known as Azariah) according to 1 Chr 3:11-12: Ahaziah, Joash, and Amaziah. Though some commentators understand the omission as deliberate because of these kings' relation to the notorious Athaliah (see 2 Kgs 11–14), the simplest explanation is similar looking and sounding names: Ahaziah/ Azariah-Uzziah.

10. *Amos*: Most manuscripts of 1 Chr 3:14 give this king's name as Amon (or Ammon). So do 2 Kgs 21:18-26 and 2 Chr 33:20-25. Amos is the name of the prophet. The idea that Matthew wished to insert psalmic (see Asaph in 1:7-8) and prophetic (Amos) strains into Jesus' genealogy is unlikely. The name Amos is best explained as an error that crept into Matthew's text or source.

11. *Jechoniah and his brothers*: In fact Josiah was the grandfather of Jechoniah. Josiah was the father of Jehoiakim, who in turn was the father of Jechoniah. Some later manuscripts restore the Jehoiakim generation, thus giving fifteen generations between David and the Babylonian exile. For an even larger omission, see Matt 1:8.

12. *Shealtiel*: According to 1 Chr 3:17, 19, Shealtiel was the son of Jechoniah but not the father of Zerubbabel (who was the son of Pedaiah, the brother of Shealtiel). Several other texts (Ezra 3:2, 8; 5:2; Neh 12:1; Hag 1:1, 12, 14; 2:2, 23) affirm that Shealtiel was the father of Zerubbabel, as does the Septuagint of 1 Chr 3:19.

13. *Abiud*: This name does not appear in the list of Zerubbabel's children in 1 Chr 3:19-20. Zerubbabel is the last figure in the genealogy for whom there is OT evidence. The remaining figures are unknown and differ from those named in Luke 3:23-27.

16. *Jacob*: According to Luke 3:23 the father of Joseph was named Eli. Luke traced Joseph's ancestry back through Zerubbabel and Shealtiel to Nathan the son of David (see Luke 3:27, 31).

Joseph . . . was born: Some Caesarean Greek manuscripts and Old Latin witnesses read: ". . . Joseph, to whom being betrothed the virgin Mary bore Jesus, who is called Messiah." This reading arose to bring the genealogy into line with Matt 1:18 and to avoid the impression that Joseph was the physical father of Jesus. The Sinaitic Syriac manuscript attests a third reading: ". . . Joseph; Joseph, to whom Mary the virgin was betrothed, begot Jesus who is called the

Messiah." While underlining Mary's virginity and alluding to Matt 1:18, this reading follows the standard genealogical pattern. The external evidence strongly favors the reading underlying our translation. The other two readings can be explained as arising from it (see *TCGNT,* 2–7).

17. *fourteen generations*: From Abraham to David there are fourteen names, and so Abraham must be counted as a generation. From David to the exile there are fourteen generations, but several generations have been omitted to yield this number (see 1:8, 11). From the exile to Jesus there are only thirteen generations; the idea that Jesus and "the Christ" constitute different generations is fanciful. The idea that the number fourteen derives from the numerical values of the consonants in David's name (daleth = 4, waw = 6, daleth = 4) is unlikely. Though the device of gematria may be present in Revelation (see 13:18), the number fourteen in Matt 1:17 is better connected with its function as a multiple of seven.

Interpretation

The first two chapters in Matthew's Gospel concern Jesus' birth and infancy. The first chapter explains who Jesus is by tracing his genealogy through Abraham and David (Matt 1:1-17), and how Joseph became his legal father without being his physical father (1:18-25). The second chapter features various place-names: the Magi come to Jerusalem (2:1-6) and then go to Bethlehem (2:7-12); Joseph, Mary, and Jesus flee into Egypt (2:13-15) to avoid the slaughter of infants in Bethlehem (2:16-18) and eventually go to Nazareth (2:19-23).

Matthew's infancy story situates Jesus within the history of Israel. The genealogy takes Abraham, David, and the Babylonian exile as its key points. Jesus is the royal Son of David. The episodes in chapter 2 echo the experiences of Moses. The divine sonship of Jesus is tied to the history of Israel ("Out of Egypt I called my son," 2:15).

Besides Jesus, the central character in Matthew's infancy narrative is Joseph. As a son of David he supplies the legal paternity of Jesus. As a model of biblical piety he trusts communications from God and acts upon them, thus allowing the child Jesus to reach maturity.

Matthew's story begins with the genealogy of Jesus. A genealogy is the account or record of the descent of a person, group, or tribe from an ancestor. A genealogy may be segmented (taking account of several figures within a single generation) or linear (moving from one generation to the next by means of a single figure in each generation).

Research on biblical genealogies in the context of oral genealogies in modern cultures and written genealogies in the ancient Near East provides some important guidelines for approaching the NT genealogies of Jesus (Matt 1:1-17; Luke 3:23-38). As Wilson (*Genealogy and History*) has shown, one must look to the domestic, political-legal, or religious function of the genealogy in the present. Genealogies are more statements about relationships in recent times than records motivated by antiquarian interest or historical curiosity. Therefore the interpreter must look to the present function of the genealogy in the domestic, political-legal, or religious sphere.

Moreover, genealogies especially in the oral stage are flexible and fluid. They may change to reflect a change in circumstances. And it is possible for a person, group, or tribe to have more than one genealogy. These may even appear side-by-side without sense of contradiction. When a genealogy is committed to writing or becomes part of a written document, it tends to lose fluidity and be taken more seriously as a historical document. There is little or no evidence for constructing genealogies simply from existing narratives or for using genealogies as the skeleton for constructing a series of narratives.

A genealogy may or may not contain solid historical information. In either case the function of the genealogy is most important: What is the genealogy saying about relationships on the domestic, political-legal, or religious levels? When that primary question has been answered, one may proceed in some cases to determine the historical accuracy of a genealogy.

The most important OT genealogies appear in the Book of Genesis and in Chronicles. Gen 4:17-26 contains two genealogies: from Cain to the sons of Lamech (4:17-24), and from Adam through Seth to Enosh (4:25-26). Genesis 5 moves from Adam to the sons of Noah. For the most part these are linear genealogies. Also listed in Genesis are the descendants of Noah (Gen 10:1-32), the generations from Shem to Abraham (Gen 11:10-32), and the descendants of Jacob (Gen 46:8-27). Exod 6:16-25 lists the descendants of Levi. The most extensive genealogical lists begin 1 Chronicles; the first nine chapters move from Adam to the descendants of Saul.

With respect to Matthew's genealogy of Jesus the most important OT sources are 1 Chronicles 2–3 (for the names from Abraham to the Babylonian exile) and Ruth 4:18-22 (for the names from Perez to David, and for the formal pattern "A was the father of B").

The OT genealogies were expanded and developed in *Jubilees* and ps.-Philo's *Biblical Antiquities*. For example, *Jubilees* 4:7-33 and 8:5-9 provide the names of the wives of the patriarchs that are absent from the biblical accounts. The early chapters of ps.-Philo's *Biblical Antiquities* fill out Genesis 4–5, 10–11, and provide smaller genealogies with names not witnessed in the biblical text. The complex linguistic processes through which both books have passed make deciphering these names difficult. To say where they came from is even more difficult. The expanded genealogies in these two examples of the "rewritten Bible" do suggest that in the first century a certain fluidity attended even biblical genealogies that had long been committed to writing.

The function of Matthew's genealogy is to trace Jesus' descent back to David and Abraham: The one whom Christians proclaim as "Messiah"

("Christ" in the Greek form) can be correctly claimed to be "Son of David." That Jesus the Christ came at the "right" time is suggested by the threefold sequence of fourteen generations: from Abraham to David, from David to Babylonian exile, and from the Babylonian exile to Jesus the Christ. The early names in Matthew's list can be traced to 1 Chronicles 2–3 and Ruth 4:18-22. The origin of the names from Abiud (1:13) to Jacob (1:16) remains a mystery.

The basic purpose of the genealogy of Jesus in Matt 1:1-17 is clear: Jesus is the Son of David (and of Abraham) and was born at an opportune time in Israel's history. For the Matthean community it served to root Jesus firmly within the history of God's people—something that was important both for Jewish and Gentile Christians.

The inclusion of five women in Jesus' genealogy (see 1:3, 5, 6, 16) breaks the formal pattern set in the Book of Ruth and elsewhere ("A was the father of B"). This unusual departure from both the form and the content of biblical genealogies was surely purposeful. But what was the purpose? Tamar (see Genesis 38) disguised herself as a harlot and conceived sons by her father-in-law, Judah. Rahab (see Joshua 2; 6) was the harlot of Jericho whose life was spared because she aided Joshua's spies. Ruth was a Moabite woman who joined herself to Israel through her husband's family. Bathsheba, referred to here simply as the "wife of Uriah," became David's wife when he arranged for Uriah's death in battle (see 2 Samuel 11–12). Mary, the mother of Jesus, was drawn into David's line through her husband Joseph, though her child Jesus was the legal rather than physical son of Joseph (as the next passage makes clear).

Efforts to find a factor common to all four OT women at the level of the biblical text or the Jewish tradition are not entirely successful. Rahab and Ruth were Gentiles, and "the wife of Uriah" may also have been a Gentile. But this does not seem to be the case for Tamar. It is possible to accuse Tamar, Rahab, and Bathsheba of sexual misconduct. But matters are not so clear in the case of Ruth. It seems best to leave the idea expressed by the inclusion of the four women at the level of "irregularity" or "departure from the ordinary." In their own distinctive ways they prepare for and foreshadow the irregular birth of Jesus that will be described in Matt 1:18-25. In the context of the formal pattern set by the genealogy ("A was the father of B") and the threefold series of fourteen generations, the four women set up the reader to expect the unexpected. At the beginning of the Gospel they function as part of a theme that runs through the entire text: the tension between tradition and newness.

The differences between the Matthean and Lukan genealogies also help to clarify the purpose of Matt 1:1-17. The clearest difference is the starting point. Luke works backward from Jesus through David and Abraham to Adam (who is called "Son of God"). Starting from Adam is consistent with Luke's emphasis on the universal character of the salvation brought by Jesus.

Matthew starts from Abraham and works through David and the exile down to Jesus. This procedure is consistent with Matthew's stress on the Jewishness of Jesus.

There are other differences. Luke adopts another OT genealogical pattern ("C the son of B, B the son of A"). He includes many more names than Matthew does, and makes no effort at dividing Israel's history into distinct periods. He traces Jesus' Davidic descent from Nathan (see 2 Sam 5:14; 1 Chr 3:5; 14:4; Zech 12:12) rather than Solomon. He gives Joseph's father's name as Eli rather than Jacob. Efforts at harmonizing the two genealogies or at appealing to an elaborate system of genealogical records have not been convincing. It seems better to respect the fluid nature of genealogies (compare Genesis 4 and 5) and to leave the problems unresolved. The chief point, however, should not be obscured. Both evangelists seek to place Jesus in line with David and Abraham (and Adam, in Luke's case). Both present Joseph as the legal father of Jesus but suggest that he was not the physical father of Jesus.

The genealogies of Jesus usually strike terror into the hearts of homilists and teachers. But once past the unfamiliar names it is possible to find in Matt 1:1-17 some important themes for actualization: the roots of Jesus in the history of Israel, the surprising instruments that God uses, the peculiar assortment of people that make up the ancestors of Jesus (and the Church in all ages), the tension between tradition and newness, the "right" time as part of God's plan for salvation, etc.

For Reference and Further Study

Johnson, M. D. *The Purpose of the Biblical Genealogies With Special Reference to the Setting of the Genealogies of Jesus.* 2nd ed. Cambridge, U.K.-London-New York: Cambridge University Press, 1988.

Orsatti, M. *Un saggio di teologia della storia. Esegesi di Mt. 1.1-17.* Brescia: Paideia, 1980.

Tatum, W. B. " 'The Origin of Jesus Messiah' (Matt 1:1, 18a): Matthew's Use of the Infancy Traditions." *JBL* 96 (1977) 523–35.

Waetjen, H. C. "The Genealogy As the Key to the Gospel according to Matthew." *JBL* 95 (1976) 205–30.

Wilson, R. R. *Genealogy and History in the Biblical World.* Yale Near Eastern Researches 7. New Haven–London: Yale University Press, 1977.

_________. "The Old Testament Genealogies in Recent Research." *JBL* 94 (1975) 169–89.

2. *The Birth of Jesus* (1:18-25)

18. Now the birth of the Messiah took place in this way. When his mother Mary had been engaged to Joseph, before they lived together, she was found to be with child—from the Holy Spirit. 19. Joseph her husband, being just but not willing to shame her, planned to divorce her quietly. 20. As he was considering this, behold an angel of the Lord appeared to him in a dream saying: "Joseph, son of David, do not fear to take home Mary your wife. For what has been begotten in her is from the Holy Spirit. 21. She will bear a son, and you will call his name Jesus. For he will save his people from their sins." 22. All this took place in order that what was spoken by the Lord through the prophet might be fulfilled: 23. "Behold the virgin will be with child and bear a son, and they will call his name 'Emmanuel' (which is interpreted 'God with us')." 24. Joseph awoke from sleep, and did as the angel of the Lord commanded him, and took home his wife. 25. And he did not know her until she bore a son. And he called his name Jesus.

Notes

18. *the birth of the Messiah*: The Greek word for birth (*genesis*) is the same as in 1:1 ("birth-record"), and joins together the two pieces. Most manuscripts read "Jesus Christ." But the presence of the definite article ("the") and the emphasis of the genealogy on Jesus as Son of David (=Messiah) suggest that "the Messiah" was original.

before they lived together: See the following explanation of Jewish marriage customs. The narrator makes clear that the marriage between Joseph and Mary had not yet been consummated before Mary became pregnant. Though Joseph is the legal father of Jesus, his birth came about in a very unusual way, without Joseph being the physical father.

from the Holy Spirit: There is no definite article in the Greek text. Also the idea of "holy spirit" implied in the text is more akin to OT ideas than to the doctrines of the Church councils. The role of the spirit of God in creation appears in Gen 1:1-2. The phrase "from the Holy Spirit" is the narrator's explanation to the readers, thus supplying them with the clue to the mystery of Mary's pregnancy that Joseph must face.

19. *being just*: The Greek term *dikaios* is best interpreted with reference to Joseph's observance of the Law. Weaker interpretations like "kindly" or "pious" do not suffice. The particular law that concerned Mary and Joseph appears in Deut 22:23-27, the case of an engaged woman found not to be a virgin. She was to be returned to her father's house and stoned to death by the men of the city on account of the disgrace brought upon her father's house.

but not willing to shame her: The Greek *kai* ("and") must have an adversative sense ("but"). The "shame" alludes to the public procedure outlined in Deut 22:23-27. Joseph decided to spare Mary this public disgrace by simply putting her through the less public procedure of divorce: "If she says 'I am defiled,' she forfeits her marriage contract and goes forth" (*m. Sot.* 1:5).

20. *an angel*: An angel also serves as a messenger of God in Matt 2:13, 19 in the context of dreams. Dreams are vehicles of divine communication in Matt 2:12, 22. So here are introduced two motifs that will be prominent in the following chapter.

Son of David: The legal Davidic paternity of Jesus was established by the genealogy. The goal of Matt 1:18-25 is to establish Jesus also as Son of God and to explain how both titles—Son of David and Son of God—can be predicated of Jesus. This task is carried out by claiming that the real instrument of Jesus' birth was the Spirit of God.

take home: By their engagement Mary was already the wife of Joseph. The point at issue is whether Joseph should go through the entire marital process and bring to his own home (or his father's) his now pregnant bride. While Joseph's instinct was to interrupt the process, the angel's advice is to go through with it as part of God's plan.

21. *you will call his name*: According to Luke 1:31 Mary was to give the name to Jesus. But for Matthew, Joseph is the focal character, and so he gives the name (see Matt 1:25). The name was customarily given at the circumcision, on the eighth day after birth (see Luke 1:59; 2:21). Either parent could give the name (see Gen 4:25-26).

Jesus: "Jesus" is a Greek form of the Hebrew name Yeshua or Yeshu, which are shortened forms of Joshua. The original meaning of Joshua was probably "Yahweh helps." But the name was connected with the Hebrew root for "save" (*yš'*) and interpreted as "God saves." The interpretation of Jesus' name connects that name with his mission in God's plan.

22. *fulfilled*: This kind of formula to introduce an OT quotation fulfilled by Jesus appears also in Matt 2:15, 17, 23; 4:14; 8:17; 13:35; 21:4; 26:56; and 27:9 (see also 2:5; 3:3; 12:17; 13:14). The device underlines the continuity between the OT and Jesus. Some manuscripts insert "Isaiah" before "the prophet," but this is probably only a later addition to the Matthean text (though it does reflect Matthew's practice elsewhere).

23. *Behold the virgin*: In the Hebrew text of Isa 7:14 the oracle refers to the imminent birth of a Davidic prince from a young woman of the royal court; that would be a sign of hope to Judah in the days of King Ahaz (ca. 735–715 B.C.). The Septuagint's use of the Greek word *parthenos* ("virgin") for *'almâ* ("young woman") indicates that she was perceived to be a virgin at the time of the oracle. But in both texts the assumption is the natural mode of conception, not virginal conception. For early Christians like Matthew, however, the appearance of *parthenos* in Isa 7:14 bolstered their already existing faith in the virginal conception of Jesus.

will be with child: lit., "have in the womb." The Septuagint reads "receive in the womb." The Matthean expression puts Jesus' conception in line with the birth stories of the OT patriarchs (see Gen 16:11; 17:17) and judges (see Judg 13:3, 7).

they will call: Matthew differs from both the Hebrew text (''she will call'') and the Septuagint (''you will call''). He may have used a variant text of Isa 7:14. Or perhaps he was looking to the ''people'' mentioned in Matt 1:21 (''he will save his people from their sins'').

Emmanuel: The Hebrew name mentioned in Isa 7:14 is given a Greek interpretation in the parenthetical phrase (''God with us''). See Isa 8:8, 10. The name as applied to Jesus is part of his identity as Son of God. It also prepares for the promise of the risen Lord to be with his disciples all days to the close of the age (see Matt 28:20).

25. *he did not know her until*: Matthew emphasizes that as a virgin Mary conceived and gave birth to Jesus. The phrase ''he did not know her'' is a biblical euphemism for sexual relations (see Gen 4:1). The text neither confirms nor denies the perpetual virginity of Mary; there is no implication about what happened after Jesus' conception and birth. For mentions of Jesus' ''brothers'' and ''sisters,'' see Matt 12:46-50 and 13:55-56.

he called: The Greek verb is ambiguous with regard to the subject (''he'' or ''she''). But the angel's instruction to Joseph in 1:21 (''you will call'') indicates that Joseph is the subject. By giving the child his name Joseph establishes Jesus' Davidic origin before the Law.

Interpretation

The story of Jesus' birth in Matt 1:18-25 can be read as the continuation of the genealogy. Whereas the genealogy established Jesus to be the Son of David through his legal father Joseph, the birth-story explains how it came to be that Jesus the Son of God conceived through the Holy Spirit was David's son. To appreciate this birth-story one must first have some basic information about Jewish marriage laws and customs, divine communication through angels and dreams, the announcement-of-birth pattern, and the use of biblical quotations in Matthew's Gospel.

Jews of Jesus' time understood marriage more in terms of a civil contract than as a religious ritual or ''sacrament.'' The OT and ancient Near Eastern evidence about marriage is summarized in R. de Vaux's *Ancient Israel: Social Institutions* (New York–Toronto: McGraw-Hill, 1965) 24–38. The rabbinic material is treated by S. Safrai in *The Jewish People in the First Century* (Philadelphia: Fortress, 1976) 752–92. For our purposes it is necessary merely to outline the procedures that are pertinent to the situation of Joseph and Mary in Matt 1:18-25.

Engagement or betrothal was taken very seriously and acknowledged to have legal consequences (see Deut 20:7; 22:23-27). The usual case seems to have been arranged through elders in the family. The parties were generally young by today's Western standards. In rabbinic times minimum ages were set for the male at thirteen and for the female at twelve. Apart from the forbidden degrees of kinship (see Leviticus 18) it was customary to marry within tribes or families.

The betrothal took place at the home of the father of the bride (where she was to stay after the betrothal ceremony). At the betrothal ceremony the husband presented the wife (and her father) with the marriage contract and the so-called bride-price. One or several years might separate the betrothal ceremony from the actual marriage ceremony. The marriage ceremony consisted in the transfer of the bride from her father's home to that of the groom's home or that of his father. When reading Matt 1:18-25 we are to envision that the betrothal ceremony between Joseph and Mary had already taken place and that they awaited the wedding ceremony. Mary remains at the home of her parents, and Joseph visits that household from time to time.

Mary's pregnancy at first sight appears to be the case outlined in Deut 22:23-27, which involves a betrothed virgin who had sexual relations with either a man in the city or a man in the country. In the first case the penalty is death for both parties, in the second case only for the man. The reason for the difference concerns the woman's ability to cry out and stop an act of rape; in the city she would be heard but not in the country. The principle underlying both cases is the assumption that the man "violated his neighbor's wife" (Deut 22:24).

It is difficult to know how rigidly this law and its punishment were carried out in ancient Israel. The assumption behind the description of Joseph in Matt 1:19 ("being just but not willing to shame her") is that he had a choice either of demanding that the procedure in Deut 22:23-27 be carried out or simply going through the usual divorce procedure. Divorce was basically a written notice signed by two witnesses that the husband had divorced his wife and that she was now free to marry someone else. Joseph's decision to divorce Mary "quietly" implies that he would not subject her to the public disgrace involved in the case covered by Deut 22:23-27.

Joseph's agonizing choice and confusion are cut short by a divine communication through a dream. The messenger is called an "angel of the Lord" (Matt 1:20), a figure well-known from the OT (see Gen 16:7-13; 22:11; Exod 3:2; Num 22:22; Judg 6:11-24; 13:3; Zech 1:11; 3:1). In many of the OT cases it is difficult to distinguish between the Lord and the angel of the Lord. The angel of the Lord appears at decisive points for God's people and makes known the will of God in this or that situation. The basic meaning of the Hebrew term *mala'k* and its Greek equivalent *angelos* is "messenger." That is the function carried out by the "angel of the Lord" in Matt 1:18-25.

Another way of expressing divine communication in biblical times was dreams. Whereas moderns look to dreams as clues to their past and present, ancients considered dreams as guides to the future. The Book of Genesis features the dreams of Jacob (Gen 28:10-17) and Joseph (Gen 37:5-11), and in the Book of Daniel the dreams of the pagan kings are interpreted with reference to the future of their empires and world history.

In ps.-Philo's *Biblical Antiquities* 9:10 the motifs of the angel of the Lord and dreams as modes of divine communication came together in connection with the birth of Moses: "And the spirit of God came upon Miriam one night, and she saw a dream and told it to her parents in the morning, saying, 'I have seen this night, and behold a man in a linen garment stood and said to me, "Go and say to your parents, 'Behold he who will be born from you will be cast forth into the water, likewise through him the water will be dried up. And I will work signs through him and save my people, and he will exercise leadership always.'"' And when Miriam told of her dream, her parents did not believe her." Miriam, the sister of Moses, knows what to do because God's will is communicated to her in a dream. A man in a linen garment (presumably an angel) announces the birth of Moses, hints at his name (by deriving it from the Hebrew root *mšh*, "draw forth"), and identifies his mission as an adult. This parallel, which comes from a work roughly contemporary with the NT, is especially interesting in light of the Moses-Jesus analogies that emerge from the stories in Matthew 2. It also prepares us to appreciate the form in which the angel's proclamation is expressed in Matt 1:20-21.

At the center of Matt 1:18-25 is the angel's announcement to Joseph regarding Jesus' birth, name, and identity. The angel's proclamation in Matt 1:20-21 follows a pattern developed in the OT with respect to the birth of a son: announcement of the birth introduced by "behold," designation of the child's name, and specification of the child's identity. The pattern applies to Ishmael (Gen 16:11-12), Isaac (Gen 17:19), Solomon (1 Chr 22:9-10), Josiah (1 Kgs 13:2), and the prince born of the young woman at Ahaz's court (Isa 7:14-17). In the case of Ishmael, the messenger is the angel of the Lord. The case of Josiah serves to illustrate the scheme: "Behold, a son shall be born to the house of David, Josiah by name; and he shall sacrifice upon you (= the altar) the priests of the high places who burn incense upon you, and men's bones shall be burned upon you" (1 Kgs 13:2). These biblical examples coupled with the Miriam-story from ps.-Philo show that this formal pattern was known and used in NT times.

The story of the announcement of Jesus' birth is accompanied by the first of many "fulfillment quotations" in Matthew (see 1:23; 2:5, 15, 17, 23; 3:3; 4:14; 8:17; 12:17; 13:14, 35; 21:4; 26:56; 27:9). They are the evangelist's device for underlining the continuity between the biblical tradition and the events in Jesus' life. The notion of "fulfillment" need not be taken to imply the end or evacuation of the OT tradition. For Matthew and his community the tradition retained its significance and found its fullness in the person of Jesus.

Each fulfillment quotation will be treated as it appears in the text. But some general observations on them are called for here. (1) Many of the quotations do not conform exactly to the wording of the Greek Septuagint or the Hebrew Masoretic text. The divergences can be explained in various ways: the use of slightly different biblical texts, scribal activity that can be described as "targumizing" (paraphrasing and/or adapting), and the editorial touches of the evangelist himself. (2) Little attention is given to the original historical setting or literary context of the biblical quotation. In most cases there is a word or an idea that is emphasized and applied to the event connected with Jesus. (3) Early Christians may have gathered anthologies of biblical quotations considered to be especially appropriate for expressing their beliefs about Jesus. And such an anthology (or florilegium) may have been used by Matthew in writing his Gospel. Long a hypothetical genre in NT study, the anthology of biblical quotations is now represented among the Dead Sea Scrolls. (4) Whatever the context of the biblical quotations may be and whatever the history of scribal activity within the Matthean community may have been, the most important task facing the reader of Matthew is to attend to what the evangelist does with the biblical texts to express his convictions about Jesus.

The central character in Matthew's account of Jesus' birth is Joseph (whereas in Luke it is Mary). Having established the legal Davidic paternity of Jesus through Joseph (Matt 1:1-17), the evangelist now in Matt 1:18-25 wants to bring together that way of looking at Jesus ("Son of David") with the early Christian confession that Jesus is Son of God. Rather than tracing Jesus' divine sonship to the resurrection (see Rom 1:4) or the baptism (see Matt 3:13-17), Matthew tries to show how Jesus was Son of God from the very time of his conception.

It is sometimes asserted that the account of Jesus' virginal conception was part of Matthew's defense against a Jewish charge that Jesus was the illegitimate son of Mary. Such charges do appear in some Talmudic texts and in an even later collection of polemics known as *Toledot Yeshu.* There the claim is made that Jesus was fathered by a Roman soldier named Panthera.

How early was this charge? Did the idea of Jesus' virginal conception in Matt 1:18-25 generate the charge of Jesus' illegitimacy, or was it a response to it? Since the textual evidence for Jesus' illegitimacy is late, it seems best to take the charge as generated by the early Christian belief in the virginal conception of Jesus. For a recent defense of the historical character of this tradition (that is, that Jesus indeed was illegitimate), see J. Schaberg's *The Illegitimacy of Jesus: A Feminist Theological Interpretation of the Infancy Narratives* (San Francisco: Harper & Row, 1987).

Actualization of Matt 1:18-25 might well focus on Joseph's confusion, trust, and subsequent enlightenment. From this perspective Joseph emerges as a major figure for the Advent season. Or attention might be given to the idea of fulfillment expressed by the quotation of Isa 7:14. It is better to point out the differences between the OT and NT texts than to cover them over. In fact the NT claims a kind of "super-fulfillment" for Jesus' birth in comparison with the birth foretold in Isa 7:14. It is important also to stress that "fulfillment" does not remove significance or meaning from the OT; it is more a matter of continuity than of discontinuity.

For Reference and Further Study

Brown, R. E. *The Birth of the Messiah,* 96–164.

Conrad, E. W. "The Annunciation of Birth and the Birth of the Messiah." *CBQ* 47 (1985) 656–63.

Davies, W. D. *Setting,* 70–72.

Fitzmyer, J. A. "The Virginal Conception of Jesus in the New Testament." *TS* 34 (1973) 541–75.

Miguens, M. *The Virgin Birth. An Evaluation of Scriptural Evidence.* Westminster, Md.: Christian Classics, 1975.

Schaberg, J. *The Illegitimacy of Jesus. A Feminist Theological Interpretation of the Infancy Narratives.* San Francisco: Harper & Row, 1987.

Soares-Prabhu, G. M. *The Formula Quotations in the Infancy Narrative of Matthew.* Rome: Pontifical Biblical Institute, 1976.

Stendahl, K. *The School of St. Matthew.* 2nd ed. Philadelphia: Fortress, 1968.

3. *The Visit of the Magi and the Flight to Egypt* (2:1-23)

1. Now after Jesus was born in Bethlehem of Judea in the days of Herod the king, behold, Magi from the East came to Jerusalem, 2. saying: "Where is the one who is born king of the Jews? For we have seen his star at its rising and have come to pay homage to him." 3. When King Herod heard this, he was disturbed, and all Jerusalem with him. 4. And he gathered all the chief priests and scribes of the people and inquired of them where the Messiah was to be born. 5. They said to him: "In Bethlehem of Judea. For so it was written by the prophet: 6. 'And you, Bethlehem, land of Judah, by no means are you least among the princes of Judah; for from you will come forth a ruler who will shepherd my people Israel.' "

7. Then Herod called the Magi secretly and ascertained from them the time when the star appeared. 8. And he sent them to Bethlehem, saying: "Go and search diligently for the child. And when you have found him, inform me, so that I too might come and pay homage to him." 9. They listened to the king and went their way; and behold, the star that they saw at its rising went before them until it came and rested over where the child

was. 10. When they saw the star, they rejoiced with extremely great joy. 11. And they went into the house and saw the child with Mary his mother, and they fell down and paid him homage, and they opened their treasure-boxes and offered him gifts—gold and frankincense and myrrh. 12. And since they were warned through a dream not to return to Herod, they returned to their own land by another route.

13. Now after they departed, behold, an angel of the Lord appeared in a dream to Joseph, saying: "Arise, take the child and his mother, and flee into Egypt, and stay there until I tell you. For Herod is going to seek out the child to destroy him." 14. He arose, and took the child and his mother by night, and departed into Egypt, 15. and was there until Herod's death in order that what was said by the Lord through the prophet might be fulfilled: "Out of Egypt I called my son."

16. Then Herod, seeing that he had been deceived by the Magi, was very angry; and he sent and killed all the male children in Bethlehem and in all its region from two years old and below, according to the time that he ascertained from the Magi. 17. Then what was said through Jeremiah the prophet was fulfilled: 18. "A voice was heard in Ramah, weeping and much lamentation, Rachel weeping for her children, and she was not willing to be consoled, because they were no more."

19. Now after Herod died, behold, an angel of the Lord appeared to Joseph in a dream in Egypt, 20. saying: "Arise, take the child and his mother, and go into the land of Israel. For those who were seeking the child's life have died." 21. He arose and took the child and his mother, and went into the land of Israel. 22. But hearing that Archelaus ruled over Judea in place of his father Herod, he was afraid to go there. Having been warned in a dream, he went away into the district of Galilee. 23. And he went and dwelt in the city called Nazareth so that what was said through the prophets might be fulfilled: "He will be called a Nazorean."

Notes

1. *Jesus was born*: In contrast to Luke 2:1-7 there is only a brief mention of Jesus' birth. Bethlehem was the ancestral home of David, and so the birth-story carries on the "Son of David" motif from chapter 1. Bethlehem of Judea is five miles south of Jerusalem; it is distinguished here from Bethlehem of Galilee, seven miles northwest of Nazareth.

   Herod the king: The most powerful member of an Idumean family that was deeply involved in Jewish affairs in the first century B.C. and A.D., Herod the Great was appointed King of the Jews by the Roman senate in 40 B.C. and gained control of Jerusalem in 37 B.C. He died in 4 B.C., and his kingdom was divided among his surviving sons. Herod the Great was a masterful politician who succeeded in playing off Roman and Jewish factions against each other. He was especially famous for his massive building projects at Caesarea Maritima, Samaria, and the Jerusalem temple. He also had many fortresses constructed, the most famous being Masada. His domestic problems and well-known cruelty to members of his own family provide the background to the incident described in Matt 2:1-12.

Magi from the East: The term "Magi" originally referred to a caste of Persian priests with special claims to interpret dreams. Here they appear as astrologers/astronomers who looked to the movement of the stars as a guide to major events. Since they do not know where the Christ is to be born, they are assumed to be Gentiles. Where in the East they came from is not clear. The term "Magi" suggests Persia, their practice of astrology indicates Babylon, and the gifts they bring point to Arabia or the Syrian Desert. The term "Magi" has been retained in the translation because the modern alternatives are not accurate: "wise men" (too generic), "kings" (inaccurate), and "astrologers" (confusing for people today).

2. *king of the Jews*: Since this was the official title of Herod the Great, the Magi's question would have been interpreted as referring to a rival of Herod. The title was used by Alexander Jannaeus (103–76 B.C.) and his successors as priest-king. Since the Idumean Herod's Judaism was suspect in some quarters (for the Idumeans had been forcibly converted to Judaism under John Hyrcanus [134–104 B.C.]), any rival claimant to the title would pose a danger to Herod. This was the title, of course, that was attached to the cross as the charge on which Jesus was crucified (see Matt 27:11, 29, 37).

his star at its rising: The idea that the births and deaths of great figures were accompanied by astral phenomena was widely accepted in antiquity. The nature of the astral phenomenon accompanying Jesus' birth has been variously interpreted as a new star (supernova), a comet, or the conjunction of the planets Jupiter and Saturn. The evidence for a planetary conjunction in 7 B.C. and its possible theological implications has been summarized by R. Rosenberg in *Bib* 53 (1972) 105–09. However, the qualifying expression "at its rising" would apply better to a supernova or a comet than to a planetary conjunction. But the motif of the star probably owes more to Num 24:17 ("a star shall come forth out of Jacob") than to such astral phenomena. Only in Matt 2:9 does the star clearly function as a guide for the Magi. For a Jewish text from the first century B.C. that accepts astrology as compatible with Judaism and climaxing in the Messiah's coming, see *Treatise of Shem* (*OTP* 1.473-86). See also the articles by J. H. Charlesworth in *HTR* 70 (1977) 183–200, and *BJRULM* 60 (1978) 376–403.

pay homage: The Greek word *proskyneō* refers to an act of submission (bowing, prostration) before a person of great dignity or authority. In this case it is to be done before a king ("king of the Jews"). The term also appears in Matt 2:8, 11, thus functioning as a major motif in the story. Since it can also describe the proper attitude of humans toward God, it may also carry forward the theme of Jesus as Son of God.

3. *all Jerusalem with him*: Here the city is personified, as it frequently is in the OT. The meaning, of course, is all the people of Jerusalem. For a similar generalization in the passion narrative, see Matt 27:25 ("all the people answered: 'His blood be on us and on our children' "). In both cases the "all" does not include every individual in Jerusalem.

4. *chief priests and scribes of the people*: The plural "chief priests" presumably covers former high priests and members of the high priestly family in addition to the current high priest. The scribes would have had expertise in the interpretation of the Scriptures and so could answer the question of the Magi regarding the birthplace of the King of the Jews. The mention of these groups here may also point forward to the enemies of Jesus during the passion story.

   the Messiah: Note that "King of the Jews" and "the Christ/Messiah" are used interchangeably (see Matt 2:2). The former title was more appropriate to Gentiles, and the latter to Jews.

5. *in Bethlehem of Judea*: That this was commonly accepted as the birthplace of the Messiah is suggested by John 7:42: "Has not the Scripture said that the Christ is descended from David, and comes from Bethlehem, the village where David was?"

   the prophet: Some manuscript witnesses try to specify the prophet as Micah or Isaiah. In fact the quotation is a combination of Mic 5:1(2) and 2 Sam 5:2.

   land of Judah: The "quotation" of Mic 5:1(2) appears in a modified version: "land of Judah" replaces "Ephrathah," probably to underscore the Messiah's descent from Judah (see Matt 1:1-2); "by no means" denies the insignificance of Bethlehem; "rulers" represents a variant pointing of the Hebrew root that also covers "clans"; and there is some abbreviation in the last line.

   who will shepherd: The end of the "quotation" comes from 2 Sam 5:2 ("you will shepherd my people Israel"). It has been modified only to bring it in line with the quotation from Micah ("who will shepherd").

8. *inform me*: Matt 2:12 implies that Herod expected the Magi to go to Jerusalem and to inform him directly. Herod's expressed desire to "pay homage" to the child contrasts with his real intentions (to be revealed in Matt 2:16-18) and with the genuine intentions of the Magi who wish only to pay homage to the newborn king of the Jews (see 2:2, 11).

9. *the star . . . went before them*: Now the movement of the star specifies where precisely the child is. The extent to which the star had served as a guide before this point had not been made clear.

10. *rejoiced*: The expression of their joy is described in very heightened terms so as to emphasize the point.

11. *the house*: Matthew seems to assume that Mary and Joseph live in a house at Bethlehem. He will go on to explain how they got from Bethlehem to Nazareth. On the contrary, Luke 2:1-7 explains how they first got from Nazareth to Bethlehem. Despite popular tradition it is not necessary to read Luke 2:7 as referring to a cave or a stable. It is more likely a reference to the part of a private house set apart for animals that could be used also as guest quarters in an emergency situation. So there is no need to see a direct contradiction between Matthew and Luke on this point. Both may well have envisioned Mary, Joseph, and Jesus in a house.

    paid him homage: Thus the Magi do what they set out to do (see 2:2) and what

Herod only feigned to do (2:8). See Matt 14:33 and 28:9, 17 for other instances of this attitude to Jesus.

gifts: It is from the list of three gifts (gold, frankincense, and myrrh) that the idea of *three* Magi arose. From a possible allusion to Ps 72:10 ("may the kings of Seba and Sheba bring gifts") emerged the idea that they were kings. The nature of the gifts suggests an allusion to Isa 60:6 ("all those from Sheba shall come; they shall bring gold and frankincense"). These places connect the Magi with Arabia or the Syrian Desert.

12. *through a dream*: For dreams as a means of divine communication, see Matt 1:20; 2:13, 19. But here (unlike the dreams of Joseph) there is no mention of "an angel of the Lord."

13. *Now after they departed*: The word "they" refers to the Magi. The Greek participial construction begins several episodes in the infancy narrative (see Matt 1:18; 2:1, 13, 19).

behold, an angel: A similar pattern appears in Matt 1:20; 2:19. The dreams featuring the angelic interpreter are the principal means of divine communication throughout the Matthean infancy story.

Egypt: Egypt, which came under Roman control in 30 B.C., was outside the jurisdiction of Herod. Egypt had been the traditional place of refuge for Jews both in biblical times (see 1 Kgs 11:40; Jer 26:21) and in the Maccabean era when the high priest Onias IV fled there.

Herod is going to seek out: The phrasing is reminiscent of Pharaoh's determination to kill Moses (see Exod 2:15). The description is consistent with Herod's ruthlessness in defending his royal prerogatives; see R. T. France, *NovT* 21 (1979) 98–120. The verb "destroy" appears again in the passion story (see Matt 27:20).

15. *until Herod's death*: Herod died in March-April of 4 B.C.

Out of Egypt: The quotation is from Hos 11:1. The wording of the quotation is much closer to the Hebrew text than to the Septuagint ("Out of Egypt I have summoned his children"). Matthew's emphasis is on Jesus as Son of God. The original context is Israel's exodus from Egypt; Israel is thus called the Son of God. Such a background for Jesus' divine sonship stresses the continuity between Jesus and Israel, for Jesus repeats the experience of Israel in the exodus generation. What is peculiar about the use of the quotation from Hos 11:1 is the direction: Whereas the quotation has God calling the son *out of* Egypt, the story has the Son going *into* Egypt. The two main points of convergence are Egypt and Son.

16. *Then Herod, seeing*: The same kind of construction introduces Herod's action in Matt 2:7. The verb *enepaichthē* ("deceived") carries the idea of ridicule or being made to look foolish. It appears again in the passion story with regard to the mockery of Jesus as king (see Matt 27:29, 31, 41).

all the male children: Since the rumor concerned the King of the Jews, Herod had only to fear male children as his rivals. The quotation from Jer 31:15 uses a more inclusive term *tekna*. According to *Testament of Moses* 6:2-7, Herod was rash and perverse, one who would "kill old and young, showing mercy to none."

from two years old and below: The model for Herod's action is supplied by Pharaoh's decree to kill all the Hebrew male children (see Exod 1:15-22). Since Herod died in 4 B.C. and the star arose some two years before, it has become customary to date Jesus' birth to 7 or 6 B.C. (see Luke 1:5; 3:23). We are to assume that Herod took all possible precautions to destroy his alleged rival.

17. *Jeremiah*: The quotation in the following verse is from Jer 31:15. Other Jeremiah quotations appear in Matt 16:14 and 27:9. Matthew may also have perceived Jeremiah as a model for Jesus, especially in the passion narrative; see R. E. Winkle, *AUSS* 24 (1986) 155–72.

18. *in Ramah*: Ramah was halfway between Bethel and Jerusalem. According to Gen 35:19, Rachel died on the way to Ephrath, which is identified as Bethlehem. The identification probably reflects movement on the part of some of the clan of Ephrath(ah) to Bethlehem. This tradition led Matthew to associate the slaughter of the innocents with Rachel's weeping.

    Rachel weeping: Whereas in Jer 31:16-17 Rachel is told to stop weeping because her children are coming back from exile, here the quotation is used in a context of unrelieved suffering. The quotation of Jer 31:15 in Matt 2:18 seems to be an independent Greek translation of the Hebrew text; it is close to the A version of the Septuagint. The OT wording has not been substantially tailored to fit the incident described in Matt 2:16.

19. *Now after Herod died*: The linguistic constructions and vocabulary of Matt 2:19-21 flow from the previous episodes and carry on a continuity with them.

20. *those who were seeking*: The principal seeker of the child's life was Herod (see Matt 2:13). The plural suggests the complicity of the "chief priests and scribes" (2:4) and perhaps even "all Jerusalem" (2:3). This expression points forward to the passion story and the enemies of Jesus there (see 26:3). There is probably also a look backward to the enemies of Moses: "Go back to Egypt; for all the men who were seeking your life are dead" (Exod 4:19).

22. *Archelaus*: On Herod's death in 4 B.C. his kingdom was divided among his three sons: Archelaus, Herod Antipas, and Philip. Archelaus was given control over Judea, Samaria, and Idumea. His rule as ethnarch was characterized by cruelty and political chaos until the Romans stepped in (A.D. 6) and began appointing their own governors (the most famous of which is Pontius Pilate).

    Galilee: Galilee (along with Perea) was given to Herod Antipas (see Luke 23:6-12). Compared to Judea, it would have been more peaceful and secure. The relative security of Galilee is the implied motive for Joseph's decision to go to Nazareth. Matthew gives no indication that Joseph and Mary came from Nazareth, as Luke does.

23. *Nazareth*: The place was an agricultural village not far from the Via Maris, the main trade route to Egypt. It is not mentioned in the OT. The reference to it in John 1:46 ("Can anything good come out of Nazareth?") underlines its insignificance.

    "He will be called a Nazorean": The alleged quotation is neither the direct quotation nor adaptation of any known OT text. The term "Nazorean" has three prin-

cipal derivations: from the place-name Nazareth, from *nāzîr* as one devoted to God (see Judg 13:5, 7), and from *nēṣer* meaning "branch" and used with reference to the Messiah (see Isa 11:1). It is likely that the readers were expected to keep all three connotations in mind rather than one alone. The latter two derivations would qualify the expression as a biblical quotation, and the first would tie them into the place in which Jesus lived.

Interpretation

Matthew 1 focused on the identity of Jesus. It first answered the question "Who is Jesus?" by relating him genealogically to Abraham and David. Then it showed how Joseph became the legal father of Jesus and how he got the name Jesus. In Matthew 2 the emphasis shifts from the identity of Jesus to a series of places. If the major concern of chapter 1 was "Who?," the major concern of chapter 2 is "Where?"

It is customary to divide Matthew 2 into four segments: the coming of the Magi (2:1-12), the flight into Egypt (2:13-15), the slaughter of the innocent children (2:16-18), and the return from Egypt (2:19-23). In fact it is probably better to divide the Magi story into two parts according to the place in which the action occurs: Jerusalem (2:1-6) and Bethlehem (2:7-12). This division in turn highlights the significance of the places in the remaining episodes: Egypt (2:13-15), Bethlehem and Ramah (2:16-18), and Egypt and Nazareth (2:19-23). Each of the final three episodes concludes with a biblical quotation that relates to the place featured in that episode. At the center of the Magi story (2:6) is a biblical quotation that focuses on Bethlehem. So the basic question dealt with in Matthew 2 is "Where?"

In Christian piety the individual stories in Matthew 2 have been mixed with the corresponding material in Luke 2 into the "Christmas story"—an often uncritical harmonization of the biblical accounts blended with popular imagination. The result has been even greater impetus to read the episodes in Matthew 2 as separate and self-contained units.

Yet when we look about for the Jewish background of the four (or five) incidents in Matthew 2, we can recapture their literary and theological unity. That unity is supplied by the birth and childhood of Moses—in both the biblical narrative in the Book of Exodus and the later elaborations of that narrative. The Moses-Jesus typology underlying Matthew 2 enables us to find the unity among the various episodes.

The question of the historical character of the narratives in Matthew 2 is a complicated issue. It is sometimes claimed that these narratives are "midrash," in the sense of being elaborations built upon biblical texts rather than real events. No matter what decision (historical or literary creations) is finally made, attention to the biblical background of these episodes in the Moses narratives will heighten the reader's appreciation of them.

For their historicity one can point to many features that are compatible with what is known from other sources: the character of Herod the Great, Jewish interest in astrology, Egypt as a place of refuge for Jews, etc. Moreover, the scriptural quotations that serve to end the last three episodes do not fit exactly: "out of Egypt," the location of Ramah, and the origin of the "Nazorean" quotation. If someone wished to create incidents out of biblical quotations, it was possible to have done a better job.

Against the historicity of these episodes stand the facts that they are not paralleled in Luke's infancy narrative nor are they mentioned elsewhere in the New Testament. Moreover, these spectacular events—the star guiding the Magi to the birthplace of the Jewish Messiah, the slaughter of many innocent children in Bethlehem and its environs—are not corroborated by extrabiblical sources. The device of dream vision and angelic appearance is not the stuff on which scientific historiography relies.

The historicity of these episodes remains an open question that probably can never be definitively decided. The more important issue is determining what these stories meant to Matthew and his community.

The early chapters of the Book of Exodus tell about the birth and youth of Moses. For the interpretation of Matthew's infancy narrative the following points are most important. Pharaoh, the wicked king of the Egyptians, decrees that Moses and all Hebrew male children be killed (Exod 1:16, 22). But Moses is saved in a marvelous way through the intervention of Pharaoh's daughter (Exod 2:1-10). Afraid of being punished for killing an Egyptian, the young man Moses flees from Pharaoh into the land of Midian (Exod 2:15). After Pharaoh's death (Exod 2:23), the Lord directs Moses to return from Midian to Egypt "for all the men who were seeking your life are dead" (Exod 4:19).

So there are parallels between the stories of Moses and Jesus: the decree of death from the wicked king, flight to escape the decree, the slaughter of innocent children, and the return after the death of the wicked king. There are of course some obvious differences. Pharaoh is king of the Egyptians, whereas Herod claims to be king of the Jews. Moses flees from Egypt into Midian, whereas Jesus flees from Judea into Egypt. The Moses story encompasses his birth and life as a young man, whereas Jesus remains an infant throughout Matthew 2. The first two differences may be deliberate contrasts with Moses, designed to draw attention to the bad leadership in Judea in Jesus' time and to the idea of Jerusalem as the place in which Jesus is rejected. We can assume that Matthew's readers would have heard echoes of the Moses-story in Matthew 2.

That the story of Moses' birth was a topic for reflection in Jesus' time is indicated by ps.-Philo's *Biblical Antiquities* 9:9-15. While much of that text is quotation or paraphrase of Exodus 2, there are some divergences that are quite like what appears in Matthew 2. The Spirit of God initiates the chain of events leading up to Moses' birth: "And the Spirit of God came upon Miriam . . . (9:10)." Both Miriam (9:10) and Pharaoh's daughter (9:15) know what to do because God has communicated with them through dreams. In Miriam's dream a "man in a linen garment" (9:10) tells her what to say to her parents about the son to be born to them. This angelic figure relates the name of Moses to his mission as an adult: "Behold he who will be born from you will be cast forth into the water; likewise through him the water will be dried up" (9:10). The slaughter of the innocents that was only threatened in Exodus 1 is actually carried out according to *Bib. Ant.* 9:12: "the king of Egypt appointed local chiefs who, when the Hebrew women gave birth, would immediately throw their male children into the river."

Another reflective expansion of the Exodus 1–2 narrative appears in Josephus' *Antiquities* 2:205-37. The persecution of the Hebrews is sparked off by a prediction about a marvelous child: "One of the sacred scribes—persons with considerable skill in accurately predicting the future—announced to the king that there would be born to the Israelites at that time one who would abase the sovereignty of the Egyptians and exalt the Israelites, were he reared to manhood, and would surpass all men in virtue and win everlasting renown" (2:205). The birth of Moses is announced to his father Amram in a dream by God: "And God . . . appeared to him in his sleep" (2:212). He also announces Moses' mission as an adult: "He shall deliver the Hebrew race from their bondage in Egypt" (2:216). The reason why Moses' mother was able to escape notice was the easiness of her giving birth to Moses: "She escaped the vigilance of the watch, thanks to the gentleness of her travail, which spared her any violent throes" (2:218).

These two examples of the "rewritten Bible" indicate that the birth of Moses was a topic of reflection among Jews of Jesus' time. They also show how the biblical narrative was embellished rather freely. Several of these embellishments have parallels in Matthew 2.

The reference to the sacred scribe of the Egyptians raises the issue about the biblical background of the Magi. Davies argues that the biblical model is supplied by the Egyptian wise men and sorcerers, the magicians, who enter into contests with Moses (see Exodus 7–8) and finally are forced to acknowledge that the "finger of God" is with Moses and Aaron (see Exod 8:19). The obvious problem here is the very negative portrayal of the Egyptian magicians in contrast to the positive presentation of the Magi in Matt 2:1-12.

A more convincing possibility (suggested by Brown) as the biblical model for the Magi is Balaam as he is portrayed in Numbers 22–24. The pagan seer prophesies good for Israel instead of bad, thus frustrating the evil plans of King Balak. The climax of his prophecies comes in Num 24:17: "a star shall come forth out of Jacob, and a scepter shall arise out of Israel." This identification is strengthened by the fact that Philo of Alexandria (*Life of Moses* 1:276) called Balaam a *magos*.

When Matthew 2 is taken as a literary whole and read against the background of Exodus 1–2, Jesus emerges as a Moses-figure. (The expression "new Moses" may convey the impression that the "old Moses" was unimportant, and therefore it is better avoided.) With the various stories in chapter 2 Matthew sought to express a continuity between Moses and Jesus: In both cases a wicked king (Pharaoh and Herod) tried to do away with them as infants; their escape was accompanied by a slaughter of innocent children; and return became possible only after those who sought the child's life had died.

While Matthew pointed his readers backward to Moses, he also pointed them forward to Jesus' passion and death. The comments above show how hints about the passion narrative are sprinkled through chapter 2 (see Matt 2:2, 3, 4, 16, 20). From the start Jesus was associated with suffering and death. Whereas for many people the story of the "holy innocents" is an anomaly in the Christmas story, for Matthew it was an integral part of Jesus' infancy.

The Moses-theme and the passion-prefiguration run through Matthew 2. The individual episodes carry subsidiary themes, especially with respect to the itinerary of Jesus. The Magi (Matt 2:1-12) come from the East to Jerusalem and ascertain where the king of the Jews is to be born. His birth at Bethlehem is determined from Mic 5:1(2) and 2 Sam 5:2 (see Matt 2:6). The flight into Egypt (Matt 2:13-15) is explained with reference to Hos 11:1 (see Matt 2:15). The slaying of the infants (Matt 2:16-18) culminates in the quotation of Jer 31:5, and the return to Nazareth (Matt 2:19-23) is said to have a basis in Scripture (see Matt 2:23). The combination of these place-names and the Scripture quotations at each point indicates that the itinerary of Jesus is "according to the Scriptures," that is, in accord with God's will as revealed in the Bible.

Another central theme concerns the Magi as models for Gentile believers. Matthew's Gospel ends with the risen Lord's command to "make disciples of all the Gentiles" (28:19). In setting that scene Matthew says that the eleven disciples "paid homage" to Jesus (28:17)—the same term that features so prominently in the Magi story (2:2, 8, 11). Matthew sets up a deliberate contrast between the Gentile Magi who sincerely wish to pay homage to the "king of the Jews" (2:2, 11) and Herod who claims to be "king of Jews" and feigns offering homage to Jesus (2:8). Thus the Magi prefigure those Gentiles who are part of Matthew's community.

The possibilities for actualizing Matthew 2 correspond to its major themes. The Moses-typology roots Jesus in the history of Israel; indeed his divine sonship is specifically tied to Israel's experience as a people ("out of Egypt

I called my son," 2:15). The references ahead to the passion narrative remind us that the mystery of the Cross was present in Jesus' life from the beginning. The theme of fulfilling God's will is carried forward by the itinerary and its scriptural warrants. The Magi's role as prefiguring the acceptance of Gentiles into the Christian community points toward the universal character of the gospel; it is meant to be shared with all peoples.

For Reference and Further Study

Brown, R. E. *The Birth of the Messiah,* 165–230.

Davies, W. D. *Setting,* 77-82.

France, R. T. "The Formula-Quotations of Matthew 2 and the Problem of Communication." *NTS* 27 (1981) 233–51.

__________. "Herod and the Children of Bethlehem." *NovT* 21 (1979) 98–120.

Gnuse, R. "Dream Genre in the Matthean Infancy Narratives." *NovT* 32 (1990) 97–120.

Schmahl, G. "Magier aus dem Osten und die Heiligen Drei Könige." *TTZ* 87 (1978) 295–303.

4. *John the Baptist* (3:1-6)

1. Now in those days John the Baptist came preaching in the wilderness
of Judea, 2. saying: "Repent, for the kingdom of heaven has drawn near."
3. For this was the one spoken about through Isaiah the prophet: "The voice
of one crying in the wilderness: 'Prepare the way of the Lord, make straight
his paths.' " 4. Now John had his clothing of camel's hair and a leather
belt about his loins. His food was locusts and wild honey. 5. Then Jerusalem and all Judea and all the region around the Jordan were going out
to him 6. and being baptized in the Jordan River by him, confessing their
sins.

Notes

1. *in those days*: An OT expression is used to mark the beginning of a new period, not to give a precise indication of time. In fact the story has moved quickly from the infancy of Jesus to his adulthood. John the Baptist arrives on the scene without introduction; in Luke, John is a major figure in the infancy narrative, and in Mark his ministry marks "the beginning of the good news."

wilderness of Judea: By adding the place-name Matthew makes explicit what is implicit in Mark. The expression refers to the area east of Jerusalem, sloping down toward the Dead Sea. In this area the Qumran community had its settlement, and there is evidence of other religious movements in the area.

2. *repent*: Matthew makes the idea of repentance part of John's direct discourse, whereas in Mark 1:4 and Luke 3:3 it is part of the narrative: "preaching a baptism of repentance for the remission of sins." The biblical idea of repentance involves a willingness to turn one's life around in the sense of a complete reorientation.

   For the kingdom of heaven has drawn near: Matthew alone supplies the reason why John preached repentance. The motive is the nearness of God's kingdom ("has drawn near"). Thus John says the exact same thing as Jesus does (see 4:17). The "kingdom of heaven" (a characteristically Matthean expression) refers to the fullness of God's power and presence that will be acknowledged by all creation. In preparation for that display and in recognition of its nearness, repentance is the proper response.

3. *Isaiah*: The quotation that follows is from Isa 40:3 (LXX). Matthew has avoided the problem posed by Mark 1:2 where the quotation of Exod 23:20/Mal 3:1 comes under the rubric of "Isaiah." Matthew uses Exod 23:20/Mal 3:1 in Matt 11:10, in another context referring to John. The introduction to the Isaiah quotation does not follow the "formula" of the fulfillment quotations throughout Matthew.

   the voice: Isa 40:3 was part of the oracle of comfort beginning the so-called Second Isaiah. In its OT context the passage refers to the return of the exiled community in Babylon to Jerusalem ca. 538 B.C. ("in the wilderness prepare the way of the Lord"). In its NT context the "voice in the wilderness" is John and the "Lord" is Jesus. Matthew follows Mark in quoting the Septuagint version but changing the end from "our God's" to "his." For the use of this quotation by the Qumran community as supplying a rationale for its life by the Dead Sea, see 1QS 8:14; 9:19.

4. *Now John*: Matthew has reversed Mark's order by placing first the personal description of John (Matt 3:4 = Mark 1:6) and then the mention of his baptizing activity second (Matt 3:5-6 = Mark 1:5). The Matthean order allows a smoother transition to the discourse material presented in Matt 3:7-12.

   camel's hair and a leather belt: With this garb John stands in line with the OT prophet Elijah (see 2 Kgs 1:8). This apparel may have marked John simply as a prophetic figure in general. But given the interest in John as a "new Elijah" (see Mal 3:1; 4:5) this outfit may have been intended more specifically with reference to Elijah (see Matt 11:7-15; 17:10-13).

   locusts and wild honey: Such food could be found in the "wilderness" where John was preaching. That John's motive in this diet was ritual purity rather than asceticism is suggested by S. L. Davies, *NTS* 29 (1983) 569–71.

5. *Jerusalem and all Judea*: For an earlier personification of Jerusalem, see Matt 2:3. Matthew has changed and expanded Mark 1:5 ("all the country of Judea and the people of Jerusalem"). Both evangelists exaggerate the impact of John by the use of "all." Matthew has prepared for John's discourse in the following sections.

6. *being baptized*: The term "baptize" evokes images of being dipped down in water and even drowning. The River Jordan was used as the place of John's ritual, which signified the intention to repent in light of the nearness of God's kingdom (see

Matt 3:2). The confession of sins accompanying the baptism relates to the repentance demanded by John and to God's willingness to forgive sins.

Interpretation

In Matt 3:1-6 we see a careful editor at work—careful to transmit the basic message of his source (Mark 1:2-6) while doing the kinds of tasks that a good editor performs: integrating the source into his own narrative ("Now in those days," 3:1), supplying explanations ("for the kingdom of heaven has drawn near," 3:2), correcting mistakes in the source ("through Isaiah," 3:3), and rearranging material to make his presentation more coherent and effective (3:4, 5-6). The evangelist is clearly respectful of his source (to the point of reusing the omitted Exod 23:20/Mal 3:1 in Matt 11:10) but free to make changes and move material around. Perhaps the most dramatic change comes in Matt 3:2 in which John says: "Repent, for the kingdom of heaven has drawn near." Thus Matthew has John say precisely the same thing that Jesus says in Matt 4:17. This device has the effect of relating the two figures by way of content and marking off a literary unit that begins with John (3:1) and leads up to Jesus' calling his first disciples (4:18-22).

In the midst of his description of the death of John the Baptist at the hands of Herod Antipas (*Ant.* 18:116-119), Josephus provides the following description of John's person and activity: "He was a good man and had exhorted the Jews to lead righteous lives, to practice justice toward their fellows and piety toward God, and so doing to join in baptism. In his view this was a necessary preliminary if baptism was to be acceptable to God. They must not employ it to gain pardon for whatever sins they committed, but as a consecration of the body implying that the soul was already thoroughly cleansed by right behavior" (117).

The remainder of Josephus' description of John will be taken up in connection with the Matthean account of John's death (Matt 14:1-12). But some general remarks about *Antiquities* 18:116-119 are in order here. The long-standing debate about the authenticity of the passage (Did Josephus write it, or has a later writer inserted it?) has moved rather firmly in the direction of accepting it as composed by Josephus. Yet acceptance of its general authenticity does not rule out the possibility that the text has been retouched by scribes in the process of transmission. Even more important is the recognition that Josephus had his own purposes and tendencies as a writer, and so his statements should not necessarily be taken at face value as an accurate record of historical events. He wrote some sixty years after the death of John. He worked at Rome under the patronage of the Flavian emperors. He aimed to explain what had gone wrong with the Jewish revolt of A.D. 66–73 and in the process to get even with his old enemies in Palestine.

Josephus' picture of John the Baptist is basically positive. John appears as a Jewish preacher whose message concerns justice toward others and piety toward God. John's ritual of baptism is described in a somewhat tortuous way, suggesting that Josephus was trying to avoid misunderstandings and misinterpretations. He insists that justice and piety were preliminaries to John's baptism and that the baptism of the body symbolized the cleansing of the soul. On the other hand, he goes out of his way to deny that John's baptism brought about the forgiveness of sins.

The style of Josephus' report about John is abstract, using terms like "justice" and "piety" that would be interpreted differently by Jews (who would understand them in a biblical context) and Gentiles (who would read them more in a philosophical context). One could say that Josephus was simply making Jewish ideas more intelligible to non-Jews. But this benign interpretation may not be entirely accurate. Another tendency in Josephus' works is to play down Jewish eschatology (see below on Matt 3:7-10) or to pass it off as dangerous and irresponsible. If we are to believe the Gospel tradition about John, the horizon for his preaching and baptism was the coming kingdom of God. Josephus appears to have stripped away this dimension from John's career and made him into a popular Jewish preacher. Then it becomes hard to understand why John was perceived by Herod Antipas as a fomentor of sedition (*Ant.* 18:118-119; see also the discussion of Matt 14:1-12).

In the Gospels (see Matt 3:1-6; Mark 1:2-6; Luke 3:1-6; John 1:19-23) John's preaching and baptism are oriented to the coming kingdom of God and to preparing the way of the Lord. His clothing ("camel's hair and a leather belt") suggests that the prophet Elijah was his model (see 2 Kgs 1:8). His baptism involved the confession of sins and repentance (see Matt 3:6, 11) as a means of escaping the "coming wrath" (3:7). At several points he plays the role of Elijah (see Matt 11:7-15; 17:10-13; Mark 9:11-13) who must come before the kingdom will appear (see Mal 4:5-6), though in John 1:21 he denies that he is Elijah.

The Lukan infancy narrative links John the Baptist and Jesus together in a family relationship (to which none of the other Gospels allude). In Luke 1–2 there is drawn an elaborate parallelism between the birth-announcements and births of the two figures that serves to highlight the superiority of Jesus over John. According to Luke, John was the son of Zechariah and Elizabeth and so from a priestly family, and a cousin to Jesus through Elizabeth's relationship to Mary (see Luke 1:36).

All the evangelists take care to distinguish Jesus from John the Baptist. Jesus' seeking out of John and requesting his baptism indicate some contact between the two in which John has the role of mentor. Yet when Jesus begins his public activity, John is off the scene (Matt 4:12; Mark 1:14; Luke 3:20; cf. John 3:23-24). There are attempts to clarify the relationship between the two (John 1:6-9; 1:19-23) with the result that Jesus' independence of and superiority to John the Baptist are emphasized.

Acts contains two stories (18:24-28; 19:1-7) that indicate the survival of John's movement after the death of its founder (and of Jesus). Apollos of Alexandria is said to have known "only the baptism of John" (Acts 18:25). The disciples at Ephesus had been baptized only "into John's baptism" (Acts 19:3). Such people need instruction from followers of Jesus and in the case of John's disciples at Ephesus baptism in the name of the Lord Jesus and the gift of the Holy Spirit (Acts 19:5-6).

The evidence about John the Baptist from Josephus and the New Testament indicates that in Matt 3:1-6 we are being introduced to an important historical character. His preaching and baptism attracted crowds of people, including Jesus. It was so popular that Herod Antipas feared an uprising and had John first imprisoned and then executed. John's reputation was such that the early Christians took pains to differentiate him from Jesus and to underline John's inferiority. The movement that he began survived his death and spread at least to Ephesus in Asia Minor.

When the Dead Sea Scrolls were discovered in the late 1940s and the first documents were published, many writers argued that John the Baptist had been a member of the group that produced those scrolls. This identification was suggested by several factors: the general location (the Judean wilderness) in which John was active and the Qumran community lived, their ascetic lifestyles, their common interest in the coming kingdom of God, and their ritual uses of water (see below on Matt 3:11-12). While John could have been a member of the Qumran community at some point (see Luke 1:80: "and he was in the wilderness until the day of his manifestation"), one should be cautious about jumping to conclusions on this matter. On the one hand, there seem to have been many religious groups and movements in the general area of the Judean wilderness. John need not have been an Essene or a member of the Qumran community. On the other hand, John differed from the Qumran community on some matters, especially about the significance of the baptism that he proclaimed.

The message to Matthew's community would have been the standard early Christian message about John the Baptist. The text supplied them with basic information about a relation to Jesus and his preaching (they say the same thing), and suggested an ultimate relationship of inferior ("the voice of one crying in the wilderness"), and superior ("Prepare the way of the Lord, make straight his paths") between John and Jesus.

In the Church year John the Baptist is most prominent in the Advent season. The role of "precursor" attributed to him by way of Isa 40:3 gets particular emphasis. Attention to the Gospel tradition and to Josephus, however, suggests that his relationship to Jesus was not so simple and untroubled as the "precursor" theme allows. Without denying this traditional role it may be useful to highlight the tensions about John's popularity and the survival of his movement so that Christians today can appreciate what was at stake in assigning the role of precursor to John the Baptist.

For Reference and Further Study

Feldman, L. H. *Josephus and Modern Scholarship (1937–1980)* (Berlin–New York: de Gruyter, 1984) 673–79.

Meier, J. P. "John the Baptist in Matthew's Gospel." *JBL* 99 (1980) 383–405.

Scobie, C. H. H. *John the Baptist.* Philadelphia: Fortress, 1964.

Wink, W. *John the Baptist in the Gospel Tradition.* SNTSMS 7. Cambridge, U.K.: Cambridge University Press, 1968.

5. *John's Preaching* (3:7-10)

7. Seeing many of the Pharisees and Sadducees coming for baptism, he said to them: "Brood of vipers, who taught you to flee from the coming wrath? 8. Produce fruit appropriate to repentance. 9. And do not think to say among yourselves 'We have Abraham as father.' For I say to you that God can raise up from these stones children to Abraham. 10. The ax already lies at the root of the trees. Therefore every tree not producing good fruit is cut down and thrown into the fire."

Notes

7. *coming for baptism*: John's address to these Pharisees and Sadducees ("brood of vipers") distinguishes them from those people described in 3:5-6 as sincere seekers after John's baptism. It is not proper to say that these Pharisees and Sadducees represent Israel. Rather they are part of Matthew's polemic against Jesus' opponents within Israel and the opponents of his own community.

   vipers: Vipers were a genus of snakes prevalent in antiquity; some were poisonous, and some were not. Since the bite of the poisonous vipers could be fatal, the term was used metaphorically for evil or evil people (see Matt 12:34; 23:33).

   coming wrath: The term refers to God's intervention on the Day of the Lord, one aspect of which is to be God's expression of his negative feeling toward sin and sinners (see Rom 2:5, 8; 5:9; 9:22). John's baptism was a sign of repentance before the Day of the Lord, thus exempting the baptized from God's wrath.

8. *produce fruit*: The Pharisees and Sadducees are warned not to imagine that the mere ritual of baptism will preserve them from God's wrath. Rather they must do the good deeds that are appropriate to genuine repentance in view of the

coming kingdom. The image of Israel as a tree from which fruit is expected appears in Hos 9:16; Isa 27:6; Jer 12:2; 17:8; Ezek 17:8-9, 23.

9. *we have Abraham as father*: Belonging to the children of Abraham will not protect those who refuse to repent and do good works. There may be an allusion here to the rabbinic idea of the "merits of the fathers" according to which the righteousness of the patriarchs is charged to the account of Israel (see S. Schechter, *Aspects of Rabbinic Theology* [New York: Schocken, 1961] 170–98).

   from these stones children: When translated from Greek to Aramaic (or Hebrew) there is a clear play on words—*'abnayyā'* ("stones") and *bĕnayyā'* ("children")—that suggests a Semitic stage in the process of transmission. The idea is that God's power far surpasses the laws of natural lineage. The Matthean community may have read a reference to the Gentile mission into this saying.

   to Abraham: In Galatians 3 and Romans 4 Paul developed arguments about the true children of Abraham and concluded that Abraham's children included those who followed his example of fidelity. The question about what constitutes a child of Abraham is contained in kernel form in Matt 3:9.

10. *the ax*: The warning about doing good deeds in the face of the coming wrath is presented and expanded with the picture of an ax used in cutting down a tree (see Isa 10:33). Destruction is so close that only producing good fruit can save the tree from being thrown into the fire. This third warning heightens the first warning.

INTERPRETATION

John's discourse begins with three warnings (Matt 3:7b-8, 9, 10) directed toward "many of the Pharisees and Sadducees." The fundamental assumption of the warnings is the closeness of the Day of the Lord (and the judgment that will be part of it). John urges them (1) not to imagine that the ritual of baptism alone will protect them, (2) not to think that belonging to the children of Abraham will protect them, and (3) not to waste the little time that is left.

Matt 3:7-10 is the first Q section in the Gospel. It is very close in wording to Luke 3:7-9, with the only significant difference coming in the audience for John's warnings: "Pharisees and Sadducees" (Matt 3:7) versus "the multitudes" (Luke 3:7). Since Luke is generally more conservative in preserving Q and since Matthew frequently uses "Pharisees and Sadducees" to designate the Jewish opponents of Jesus, Luke 3:7 may represent the reading of Q. Or it is possible that Q mentioned no audience, and each evangelist constructed his own characteristic framework, with Luke opting for the generalizing "multitudes" and Matthew for the more specific "Pharisees and Sadducees."

In Matthew this text presents the first encounter with the Jewish groups that will constitute chief rivals of Jesus during his public ministry. The

Pharisees were most likely the chief rivals of Matthew and his community after the destruction of Jerusalem and its Temple in A.D. 70. It is also likely that Matthew has sharpened and even exaggerated the negative portrayal of the Pharisees during Jesus' time in light of his experiences with them after A.D. 70.

The Pharisees were a Jewish group active in Palestine from the second century B.C. to the first century A.D. Their name probably has some connection to the Hebrew word for "separate" (*pāraš*); they are the "separated ones." The Pharisees developed traditions on how to live out the Torah in everyday life. They emphasized ritual purity, food tithes, and Sabbath observance. They were admired by the people, and at times held social and even political power. Their specific teachings will be treated in the course of the commentary as we move into passages that present them in controversy with Jesus.

The Sadducees were active in Palestine up to the destruction of the temple in A.D. 70. They took their name from the high priestly family of Zadok (1 Kgs 1:26), or possibly from the "just ones" (*ṣaddîqîm*). They rivalled the Pharisees for power and influence, and are generally thought to have dominated the temple personnel, the wealthy, and the political elite. They differed from the Pharisees with regard to the latter's approach to tradition and with respect to their convictions about immortality and Divine Providence.

It is doubtful that John's message was directed specifically to the Pharisees and Sadducees. By so directing it Matthew has introduced the chief Jewish rivals of Jesus (and of his own community) and suggested that John's message had particular relevance for them.

By directing John's warnings to the Pharisees and Sadducees, Matthew has not only fulfilled the literary function of introducing the antagonists of Jesus but also insinuated some charges against them. These charges include failure to take appropriate action (3:8, 10) and excessive reliance upon physical descent from Abraham (3:9). Such charges, especially against the Pharisees, will be repeated and expanded as the Gospel proceeds, and will reach their climax in chapter 23. To Matthew's community, which was locked in a religious conflict with the Pharisaic movement after A.D. 70, this version of John's preaching would have summarized some of their complaints about the Pharisees.

Attention to Matthew's editorial achievement and its significance for late first-century Christians should not distract from the positive content of John's message as it is presented in Matt 3:7-10. The horizon of John's message is the coming kingdom of God and the judgment that accompanies it. John urges action that is appropriate to repentance, for the time is short. The themes of the nearness of God's kingdom and the kind of action that is appropriate to it will be developed as the Gospel proceeds. They remained major concerns for Matthew and his community.

In preaching or teaching on this passage one might accent the relation between God's kingdom and appropriate action. This point, which is the perennial concern of Christian ethics, has its basis in the Jewish apocalypticism represented by John the Baptist and taken over as a theological framework by Jesus and early Christians such as Matthew.

In dealing with Jesus' opponents several strategies are possible. One can stress the historical situation of the Matthean community after A.D. 70 and treat the polemic of the Gospel as bound to that set of circumstances. Or one might balance off the negative Gospel portraits of the Pharisees (and Sadducees) with some positive material from Jewish sources that give a better idea of their goals and programs. Or one may do what preachers and teachers of many ages have done: "spiritualize" or "moralize" by regarding Jesus' opponents as serious religious people who have gotten their priorities confused. At any rate, one must be sensitive to the anti-Semitic potential involved in identifying the "Pharisees and Sadducees" of Matthew with the Jewish people as a whole either only in antiquity or throughout history and today.

For Reference and Further Study

LeMoyne, J. *Les Sadducéens.* Paris: Gabalda, 1972.

Menahem, R. "A Jewish Commentary on the New Testament: A Sample Verse." *Immanuel* 21 (1987) 43–54.

Neusner, J. *From Politics to Piety.* Englewood Cliffs, N.J.: Prentice-Hall, 1973.

Rivkin, E. *The Hidden Revolution.* Nashville: Abingdon, 1978.

Saldarini, A. J. *Pharisees, Scribes and Sadducees in Palestinian Society. A Sociological Approach.* Wilmington: Glazier, 1988.

6. *The Baptisms of John and Jesus* (3:11-12)

11. "I baptize you in water for repentance. The one who comes after me
is mightier than I am; I am not worthy to carry his sandals—he will baptize
you in the Holy Spirit and fire. 12. His winnowing fork is in his hand; and
he will clear his threshing floor and will gather his wheat into the barn;
but the chaff he will burn with an unquenchable fire."

Notes

11. *I baptize you*: The saying shows a chiastic structure: A—baptism of water, B—person of John, B[1]—person of Jesus, A[1]—baptism in the Holy Spirit and fire.

As a person Jesus is mightier than John; likewise Jesus' baptism is more powerful than John's baptism.

for repentance: In Matt 3:2 this expression was avoided (cf. Mark 1:4; Luke 3:3). Here it is taken up and used without embarrassment (cf. Matt 3:13-17). The context of repentance is preparation for the eschaton; the baptism in the Holy Spirit and fire signals the presence of the eschaton, thus underscoring the superiority of Jesus' baptism.

mightier: Out of context or in another context it might be possible to interpret this expression as a reference to God the Father. But here (and in Luke 3:16) it surely refers to Jesus. The superiority of Jesus to John the Baptist is a major theme in the Lukan infancy narrative.

to carry his sandals: John professes that he is not worthy even to perform a service appropriate to a slave for Jesus. Both Mark 1:7 and Luke 3:16 use a slightly different image: "to loosen the strap of his sandals."

in the Holy Spirit and fire: For the refining fire of the Day of the Lord see Zech 13:9; 1 Cor 3:13-15. Mark 1:8 simply reads "the Holy Spirit." An earlier form of the saying may have read "wind and fire," a reference to two symbols of the coming of God's kingdom; see J. D. G. Dunn, *NovT* 14 (1972) 81–92.

12. *winnowing fork*: The term refers to the hand device used by a farmer to throw into the air the shredded grain and straw. The wind would then carry away the lighter chaff, and the grain would fall back to the ground. The "threshing floor" was the flat surface on which this procedure was carried out. The winnowed grain was stored in barns, and the chaff was burned. Jer 15:7 uses the image to describe God's judgment against Jerusalem: "I have winnowed them with a winnowing fork." In Matt 3:12 the image refers to God's coming eschatological judgment, which will include a separation between good and evil people as well as reward and punishment for them (see Matt 13:30, 40-43, 49).

Interpretation

The second part of John's discourse (Matt 3:11-12) compares John and Jesus (and their baptisms) and then issues another warning about the coming judgment. The material is from Q (see Luke 3:16-17), though there are overlaps between Matt 3:11-12/Luke 3:16-17 and Mark 1:7-8.

The baptism of John both differs from and is similar to other Jewish water rituals. With regard to rituals in the tent of meeting and then the Jerusalem Temple, priests were expected to perform washings before offering sacrifice (see Exod 40:12). On the Day of Atonement the high priest is directed to wash before (Lev 16:4) and after (Lev 16:24) the sacrifice. While such washings are superficially like John's baptism, there are obvious differences: The Temple rituals are self-administered, concern ritual rather than moral purity, and have no eschatological dimension.

The Qumran community practiced ritual washings as part of their daily routine. In fact they even constructed an elaborate system of water channels that made possible bathing in non-stagnant water. As in the case of the Temple rituals the Qumran washings were self-administered, repeatable, and concerned with ritual purity. Since the major figure in the community's early days was the Teacher of Righteousness (whose legitimate claim to the high priesthood had been ignored) and since the spirituality of the community was "priestly" (see 1QS 9:3-7), it is not surprising that its members adapted Temple rites to their new life in the Judean wilderness. There is some evidence, however, that at Qumran this community stressed the interior dispositions of the one undergoing the washing and the role of the Spirit in cleansing from sin. That such washings should be connected to moral purity is not surprising (see Isa 1:16-17; Jer 4:14; Ezek 36:25): "By his soul's humility toward all the precepts of God shall his flesh be cleansed when sprinkled with lustral water and sanctified in flowing water" (1QS 3:8-9).

Rabbinic sources also allude to the institution of proselyte baptism. When a Gentile decided to become a Jew, he or she underwent a ritual immersion that signified separation from "uncircumcision" (see *m. Pesah.* 8:8; *m. Eduy.* 5:2; *b. Yebam.* 46-47). A male convert was also circumcised. Though the Jewish institution of proselyte baptism may have influenced Christian baptism (with its idea of conversion-initiation as in 1 Pet 2:9-10), it probably had little to do with John's baptism. Indeed it is not clear how early this ritual was practiced.

Though John should not be taken in isolation from biblical, Qumran, and rabbinic analogies and though it is even possible to speak of a "Baptist movement" in the region of the Jordan River around John's time, it is important to grasp the unique character of John's baptism. It was administered by another, occurred only once, and prepared one for the coming of God's kingdom and the judgment. Its emphasis was moral purity and conversion rather than ritual purity.

John's baptism served as the prototype for Christian baptism. The chief difference is that Christian baptism is "in the name of Jesus" and takes its direction and meaning especially from Jesus' death and resurrection.

It is possible to read Matt 3:11-12 as a contrast between John's baptism and the "cleansing" to be brought about by God on the Last Day. Thus John would simply be carrying out his "Elijah" role. But for Matthew and his community the contrast was surely between John and Jesus (and their baptisms). And the reference is not so much to the Christian sacrament of baptism as it is to the eschatological significance of Jesus who will come as judge for all the nations (see Matt 25:31-46).

For Matthew's community the focus of Matt 3:11-12 would have been the identification of Jesus as "the one who comes after me." The early chapters in the Gospel have as one of their functions introducing the person of Jesus. In the infancy narrative Jesus was related to Abraham and David. In Matt 3:13-17 Jesus will be revealed as Son of God (with Davidic overtones), an Isaac-figure, and God's Servant. The thrust of the intervening material (Matt 3:1-12) is to place Jesus in relation to John the Baptist. After introducing John and his activity (3:1-6) and giving a sample of his preaching (3:7-10), now Matthew uses a piece of tradition that brings John together with Jesus and insists on Jesus' superiority to John. By identifying Jesus as the one who comes after John, Matthew also prepares for the many texts in his Gospel that stress the eschatological significance of Jesus and portray him as judge or preacher of judgment.

The context and content of Matt 3:11-12 indicate a direct focus on the person of Jesus and an emphasis on his superiority to John. The text also points toward the role of Jesus in the events of the Last Day.

For Reference and Further Study

Betz, O. "Die Proselytentaufe der Qumransekte und die Taufe im NT." *RQ* 1 (1958) 213-34.

Gnilka, J. "Die essenischen Tauchbäder und die Johannestaufe." *RQ* 3 (1961) 185-207.

Lohfink, G. "Der Ursprung der christlichen Taufe." *TQ* 156 (1976) 35-54.

Neusner, J. *The Idea of Purity in Ancient Judaism.* Leiden: Brill, 1973.

Thomas, J. *Le mouvement baptiste en Palestine et Syrie (150 a. J.-C.-300 apr. J.-C.).* Gembloux: Duculot, 1935.

7. *Jesus Made Manifest* (3:13-17)

13. Then Jesus came from Galilee to the Jordan to John, to be baptized by him. 14. But John tried to prevent him, saying: "I have need to be baptized by you, and you come to me?" 15. Jesus answered and said to him: "Let it be for now! For thus it is fitting for us to fulfill all righteousness." Then he agreed. 16. Once he had been baptized, Jesus emerged immediately from the water. And behold, the heavens were opened, and he saw the Spirit of God, descending dove-like, coming upon him. 17. And behold, a voice from the heavens was saying: "This is my son, the beloved, with whom I am well pleased."

Notes

13. *Jesus came*: In comparison with Mark 1:9 and Luke 3:21, Matt 3:13 supplies the fullest information about Jesus' movement and why he came to John. Luke is

particularly obscure, since John is already in prison (see Luke 3:20); one would hardly guess that Jesus was baptized by John. Such obscurity does not exist in Matt 3:13.

14. *tried to prevent him*: The dialogue between John and Jesus appears only in Matt 3:14-15 and indicates some embarrassment over Jesus' baptism. The embarrassment can be traced either to the intrinsic superiority of Jesus and his baptism to John (see Matt 3:11) or to the character of John's baptism "for repentance" (see Matt 3:11). John's explanation in Matt 3:14 is ambiguous, and so the text is not a clear statement of Jesus' sinlessness.

15. *to fulfill all righteousness*: The phrase is best not taken as referring to Christian baptism (see Rom 6:1-11) or to the economy of the Old Covenant (as in the Matthean fulfillment quotations). Rather it probably alludes to the way of life appropriate to one baptized by John ("producing good fruit"). Recognizing the superiority of his own baptism, Jesus nevertheless pledges to act in accord with John's baptism.

16. *the heavens were opened*: The opening of the heavens signifies the new possibility of communication between God and humankind (see Ezek 1:1; 2 Macc 3:24 ff.; *2 Baruch* 22; Jn 1:51; Acts 7:55-56; 10:11; Rev 11:19; 19:11-21).

    he saw: It is reading too much into this phrase in Matt 3:16 to argue that Jesus' experience was a private vision. Matthew most likely understood it as a public event accessible to others (as in Mark 1:10-11 and Luke 3:21-22).

    descending dove-like: The idea of open communication between God and humankind is further developed by the descent of the Holy Spirit upon Jesus. The description of the Spirit's descent is presented in an adverbial phrase ("dove-like = like a dove does") that may evoke the OT creation account ("the Spirit of God was moving over the face of the waters," Gen 1:2).

17. *a voice from the heavens*: The phrase may reflect or be connected with the rabbinic *bat qôl* ("a daughter of a voice," i.e., an echo of a word uttered in heaven), another image for the opening up of communication between God and humankind.

    this is my son: The three images for open communication—the opening of the heavens, the dove-like descent of the Spirit, the heavenly voice—prepare for the identification of God's Son. The identification is made in the third person ("This is . . .") as opposed to Mark 1:11 and Luke 3:22 ("you are . . ."). The heavenly voice combines phrases from the OT: "my Son" (Ps 2:7 = the Davidic king as the adopted son of God), the "beloved" (Gen 22:2 = Isaac), and "with whom I am well pleased" (Isa 42:1; 44:2 = God's Servant). At the outset of Jesus' public ministry he is identified in terms of biblical figures that provide types for his own person and activity.

Interpretation

In the account of Jesus' baptism by John, Matthew rejoins his Markan source (see Mark 1:9-11; Luke 3:21-22). He has inserted into it a dialogue between John and Jesus (Matt 3:14-15) that explains why Jesus underwent baptism by John. The narrative ends with an identification of Jesus in terms of prominent biblical figures: Son of God, Isaac, and God's Servant.

That Jesus was baptized by John is among the most certain historical facts in the Gospel tradition. Since it assumes a dependence upon and inferiority to John on Jesus' part, it is clearly not the kind of story that early Christians would have invented. The dialogue inserted in Matt 3:14-15 indicates that early Christians felt some embarrassment about the episode and needed an explanation of how it came about.

When modern Christians read Matt 3:13-17 and parallels, they instinctively draw connections between the baptism of Jesus and Christian baptism, thus treating Jesus' baptism as supplying the prototype of their own. This ecclesiastical approach leads to debates about the relation between water-baptism and Spirit-baptism as well as other theological controversies.

Rather than focusing on the historicity of Jesus' baptism or its significance for Christian baptism, it is better to recognize that the focus for Matthew and the other evangelists was the person of Jesus. More specifically Matt 3:13-17 serves to establish Jesus' identity before he begins his public ministry. It does so by having the heavenly voice make clear who he is and why he is significant.

The literary form of "interpretative vision" appears in the targums of Gen 22:10 and 28:12 (see Lentzen-Deis, *Die Taufe Jesu*). To the biblical account of Abraham's willingness to sacrifice Isaac *Targum Neofiti* (and *ps.-Jonathan*) of Gen 22:10 adds the idea that Isaac willingly accepted this arrangement to the point of requesting that he be tied more tightly. The text continues with an interpretative vision: "The eyes of Abraham were on the eyes of Isaac, and the eyes of Isaac were scanning the angels on high. Abraham did not see them. In that hour a voice came forth from the heavens and said: 'Come, see two singular (=just) (persons) who are in my world; one sacrifices and the other is sacrificed; he who sacrifices does not falter and he who is sacrificed stretches forth his neck.' "

Another interpretative vision is attached to Jacob's dream in Gen 28:12. To the biblical account *Targum Neofiti* (and *ps.-Jonathan*) adds the following: "Behold, the angels that had accompanied him from the house of his father ascended to bear good tidings to the angels on high, saying: 'Come and see a just man whose image is engraved in the throne of glory, whom you desired to see.' And behold, the angels from before the Lord were ascending and descending and observed him."

There are serious problems involved in dating the two "Palestinian" targums in which these visions appear. The manuscripts are comparatively late, and they contain some obviously late material. They also contain material witnessed in other texts from around the time of Jesus. And so it is difficult to know how far back in history any specific passage can be traced. The prudent course when using targumic material in NT study is to talk about parallels and perhaps common traditions, and not to assume a relation of direct dependence.

Having issued that methodological caution, we can look again at the parallels between the targumic interpretative visions and Matt 3:13-17. In all three cases (Isaac, Jacob, Jesus) the hero is at an early point in his public or adult career. Communication between heaven and earth is opened up, by angels in the targums and by various means (the opening of the heavens, the dove-like descent of the Spirit, the voice) in Matt 3:13-17. The voice from the heavens points out the hero and declares something about his identity: "two singular (=just) (persons) who are in my world" (Abraham and Isaac); "a just man whose image is engraved in the throne of glory" (Jacob); and "my son, the beloved, with whom I am well pleased" (Jesus). Familiarity with the Jewish interpretative vision helps the reader to recognize where the spotlight in the text rests.

In entitling this episode "Jesus made manifest" an attempt has been made to be faithful to the focus of the biblical account—the manifestation of Jesus' identity at the very beginning of his public ministry. The baptism of Jesus by John in the Jordan River is the occasion for the identification of Jesus by the voice from heaven. Matthew agreed with the other evangelists in this Christological emphasis.

The particular contribution of Matthew comes in the dialogue between John and Jesus in Matt 3:14-15. That dialogue seeks to deal with some embarrassment caused by the fact that Jesus submitted to John's baptism. The embarrassment may have arisen from tension with Christian claims about the superiority of Jesus over John. Or it may have stemmed from the connection of John's baptism with repentance and forgiveness of sins on the one hand and Christian claims about the sinlessness of Jesus (see Heb 4:15). Whether such embarrassment originated with the Matthean community (from the sheer logic of events) or from outside (followers of John, Pharisees, etc.) cannot be known.

There is a line of interpretation that connects the terms used by the heavenly voice ("my son, the beloved, with whom I am well pleased") with Israel and suggests that Jesus is being represented as the replacement for Israel, i.e., the new Israel. It is possible to relate the three titles to Israel taken as a collectivity. But the "replacement" idea is not really necessary or advisable. It is better to add the three titles to the list of titles already developed in the first two chapters and to approach Matt 3:13-17 as a further effort to express the extraordinarily rich identity of Jesus.

Any actualization of the text should concentrate on the person of Jesus and his identity as he embarks on his public ministry. The theme of Christian baptism should take second place. The embarrassment encountered in the dialogue (3:14-15) might be pursued as a means of clarifying what precisely is going on in the narrative. It might also be used to shed light on the tensions between early Christian claims and the objections of their fellow Jews to them.

For Reference and Further Study

Dunn, J. D. G. *Baptism in the Spirit.* (Naperville, Ill.: Allenson, 1970) 23-37.
Keck, L. E. "The Spirit and the Dove." *NTS* 17 (1970) 41–67.
Lentzen-Deis, F. "Das Motiv der 'Himmelsöffnung' in verschiedenen Gattungen der Umweltliteratur des Neuen Testaments." *Bib* (1969) 301–27.
__________. *Die Taufe Jesu nach den Synoptikern. Literarkritische und gattungsgeschichtliche Untersuchungen.* Frankfurt: Knecht, 1970.

8. *The Testing of God's Son* (4:1-11)

1. Then Jesus was led up into the wilderness by the Spirit to be tested by the devil. 2. And after fasting forty days and forty nights, at last he was hungry. 3. And the tester approached him and said to him: "If you are the Son of God, say that these stones become bread." 4. But he answered and said: "It is written: 'Not by bread alone shall a man live, but by every word coming forth through the mouth of God.' "

5. Then the devil took him into the holy city and set him upon the "wing" of the temple, 6. and said to him: "If you are the Son of God, cast yourself down. For it is written that 'to his angels he has given charge of you' and 'on their hands they will bear you up, lest you strike your foot upon the rock.' " 7. Jesus said to him: "Again it is written: 'You shall not test the Lord your God.' "

8. Again the devil took him to a very high mountain, and showed him all the kingdoms of the world and their glory. 9. And he said to him: "All these things I will give to you if you fall down and pay homage to me." 10. Then Jesus said to him: "Go away, Satan. For it is written: 'You shall pay homage to the Lord your God and worship him alone.' "

11. Then the devil left him, and behold angels came and served him.

Notes

1. *wilderness*: In the narrative sequence after the baptism the reader would naturally think of the Judean Desert. But more important than precise geographical location is the biblical motif of the wilderness as the place in which Israel was tested (see Deut 8:2).

to be tested: In the OT "testing" refers to the process by which the covenant partner is scrutinized to determine his fidelity in keeping the agreement. In the context of Israel's relationship with God the process will reveal whether Israel is faithful or not. God can test Israel, but Israel must not test God. Here the testing will show forth the fidelity of the Son of God.

by the devil: "Devil" is the English equivalent of the Greek *diabolos*, which serves as a synonym for Satan ("tester, tempter"). Whereas in pre-exilic times God tests Israel, in post-exilic times that function is given over to Satan (see Job 1–2; Zech 3:1-2; 1 Chr 21:1). The assumption is that the devil remains under God's ultimate control. In the case of Jesus the Spirit of God leads him into the wilderness, and so makes the testing possible.

2. *forty days and forty nights*: Once in the wilderness Jesus abstained from food. His fasting may reflect a phrase in Deut 8:2 ("that he might humble you") in which the verb "humble" can carry the idea of fasting. The number "forty" may relate to the forty years in the wilderness during which Israel was tested (see Deut 8:2), though it more directly refers to the forty-day fasts undertaken by Moses (see Deut 9:18) and Elijah (see 1 Kgs 19:8).

3. *the tester*: Matthew uses a different Greek word (*peirazōn*) from *diabolos*, thus tying in the devil's activity with the purpose of Jesus' being led to the wilderness ("to be tested"). Luke 4:3 retains the term *diabolos*.

If you are the Son of God: The phrase also prefaces the second test (Matt 4:6); it expresses the content of all three tests, which attempt to determine what kind of Son of God Jesus is. The "Son of God" title also relates the experience of Jesus to that of Israel (see Hos 11:1; Matt 2:15).

that these stones become bread: The challenge is not to perform a "show-miracle," since there is no audience in the wilderness. Rather the background is God's feeding Israel during its wandering in the wilderness (see Deut 2:7). God's provision of manna for Israel frequently met with grumbling and craving for earthly food (see Ps 78:18-20). Will Jesus the Son of God fail the test (as Israel did) or persevere in trust toward God?

4. *"Not by bread alone"*: The Son of God's response to the first test is a quotation of Deut 8:3, which supplies a reason for the manna: That Israel might know the Word of God as the true source of its life. The Son of God already knows this, and so is able to resist and overcome the first test. The quotation corresponds to the Septuagint of Deut 8:3.

5. *the holy city*: Luke 4:9 calls it by its name Jerusalem and places the second Matthean test third in sequence. The city was considered "holy" primarily because of the Temple in which God was believed to dwell in a special way. There is no reference to crowds of people frequenting the Temple, and so the test should not be taken as incentive to perform a public "show-miracle."

the "wing" of the Temple: The Greek diminutive form *pterygion* derives from the word for "wing." It refers to some (otherwise unknown) point in the Temple or Temple area that is prominent and juts out. The usual English translation is "pinnacle." There is probably some connection with the OT motif of God's protecting "wing," which is present in Psalm 91: "he will cover you with his pinions, and under his wings you will find refuge" (Ps 91:4). There may be a play on a popular name given to a point in the Temple and Psalm 91, which will supply in Matt 4:6 the "biblical foundation" for the reckless action that is proposed to Jesus.

6. *If you are the Son of God*: The same challenge as in 4:3. Though lacking in the third test (4:8), the idea is assumed there and is the basis for the entire narrative.

   to his angels: The "biblical foundation" consists of phrases from Psalm 91, which joins the themes of God's protection with the Temple as the place of God's presence. The quotations conform to the Septuagint of Psalm 90:11-12, with the omission of the second part of v. 11 ("to guard you in all your ways"). The tempter suggests that Jesus test out the validity of these promises about divine protection.

7. *You shall not test the Lord*: Jesus' response comes from Deut 6:16. The test again follows the Septuagint; the second half of the verse ("as you tested him at Massah") is omitted, since allusion to the incident at Massah (see Exod 17:1-7) may have seemed extraneous. Nevertheless that incident is the model for Israel's testing the Lord. The name derives from the Hebrew root for "test" (*nsh*). Jesus refuses to do what ancient Israel did.

8. *a very high mountain*: Efforts to identify a mountain from which all the kingdoms of the world could be seen are pointless. The picture may have been influenced by the descriptions of Moses' looks at the Holy Land from Mount Pisgah (Deut 3:27) and Mount Nebo (Deut 34:1-4). In Jesus' case, however, he is invited to look at all the kingdoms of the world.

9. *pay homage to me*: The devil uses the word that was so prominent in the Magi story (Matt 2:2, 8, 11) and will appear with reference to the risen Jesus in Matt 28:17. For Jesus to pay homage to the devil would amount to a reversal of roles, for others should pay homage to Jesus. But this is the alleged price that he must pay to gain power over all the kingdoms: paying homage to Satan.

10. *Go away, Satan*: Jesus uses a similar phrase in Matt 16:23 when Peter refuses to accept the truth of the passion prediction in 16:21. The Lukan parallel (4:8) does not contain the phrase, suggesting that Matthew saw a connection between the two incidents.

    You shall pay homage to the Lord: The Hebrew of Deut 6:13 reads: "You shall fear the Lord your God and serve him." Most Septuagint manuscripts reflect the same text. Luke 4:8 agrees with Matt 4:10, except in order. The differences from the Septuagint are "pay homage" instead of "fear" and the addition of "alone." They may reflect a different textual tradition of Deut 6:13 or early Christian scribal activity.

11. *the devil left him*: Jesus' responses to the three tests have made clear what kind of Son of God he is. There is nothing left for the "tester" to do, and so it is fitting that an angel minister to Jesus. At this point the Q narrative rejoins the Markan narrative ("and the angels served him").

Interpretation

The customary title for Matt 4:1-11 and its parallels (Mark 1:12-13; Luke 4:1-13) is the "Temptation of Jesus." A better title, one more appropriate to the biblical basis of the narrative in the Book of Deuteronomy, is the "Testing of God's Son." The concern of the passage is not so much whether the devil can lure Jesus into this or that sin as it is the portrayal of Jesus as God's Son "who in every respect has been tested as we are, yet without sin" (Heb 4:15). Where Israel in the wilderness failed, Jesus passes every test.

The Markan version (Mark 1:12-13) is very short in comparison with Matt 4:1-11 and Luke 4:1-13; it is a straightforward narrative, without the lengthy dialogues of the other Gospels. The Matthean and Lukan versions are clearly related. Since they depart from Mark and are closely parallel, they are usually attributed to Q (though by length and complexity they stand out from the simple sayings-material characteristic of Q).

After a narrative introduction (Matt 4:1-2), the Matthean version consists of three dialogues between the devil and Jesus (4:3-4, 5-7, 8-10) and a narrative conclusion (4:11). Each dialogue has the devil offering a test and Jesus responding with a quotation from Deuteronomy 6–8. The biblical quotations correspond closely to the Septuagint, indicating that the present text at least was composed in Greek on the basis of the Greek Bible. Whether the story goes back to Jewish-Christian scribes (as Gerhardsson argues) or to Jesus himself (as Dupont claims) cannot be determined.

The three biblical quotations in which Jesus' responses are expressed come from Deuteronomy 6–8 (8:3; 6:16; 6:13). In those chapters Moses addresses the people of Israel near the end of their wandering in the wilderness and before their entrance into the promised land. The underlying motif of the Book of Deuteronomy is the covenant. In chapters 6–8 Moses supplies the historical foundations for God's relationship with Israel and presents exhortations on that basis. This material is reminiscent of the "historical prologue" in the covenant formula. For a full discussion of covenant, see D. J. McCarthy, *Treaty and Covenant* (Rome: Biblical Institute Press, 1978).

The premise of Moses' speech is God's love for and election of Israel: "The Lord your God has chosen you to be a people for his own possession . . . because the Lord loves you" (Deut 7:6-7). The relationship between God and Israel takes the form of a covenant: "the faithful God who keeps covenant and steadfast love with those who love him and keep his commandments" (Deut 7:9). Woven through the speech are references to Israel's wanderings in the wilderness and the challenges related to its entrance into the promised land. These are placed in the context of a father-son relationship: "As a man disciplines his son, the Lord your God disciplines you" (Deut 8:5). The motif of Israel as God's son appears elsewhere in this book (see Deut 1:31; 14:1; 32:5-6, 18-20) and other OT writings (see Exod 4:22-23; Hos 11:1).

Israel's experience in the wilderness is expressed in terms of a test from God: "And you shall remember all the way which the Lord your God has led you these forty years in the wilderness, that he might humble you, testing you to know what was in your heart, whether you would keep his commandments, or not" (Deut 8:2). Besides the testing motif this verse contains several other themes developed in Matt 4:1-11: Israel's being led by God, the number forty, the wilderness, and perhaps even the notion of fasting in the verb "humble" (*'nh*).

Whereas God may test Israel, Israel should not test God: "You shall not put the Lord your God to the test, as you tested him at Massah" (Deut 6:16). By quoting this verse in Matt 4:7 Jesus aligns himself with Israel as it should be and in contrast to Israel as it was at Massah and Meribah (see Exod 17:1-7).

So Deuteronomy 6–8 not only supplies the three biblical quotations attributed to Jesus in Matt 4:1-11 but also provides the key terms "Son of God" (see Matt 4:3, 6) and "test." Moses challenges Israel to learn from its past mistakes in the wilderness and to act faithfully as it enters the Promised Land. Matthew (following Q) presents Jesus as the true Son of God who passes the tests set forth by the devil and emerges as the model of covenant fidelity.

If we grant that Matthew took over his version of the "Testing of God's Son" from Q, it was an especially congenial text for him and his audience. In form it resembles a rabbinic debate in which great teachers trade quotations from Scripture and settle arguments by them. In content it carries on Matthew's attempt to identify Jesus before the beginning of his public ministry. The idea of Jesus as God's Son had already been raised in Matt 1:20; 2:15; and 3:17. The testing narrative allows Matthew to connect Jesus' divine sonship with the experience of Israel. Israel in the wilderness failed the testing; Jesus passes it.

The contrast between the wilderness generation and Jesus need not lead to talk about Jesus as the "new Israel." Rather Jesus stands with Israel in accepting the challenges posed by Moses in Deuteronomy 6–8. As in Heb 3:7–4:10 the wilderness generation is a negative example to be avoided. Far from replacing Israel, Jesus takes his identity from Israel. Behind the early Christian claims about his divine sonship is his solidarity with the Israel addressed by Moses. He accepts the testing from God and refuses to test God.

The Matthean order of tests—wilderness, Temple, mountain—is generally considered to reflect the order of Q. Luke's order—wilderness, mountain, Temple—is usually explained in light of Luke's special interest in geography in general and in Jerusalem and its temple in particular. But it is possible that Matthew has changed the order to foreshadow future events in his Gospel so that there is a correspondence between the first temptation (4:2-4), and the miraculous feedings (14:13-21; 15:32-39), the second temptation (4:5-7) along with the baptism (3:13-17) and the transfiguration (17:1-13), and the third temptation and the conclusion of the Gospel (28:16-20).

In the Church's calendar, Matt 4:1-11 becomes prominent at the beginning of Lent. Understanding this text against the background of Deuteronomy 6–8 allows one to go beyond the narrow themes of fasting and temptation to the level of Christology. As is the case with all the material in the opening chapters of Matthew, the focus of attention is the identity of Jesus. Understanding it as the testing of God's Son allows one to see the nature of Jesus' divine sonship and its relation to Israel as God's Son.

For Reference and Further Study

Dupont, J. *Les tentations de Jésus au désert.* Bruges: Desclée de Brouwer, 1968.

Gerhardsson, B. *The Testing of God's Son (Matt 4:1-11 & Par.). An Analysis of an Early Christian Midrash.* Lund: Gleerup, 1966.

Przybylski, B. "The Role of Matt 3:13–4:11 in the Structure and Theology of the Gospel of Matthew." *BTB* 4 (1974) 222–35.

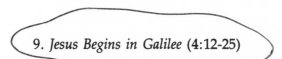

9. *Jesus Begins in Galilee* (4:12-25)

12. On hearing that John had been handed over, he withdrew into Galilee. 13. And on leaving Nazareth he came and dwelt in Capernaum by the sea in the territories of Zebulon and Naphtali, 14. in order that what was said through Isaiah the prophet might be fulfilled: 15. "Land of Zebulon and land of Naphtali, toward the sea, beyond the Jordan, Galilee of the Gentiles, 16. the people dwelling in darkness has seen a great light; and for those dwelling in the land and in the shadow of death, a light has risen for them." 17. From then on Jesus began to preach and to say: "Repent. For the kingdom of heaven has drawn near."

18. While walking by the Sea of Galilee he saw two brothers, Simon called Peter and Andrew his brother, casting a net into the sea. For they were fishermen. 19. And he said to them: "Come after me, and I will make you fishers of men." 20. They immediately left their nets and followed him. 21. And he went on from there and saw two other brothers, James the son of Zebedee and John his brother, in the boat with Zebedee their father; they were mending their nets. And he called them. 22. And they immediately left the boat and their father, and followed him.

23. And he went about in all of Galilee, teaching in their synagogues and preaching the good news of the kingdom and healing every disease

and infirmity among the people. 24. And his fame went forth in all Syria. And they brought to him all those faring badly, those afflicted by various diseases and pains, demoniacs and the moonstruck and paralytics; and he healed them. 25. And there followed him great crowds from Galilee and Decapolis and Jerusalem and Judea and beyond the Jordan.

Notes

12. *John had been handed over*: After Jesus' baptism but before his public ministry, John is off the scene. The full story of his imprisonment and death is told in Matt 14:1-12 by way of the flashback technique. Matthew follows Mark in using the verb "hand over," which becomes prominent in the passion narrative (see Matt 26:15, 16, 21, etc.). Thus the fate of John foreshadows the fate of Jesus.
withdrew: This characteristically Matthean verb appeared in Matt 2:14, 22 (see also 12:15; 14:13; 15:21). Since John had been handed over to Herod Antipas (see 14:1-12) and the same Herod ruled over Galilee, Jesus' decision to "withdraw" to Galilee from the Judean wilderness is puzzling. At any rate, Galilee is the scene for the beginning of Jesus' public ministry.

13. *Capernaum*: The place takes its name from the Hebrew for "village of Nahum." It is on the northwest shore of the Sea of Galilee ("by the sea") in the general area allotted to the tribes of Zebulon and Naphtali. It is a substantial distance from Nazareth, which is in the center of Lower Galilee. If any city can be called the home-base of Jesus' ministry in Galilee, it was Capernaum. See, however, Jesus' negative judgment upon Capernaum in Matt 11:23.

14. *through Isaiah*: The fulfillment quotation comes from Isa 8:23–9:1 (9:1-2 in English). But it is a rather loose adaptation of the Septuagint text, designed to show that the beginning of Jesus' public ministry in Galilee was in accordance with the Scriptures. In Isaiah the text expressed an oracle of hope after the overrunning of Galilee by the Assyrians in 732 B.C.

15. *Galilee of the Gentiles*: The OT epithet may allude to the fact that after the Assyrian conquest in 732 B.C. the region of Galilee became known as the Assyrian province of Megiddo. In the Matthean community the description probably was taken as a reference to the Gentile population of the area and a foreshadowing of the risen Lord's command to "make disciples of all the Gentiles" (Matt 28:19). Nevertheless the emphasis of the fulfillment quotation is Galilee, not Gentiles.

16. *a light has risen*: The change of the Septuagint's *lampsei* ("will shine") to *aneteilen* ("has risen") probably stresses the beginning (= dawn) made by Jesus in his public activity. The RSV uses "sat" instead of "dwelling"; "sat" is closer to the Greek, but the Greek is merely an overly literal translation of the underlying Hebrew root *yšb* in the biblical quotation.

17. *the kingdom of heaven has drawn near*: Matt 4:17 is a simplified version of Mark 1:14b-15, using the characteristically Matthean "kingdom of heaven." The content of Jesus' message as summarized here is exactly the same as that of John

the Baptist (see Matt 3:2). The "kingdom of heaven" refers to that time when God's power and judgment will be made fully manifest and acknowledged by all creation. It is said to "have drawn near"—not yet a full reality but very close to the point that it can be called inaugurated. For a recent survey see B. T. Viviano, *The Kingdom of God in History* (Wilmington: Glazier, 1988).

18. *by the Sea of Galilee*: Jesus encounters his first disciples at their place of work as fishermen. The Sea of Galilee (see Matt 15:29) is a harp-shaped body of fresh water, eight miles at its widest point and thirty-two miles around, in northern Galilee. The trade route known as the *Via Maris* ("way of the sea") followed its western shore in part, thus giving the area commercial importance. Other names applied to the sea were the Sea of Chinnereth, Sea of Tiberias, and Lake of Gennesaret.

two brothers: At several points Matthew supplies information about the characters: "called Peter" (4:18), "two other brothers" (4:21), and "with Zebedee their father" (4:21). This information is readily deducible from Mark 1:16-20. As a careful editor Matthew has merely made it explicit, to help the reader grasp relationships more easily.

they were fishermen: The perception of the opponents of Peter and John in Acts 4:13 ("uneducated, common men") should not be taken too literally. Fishing was a major industry on the Sea of Galilee, and the first disciples owned the equipment necessary (nets and boats) to take part in this kind of work. There is no reason to assume that they were illiterate (see W. Wuellner, *The Meaning of "Fishers of Men"* [Philadelphia: Westminster, 1967]).

19. *fishers of men*: The word-play is generated by the occupation of the first disciples; their new calling has the element of mission from the start. In light of the importance of the fishing business at the Sea of Galilee it is clear that the first followers of Jesus were leaving behind a secure and stable lifestyle. There may have been an allusion to Jer 16:16 ("Behold, I am sending for many fishers, says the Lord, and they shall catch them").

20. *followed*: The response of the first two persons summoned by Jesus is described with the NT technical term for discipleship (*akoloutheō*). The lack of preparation (there is no indication they knew about Jesus beforehand) and the quickness of their response ("immediately") highlight the attractiveness and persuasiveness of Jesus.

21. *James . . . and John*: In 4:18 Matthew clearly identified Simon as Peter ("called Peter"), who along with James and John form an inner circle among Jesus' disciples (see Matt 17:1 and 26:37). James the son of Zebedee is to be distinguished from James the son of Alphaeus (Matt 10:3) and James the "brother of the Lord." At the start of Jesus' public ministry Matthew has introduced some of the key figures who accompany Jesus throughout his career.

23. *in all of Galilee*: Matthew clearly adapted the summary in Mark 1:39 by adding some characteristic touches: Jesus "teaches," preaches the "good news of the kingdom," and acts as a healer and not just an exorcist. In the Matthean context the reference to "their synagogues" begins a motif that runs through the Gospel and serves to distance Jesus' followers from other Jews.

24. *Syria*: Here the term most likely refers to the Roman province of Syria, which included Palestine and the places named in 4:25 (see Luke 2:2; Acts 15:23, 41; 18:18; 20:3; 21:3; Gal 1:21). For the history of the term, see L. R. Shehadeh, "Syria I: The Graeco-Roman Period. A Geo-Historical Study," *NEST Theological Review* 8 (1987) 9–23. Syria may have been the home of the Matthean community.

    demoniacs and the moonstruck: The "demoniacs" were believed to be under the control of spiritual beings ("demons"), who entered the body and caused mental or physical suffering. The "moonstruck" is usually taken as a reference to epileptics (whose illness was thought in antiquity to be related to the phases of the moon). But the term probably included more than epileptics—all those under the harmful influence of the moon.

25. *great crowds*: Matthew adapts the Markan summary in Mark 3:7-13, shortening it considerably and reversing the order by placing the healings first and the list of places second. From Mark's list he omitted Idumea as well as Tyre and Sidon; he added the Decapolis. The new list supplies the audience for the Sermon on the Mount. Were they Jews only (Lohfink), or Jews and Gentiles (Krieger)?

    Decapolis: The term means "ten cities." It refers to the ten cities of Hellenistic culture east of Galilee and Samaria. Pliny the Elder gave the following list: Damascus, Philadelphia, Raphana, Scythopolis, Gadara, Hippos, Dion, Pella, Gerasa, and Canatha. Almost all of them are on the eastern side of the Jordan.

Interpretation

The beginning of Jesus' ministry takes place in Galilee. The three pericopes in Matt 4:12-23 describe how Jesus came back to Galilee after his baptism by John (4:12-17), how he called his first four disciples by the Sea of Galilee (4:18-22), and how crowds from all over the area came to Galilee to hear his preaching and to be healed by him (4:23-25).

Matthew's source in this section is Mark. His use of Mark here illustrates some of his editorial techniques. In the first pericope (4:12-17) Matthew has shaped the account of Jesus' movement from Nazareth to Capernaum from Mark 1:14a and 1:21, reinforced the idea of that movement as being in accord with God's will by the quotation from Isa 8:23–9:1, and shortened Mark 1:14b-15 and brought it into line with the summary of John's preaching (Matt 3:2). In the second pericope (4:18-22) Matthew followed Mark 1:16-20 quite closely and added only a few editorial clarifications to help readers to identify the characters. The third pericope (4:23-25) has been created by Matthew from phrases in Mark 1:39 and 3:7-13 to serve as an introduction to the Sermon on the Mount. This section indicates that Matthew acted as editor in a variety of ways—from basic reproduction of material in his source to freely creating from phrases and motifs in his sources.

Galilee is the place in which Jesus' public ministry began. Except for the final days in Jerusalem his ministry was confined to Galilee according to the Synoptic Gospels; John presents Jesus going back and forth between

Galilee and Jerusalem. In Jesus' time Galilee was a small area (about forty-five miles from north to south) bounded on the east by the Jordan River and the Sea of Galilee, on the south by Samaria, and on the north and west by Syro-Phoenicia. A major highway from Syria to Egypt—the Way of the Sea—ran through it from north to south. It is customary to divide the district in two parts: Upper Galilee and Lower Galilee.

In Jesus' time Galilee was under the political control of Herod Antipas, a son of Herod the Great, who also ruled over Perea, a strip of land to the east of the Jordan and to the south of Galilee. After A.D. 6 when Archelaus, the brother of Herod Antipas, was relieved of his control over Judea, that district was administered by a series of Roman governors, the most famous of which was Pontius Pilate (A.D. 26–36).

The major industries of Galilee were farming and fishing, settings frequently presupposed in Jesus' parables (see Matt 13:1-52). The base for Jesus' ministry in Galilee was Capernaum, on the northwestern shore of the Sea of Galilee. In those days the way in which religious or philosophical doctrines were spread was by means of travelling preachers (as in Matt 10:1-42). So while Capernaum served as "home-base," the Gospels indicate that Jesus and his disciples were moving about Galilee, preaching the message of the kingdom.

Though under politically separate control, Galilee and Judea were linked together by religious practice over against Samaria. Whereas the Samaritans took Mount Gerizim as their sacred site (see John 4:20), the Galileans and Judeans worshipped at the Jerusalem temple. There are indications, nonetheless, of tensions between Galileans and Judeans. The Judeans probably looked upon the Galileans as "country bumpkins" or "hicks," and the Galileans seem to have resented the special status of Jerusalem as a pilgrimage site. For further information about Galilee see S. Freyne, *Galilee from Alexander the Great to Hadrian, 323 B.C.E. to 135 C.E. A Study of Second Temple Judaism* (Wilmington: Glazier, 1980); and E. M. Meyers and J. F. Strange, *Archaeology, the Rabbis, and Early Christianity: The Social and Historical Setting of Palestinian Judaism and Christianity* (Nashville: Abingdon, 1981).

Matthew has repeated and reshaped Markan materials to portray the beginning of Jesus' ministry in Galilee. Since his community probably lived near (or even in) Galilee, this geographical setting would have carried special significance for Matthew's readers.

First in 4:12-17 Matthew shows that Jesus' return to Nazareth after John's arrest was in accordance with God's will. This is done most obviously by means of the fulfillment quotation of Isa 8:23–9:1 in Matt 4:15-16. There is an important subsidiary theme also: the close relation between John and Jesus in their preaching (3:2=4:17) and their destiny (4:12).

Then in 4:18-22 Jesus calls his first disciples: Simon Peter and Andrew, James and John. The lack of preparation, the simple commands given by

Jesus, and the immediate responses all underline the attractiveness of Jesus. The pericope also serves to introduce the members of Jesus' inner circle, who will accompany him to Jerusalem and be accorded appearances of the risen Lord. To a Jewish audience the dynamics of the call of the first disciples would have seemed unusual. It was customary in Jewish circles that disciples should search out a teacher (as in John 1:35-42). Here, however, Jesus takes the initiative by choosing and summoning those whom he wanted to be his disciples.

The third pericope (4:23-25) served the practical purpose of providing an audience for the Sermon on the Mount. By naming places in which the Gospel of Matthew most likely first circulated (Syria, Galilee, the Decapolis, Jerusalem and Judea, beyond the Jordan) Matthew set up a natural identification between his text and its readers.

While modern readers cannot experience the same kind of geographical identification that Matthew's first readers did, they can appreciate the major theological themes of Matthew's account of Jesus' early ministry in Galilee: the close relation between John and Jesus, Jesus' movements in accord with God's will, the extraordinary attractiveness of Jesus in calling his first disciples, and the positive response to him from many different areas. Nevertheless the geographical dimension should not be neglected in preaching and teaching, for it is part of the Christian doctrine of the incarnation. Without attention to the concrete historical circumstances of Jesus' ministry, Christian faith runs the risk of being misperceived as a body of abstract propositions. All Christians need a basic familiarity with the land of Israel.

For Reference and Further Study

Krieger, K. S. "Das Publikum der Bergpredigt (Mt 4, 23-25). Ein Beitrag zu der Frage: Wem gilt die Bergpredigt?" *Kairos* 28 (1986) 98–119.

Lohfink, G. "Wem gilt die Bergpredigt? Eine redaktionskritische Untersuchung von Mt 4, 23–5, 2 und 7, 28 f." *TQ* 163 (1983) 264–84.

Luz, U. "Die Jünger im Matthäusevangelium." *ZNW* 62 (1971) 141–71.

Ross, J. M. "Epileptic or Moonstruck?" *BT* 29 (1978) 126–28.

Soares-Prabhu, G. M. "Matthew 4:14-16. A Key to the Origin of the Formula Quotations of Matthew." *Indian Journal of Theology* 20 (1971) 70–91.

THE SERMON ON THE MOUNT

Although Mark portrays Jesus as a powerful teacher, he gives relatively few substantial blocks of Jesus' teaching. A major motive for Matthew to write his Gospel was to present large sections of Jesus' teaching. These teaching sections appear most obviously in the five major speeches in Matthew 5–7, 10, 13, 18, and 24–25. Matthew composed these discourses out of source material available to him from Q, Mark, and his special source M.

The first and longest of the five speeches is commonly known as the Sermon on the Mount. There are many outlines of it, though no one seems to satisfy all scholars. The problem begins in 6:19 where the neat structures of the first sections break down into the loose pattern of the OT wisdom books. The commentary adopts the following general outline: A. Introduction (5:1-20); B. The Antitheses (5:21-48); C. Three Acts of Piety (6:1-18); D. Other Teachings (6:19–7:12); E. Warnings about Judgment (7:13-29).

To whom is the Sermon on the Mount addressed? The story-line of Matthew's Gospel indicates that it was addressed to all Israel gathered to hear Jesus. The teaching and healing ministry that Jesus had exercised in Galilee drew people to him from all over (4:23-25). While the disciples have a prominent place (5:1), Jesus addresses the crowds. At the end Matthew notes that the crowds were astonished at his teaching (7:28-29). According to Matthew, Jesus placed before Israel his teachings and challenged it to accept them and act upon them. The basic theme of the sermon is that Jesus came not to abolish the Law and the Prophets but to fulfill them (5:17). We must assume that for the evangelist everything in the sermon illustrates or is coherent with this basic principle.

The history of the sermon's interpretation is a miniature history of Christianity. To the present day there are sharply conflicting approaches to it. Rather than attempt to summarize that long and complicated history, I will state some theses that express my own approach: (1) Matthew places Jesus' teaching in an eschatological framework (see 5:3-12; 7:13-27). Nevertheless, much of Jesus' teaching concerns appropriate behavior in the present. (2) The sermon is neither a strictly individual ethic nor a blueprint for a social Utopia. Nevertheless it has implications for both personal and communal life. (3) The sermon is not addressed only to a Christian elite, nor is it so impossible to practice that its only function is to remind people of their status as sinners and their need for God's grace. (4) The sermon places a compendium of Jesus' teachings before Jews primarily. The goal is to show how Jesus fulfills the Law and the Prophets, not to prove the superiority of his teaching to the Jewish Scriptures or tradition. (5) In it Jesus presents what is for Christians an authoritative interpretation of the Torah. The sermon is more concerned with principles and attitudes than with deciding halakic matters or laying down laws.

For Reference and Further Study

Bauman, C. *The Sermon on the Mount. The Modern Quest for Its Meaning.* Macon, Ga.: Mercer University Press, 1985.

Betz, H. D. *Essays on the Sermon on the Mount.* Philadelphia: Fortress, 1985.

Friedlander, G. *The Jewish Sources of the Sermon on the Mount.* New York: Ktav, 1969.

Guelich, R. "Interpreting the Sermon on the Mount." *Int* 41 (1987) 117–30.

Guelich, R. A. *The Sermon on the Mount. A Foundation for Understanding.* Waco, Tex.: Word, 1982.

Kissinger, W. S. *The Sermon on the Mount: A History of Interpretation and Bibliography.* Metuchen, N.J.: Scarecrow Press, 1975.

Lambrecht, J. *The Sermon on the Mount. Proclamation and Exhortation.* Wilmington, Del.: Glazier, 1985.

Lapide, P. *The Sermon on the Mount. Utopia or Program for Action?* Maryknoll, N.Y.: Orbis, 1986.

Strecker, G. *The Sermon on the Mount: An Exegetical Commentary.* Nashville: Abingdon, 1988.

10. *The Introduction* (5:1-20)

1. Seeing the crowds he went up on the mountain. And when he sat down,
his disciples approached him. 2. And he opened his mouth and taught them,
saying: 3. "Blessed are the poor in spirit, for theirs is the kingdom of heaven.
4. Blessed are the mourners, for they will be comforted. 5. Blessed are the
meek, for they will inherit the land. 6. Blessed are those who hunger and
thirst for righteousness, for they will be satisfied. 7. Blessed are the merciful, for they will obtain mercy. 8. Blessed are the pure in heart, for they
will see God. 9. Blessed are the peacemakers, for they will be called sons
of God. 10. Blessed are those who have been persecuted for righteousness'
sake, for theirs is the kingdom of heaven.

11. "Blessed are you when they revile you and persecute and speak every
evil against you falsely on my account. 12. Rejoice and be glad, for your
reward is great in heaven. For so they persecuted the prophets before you.

13. "You are the salt of the earth. But if the salt has lost its taste, in what
way will it be salted? It is no longer good for anything except to be thrown
outside and walked upon by people. 14. You are the light of the world.
A city set upon a mountain cannot be hidden. 15. Nor do people light a
lamp and put it under a bushel, but on a lampstand, and it gives light to
all in the house. 16. So let your light shine before people, in order that they
may see your good works and glorify your Father who is in heaven.

17. "Do not think that I came to destroy the Law or the Prophets. I did
not come to destroy but to fulfill. 18. For Amen I say to you: Until heaven
and earth pass away, neither one yodh nor one hook will pass away from
the Law until all these take place. 19. Whoever therefore relaxes one of these
least commandments and teaches people to do so, will be called least in

the kingdom of heaven. But whoever does them and teaches, this one will be called great in the kingdom of heaven. 20. For I say to you that unless your righteousness exceeds that of the scribes and Pharisees, you will not enter the kingdom of heaven.''

Notes

1. *crowds*: The reference to the crowds at the beginning (5:1) and end (7:28-29) of the sermon provides a framework for Jesus' teaching of Israel. The mention of the disciples in 5:1 need not exclude the crowds. The teaching of the sermon is not intended simply for the inner core of disciples (who in any case need not be limited to the ''twelve apostles''). See G. Lohfink, ''Wem gilt die Bergpredigt?'' *TQ* 163 (1983) 264–84.

   mountain: Readers are expected to picture the hills on the western shore of the Sea of Galilee, but attempts at determining the exact site are useless. In the ancient Near East mountains were considered the homes of the gods and sacred sites. In Exodus 19ff. the Torah is revealed to Moses on Mount Sinai. Just as Moses received God's commandments on Sinai, Jesus reveals God's will on the mountain. In Matthew important events in Jesus' life take place on mountains: temptation (4:8-10), feeding of four thousand (15:29-39), transfiguration (17:1-9), arrest (26:30-35), and final commission (28:16).

   he sat down: In Jewish schools the teacher sat on a bench with the students on the ground before him. In Matthew Jesus sits to teach in a boat (13:2) and on the Mount of Olives (24:3). Matthew also speaks (literally or symbolically) of the (authoritative) ''seat of Moses'' (23:2). Luke has Jesus sit down to teach in the synagogue at Nazareth (4:20).

2. *he opened his mouth*: This is a Semitic expression used of one who is about to begin a public address (Job 3:1-2), a public teaching (Ps 78:2), or a solemn commitment (Judg 11:35-36). See D. A. Black, ''The Translation of Matthew 5.2,'' *Bible Translator* 38 (1987) 241–43. The term ''teach'' (*didaskō*) is used only in regard to this sermon in Matthew, here and in 7:29.

3. *Blessed*: Each ''Beatitude'' states that the possessor of this characteristic will be ''blessed'' by God. A formal ''blessing'' is a divine action, sometimes brought about through an intermediary (priest, king, parent, etc.). Beatitudes are common in OT wisdom books (Prov 3:13; 28:14). The NT Beatitudes refer to a future (or eschatological) reward, whereas the wisdom beatitudes assume that the reward is already present.

   poor in spirit: Luke 6:20 simply has ''the poor.'' The word *ptōchos* denotes a ''beggar,'' not just a poor person with few possessions. The Beatitudes should be read against the OT tradition of God's special care for the poor (see Exod 22:25-27; 23:11; Lev 19:9-10; Deut 15:7-11; Isa 61:1). Matthew's qualification ''in spirit'' further defines the ''poor'' as those who recognized God's kingdom as a gift that cannot be forced. The expressions ''poor'' and ''poor in spirit'' were used by members of contemporary Jewish communities to describe themselves as *Psalms of Solomon* 10:6; 15:1 and the Qumran *War Scroll* 14:7 show, respectively.

kingdom of heaven: Kingdom refers to God's reign or sovereignty. Here its eschatological meaning is dominant, though present recompense is not excluded. The term "heaven" is a Jewish substitute for "God" (see 1 Maccabees), apparently intended to avoid using the term "God" too freely. Note the parallelism is in the second parts of the first and the eighth Beatitudes (5:3, 10).

4. *the mourners*: The background is Isa 61:2-3 where the prophet's mission involves comforting all those who mourn in Zion. The occasion for their mourning is the devastation of the First Temple in Jerusalem in 587 B.C. According to Sir 48:24, Isaiah "consoled the mourners of Zion."

5. *the meek*: The background is Ps 37:11: "But the meek shall possess the land, and delight themselves in abundant prosperity." The Hebrew word for "the meek" (*'anāwîm*) is basically the same as the term for "the poor (in spirit)" in Matt 5:3. The Qumran community took Ps 37:11 as a prophecy of their struggle with their enemies (4QpPs[a]). The "land" is not necessarily limited to the land of Israel. In apocalyptic literature (see 1 Enoch 5:7) the promise is widened to include the gift of the whole world to the just: "To the elect there shall be light, joy, and peace, and they shall inherit the earth." Some manuscripts place 5:5 immediately after 5:3, thus joining the two Beatitudes on the *'anāwîm* and the heaven/earth pair.

6. *hunger and thirst for righteousness*: The background is Ps 107:5, 8-9, which describes God as satisfying the hungry and thirsty. Matthew has expanded the Q form (Luke 6:21) by adding "thirst" (to bring out the background in Psalm 107) and "for righteousness" (to clarify the nature of the hunger and thirst). Righteousness refers first to God's justice and then to human relationships and behavior. In an apocalyptic context righteousness refers to the vindication of the just at the last judgment. The satisfaction promised in the Beatitude is first and foremost eschatological.

7. *the merciful*: The background is Prov 14:21; 17:5 (LXX), where "blessing" is the reward for kindness to the poor. Mercy is first of all an attribute of God, who in turn desires mercy from human beings. Matthew twice quotes Hos 6:6 on God's desire for mercy (9:13; 12:7) and calls mercy a weighty matter of the Law (23:23). The mercy to be obtained will be at the last judgment.

8. *the pure in heart*: The background is Ps 24:3-4, which describes among those who can ascend "the hill of the Lord" (Mount Zion) those who have "clean hands and a pure heart." Neither a reference to sexual-ritual purity nor to singleheartedness, "pure in heart" characterizes people of integrity whose moral uprighteousness extends to their inmost being and whose actions and intentions correspond. "Seeing God" here refers no longer to visiting the Jerusalem temple but rather to the last judgment. See M. Barré, "Blessed Are the Pure of Heart," *Bible Today* 22 (1984) 236-42.

9. *the peacemakers*: The background is the OT idea of *shalom* as the fullness of God's gifts. Although all peace comes from God and perfect peace will be realized only in God's kingdom, following Jesus in the present demands the active pursuit of peace. The peacemakers will be invited to join the angels ("sons of God,"

see Gen 6:1-4) at the last judgment. A gender-neutral translation such as "children" might obscure the allusion to joining the angels in God's kingdom.

10. *persecuted for righteousness' sake*: The reference to "righteousness" echoes the fourth Beatitude (5:6) and prepares for the demand for a better righteousness (5:20). The reward ("theirs is the kingdom of heaven") links this Beatitude with the first one. Matthean community members might take this Beatitude as a description of the discipline and social ostracism that they endured for their unusual way of living Judaism.

11. *when they revile you*: The language shifts from the third person of Matt 5:3-10 to the second person plural (as in the Q Beatitudes of Luke 6:20-23). The verbs in Matt 5:11 ("revile . . . persecute . . . speak") in comparison with Luke 6:22 ("hate . . . exclude . . . revile . . . cast out") indicate a more active conflict with regard to Matthew's community, whereas the Lukan verbs suggest that a separation has already occurred.

    falsely: The participle *pseudomenoi* ("falsely") is not in Luke 6:20 and in Western texts of Matt 5:11. It may have been inserted by a scribe to limit the generalization. But the evangelist could have done this too; see M. W. Holmes, "The Text of Matthew 5.11," *NTS* 32 (1986) 283–86.

12. *your reward*: The idea of God rewarding the persecuted appears in Jewish works (1 Enoch 108:10; 4 Ezra 7:88-101). Christians are persecuted on Jesus' account (see 5:11), whereas those rewarded in 4 Ezra 7 suffered to "keep the Law of the Lawgiver perfectly" (7:89). The motif of the earlier persecution of the prophets recurs in Matt 23:29-30. See 2 Chr 36:16: "but they kept mocking the messengers of God, despising his words, and scoffing at his prophets, till the wrath of the Lord arose against this people, till there was no remedy." In a post-A.D. 70 setting this commentary on the destruction of the First Temple would have been particularly appropriate.

13. *salt of the earth*: Salt was used to give flavor to food (see Job 6:6), to preserve it, to purify, and as part of sacrifices (see Lev 2:13; Ezek 43:24). The second person plural forms carry on the mode of address begun in 5:11-12. Though salt does not lose its taste, it may become adulterated so that its taste is weakened (see Pliny, *Natural History* 31.44, 95).

14. *light of the world*: The background is Isa 2:2-5. The light image is part of the invitation to Israel: "O house of Jacob, come, let us walk in the light of the Lord" (2:5). In Isa 42:6; 49:6 Israel's vocation is to be a "light to the nations." Paul picked up this theme of Israel's vocation in Rom 2:19 ("a light to those who are in darkness"). The light imagery is developed in the sayings in 5:15-16 in which Jesus' followers are challenged to active engagement in their "good works." The goal of these works is that other people might come to praise God (5:16). The epithet "your Father who is in heaven" (5:16) is characteristically Matthean in comparison with the other NT writers and is a typical Jewish way of talking about God in prayer.

    city set upon a mountain: If there is an allusion to Isa 2:2-5, there is also an allusion to Jerusalem built upon Mount Zion. The OT envisions all nations coming to the city of Jerusalem to learn the Torah, with the result being perfect peace.

See K. M. Campbell, "The New Jerusalem in Matthew 5.14," *SJT* 31 (1978) 335–63.

17. *the Law and the Prophets*: Matthew uses this expression to refer to the OT as a whole (see 7:12; 11:13; 22:40). In later Jewish parlance the OT consists of the Torah, the Prophets, and the Writings.

to fulfill: In what sense does Jesus fulfill the Law and the Prophets? It could be a reference to (1) his obedience toward its precepts during his earthly life, (2) his role in fulfilling the Scriptures emphasized in Matthew 1–2 and elsewhere in the Gospel, or (3) the thrust of his teaching expressed in the love-commandment (22:40) from which the other commandments take their meaning and force.

18. *Until heaven and earth pass away*: The saying is introduced with great solemnity: "For Amen I say to you." The passing away of heaven and earth is another way of describing the coming of God's kingdom in its fullness. The thrust is that the Law and the Prophets remain in force until then. According to Matt 24:35 Jesus' works will even outlast the Law and the Prophets.

neither one yodh nor one hook: The Greek *iota* is the equivalent of the Hebrew letter *yodh*, the smallest letter in the alphabet. The "hook" may refer to a decorative stroke added to certain letters. This may be a case of hendiadys: the smallest part of the smallest letter. Thus the point would be that nothing of the Law and the Prophets will pass away.

until all these take place: The occurrence of a second "until" clause in one sentence is peculiar. If "all" refers to eschatological events, the clause adds nothing to the first. If it refers to Jesus' death and resurrection, then all of Matt 5:17-19 would be only of historical interest for early Christians.

19. *least commandments*: It was customary for rabbis to distinguish between grave commandments such as honoring one's parents (Deut 5:16) and light commandments such as the law of the bird's nest (Deut 22:6-7), though the reward for both is the same ("that it may go well with you, and that you may live long").

does them and teaches: Matthew recognizes the distinction between grave and light commandments but urges that all be practiced. The close connection between teaching and doing is one of Matthew's favorite themes. Rabbi Judah in *m. 'Abot* 2:1 teaches: "Be heedful in a light precept as in a grave one."

20. *scribes and Pharisees*: The statement points ahead to the critique of the scribes and Pharisees in Matthew 23 where the major charge is their not practicing what they preach (23:3), in contrast to the ideal of teaching and doing enunciated in 5:19. The "righteousness" involves fidelity to God's will revealed in the Torah and Jesus' interpretation of it.

Interpretation

The introduction to the Sermon on the Mount contains four sections: the setting (5:1-2), the Beatitudes (5:3-12), the identity of Jesus' followers (5:13-16), and the teaching about the Law (5:17-20).

The setting (5:1-2) on the mountain stands in contrast to the plain that serves as the setting of the Lukan sermon (Luke 6:17-20a). By placing this first and most dramatic instance of Jesus' teaching on the mountain, Matthew sought to evoke biblical ideas about mountains as places of divine revelation and about Mount Sinai as the place where God's will for Israel was revealed. But note that Jesus gives the teaching; he does not receive it as Moses did.

Though the disciples are mentioned as constituting part of the audience (5:1), it seems that Jesus' teaching was meant to take in all Israel being gathered by Jesus. This larger audience is suggested by the framework in which the sermon as a whole is set (4:23-25; 7:28-29). Thus the content of the sermon is not intended simply for those who are already Jesus' disciples or for humankind in general (as if it were some kind of natural law). Rather the sermon challenges Israel to find in Jesus' teaching the authentic interpretation of God's will revealed in the Torah.

The Beatitudes (5:3-12) contain eight blessings in the third person plural ("Blessed are the poor in spirit") and one blessing in the second person plural ("Blessed are you . . ."). The first eight form a structural package. The first and eighth Beatitudes offer the same reward ("for theirs is the kingdom of heaven"). The fourth and the eighth Beatitudes mention "righteousness."

The Matthean Beatitudes are an expansion of the set of four Q Beatitudes found in Luke 6:20-23. Luke expanded the set of four by constructing a corresponding set of four woes (Luke 6:24-26), whereas Matthew (or his sources) has filled out the list of Beatitudes to make nine.

The Beatitude form is familiar from the Hebrew Bible, especially the wisdom writings. Psalm 1 is an extended example of the Beatitude form in which someone is declared "blessed" or "happy": "Blessed is the man who walks not in the counsel of the wicked. . . ." The third-person form is more common than the second person. And so Matthew's third person reformulation of the second person Q form is consistent with the usual Jewish style for expressing a Beatitude.

The most striking deviation of the NT Beatitudes from the pattern of the wisdom books comes in the timing of the reward. The assumption of the wisdom books is that virtue or good actions are rewarded in the present. The NT Beatitudes promise fullness of life in God's kingdom. They are primarily eschatological, though there may be some anticipation of the reward in the present. When God's kingdom comes, the kind of people who possess the virtues listed in the Beatitudes or do what they entail will be rewarded. Even those who "inherit the land" (5:5) will inherit the "new earth" accompanying the "new heaven" when God's kingdom comes in its fullness. Thus the Beatitudes function not as "entrance requirements" but rather as a delineation of the characteristics and actions that will receive their full and appropriate eschatological reward. The promise of God's kingdom frames the eight Beatitudes (5:3, 10), and the intervening promises (comfort, inheriting the land, satisfaction, obtaining mercy, seeing God, being called "sons of God") refer to the final judgment, the vindication of the just, and the establishment of God's perfect kingdom.

The content of the first parts of the Beatitudes is established often by the biblical texts to which they allude: poor in spirit (Isa 61:1-3), the mourners (Isa 61:1-3), the meek (Ps 37:11), those who hunger and thirst for righteousness (Ps 107:5, 8-9), etc. While the OT roots of the Beatitudes provide a firm principle for their interpretation, it must be admitted that their language is so general that various applications can be made. One clue toward how Matthew understood them is provided by his characteristic additions in 5:6 ("for righteousness") and 5:10 ("for righteousness' sake"). That was Matthew's way of describing the Jewish tradition made concrete in Jesus' teaching (see 5:20). When read against a background of the conflict between Matthew's community and other Jews, the Beatitudes sketch the attitudes that the Matthean Christians should manifest and allude to the suffering that they endured (5:4, 10-11).

The third unit of the introduction (5:13-16) continues the second person plural style of the final Beatitude ("you are . . ."). The sayings about salt and light are Matthew's formulation of sayings found elsewhere in the Synoptic tradition (Mark 9:49-50/Luke 14:34-35 for salt, and Mark 4:21/Luke 8:16 for light). Along with the image of the "city set upon a mountain," they serve to define the identity of those who follow Jesus faithfully. That identity is firmly rooted in Israel's identity as God's people (Isa 2:2-5). It also has significance for the world as a whole: "the salt of the earth," "the light of the world" that "gives light to all in the house," and the "city set upon a mountain" that is visible to all.

The final part of the introduction (5:17-20) affirms an organic relation between Jesus' teaching and the Torah. That relation is expressed as "fulfillment" (5:17). There is no direct parallel to any other Synoptic text (see Luke 16:16-17 for a vaguely similar saying). Within the passage there are tensions (the two "until" clauses in 5:18), and there are also tensions with the apparent abrogations of the Torah in 5:31, 33, 38. Nevertheless, the thrust of the passage as it stands is that Jesus' fulfillment affirms and establishes the Torah rather than nullifies it. It uses the "light-heavy" distinction among the commandments that is well known from the rabbinic writings only to reject it in practice (as Rabbi Judah did). It challenges Jesus' followers to a righteousness superior to that taught by the scribes and Pharisees.

Whatever the origins and history of the material contained in Matt 5:17-20, its present form expressed the convictions of the Matthean community. The Torah remains in force. Jesus came not to destroy it but to fulfill it. Jesus' program for interpreting and practicing the Torah is superior to that of the scribes and Pharisees (see ch. 23 for a critique of their program).

The Beatitudes (5:3-12) are often presented in preaching and teaching as Jesus' distinctive contribution to defining the elements of good character or as a list of Jesus' values in opposition to those of the world. Or they are sometimes taken as part of an "ethics of discipleship" intended only for those who follow Jesus already. But the Beatitudes are neither philosophical nor sectarian ethics. The Beatitudes are thoroughly Jewish in form and content. They challenged those who made up "Israel" in Matthew's time by delineating the kinds of persons and actions that will receive their full reward when God's kingdom comes. They remind Christians today of the Jewish roots of their piety and challenge each generation to reflect on what persons and actions they consider to be important or "blessed."

The "challenge" theme of the introduction is carried on in the images of salt, light, and the city upon the mountain (5:13-16). Based firmly on Jewish life and Scripture, these images also challenge Christians to reflect upon their significance for the world as a whole. Those who carry forth Judaism to the Gentiles in fidelity to Jesus' teaching are important for the world at large. Without them the world is a dark and dismal place.

The sayings about the abiding validity of the Torah as interpreted by Jesus (5:17-20) serve as a further reminder of the organic relation between Judaism and Matthean Christianity. They remind us that at least some Christians in the late first century A.D. found no contradiction in following both the Torah and Jesus' teaching. This fact should forestall mindless attacks against "Jewish legalism." On the other hand, these sayings refer to the Torah—the revelation of God's will to Israel on Sinai, not law in general. In all the texts of the introduction to the sermon it is important to cut a pathway between philosophical generalities and sectarian anti-Judaism. That pathway involves a respect for the Jewish background and setting in which these texts originated.

For Reference and Further Study

Banks, R. "Matthew's Understanding of the Law. Authenticity and Interpretation in Matthew 5:17-20." *JBL* 93 (1974) 226–42.

Dupont, J. *Les Béatitudes*. 3 vols. Paris: Gabalda, 1969, 1973.

Guelich, R. A. "The Matthean Beatitudes: 'Entrance Requirements' or Eschatological Blessings?" *JBL* 95 (1976) 415–34.

Hamerton-Kelly, R. "Attitudes toward the Law in Matthew's Gospel: A Discussion of Matthew 5:18." *BR* 17 (1972) 19–32.

Luz, U. "Die Erfüllung des Gesetzes bei Matthaus (Mt 5, 17–20)." *ZTK* 75 (1978) 398–435.

11. *Six "Antitheses"* (5:21-48)

21. "You have heard that it was said to the ancients: 'You shall not kill. But whoever does kill will be liable to judgment.' 22. But I say to you that everyone who is angry at his brother will be liable to judgment. Whoever says to his brother 'empty-head' will be liable to the Sanhedrin. Whoever says 'fool' will be liable to the Gehenna of fire. 23. So if you are offering your gift at the altar and there you remember that your brother has something against you, 24. leave your gift there before the altar and go, first be reconciled to your brother, and then go and offer your gift. 25. Be well disposed toward your enemy quickly, while you are with him on the way, lest the enemy hand you over to the judge and the judge to the guard, and you be put in prison. 26. Amen I say to you, you will not come out of there until you have paid the last cent.

27. "You have heard that it was said: 'You shall not commit adultery.' 28. But I say to you that everyone who looks at a woman so as to lust after her has already committed adultery with her in his heart. 29. But if your right eye leads you into sin, pluck it out and cast it from you. For it is better for you to lose one of your members and not have your whole body thrown into Gehenna. 30. And if your right hand leads you into sin, cut it off and cast it from you. For it is better for you that one of your members be lost and your whole body not go off to Gehenna.

31. "It was said: 'Whoever divorces his wife, let him give her a document.' 32. But I say to you that everyone who divorces his wife apart from sexual irregularity makes her an adultress; and whoever marries a divorced woman commits adultery.

33. "Again you have heard that it was said to the ancients: 'You shall not swear falsely; but you shall carry out your oaths to the Lord.' 34. But I say to you not to swear at all—neither by heaven because it is the throne of God, 35. nor by the earth because it is the footstool of his feet, nor by Jerusalem because it is the city of the Great King, 36. nor shall you swear by your head because you cannot make one hair white or black. 37. But let your word be "yes, yes" "no, no." Anything more than these is from the Evil One.

38. "You have heard that it was said: 'Eye for eye' and 'Tooth for tooth.' 39. But I say to you not to resist an evil doer. But whoever strikes you on

your right cheek, turn to him the other also. 40. And to whoever wishes to sue you and to take your shirt, let him have your coat also. 41. And whoever forces you to go one mile, go two with him. 42. Give to whoever asks you, and do not turn away whoever wishes to borrow from you.

43. "You have heard that it was said: 'You shall love your neighbor and hate your enemy.' 44. But I say to you: 'Love your enemies and pray for those who persecute you, 45. in order that you may be sons of your Father in heaven, because he makes his sun rise on evil and good, and he rains upon righteous and unrighteous. 46. For if you love those who love you, what reward do you have? Do not even the tax collectors do the same? 47. And if you greet your brethren only, what more do you do? Do not even the Gentiles do the same? 48. You therefore be perfect as your heavenly Father is perfect."

Notes

21. *it was said to the ancients*: The use of the "divine passive" (it was said = God said) to describe statements in Scripture appears frequently in rabbinic literature. The "ancients" probably refers to Moses and the Sinai generation, though "elders" can refer to Joshua and his contemporaries or to the post-biblical phase of the oral tradition (see *m. 'Abot* 1:1).

    you shall not kill: The commandment not to murder is taken from Exod 20:13/Deut 5:18. The sanction ("liable to judgment") does not accompany the commandment; it may derive from Exod 21:12; Lev 24:17; Num 35:16. The commandment refers to murder understood as the unjust taking of another's life.

22. *who is angry*: Anger is taken as the root of or first step toward murder. If one restrains anger, murder becomes impossible. Some manuscripts add a qualification "without cause" (*eikē*), but this limitation is probably a later scribal addition; cf. D. A. Black, "Jesus on Anger: The Text of Matthew 5:22a Revisited," *NovT* 30 (1988) 1–8.

    his brother: The expression is best taken generically as "fellow Israelite" or "fellow human being." There is no need to narrow it down to other members of the Matthean community. The three examples in 5:22 all make the same point about restraining anger. There is probably no progression intended in the three examples with regard either to the offense or to the punishment.

    judgment: In 5:21 the word *krisis* refers to the legal process or to a court. In 5:22 the tribunals ("judgment . . . Sanhedrin . . . Gehenna of fire") probably allude to the last judgment. Gehenna, originally the Valley of Hinnom to the west and south of Jerusalem, in the NT designates the place of final punishment for the wicked. The word "judgment" can be taken in an eschatological sense. For Sanhedrin, see C. S. Keener, "Matthew 5:22 and the Heavenly Court," *ExpTim* 99 (1987) 46.

23. *if you are offering your gift*: The two examples (5:23-24, 25-26) following the first antithesis are only loosely related by their theme of reconciliation. The first ex-

ample presupposes the existence of the Jerusalem Temple. There is criticism of one's attitude during the Temple worship, not of the Temple itself. The destruction of the Temple in A.D. 70 would not have rendered the warning meaningless. The Mishnah (compiled around A.D. 200) speaks as if the Temple were still functioning.

26. *the last cent*: The Greek word *kodrantēs* is a loan-word from the Latin *quadrans*, which was the smallest coin of the Roman currency. The final line implies that the case involved unpaid debts. But imprisonment for unpaid debts was not customary among Jews, and so the example seems to presuppose Roman law. The second example carries on the theme of willingness to be reconciled that was raised in the first example.

27. *'You shall not commit adultery'*: The text quotes Exod 20:14/Deut 5:18. Adultery referred to sexual relations between a married (or engaged woman) and a man other than her husband. The offense was against the husband of the adulterous woman and was to be punished by the death of both parties (Deut 22:22-24). Though there is doubt whether such a punishment was enacted, it is assumed in the story of Jesus and the adulterous woman in John 7:53–8:11.

28. *so as to lust after her*: This "antithesis" deepens the content of the sixth commandment (5:27) by alluding to the ninth (in its Greek form). The dynamic is the same as the first antithesis: Just as anger is the root of murder, lust is the root of adultery. The lustful look is the beginning of the process of possessing the wife of another man (see Exod 20:17).

29. *your right eye*: The connection between 5:27-28 and 5:29-30 is lustful look/right eye leading one into sin. A three-part warning (hand-foot-eye) appears in Mark 9:43-48. The right side was considered the more respectable in antiquity. Whether the right hand (5:30) is assumed to carry any sexual connotation is not clear.

31. *It was said*: The third antithesis is introduced by a very compressed formula in comparison with the others. It carries on the theme of marriage and adultery found in 5:27-28.

    Whoever divorces his wife: The alleged text is in fact a summary of Deut 24:1, which outlines the divorce process: "he writes her a bill of divorce and puts it in her hand and sends her out of his house, and she departs out of his house." The document stated that the husband had divorced the woman, and so she was free to marry someone else without incurring the charge of adultery. The divorce proceeding was initiated by the husband.

32. *who divorces his wife . . . makes her an adulteress*: Whereas Luke 16:18 defines the adultery as divorce and remarriage, Matt 5:32 makes divorce itself the equivalent of adultery. For a full treatment of the divorce pericopes, see the interpretation of Matt 19:1-12.

    apart from sexual irregularity: The exceptive clause (see Matt 19:9) comes from Matthew or his community. It was probably motivated by the idea that in the case of adultery the man had to divorce his wife. The precise meaning of *porneia* here translated as "sexual irregularity" is much debated. The two most common explanations are (1) sexual misconduct on the woman's part and (2) illicit marital union within the degrees of kinship proscribed in Lev 18:6-18 (see Acts 15:20, 29). The first explanation is more likely. For a defense of the second, see J. A. Fitzmyer, "The Matthean Divorce Texts and Some New Palestinian Evidence," *TS* 37 (1976) 197–226.

33. *'You shall not swear falsely'*: The fourth antithesis is introduced by "again," which marks a beginning after the two antitheses on marriage and divorce. Though there is some connection with the eighth commandment ("You shall not bear false witness against your neighbor," Exod 20:16; Deut 5:20), the more likely background is Lev 19:12: "You shall not swear by my name falsely."

34. *not to swear at all*: Jesus' prohibition of swearing has the effect of the preceding antithesis: It guards against swearing falsely by forbidding any kind of swearing at all. This move has the consequence of rendering the Torah passages about oaths useless. Yet this need not be taken as abrogation or criticism of the "old Law." Rather it is a sharpening that Matthew understood as fulfillment.

neither by heaven: See the parallel tradition in Jas 5:11. The substitutes for the name of God in oaths are all related to God: "Heaven is my throne, and the earth is my footstool" (Isa 66:1). For Jerusalem as the city of the Great King (=God), see Ps 48:3.

36. *by your head*: For swearing "by the life of your head" see *m. Sanh.* 3:12. The use of hair coloring was well known in antiquity. The comment is ironic, to the effect that underneath the coloring the original shade remains. Thus the weakness of human beings to change nature is emphasized.

37. *"yes, yes" "no, no"*: In later rabbinic writings a double "yes" or a double "no" could be construed as an oath (see Lachs, 102-03) in its own right. But that is not the case here, where all oaths are prohibited. It is not clear whether "the Evil One" refers to Satan or to evil in general. See P. S. Minear, "Yes or No: The demand for honesty in the early Church," *NovT* 13 (1971) 1-13.

38. *'Eye for eye'*: The "law of retaliation" is expressed in Exod 21:24; Lev 24:20; and Deut 19:21. The goal of the law was to keep revenge within certain boundaries, and to avoid the escalation of violence. Its OT formulations affirm personal responsibility for one's actions, the equality of persons before the law, and just proportion between crime and punishment. It is doubtful that this law was in effect in Jesus' time.

39. *not to resist an evildoer*: Jesus' teaching moves out of the realm of civil law and judicial principles. The term *ponēros* is ambiguous. Since one must resist the Evil One (Satan) and evil itself, the word most likely refers to one who does evil. The setting of the saying is personal relations on a small scale. Whether it can be transposed to the social or political realms is a matter of ongoing debate.

right cheek: Unlike Luke 6:29 Matthew specifies it as the "right" (cheek). The specification indicates the blow comes from the back of the assailant's left hand, and therefore constitutes an insult rather than a violent assault. It is possible that "the other" is a misunderstanding of "back" in Aramaic (*'uḥrâ/'aḥōrâ*) and that the idea is that, when insulted by a slap on the cheek, you should simply turn away and not retaliate.

40. *shirt . . . coat*: The *chitōn* was the garment worn next to the skin, and the *himation* was the outer garment. The *chiton* (translated here as "shirt") covered the whole body. Whereas in Luke 6:29 to someone who is taking the coat one should give the shirt, in Matt 5:40 the context is the legal case about the "shirt" in Exod 22:26-27: "If ever you take your neighbor's garment in pledge, you shall restore it to him before the sun goes down; for that is his only covering."

41. *forces you*: The third example refers to the legal right of Roman soldiers to press civilians into service. For example, Simon of Cyrene is pressed into service to carry the beam of Jesus' cross (Matt 27:32). Instead of resisting this imposition, Jesus urges a doubling of the service. The service probably consisted in carrying baggage from one place to another.

42. *give*: The final examples move out of the realm of force and deal with a beggar and one seeking a loan. The injunctions to give alms and lend without concern for repayment are based on Deut 15:7-11: "You shall give to him freely, and your heart shall not be grudging when you give to him."

43. *love your neighbor*: The commandment appears in Lev 19:18 where the context is the congregation of the people of Israel (19:1). There is no OT commandment to hate one's enemy. In the Qumran scrolls there are directives to "hate all the sons of darkness" (1QS 1:10) and "everlasting hatred for all the men of the Pit" (9:21). These directives are rooted in the dualism of the Qumran community: Those who oppose the angel of Light, the children of light, and the deeds of light deserve the enmity of the community.

44. *love your enemies*: The effect of Jesus' teaching is to break through limitations imposed on the object of one's love. It relates back to the fifth antithesis with its emphasis on breaking the cycle of hatred and violence. While there is not a direct parallel in the OT or rabbinic writings, many biblical and rabbinic teachings point in the same direction as Jesus' teaching does.

45. *that you may be sons*: Matthew places the motivation earlier than Luke does (see Luke 6:27, 35). The form is typical of the Pentateuch, especially Deuteronomy. The content is also from Deuteronomy: "You are the sons of the Lord your God" (14:1). Since God supplies sun and rain for all kinds of people, the challenge is to work from a God-ward perspective of care and love for all.

46. *tax collectors*: The cases in 5:46-47 illustrate the superior righteousness (5:20). It does not require much virtue to love those who love you or to greet one's brethren only. Tax (or toll) collectors were suspected of dishonesty and collaboration with the Romans. They are paired with Gentiles in Matt 18:17 and also with sinners (9:10) and harlots (21:31-32). Thus they constitute a class of disreputable people within Israel. Luke 6:32-33 reads "sinners."

47. *Gentiles*: The most obvious meaning is "those outside of Israel." Efforts to link them to the "people of the land" (i.e., nonobservant Jews) are not convincing. The perspective of the teaching is thoroughly Jewish. There is no contradiction between the somewhat disparaging comments about the *ethnikoi* here (and 18:17) and the command to carry the Gospel to the Gentiles in 28:19.

48. *be perfect*: Luke 6:36 has "Be merciful as your Father is merciful." The idea of God as "perfect" does not appear in the OT and lends itself to abstraction. The background is probably in OT sayings about God's holiness: "You shall be holy; for I the Lord your God am holy" (Lev 19:2; see 20:26; 21:8). The word "perfect" (*tam*) refers to the "wholeness" of God who cares for all peoples.

Interpretation

Matt 5:21-48 consists of six sections that follow the same basic pattern in their beginning: "You have heard that it was said . . . But I say to you." They are traditionally called "antitheses," which means "contrasts" or "oppositions." As a rhetorical pattern an antithesis consists of two parts in which one is set over against or contradicts the other. When applied to Matt 5:21-48 the word "antithesis" fits the rhetorical pattern but not the content. In some cases Jesus expresses agreement with the biblical teaching but urges his followers to go deeper or to the root of the commandment (murder→anger, adultery→lust, retaliation→nonresistance). In other cases Jesus' teaching can seem to go so far as to make the biblical commandment useless (divorce, oaths, love of neighbor).

Christians often overemphasize the difference between the OT teachings quoted in the first part of the antithesis and Jesus' instruction in the second part. They talk about the opposition between law and gospel, or refer to the "new Law" promulgated by Jesus. But the Matthean context in which the antitheses appear cautions against drawing sharp contrasts between Jesus and the Torah.

Since the antitheses follow Matt 5:17-20 which affirms that Jesus came not to abolish but to "fulfill" the Law and the Prophets, it would seem that the antitheses are intended to illustrate in what that fulfillment consists. Matthew himself appears to have been responsible for the antithesis form. Therefore in interpreting them from a Matthean perspective we should focus on their function as fulfilling the Torah rather than abrogating it. Matthew did not take them as rendering the OT commandments obsolete or useless. Rather he wanted to show that Jesus interpreted the Torah in such a way as to lead it to its goal and its fullness.

Much of the material in Matt 5:21-48 appears as separate pieces in Luke (Q) and Mark: Matt 5:25-26 = Luke 12:57-59; Matt 5:29-30 = Mark 9:43, 45, 47; Matt 5:32 = Luke 16:18; Matt 5:39-42 = Luke 6:29-30; Matt 5:43-48 = Luke 6:27-28, 32-36. The antithesis form does not appear in the parallel material. Some trace that form back to Jesus or the pre-Matthean tradition, but others attribute it to the evangelist. At any rate, even if he was not entirely responsible for the pattern, Matthew certainly made it his own and used it to illustrate how Jesus came not to abolish but to fulfill the Law and the Prophets.

The English term "Law" can distort the Jewish understanding of Torah. The word "Torah" derives from the Hebrew verb "instruct" (*yrh*) and refers to the teaching or instruction presented in the Scriptures, especially the Pentateuch. For Jews the Torah was (and is) the revelation of God's will, a kind of divine blueprint for action. It is a gift and a privilege given to Israel, not a burden. Acting upon the Torah is the privileged way of responding to the Creator God who has entered into covenant relationship with Israel. It presupposes the prior manifestation of God's love. The Greek translation of Torah (*nomos*) is not incorrect since the Torah is concrete and demands action. But the theological context of covenant can never be forgotten if distortion is to be avoided.

Matthew presents the six antitheses as examples of the principle that Jesus came not to abolish but to fulfill the Law and the Prophets. Efforts to discern structural principles beyond the obvious pattern of six antitheses are not convincing. Some find two sets of three, with a break signalled by "again" in 5:33. There are connections of content in the second and third antitheses (marriage-divorce) and the fifth and sixth antitheses (nonresistance-love of enemies).

The biblical and Jewish background of the six antitheses has been spelled out in the notes. The task here is to consider what message Matt 5:21-48 would have conveyed in the Matthean community's contest with other Jews about the true nature of Judaism after A.D. 70. At least one group—the early rabbinic movement—placed great emphasis on studying and living the Torah. Matthew's task was to show that Jesus (and his followers), far from being an enemy of the Torah, fulfilled it in his teaching and action, and thus gave to it the appropriate interpretation for the changed situation of Judaism. The usual Christian categories of intensification (antitheses 1, 2, 5) and abrogation (antitheses 3, 4, 6) do not apply to Matthew's situation. For him, the operative word was "fulfillment." The biblical text in each case is the starting point, and one can find early Jewish rabbis who agree with Jesus at almost every point (see Lachs).

The dynamic of the antitheses is one of sharpening the Torah, getting to the root of what it teaches, moving into the realm of internal dispositions from which evil actions proceed. The first antithesis (Matt 5:21-22) attacks anger as the root of murder. The two loosely connected illustrations (5:23-24, 25-26) stress the value of reconciliation with an enemy. The second antithesis (5:27-28) attacks lust as the root of adultery. The loosely connected sayings about the right eye and the right hand as causes of scandal (5:29-30) are further instances of going to the sources of sin.

The third antithesis (5:31-32) presents Jesus' prohibition of divorce as a way of avoiding the divorce procedure outlined in Deut 24:1. The exceptive clause ("apart from sexual irregularity") suggests that Matthew was part of the Jewish debate about the grounds for divorce involving the interpretation of the phrase "some indecency" in Deut 24:1. Whereas Hillel gave it a wide interpretation, Shammai narrowed it down to mean unchastity (*m. Gittin* 9:10). If *porneia* refers to sexual misconduct on the woman's part, then Matthew makes Jesus agree with Shammai. If it refers to marriages within the degrees of kinship forbidden by Lev 18:6-18, then Matthew brings Jesus' authority to bear on what may have been a problem especially for Gentile converts and presents him again as upholding the Torah.

The antithesis (5:33-37) about oaths carries on the same dynamic: To avoid swearing falsely avoid oaths entirely. Again the development of the antithesis suggests that Matthew was embroiled in a debate about the propriety of making oaths and vows, and about the formulas associated with such oaths and vows.

The antithesis on nonretaliation (5:38-39a) also urges Jesus' followers to opt out of the process of revenge through violence. The four illustrations (5:39b-42) follow a two-part structure ("whoever . . . to whoever"). They not only prohibit violence but also demand that brutality and force be met with abounding goodness.

The final antithesis (5:43-48) concerns the definition of the "neighbor." It urges that love include even enemies and uses the example of God's care for all creatures to challenge us to avoid restricting love only to those who can benefit us or already love us.

The topics treated in the six antitheses—murder and anger, adultery and lust, divorce, oaths, responding to evil, loving friends and enemies—remain among the most important and controversial matters for religious people. Teachers and preachers who raise them can be sure of arousing interest and discussion. The preceding interpretation has focused on the theological framework in which the topics are presented by Matthew. The context is the debate within Judaism about the authoritative interpretation of the Torah. Matthew and other Jewish Christians viewed the Torah as divine revelation and the appropriate response to the God of covenant, not as something obsolete and burdensome. Their concern was to show how Jesus came *to fulfill* rather than *to abolish*. Even if at points the framework gets strained, it ought not to be abandoned in favor of sharp contrasts between (Jewish) legalism and (Christian) gospel love.

For Reference and Further Study

Fitzmyer, J. A. "The Matthean Divorce Texts and Some New Palestinian Evidence." *TS* 37 (1976) 197–226.

Horsley, R. A. "Ethics and Exegesis: 'Love Your Enemies' and the Doctrine of Nonviolence." *JAAR* 54 (1986) 3–31.

Lambrecht, J. "The Sayings of Jesus on Nonviolence." *Louvain Studies* 12 (1987) 291–305.
Lohfink, G. "Der ekklesiale Sitz im Leben der Aufforderung Jesu zum Gewaltverzicht (Mt 5,39b-42/Lk 6,29f)." *TQ* 162 (1982) 236–53.
Minear, P. S. "Yes or No: The demand for honesty in the early Church." *NovT* 13 (1971) 1–13.
van Boxel, P. W. "You have heard that it was said." *Bijdragen* 49 (1988) 362–77.
Witherington, B. "Matthew 5:32 and 19:9—Exception or Exceptional Situation." *NTS* 31 (1985) 571–76.

12. *Three Acts of Piety* (6:1-18)

1. "Be careful not to practice your righteousness before people to be seen by them. If not, you have no reward from your Father in heaven.

2. "When you give alms, do not sound a trumpet before you as the hypocrites do in the synagogues and in the alleys in order that they may be glorified by people. Amen I say to you, they have their reward. 3. But when you give alms, let not your left hand know what your right is doing, 4. in order that your almsgiving might be in secret. And your Father who sees in secret will pay you back.

5. "And when you pray, do not be like the hypocrites because they love to stand praying in the synagogues and on the street-corners in order to make an appearance before people. Amen I say to you, they have their reward. 6. But you when you pray, go into your inner room and close your door to pray to your Father who is in secret. And your Father who sees in secret will pay you back. 7. When you pray, do not babble on like the Gentiles, for they think that they will be heard for their many words. 8. Do not be like them. For your Father knows what need you have before you ask him. 9. So you pray in this way: 'Our Father who is in heaven, may your name be made holy. 10. May your kingdom come. May your will be done—as it is in heaven, so also on earth. 11. Give us today our bread for the coming day. 12. And forgive us our debts as we also have forgiven those who owe us. 13. And do not bring us into the test but rescue us from the Evil One.' 14. For if you forgive people their transgression, your heavenly Father will forgive you also. 15. But if you do not forgive people, neither will your Father forgive your transgressions.

16. "When you fast, do not be like the hypocrites—with a gloomy look, for they disfigure their faces in order to appear to people as fasting. Amen I say to you, they have their reward. 17. But you, when you fast, anoint your head and wash your face 18. in order not to appear to people as fasting but to your Father who is in secret. And your Father who sees in secret will pay you back."

Notes

1. *righteousness*: The term is best taken in a general sense (as in Matt 3:15; 5:20). It is a heading for 6:2-18.

   If not: The elliptical statement can be filled out ("If you are not careful"). The heading draws a disjunction between a reward from human beings and one from God, between an earthly reward and a heavenly one.

2. *When you give alms*: The term for almsgiving is *eleēmosynē*, which can also mean "mercy" (see Matt 9:13; 12:7). The context demands the specific, concrete meaning. Kindness to the poor is praised in Prov 14:21, 31; Isa 58:6-8. The Torah also institutionalized procedures for feeding the poor (Deut 14:28-29; 24:19-22). Nevertheless, the personal, spontaneous giving of alms was considered one of the marks of the pious (see Job 29:12, 16).

   trumpet: The expression should be taken as hyperbole and metaphor. It is possible that someone actually did this. But the point is to caricature the ostentatious behavior captured by the image of blowing a horn to advertise one's almsgiving. Another approach to the text is to envision the receptacles set up in the Temple courts. The idea would be to avoid making those "trumpets" resound when putting in coins. See N. M. McEleney, "Does the Trumpet Sound or Resound? An Interpretation of Matthew 6:2," *ZNW* 76 (1985) 43–46. But this interpretation lessens the caricature and presupposes a setting in the Jerusalem Temple.

   hypocrites: The term derives from the Greek *hypokritēs*, which designated an actor who performed behind a mask. Its metaphoric use here would refer to someone who pretended to be something he is not. But in Matthew the word (see also ch. 23) has a wider meaning and describes pretentious, ostentatious people.

3. *your left hand*: This sounds like a proverb, though no such proverb has survived from antiquity. The idea seems to concern giving in secret, but the precise applicability remains somewhat obscure. In the context, however, of reward from humans (glory) and from God it may refer to letting no one else know, not even your closest friend (one as close as your left hand).

4. *will pay you back*: For God as the one who rewards good deeds done in secret, see Prov 24:12: "and will he not requite man according to his work?" It is grammatically possible to take "in secret" with the verb "pay back," though it goes more smoothly with "sees."

5. *stand praying in the synagogues*: Jesus is not criticizing public prayer in groups, but rather (it seems) private prayer made into a public display. The formal prayer (the Eighteen Benedictions) was carried out in a group, while standing, and in synagogues. The behavior criticized here makes an informal, private activity into a public display.

6. *inner room*: The Greek word *tameion* can refer to a "storage room" or "pantry," or the innermost room in the house. In either case the idea is the room least likely to attract public notice. Perhaps such a room had no windows.

7. *do not babble*: The precise etymology and meaning of the verb *battalogeō* remain disputed. The usual English translation "babble" takes it as onomatapoeia. Its

context in Matt 6:7 alludes to a flood of word and formulas. It should be distinguished from NT exhortations to pray with perseverance (Luke 11:5-8; 18:1-8) and without ceasing (1 Thess 5:17).

8. *your Father knows*: The pagan idea of a God who can be manipulated by a flood of words stands in contrast to Israel's heavenly Father who says: "Before they call I will answer, while they are yet speaking I will hear" (Isa 65:24).

9. *Our Father who is in heaven*: The Matthean version uses the long form of address (cf. "Father" in Luke 11:2) that is also common in Jewish prayer, whereas the simple "Father" is not. It not only brings the prayer into line with typical Jewish prayer forms but also prepares for the petition in 6:10b.

   may your name be made holy: The phrase has a parallel in the Jewish *Kaddish* prayer: "May thy great name be magnified and hallowed." For the hallowing of God's name in the OT see Lev 22:32; Deut 32:51; Isa 8:13; 29:23. In later Judaism the phrase is used in connection with suffering martyrdom for religious principles.

10. *kingdom come*: The second petition expresses the central concern of the entire prayer—the coming of God's kingdom in its fullness. The reference is to the future, eschatological kingdom. When it comes all creatures will "hallow" God's name and God's will will be done perfectly on earth. For some Jewish scenarios of the coming kingdom, see *Testament of Moses* 10 and *1 Enoch* 91, 93.

    your will be done: Matthew's additional petition (cf. Luke 11:2) looks forward to what will happen after God's kingdom comes—a perfect harmony between the way in which heaven and earth run. Understood in this eschatological sense, the petition does not add new content to the second petition. The petition is anticipated in the way in which God is addressed: "who is in heaven."

11. *bread for the coming day*: The Greek word *epiousios* is taken to mean "coming." Thus it might refer to the eschatological Day of the Lord (as the previous petitions suggest), or as a morning prayer it could allude to the food necessary to survive for the rest of the day. The Latin tradition of *supersubstantialis*, frequently connected with the Eucharist in Christian piety, may carry an allusion to the manna provided for Israel in the wilderness.

12. *our debts*: Luke 11:4 reads "our sins." In fact, both texts say the same thing. The image of "debts" to describe sins against God is common in Jewish writings. The idea of granting a release of debts because God has released one's own debts appears in Deut 15:1-2. The idea of forgiving others in connection with being forgiven oneself is underscored in Matt 6:14-15.

13. *the test*: For the idea of God as the one who tests or tries, see Pss 11:5; 26:2. The test in view here is the final, eschatological testing through which all must pass. The petition is that God not let us fall in this testing. The word *ponēros* is ambiguous; it can be taken as "evil" or "the Evil One." If the eschatological interpretation is correct, it is better to take *ponēros* as referring to Satan. Some manuscripts add a conclusion such as the following: "For thine is the kingdom and the power and the glory, forever. Amen." The addition is clearly based on 1 Chr 29:11-12 and fits in with the Jewish practice of "sealing" a prayer. But it does not seem to have been part of the earliest versions of Matthew's Gospel and must be viewed as a later addition.

14. *if you forgive*: The parallel sayings in 6:14-15 represent an underscoring of the idea introduced in 6:12. The theme of a close relation between our willingness to forgive others and God's willingness to forgive us appears in Sir 28:1-2. For "transgressions" the Greek text has *paraptōmata*, a different word from "debts" (*opheilēmata*) found in 6:12.

16. *when you fast*: The only fast enjoined in the Torah is on the Day of Atonement (see Lev 16:31; 23:26-32). Public fasts were called in remembrance of national disasters or in times of great need, such as droughts. What is criticized in Matt 6:16-18 is ostentatious behavior during private fasts. According to *Didache* 8:1 the "hypocrites" fasted on Monday and Thursday.

a gloomy look: The Greek term is *skythrōpos* (see Luke 24:17). The assumption is that such persons fast. The problem is that it is all for public show: They disfigure (*aphanizousin*) themselves to appear (*phanōsin*) as fasting. The public recognition of their fasting is the only reward they deserve and receive. For criticism of external show in fasting see Isa 58:1-4.

17. *anoint your head*: To put oil on one's head was a sign of joy and festivity; see Isa 61:3 ("the oil of gladness instead of mourning").

Interpretation

The third part of the Sermon on the Mount (6:1-18) consists of an introductory statement of principle (6:1), along with teachings on three acts of piety: almsgiving (6:2-4), prayer (6:5-8), and fasting (6:16-18). The section on prayer includes the text of the Lord's Prayer (6:9-13) and a teaching on forgiveness of sins (6:14-15).

The teachings on the three acts of piety follow the same literary pattern: the act of piety, the criticism of inappropriate behavior, the "but I say to you" sentence defining public recognition as the reward, instruction on appropriate behavior that avoids public display, and the promise of a reward from God. These teachings have no direct parallels in other Gospels, and so we must assume that they had special meaning for the Matthean community.

The three acts of piety—almsgiving, prayer, fasting—were important aspects of Jewish religious life in Jesus' time. The Matthean Jesus is not criticizing the acts of piety as such, nor is he speaking against public manifestations of piety. In each case it is a matter of a private act of piety—not the Jewish daily prayers, nor the fast of the Day of Atonement. His target is the aberrant style of those who make acts of personal piety such as almsgiving, prayer, and fasting into public displays. It is ostentatiousness in personal piety that is criticized here: drawing public attention to almsgiving, praying in public places so as to be seen, and calling attention to one's fasting. Such people will have to be satisfied with public recognition as their reward. They will get no reward from God. On the other hand, God will reward those who keep secret their private acts of piety.

In their Matthean context these teachings about true and false piety would have been taken as criticisms of the rival Jews who controlled "their synagogues," the "synagogue of the hypocrites." The description of those who practiced this false piety as "hypocrites" (6:2, 5, 16) and the references to "the synagogues" (6:2, 5) make this certain. When read alongside the polemic in Matthew 23, Matt 6:1-18 functions as part of the attack against the Jewish opponents of the Matthean community. The positive message of the text is that Jesus' followers are to avoid public displays of private piety. The conflict was not over the practices of piety but about the way in which they should be carried out. The claim is that in Jesus' community these practices are carried out correctly, in accordance with God's will.

The section on prayer (6:5-15) differs from the other two sections by its inclusion of the Lord's Prayer (6:9-13) and the instruction on forgiveness (6:14-15) that serves as a commentary on 6:12. From one perspective the Lord's Prayer can be viewed as an intrusion or interruption in a carefully structured triad. But it can also be taken as the center of the entire text (6:1-18) and thus as the "spiritual heart" of the piety that ought to animate Jesus' followers.

The Matthean version of the Lord's Prayer consists of an address to God (6:9b), three "you" petitions (6:9c-10), and three "we" petitions (6:11-13). The petitions are short and express the needs of those awaiting the coming of God's kingdom. The central petition is "May your kingdom come" (6:10a). The "you" petitions that frame it express hopes for what conditions will be when God's kingdom comes—all creatures will declare the holiness of God, and God's will is to be done perfectly on earth. The three "we" petitions also presuppose eschatological expectation: sustenance for the "coming day" (6:11), forgiveness of sins (6:12), and divine protection in the eschatological testing (6:13). Thus in its content focusing on the coming Day of the Lord the Lord's Prayer is thoroughly Jewish, typical of at least one theological style in first century Judaism.

The Matthean version of the Lord's Prayer is especially Jewish, in comparison with the shorter (and more primitive) version in Luke 11:2-4. The longer address to God as "Our Father who is in heaven" (Matt 6:9b) instead of the simple "Father" in Luke 11:2 involves the substitution of a standard Jewish formula of address to God in prayer for a highly unusual one. The insertion of a third "you" petition (6:10b) and a third "we" petition (6:13) is typical of the flexibility of Jewish prayer. The metaphor of "debts" (6:12) as a way of talking about sins is characteristically Jewish. Whereas the Lukan version is sometimes described as the Lord's Prayer for Gentiles, the Matthean version with its additions is clearly most appropriate for Jewish Christians. Indeed there is nothing in it that a pious Jew of the first century or today could not say. Of course, the context of the prayer in the NT and the history that has surrounded it over the centuries have made it into the Christian prayer par excellence and therefore suspect among Jews.

The Jewish character of the Lord's Prayer is also clear from a comparison with the Jewish Eighteen Benedictions recited three times a day. The prayer is also known as the 'Amidah, from the Hebrew root *'md* ("stand up"), since it is customary to recite the prayer while standing. The Eighteen Benedictions consists of three introductory praises, twelve petitions for personal and communal needs, and three concluding praises. It is, of course, much longer and more developed than the Lord's Prayer is. But practically every phrase in the Lord's Prayer appears in the Eighteen Benedictions.

The precise relation between the two prayers is unclear. Some have argued that the Lord's Prayer is a simplified version of the Eighteen Benedictions. We do know that in some early Christian circles (probably Antioch in Syria) the Lord's Prayer functioned as the Christian alternative to the Jewish Eighteen Benedictions: "Three times in the day you are to so pray (the Lord's Prayer)" (*Didache* 8:3). Since *Didache* comes from roughly the same place and time as Matthew's Gospel, it is possible that the Lord's Prayer also functioned in this way in the Matthean community.

The following texts provide a sample of the style and content of the Eighteen Benedictions:

1. Blessed art thou, O Lord,
   Our God and God of our fathers,
   God of Abraham, God of Isaac, and God of Jacob,
   Great, mighty, and awesome God,
   God Most High, creator of heaven and earth,
   Our shield and shield of our fathers,
   Our refuge in every generation.
   Blessed art thou, O Lord, shield of Abraham.
2. Thou art mighty - humbling the haughty,
   Powerful - calling the arrogant to judgment,
   Eternal - reviving the dead,
   Causing the wind to blow and the dew to fall,
   Sustaining the living, resurrecting the dead -
   O cause our salvation to sprout in the twinkling of an eye!
   Blessed art thou, O Lord, who revivest the dead.
3. Thou art holy and thy name is awesome
   And there is no god beside thee.
   Blessed art thou, O Lord, the Holy God.
4. Graciously favor us, our Father, with understanding from thee,
   And discernment and insight out of thy Torah.
   Blessed art thou, O Lord, gracious bestower of understanding.

5. *Turn us to thee, O Lord, and we shall return*
   Restore our days as of old (Lam. 5:21).
   Blessed art thou, O Lord, who desirest repentance.
6. Forgive us, our Father, for we have sinned against thee,
   Erase and blot out our transgressions from before thine eyes,
   For thou art abundantly compassionate.
   Blessed art thou, O Lord, who forgivest readily.
7. Behold our afflictions and defend our cause,
   And redeem us for thy name's sake.
   Blessed art thou, O Lord, Redeemer of Israel.

The benedictions continue in the same vein until the eighteenth is reached. The Lord's Prayer and the Eighteen Benedictions use the same phrases, arose at roughly the same time and place, feature the prayer of petition along with praise and thanksgiving, and were recited three times daily. The Lord's Prayer is much shorter and more consistently eschatological in its theology.

Perhaps the Matthean community did use the Lord's Prayer as its alternative to the Eighteen Benedictions. This hypothesis, which is suggested by *Didache* 8:3, is strengthened by the polemical context (Matt 6:1-18) in which the "hypocrites" and their synagogues are roundly criticized for their style of ostentatious piety. In such a situation the terse and modest Lord's Prayer with its recognition of God's omnipotence and its unwavering hope for the coming kingdom of God would have been an appropriate vehicle for fostering the identity of the Matthean community vis-à-vis the early rabbinic movement.

Teachers and preachers need to emphasize that the Matthean Jesus in 6:1-18 does not attack public piety (something unthinkable for a first-century Jew) but rather criticizes ostentatious displays of what should be private religious acts. They need also to be sensitive to the "eschatological" orientation of the Lord's Prayer as well as to its thoroughly Jewish language and content.

For Reference and Further Study

Carmignac, J. *Recherches sur le "Notre Père."* Paris: Letouzey & Ane, 1969.

Dorneich, M., ed. *Vater-Unser Bibliographie—The Lord's Prayer, a Bibliography.* Freiburg: Herder, 1982.

Harner, P. B. *Understanding the Lord's Prayer.* Philadelphia: Fortress, 1975.

Mangan, C. *Can We Still Call God "Father?" A Woman Looks at the Lord's Prayer Today.* Wilmington: Glazier, 1984.

13. *Other Teachings* (6:19–7:12)

19. "Do not lay up treasures for yourselves on earth, where moth and rust destroy and where thieves break through and steal. 20. But lay up treasures for yourselves in heaven, where neither moth nor rust destroy and where thieves do not break through and steal. 21. For where your treasure is, there also your heart will be.

22. "The lamp of the body is the eye. If your eye be healthy, your whole body will be radiant. 23. But if your eye be diseased, your whole body will be dark. If the light that is in you is darkness, how great the darkness!

24. "No one can serve two masters. For either he will hate the one and love the other, or he will be devoted to one and despise the other. You cannot serve God and Mammon.

25. "Therefore I say this to you: Do not be concerned about your life as to what you will eat or what you will drink, nor about your body as to what you will wear. Is not your life more than food and your body more than clothing? 26. Look at the birds of the heaven, because they do not sow, nor harvest, nor gather into barns, and your heavenly Father feeds them. Are you not superior to them? 27. Which of you by being anxious can add to his stature one measure? 28. And why are you anxious about clothing? Consider the lilies of the field how they grow. They do not labor and do not spin. 29. But I say to you that not even Solomon in all his glory was dressed like one of these. 30. If God so clothes the grass of the field, which lives today and tomorrow is thrown into the oven, how much more will he care for you, people of little faith? 31. So do not be anxious, saying: 'What will we eat?' or 'What will we drink?' or 'What will we wear?' 32. For all these things the Gentiles seek. Your heavenly Father knows that you need all these. 33. But seek first the kingdom of God and his righteousness, and all these will be added on for you. 34. Do not be anxious about tomorrow, for tomorrow will be anxious for itself. Enough for each day is its own trouble.

7:1. "Do not judge, in order not to be judged. 2. For with the judgment you judge you will be judged, and with the measure you measure it will be measured out for you.

3. "Why do you see the speck in the eye of your brother, but you do not notice the beam in your own eye? 4. Or how can you say to your brother: 'Let me take out the speck from your eye,' and behold the beam is in your eye? 5. Hypocrite, take out first the beam from your eye, and then you can see to take out the speck from the eye of your brother.

6. "Do not give what is holy to dogs, nor throw your pearls before pigs, lest they trample them with their feet and turn on you and tear you apart.

7. "Ask and it will be given to you. Seek and you will find. Knock and it will be opened to you. 8. For everyone who asks receives, and whoever seeks finds, and to one who knocks it will be opened. 9. Or which one of you, who when his son will ask for bread will give to him a stone? 10. Or when he asks for a fish will give to him a serpent? 11. If you being evil

know how to give good gifts to your children, by how much more will your heavenly Father give good things to those who ask him.

12. "Therefore everything that you wish that people would do to you, so also do to them. For this is the Law and the Prophets."

Notes

19. *moth and rust*: The treasure destroyed by the moth (*sēs*) would consist of cloth. The precise meaning of *brōsis* (literally, "eating") is disputed. If properly translated "rust," the treasure is metal. But it may refer to an insect, and so the treasure could be cloth or food. The thieves can "break through" the mud-brick walls of a house and steal.

20. *treasures . . . in heaven*: For the idea of treasures in heaven see 4 Ezra 7:77; 8:33, 36; 2 Baruch 14:12; 24:1; Tob 4:8-9. Typical is 4 Ezra 7:77: "For you have a treasure of works laid up with the Most High; but it will not be shown to you until the last times." See also the statement of Monobaz (who converted to Judaism in Jesus' time): "My fathers gathered treasures for below, I have gathered treasures for above" (*t. Pe'a* 4:18).

21. *where your treasure is*: The idea is that your goal or what you consider important will determine the course of your activity and your commitment. The saying remains somewhat obscure in meaning and only loosely connected with 6:19-20. What joined the two units may simply have been the two words "where" and "treasure."

22. *If your eye be healthy*: Two lines of interpretation are possible. The "physiological" approach (reflected in the translation) takes the eye as the lamp of the body. Depending on the health of the eye, one will experience the world around as either light or darkness. Building on this is the "moral" interpretation more at home in Judaism. There the contrast may be between generous and jealous/stingy people. Or perhaps it is between the children of light and the children of darkness.

23. *diseased*: The Greek word is *ponēros* ("evil"). If the "moral" interpretation is present, there may be a reference to Deut 15:9: "Take heed lest . . . your eye be hostile to your poor brother." The image of "evil eye" in this context refers to lack of generosity.

24. *hate . . . love*: The sharp opposites reflect the language of Deut 21:15-17. Some cases in rabbinic writings (*b. Qidd.* 90a; *m. Gitt.* 4:5; *m. 'Eduy.* 1:13) presuppose situations in which a slave was owned by more than one master.

Mammon: The term appears in Hebrew and Aramaic texts to mean "wealth, money, property." It is usually derived from *'mn* ("believe, trust") and taken to mean "that in which one places trust." Others derive it from *mwn* ("supply with nourishment"). The term becomes negative only in context (as here) or in combination with another term (see Luke 16:9, "mammon of unrighteousness").

25. *Therefore*: The introduction to Matt 6:25-34 has the effect of linking the unit to the preceding saying about the whole-hearted service of God (6:24), and thus provides a theological context of trust in God (rather than laziness or impracticality) for the command "do not be concerned."

your life: The Greek word *psychē* can be translated "soul." But it would be a misunderstanding of the Semitic anthropology if "soul" were taken as the spiritual part of the person in contrast to the material part ("body"). The *nepeš* ("gullet") needs food and drink in order that the body may be healthy. The reasoning moves from the "light" (food and clothing) to the "heavy" (life and body).

26. *birds of the heaven*: Luke 12:23 has "crows, ravens." Matthew may have changed the wording because "ravens" were considered unclean animals (see Lev 11:15; Deut 14:14). The more general expression also allows the saying to take in more members of the animal kingdom.

27. *one measure*: The measure *pēchys* was originally a forearm, i.e., from the elbow to the tip of the finger (about eighteen inches). The term that it modifies (*hēlikia*) can refer either to the time of life (age) or to bodily stature (height). So the saying could concern adding to one's time of life.

28. *lilies*: The word may be as generic as "birds" in 6:26, intended to describe various flowers and plants. Some even think that "beasts" (*thēria*) would be more appropriate in the context. The first verb that describes their (in)activity as "labor" (*kopiōsin*) is odd and thus has attracted many emendations, e.g., *kopanizousin* ("beat" flax) from Lachs, p. 133.

29. *Solomon*: For OT descriptions of Solomon's great wealth, see 1 Kgs 10:4-5; 2 Chr 9:13-22, though nothing is said there about the splendor of his clothing.

30. *the grass of the field*: For the transitory character of flowers and grass (in comparison with God's word) see Isa 40:6-8: "The grass withers, the flower fades."

people of little faith: In Matt 8:26; 14:31; 16:8 the term *oligopistos* is applied to the inner circle of Jesus' disciples. While not a positive term in that context, it does at least soften the negative portrayal of Jesus' disciples in Mark. Here it appears in a wider context and apparently has been taken over from Q (as Luke 12:28 indicates).

32. *Gentiles*: The word *ethnē* ("nations") describes people outside Israel. It appears in Luke 12:30 also and so was taken over from Q. In its present Matthean context the term may affirm that the audience for the Sermon on the Mount is Israel gathered to hear Jesus' teaching.

33. *his righteousness*: This major Matthean word does not appear in Luke 12:31. It may have been suggested, however, by 12:32 ("it is your Father's good pleasure to give you the kingdom"). But Matthew's emphasis is active rather than passive. God's righteousness is revealed in Jesus' teaching (see Matt 5:6, 10, 20).

34. *tomorrow*: The aphorism added to the Q section has parallels in wisdom teachings: "Do not boast about tomorrow, for you do not know what a day may bring forth" (Prov 27:1; see also Qoh 2:23). The Greek *kakia* (here translated "trouble") could also be taken in a moral sense as "evil" or "wickedness."

7:1. *Do not judge*: In form the imperative continues the pattern set up in 6:25 ("Do not be concerned"). Although the verb *krinō* frequently presupposes a judicial setting, here it carries the wider sense of "pass judgment upon." For a more complicated version of this teaching see Jas 4:11-12.

2. *judgment . . . measure*: Similar ideas are expressed in rabbinic sayings: "In the measure with which a man measures it is meted out to him" (*m. Sot.* 1:7); "in the pot in which they cooked they were cooked" (*Exod. Rabb.* 1). The one who will judge or measure in the Gospel sayings is God.

3. *speck . . . beam*: The fantastic images of the wood chip and the beam illustrate the process of fraternal correction based on Lev 19:17: "you shall reason with your neighbor." The advice is given to the one who offers the correction that he should be of perfect integrity himself and not a "hypocrite" (7:5). The same image is used in a rabbinic saying (*b. Arak.* 16b) but with the roles reversed: "Rabbi Tarfon said: 'I wonder whether there is anyone in this generation who accepts reproof, for if one say to him: "Remove the mote from between your eyes," he would answer, "Remove the beam from between your eyes."' "

6. *What is holy*: The "holy" food is meat sacrificed in the Temple. To feed this to dogs is inappropriate behavior, and you run the risk of being attacked and torn apart by them. Likewise to place pearls before swine invites oneself to be trampled. The saying follows a chiastic pattern (ABB^1A^1) structure. The point is that if you behave inappropriately toward others, you must reckon with the corresponding reactions and consequences. See H. von Lips, "Schweine füttert man, Hunde nicht—ein Versuch, das Rätsel von Matthäus 7:6 zu losen," *ZNW* 79 (1988) 165–86. Later the saying was used to prevent the unbaptized from partaking in the Eucharist (*Didache* 9:5). Rabbinic parallels exist in which the Law is to be kept from non-Jews.

7. *Ask*: The three verbs (ask, seek, knock) appear in both vv. 7 and 8. Again as in 7:1-2 it is assumed that God will give the response (=divine passives). The idea that God will hear the prayers of the people is especially prominent in the OT prophets (Isa 30:19; 58:9; 65:24; Jer 29:12-14; Hos 2:23; etc.).

9. *bread . . . stone*: The bread and fish analogies assume a father-son relation. Luke 11:11-12 contains the fish analogy but uses a situation in which the child asks for an egg and is given a scorpion. Matthew has omitted the second Q analogy (perhaps because it was so much like the fish-serpent one) and placed first the bread-stone analogy (perhaps because bread was so important and because the combination already appeared in Matt 4:3).

11. *being evil*: The assumption is that in comparison with God humans are "evil." Matthew has changed the odd expression in Luke 11:13 "the Father who is from heaven" to his more usual "your Father who is in heaven." He preserves the original wording of Q ("good things") where Luke substitutes "Holy Spirit."

12. *everything that you wish*: A full treatment of this saying appears below. Here it is sufficient to call attention to (1) the positive formulation of the Golden Rule and (2) the Matthean additional comment about it being "the Law and the Prophets" (see 5:17).

Interpretation

The introduction (5:1-20) and the first two major parts (5:21-48; 6:1-18) of the Sermon on the Mount display clear structures: nine Beatitudes, six antitheses, and three acts of piety. The third major part (6:19–7:12) has no obvious structure. Rather it is put together like a wisdom book (see Proverbs, Sirach, Qoheleth) in which short units are placed side by side because of their similar content or because of external principles (catchwords, etc.). It features commands, illustrations, reflections, and a summary conclusion (7:12). The OT sources and rabbinic parallels have been mentioned in the notes. The focus of the interpretation here is to follow how the sayings have been put together to form a unit. Particular attention will be given to the final saying (7:12), especially its background and function in the sermon.

The section about treasures (6:19-21) first contrasts earthly (perishable) treasures and heavenly (imperishable) treasures (6:19-20), and adds a reflection on the relation between one's treasure and one's heart (6:21). The units seem to have already been joined in Q (see Luke 12:33-34), probably on the basis of the word "treasure."

The sayings concerning the eye (6:22-23; see Luke 11:34-36) take as their starting point current ideas about the eye as the "lamp" of the body and move in a "moral" direction—to contrast either generous and stingy people, or good and evil people. They were joined to 6:21 because of their theme of intention determining the whole direction of one's life.

The saying about not serving two masters (6:24; see Luke 16:13) moves the theme of total commitment forward by imagining an attempt at divided commitment and judging it impossible.

The reflection on trust in God's power (6:25-34; see Luke 12:22-32) states a basic principle (6:25), gives two illustrations regarding food (6:26-27) and clothing (6:28-30), restates the principle (6:31-32), draws a conclusion (6:33), and adds a final consideration (6:34). It is vaguely connected to the preceding by its theme of whole-hearted service of God. To the Q version Matthew has appended his characteristic concern about God's righteousness (6:33) and what sounds like a popular aphorism (6:34).

In form ("do not") the saying about not passing judgment on others (7:1-2; see Luke 6:37-38) follows on the reflection about trust. In content it prepares for the reflection on fraternal correction (7:3-5; see Luke 6:39-42), a join already made in Q. It urges those who would correct others to have their own lives in order first.

The mysterious saying about not giving what is holy to dogs (7:6) is surely traditional, even if there is no Synoptic parallel and so it probably cannot be assigned to Q. Many interpretations are possible. But given the "wisdom" context, one that focuses on inappropriate behavior toward others and the responses to such behavior fits best: If you feed sacred food to dogs, they may attack you and tear you apart; if you put pearls before pigs, they may trample them under foot and the pearls will be lost. Attempts at identifying "what is holy" and the pearls as well as the dogs and pigs arose when the saying's context was lost. The Matthean text need not be allegorized to make sense. Rather it fits in vaguely with the preceding two sections on interpersonal relations.

The teaching about prayer of petition (7:7-11; see Luke 11:9-13) consists of the following elements: three imperatives and their consequences (7:7), the development of each of the three verbs (7:8), two illustrations about a father who gives good gifts to his children when they ask for something (7:9-10), and a concluding reflection (7:11). The emphasis throughout is on the almost automatic efficacy of the prayer of petition. This belief is anchored in the image of God as a kindly father willing and eager to answer the prayers of his children.

This analysis of the sayings in Matt 6:19–7:11 shows several things: They are loosely joined together on principles of form and content; they are traditional (mostly from Q); they are rooted in the Jewish tradition, especially as presented in Wisdom literature; and they are hard to locate concretely within the inner-Jewish conflict between the Matthean community and other Jews (though one can imagine their relevance at some points).

The third section ends with the so-called Golden Rule: "Therefore everything that you wish that people would do to you, so also do to them. For this is the Law and the Prophets" (7:12). What is often put forward as unique to Jesus is in fact rooted in the Hebrew Scriptures and has many parallels in Jewish writings from Jesus' time. The theological root of the Golden Rule is Lev 19:18: "You shall love your neighbor as yourself." A negative form of the Golden Rule appears in the book of Tobit 4:15: "Do to no one what you yourself dislike."

The most enlightening parallel concerns two teachers roughly contemporaneous with Jesus: "A certain heathen came before Shammai and said to him: 'Make me a proselyte on condition that you teach me the whole Torah while I stand on one foot.' Thereupon he repulsed him with a builder's cubit which was in his hand. When he went before Hillel, he said to him: 'What is hateful to you do not to your neighbor; that is the whole Torah, while the rest is commentary on it; go and learn it' " (*b. Šabb.* 31a). This parallel is important because Hillel uses the Golden Rule as his summary of the whole Torah, just as Jesus does according to Matt 7:12. The negative form in which Hillel formulates the rule need not be taken too seriously since early Christians seeking to repeat Jesus' teaching did the same (see *Didache* 1:2; and the Western manuscripts of Acts 15:29).

The Golden Rule appeared in Q (see Luke 6:31). To the Q form Matthew added the introductory particle "therefore," thus giving the Golden Rule the status of a conclusion. He also appended the comment: "For this is the Law and the Prophets,''thus making it into a summary of the Law and the Prophets (see also Matt 22:40, where the whole Law and the Prophets ''depend'' on the commandments to love God and one's neighbor). By his additions Matthew has introduced some coherence and significance into the various Wisdom teachings in Matt 6:19–7:11.

In the struggle in which the Matthean community found itself the Golden Rule served as Jesus' summary of the Law and the Prophets. Perhaps the followers of other Jewish teachers put forth similar summaries. Matthew does not declare the rest of the Torah obsolete and useless in the light of Jesus' summary (nor does Hillel). The idea is that the summary gives direction to the whole Torah: If you are guided by the summary statement, you will surely be faithful to the whole Torah.

Each unit within this third section of the sermon can be taken on its own in preaching or teaching. One needs to be aware of the loose structure and external connections in the text. The units are something like pearls on a string. What unity there is is supplied by the final statement of the Golden Rule (7:12), which draws us back to Matthew's fundamental conviction about Jesus the teacher: He came not to abolish but to fulfill (5:17). While Matthew considered Jesus to represent the best in Judaism, he quite definitely understood his teaching as firmly rooted within Judaism. The many references to its sources in the Hebrew Bible and to its parallels in other Jewish writings illustrate the continuity that existed between Jesus and Judaism according to Matthew.

For Reference and Further Study

Allison, D. C. ''The Eye Is the Lamp of the Body (Matthew 6:22-23 = Luke 11:34-36).'' *NTS* 33 (1987) 61–83.

Maxwell-Stuart, P. G. '' 'Do not give what is holy to the dogs' (Mt 7.6).'' *ExpTim* 90 (1979) 341.

Olsthoorn, M. F. *The Jewish Background and the Synoptic Saying of Mt 6, 25-33 and Lk 12, 22-31.* Jerusalem: Franciscan Printing Press, 1975.

Safrai, S. and Flusser, D. ''The Slave of Two Masters.'' *Immanuel* 6 (1976) 30–33.

14. *Warnings about Judgment* (7:13-29)

13. "Enter through the narrow gate. For wide is the gate and spacious the way that leads to destruction, and many are entering through it. 14. How narrow is the gate and hard the way that leads to life, and few are those who find it.

15. "Be careful of false prophets, who come to you in sheep's clothing, but inside they are ravenous wolves. 16. From their fruits you will know them. Do people gather grapes from thorns or figs from thistles? 17. So every good tree produces fine fruits, but the bad tree produces evil fruits. 18. A good tree cannot produce evil fruits, nor a bad tree produce fine fruits. 19. Every tree not producing fine fruit is cut down and thrown into the fire. 20. So from their fruits you will know them.

21. "Not everyone who says to me 'Lord, Lord' will enter the kingdom of heaven, but whoever does the will of my Father in heaven. 22. On that day many will say to me: 'Lord, Lord, did we not prophesy in your name, and did we not cast out demons in your name, and did we not do many mighty works in your name?' 23. And then I will declare to them that I never knew you; depart from me, you who are doers of lawlessness.

24. "Everyone who hears these words of mine and does them, will be like a prudent man who built his house upon stone. 25. And the rain came down, and the rivers came, and the winds blew and beat upon that house, and it did not fall, for it had been founded upon rock. 26. And everyone who hears these words of mine and does not do them, will be like a foolish man who built his house upon the sand. 27. And the rain fell, and the floods came, and the winds blew and beat against that house, and it fell down; and its fall was great."

28. And it happened when Jesus finished these words, the crowds were astonished at his teaching. 29. For he was teaching them as one having authority and not as their scribes.

Notes

13. *the narrow gate*: The image is probably that of a city gate through which people would enter the city. Since the topic of the sermon is entering the kingdom of God, the point behind the images of the narrow gate and the hard way is the difficulty involved in bringing the task to its (eschatological) conclusion.

spacious way: The Greek *eyrychōros* means "roomy, broad, spacious." The two-way tradition is rooted in such texts as Deut 11:26; 30:15; Jer 21:8. It is prominent in various Jewish writings (Wis 5:6-7; Prov 28:6, 18; 4 Ezra 7:3-15; 1QS 3:18–4:26). It also appears in early Christian writings (*Didache* 1–6; *Barnabas* 18–20).

14. *hard*: The Greek *tethlimmenē* derives from *thlipsis* ("tribulation"), which is frequently used in connection with end-time tribulations (see Acts 14:22). Here it functions as the opposite of *eyrychōros* and carries the idea of "crowded, hard-

pressed." The scene is a warning to the audience that to enter the kingdom is hard and only a few do so (see 4 Ezra 7:20, 47; 8:1; 9:15, 22; 2 Bar 44:15; 48:33).

15. *sheep's clothing*: The images contrast a harmless appearance (sheep) and a dangerous reality (wolves). In the background is the image of Israel as God's flock of sheep (see Ezek 34:10; Zech 11:17; 13:7; Ps 74:1). The image of the ravenous wolf appears in Gen 49:27; Ezek 22:27. In the Matthean context the warning concerns false prophets who lead Israel astray (see Deut 13:1-5). In the early Church the imagery was used to describe situations within the Church (see Acts 20:29).

16. *From their fruits*: The sentence is repeated in 7:20, thus forming an inclusion. For the comparison of a human and a tree in a Wisdom context see Psalm 1. The criterion for recognizing the false prophet is the deeds of the prophet (see Isa 3:10; Jer 17:10).

grapes . . . figs: Sweet and nourishing fruits do not come from thorns and thistles. Luke 6:44 reverses the order: figs from thorns, and grapes from a bramble bush. The next two verses (7:17-18) make the basic point in two different ways: good trees produce good fruit, and bad trees produce bad fruit.

19. *every tree not producing*: Matthew had already used this saying in his summary of John the Baptist's preaching (3:10). He inserted it in Q (see Luke 6:43-45) because it fit so well in theme and wording. Moreover, it gives the unit (7:15-20) a more explicit eschatological orientation than it would otherwise have had.

21. *"Lord, lord:"* The term was first a term of respect applied to teachers ("master"), only secondarily a Christological title. The true disciple of Jesus must not only claim him as teacher but also put his teaching into practice.

enter the kingdom: Matthew makes clear the eschatological dimension of the choice at hand. Compare Luke 6:46: "Why do you call me 'Lord, lord,' and not do what I tell you?"

22. *did we not prophesy in your name*: The expression "on that day" refers to the last judgment. The scene anticipates the great judgment scene in Matt 25:31-46. The scene may be Matthew's version of Mark 8:38-39 (see Luke 9:49-50), which does not appear elsewhere in Matthew. If it is, Matthew has developed the story and moved the situation into the final judgment.

23. *I never knew you; depart from me*: The first formula anticipates Peter's denial of Jesus in Matt 26:72. The second anticipates the Son of Man's judgment in Matt 25:41.

doers of lawlessness: The term *anomia* derives from *nomos* ("law"), which is preceded by the "alpha privative." In 23:28 the scribes and Pharisees are accused of being full of hypocrisy and *anomia*. From the Matthean perspective *anomia* describes those who do not follow the Torah as interpreted by Jesus.

24. *hears these words of mine and does them*: The reference to Jesus' words is emphatic, endowing them with special importance. For the close relation between hearing and doing see Deut 31:12: "that they may hear . . . and be careful to do all the words of this law." This in turn becomes the criterion by which one is judged to be a "prudent" man, a term that takes in the Wisdom tradition.

built his house upon stone: Luke 6:48 gives more attention to the process of building the foundation: "who dug and went deep and laid the foundation." See also Luke 6:49 ("a house on the ground without a foundation") in comparison with Matt 7:26 ("his house upon the sand"). Similar pictures of those who study Torah and do good works appear in *m. 'Abot* 3:18 and *ARN* 24 (see Lachs, p. 151).

25. *rain came down*: The Matthean descriptions of the storm (see 7:25, 27) are presented in short sentences that give a sense of the storm (cf. Luke 6:48, 49). In fact, Luke is only interested in the effects of a flood, whereas Matthew gives a dramatic description of a rain storm. The storm is a way of talking about the trials and tribulations that will accompany the coming of the kingdom.

28. *when Jesus finished these words*: The same formula appears at the end of each of the five major speeches in Matthew (see 11:1; 13:53; 19:1; 26:1). The formula is based on Deut 32:45: "When Moses had finished speaking all these words to all Israel" (see also Deut 31:1, 24).

the crowds were astonished: The reaction reminds us about the nature of the audience (see 4:23–5:2). Matt 7:28b-29 is based on Mark 1:22. Its placement here has the effect of distancing Jesus' teaching from that of "their scribes."

Interpretation

The units in the concluding section of the Sermon on the Mount (7:13-27) are connected by two elements: the sharp contrast between two kinds of people, and the warning that both will have to face judgment before God. Each unit has a parallel in Luke, suggesting that both evangelists had access to Q. Most of the parallels appear in Luke's Sermon on the Plain (Luke 6:43-49).

The four units develop wisdom themes in an eschatological framework. Only the narrow gate and the hard way (7:13-14; see Luke 13:23-24) lead to "life," whereas the wide gate and the spacious way lead to destruction. Just as a tree is known by the kind of fruit it produces, so prophets will be known at the last judgment (7:15-20; see Luke 6:43-45); the tree bearing bad fruit will be burned in the fire. Only those who do the Father's will (7:21-23) can expect to enter the kingdom of heaven, whereas those who do not—whatever other achievements they have—will not enter. Hearing Jesus' words and doing them (7:24-27) provides a firm foundation for the "storm": those lacking such a foundation will experience a great fall.

So each unit contrasts two kinds of people: the two ways, the two trees, those who do God's will and those who do not, and the two foundations. In each unit there is a hint that in the last judgment these two kinds of people will be rewarded or punished: destruction-life, fine fruits-evil fruits (thrown into the fire), enter the kingdom-told to depart, and stands-falls.

The division of humankind into two kinds of people is a commonplace in Wisdom literature. The joining of this motif to the idea of the last judgment is also common in Jewish writings of Jesus' time. A major premise of the Wisdom books is the law of retribution: The good are rewarded, and the wicked are punished. But life is not so neat. Around Jesus' time there was a strong tendency to put off the ultimate rewards and punishments until the end of human history as we know it. And so it was inevitable that the division of humankind and the last judgment would be combined.

A dramatic example of the combination appears in the Qumran *Manual of Discipline* (or *Community Rule*), columns 3–4, in a section called the "instruction on the two spirits." The text first establishes the sovereignty of God the Creator and observes that "he allotted unto man two Spirits that he should walk in them until the time of his visitation" (3:18). The "sons of light" walk in the ways of light under the guidance of the Prince of Light, whereas the "sons of darkness" walk in the ways of darkness under the guidance of the Angel of Darkness. The two ways are characterized by sharply different characters and actions. The way of light (4:2-8) features humility, forbearance, mercy, goodness, understanding, etc., while the way of darkness (4:9-11) features cupidity, slackness, impiety, falsehood, pride, etc. Representatives of these two ways fight it out "until the final end" (4:17) when God will put a stop to perversity and all lying abominations and the just be rewarded with the knowledge of the Most High.

The warnings about judgment in Matt 7:13-27 presuppose this kind of schema according to which people are divided into two groups to be rewarded or punished at the last judgment. As in the Qumran *Manual of Discipline,* the division is not between Jews and Gentiles. Nor is it between Christians and Jews as if they already represented different and separate religions. Rather, here the division is between Jews who accept Jesus' interpretation of the Torah and those who do not.

It has become customary among exegetes to find in Matt 7:13-27 indications of rivalries and scandals within the Matthean community. But that inner-church reading of the text is not necessary. The texts make better sense when taken as part of the struggle between the Matthean community and its Jewish rivals. This inner-Jewish approach is true to the framework of the sermon in which Israel is addressed and asked to accept Jesus' teaching as the fulfillment of the Torah.

It is also true to the content of the various parts of 7:13-27: The audience is asked to choose Jesus' narrow gate and hard way that leads to life over the wide gate and spacious way that leads to destruction (7:13-14). They are warned against false prophets; from their fruits (=bad fruits) they will be known (7:15-20). Even those who do marvelous deeds in Jesus' name (see Mark 9:38-39) must do God's will to enter the kingdom (7:21-23). The teachings of Jesus ("these words of mine") provide the rock on which one might build one's house (7:24-27). All these teachings make perfect sense when read as part of the conflict within Judaism after A.D. 70. Matthew presents Jesus' teaching as the authoritative interpretation of the Torah and rejects his rivals and their interpretation.

The conclusion (7:28-29; see Mark 1:22) contains the first instance of a formula that appears at the end of each major discourse in the Gospel. That formula ("when Jesus finished these words") is reminiscent of several texts near the end of Deuteronomy, thus giving the teachings of Jesus a very high status.

Matthew's use of Mark 1:22 served a twofold purpose. It reminded his readers about the nature of the audience for the sermon (see Matt 4:23–5:2). These teachings are laid before all Israel; people must choose to accept or reject them (see 7:13-27). It also contrasts Jesus' authority as a teacher with that of other Jewish teachers ("not as their scribes"), probably related to the teachers who were the Jewish rivals of Matthew's community. Thus the conclusion confirms the fact that all Israel is addressed in the sermon and that the content of the sermon is based on the authority of Jesus which is superior to that of "their scribes."

The thesis of the Sermon on the Mount is that Jesus came not to abolish but to fulfill the Law and the Prophets. Matthew's compendium of his teaching seeks to show what fulfillment entails. It clearly does not mean doing away with the Torah. In some cases it involves going to the root of the Torah's teachings or going beyond the letter. The sermon emphasizes internal dispositions and attitudes that will structure the appropriate enactment of the Torah.

The materials contained in Matt 7:13-27 provide a fitting conclusion, which can be adapted easily by preachers and teachers. The division of humankind and the promise of final judgment are rich themes. An application to the Church or community is appropriate as long as interpreters recognize that this was probably not Matthew's original perspective. As in Matthew 13 the promise of the final judgment where rewards and punishments will be carried out by God provides a restraint upon active hostility in the present. Biblical teaching need not be used as theological justification for acting upon one's prejudices.

For Reference and Further Study

Betz, H. D. "Eine Episode im Jüngsten Gericht (Mt 7,21-23)." *ZTK* 78 (1981) 1–30.

Hill, D. "False Prophets and Charismatics: Structure and Interpretation in Matthew 7, 15-23." *Bib* 57 (1976) 327–48.

Krämer, M. "Hütet euch von den falschen Propheten." *Bib* 57 (1976) 349–77.

Mattill, A. J. "The Way of Tribulation." *JBL* 98 (1979) 531–46.

15. *Jesus the Healer* (8:1-17)

1. When he came down from the mountain, many crowds followed him. 2. And behold a leper approached and did him homage, saying: "Lord, if you are willing, you can make me clean." 3. And he stretched out his hand and touched him, saying: "I so wish. Be made clean." 4. And Jesus said to him: "See to it that you tell no one; but go, show yourself to the priest and offer the gift that Moses commanded as a witness to them."

5. As he entered Capernaum, a centurion approached him and begged him 6. and said: "Lord, my servant is laid up at home paralyzed, suffering terribly." 7. And he said to him: "Shall I come and heal him?" 8. And the centurion answered and said: "Lord, I am not worthy that you should enter under my roof, but only say the word, and my servant will be healed. 9. For I am a man under authority, having soldiers under me. And I say to this one: 'Go' and he goes. And to another: 'Come,' and he comes. And to my servant: 'Do this' and he does it." 10. And when Jesus heard this, he was amazed and said to those following him: "Amen I say to you, I have not found such faith among anyone in Israel. 11. I say to you that many from East and West will come and recline with Abraham and Isaac and Jacob in the kingdom of heaven, 12. but the sons of the kingdom will be cast out into the darkness outside. There will be weeping and gnashing of teeth." 13. And Jesus said to the centurion: "Go. As you have believed, let it be done to you." And his servant was healed in that hour.

14. And Jesus came into Peter's house and saw his mother-in-law laid up and feverish. 15. And he touched her hand, and the fever left her, and she was raised up and served him. 16. That evening they brought to him many people possessed by demons. And he cast out the spirits by word and healed all those faring badly, 17. so that what was said through Isaiah the prophet was fulfilled: "He has taken our sicknesses and borne the diseases."

Notes

1. *from the mountain*: The entire verse was created by Matthew as an editorial bridge between the Sermon on the Mount and the healing story in Mark 1:40-45. The idea of many crowds following Jesus stands in tension with Jesus' command in Matt 8:4 not to tell anyone about his healing.

2. *a leper*: The regulations about lepers are given in great detail in Leviticus 13–14. The condition in antiquity covered various skin diseases, and was not the same as the modern form of leprosy known as Hansen's disease. This condition involved segregation from the community so that further infection might be prevented.

   did him homage: The leper approaches Jesus in the same way as the Magi did (2:2, 8, 11)—by doing him the homage owed to a royal or divine figure. Mark 1:40 reads: "beseeching him and kneeling."

Lord: Matthew inserts an honorific address, which can mean both "sir" and "Lord" (*kyrie*). The request "you can make me clean" could conceivably be a request for Jesus' declaration of the man's return to health (see Leviticus 13–14). But Jesus actually heals the man and then urges that he follow the procedure outlined in Scripture about getting himself declared clean.

3. *he stretched out his hand*: Matthew omits the references to the emotions of Jesus in Mark 1:41 ("moved with pity [or, anger]") and 1:43 ("he sternly charged him"). This is part of Matthew's editorial policy of omitting extraneous details as well as his lack of interest in the "emotions" of Jesus.

   touched him: According to Lev 5:3 Jesus himself might contract ritual uncleanness by touching the sources of uncleanness. But the NT account makes nothing of that idea. Instead Jesus' touch is presented as the means by which the cure of the leper is brought about.

4. *that you tell no one*: Here and elsewhere (see Matt 9:30; 12:16; 16:20; 17:9) Matthew takes over the injunction-to-silence motif from Mark. But the motif does not function as part of the "messianic secret" as in Mark. Also there is some tension with the "many crowds" (Matt 8:1) that accompany Jesus down from the mountain.

   that Moses commanded: The procedure for declaring a leper clean is outlined in Leviticus 14. Although Matthew took over this idea from Mark 1:44, it takes on special meaning after the Sermon on the Mount, with its theme of Jesus fulfilling the Law and the Prophets (5:17). Matthew also omitted the (potentially) confusing Mark 1:45 where the identity of "he" causes problems.

5. *Capernaum*: For Capernaum as the seat of Jesus' public activity see Matt 4:13. For the inadequate response by Capernaum to the miracles done by Jesus see Matt 11:23.

   centurion: A centurion was the commander of a hundred men in a Roman legion. From the story we are to assume that he was a Gentile, though probably not a Roman. It is not clear whether we are to imagine him as being on duty with a garrison in Capernaum or as having settled there upon retirement.

6. *Lord*: Unlike Luke 7:1-5, the centurion addresses Jesus directly (without intermediaries) and prefaces his request with the honorific "Lord = Sir." For Christian readers who refer to Jesus as "Lord," this title would have taken on greater significance than an expression of politeness.

   my servant: The Greek term *pais* is ambiguous; it can mean both "child" and "servant." This ambiguity is mirrored in the parallel accounts: "slave" (*doulos*) in Luke 7:2, and "son" (*hyios*) in John 4:46. Matthew's description of the servant's condition is given in much greater detail than in the other Gospels.

7. *Shall I come*: The usual translation presents Jesus' response to the centurion as a promise or an offer ("I will come"). The sentence can also be taken as a question ("Shall I come?"), which could express positive involvement on Jesus' part or even annoyance on his part.

8. *I am not worthy*: The centurion's reply suggests that Jesus' statement in 8:7 be taken as an annoyed question asking whether Jesus as a Jew would be expected

to enter the house of a Gentile and so transgress rules forbidding such free dealings with Gentiles. The centurion's response is a model of politeness, and offers an alternate way for Jesus to heal his servant ("only say the word").

9. *a man under authority*: The point of the comparison in 8:9 is that just as the centurion exercises authority in the military sphere, so Jesus exercises authority in the spiritual sphere (by controlling the evil spirits who cause the disease). The expression "under authority" is difficult, since the idea is that the centurion exercises authority. Perhaps he means that just as the commander or emperor gave him military authority, so God gave Jesus authority over sickness.

10. *such faith*: The Gentile's recognition of Jesus' power and its source in God provides a model for all believers, especially the Gentiles among the early Christians. It occasions the insertion of the Q saying (see Luke 13:28-29) about Gentiles coming to the banquet in God's kingdom.

11. *many from East and West*: The image of the non-Jews coming to Jerusalem to worship the God of Israel is common in prophetic literature (see Isa 2:2-4; 25:6; Mic 4:1-4; Zech 2:11-12; 8:20-23). Here the scene shifts to the banquet in God's kingdom. For a negative fate visited upon the Gentiles, see Zeph 3:8.

12. *the sons of the kingdom*: These are Jews to whom the kingdom has been offered. Of course, the expression does not include all Jews, since Abraham, Isaac, and Jacob preside at the banquet. For "weeping and gnashing of teeth" see Matt 22:13; 24:51; 25:30.

13. *As you have believed*: The expression falls short of making the healing of the servant the *result* of the centurion's faith. It can carry the idea that things will happen *as* the centurion hoped and requested.

his servant was healed: For the story of a healing at a distance in rabbinic literature see *b. Ber* 34b in which Hanina ben Dosa prays on behalf of the son of Rabban Gamaliel who is cured at the very moment when Hanina prays. But Hanina is just a mediator, whereas Jesus appears as powerful by his very word alone.

14. *Jesus came into Peter's house*: Matthew omits several details in Mark 1:29-30: that they came out of the synagogue, that four apostles accompanied him, and that they informed Jesus about Peter's mother-in-law's condition. The effect of Matthew's editing is to place the spotlight directly on Jesus. It is possible that Matthew's omission of Mark's report that they came out of the synagogue was related to his own hostility toward the Jewish leaders in control of "their synagogues."

15. *she was raised up and served him*: The healing of the woman's fever is immediate and complete. Her restoration is described with the term reserved for the resurrection of Jesus (*ēgerthē*). Whereas in Mark 1:31 she serves "them," here she serves "him."

16. *by word*: Matthew has shortened the overblown summary in Mark 1:32-34, without omitting much of significance. Thus he omitted the second time expression ("when the sun set"), the repetitious descriptions of who was healed, and the secrecy motif. He added the note "by word" to take in the story of the centurion's servant (Matt 8:5-13).

17. *Isaiah*: The fulfillment quotation is taken from Isa 53:4, the famous Suffering Servant text. The Servant's assumption of sickness and diseases is part of his suffering. Thus the quotation places Jesus' healing ministry in the context of his passion; it is not merely a matter of displaying power.

INTERPRETATION

Having shown Jesus to be powerful in word with the Sermon on the Mount, Matthew now portrays him as powerful in deed with a series of miracle stories (chs. 8–9). His mighty deeds include both healings and displays of power over nature.

The first part in the series (Matt 8:1-17) consists of the healing of a leper (8:1-4), the healing of the paralyzed servant of a centurion (8:5-13), the healing of Peter's mother-in-law from a fever (8:14-15), and the healing of many sick persons (8:16-17). These stories for the most part follow the same general outline. We are informed about a physical problem (leprosy, paralysis, fever). There is a contact between Jesus and the sick person. The cure is instantaneous and complete. The Gospel miracle stories usually mention the great faith of the sick persons or their friends. The goal of the healing is not spectacular display. Rather it is to engender questions about Jesus ("Who is this?") and the source of his power. The miracles are signs pointing beyond themselves to Jesus and his heavenly Father.

Throughout Matt 8:1-17 Matthew depends on Mark or Q. Not content to repeat his sources, Matthew shows himself to be a skillful editor by omitting what he perceived to be extraneous details and by giving new dimensions to existing material.

In the story of the leper (8:1-4; see Mark 1:40-45) Matthew has constructed an editorial bridge (8:1) between the Sermon on the Mount and the cycle of miracle stories. He has highlighted the prayerful attitude of the leper and omitted the references to Jesus' emotions. Matthew's telling of the story brings out Jesus' command to the leper that he should fulfill the instructions laid down in Leviticus 14, thus showing once again that Jesus came not to abolish but to fulfill the Law and the Prophets.

The healing of the centurion's servant (8:5-13) also appears in Luke 7:1-10 but in a longer and more complicated form in which the "elders of the Jews" serve as intermediaries between the centurion and Jesus. Whether the Q form contained these intermediaries is unclear. Luke may have added them in keeping with his conviction that Jews and their synagogues served as intermediaries in the Gentile mission of the early Church. Or Matthew may have deleted them in light of his editorial policy of omitting unnecessary details and his antipathy toward "their synagogues." At any rate, the effect of the short version in Matthew is to highlight the prayerful dialogue between the centurion and Jesus. This dialogue provides the occasion for Matthew to insert the Q saying (8:11-12; see Luke 13:28-29) as a general comment on Gentiles sharing in the kingdom of heaven.

The story of Peter's mother-in-law (8:14-15; see Mark 1:29-31; Luke 4:38-39) has been greatly simplified by suppressing unnecessary characters and information. The result is a short narrative in which the feverish woman and Jesus the healer are the only figures. The summary account of the many healings (8:16-17; see Mark 1:32-34; Luke 4:40-41) has been shortened to avoid repetition and expanded to include Isa 53:4 as a fulfillment quotation.

From this first part of the miracle-cycle we can draw some conclusions about Matthew as an editor of narrative material. His most obvious tendency is abbreviation and omission of unnecessary details. The effect of this process is greater emphasis on the encounter between Jesus and the sick person. Those encounters frequently turn into "prayer dialogues" with Jesus. Matthew also feels free to add material to his sources (as in 8:11-12, 17). Though this material was traditional, its insertion placed the existing accounts in a new perspective—a perspective of great significance for Matthew's theological program.

The stories in Matt 8:1-17 portray Jesus as a doer of miracles and a powerful healer. As such he was not unique in the Jewish tradition or in the Greco-Roman world. The accounts of Elijah and Elisha in the OT books of Kings provided ancient models for understanding the exploits of Jesus. Certain charismatic Jewish teachers like Hanina ben Dosa achieved fame as miracle-workers around Jesus' time. And somewhat later, miracle stories were told about the pagan Apollonius of Tyana. Even Jesus' Jewish opponents and detractors did not deny his ability to work miracles; their contention was that he did these things out of Satan's power (Matt 9:32-34; 12:22-30).

The story of Jesus healing the centurion's servant (Matt 8:5-13) has a striking parallel in rabbinic literature about a contemporary of Jesus:

> Our Rabbis taught: Once the son of R. Gamaliel fell ill. He sent two scholars to R. Hanina b. Dosa to ask him to pray for him. When he saw them he went to an upper chamber and prayed for him. When he came down he said to them: Go, the fever has left him. They said to him: Are you a prophet? He replied: I am neither a prophet nor the son of a prophet, but I learnt this from experience. If my prayer is fluent in my mouth, I know that he is accepted: but if not, I know that he is rejected. They sat down and made a note of the exact moment. When they came to R. Gamaliel, he said to them: By the temple service! You have not been a moment too soon or too late, but so it happened: at that very moment the fever left him and he asked for water to drink (*b. Ber.* 34b).

Both the Gospel story and the rabbinic account involve the strange motif of healing at a distance. The chief difference is what is claimed about the central character. Hanina exemplifies the kind of a prayer heard by God;

God heals in response to his prayer. Jesus heals in virtue of his own power; his word is powerful. The parallel illustrates that the claims made about Jesus in the Gospels go beyond the limitations set by the rabbinic writings. These claims contain an "implicit Christology" in that Jesus does what only God can do. He is more than a mediator of God's power.

Matthew's work as an editor was not merely a literary undertaking. Rather it was an essential part of his theological program as he and his community sought to define its brand of (Christian) Judaism vis-à-vis other Jews. The healing of the leper (8:1-4) reaches its climax in Jesus' command to the leper to obey Leviticus 14, thus confirming the master thesis of the Sermon on the Mount that Jesus came to fulfill the Law and the Prophets. The great faith of the centurion (8:5-13) shows the basis on which non-Jews could be admitted to the people of God according to early Christian theology. The fulfillment quotation (Isa 53:4) in 8:17 ties in Jesus' healing activity to his passion and death. The latter two points are new at this stage in the Gospel.

Up to this stage of the Gospel Jesus has ministered to and addressed Israel. Now in 8:5-13 he ministers to a non-Jew on the basis of his display of faith in Jesus' power. This provides the occasion for Matthew to insert a prophecy about Gentiles sharing in the banquet of God's kingdom while some Jews are shut out of it (8:11-12). Matthew here says some of the things Paul says in Romans 11—about how Gentiles might become part of God's people and what happens to Jews who reject the gospel. Given the situation of the Matthean community facing hostility from other Jews about the role of their Gentile associates, the story of the Gentile centurion would have been especially significant.

The use of Isa 53:4 ("He has taken our sicknesses and borne the diseases") in Matt 8:17 places Jesus' acts of power in a peculiar perspective. As the comparison between the healings performed by Jesus and Hanina ben Dosa shows, the Gospels make some exalted (even if implicit) claims about Jesus' power. But just at the point where all the emphasis seems to be on the spectacular aspects of Jesus, the evangelist introduces an OT fulfillment quotation that portrays Jesus as the Suffering Servant who takes upon himself the sins of the people. The miracles become part of Jesus' passion—a subtle reminder of what was the goal of his public ministry and a subtle criticism of those who so focus on Jesus' miracles as to ignore his suffering and death.

Despite Matthew's careful use of sources, Matt 8:1-17 contains some fresh insights for teachers and preachers. The first two stories offer a snapshot of early Christians like Matthew—trying to follow Jesus as the one who fulfills the Law and Prophets while making room for Gentiles on the basis of their faith in Jesus. The use of Isa 53:4 as a fulfillment quotation in 8:17 gives an important twist in the way we look at Jesus' miracles: These signs of God's power at work point to the passion.

For Reference and Further Study

Kingsbury, J. D. "Observations on the 'Miracle Chapters' of Matthew 8-9." *CBQ* 40 (1978) 559–73.

Thompson, W. G. "Reflections on the Composition of Mt 8:1–9:34." *CBQ* 33 (1971) 365–88

Wegner, U. *Der Hauptmann von Kafarnaum (Mt 7, 28a, 8:5-10.13 par Lk 7, 1-10)*. Tübingen: Mohr-Siebeck, 1985.

Zeller, D. "Das Logion Mt 8,11f/Lk 13,28f und das Motiv der 'Völkerwallfahrt.'" *BZ* 15 (1971) 222–37, 16 (1972) 84–93.

16. *More Acts of Power* (8:18–9:8)

18. When Jesus saw the crowd around him, he gave orders to go over to the other side. 19. And a certain scribe approached him and said: "Teacher, I will follow you wherever you go." 20. And Jesus said to him: "The foxes have fox-holes, and the birds of the heaven nests, but the Son of Man does not have anywhere he might lay his head." 21. Another of his disciples said to him: "Lord, allow me first to go off and bury my father." 22. But Jesus said to him: "Follow me, and leave the dead to bury their dead." 23. And when he entered the boat, his disciples followed him. 24. And behold there was a great storm on the sea, so that the boat was being swamped by the waves. But he was asleep. 25. And they came and awoke him, saying: "Lord, save [us]. We are perishing." 26. And he said to them: "Why are you fearful, men of little faith?" Then he arose and rebuked the winds and the sea, and there was great calm. 27. The men were amazed and said: "What kind of man is this, that both the winds and the sea obey him?"

28. And when he came to the other side, into the land of the Gadarenes, two men possessed by demons came forth from the tombs and met him; they were very fierce, so that no one could pass by through that way. 29. And behold they shouted, saying: "What is there between us and you, Son of God? Have you come here before time to torment us?" 30. Now at a distance from them a herd of many pigs was feeding. 31. The demons begged him, saying: "If you cast us out, send us away into the herd of pigs." 32. And he said to them: "Go." They came out and went into the pigs. And behold the entire herd rushed down the steep bank into the sea, and they died in the waters. 33. The herdsmen fled, and going away into the city they told everything and what happened to the men possessed by demons. 34. And behold the whole city went out to meet Jesus, and on seeing him they begged him to leave their district.

9:1. And he got into the boat and crossed, and he came into his own city. 2. And behold they brought to him a paralytic laid out on a bed. And on seeing their faith Jesus said to the paralytic: "Take courage, son; your sins are forgiven." 3. And behold some of the scribes said among themselves: "This one blasphemes." 4. And Jesus knew their thoughts and said: "Why are you thinking evil thoughts in your hearts? 5. For which is easier—to say 'your sins are forgiven,' or to say 'arise and walk?' 6. But that you may know that the Son of Man has power to forgive sins on earth"—then he said to the paralytic: "Arise, take up your bed and go to your house." 7. And he arose and went away to his house. 8. When the crowds saw this, they were afraid and glorified God who gave such power to human beings.

Notes

18. *he gave orders*: Whereas in Mark 4:35 Jesus makes a suggestion ("Let us go across"), here he takes the initiative and the disciples follow along (see 8:23). The "other side" would have been the eastern side of the Sea of Galilee.

19. *teacher, I will follow you*: Although scribes usually form (along with the Pharisees) the opposition to Jesus, this scribe seems initially sincere in his desire to become a disciple (see 13:52; 23:34 for positive references to scribes). His address to Jesus as "teacher" (*didaskale*) also seems genuine (as in 19:16), though the title is used often by Jesus' opponents (see 12:38; 22:16, 24, 36). His statement "I will follow you" is the equivalent of "I wish to become your disciple."

20. *the Son of Man*: In response to the scribe whose occupation would have demanded the stable lifestyle of a home, Jesus offers only the life of a wandering preacher. The "Son of Man" here for Matthew was Jesus. The saying is not a generic statement about the human condition. Rather it is about the lifestyle of Jesus and his followers. For Jesus as a wandering charismatic, see G. Theissen, *Sociology of Early Palestinian Christianity* (Philadelphia: Fortress, 1978).

21. *Another of his disciples*: The second questioner has already become a disciple (see Luke 9:59), and so the issue here is an obstacle to a discipleship already undertaken. His request is at least reminiscent of that made by Elisha to Elijah: "Let me kiss my father and my mother, and then I will follow you" (1 Kgs 19:20).
bury my father: For the importance of burying the dead as a religious act, see Tobit 1:16-20; 4:3; 6:15. In rabbinic law the duties connected with burying a close relative override the obligations to make the daily prayers at the proper times (see *m. Ber.* 3:1).

22. *leave the dead to bury their dead*: The point of the saying is that following Jesus and sharing his ministry of preaching and healing override even the solemn obligation of burying one's father. The various attempts at softening the saying by alternative translations (e.g., "leave it to the buriers to bury their dead") still come back to the same basic point. The saying is probably to be taken as deliberate hyperbole intended to shock the hearers.

23. *his disciples followed him*: After the interlude in 8:19-22, the main story is rejoined. Those who accompany Jesus have made their decision about the challenges expressed in the interlude. Jesus takes the initiative (see 8:18), and they follow

him. The verb "follow" (*akolouthō*) becomes a technical term in the Gospels for following Jesus.

24. *storm*: Matthew's Greek term is *seismos* ("earthquake"), which probably carries an apocalyptic overtone: "On that day there shall be a great shaking in the land of Israel" (Ezek 38:19). The boat later became a symbol for the Church. But it is hard to know whether Matthew's readers were yet sensitive to such symbolism. Jesus' sleep implies his trust in God, not his disinterest or insensitivity.

25. *Lord, save* [*us*]. *We are perishing*: Compare Mark 4:38 "Teacher, do you not care if we perish?" Matthew has turned the disciples' statement into a prayer in which Jesus is addressed as "Lord" (*kyrie*) and asked to act in terms that go beyond the immediate danger at hand.

26. *men of little faith*: Compare Mark 4:40: "Have you no faith?" Matthew softens the harsh critique of the disciples in Mark and introduces his characteristic assessment of Jesus' disciples as *oligopistoi* (see 14:31; 16:8; 17:20): They have some faith, but their faith is far from perfect.

rebuked the winds and the sea: Jesus does what Ps 107:29 attributes to Yahweh: "He made the storm be still, and the waves of the sea were hushed." His action generates the question expressed in 8:27: "What kind of man is this?"

28. *Gadarenes*: The reading in Mark 5:1 appears to have been "Gerasenes." Gerasa is more than thirty miles southeast of the Sea of Galilee. Matthew changed it to Gadara, some five to six miles southeast of the Sea of Galilee. Its population was mainly pagan, and so there would be no objection to herds of pigs there. Even with the change there remains the problem of how the pigs were driven into the sea, unless there is a vague sense of "Gadarene territory."

two men: Mark 5:2 (see Luke 8:27) mentions only one man. Matthew also has two blind men healed in 9:27-31 (see Mark 10:46-52). He also doubles the asses in 20:29-34 at Jesus' Palm Sunday entrance into Jerusalem. It is not clear whether we are to imagine them to have been Gentiles (the majority of the population) or Jews.

very fierce: Matthew summarizes the lengthy and graphic description of the demoniac's behavior in Mark 5:2-5. The dwelling in the antechamber of tombs may have had some connection with the idea of a kinship between the dead and evil spirits. There may also be some connection with Isa 65:4: "who sit in tombs . . . who eat swine's flesh."

29. *before time*: The binding and defeat of the demonic forces was understood to be part of the "last days." The demons recognize Jesus for who he is ("Son of God") but are puzzled that he is anticipating the arrival of the kingdom by his exorcism. Their initial question to him ("What is there between us and you") expresses their conviction that as yet they have no business together (see Mark 1:24; John 2:4).

30. *a herd of many pigs*: In the OT pigs are unclean animals because they have cloven hooves but no ruminant stomach (see Lev 11:7; Deut 14:8). None of the usual explanations fully satisfies: pigs were sacred in certain pagan cults; fear of disease; etc. In pagan territory such as Gadara their presence would be quite com-

mon. To Jews the destruction of a herd of pigs would have been somewhat humorous. Matthew's note that the herd was "at a distance from them" may have been generated by Matthew's awareness of the distance between Gadara and the Sea of Galilee.

31. *into the herd of pigs*: Matthew omits the name of the demon(s) as "Legion," probably because it could be construed as a criticism of the Romans and their military presence (see Mark 5:9). The assumption behind the demon's request is that they need a dwelling place where they might spend their destructive energy (see Josephus, *Ant.* 8:48).

32. *down the steep bank*: The problem of the distance of Gadara from the Sea of Galilee remains. We are to assume that with the drowning of the pigs the demons also were destroyed or at least their force was spent. That Jesus would destroy property has long been a source of scandal. But to Jews the loss of a herd of pigs would be something like the destruction of rats or mice today.

34. *to leave their district*: Matthew omits the description in Mark 5:15-20 about the healed demoniac, his effort at following Jesus, and his preaching in the Decapolis. Matthew merely alludes to the demoniacs (8:33) but keeps the focus on Jesus. The Gentiles even ask Jesus to leave their territory. The Matthean story is proof of Jesus' power over demons.

9:1. *his own city*: Jesus' own city now is Capernaum, the center of his ministry in Galilee (see Matt 4:13). Matthew apparently saw no conflict between this statement and the saying in 8:20: "The Son of Man does not have anywhere he might lay his head." He does omit, however, Mark's comment (2:1) that Jesus was "in the house," which might be construed as his own.

2. *they brought*: Matthew omits the graphic details of what the friends did in order to get the paralytic in contact with Jesus (see Mark 2:3-4). The result is that the role of Jesus is highlighted and the theme of the forgiveness of sins is emphasized. Jesus is impressed, however, by the faith of the friends ("on seeing their faith").

take courage: The address in Mark 2:5 is strengthened by the addition of this imperative (see also 9:22; 14:27). By declaring the paralytic's sins forgiven Jesus may be appealing to cultural assumptions about the relation between sickness and sin (see John 9:2).

3. *blasphemes*: The technical biblical meaning of blasphemy consists in misusing the divine name Yahweh (see Lev 24:15-16; Num 15:30). By declaring the man's sins forgiven, Jesus usurps the divine prerogative of forgiving the sins of others. For another nontechnical use of the term "blasphemy" see Matt 26:65.

4. *Jesus knew their thoughts*: The power to read hearts is customarily attributed to God (see Jer 11:20; Ps 7:9; 2 Chr 6:30; Sir 43:18-19). This ability to know what is going on behind the appearances is a major motif in the Matthean passion account.

5. *which is easier*: It is easier to *say* "your sins are forgiven," since the effect could not be verified by empirical means. The logic of the story is that, if Jesus has

power over the paralysis, he also has power over the sins. By proving the former, he at least makes the latter more plausible.

6. *the Son of Man*: In this context the title refers to Jesus. There is no text in Jewish literature that attributes to the Son of Man power to forgive sins. The prerogative relates more to the person of Jesus than it does to the title. The instantaneous and complete cure of the man establishes the extraordinary authority of Jesus and renders at least plausible his power over sins.

8. *they were afraid*: Whereas according to Mark 2:12 the crowds were amazed, Matthew says "they were afraid." This reaction of awe also appears in connection with the transfiguration (17:6) and the resurrection (28:5, 10), as well as the anticipation of the general resurrection (27:54).

   to human beings: This power refers first and foremost to the Son of Man. It may also allude to the practice of forgiving sins within the early Christian community (see Matt 16:19; 18:18; Jas 5:16).

Interpretation

The second series of miracle stories (Matt 8:18–9:8) also shows some of Matthew's characteristic moves as an editor. He not only shortens the Markan accounts by omitting unnecessary details but also brings out themes by subtle additions.

In Matthew's version of the stilling of the storm (8:18-27; see Mark 4:35-41) Jesus takes charge of matters from the start by giving orders (8:18) and leading the way for his followers (8:23). Between those two verses Matthew introduces the double dialogue about discipleship from Q (8:19-22), thus highlighting discipleship as an ancillary theme along with Christology. His description of the storm as a *seismos* (8:24) gives the event greater eschatological significance (see 27:51-53). The disciples' address to Jesus in 8:25 ("Lord, save [us]. We are perishing") takes the form of a prayer. Jesus' address to them as "men of little faith" (8:26) is more positive than Mark 4:40 ("Have you no faith?"). Whereas Mark in his account focuses almost entirely on Jesus, Matthew by his additions, deletions, and changes provides a double focus on Jesus and the disciples.

Matthew's account of the healing of the two demoniacs in 8:28-34 is considerably shorter than Mark 5:1-20 is. Apparently sensitive to the geographical problem posed by Gerasa (Mark 5:1), Matthew shifted the location to Gadara, which was nearer to the Sea of Galilee. The overall effect of the severe editing applied to Mark 5:1-20 is a less colorful but tighter story that highlights the conflict between the demons and the Son of God. The Matthean version turns around the demons' questions in 8:29: "What is there between us and you, Son of God? Have you come here before time to torment us?" Matthew shows no interest in what became of the men who were healed (cf. Mark 5:18-20), perhaps because he assumed that they were Gentiles and the time for the Gentile mission had not come (see Matt 10:5; 28:19).

Again in the healing of the paralytic (9:1-8; see Mark 2:1-12) Matthew omits certain colorful yet ultimately unnecessary details such as the size of the crowd (Mark 2:2) and the friends' efforts at lowering the paralytic into the house (Mark 2:4). Again the result of these omissions is to highlight the central concerns of the text: Jesus the healer has the power to forgive sins. The secondary characters (here the friends) are set even further in the background than in Mark, and the result is further emphasis on the encounter between Jesus and the paralytic.

Whereas in Matt 8:1-17 Jesus showed his power as a healer of various diseases, in Matt 8:18–9:9 he shows his power over even more formidable obstacles: a storm at sea (8:18-27), demons (8:28-34), and sin (9:1-8). These foes all belong to the kingdom of children of darkness (see the discussion of Matt 7:13-27).

The background for the stilling of the storm is the ancient Near Eastern idea that the sea (especially a storm at sea) symbolized the powers of chaos and evil over against God. By making the storm subside and controlling the sea Jesus defeats the forces of chaos and evil. Some see the episode as rooted in Psalm 107:23-30:

> Some went down to the sea in ships, doing business on the great waters;
> they saw the deeds of the Lord, his wondrous works in the deep.
> For he commanded, and raised the stormy wind, which lifted up the waves of the sea.
> They mounted up to heaven, they went down to the depths; their courage melted away in their evil plight;
> they reeled and staggered like drunken men, and were at their wits' end.
> Then they cried to the Lord in their trouble, and he delivered them from their distress;
> he made the storm be still, and the waves of the sea were hushed.
> Then they were glad because they had quiet, and he brought them to their desired haven.

By showing power over the sea Jesus does what God does according to Pss 74:13-14; 89:10-12. Indeed in apocalyptic texts the sea monsters Leviathan (Ps 74:14) and Rahab (Ps 89:10) become symbols of the evil powers defeated when God's kingdom comes in its fullness (see 2 Baruch 29:4).

The dualistic framework sketched in Matt 7:13-27 also seems to be the assumption of the remaining stories in the second series. In the NT demons are evil spirits, opposed to God and to God's people. They are under the leadership of Satan, "the evil one," or the devil—however their chief may be named. The exorcism of the demons in Matt 8:28-34 constitutes another victory for Jesus over the forces of evil and thus another step toward the fullness of the kingdom. The demons recognize this fact, though in a confused way: "What is there between us and you, Son of God? Have you come here before time to torment us?"

It is possible that the healing of the paralytic and the debate about forgiveness of sins were originally two independent stories (Mark 2:1-5a, 10b-12; 2:5b-10a). But in Mark they had become one story, whose point was the relationship between Jesus' power to heal and his power to forgive sins. Matthew took over that same point. What led Matthew to place this story alongside the other two was probably the cultural assumption that there was a causal connection between sickness and sin. So in John 9:2 Jesus' disciples ask him: "Rabbi, who sinned, this man or his parents, that he was born blind?" More important than the causal connection was the conviction that "sin" often personified as a powerful figure (see Romans 5–8) belonged on the side of the forces of "the evil one." The healing of the paralytic and the forgiveness of sins constituted another blow against the powers of evil and another step toward God's reign.

In these three episodes Jesus does actions that no ordinary human person can do. By subduing the storm at sea, by exorcising the demons, and by forgiving sins Jesus goes beyond the powers attributed to rabbis and Jewish leaders. The Christian claim about Jesus places him in a position like that of the Angel of Light in the Qumran *Manual of Discipline* 3–4. In fact, by doing such deeds Jesus does things attributed to God in the Jewish Scriptures. In these stories are the roots of the later Christian confession about the divinity of Jesus.

For the Matthean community these three stories helped to answer the disciples' question: "What kind of man is this?" (8:27). He is clearly no ordinary man. Besides the basic christological message that was central to Matthew the stories carried subthemes that may have enabled the Matthean community to reach greater charity about its identity.

Matthew's retelling of the stilling of the storm (8:18-27) provides a model for a Church under pressure. The Q sayings emphasize the tough conditions faced by disciples and the overriding importance of following Jesus (8:19-22). The body of the story stresses the power of Jesus and how the disciples should approach him in a spirit of prayer (8:25). The basic message is trust in Jesus' power.

The reshaping of the story about the demons (8:28-34) probably had some connection with Matthew's understanding of the mission of the earthly Jesus to Israel (see 10:5; 28:19). Only after the resurrection is the Gentile mission operative. Matthew shows hardly any interest in the demoniacs. His real concern is with Jesus' victory over the demons.

The final story (9:1-8) may have echoed Christian beliefs about the forgiveness of sins in baptism (see Rom 6:1-14) and about baptism bringing about the end of the dominion of sin and death over the Christian. It is possible that the last line in the story ("and glorified God who gave such power to human beings") presupposes that forgiveness of sins was practiced within the community (16:19; 18:18).

Each of the three texts emphasizes in its own way the power of Jesus. Matthew's reworking of his Markan sources heightens the role of Jesus. Attention to the dualistic, eschatological framework in which these stories are told adds to our appreciation of the significance of Jesus' actions. They are not merely spectacular displays. Rather they are undertaken as part of his proclamation of the coming kingdom of God. One by one—the storm at sea, demons, disease, and sin—are defeated by one who is capable of deeds usually assigned to divine power. The stories about his exploits lead us too to ask: "What kind of man is this?"

For Reference and Further Study

Annen, F. *Heil für die Heiden.* Frankfurt: Knecht, 1976.

Bornkamm, G. "The Stilling of the Storm in Matthew," in *Tradition and Interpretation,* 52–57.

Casey, M. "The Jackals and the Son of Man." *JSNT* 23 (1985) 3–22.

Hengel, M. *The Charismatic Leader and His Followers.* New York: Crossroad, 1981.

17. *Interlude* (9:9-17)

9. And Jesus passed on from there and saw a man called Matthew seated at the tax office, and he said to him: "Follow me." And he stood up and followed him. 10. And it happened when he was reclining in the house, behold many tax collectors and sinners came and reclined along with Jesus and his disciples. 11. And the Pharisees who were looking on said to his disciples: "Why does your teacher eat with tax collectors and sinners?" 12. On hearing them he said: "Those who are well have no need of a physician, but those who are sick. 13. Go, learn what this means: 'I wish mercy and not sacrifice.' For I came not to call the righteous but sinners."

14. Then the disciples of John approached him and said: "Why do we and the Pharisees fast, but your disciples do not fast?" 15. And Jesus said to them: "Can the attendants of the bridegroom mourn as long as the bridegroom is with them? The days will come when the bridegroom will be taken away from them, and then they will fast. 16. No one puts a piece of unshrunk cloth on an old garment. For its patch tears away from the garment, and the tear becomes worse. 17. Neither do people put new wine into old skins. Otherwise, the skins burst, and the wine is poured out, and the skins are destroyed. But people put new wine into new skins, and both are preserved."

Notes

9. *Jesus passed on*: Matthew omits the (unnecessary) information in Mark 2:13 and proceeds directly to Jesus' encounter with Matthew. We are probably to imagine the "tax office" (*telōnion*) as a tollbooth at which fees were collected on goods (most likely fish) as they were transported out of the region of the Sea of Galilee.

   Matthew: The name Matthew is the Greek form of a Hebrew name meaning "gift of God." In Mark 2:14 the same story is told about "Levi, the son of Alphaeus." Why the change in names? Some argue that Levi had two names, Levi and Matthew. Others claim that "Matthew" had special significance for this community as its founding apostle, its "patron saint," or the source of its traditions. Or it may be a play on the Greek word for "disciple" (*mathētēs*), which is so prominent in Matt 9:9-13.

10. *in the house*: The "reclining" position refers to the posture taken for eating a meal; one "reclined" on a couch (see Matt 26:20). Mark 2:15 reads "in his house," which could suggest that it was Jesus' house, though most likely Mark meant to refer to Levi's house. Matthew does not really resolve the ambiguity; he only makes it somewhat less noticeable.

    many tax collectors and sinners: Those who collected taxes and tolls (*telōnai*) were suspected of overcharging and of being in the employ of the Romans. The "sinners" were those who because of their lifestyle or occupation or actions were looked upon as failing to meet proper religious standards. Matthew notes that they "came" to eat with Jesus (cf. Mark 2:15). He also omits the concluding note in Mark 2:15 ("for there were many who followed him"). In Matthew's scenario they are just becoming disciples.

11. *the Pharisees*: Mark 2:16 reads "the scribes of the Pharisees." It also states their question twice, first indirectly and then directly. Matthew has tightened the verse considerably. He also has the Pharisees refer to Jesus as "teacher."

12. *physician*: There are sayings in Greek literature about a physician not being around the healthy (Stobaius 3.462.14). And the saying in Matt 9:12 does sound like a proverb. In the background may be OT texts about God as healer (see Jer 8:22; Exod 15:26). Here, however, the focus is on those "who are sick" (=tax collectors and sinners), as the end of Matt 9:13 makes clear.

13. *I wish mercy and not sacrifice*: The quotation of Hos 6:6 follows the Septuagint. The same quotation is used in Matt 12:7 in the context of debate about Sabbath observance. It seems that "sacrifice" in the Matthean context carries connotations of the program of ritual purity and Sabbath observance proposed by the opponents of the Matthean community.

14. *the disciples of John*: Matthew omits the Pharisees as questioners (see Mark 2:18) but includes them in the direct question. The fasts in question were most likely private fasts undertaken for devotional purposes (as in Matt 6:16-18). According to *Didache* 8:1 the "hypocrites" fast on Monday and Thursday. Therefore Christians should fast on Wednesday and Friday.

15. *the attendants of the bridegroom*: The Greek has "the sons of the bridegroom." The point is that mourning rituals are not appropriate to a wedding celebration. In the Matthean context Jesus is the bridegroom (see Matt 22:2; 25:1). Matthew omits the unnecessary repetition in Mark 2:19b ("as long as . . ."). With Jesus' death it became appropriate again for Christians to fast and apparently the Matthean community did so.
16. *a piece of unshrunk cloth*: The idea is that, when washed, the cloth will shrink and make the hole in the old garment worse. The same dynamic applies (though in an opposite direction) to the new wine in the old skins. The fermenting wine will expand and burst the skins and both will be lost.
17. *both are preserved*: This concluding note was added by Matthew and expresses his interpretation of the two parables (cf. Mark 2:22). The point of the parables would seem to be the incompatibility of new and old. Matthew suggests that the old can be preserved only by means of the new, an approach quite fitting in his situation.

Interpretation

The material contained in Matt 9:9-17 functions as an interlude between the second and third cycles of miracle stories. It consists of the call of Matthew and the defense of Jesus' eating with tax collectors and sinners (9:9-13) as well as an explanation of why Jesus' disciples did not fast (9:14-17). The sequence, which is taken over from Mark 2:13-22, exhibits a loose logic based on related ideas. After the debate about Jesus' power to forgive sins (Matt 9:1-8), the Gospel considers why Jesus could eat with sinners (9:9-13) and why his disciples could eat at all while other pious people fasted (9:14-17).

Among the many changes that Matt 9:9-13 introduces in comparison with Mark 2:13-17, the most substantive is the insertion of the biblical quotation from Hos 6:6 ("I wish mercy and not sacrifice") in Matt 9:13. Besides tightening the Markan account (see the notes for details) only Matt 9:9 identifies the tax collector who is called to follow Jesus as Matthew. Moreover, the Pharisees in 9:11 refer to Jesus as "teacher" (*didaskalos*).

In the second episode (Matt 9:14-17) the evangelist followed Mark 2:18-22, omitting only extraneous or repetitious material and thus providing a tighter account. The major departure comes only at the very end of the double parable on the cloth and the wine skins: "and both are preserved" (9:17).

After a narrative setting (9:9-11a), the rest of the text consists of a debate between the opponents (9:11b, 14) and Jesus (9:12-13, 15-17). The opponents (Pharisees, disciples of John) raise questions, and Jesus supplies answers.

After calling to discipleship Matthew the tax collector, Jesus is challenged for eating with tax collectors and sinners. In the Roman empire contracts for collecting taxes and tolls were often put out to bid. The highest bidder in turn hired local people to collect the fees. In this system the bidder and his employees were responsible for paying the taxes to the government. But they could also try to get extra taxes from the people in order to increase their personal profit. Even if they were not skimming off the top, they were suspected of doing so. Thus by the nature of the tax system tax collectors were suspected of dishonesty. In Judea in Jesus' time they may also have been looked upon as collaborators with the Roman officials and therefore as disloyal. Moreover, the nature of their work and its contacts with non-Jews may have rendered tax collectors religiously suspect in the eyes of the pious.

The term "sinners" is harder to pin down. It may include people notorious for their immoral activities such as thieves, prostitutes, and brawlers. But it may also have involved people who by their very professions (tax collectors, peasant farmers, etc.) could not be expected to live a full Jewish religious life. Whether "sinners" can be equated with the *'am hā-āreṣ* ("people of the land") in rabbinic literature is debatable.

For the Pharisees who ask about Jesus' practice of eating with tax collectors and sinners (9:11), the meal was an important occasion and sign of fellowship. Their banquets were opportunities to share one another's company and food under religiously controlled circumstances. The fact that Jesus openly shared meals with tax collectors and sinners was scandalous behavior according to the Pharisees' perspective.

The second issue for debate (Matt 9:14-17) concerned private fasts undertaken as acts of piety, not the solemn fast of the Day of Atonement (see Lev 16:31-34) or public fasts proclaimed in times of national emergency. It seems that Jesus did not instruct his disciples to observe a regimen that included religious fasting at specific times. In Matthew's account the questioners are the followers of the ascetic John the Baptist. Other Jews are known to have fasted regularly on Mondays and Thursdays (see *Didache* 8:1). Furthermore, it seems that after Jesus' death early Christians also adopted a similar pattern of fasting. The Christian solution to this tangle was that the public ministry of Jesus constituted a special time—the time of the bridegroom—and that therefore fasting was inappropriate. But after Jesus' death fasting was again acceptable for Christian Jews.

The interlude between the second and third cycles of miracles contains basic teaching about discipleship, connected by theme to the little Q piece on discipleship in Matt 8:19-22. It explains who could be Jesus' disciples (just about anyone) and what kind of actions were fitting (not necessarily those usually done by pious people).

For the Matthean community this interlude could supply guidance in dealing with their own situation in the late first century. Just as Jesus shared meals with social outcasts, so the fellowship of the Matthean community could be extended to all kinds of people. This openness may well have contrasted with the exclusivity practiced by the Jewish rivals of the Matthean community as they took over some of the ideals and practices of the Pharisees. Indeed Hosea 6:6 ("I wish mercy and not sacrifice") may have functioned as the Matthean slogan in this conflict. The quotation appears twice—once in the context of meals (9:11), and once in the debate about Sabbath observance (12:7). It is possible that "sacrifice" alluded to the Pharisaic program of extending the rules of ritual purity for priests in the Jerusalem Temple to all Israel, or at least as much of Israel that wished to participate in the religious renewal constituted by Pharisaism. Thus Matthew would be using the Hosea text to criticize the program of his rivals.

The debate about fasting (9:14-17) follows the argument of its Markan model until the very end ("and both are preserved"). The fundamental point is that the time of Jesus is a special moment in which fasting is inappropriate. This point is strengthened by the double parable (9:16-17), which seems to stress the incompatibility of the old (garment, wineskins) and the new (patch, wine). The double parable is usually cited as proof of the discontinuity between Judaism and Christianity; they do not fit together.

Whether the usual interpretation of the double parallel is correct, Matthew gave it a different twist by his additional comment "and both are preserved" (9:17). Matthew does not want to lose the old. If we assume that "the old" relates to pre-A.D. 70 Judaism (the Hebrew Bible, Israel's history, the Temple, the land, and so forth), the addition may reflect Matthew's conviction that the tradition of pre-70 Judaism is best preserved by the movement centered around Jesus. For him and other Jewish Christians the only way to move into the future without the Temple and without direct control of the land of Israel was to take Jesus and his teaching as the guide. What appeared to some Jews as scandalous novelty was in fact the way in which "both (old and new) are preserved."

The problems about who may be part of a religious community and what kinds of religious practices are appropriate at any given time are always matters of controversy. They were such in Jesus' time and in Matthew's time, and remain such today. The texts in Matt 9:9-17 show us that such controversies are not new.

The emphasis on Jesus as the bridegroom and on his public ministry as a unique period adds a fresh Christological perspective to what had been developed up to this point in the Gospel.

The passage also provides an important perspective on how Matthew perceived the Christian movement with respect to Judaism. For him it was the way in which Judaism could be preserved (9:17). Its preservation could happen only if the program of "mercy" was followed and not the program of "(Temple) sacrifices" (9:13).

For Reference and Further Study

Donahue, J. R. "Tax Collectors and Sinners." *CBQ* 33 (1971) 39–61.
Hill, D. "On the Use and Meaning of Hosea vi.6 in Matthew's Gospel." *NTS* 24 (1977) 107–19.
Kee, A. "The Question about Fasting." *NovT* 11 (1969) 161–73; "The Old Coat and the New Wine." *NovT* 12 (1970) 13–21.
Kiley, M. "Why 'Matthew' in Matt 9,9-13?" *Bib* 65 (1984) 347–51.

18. *More Healings* (9:18-34)

18. While he was saying these things to them, behold an official approached him and did him homage and said: "My daughter has just died. But come and lay hands on her, and she will live." 19. And Jesus arose and followed him, with his disciples. 20. And behold a woman who suffered from bleeding for twelve years came up behind him and touched the hem of his garment. 21. For she said to herself: "If only I touch his garment, I will be healed." 22. But when Jesus turned around and saw her, he said: "Take courage, daughter. Your faith has healed you." And the woman was healed from that hour. 23. And Jesus came into the house of the official. And when he saw the flute-players and the crowd making a din, 24. he said: "Go away. For the girl is not dead, but she is only asleep." And they laughed at him. 25. But when the crowd had been put outside, he went in and took her hand, and the girl arose. 26. And this story went forth in all that land. 27. And as Jesus passed on from there, two blind men followed him, shouting and saying: "Have pity on us, Son of David." 28. When he came into the house, the blind men approached him. And Jesus said to them: "Do you believe that I can do this?" They said to him: "Yes, Lord." 29. Then he touched their eyes and said: "According to your faith let it be done to you." 30. And their eyes were opened. And Jesus sternly charged them, saying: "See that no one knows this." 31. But they went out and spread his fame in all that land.

32. As they were going out, behold they brought to him a mute man possessed by a demon. 33. And when the demon had been cast out, the mute man spoke. And the crowds were amazed, saying: "Never was anything like this seen in Israel." 34. But the Pharisees said: "By the prince of demons he casts out demons."

Notes

18. *official*: Matthew uses a generic term to describe the man. According to Mark 5:22 (also Luke 8:41) he was a "ruler of the synagogue," perhaps its president,

and his name was Jairus. From Matthew's bland "an official" one would hardly know that the man was Jewish. Perhaps Matthew played down the connection with the synagogue because of his own community's strained relationship with "their synagogues."

did him homage: Matthew simplifies the long description in Mark 5:21-22 by using the verb *proskyneō* ("do homage") that typically describes the proper posture in Jesus' presence (see Matt 2:2, 8, 11; 8:2).

has just died: According to Mark 5:23 the man's daughter was at the point of death; only later (in Mark 5:35) does word arrive that she has died. By stating early on that the girl had died, Matthew can omit the subsequent episode and thus produce a tighter account. He also makes the ruler's faith all the more remarkable and highlights Jesus' confidence in his powers as a healer.

lay hands on her: Of the several meanings attached to this gesture (imparting a blessing, ordination, sacrificial ritual) the most obvious here is the transfer of physical and spiritual health or wholeness. For this action in the context of an exorcism see *Genesis Apocryphon* 20:28-29 where Abraham says: "and I laid my hands upon his head. And the plague was removed from him. . . ."

19. *with his disciples*: The additional and awkward phrase is unusual in an account in which Matthew's major concern appears to be abbreviation. It has the effect of drawing Jesus' disciples into the third cycle of miracle stories. That the disciples were there is derived from Mark 5:31.

20. *bleeding*: Matthew summarizes the complicated description of the woman's condition and the unsuccessful attempts at healing her in Mark 5:25-26. The condition is diagnosed by J. D. M. Derrett (*Bib* 63 [1982] 474–505) as menorrhagia or perhaps vaginal bleeding from fibroids.

hem of his garment: Whereas Mark 5:27 has simply "garment," Matt 9:20 (and Luke 8:44 perhaps) adds the term *kraspedon*, which refers to the edge or border of a garment. Given the Jewish environment of Matthew, the word may have described the fringes or tassels worn at the edge of one's garment in accord with Num 15:38-39; Deut 22:12. See Matt 23:5 for a reference to such tassels worn by Pharisees.

21. *If only I touch*: The woman's plan is the reverse of Matt 9:18, where the assumption is that Jesus' powerful touch can heal. Here the assumption is that the sick person can be healed by touching the powerful man. It is not so much an element of magic as it is a proof of the woman's faith in Jesus' power to heal her.

22. *has healed you*: Matthew omits the description of the healing and the search for the one who touched Jesus' garment (Mark 5:29-33). Instead his summary revolves around the word *sōzō*, which can mean "heal" and "save": "I will be healed" (v. 21), "Your faith has healed you" (v. 22), and "the woman was healed" (v. 22). While the primary healing was physical, the spiritual aspect of healing (salvation) is also present.

23. *he saw the flute-players*: Since he said in 9:18 that the girl was already dead, Matthew could omit the message about her death (Mark 5:35-37). Matthew added the note about the presence of the flute-players: "Even the poorest in Israel must

not furnish less than two flutes and one woman wailer (at the funeral of his wife)'' (*m. Ketub.* 4:4). The presence of the flute-players confirms that the girl already died.

24. *she is only asleep*: It is possible that the story concerns Jesus' superior insight into the girl's condition (she was unconscious or in a coma). But it is more likely to be taken as a resuscitation of a dead person, a sign pointing toward the resurrection of Jesus. This second line of interpretation is strengthened by 9:25 (''and the girl arose''), which uses the standard term for resurrection, *ēgerthē*.

26. *this story*: Some manuscripts read ''her story.'' This ending contrasts sharply with Mark 5:43 (''he strictly charged them that no one should know this''). Matthew also omits Jesus' command that the girl be given something to eat—a proof of her complete restoration to life.

27. *two blind men*: The story is roughly based on the healing of blind Bartimaeus in Mark 10:46-52. Another version appears in Matt 20:29-34. For another example of Matthew having two persons healed instead of one, see the story of the two demoniacs in Matt 8:28-34.

 Son of David: The Christological focus of this text is Jesus as Son of David (see Matt 20:31; Mark 10:47). For the Son of David as a healer see D. C. Duling, ''The Therapeutic Son of David: An Element in Matthew's Christological Apologetic,'' *NTS* 24 (1978) 392–410.

28. *Do you believe*: The addition of this term and the sentence in 9:29 (''According to your faith let it be done to you'') highlights the theme of faith only implicit in Mark 10:46-52 and Matt 20:29-34 (see ''your faith has healed you'' in Mark 10:52).

30. *See that no one knows this*: Matthew often suppresses Jesus' commands to silence but here he inserts one on the basis of Mark 1:43-45. Compare Matt 8:3-4.

31. *spread his fame*: The motif of the growing reputation of Jesus as the result of his healings runs through the third cycle (9:26, 31, 33).

32. *a mute man possessed by a demon*: The Greek term *kōphos* can have several meanings: unable to speak, unable to hear, or both. Since the sign of the healing is the fact that the man could speak (9:33), the translation ''mute'' seems most appropriate. The condition is attributed to possession by a demon; the healing consists in driving out the demon.

33. *crowds*: The reaction of the crowds is amazement. Their response (cf. Matt 12:23) emphasizes the location of Jesus' mighty deeds ''in Israel.''

34. *Pharisees*: Matthew's source (Mark 3:22) labels Jesus' opponents here as ''the scribes who were from Jerusalem.'' Both here and Matt 12:24 call them ''the Pharisees,'' an example of Matthew's tendency to give special prominence to the Pharisees as the opponents of Jesus. The Pharisees do not deny Jesus' power as a healer; they claim that this power is from Satan.

Interpretation

The four miracle stories in Matt 9:18-34 continue the theme of Jesus' power. He heals the daughter of an official (9:18-19, 23-26), the woman with the bleeding (9:20-22), two blind men (9:27-31), and the mute demoniac (9:32-34). The actions prepare for Jesus' willingness to share his healing powers with his disciples (10:1) and for his self-description to John's disciples (11:4-6). The emphasis on Jesus' growing fame (9:26, 31, 33) and the opposition to him (9:34) prepares for the theme of accepting and rejecting Jesus that dominates chapters 11–15.

In editing his sources Matthew was chiefly concerned to preserve only what he considered to be essential details, thus allowing the most important themes to shine forth. Matthew found the healings of the official's daughter and the bleeding woman already intertwined in Mark 5:21-43. While maintaining Mark's basic outline in 9:18-26, Matthew has greatly abbreviated his source (see the notes for details). His editing leaves the source material primarily in the form of a conversation that emphasizes the faith of the official and the woman. The vocabulary of salvation (9:21-22) and resurrection (9:25) link these stories to the broader concerns of early Christian theology. Since from the start the girl was dead (9:18), her restoration to life becomes a sign pointing toward the resurrection (9:25).

The healing of the two blind men (9:27-31) is a loose adaptation of the Bartimaeus story (Mark 10:46-52) coupled with details from other texts. It forms a doublet with Matt 20:29-34 and is an example of Matthew's peculiar practice of doubling characters (as in 8:28-34). The Matthean version of the miracle revolves around the scrutiny of faith in 9:28: "Do you believe that I can do this?" Their faith is an essential element in their healing.

The healing of the mute demoniac (9:32-33a) is told so quickly that one gets the impression that Matthew's real interest lay in contrasting the reactions of the crowd (9:33b) and the Pharisees (9:34). The contrast prepares for several sayings in the following discourse as well as the more extended treatment of opposition to Jesus in chapters 11–15.

Attention to Matthew's editorial practices in chapters 8–9 has shown him to be a careful editor, eager to prune away unnecessary details. While remaining essentially faithful to the content of his sources, Matthew did not hesitate to make changes, to bring out themes more sharply, and even to introduce new aspects. His miracle stories tend toward becoming dialogues or conversations in which the suppliant's faith is central.

Matthew and the other evangelists portray Jesus as a miracle-worker. In the biblical sense of miracle such a figure is a vehicle through which God's power shines forth. The most prominent biblical miracle-worker (besides Jesus) is the prophet Elisha. According to the cycle of stories in 2 Kings 2–6 Elisha performs the following "miracles": He purifies the water (2:19-22), provides water for Israel's army (3:20), supplies oil for the poor widow (4:1-8), restores to life the son of the Shunammite woman (4:18-37), finds the antidote for a poisonous stew (4:38-41), multiplies barley loaves (4:42-44), heals Naaman the Syrian of leprosy (5:1-19), and recovers the borrowed ax-head (6:1-7). In many respects the ninth-century B.C. prophet Elisha is the most obvious biblical prototype of Jesus the miracle-worker.

In the interpretations of Matt 8:1-17 and 8:18–9:8 the focus of the background section has been on a rabbinic contemporary (Hanina ben Dosa) and the apocalyptic context in which Jesus' miracles appear in the Gospels, respectively. Here we remind the reader that even in the early biblical tradition the miracles of Jesus have parallels and precedents. The most famous OT miracle-worker was Elisha, and it is possible that Elisha served as a model both for Jesus and for those who wrote about him.

There are, however, some noteworthy differences. In the Jesus tradition there is more emphasis on healing persons, and in nearly every case there is reference to faith on the part of the sick person or those close to him or her. In the Elisha tradition the prophet is more clearly an instrument of God's power, whereas Jesus seems to act upon his own power and authority as God's Son. Some of the deeds done by Elisha affect the lives of many people (2:23-25) and even an army (3:20).

Another new element in the tradition of miracles is the idea that in many cases Jesus must exorcise a demon in order to heal. The assumption is that demons cause some diseases (9:32). By his exorcisms and healings Jesus strikes a decisive blow against the kingdom of Satan. The themes of routing demons and defeating the apocalyptic forces of evil are absent from the Elisha cycle. The material supplied in the background sections of the three miracle cycles in Matthew 8–9 provides a framework for understanding the Gospel miracles: their structure, their prototypes and parallels, their apocalyptic context, and their special themes (faith, salvation, resurrection).

The element most pertinent to the situation of the Matthean community comes in Matt 9:33b-34: the notice of the split between the crowds and the Pharisees in their assessment of Jesus' miracles. The reaction of the crowd (which is uniquely Matthean) situates Jesus' miracles squarely within Israel: "Never was anything like this seen in Israel." The reaction of the Pharisees ("By the prince of demons he casts out demons") does not contest the fact of Jesus' healings and exorcism. The point at issue is the source of his power. Here the Pharisees may well be spokesmen for one Jewish assessment of Jesus' miracles in the late first century.

In his editing of Mark 5:21-43 Matthew may have deliberately avoided connecting the official to the synagogue, lest the impression be given that it was one of "their synagogues." On the other hand, Matthew has heightened the "Jewishness" of the account by suggesting that Jesus wore tassels (9:20) and by stating that flute-players were present in the official's house

(9:23). Thus Matthew carries on his project of situating Jesus within Israel while placing him over against certain other factions within Israel.

At the center of the third cycle of Jesus' miracles is the cry of two blind men: "Have pity on us, Son of David" (9:27). Son of David is the chief Christological title in this cycle. Immediately following is Jesus' testing of the men's faith (9:28-29). Elsewhere we have called attention to the vocabulary of salvation and resurrection.

Though it is important to be sensitive to the theological dimensions of these accounts, they need not be turned into allegories designed to illustrate abstractions. Even Matthew, who systematically removes unnecessary details, never departs from the concrete situation of first-century Palestine in which Jesus acted.

The concluding statement of the Pharisees (9:34) reminds us that Jesus' miracles are always subject to interpretation and that much depends on the theological and philosophical assumptions that one brings to them. This applies not only to the crowds and the Pharisees of the first century but also to the fundamentalists and the skeptics of today.

For Reference and Further Study

Hutter, M. "Ein altorientalischer Bittgestus in Mt 9,20-22." *ZNW* 75 (1984) 133–35.

Robbins, V. K. "The Woman Who Touched Jesus' Garment: Socio-Rhetorical Analysis of the Synoptic Accounts." *NTS* 33 (1987) 502–15.

19. *Setting* (9:35–10:4)

35. And Jesus went about all the cities and villages, teaching in their synagogues and preaching the gospel of the kingdom and healing every disease and every infirmity. 36. When he saw the crowds, he took pity on them, because they were harassed and torn apart, like sheep not having a shepherd. 37. Then he said to his disciples: "The harvest is large, but the workers are few. 38. Therefore beg the Lord of the harvest that he send out workers into his harvest."

10:1. And he summoned his twelve apostles and gave them power over unclean spirits to cast them out, and to heal every disease and every infirmity. 2. These are the names of the twelve apostles: First Simon who is called Peter, and Andrew his brother, and James the son of Zebedee and John his brother, 3. Philip and Bartholomew, Thomas, and Matthew the tax collector, James the son of Alphaeus, and Thaddeus, 4. Simon the Cananean and Judas Iscariot, the one who handed him over.

NOTES

35. *Jesus went about*: The summary of Jesus' activity combines material from Mark 6:6 ("And he went about the villages, teaching") and phrases already used in Matt 4:23. The use of the same formula in Matt 4:23 and 9:35 mark off the intervening material as a unit. Part of that formula is "in their synagogues"—an unusual phrase in light of Matthew's antipathy toward "their synagogues."

36. *like sheep not having a shepherd*: The image of Israel as the lost sheep (see Matt 10:6) is rooted in many OT texts (Num 27:17; 1 Kgs 22:17; 2 Chr 18:16, Ezek 34:5; Zech 13:7). Jesus shows compassion toward his people (see Matt 14:14; 15:32; 20:34) and wishes to serve as their shepherd. The need of the flock is stressed by the addition of the two participles "harassed and torn apart."

37. *harvest*: In Matt 13:39 the harvest is defined as "the close of the age." This identification is based on OT texts (Isa 24:13; 27:12; Joel 3:13) and appears also in 2 Bar 70:2; 4 Ezra 4:39. The close of the age will witness a coming together of all peoples for judgment. The "workers" can help people prepare for the harvest.

38. *the Lord of the harvest*: This figure clearly is God. But by preparing his twelve apostles to share in the mission of preparation Jesus acts as the representative of God.

10:1. *gave them power*: Having demonstrated Jesus' power in chapters 8–9, Matthew portrays Jesus as sharing those powers with the Twelve. The expression "to heal every disease and every infirmity" links Matt 10:1 back to 9:35, thus suggesting that the two pieces (9:35-38 and 10:1-4) form an introduction to the mission discourse.

2. *the names of the twelve apostles*: An "apostle" is one who is sent or commissioned. Only here in Matthew are the Twelve called "apostles." In early Christianity the term was more flexible than the traditional concept of the twelve apostles allows. Other lists of apostles appear in Mark 3:16-19; Luke 6:14-16; and Acts 1:13. In Matthew's list the names come in six pairs.

First Simon: The adjective *protos* ("first") recognizes the role of Simon Peter as spokesman for the group (see 15:15; 16:16; 17:4; 18:21; 19:27) as well as his status as one of the first two disciples (see Matt 4:18-20). Matthew tidies up Mark 3:16b-18a by joining Simon and Andrew and by omitting the information about the name "Boanerges."

3. *Thomas and Matthew the tax collector*: Matthew has placed Thomas first in this pair (cf. Mark 3:18; Luke 6:15). He has also identified Matthew as the *telōnēs* (see Matt 9:9).

4. *Simon the Cananean*: Although "Cananean" could be a geographical designation, Luke 6:15 translates the term into Greek as *zēlōtēs*. It is not clear whether Simon should be understood as "zealous" in the religious sense or as a part of a political-religious revolutionary movement known as the Zealots.

Judas Iscariot: The surname Iscariot is usually taken in its geographical sense: "A man from Keriot" (see Josh 25:25). Other interpretations include these: liar or hypocrite, ruddy, assassin, member of the Sicarii, and man of Issachar or of Sychar.

INTERPRETATION

The setting (9:35–10:4) that Matthew constructed for the mission discourse serves as a bridge between the displays of Jesus' power in chapters 8–9 and his instructions to those who share his mission in chapter 10. This bridge has two parts that feature Jesus' saying about the sheep without a shepherd (9:35-38) and the list of the twelve apostles (10:1-4). The two parts are joined by the expression "healing every disease and every infirmity" in 9:35 and 10:1.

The first part (9:35-38) has been constructed out of pieces taken from a variety of sources: verse 35 out of Mark 6:6 and Matt 4:23; verse 36 out of Mark 6:34; and verses 37-38 out of the Q-saying also found in Luke 10:2. Thus Matthew illustrates his ability to draw something new out of the old (see Matt 13:52). The most obvious Matthean addition serves to heighten the plight of the sheep as "harassed and torn apart" (9:36).

The second part (10:1-4) begins with material from Mark 6:7 and 3:13-15, accompanied by the characteristic Matthean expression "to heal every disease and every infirmity" (see 4:23; 9:35) in 10:1. The list of disciples in 10:2-4 is an edited version of Mark 3:16-19. Matthew has arranged the twelve names in six pairs and provided further information in a few places: Simon Peter is "first"; Andrew is "his brother"; and Matthew is the "tax collector." The confusing note about the "sons of thunder" in Mark 3:17 is omitted entirely.

Another element that ties together Matt 9:35-38 and 10:1-4 is the theme of Israel as the missionfield of Jesus and the twelve apostles. Jesus the Good Shepherd is sent to the "harassed and torn" flock to prepare them for the harvest. He in turn sends forth his twelve apostles to carry on and extend his mission. The theme of Israel is expressed especially in the image of the flock and in the concept of twelve apostles.

The image of Israel as a flock is common in the Hebrew Bible. A subcategory of such imagery appears in texts that concern the relation between flock and shepherd. In fact, Matt 9:36 alludes to Num 27:17: "that the congregation of the Lord may not be as sheep without a shepherd." Matthew's heightening of their condition as being "harassed and torn apart" (9:36) may reflect other texts: "I saw all Israel scattered upon the mountains, as sheep that have no shepherd" (1 Kgs 22:17; 2 Chr 18:16). The prophets used this imagery to describe the exile ("they were scattered because there was no shepherd," Ezek 34:5) and the Day of the Lord ("Strike the shepherd that the sheep may be scattered," Zech 13:7).

Another Israel-image is contained in the idea of "twelve" apostles. Ancient Israel, of course, understood itself to be a confederation of twelve tribes descended from Jacob/Israel and his wives (Leah and Rachel) and concubines (Zilpah and Bilhah): Reuben, Simeon, Levi, Judah, Issachar, Zebulun, Joseph (=Ephraim and Manasseh), Benjamin, Gad, Asher, Dan, and Naphtali. Even after the twelve-tribe structure ceased to carry political meaning, people remained aware of their ancestry. In the "restored Israel" the twelve-tribe structure was expected to have meaning again (see Rev 21:12-14).

It is quite likely that the idea of "twelve" disciples goes back to the ministry of the earthly Jesus. The promise made in Matt 19:28 ("you who have followed me will also sit on twelve thrones, judging the twelve tribes of Israel") suggests that the "twelve" were symbolic of Jesus' hope for a restored Israel when God's kingdom comes. The fact that little is known about most of the figures on the list and there are even some manuscript variants about their names only strengthens the likelihood that the "twelve" was deeply rooted in early Christian consciousness.

With the images of the sheep without a shepherd and the twelve apostles Matthew prepares for Jesus' instructions regarding the mission to Israel (see 10:6). He comments on the present state of Israel as "harassed and torn apart" (9:36)—a description even more appropriate after the events of A.D. 70. He charts out the place of Jesus' followers in the story of salvation: The harvest (=final judgment) is approaching; Israel the flock needs leadership that only Jesus and his disciples can provide; and on their leadership depends the restoration of Israel.

The distinctively Matthean way of listing the twelve apostles in six pairs may reflect some contact with the early rabbinic movement. In *m. 'Abot* the great teachers of Israel from the second century B.C. to the first century A.D. are listed in pairs: Jose ben Joezer and Jose ben Yohanan, Joshua ben Perachiah and Nittai the Arbelite, Judah ben Tabbai and Simon ben Shetach, Shemaiah and Abtalion, and Hillel and Shammai (1:4-15). A list of disciples is presented in connection with Yohanan ben Zakkai in *m. 'Abot* 2:8: "Rabban Yohanan ben Zakkai had five disciples: Rabbi Eleazar ben Hyrcanus, and Rabbi Joshua ben Hananiah, and Rabbi Jose the priest, and Rabbi Simon ben Nathaniel, and Rabbi Eleazar ben Arak." Whether there is any direct contact between Matt 10:2-4 and *m. 'Abot* is not certain. But it is noteworthy that both texts contain lists of disciples and place figures in pairs. Since the device is more important in Judaism, it is possible that Matthew was giving his own Jewish-Christian version.

These bridge texts contain rich subthemes: Jesus as preacher and healer (9:35), the good shepherd (9:36), sharing in Jesus' power (10:1), and the apostles as carrying on Jesus' mission (10:2-4). But the main theme is Israel. The passage comments on the state of Israel's leadership and situates Jesus and his first followers in relation to Israel's spiritual well being. The goal of their mission is a "restored Israel." How that can come about is sketched in the mission discourse in 10:5-42.

For Reference and Further Study

Beare, F. W. "The Mission of the Disciples and the Mission Charge: Matthew 10 and Parallels." *JBL* 89 (1970) 1–13.

Brown, S. "The Mission to Israel in Matthew's Central Section (Mt 9:35–11:1)." *ZNW* 69 (1978) 73–90.

Grassi, J. A. "The Last Testament-Succession Literary Background of Matthew 9:35–11:1 and Its Significance." *BTB* 7 (1977) 172–76.

Morosco, R. E. "Matthew's Formation of a Commissioning Type Scene Out of the Story of Jesus' Commissioning of the Twelve." *JBL* 103 (1984) 539–56.

Weaver, D. J. *Matthew's Missionary Discourse. A Literary Critical Analysis.* Sheffield, U.K.: JSOT, 1990.

20. *Mission to Israel* (10:5-15)

5. These twelve Jesus sent out and charged them, saying: "Do not go among the Gentiles, nor enter into the city of the Samaritans. 6. Rather, go to the lost sheep of the house of Israel. 7. Go and proclaim, saying that 'the kingdom of heaven has drawn near.' 8. Heal the sick, raise the dead, cleanse lepers, cast out demons. You have received without cost, so give without cost. 9. Do not acquire gold or silver or copper for your belts, 10. no bag for the journey, nor two tunics, nor sandals, nor staff. For the worker is worthy of his food. 11. Into whatever city or village you enter, find out who in it is worthy and stay there until you depart. 12. When you enter the house, salute it. 13. And if the house be worthy, let your peace come upon it. But if it not be worthy, let your 'peace' return to you. 14. And whoever may not receive you or listen to your words, go out of that house or that city and shake the dust off your feet. 15. Amen I say to you, it will be easier for the land of Sodom and Gomorrah in the day of judgment than for that city."

Notes

5. *among the Gentiles*: The literal translation would be "in the way of the Gentiles," which would mean "in the direction of the Gentiles." The "city" of the Samaritans could refer to Samaria-Sebaste or to Mount Gerizim. But there may be a confusion stemming from the Aramaic word *mĕdînâ'*, which can signify both "city" and "district."

6. *the lost sheep*: The expression refers to all Israel, not simply one group within Israel. This is suggested by the collective nouns in 10:5 (Gentiles, Samaritans), other Matthean texts (9:36; 15:24), and OT texts such as Ezekiel 34.

7. *the kingdom of heaven:* The Twelve are to share in Jesus' mission of proclaiming God's kingdom by repeating his words in Matt 4:17, which were in turn the same as the message of John the Baptist in 3:2. Thus there is a continuity between John, Jesus, and the twelve.

8. *Heal the sick*: The four commands ("heal . . . raise . . . cleanse . . . cast out") correspond to actions done by Jesus in chapters 8–9, thus establishing a continuity between the deeds of Jesus and those of his closest disciples. They also prepare for the summary of Jesus' activities in Matt 11:4-6.

   without cost: Just as the message of the coming kingdom and the power to heal have been given to the Twelve by God, so they should give those gifts to others. This idea is also found in rabbinic writings: "Just as you (Moses) received it (the Torah) without payment, so teach it without payment" (*b. Ber.* 29a). And Hillel warned that "one who makes worldly use of the crown (of the Torah) shall waste away" (*m. 'Abot* 1:13). See also Paul's boast in 2 Cor 11:7: "I preached God's gospel to you without cost."

9. *do not acquire gold*: Since the previous sentence established the principle of gratuity, here the idea is most likely a warning against making provisions before the mission. The listing of different metals (gold, silver, copper) gives added emphasis in comparison with Mark 6:8 and Luke 9:3. The "money belt" was worn under the outer garment.

10. *nor sandals, nor staff*: Matthew goes beyond the prohibitions of a food-bag and two tunics (in addition to what one wore?) to forbid sandals and a staff. Mark 6:9 says that the disciples are to wear sandals. Since going barefoot in rocky Palestine would be nearly impossible, perhaps the idea is a second pair of shoes. The staff was intended as a defense against wild animals. The idea is not to be so encumbered that one's baggage holds one back in travelling.

    the worker is worthy of his food: See Luke 10:7: "the laborer deserves his wages," though in context the meaning is the same as Matt 10:10. See also 1 Cor 9:14: "In the same way the Lord commanded that those who proclaim the gospel should get their living by the gospel." Paul did not follow this principle in his own ministry, but deliberately supported himself lest he be a burden to local communities.

11. *stay there until you depart*: A "worthy" person receives the message of the kingdom and its apostle. The prohibition about going from house to house was intended to prove the apostle's dedication to the mission rather than to his physical surroundings.

13. *'peace'*: The greeting mentioned in 10:12 was "Peace (= Shalom) to this house." The acceptance or rejection of the "Shalom" determines whether the householder is worthy and one should stay at that house. *Didache* 12 places a two- or three-day limit on the stay of a travelling prophet. For "peace" as the greeting of God's messenger, see Isa 52:7.

14. *shake the dust off your feet*: When Jews returned from foreign lands, they shook off the dust from their feet as a symbolic rejection of pagan lands (see Lachs, 180). This symbolic action by missionaries of the Jesus movement is applied here to Jewish cities (see 10:5b-6).
15. *Sodom and Gomorrah*: For the wickedness and evil fate of Sodom and Gomorrah, see Genesis 19. For the two cities as emblematic of wickedness see Deut 29:22-23; Isa 1:9; 13:19; Jer 49:18; 50:40. The NT writings also pick up this theme (see Rom 9:29; 2 Pet 2:6; Jude 7; Rev 11:8).

Interpretation

Matthew has constructed the first part of Jesus' missionary discourse to the twelve apostles (10:5-15) out of material in Mark 6:8-11 and Q (see Luke 9:2-5; 10:2-12). After developing a narrative framework (10:5a), he has Jesus speak about the mission to Israel (10:5b-6), the message of God's kingdom (10:7), the tasks of healing (10:8), the need for travelling "light" (10:9-10), dealing with acceptance and rejection (10:11-14), and the coming judgment (10:15).

Much of this material was already in Matthew's sources. His major contribution was using it in the framework of the disciples' mission to Israel: "Go to the lost sheep of the house of Israel" (10:6). Though it is likely that Matt 10:5b-6 was present in the evangelist's special tradition (M) and probably goes back to a saying of the earthly Jesus, Matthew has used it as the heading for all the missionary instructions in chapter 10.

Besides placing these instructions in a framework Matthew has emphasized the continuity between the preaching and activity of Jesus and those of the Twelve. They are to say what Jesus said: "The kingdom of heaven has drawn near" (10:7 = 4:17). They are to do what Jesus did: "Heal the sick, raise the dead, cleanse lepers, cast out demons" (10:8 = 8:1–9:38). Thus the mission of the Twelve to Israel is the continuation and prolongation of Jesus' mission.

In the body of the instructions (10:9-14) Matthew heightens the simple lifestyle demanded of the Twelve: "no gold or silver or copper" (10:9); "nor sandals nor staff" (10:10). For the instructions about dealing with acceptance and rejection (10:11-14) Matthew generally follows Mark 6:10-11 and Q (Luke 10:5-11). The Sodom-Gomorrah threat (10:15) is based on Q (Luke 10:12); Matthew has added the name "Gomorrah" and used the saying to move forward the idea of a mission to Israel raised in 10:5b-6.

It is possible to find biblical models for Jesus' missionary discourse in Matthew 10. Those models include Jacob's last testament in Genesis 49 and

God's commissioning of Moses in Exodus 3–4. But in Matthew 10 we are dealing with what in the first century were living realities rather than the sophisticated products of religious imagination.

In the ancient Mediterranean world the primary way in which philosophical and religious teachings were spread was through travelling missionaries. The Cynics were known especially for their street-corner oratory and for their ascetic lifestyle. The true Cynic, according to Epictetus (3.22.19-26), knows that "he is sent as a messenger from God to men concerning things good and evil, to show them that they have gone astray and are seeking the true nature of good and evil where it is not to be found, and take no thought where it really is." The Cynic missionary takes no account of the dangers of travel in the ancient world (see 2 Cor 12:25-27): "Death? Let it come when it will, whether to my whole body or to part of it. Exile? Can one be sent into exile beyond the universe?"

The basic assumption behind Jesus' missionary discourse to the Twelve is that Jesus' teaching is to be spread by travelling missionaries. Before modern communications and when writing materials were scarce, there was hardly any other way imaginable. Jesus himself was this kind of teacher. Using Capernaum as a base, Jesus and his followers moved around Galilee and finally went up to Jerusalem where he met his death. In Syria and Palestine the mission of Jesus was carried on by other travelling preachers. For an analysis of earliest Christianity as a movement spread by wandering charismatics, see Gerd Theissen, *Sociology of Early Palestinian Christianity* (Philadelphia: Fortress, 1978). It is important, however, not to romanticize or exaggerate this aspect of early Christianity. The cities and towns in ancient Palestine and Syria were not far apart. As the instruction indicates, what was most important is what happened when the travelling missionaries arrived at their destination.

Then (as today) the possibility for fraud in exploiting philosophy or religion was always present. The instructions in Matt 10:7-15 would have provided a checklist for people in Palestine and Syria (10:5b-6) whereby they could distinguish genuine representatives of the Jesus movement from frauds: Do they say and do what Jesus said and did? Do they demand a fee for the gospel? Do they cart around large supplies of food and clothing? Do they spend their energies in seeking out the best accommodations? How do they handle rejection?

That travelling missionaries caused problems in the early church in Syria is indicated by *Didache* 11–13. Written in roughly the same area and time as Matthew's Gospel, this handbook of Christian living contains elaborate instructions on how to deal with travelling apostles and prophets. Some of these instructions suggest negative experiences from such figures. For example, an apostle is "to be received as the Lord." He may stay one or even two days. But if he stays three days, he is a false prophet.

In the Matthean community the missionary instructions in 10:5b-15 would have provided guidance not only for early Christian missionaries who spread the gospel but also for those who facilitated their mission in various locales. Both the missionaries and those who received them knew what to expect.

Matthew placed these instructions about lifestyle in the framework of the mission to Israel. Just as Jesus was sent to the lost sheep of the house of Israel, so his disciples were sent on the same mission. For the Matthean community, which perceived itself as having a special role within Israel to show other Jews that theirs was the authentic way of Judaism after A.D. 70, these instructions were especially significant. In Matt 28:19 Jesus urges the "eleven" to make disciples of "all the Gentiles." Thus Matthew locates the beginning of the Gentile mission in the commission of the risen Lord. But the opening up of the Gentile mission did not mean that the mission to Israel was entirely over. The Gentile mission did not exclude a Jewish mission. The aim of the Jewish mission was not to convert Jews to Christianity as from one religion to another. Rather it was to suggest that after A.D. 70 Christian Judaism was the best way to carry on the Jewish tradition.

In his instructions (taken over from Q) Matthew gives much attention to dealing with acceptance and rejection (10:11-15). Though this was a theme in all missionary teaching, it had particular relevance for the Matthean community. Embroiled in a contest with other Jewish groups in the late first century, the missionaries of the Matthean community necessarily dealt with rejection. Their instructions are clear: When you encounter rejection, do not react violently. Rather write those people off ("shake the dust off your feet") and leave their fate to the justice of God on the last day.

The eschatological saying 10:15 ("it will be easier for the land of Sodom and Gomorrah . . .") connects the discourse to Israel's history (see Genesis 19). It also places the mission to Israel in an eschatological framework (see 10:23). Moreover, it indicates the appropriate strategy for Christians to deal with those who reject them: Leave their fate to God's judgment.

The first part of the mission discourse (10:5b-15) emphasizes the continuity between Jesus' mission and that of the twelve. They are to say and do as Jesus said and did. Their simple lifestyle was not so much an exercise in asceticism as it was a testimony to the overriding importance of proclaiming God's kingdom. The mission to Israel was undertaken against an eschatological horizon.

Christianity's continuing mission to Israel remains a very delicate matter in Christian-Jewish relations. On the one hand, the mission to the Gentiles (Matt 28:19) does not exclude the mission to Israel (10:5b-6). Indeed if Christians are convinced of the rightness and importance of the gospel, they are obliged to share it with others, including and especially Jews. On the other hand, the history of the Christian mission to Israel with its persecutions, forced conversions, and insensitive approaches to evangelization have correctly made most Jews suspicious of such a mission. In its third millennium Christianity needs to find a better way both to be faithful to the gospel mandate and to be sensitive in its efforts in carrying out that mandate.

For Reference and Further Study

Bartnicki, R. "Der Bereich der Tätigkeit der Jünger nach Mt 10,5b-6." *BZ* 31 (1987) 250–56.

Hooker, M. D. "Uncomfortable Words: X: The Prohibition of Foreign Missions (Mt 10:5b-6)." *ExpTim* 82 (1971) 361–65.

21. *Future Sufferings* (10:16-25)

16. "Behold I send you like sheep in the midst of wolves. Therefore be shrewd like serpents and simple as doves. 17. Beware of people. For they will hand you over to sanhedrins, and in their synagogues they will scourge you. 18. And to governors and kings you will be dragged for my sake, as a witness to them and to the Gentiles. 19. But when they hand you over, do not be anxious about how and what you will say. For it will be given to you in that hour what you will say. 20. For you will not be speaking, but the Spirit of your Father speaking in you. 21. Brother will hand over brother to death, and father child; and children will rise up against parents and put them to death. 22. And you will be hated by all on account of my name. But whoever endures to the end, this one will be saved. 23. When they persecute you in one city, flee into another. For Amen I say to you, you will not have gone through the cities of Israel before the Son of Man comes. 24. For a disciple is not above the teacher, nor a slave above his master. 25. It is enough for the disciple to become like his teacher, and the slave like his master. If they called the master of the house 'Beelzebul,' by how much more those of his household."

Notes

16. *like sheep*: For the pious within Israel depicted as sheep, see 1 Enoch 90:6-30. The image of sheep among wolves highlights the dangers surrounding the disciples' mission. One way of depicting the wonders of the messianic age uses these two images: "The wolf shall dwell with the lamb" (Isa 11:6).

shrewd like serpents: The serpent of Gen 3:1 is called "shrewd." The adjectives and nouns occur together in the midrash on Canticles 2:14: "Rabbi Judah said in the name of Rabbi Simeon: 'With me they are innocent as doves, but with the nations of the world they are like cunning serpents.' " The "they" in the quotation refers to Israel.

17. *sanhedrins*: The expression refers to local councils of Jewish leaders, not to the supreme court of chief priests and elders in Jerusalem (see Matt 26:59). The members would have been in charge of seeing after the welfare and good order of the Jewish community.

in their synagogues: The synagogue was the place of meeting for Jews. The qualification "their" places a distance between the Matthean Christians and those who control "their synagogues." Nevertheless, Jesus' disciples are subject to punishment in "their synagogues." For flogging as a Jewish punishment, see Deut 25:1-3; for its application to early Christians, see Acts 22:19; 2 Cor 11:24-25.

18. *to governors and kings*: The governors would be the Roman prefects of Judea such as Pilate, Felix, and Festus. The "kings" would be the Herodian princes such as Antipas, Agrippa I, and Agrippa II. It is not clear whether Jews were the ones who would be dragging the disciples to these governors and kings.

a witness to them: These persecutions provide the opportunity for the disciples to give witness to Christ before the authorities. The term "them" is ambiguous; it could refer to the Jews who frequent "their synagogues," or to the "governors and kings," or to the Gentile officials (as opposed to Gentiles in general).

19. *it will be given to you*: That is, God will give to you; a case of the divine passive. For early Christians unaccustomed to public speaking, the prospect of mounting a defense would have been a frightening prospect. Here they are assured the help of the Holy Spirit (10:20). It is unusual to talk about the availability of the gift of the Spirit to the disciples, since during his ministry Jesus is the primary bearer of the Spirit.

21. *Brother will hand over brother*: The division of the family was an apocalyptic commonplace. It has a basis in Micah 7:6. As a sign of the end-time, see 2 Bar 70:3; 4 Ezra 5:9; Jub 23:19; 1 Enoch 100:1-2. Its literary history, of course, does not preclude a historical basis in the experience of the Matthean community.

22. *whoever endures to the end*: The endurance is patient acceptance rather than active resistance. The "end" must not be death by martyrdom but rather the end of the sufferings associated with the coming of God's kingdom. This eschatological interpretation is suggested by Matt 10:23.

23. *before the Son of Man comes*: The most obvious interpretation is that the disciples will not have carried out their mission to Israel before the (eschatological) Son of Man (=Jesus) comes (in glory to judge). Some interpreters doubt that an eschatological figure is meant. Others argue that the Son of Man's coming refers to an event within history: Jesus' death and resurrection, the gift of the Spirit at Pentecost, or the destruction of Jerusalem in A.D. 70.

24. *a disciple is not above the teacher*: The images represent the school (disciple/teacher) and home (slave/master). According to *b. Ber.* 58b "it is sufficient for the servant to be like his master." The point is that the disciples share the same fate as their master Jesus did.

25. *Beelzebul*: For a full treatment of this charge, see the material on Matt 12:22-37; for the name Beelzebul, see the note on Matt 12:24. The logic is the Jewish *qal wĕḥômer*: If they accuse Jesus of acting through Satan's power, by how much more the servants!

Interpretation

In the second part of the missionary discourse (Matt 10:16-25) Jesus promises sufferings to the twelve during their mission and explains those sufferings as necessarily connected with following him. After the opening statement (10:16), there are two dangerous situations described (10:17-18; 10:21-22) along with two promises of help (10:19-20; 10:23-24) and a concluding reassurance (10:25). The two dangerous situations involve persecutions by outsiders and divisions within the family. In the first case the aid of the Holy Spirit is promised; in the second case the coming of the Son of Man is promised. The fundamental theological principle underlying this part of the discourse is "like teacher/master, so disciple/slave." Just as Jesus suffered persecution and division, so the disciple must expect the same.

The framework of Matt 10:16-25 consists of sayings based on Q (10:16 [see Luke 10:3]; 10:24a [see Luke 6:40]). The core of the passage is taken from Mark 13:9-13, part of the eschatological discourse, some of which is reused in Matt 24:9-14. By taking this eschatological material out of its context in Jesus' last speech and making it part of Jesus' instruction regarding his disciples' mission to Israel, Matthew has imbued the mission with eschatological significance (see Matt 10:23!) and made the eschatological instructions applicable to the historical experiences of his community. In this passage Matthew's editorial skill shines forth in the structure that he has imposed on the material and in the literary-historical setting in which he used the material.

The two situations envisioned in Matt 10:16-25 involve persecution from outside the band of disciples and division within families. In both cases literary conventions and harsh realities mix.

In the Hebrew Bible there is a long literary tradition of talking about Israel's sufferings. It takes in the oppression before the exodus, the wandering in the wilderness, the crisis that led to the monarchy, the destruction of the First Temple in 587 B.C., and the slow progress in restoration. In Maccabean times (167-164 B.C.) we get a glimpse of what to some looked like a religious persecution against Jews in the land of Israel by an alliance of foreigners and other Jews. In early Christianity Paul goes out of his way to "boast" about the persecutions he suffered (see 2 Cor 11:23-27). Thus there was at hand for Jews in Jesus' time and for early Christian writers a fund of experience and a vocabulary that they could use when talking about persecution.

Matt 10:17-18 describes the persecution of the disciples at the hands of Jews (10:17) and the secular (Gentile) authorities (10:18). That local Jewish councils (sanhedrins) and synagogues could punish recalcitrant Jews is well known. There is, however, some question about the extent and systematic character of Jewish persecution of Christians in the first century A.D. The evidence is gathered and evaluated by D. R. A. Hare in *The Theme of Jewish Persecution of Christians in the Gospel according to St. Matthew* (SNTSMS 6; Cambridge, U.K.: Cambridge University Press, 1967). Hare gives a "minimalist" reading of the evidence and finds little evidence for an extensive and systematic persecution of early Christians by Jews in the first century. The same conclusion is generally reached in investigations of pagan persecution of Christians in the first century. What persecution there was seems in both cases to have been local and sporadic—but nonetheless real for those who suffered.

The theme of tensions within the family is expressed clearly in Mic 7:6: "the son treats the father with contempt, the daughter rises up against her mother, the daughter-in-law against her mother-in-law, a man's enemies are the men of his own house." These household divisions were reckoned in many Jewish apocalyptic writings (see the note on Matt 10:21) as a sign of the end-time. The possible negative effect of discipleship on family relationships runs like a thread through early Christian writings (see Matt 4:22; 8:21-22). The tension between religious commitment and family obligations has always been part of Christian history. Matt 10:21-22 envisions the process of delation, whereby one member of a family accuses another to the officials and hands that person over to the punishment of death. Again we can be sure that such things happened, but how frequently and in what areas we do not know. In reading Matt 10:17-18 and 10:21-22 one must be sensitive to both literary convention and actual experience.

The twelve are promised in Matt 10:23 that "you will not have gone through the cities of Israel before the Son of Man comes." The promise would appear to be that before the mission to Israel will be completed the Son of Man will come. In its Matthean context the saying looks forward to the coming of the Son of Man in a short time. Every element in the saying has been picked over and argued: (1) Is the Son of Man Jesus? Or is he some apocalyptic figure other than Jesus? (2) Does the coming of the Son of Man refer to the eschaton, or to Jesus' death and resurrection, or to the destruction of Jerusalem in A.D. 70? (3) Do the "cities of Israel" refer to the land of Israel or to all places in the world in which Jews live?

For Matthew the "Son of Man" must have been Jesus. It is possible that the evangelist viewed Jesus' death and resurrection to be the "beginning of the end," as the portents described in Matt 27:51b-53 suggest, though the coming of the Son of Man is part of the fullness of God's kingdom (as Matthew 24–25 indicate). The "cities of Israel" were probably understood by Matthew to include those in the land of Israel or perhaps Syria too. But the idea of a worldwide mission to Diaspora Jews seems unlikely.

Matthew intended a parallelism between the mission of the twelve apostles and the mission of his own community. Within this parallelism Matt 10:16-25 offered a realistic preview of hardships and a word of consolation. The language of persecution at the hands of Jews and Gentiles bears witness at least to the experience of some Christians. It suggests that Christian missionaries working within Israel met violent opposition at some points. Also poignant is the reference to tensions within families in Matt 10:21-22. In the particular Matthean situation of rivalry within Judaism after A.D. 70 regarding the survival and continuation of Judaism such tensions within families were more than literary conventions.

The promise of consolation (10:19-20, 23-24) involves the gift of the Spirit and the coming of the Son of Man. In the Jewish context these gifts were proper to the eschaton. Their appearance before the eschaton suggests that, for Matthew, the end-time was already breaking into the present.

The chief Christological theme in Matt 10:16-25 is the identity between Jesus and his disciples in persecution and suffering. This identity carries both challenge and consolation. The saying about the coming of the Son of Man (10:23) contains many problems. If it means that Jesus thought that the Son of Man would come before the mission in Israel was completed, was he mistaken? If he was mistaken, what does this error say about the consciousness of Christ?

One classic way of avoiding the attribution of error to Jesus is to interpret the "cities of Israel" as referring to all Jews wherever they may live. This interpretation would push back the date until first-century missionaries could reach the more remote areas in which Jews dwelt. In Christian history this idea has developed into the Church's mission to Israel: When that mission is completed, then the Son of Man will come. This conviction has led some Christians to give utmost attention and zeal to the mission to Israel as a means of causing or occasioning the Son of Man's coming. But the exegetical basis of this approach in Matt 10:23 is very slight.

Jewish persecution of early Christians should not be exaggerated. By no means does it equal Christianity's record in persecuting Jews over the centuries. Moreover, the "persecution" alluded to in Matt 10:17 pitted Jew against Jew; it took place within Judaism and was not the action of one religion against another.

For Reference and Further Study

Bartnicki, R. "Das Trostwort an die Jünger in Mt 10, 23." *TZ* 43 (1987) 311–19.
Crawford, B. "New Expectation in the Sayings of Jesus." *JBL* 101 (1982) 228–44.
Kunzi, M. *Das Naherwartunglogion Matthäus 10, 23. Geschichte seiner Auslegung*. BGBE 9. Tübingen: Mohr-Siebeck, 1970.
MacLaurin, E. C. B. "Beelzeboul." *NovT* 20 (1978) 156–60.
McDermott, J. M. "Mt. 10:23 in Context." *BZ* 28 (1984) 230–40.
Sabourin, L. " 'You will not have gone through all the towns of Israel before the Son of Man comes.' " *BTB* 8 (1977) 5–11.

22. *Other Instructions* (10:26-42)

26. "So do not fear them. For there is nothing hidden that will not be revealed, and secret that will not be known. 27. What I say to you in the darkness, you tell it in the light. And what you hear in the ear, proclaim on the housetops. 28. And do not fear those who kill the body but cannot kill the soul. Fear rather one who can destroy both soul and body in Gehenna. 29. Are not two sparrows sold for a cent? And not one of them falls upon the ground without your Father. 30. But even all the hairs of your head are numbered. 31. So do not fear. You are worth more than many sparrows.

32. "Everyone who acknowledges me before people, I will acknowledge him before my Father in heaven. 33. But whoever denies me before people, I too will deny him before my heavenly Father.

34. "Do not suppose that I have come to bring peace on earth. I have come to bring not peace but the sword. 35. I have come to divide a man against his father and a daughter against her mother and a daughter-in-law against her mother-in-law. 36. And a man's enemies will be members of his own household.

37. "Whoever loves father or mother more than me is not worthy of me. And whoever loves son or daughter more than me is not worthy of me. 38. And whoever does not take his cross and follow after me, is not worthy of me. 39. Whoever finds his life will lose it, and whoever loses his life for my sake will find it.

40. "Whoever receives you receives me, and whoever receives me receives him who sent me. 41. Whoever receives a prophet in a prophet's name will receive a prophet's reward, and whoever receives a righteous one in a righteous one's name will receive a righteous one's reward. 42. And whoever gives one of these little ones a cup of cold water only in the name of a disciple, Amen I say to you, that one will not lose his reward."

Notes

26. *do not fear*: This command serves as the unifying principle for the disparate material in Matt 10:26-31. It appears in verses 26, 28, and 31.

    nothing hidden: The sayings in Matt 10:26-27 appear in the context of the disciples' mission to Israel: They are to proclaim what they have learned from Jesus. In Luke 12:2-3 they occur in the context of unmasking the hypocrisy of the Pharisees, and in Mark 4:22 they refer to Jesus' teaching in parables. For similar ideas see Eccl 10:20 and *m. 'Abot* 2:4.

27. *you hear in the ear*: In other words, "what is whispered to you." The "housetops" would represent the highest points in a city from which voices could carry from place to place. The thrust of Matt 10:26-27 is that Jesus' teaching is not esoteric, the preserve of the initiated few. Rather it was intended from the start to be public property.

28. *body . . . soul*: The saying presupposes an anthropology in which the soul (*psychē*) is one's real self and the body (*sōma*) is the perishable shell. The only one capable of killing both soul and body is God. The point is: Fear God rather than human beings. "Gehenna" refers to the place of final punishment for the wicked—over which God exercises ultimate control.

29. *Two sparrows sold for a cent*: The Greek word *assarion* derives from the Latin *as* or *assarion*, a Roman copper coin worth about 1/16 of a denarius. The sparrow, a small bird eaten by the poor, was the cheapest meat that one could buy at the market. The sparrow's "fall to the ground" describes its death—which does not occur without God's knowledge and care. If God cares for sparrows, how much more does God care for humans (see v. 31).

30. *all the hairs*: According to *b. Bab. B.* 16a God created for every hair a separate follicle. The saying interrupts the natural sequence of 10:29, 31, but it makes the same basic point about God's care for human beings.

32. *acknowledges*: Though there is a forensic element to 10:32-33 (earthly trial-last judgment), it is not necessary to limit confession and denial to legal situations. See the case of Peter in Matt 26:69-75. For the Son of Man presiding at the last judgment see Matt 25:31-32.

    I will acknowledge: Matthew made two changes in the Q version (=Luke 12:8): "I" instead of "Son of Man" (to avoid the impression that Jesus and the Son of Man are different characters); and "my heavenly Father" rather than "the angels of God" (the same change occurs in Matt 10:33/Luke 12:9).

34. *not peace but the sword*: After the Beatitude on the peacemakers (5:9) and the call to love one's enemies (6:44), Matthew could hardly have understood the saying as a call for (eschatological) warfare. Rather the saying simply calls attention to the decision required for or against the gospel, and the division among people that is a consequence of that decision. Luke 12:51 reads "division" instead of "sword," a correct though nonpoetic rendering.

35. *a man against his father*: Matthew has aligned the Q saying (Luke 12:53) more closely with Mic 7:6, though what precise version he used remains debatable.

For the background of this idea of division within the family and its eschatological significance, see the note on Matt 10:21.

36. *members of his own household*: The term *oikiakoi* refers not to slaves or servants but rather to other relatives who live in the house. The Greek of Mic 7:6 has "those in his house."

37. *is not worthy of me*: The Greek adjective *axios* here has the sense "does not deserve to belong to me." Matthew has removed the word "hate" from the Q saying (Luke 14:26) in favor of "loves . . . more than me." The content of the saying flows from Matt 10:34-36: A decision for Jesus may rend family ties. The monastic life of the Qumran Essenes involved such a sharp break. Rabbinic teachings insist on following God (*b. Yebam.* 5b) or the teacher (*m. Bab. M.* 2:11) rather than one's parents.

38. *take his cross*: Crucifixion was well known to Jews of Jesus' time, and there is no decisive reason why the earthly Jesus could not have uttered such a saying. Here there is no reference to the cross of Jesus (cf. Matt 16:24). The saying warns of suffering and even painful death as part of the disciple's lot. Of course, the saying takes on deeper meaning in the light of Jesus' death and resurrection.

39. *his life*: The Greek word *psychē* is here best translated "life" since a Semitic anthropology is presupposed, whereas in 10:28 a Greek anthropology demands that *psychē* be rendered as "soul." Though the combination with 10:38 suggests that martyrdom is at issue, the saying probably has a broader application to self-denial and wholehearted acceptance of the demands of being a disciple.

40. *receives me*: The rabbinic principle was that "the representative of a person is like himself" (*m. Ber.* 5:5). The idea of Jesus as the representative of God and of the disciples as representatives of Jesus is developed especially in the Fourth Gospel (see John 11:44-45; 13:20). The use of "who sent me" as an epithet for God implies that the disciples mentioned here are "apostles."

41. *prophet*: For problems in discerning true from false prophets, see Matt 7:15-20 (see also *Didache* 11–13). The discourse has returned to the theme of the travelling missionaries (see 10:11-14), but here the focus is on the reward for receiving the true prophet (and his message). Whether there existed a class of people known as the "righteous" is not clear.

42. *these little ones*: In the context of Matthew 10 the expression refers to the twelve apostles. But Matt 18:6, 10, 14 suggests that "little ones" was also a designation for the Matthean community, thus suggesting again a parallelism between the twelve apostles and the Matthean Christians.

Interpretation

The third part of the mission discourse (Matt 10:26-42) is a collection of disparate sayings. They are connected only loosely with each other and with the themes of mission and suffering in the first two parts. Most of the material appeared in Q—in separate contexts if Luke can be used as a guide in this matter: Matt 10:26-33 = Luke 12:2-9; Matt 10:34-36 = Luke 12:51-53; Matt 10:37-39 = Luke 14:26-27; 17:33; Matt 10:40-42 = Luke 10:16/Mark 9:41. Matthew's editorial contribution here is using these disparate materials in the context of the mission discourse.

Some commentators complain that in this third section (which can be divided into subsections) Matthew lost sight of his mission context and drew in the sayings from Q without much purpose. But suppose we assume that Matthew did deliberately use these Q materials as part of his mission discourse. What message comes forth on this supposition?

First in 10:26-31 the disciples are urged: "Do not fear" (10:26, 28, 31). In their mission they continue the process of making public the message of Jesus, which is not hidden or esoteric (10:26-27). They are to fear God alone, not human beings (10:28). They are to trust in God's care for them (10:29-31). Then in 10:32-33 they are reminded that their steadfast confession of Jesus will be rewarded and their denial of him will be punished. Though these sayings came as a package in Q (see Luke 12:2-9), they originated as small, independent units. Taken individually, they are difficult to interpret because we do not know their context. Whatever their original context may have been, Matthew has given them a new context in his mission discourse. In that context they take on a certain meaning.

The rest of the discourse can be interpreted in the same key. The disciples should expect to meet division within families (10:34-36), for in this way Mic 7:6 is fulfilled. They must not value their family ties (10:37) or even their own lives (10:39) above their following Jesus; their discipleship will surely involve suffering (10:38).

The discourse ends in 10:40-42 with material that has some vague parallels in Luke 10:16 and Mark 9:41 but is really distinctively Matthean. The closing section talks about rewards for receiving the apostles, prophets, righteous, and "little ones." The basic theological principle is stated in 10:40: "Whoever receives you receives me, and whoever receives me receives him who sent me."

One of the peculiarities of Matthew's mission discourse is that, after this long speech, we hear nothing about the mission itself or its outcome. In Matt 11:1 nothing is said about the conduct of the mission. The disciples suddenly reappear in the Galilean grainfields in Matt 12:1. Again, some maintain that Matthew lost sight of his own context. Others argue that Matthew deliberately left open the mission of the disciples to Israel, thus suggesting that the mission itself continues and that the instructions directed at the twelve apostles have meaning for all those who take up the missionary task.

Since the material in Matt 10:26-42 is so disparate, no one point of background information opens up the text. A central theme—division within families—has already been treated in connection with Matt 10:16-25. There are two further points that deserve comment here: the differing anthropologies in 10:28 and 10:39, and the relation between the sender and the one sent in 10:40.

The saying in Matt 10:28 presupposes a sharp division between body (*sōma*) and soul (*psychē*) in which the "soul" is the more important, immortal part. Humans can kill the body but not the soul; only God can destroy both body and soul. This distinction has its roots in Greek thought but quickly became part of Hellenistic thinking. Its appearance in a first-century Jewish text from Palestine or Syria is not at all surprising.

The saying in 10:39 about losing and finding one's life (*psychē*) is more in line with the anthropology of the Hebrew Bible. When it talks about the *nepeš* (*psychē* in Greek), it means the whole person, not soul versus body. In both 10:28 and 10:39 the Greek word (*psychē*) is the same. But because one presupposes a "Greek" anthropology and the other a "Hebrew" anthropology they should be translated differently as "soul" and "life."

The second background point involves apostleship. The rabbinic principle was that "the representative of a person is like himself" (*m. Ber.* 5:5). It was customary in the past to trace the institution of apostleship to the system of messengers sent by Jewish communities or synagogues to other communities or synagogues. But doubt has arisen about when this system arose. Even without such a developed system, it is clear that in antiquity messengers were a standard way of communicating and that around them certain rules built up. One such rule was "the representative of a person is like himself." This principle underlies Matt 10:40: "Whoever receives you receives me. . . . " The NT writers take the principle further by presenting Jesus as the one sent from God: "Whoever receives me receives him who sent me" (10:40b; see also John 5:23; 12:44-45; 13:20).

The most distinctively Matthean section is Matt 10:40-42. The titles implied or used there—apostle, prophet, righteous one, "little ones"—are often taken as indicating roles or offices within the Matthean community. That there were Matthean apostles and prophets seems likely. Whether a class of people was known as the "righteous ones" is doubtful. The "little ones" may have described the Matthean community as a whole or a group of simple but pious people within it (see 18:6, 10, 14). Though Matt 10:40-42 does not allow a clear look at the structure of the Matthean community, it does at least give us a glimpse into it.

The materials gathered from Q in Matt 10:26-39 as part of Jesus' instruction on the mission to Israel would have been meaningful to the Matthean community in its struggle with its Jewish rivals. The way by which the message of the Matthean community was spread was apostles and prophets (see *Didache* 11–13). The Q sayings provided such missionaries with encouragement, consolation, and challenge. They warned them beforehand to expect resistance and factions even within their own families. They reminded them of the incomparable value of their commitment to Jesus. The theological basis for their mission is the identification between the apostle and the one who sent them (10:40).

In the context of the Matthean missionary discourse the most important Christological statement comes in 10:40: "Whoever receives you receives me, and whoever receives me receives him who sent me." This "sending" Christology, though more developed in John, appears also in Matthew. It serves as the basis for the idea of Jesus' identification with the "little ones" in Matt 25:31-46. It gives rise to viewing Christian life as a "chain" of mission: As the Father sends the Son, so the Son sends the disciples.

The "traditional" character of the material in 10:26-42 reminds us that there is a continuity within discipleship. The sayings originated as small units, were taken into Q, were used by Matthew in his particular situation, and have been adapted by Christians through the centuries. There is thus a line of thinking about being a follower of Jesus. At the same time there is a flexibility or adaptability to discipleship; these instructions have been meaningful to very different groups at different times and remain so because of the "general" nature of their language.

For Reference and Further Study

Allison, D. C. " 'The hairs of your head are all numbered.' " *ExpTim* 101 (1990) 334–36.

Black, M. "The Violent word." *ExpTim* 81 (1970) 115–18.

Marshall, I. H. " 'Fear him who can destroy both soul and body in hell' (Mat 10:28 R.S.V.)." *ExpTim* 81 (1970) 276–80.

23. *John and Jesus* (11:1-19)

1. And when Jesus finished giving orders to his twelve disciples, he passed over from there to teach and preach in their cities. 2. John who was in prison heard of the works of the Christ and sent through his disciples and said to him: 3. "Are you the one who is to come, or shall we wait for another?" 4. Jesus answered and said to them: "Go, announce to John what you hear and see. 5. The blind see and the lame walk, lepers are cleansed and the deaf hear, and the dead are raised and the poor have good news preached to them. 6. And blessed is the one who does not take offense at me."

7. As they were going Jesus began to say to the crowds about John: "What did you go out into the wilderness to see? A reed shaken by the wind? 8. But what did you go out to see? A man clothed in soft garments? Behold those wearing soft garments are in the houses of kings. 9. But why

did you go out? To see a prophet? Yes, I say to you, and more than a prophet. 10. This is the one about whom it is written: 'Behold I send my messenger before you, who will prepare your way before you.' 11. Amen I say to you, there has not risen among those born of women greater than John the Baptist. But the least in the kingdom of heaven is greater than he is. 12. From the days of John the Baptist until now the kingdom of heaven suffers violence, and the violent seize it. 13. For all the prophets and the Law until John prophesied. 14. And if you are willing to accept it, he is Elijah who is to come. 15. Whoever has ears, let him hear.

16. "To what shall I compare this generation? It is like children sitting in the market-places who call out to others, 17. saying: 'We piped for you, and you did not dance. We lamented, and you did not mourn.' 18. For John came neither eating nor drinking, and they said: 'He has a demon.' 19. The Son of Man came eating and drinking, and they said: 'Behold a glutton and a wine-drinker, a friend of tax collectors and sinners.' And wisdom is justified by all her deeds."

Notes

1. *Jesus finished*: The end of the second major discourse is signalled by the verb *teleō* used to mark the end of the other discourses (Matt 7:28; 13:53; 19:1; 26:1). Matthew says nothing about the disciples' return after being sent forth on their mission (cf. Mark 6:30). But they reappear with Jesus in Matt 12:1-8. The lack of an ending gives the impression that the missionary discourse has abiding value.

2. *John who was in prison*: According to Josephus (*Ant.* 18:116-119) John was imprisoned at Herod Antipas' fortress at Machaerus, east of the Jordan. The story of John's death appears in Matt 14:1-12, though notice of his arrest had been given in Matt 4:12. The text here assumes that John could receive visits from his disciples and through them communicate with the outside world. Matthew has created the scene for the Q text.

   the works of the Christ: Some manuscripts read "Jesus" instead of "the Christ," but that looks like a way of avoiding the historical awkwardness caused by "the Christ." Is "the Christ" to be understood as a title (the Messiah) or a second name given to Jesus by early Christians. In other words, is John inquiring about the "works of the Messiah" or "the works of Jesus?" The former interpretation seems more likely.

3. *the one who is to come*: John's question about Jesus' identity seems to be at odds with the account of Jesus' baptism by John (see Matt 3:13-17) if that incident is interpreted as a public event. The "one who is to come" is generally identified as the Messiah; Elijah is a less likely figure in this context. The "one who is to come" is not a known messianic title, but see Isa 59:20 where the verb refers to God: "He will come to Zion as Redeemer."

4. *Jesus answered*: Jesus does not answer John's question directly. Instead he tells his questioners to report to John what they have seen and heard. Two interpre-

tations are possible: (1) Jesus does the deeds of the Messiah (see 11:2), and his works answer John's question in the affirmative. (2) Jesus demands a reinterpretation of the signs by which the "one who is to come" is to be discerned—by deeds of healing, not military exploits.

5. *the blind see*: The list of the recipients of Jesus' deeds corresponds to the content of Matthew 8–9: blind (8:27-30), lame (8:5-13; 9:1-7), leper (8:1-4), deaf (8:32-34), dead (9:18-26), and poor (5:3). The term for "deaf" (*kōphos*) can also mean "mute," as in 8:32-34. Because of this context Matthew had no need to list the healings done by Jesus as in Luke 7:21. See Isa 26:19; 35:5-6; 61:1 for the OT roots of the list.

6. *does not take offense*: The Greek verb is *skandalizō*. Its appearance here expresses the theme of the next few chapters in which people (Pharisees and Jesus' own family) do take offense at him (ch. 12), and Jesus explains the mixed reception he receives by means of parables (ch. 13). Perhaps the saying also suggests that Jesus realized that even John would not wholly approve of him; see C. L. Mitton, "Uncomfortable Words: IX. Stumbling-block Characteristics in Jesus," *ExpTim* 82 (1971) 168–72.

7. *a reed shaken by the wind*: The word "reed" (*kalamos*) refers to tall, hollow grasses growing in shallow water near the Jordan (where John baptized). The basic level of Jesus' question is: What did you go out to see—John or the grass? The way in which the reed is described ("shaken by the wind") may imply a contrast between the flexible reeds and the unbending prophet John. The symbol of the reed appeared on coins minted under Herod Antipas on the occasion of his founding Tiberias ca. A.D. 19. The image of the shaking reed may allude to Herod Antipas; see G. Theissen, "Das 'schwankende Rohr' in Mt. 11, 7 und die Gründungsmünzen von Tiberias. Ein Beitrag zur Lokalkoloritforschung in den synoptischen Evangelien," *ZDPV* 101 (1985) 43–55.

8. *clothed in soft garments*: There is probably a reference back to John's Elijah-like clothing of camel's hair and a leather belt (Matt 3:4). There may also be a look forward to John's death in the court of Herod Antipas (Matt 14:1-12), as the second part of Matt 11:8 suggests. Again the "tough" figure of the prophet contrasts with the "soft" courtiers of Herod Antipas.

9. *more than a prophet*: By his lifestyle (see Matt 3:4) and his message John encouraged the identification of himself as a prophet. Jesus uses this popular perception of John as an occasion to move beyond that identification to identify him as Elijah, the precursor of the Messiah.

10. *Behold I send my messenger*: At this point Matthew uses the quotation in Mark 1:2 that he omitted in Matt 3:3, probably because it did not come from the book of Isaiah. The quotation combines Mal 3:1 and Exod 23:20. The speaker is God, "you" is Jesus, and the messenger is John. The final words "before you" constitute an addition that serves to clarify the relationships. The quotation evokes Mal 4:5 (3:23 in the Hebrew text): "I will send you Elijah the prophet before the great and terrible day of the Lord comes." This quotation plus John's lifestyle (see 3:4; 11:8) prepares for the explicit equation of John with Elijah in Matt 11:14.

11. *greater than John*: The assessment of John is prefaced by "Amen"—an indicator of special solemnity on Jesus' part. His saying assumes that John does not participate in the kingdom of heaven, that is, he belongs to a different stage in the history of salvation (see Luke 16:16 for a similar schema). John may be the greatest figure of the past. But from Jesus' perspective he belonged to another age.

12. *the kingdom of heaven suffers violence*: The nature of the "violence" and the identity of the "violent" have long been topics of scholarly debate. The Matthean context—with John in prison under the order of Herod Antipas, and the allusions to Herod Antipas in 11:7-8—suggests that here the "violent" include Herod and his followers and the "violence" refers to the actions taken against John. There is some tension with Matt 11:11, for Matt 11:12 suggests that in John's day the kingdom was enough of a present reality to suffer opposition from the "violent," and that thus John somehow belonged to the age of the kingdom.

13. *all the prophets*: Luke 16:16 is generally acknowledged to be closer to Q: "The Law and the prophets were until John." Matthew has modified the Q version by adding "all" and "prophesied," thus avoiding placing John in the period of the Old Testament (see Matt 11:11) and carrying on the basic idea that the Scriptures are a book of prophecy finding their fullness in Jesus. For recent treatments of Matt 11:12-13 see P. S. Cameron, *Violence and the Kingdom. The Interpretation of Matthew 11:12* (Frankfurt-Bern-New York: Lang, 1984); and D. Kosch, *Die Gottesherrschaft im Zeichen des Widerspruchs* (Frankfurt-Bern-New York: Lang, 1985).

14. *he is Elijah*: The identification of John with Elijah has been carefully set up by the quotation in Matt 11:10. Nevertheless the framework in which the identification is placed ("And if you are willing to accept it . . . Whoever has ears, let him hear") indicates some hesitation about the identification. This hesitation may reflect the fact that Elijah was understood to be the forerunner of God's kingdom (see Mal 4:5-6 = 3:23-24), not the forerunner of the Messiah. See the debate among M. M. Faierstein, *JBL* 100 (1981) 75-86; D. C. Allison, 103 (1984) 256-58; and J. A. Fitzmyer, 104 (1985) 295-96 about whether the Jewish tradition considers Elijah to be the forerunner of the Messiah.

16. *this generation*: The word *genea* appears in a negative sense to describe the opponents of Jesus and John. For similar uses of the term see Matt 12:39-42; 16:4; 17:17; 23:36; 24:34. The thrust of the parable is to shift blame from the alleged inappropriate behavior of John and Jesus to the genuinely inappropriate responses of their opponents (= "this generation").

    children: The scene of the parable is set by the picture of children playing "make-believe" games. One group (the active group) complains that the other group (the passive group) refuses to respond to either the wedding game ("we piped for you") or the funeral game ("we lamented").

18. *John came*: John's ascetic lifestyle identifies him with the "funeral" game. Instead of repenting in response to John's preaching, the opponents claimed that he had a demon and so could be ignored as "crazy" and even possessed. According to John 7:20; 8:48; 10:20 the same charge was made about Jesus.

19. *The Son of Man came*: Jesus' nonascetic lifestyle identifies him with the "wedding" game. For the significance of Jesus' meals with tax collectors and sinners, see N. Perrin, *Rediscovering the Teaching of Jesus* (New York–Evanston, Ill.: Harper & Row, 1967) 102–08. Instead of rejoicing that sinners were sharing in the banquet that foreshadowed life in God's kingdom, the opponents made personal attacks on Jesus' character.

wisdom is justified: The closing comment is obscure. It should probably be taken as a general comment on the results of the teaching of John and Jesus, something like "you will know them by their fruits" (Matt 7:20). Instead of "deeds," Luke 7:35 reads "children"; the point is just about the same in both cases. Another line of interpretation takes "wisdom" as a personal figure and identifies Wisdom and Jesus (see M. J. Suggs, *Wisdom, Christology, and Law in Matthew's Gospel* [Cambridge, Mass.: Harvard University Press, 1970]). This identification is clear enough in Matt 11:25-30, but is not as convincing for Matt 11:19.

Interpretation

The core of Matt 11:1-19 consists of three units taken from Q that pertain to relations between Jesus and John the Baptist. The first unit (Matt 11:2-6; Luke 7:18-23) concerns John's question to Jesus: "Are you the one who is to come?" The second unit (Matt 11:7-11; Luke 7:24-28) conveys Jesus' assessment of John. The third unit (Matt 11:16-19; Luke 7:31-35) is a parable about the negative responses to both John and Jesus. Since the units follow the same order in both Matthew and Luke, we may assume that this was also their order in Q. Although the three units all deal with the relationship of Jesus to John, in fact they are quite different in content and style, leaving the impression that three originally unconnected units were joined in Q on the basis of their dealing with the same general topic.

Comparison with Luke 7:18-35 indicates that Matthew has followed the wording and order of Q closely. He has, however, constructed a transition (Matt 11:1) from the missionary discourse (Matt 10:1-42) that features the verb "finished" (*teleō*) and moves Jesus into a new situation. Nothing is said about the success of the disciples' mission or about their return (though they are on the scene in Matt 12:1-8). Matthew has also located John in prison (11:2). Since he noted in 4:12 that John had been arrested, it is likely that the location is the result of Matthew's desire for editorial consistency rather than new information present in Q but suppressed by Luke. In fact, such a location fits Luke's narrative even better than Matthew's (see Luke 3:19-20) and surely would have been used by Luke if it had been present in Q.

The largest Matthean addition occurs in Matt 11:12-15 where Matthew presents a modified version of the saying found in Luke 16:16 (Matt 11:12-13), the identification of John as Elijah (Matt 11:14; see Matt 17:12; Mark 9:13), and the conventional summons to pay attention (Matt 11:15).

The result of Matthew's use of the Q material and his editorial activity is a narrative that features various speech forms: a conversation between John's disciples and Jesus (11:2-6), a series of public declarations by Jesus (11:7-15), and a parable uttered by Jesus (11:16-19). While the general topic of these units is the relationship between John the Baptist and Jesus, each one makes a slightly different point and is expressed from a different angle. They concern the works of Jesus (11:2-6), John's character and his place in salvation history (11:7-15), and the similar (negative) receptions accorded to both John and Jesus (11:16-19).

The first unit concerns the "works of the Christ" (11:2-6). The note on Matt 11:2 drew attention to the ambiguity inherent in the passage: Does Jesus affirm that his works are indeed the works of the Messiah and therefore he is the "one who is to come?" Or does Jesus suggest that, even though his works may differ from those expected of the Messiah, he is nevertheless the "one who is to come?"

If Jesus affirms that his works are those of the Messiah, then the background for his claim would be a text like Isa 35:5-6: "Then the eyes of the blind shall be opened, and the ears of the deaf unstopped; then shall the lame man leap like a hart, and the tongue of the dumb sing for joy." Isaiah 34–35 is usually placed in a post-exilic context like that of Second Isaiah. It looks forward to the Lord's day of vengeance and year of recompense for Zion (34:8). God's intervention will be accompanied by miraculous healings as in Isa 35:5-6. No mention is made of a Messiah or any other powerful champion than the Lord. But it is a short step from such a historical scenario (which remained unfulfilled) to projecting such events onto the final day of the Lord and looking forward to them as the blessings of the messianic era. In that case, since Jesus does the deeds of the Messiah as set forth in Isa 35:5-6, therefore the messianic era is upon the people of his generation and he is the "one who is to come."

An alternate approach to Matt 11:2-6 is to take it as Jesus' reinterpretation of the Jewish messianic expectations of his day. It is important to observe here that there was no single Jewish idea of the Messiah in Jesus' time. Rather ideas about the Messiah varied with time and social setting—so much so that a recent collection of articles on the topic is entitled *Judaisms and Their Messiahs at the Turn of the Christian Era,* ed. J. Neusner, W. S. Green, and E. S. Frerichs (Cambridge, U.K.-New York: Cambridge University Press, 1987). Note the plurals in the book's title: "Judaisms" and "Messiahs." The point is that there was no uniform or even dominant idea of the Messiah in first-century Judaism, nor in fact was there a uniform or dominant form of Judaism.

One messianic scenario at odds with the lifestyle of Jesus is laid out in *Psalms of Solomon* 17–18. Composed in the first century B.C. in Jerusalem, *Psalms of Solomon* contains an unusually sharp portrayal of the Messiah as a future descendant of David who will be first and foremost a military leader and who will purge and renew Israel as a this-worldly kingdom, thus restoring it to the (real or imagined) glories of David's time.

The Davidic Messiah of *Psalms of Solomon* 17 will reign over Israel (17:21), purge Jerusalem from its Gentile conquerors (17:22-25), gather a holy people and judge the tribes (17:26-27), and restore the tribal boundaries (17:28-29). This righteous king will avoid the errors and sins committed by Israel's kings in the past, for he will rely on the God who made him powerful in the holy spirit (17:37). The day when the Messiah will reign is "the day of mercy in blessing" (18:5). This Messiah is the ideal Jewish king of the future who is primarily a military and political leader.

It is possible that Jesus' list of the "works of the Christ" deliberately contrasts with the kind of messianic expectations expressed in circles such as those that produced *Psalms of Solomon*. Then Jesus would be saying: "I do the works of the Messiah, but not necessarily those of the military-political Messiah. Nevertheless, I do the works of the Messiah, and therefore I am the 'one who is to come.' "

Whatever interpretation of Matt 11:2-6 is taken—the one that takes Isa 35:5-6 as the background, or the one that takes *Psalms of Solomon*—the basic contention is that Jesus is the "one who is to come." The problem with the first background is that Isa 35:5-6 makes no mention of the Messiah. The problem with the second line of interpretation is that we do not know how widespread the military-political concept of the Messiah was in Jesus' time. Was it so well known that Jesus needed to react against it?

The second unit (Matt 11:7-15) contains a similar problem when it reaches its Matthean climax "he (John) is Elijah" (11:14). The Q material is clear enough (Matt 11:7-11; Luke 7:24-28). It begins by denying that John is a "reed shaken by the wind" (11:7) or someone "clothed in soft garments" (11:8), perhaps deliberately contrasting John with people like Herod Antipas. It goes on to assert that John is a prophet and "more than a prophet" (11:9) and then applies Mal 3:1; Exod 23:20 to situate John in reference to Jesus: He is the messenger sent by God to prepare the way for Jesus (11:10).

Then two problems arise, most likely from putting together materials that were originally separate. The first problem is, Where does John stand with regard to the kingdom of heaven? According to Matt 11:11, for all his greatness, John is still less than the least in the kingdom of heaven. That statement seems to exclude John from the kingdom of heaven and imply that a wholly new period in salvation history has begun with Jesus as the inaugurator or present dimension of the kingdom. The next statement (Matt 11:12), which Matthew probably took from another context in Q (see Luke 16:16), emphasizes the kingdom as enough of a present reality to suffer violence and suggests that this period began in the days of John the Baptist. It would seem to place John in the same era as Jesus. Matthew's rewriting of the Q statement in Matt 11:13 is finally ambiguous. It can be read so as to include John among the "all the prophets and the Law" or to make John the goal or final point ("until John") and so as to exclude him by making him part of the new age with Jesus. It is possible that Matthew was disturbed by the Q saying in Matt 11:11 and sought to modify it or blunt its impact by placing it beside the material in Matt 11:12-13. For a similar juxtaposition of contrasting statements, see Matt 24:34, 36.

The second problem concerns the identification of John the Baptist as Elijah ("he is Elijah," Matt 11:14). Whereas Mal 4:5-6 (=3:23-24 in the Hebrew text) makes Elijah the forerunner of the "great and terrible day of the Lord," almost no Jewish evidence indicates that the idea of Elijah as the forerunner of the *Messiah* was widely known or commonly accepted in the first century A.D. The only Jewish text that knows of Elijah as forerunner of the Messiah is the baraita in *b. 'Erub.* 43a-b. Even there the writer of that third-century A.D. text may have known the Gospel tradition. So it is possible that the idea of John's role as Elijah preparing the way for the Messiah was a Christian adaptation of Mal 4:5-6 rather than a direct appropriation of a familiar Jewish pattern.

The problem of the roles properly attributed to John the Baptist and Jesus gets a new twist in the parable of the children playing in the marketplace (11:16-19). The parable envisions two kinds of games—wedding dances and funeral laments. In the case of weddings the atmosphere should be joyful, whereas in the case of funerals it should be sadness and lamentation. The application of the parable associates Jesus with the happy game and John with the sad game. The point is that there is no positive response to either Jesus or John by their opponents. Thus the parable explains why for all their differences in lifestyle both Jesus and John were rejected by many of their fellow Jews. The parable shifts the focus of the problem of roles from the nature of the roles themselves to the mean-spiritedness and blindness of the opponents of John and Jesus.

The historical fact of the rejection of John and Jesus by many of their contemporaries provided a parallel and a model for the rejection of the gospel by other Jews in Matthew's day. Just as not all Jews accepted the messages of John and Jesus, so not all Jews accepted the good news proclaimed in and by the Matthean community. Thus the concluding parable and what leads up to it gave the Matthean community a way to understand its own lack of total success in proclaiming its message. It also gave them a means of "understanding" their Jewish opponents, for the opponents are assumed to be mean-spirited and spiritually blind.

Besides the obvious value of Matt 11:1-19 (especially 11:16-19) in helping the Matthean community situate itself with regard to its Jewish opponents, it also enabled it to situate itself with reference to John the Baptist. As we know from Josephus (*Ant.* 18:116-119), John the Baptist seems to have gathered a significant following among Jews of his day. At the beginning of his public career Jesus himself was part of this movement (see Matt 3:1–4:17), and it is likely that the movement begun by John survived his death for at least some time. Whether it survived in the time and place where Matthew's Gospel was composed is not known. If it did, then Matthew has provided in 11:1-19 a guide to relations between the two groups from the perspective of the Jesus movement: Jesus is the Messiah, and John was his Elijah; John is subordinated to Jesus. If John's movement was only a historical memory for Matthew's community, the message remains the same: In God's scheme of things John was subordinate to Jesus.

While Matt 11:1-19 served sociological and ecclesiological functions in helping the Matthean community to locate itself vis-à-vis the Pharisees and the Baptist movement, it also fulfilled a Christological function. It tells us that Jesus did "the deeds of the Christ" and that therefore he is the Christ. It tells us that his appearance marked a new stage in God's dealings with Israel and that in it God's kingdom was a present reality. It tells us that the rejection that Jesus and John experienced was due to no fault of theirs but was the result of the mean-spiritedness and spiritual blindness of their opponents.

The Christological function of Matt 11:1-19 provides a clue toward its actualization. Jesus did the works of the Christ, or may even have redefined the meaning of messiahship. In either case, his miracles and preaching served to herald the breaking-in of God's reign. The figure of John the Baptist—the ascetic prophet true to his convictions even to the point of imprisonment—provides a positive model for people today. The figure of Jesus—accused of enjoying himself too much with the wrong kinds of people—balances off the picture of John.

The ecclesiological function of the text can also help Christian communities today deal with the phenomenon of rejection. The message is the same as it was for the Matthean community: John and Jesus before us suffered rejection. One should, of course, be careful about suggesting an equation between the opponents criticized in Matt 11:16-19 and Jews today. This is another instance of giving anti-Semitic potential to a text in Matthew by taking it out of its historical setting.

For Reference and Further Study

Verseput, D. *The Rejection of the Humble Messianic King. A Study of the Composition of Matthew 11–12.* Frankfurt-Bern-New York: Lang, 1986.

24. *Threats against the Unrepentant Cities* (11:20-24)

20. Then he began to reproach the cities in which his many miracles had taken place, because they did not repent: 21. "Woe to you, Chorazin. Woe to you, Bethsaida. For if the miracles that have taken place in you had taken place in Tyre and Sidon, long ago they would have repented in sackcloth and ashes. 22. But I say to you, it will be more tolerable for Tyre and Sidon on the day of judgment than for you. 23. And you, Capernaum, will you be lifted up to heaven? You will go down to the underworld. For if the miracles that have taken place in you had taken place in Sodom, it would have remained until this day. 24. But I say to you that it will be more tolerable for the land of Sodom on the day of judgment than for you."

Notes

20. *reproach the cities*: The narrative framework supplied by Matthew also has the effect of summarizing the content of what follows. The cities in which Jesus performed his miracles have not repented in response to them. There may be some link between wisdom's "deeds" (11:19) and Jesus' miracles or "mighty acts" (11:20). The unresponsive cities deserve their reproach.

21. *Chorazin*: This town in Upper Galilee is located two miles north of Capernaum, in from the Sea of Galilee. Recent excavations there (see Z. Yeivin, "Ancient Chorazin Comes Back to Life," *BAR* 13/5 (1987) 22-36) have revealed a "medium-size town" that existed around Jesus' time. The center part of the city featured a public building and a synagogue (built at the end of the third or beginning of the fourth century A.D.).

    Bethsaida: The name is usually interpreted to mean "house of the fisherman." The place is generally located at the northeastern corner of the Sea of Galilee where the Jordan flows in. Sometime before 2 B.C. it was raised to the dignity of a city by the tetrarch Herod Philip and named Bethsaida-Julias to honor the daughter of the emperor Augustus. According to Jn 1:44; 12:21 Bethsaida was the hometown of Philip, Andrew, and Peter.

    Tyre and Sidon: Both cities were on the Mediterranean coast in southern Lebanon, with Sidon twenty-two miles north of Tyre. The cities are mentioned several times in prophetic literature (Isa 23:1-12; Jer 25:22; Ezek 28:11-23; Zech 9:1-4; Joel 3:4), often in the context of destruction. If the destruction prophesied of Tyre and Sidon was bad, how much worse will be that of Chorazin and Bethsaida!

    sackcloth and ashes: Sackcloth was a dark-colored material of camel or goat hair used for making bags and other containers. A garment made of sackcloth would have been uncomfortable; it was used by those facing the threat of calamity or as a sign of mourning. Ashes were the residue from a fire, similar in appearance to dust. To sit on ashes or to put them on one's head was a sign of repentance in the face of catastrophe or of mourning. See the example of Nineveh in Jon 3:5.

22. *on the day of judgment*: The assumption is that both the good and the wicked face the judgment of the eschaton. The wicked Gentile cities will fare better than the largely Jewish cities that failed to repent in response to Jesus' mighty deeds.

23. *Capernaum*: The place derives its name from the Hebrew "village of Nahum." It is located on the northwest shore of the Sea of Galilee, two and a half miles from the mouth of the Jordan River. It served as the geographical center of Jesus' ministry in Galilee, and is probably to be identified as "his city" in Matt 9:1. Recent excavations in Capernaum have revealed a first-century basalt synagogue beneath the later limestone synagogue as well as a church complex built over what has been called "Peter's House."

    you will go down: The language is taken from the taunt against the king of Babylon in Isaiah 14 in which there is a contrast between the king's pretensions to ascend to heaven above the stars of God (14:13) and the decree that he will be brought down to Sheol (14:11-12, 14-15). The text thus places Capernaum on the same level as Babylon.

    Sodom: One of the five "cities of the valley" (Gen 19:29), Sodom is usually located at the southern end of the Dead Sea. From Genesis 19 it emerges as a negative example of inhospitality and sexual perversity. It then functions in warnings about the destruction of cities (Deut 29:33; Isa 1:9-11; Amos 4:11).

24. *more tolerable for the land of Sodom*: The same saying also appeared in Matt 10:15 (Luke 10:12). For Sodom as a negative example in the NT, see also Rom 9:29; 2 Pet 2:6; Jude 7.

Interpretation

The Sodom-saying (Matt 11:24) appears as part of the Lukan mission charge to the seventy-two disciples (Luke 10:1-12). In Luke 10:13-15 the threats against the unrepentant cities follow directly on the Sodom-saying, suggesting that in Q the two pieces (=Luke 10:1-12; 10:13-15) were juxtaposed. Matthew then has departed from the order of Q. This departure allowed him to reuse and expand the Sodom-saying already used in the missionary discourse (Matt 10:15) at the end of the threats against the unrepentant cities (Matt 11:23b-24).

Matthew has also supplied a narrative framework for the threats with Matt 11:20, which contains a summary of their content: Jesus' miracles should have served as signs inspiring repentance. The threats also carry on the theme of rejection that Matthew has been developing in chapter 11 and will continue through chapters 12–13.

In making these threats Jesus addresses the cities directly (personification) and uses the literary forms and language patterns of the biblical prophets. The difference is that Jesus uses these conventions to threaten largely Jewish cities and promises even worse calamities to them than will happen to Israel's enemies of the past.

The biblical background for Jesus' threats against the unrepentant cities is to be found in the book of Isaiah and other prophetic writings. The oracle against Tyre and Sidon in Isa 23:1-12 uses the device of personification and addresses Sidon directly: "Be still, O inhabitants of the coast, O merchants of Sidon (v. 2) . . . Be ashamed, O Sidon, for the sea has spoken (v. 4) . . . You will no more exult, O oppressed virgin daughter of Sidon (v. 12)." It reflects on the destruction of Tyre ("Tyre is laid waste, without house of haven," v. 1) and threatens Sidon with the same fate. Ezekiel 28 contains a reflection on the fall of Tyre and its prince as the result of the arrogance displayed by the prince.

Jesus' threat against Capernaum (Matt 11:23) echoes the taunt against the king of Babylon in Isaiah 14. His arrogance consisted in trying to be lifted up to heaven: "I will ascend to heaven; above the stars of God I will set my throne on high" (v. 13). But the result of his arrogance is that he is brought down to Sheol: "You are brought down to Sheol, to the depths of the Pit" (v. 15; see also vv. 9, 11, 19). The effect of this kind of language is to draw a connection between Babylon of old and Capernaum of Jesus' day.

The link between Sodom and Capernaum is also made in Matt 11:23. Isaiah 1 calls on Sodom as an example of both a destroyed and sinful city: "If the Lord of hosts had not left us a few survivors, we should have been like Sodom, and become like Gomorrah. Hear the word of the Lord, you rulers of Sodom" (Isa 1:9-10a).

Matt 11:20-24 criticizes three Galilean cities–Chorazin, Bethsaida, and Capernaum–for the failure to respond correctly (with repentance) to Jesus' miracles that had been performed in them or their vicinity. The three Galilean cities are threatened in terms familiar from Isaiah and other prophets. It is possible that members of the Matthean community were familiar with the Galilean cities and perhaps with Tyre and Sidon. For them Jesus' threats would have been "close to home" and thus a stimulus to examine their own efforts at repentance.

Jesus' threats against the unrepentant cities would have also illuminated the Matthean community's experience of rejection in its own day. Just as many did not respond correctly to the gospel in the late first century, so many had not responded correctly to the earthly Jesus. But on the Day of Judgment such cities and their unrepentant citizens will receive their just punishments. Leaving to God the punishment of the gospel's opponents is a prominent theme in some of the parables and interpretations in Matthew 13.

The theological assumption of Matt 11:20-24 is that Jesus' miracles were not intended merely as displays but rather demanded the response of repentance in the face of the coming kingdom of God. Those who fail to make that connection are threatened with eschatological punishment. The passage also roots Jesus' threats in the historical experience and theological language of ancient Israel by summoning the examples of Tyre and Sidon, Babylon, and Sodom. But it turns these examples against Israel itself: What Israel saw as the just punishment of its enemies remains a possibility for Israel itself if it fails to respond correctly to Jesus' miracles. For all Jews, including Jewish Christians, the text is a warning not to stand on one's spiritual privileges.

For Reference and Further Study

Comber, J. A. "The Composition and Literary Characteristics of Matt 11:20-24." *CBQ* 39 (1977) 497–504.

25. *Revelation and Its Recipients* (11:25-30)

25. In that time Jesus answered and said: "I give you thanks, Father, lord of heaven and earth, because you have hidden these things from the wise and understanding, and revealed them to infants. 26. Yes, Father, for such was your good pleasure. 27. All things have been handed over by my Father, and no one knows the Son except the Father, and no one knows the Father except the Son and anyone to whom the Son wishes to reveal him. 28. Come to me all you who toil and are burdened, and I will refresh you. 29. Take my yoke upon you and learn from me, for I am meek and humble in heart, and you will find rest for your souls. 30. For my yoke is easy, and my burden is light."

Notes

25. *In that time*: The same phrase occurs in Matt 12:1 and 14:1. Here it links Matt 11:25-30 with what has preceded in Matt 11:1-24. Though the theme of the surrounding material is the rejection of Jesus, this pericope emphasizes the positive dignity of Jesus. The narrative frameworks in both Matt 11:25 and Luke 10:21 ("In that hour Jesus rejoiced in the Holy Spirit and said") can be attributed to the evangelists.

I give you thanks: In this prayer context the verb *exomologeō* can be translated "give thanks," "praise," or "confess." The Hebrew equivalent appears frequently in the Qumran Thanksgiving Psalms (*Hodayot*) as an introduction to a recital of what God has done for the speaker (see 1QH 7:26-27; 10:14; 11:3-4; 11:15). The prayer is a public proclamation of praise and thanks for what God has done.

Father, lord of heaven and earth: The address combines a title that implies Jesus' special intimacy with God ("Father") with the acknowledgment of this God as lord of both heaven and earth. It also prepares for the saying in which the special relationship between Father and Son is expressed.

from the wise and understanding: The phrase most clearly refers to scribes and Pharisees who reject Jesus. But given the context (Matthew 11–13) in which the rejection of Jesus is the major theme, it could also include others (as, for example, the inhabitants of the unrepentant cities in Matt 11:20-24). What God has hidden from them is the significance of Jesus' deeds and the presence of God's kingdom in his ministry (11:1-19).

infants: The *nēpioi* are Jesus' disciples who hear him and perceive his significance. The term is similar to "little ones" as a way of referring to Jesus' followers. Despite their lack of social standing and expertise in religious matters (the domain of the wise and understanding) the "infants" perceive and understand. Matthew 13 will develop this contrast.

26. *good pleasure*: The Greek *eudokia* is the equivalent of Hebrew *raṣôn,* which conveys the idea of God's gracious will guiding and directing affairs. As a comment on Matt 11:25, the verse expresses Jesus' assessment of the hiding and revealing as part of God's grace.

27. *All things have been handed over*: If "all things" points backward to "these things" in Matt 11:25 and to the earlier parts of Matthew 11, then it includes Jesus' mighty deeds and his role in the present dimension of the kingdom. If it points forward to what follows in Matt 11:27, then it has to do with Jesus' sonship and the authority that flows from it.

no one knows the Son: "Father" and "Son" are used absolutely here: "the Father" and "the Son" (see Matt 24:35; 28:19). It is not simply a parable about mutual knowledge between a father and a son (though such an analogy is at the root of the saying). The absolute use of Father and Son and the theme of mutual knowledge between them have affinities with the Johannine tradition, though there is no need to posit a direct literary relation between the two traditions here.

no one knows the Father: Some patristic writers place this and the preceding verb "know" in the aorist (*egnō*), thus suggesting that before the Son no one knew God. The use of the present *epignoskei* averts that misunderstanding and is at least consistent with Matthean thought. Justin Martyr (*Apol.* 1.63.11) reverses the order of the two clauses, but there is little other support for that sequence.

to whom the Son wishes: The mutual knowledge between the Father and the Son is opened up by Jesus' role as the revealer. The verb "reveal" provides a link with the saying in Matt 11:25.

28. *all you who toil and are burdened*: Jesus' invitation is addressed to those still outside the circle of his disciples. The description of the scribes and Pharisees in Matt 23:4 ("they bind heavy burdens") suggests that Matt 11:28 is a call to leave behind those Jewish teachers and to follow Jesus whose "burden is light" (Matt 11:30).

I will refresh you: The future tense need not be taken to imply that refreshment and rest occur only after death or in the distant future. In fact, refreshment and rest are part of following Jesus' teaching in the present. The promise of rest in Matt 11:29 ("you will find rest") suggests a more active stance than in Matt 11:28: One finds rest by taking Jesus' yoke upon oneself.

meek and humble in heart: The two terms *praus* and *tapeinos* are practically interchangeable in meaning. They tie Jesus to the kinds of people whom he holds up as examples (see Matt 5:5). They also prepare for later descriptions of Jesus in such terms (Matt 12:15-21; 21:5).

29. *Take my yoke upon you*: The image is that of an animal harnessed to do work; the yoke provides discipline and direction. In Judaism the yoke-image was used in connection with wisdom and the Torah. In Sirach 51:26 the sage invites prospective students to "put your neck under the yoke, and let your souls receive instruction." In Matt 11:29 the image is tied directly to Jesus ("learn from me, for I am meek and humble").

30. *my yoke is easy*: The easiness of the yoke and the lightness of the burden are based on relationships with the meek and humble Jesus, which brings rest in the present. Though Jesus can hardly be accused of laxity, his teachings about Sabbath observance in the following pericopes (Matt 12:1-8, 9-14) distinguish him from the Pharisees by their "lightness" of burden (see Matt 23:4).

Interpretation

In the midst of a section (Matthew 11–13) largely devoted to the rejection of Jesus and his message, Matthew presents a group of sayings that highlight the revelation that Jesus brings and the kinds of people who accept it. The revelation concerns Jesus and his Father, and those who accept it are the "infants" (*nēpioi*) rather than the professionally wise.

The first part (Matt 11:25-27) is paralleled in Luke 10:21-22, and so we can assume that both evangelists knew it from Q. In both Gospels it follows closely after Jesus' threats against the unrepentant cities (Matt 11:20-24; Luke 10:12-15), and so we can assume that already in Q the two texts were joined. Luke interrupted the sequence to report on the triumphant return of the seventy-two disciples (Luke 10:17-20). It is likely that Matt 11:25-26 (Luke 10:21) and Matt 11:27 (Luke 10:22) were originally independent sayings; they were joined either by the editor of Q or an earlier "editor" on the basis of their common theme of revelation.

The second part (Matt 11:28-30) is without parallel in Luke (or Mark) and is generally attributed to the special Matthean tradition (M). Matthew most likely is responsible for having linked that saying to the others on the basis of its themes of Jesus as revealer and the recipients of his revelation.

All three sayings (Matt 11:25-26, 27, 28-30) can be classified as "revelation sayings," but they take somewhat different forms: The first saying

(11:25-26) is a public confession of praise and thanks to God for having revealed "these things" to the "infants." The second saying (11:27) is a declaration by Jesus about his special relationship to the Father and his willingness as Son to share that relationship with others. The third saying (11:28-30) is an invitation to those outside the circle of Jesus' disciples to share in his Wisdom teaching. It unfolds according to a chiastic pattern: A–"burdened" (11:28a), B–"refresh" (11:28b), C–"my yoke" (11:29ab), B^1–"rest" (11:29c), A^1–"burden" (11:30).

It is possible also to find something of a chiastic structure in Matt 11:25-30 as a whole: A–recipients of revelation (11:25-26), B–revelation itself (11:27), and A^1–recipients of revelation (11:28-30).

The "thanksgiving" in Matt 11:25-26 follows a typical Jewish prayer pattern well known from the Qumran *Thanksgiving Hymns* and other Jewish writings from the turn of the era. It begins with a first person declaration ("I give you thanks"), addresses God directly ("Father, lord of heaven and earth"), and gives the reason for the praise and thanks ("because you have . . ."). In light of the obvious parallels between Matt 11:28-30 and Sirach 51:23-30, the case of the thanksgiving prayer in Sirach 51:1-12 emerges as a very important parallel to the form of the prayer in Matt 11:25-26: "I will give thanks to thee, O Lord and King, and will praise thee as God my Savior. I give thanks to thy name, for thou hast been my protector and helper . . ." (Sir 51:1-2a).

Those who receive the revelation are described as *nēpioi* ("infants"), which seems to be a way of referring to the disciples of Jesus both during his earthly ministry and in the Matthean community. They are contrasted with "the wise and understanding." In fact, in most Jewish writings of the time the recipients of divine revelations are wise and understanding: the great heroes of old (Pseudepigrapha), community leaders (Qumran scrolls), all Israel (rabbinic literature), the individual sage (Philo), the righteous one (Wisdom), etc. Matt 11:25 is closest to the Jewish and early Christian celebration of the "humble" or "lowly" that is expressed so dramatically in Mary's Magnificat (Luke 1:46-55).

The saying about revelation itself (11:27) is distinctively Christian, with its use of the absolute forms "the Father" and "the Son" and its idea of the Son as the revealer of the Father. On the one hand, it has been linked to the Johannine tradition because it sounds so much like statements that are common in the Fourth Gospel. On the other hand, some scholars have queried whether the earthly Jesus could have said something like this, and proceeded either to attribute it to the early Church or to reduce it to an analogy regarding relations between a father and a son.

Nevertheless, in the background of the Father-Son saying in Matt 11:27 is the Jewish (and early Christian) debate about what and where wisdom is. The tradition of wisdom as a (female) person had been well established since Proverbs 8. The question at issue was, What is wisdom, and where is she to be found? The answers were quite diverse: Wisdom is the Law of the Most High (Sir 24:23), the heavenly mysteries (1 Enoch 42:1-3), or Christ (Col 1:15-20; John 1:1-18). Wisdom is to be found in the Jerusalem Temple (Sir 24:8-12), everywhere in the cosmos (Wis 7:24-26), in heaven (1 Enoch 42:1-3), and in the Church (Col 1:18). Matt 11:27 presents Jesus as divine wisdom incarnate. Those who know him know the Father—which is after all the ultimate in wisdom.

Matt 11:28-30 returns to the subject of the recipients of the revelation. Jesus' invitation echoes Sirach 51:23-30, which is a kind of advertisement for a school ("lodge in my school," 51:23). The most pertinent verses are Sir 51:26-27: "Put your neck under the yoke, and let your souls receive instruction; it is to be found close by. See with your eyes that I have labored little and found for myself much rest." The keywords of Matt 11:28-30 ("yoke," "labor," "rest") appear in Sir 51:26-27. Whether there was a direct literary relation is unclear. At least the parallel establishes that in Matt 11:28-30 Jesus uses the language of teachers in a wisdom school.

We may assume that the Matthean community was familiar with the debate about what wisdom is and where it is to be found. For them the Q saying (Matt 11:25-27) and the M saying (Matt 11:28-30) would have provided them with their "Jewish-Christian" answer: Wisdom is the person of "the Son" and his teaching; wisdom is to be found at the "school" of Jesus. The reference to "burden" (11:28, 30) probably also provided the Matthean community with their way of assessing the Pharisees' approach to wisdom (see Matt 23:4) in comparison with the "light burden" of Jesus' teaching.

The promise of "rest" has appealed to Christians through the ages, as it does to all human beings. In teaching about Jesus' promise of rest it is essential to look at Matt 11:25-30 as a whole and to relate the promised rewards attached to Jesus' wisdom directly to his person. The Matthean text transcends the inner-Jewish debate about the nature and place of wisdom. It really concerns Christology: More than a wisdom teacher (though he is that), Jesus is "the Son" of "the Father." Whoever knows him knows the Father, which is the highest form of wisdom. The recipients of this revelation are not necessarily the professional sages but rather the marginal ("babes"). To such is offered the promise of rest.

For Reference and Further Study

Bacchiocchi, S. "Matthew 11:28-30: Jesus' Rest and the Sabbath." *AUSS* 22 (1984) 289–316.

Deutsch, C. *Hidden Wisdom and the Easy Yoke: Wisdom, Torah and Discipleship in Matthew 11:25–30.* JSNT Sup 18. Sheffield: JSOT, 1987.

_________. "Wisdom in Matthew: Transformation of a Symbol." *NovT* 32 (1990) 13–47.

Kloppenborg, J. S. "Wisdom Christology in Q." *LavThPh* 34 (1978) 129–47.

López Fernández, E. "El yugo de Jesús (Mt 11,28–30). Historia y sentido de una metafora." *Studium Ovetense* 11 (1983) 65–118.

Maher, M. " 'Take my yoke upon you' (Matt. xi. 29)." *NTS* 22 (1975) 97–103.

Stanton, G. N. "Salvation Proclaimed: X. Matthew 11:28-30." *ExpTim* 94 (1982) 3–9.

26. *Two Sabbath Controversies* (12:1-14)

1. In that time Jesus went on the Sabbath through the grainfields. His disciples were hungry, and they began to pick the heads of wheat and to eat. 2. But the Pharisees saw this and said to him: "Behold your disciples are doing what is not allowed to do on the Sabbath." 3. He said to them: "Have you not read what David did when he and those with him were hungry? 4. How he went into the house of God, and they ate the bread of the presence, which it was not lawful for him to eat nor for those with him, except for the priests alone? 5. Or have you not read in the Law that on the Sabbath the priests in the temple profane the Sabbath and are without guilt? 6. But I say to you that there is greater than the temple here. 7. If you had known what this is—I wish mercy and not sacrifice—you would not have condemned those who are without guilt. 8. For the Son of Man is lord of the Sabbath."

9. And we went from there and came into their synagogue. 10. And behold there was a man having a withered hand. And they asked him, saying: "Is it allowed to heal on the Sabbath?," in order to bring charges against him. 11. But he said to them: "Which one of you who has one sheep and if it falls into a pit on the Sabbath will not take hold of it and raise it up? 12. How much more is a human being superior to a sheep! Therefore it is allowed to do good on the Sabbath." 13. Then he said to the man: "Stretch out your hand." And he stretched it out, and it was restored as healthy as the other. 14. And the Pharisees went out and took counsel against him in order to destroy him.

Notes

1. *In that time*: The temporal indicator, not present in Mark 2:23 or Luke 6:1, may look back to Matt 11:25 ("In that time") and thus link this passage with the preceding. If this is so, the two Sabbath pericopes in Matt 12:1-8, 9-14 may be put forward by Matthew as examples of the "light burden" imposed by Jesus (see 11:30).

His disciples were hungry: Only Matthew supplies a motive for the disciples' behavior (see Mark 2:23; Luke 6:1), though he does not go so far as to suggest that there was any danger of death.

to pick the heads of wheat and to eat: The disciples' action follows Deut 23:25: "When you go into your neighbor's standing grain, you may pluck the ears with your hand, but you shall not put a sickle to your neighbor's standing grain." Such humanitarian legislation (see Deut 23:24) was intended to sustain the needy without giving them permission to pile up supplies. There is, however, no mention of the Sabbath in these cases.

2. *what is not allowed to do on the Sabbath*: The Pharisees' complaint against Jesus' disciples interprets their action as infringing upon Exod 34:21 ("on the seventh day you shall rest"). In *m. Šabb.* 7:2 there is a list of thirty-nine labors that are prohibited on the Sabbath. The labor that best corresponds to what the disciples did is "reaping" (*haqqôsēr*). Matthew has turned the Pharisees' question in Mark 2:24 into a direct statement.

3. *what David did*: The incident of David and his men eating the bread of the presence from the sanctuary at Nob is narrated in 1 Sam 21:1-6. There is no mention of the Sabbath in that text. The point in common between 1 Sam 21:1-6 and Matt 12:3-4 is satisfying the hunger of the followers of David/Son of David. Matthew has excised the name of the high priest Abiathar (Mark 2:26), since the priest's name according to 1 Sam 21:1-6 was Ahimelech.

4. *the house of God*: The expression could suggest that it was the Jerusalem Temple. Of course, the Temple had not yet been built. The "house of God" is the shrine of the ark of the covenant then at Nob, in the territory of Benjamin. Nob developed as a cultic center in the late eleventh century B.C., after the destruction of Shiloh.

the bread of the presence: The ritual surrounding the bread of the presence (or "shewbread") is described in Lev 24:5-9. Twelve cakes were set out in the sanctuary. They were finally consumed by the priests ("Aaron and his sons"). Other references to the bread of the presence appear in Exod 25:30; 39:36; 40:23. Not being from the sons of Aaron, David had no right to consume these breads.

5. *the priests in the Temple profane the Sabbath*: There are rules in the Torah itself that allow priests to do work in the Temple on the Sabbath: setting out the bread of the presence (Lev 24:8), and doubling the daily burnt offering (Num 28:9-10). By finding precedents within the Torah Matthew places the activity of Jesus' disciples on the Sabbath within the confines of Jewish law.

6. *there is greater than the Temple here*: The reasoning is from "light" to "heavy" (*qal wĕḥômer*)—from the case of the priests in the Temple to the case of Jesus' disciples. This is an extraordinary claim about the community surrounding Jesus! The "greater" is a matter of dispute: Is it Jesus, or the kingdom of God inaugurated by Jesus, or the community around Jesus? All three aspects are probably present, with the idea of Jesus' community being most prominent.

7. *I wish mercy and not sacrifice*: The quotation from Hos 6:6 was used previously in Matt 9:13. Given the Temple context set up in Matt 12:5-6, the reference to

''sacrifice'' is appropriate here but leads into a wider framework of ritual behavior, including strict Sabbath observance. The ''mercy'' is demanded from humans, as in showing compassion toward those in need on the Sabbath day.

8. *the Son of Man*: Though it is possible that at some point in the saying's tradition history (see Mark 2:28; Luke 6:5), ''son of man'' may have been a generic term for humankind, in Matt 12:8 it was surely meant by Matthew as a title for Jesus. The radical saying of Mark 2:27 (''The Sabbath was made for man and not man for the Sabbath'') is omitted by both Matthew and Luke.

9. *their synagogue*: Mark 3:1 and Luke 6:6 simply have ''the synagogue.'' Matthew's expression probably reflects his own time, when there was a division between ''their synagogue'' and ''our (Christian) synagogue.'' By this expression the evangelist set up a continuity between Jesus and the Matthean community on the one hand and Jesus' opponents and the opponents of the Matthean community on the other hand.

10. *withered hand*: The Greek term is *xēros* (''dry'' as in xerox). The man's hand was stunted in growth and paralyzed. We are to assume that this was a long-term condition (perhaps even from birth) and not a life-threatening illness that demanded immediate action on the Sabbath.

    Is it allowed to heal on the Sabbath?: All the evangelists note that the opponents' question was a trap set for Jesus (''in order to bring charges against him''), but only Matthew gives the question. The rabbinic approach to this question appears in *m. Yoma* 8:6: ''A case of risk of loss of life supersedes the Sabbath (law).'' Since the withered hand was presumably a long-term non-life-threatening condition, the rabbinic principle is not followed by Jesus.

11. *it falls into a pit on the Sabbath*: The case is taken up in *Damascus Document* 11:13-14: ''If (a beast) falls into a cistern or into a pit, let it not be lifted out on the Sabbath.'' An opinion more in line with that of Jesus is found in the rabbinic writings (*b. Šabb.* 128b; *b. Mez.* 32b). Jesus assumes that his questioners agree with him on this matter and do not hold the stricter view of the Essenes. Only Matthew includes this case (see Mark 3:3; Luke 6:8).

12. *How much more*: The argument again takes the *qal wĕḥômer* structure: If so with sheep, by how much more with a human being! The case is then turned into the rationale for Jesus' doing good on the Sabbath in healing the man with the withered hand (and for the Matthean community's own attitude toward Sabbath observance). The general principle is that it is permitted to do good on the Sabbath. This principle assumes that the Sabbath is still observed by the Matthean Christians (see 24:20) but that Sabbath regulations can be overridden by the need to ''do good'' (there may be an allusion to the love-commandment of Matt 22:40).

13. *it was restored*: The healing of the withered hand comes almost as an afterthought, since Matthew has placed the debate about Sabbath observances at the center of attention. Only Matthew has the vivid phrase ''as healthy as the other (hand).''

14. *the Pharisees*: Only at the end of the pericope are we told that Jesus' opponents were Pharisees (see 12:2). They control ''their synagogue'' (12:9). Unlike Mark

3:6, there is no mention of the "Herodians" plotting with the Pharisees. Jesus' free attitude toward the Pharisees' Sabbath traditions provokes opposition and leads to a plot against Jesus' life.

Interpretation

With the two Sabbath controversies about plucking grain (Matt 12:1-8) and healing (Matt 12:9-14), Matthew rejoins the series of controversies found in Mark 2:1–3:6. In Matt 9:1-17 Matthew had given his versions of the first three Markan controversies (Mark 2:1-22). After a long interruption (Matt 9:18–11:30) he returns to give his versions of the final two Markan controversies (Mark 2:23–3:6). By placing the two Sabbath controversies after Jesus' declaration regarding his own identity and the nature of his teaching ("My yoke is easy, and my burden is light," Matt 11:30) Matthew presents the incidents as examples of Jesus' authority as a teacher and his approach to the Pharisees' traditions.

The first episode (Matt 12:1-8) concerns the disciples' picking grain on the Sabbath and eating it. The debate concerns whether they were allowed to do this on the Sabbath, or whether it constitutes the equivalent of reaping—something forbidden as work on the Sabbath day. That the disciples were permitted to pick the grain in someone else's field is not disputed (see Deut 23:25). The issue is their doing it on the Sabbath.

In broad outline Matthew follows Mark 2:23-28. The disciples' action sets the scene for the Pharisees' objection and Jesus' appeal to the precedent set by David in 1 Sam 21:1-6 and his concluding claim about the Son of Man as lord of the Sabbath. But there are loose ends in the Markan account—the chief one being the fact that 1 Sam 21:1-6 makes no mention of the Sabbath.

Matthew has tightened up Mark's account by explaining the reason for the disciples' action (they were hungry, 12:1); turning the Pharisees' statement into a direct assertion rather than a question ("your disciples are doing what is not allowed"); deleting the erroneous mention of the high priest Abiathar (see Mark 2:26; Matt 3:4); and adding the example about kinds of work allowed in the temple on the Sabbath (Matt 12:5-7). It is possible also that Matthew has deleted the radical saying about the Sabbath being made for man and not man for the Sabbath (Mark 2:27), though its omission in Luke 6:5 makes one wonder if that radical saying appeared in the version of Mark used by the other two evangelists. If it was so present, its omission by Matthew would have been part of his more conservative attitude toward the Sabbath and Jewish institutions in general.

In the episode of Jesus healing the man with the withered hand on the Sabbath (Matt 12:9-14) Matthew has pushed what in Mark 3:1-6 is part debate and part healing story even further in the direction of a debate. The

Matthean debate takes place in "their synagogue" (12:9). The opponents put the question directly: "Is it allowed to heal on the Sabbath?" Jesus uses a case that was debated in his time—the case of an animal that falls into a pit on the Sabbath—and argues according to the *qal wĕḥômer* pattern ("from the light to the heavy") that it is allowed to heal on the Sabbath (12:11-12). Finally he notes that the Pharisees (without the Herodians, see Mark 3:6) plotted to destroy Jesus. Thus Matthew has preserved the basic structure of the healing story (Matt 12:10a, 13) but shifted the focus even more than in Mark 3:1-6 to the debate about healing on the Sabbath. He has not only sharpened the issue under debate and supplied an argument (Matt 12:10b-12) but also narrowed Jesus' opponents down to the Pharisees (12:14) and connected them with those who frequent "their synagogue" (12:9).

Was the Sabbath made for man or man for the Sabbath? Even though Matthew has omitted (or perhaps did not know) the radical saying in Mark 2:27 in which Jesus asserts that the Sabbath was made for man, there remain tensions regarding the Sabbath. In fact, these tensions reach back to the earliest biblical texts about the Sabbath. In Exod 23:12 the command to rest on the seventh day is placed in a "humanitarian" context: "that your ox and your ass may rest, and the son of your bondmaid, and the alien, may be refreshed." In Exod 34:21 the same commandment ("on the seventh day you shall rest") appears in the context of various cultic obligations—suggesting that man was made for the Sabbath, that is, that the Sabbath observance was part of Israel's worship of God.

The Sabbath commandments in the Decalogue (Exod 20:8-11; Deut 5:12-15) agree that the seventh day is a Sabbath to the Lord for the entire household. But they disagree regarding the theological root of the Sabbath. Whereas according to Exod 20:11 the Sabbath is a remembrance of creation ("for in six days the Lord made heaven and earth, the sea and all that is in them, and rested on the seventh day"), in Deut 5:15 it is a remembrance of the exodus from Egypt ("You were a servant in the land of Egypt, and the Lord your God brought you out thence with a mighty hand and an outstretched arm"). The "creation" motif for Sabbath observance, of course, underlies the Priestly creation story in Gen 1:1–2:4a in which the Sabbath is said to be woven into the very fabric of creation.

Although references to Jewish observance of the Sabbath can be found in almost every phase of Israel's history, there seems to be no doubt that Sabbath observance became especially prominent before, during, and after the Exile in Babylon. Deprived of its Temple, capital city, and homeland, the Jewish exiles emphasized the Sabbath as a very important religious obligation (see Isa 56:2; 58:13-14; Jer 17:21-27; Ezek 20:11-21). Observance of the Sabbath was not dependent on the existence of the Temple. While not a rival to the Temple cult, Sabbath observance was at least something of a substitute for the Temple cult when the Jerusalem Temple lay in ruins or was not accessible to Jews. The Sabbath along with circumcision and dietary regulations made Jews different from the peoples around them and helped to nourish Jewish identity.

The biblical texts about the Sabbath are surrounded by tensions: Is the Sabbath made for human beings, or is it for the worship of God? Is the Sabbath a remembrance of creation or of the exodus? Is the Sabbath part of or a rival to worship in the Jerusalem Temple? Despite these tensions it is clear that by NT times the Sabbath was such an essential part of Jewish life and piety that the chief concern was trying to determine what constituted "work" on the day of rest. A major innovation made by Mattathias (the father of the Maccabees) and his friends around 165 B.C. made it possible for Jews to undertake defensive warfare on the Sabbath day: "Let us fight against every man who comes to attack us on the Sabbath day" (1 Macc 2:41). On the other hand, the Essenes represented by *Damascus Document* 10:14–11:18 laid down very strict rules for observing the Sabbath—far stricter than those later codified by the rabbis. A similar strictness is present in Jubilees 50. The mishnaic tractates—*Shabbat* and *Erubin*—reflect an even later, more refined stage in the debate. But the basic question is the same: What may and may not be done on the Sabbath?

Matthew knew well the shape of the Sabbath debate in his own time. He seems also to have known that Jesus had taken a somewhat free attitude regarding what may and may not be done on the Sabbath. The other Gospels agree that Jesus healed on the Sabbath as in the case of the woman "who had a spirit of infirmity for eighteen years" (Luke 13:10-17) and the paralytic at the Bethesda pool (John 5:1-18). These were long-term illnesses, and both healings presumably could have been deferred until after the Sabbath. The incident recounted in Mark 2:23-28/Matt 12:1-8 suggests that Jesus did not stop his disciples from doing what some Jews regarded as reaping on the Sabbath.

As a follower of Jesus, Matthew was obliged to defend this rather free attitude toward Sabbath observance. It is important to remember that this topic was very much under debate in the first century and that the clarity arrived at in the Mishnah still belonged to the future. Besides defending Jesus' attitude Matthew had also to address the concerns of his largely Jewish-Christian community that by and large observed the Jewish Sabbath. The ways in which Matthew reshaped his Markan sources show how he managed to enter into the larger Jewish debate of his day, remain faithful to the example of Jesus, and minister to his own community.

Matthew entered into the larger Jewish debate by sharpening the debating partners. They are Pharisees according to Matt 12:2, 14, who are prominent in "their synagogue" (12:9). Thus Matthew has drawn a direct line between the opponents of Jesus and the rivals of his own community some fifty or sixty years later. He has also strengthened greatly the weak argument found in Mark 2:25-26 about David and his men eating the bread of the presence. That precedent was irrelevant to the Sabbath, and Matthew knew it. So he added the consideration about the "work" done by priests in the Temple on the Sabbath (Matt 12:5).

In the second incident (Matt 12:9-14) Matthew has Jesus cite a case that was debated among Jews of Jesus' and his own day. The Essenes had a strict view on this matter: "If (a beast) fall into a cistern or into a pit, let it not be lifted out on the Sabbath" (*Damascus Document* 11:13-14). The way in which Jesus speaks in Matt 12:11 seems to presume that he and the Pharisees agree over against the Essenes that it is allowed to raise an animal out of a pit on the Sabbath.

Matthew appears to remain faithful to Jesus' own attitude toward the Sabbath. In his own day Jesus seems to have been more liberal on this matter than even the relatively liberal and flexible Pharisees were. And so Matthew presents Jesus as allowing his disciples to feed themselves on the Sabbath and as healing someone in no danger of death on the Sabbath. But Matthew also breaks out of the Jewish debate by giving the two stories a Christological dimension.

Jesus is the authoritative teacher; his teaching and example are to be followed. Jesus is the healer; he has authority over the Sabbath regulations. The saying that links the two episodes together is the assertion: "The Son of Man is lord of the Sabbath" (Matt 12:8). With his presence something "greater than the temple is here" (12:6). So when Matthew's Jewish rivals criticize the Matthean community's laxness regarding the Sabbath, the response is rooted in the example of Jesus, who for the Matthean Christians is the authoritative teacher.

Matthew also sought to minister to his own largely Jewish-Christian community on the matter of Sabbath observance. It would appear that the Matthean community continued to observe the Sabbath (see 24:20). At least there is no indication to the contrary, and Sabbath observance would have been quite natural for a largely Jewish-Christian group. The question for the Matthean community—and the pastoral problem that Matthew had to address—was the manner in which the Sabbath was to be observed. The principles derived from the two episodes in Matt 12:1-14 are compassion toward others ("I wish mercy and not sacrifice," 12:7) and doing good ("it is allowed to do good on the Sabbath," 12:12). The second principle ("it is allowed to do good on the Sabbath") served as the basis for the Matthean community's behavior on the Sabbath. That principle may well have carried an allusion to the summary of the Torah as loving God and neighbor (Matt 22:34-40). At any rate, the criterion placed before the Matthean community as it struggled to deal with the complicated discernment of what one may or may not do on the Sabbath is doing good.

The tensions that the Matthean community experienced regarding the

Sabbath may not have come only from the members of "their synagogue." They may have also come from other Christians. There were objections from Paul in Gal 4:10 and from the Pauline admirer who wrote Colossians (see 2:16) to Gentile Christians being forced to observe the Jewish calendar and its Sabbath. Moreover, as the first century A.D. progressed, the Lord's day—Sunday—became a more important and more distinctively Christian institution. The first day of the Jewish week, which began at sundown on Saturday after the Sabbath, was linked from the first Easter with the resurrection of Jesus (see Matt 28:1 parr.). The first day of the week was a special time for Christians to gather in order to take up collections for the Jerusalem community (1 Cor 16:2) and to break bread and hear an edifying sermon (Acts 20:7). In Rev 1:10 it is called "the Lord's day," the only occurrence of this expression in the New Testament.

The Apostolic Fathers add to our picture of "the Lord's day" as a special time for Christian celebration. The *Didache*, which was probably composed in Syria in the late first century—the same place and time customarily assigned to the composition of Matthew—speaks of the Lord's day as a time for Christians to gather and break bread and give thanks (14:1). Ignatius, bishop of Antioch in Syria in the early second century, urged that Christians put aside Sabbath observance and keep the Lord's day instead: "no longer observing Sabbaths but fashioning their lives after the Lord's day" (*Magnesians* 9:1).

There is no explicit evidence in Matthew's Gospel of a rivalry between proponents of the Sabbath and proponents of the Lord's day. Matthew and his community may have seen no conflict at all and may have observed both the Sabbath and the Lord's day. Nevertheless, there are hints within the New Testament of a growing interest in the Lord's day among some Christians. Even more striking is the fact that both *Didache* and Ignatius of Antioch, representing the same geographical area as Matthew but a little later, are among the strongest pieces of evidence for a firm Lord's day tradition and a rivalry with the Sabbath.

What are Christians today to make out of Matthew's Sabbath teachings? After all, Matthew and his community celebrated the Sabbath, while most of us take the Lord's day (Sunday) as our time of prayer and rest. Matthew 12:1-14 is fascinating on several counts. It shows how Jewish Christians struggled to integrate their new faith in Jesus with their Jewish traditional observances. It shows how Christian convictions about Jesus as lord of the Sabbath and the principle of doing good on the Sabbath shaped Matthew's presentation.

The framework of the Jewish debate about the Sabbath—what one may or may not do on the Sabbath—was narrow, what Christians are in the unfortunate habit of calling "legalistic." The narrowness of the debate in Matthew's time ought not to obscure the fact that Jews by and large enjoyed the Sabbath as a time of prayer and rest. While it is problematic to equate the Jewish Sabbath and the Christian Sunday and to surround Sunday with Sabbath regulations, at least the Christian day of prayer and rest should have reference to Jesus as lord of the Sabbath and whatever works are done on it should be measured by the criterion of doing good.

For Reference and Further Study

Barth, G. *Tradition and Interpretation in Matthew,* 79, 81–83.

Cohen, M. "La controverse de Jésus et des Pharisiens à propos de cueillette des épis, selon l'Evangile de saint Matthieu." *MScRel* 34 (1977) 3–12.

Cohn-Sherbok, D. M. "An Analysis of Jesus' Arguments Concerning the Plucking of Grain on the Sabbath." *JSNT* 2 (1979) 31–41.

Hicks, J. M. "The Sabbath Controversy in Matthew: An Exegesis of Matthew 12:1-14." *Restoration Quarterly* 27 (1984) 79–91.

Levine, E. "The Sabbath Controversy according to Matthew." *NTS* 22 (1976) 480–83.

27. *Jesus As God's Servant* (12:15-21)

15. But Jesus knew this and departed from there, and many followed him,
and he healed them all. 16. And he ordered them not to make him manifest, 17. in order that what was said through Isaiah the prophet might be
fulfilled: 18. "Behold my servant whom I have chosen, my beloved one
with whom my soul is well pleased. I will put my spirit upon him, and
he will announce judgment to the Gentiles. 19. He will not wrangle or cry
aloud, nor will anyone hear his voice in the streets. 20. He will not break
a bruised reed or quench a smouldering wick until he brings justice to victory. 21. And in his name the Gentiles will hope."

Notes

15. *departed from there*: Matt 12:15-16 summarizes Mark 3:7-12 by using only the keywords of the latter text ("departed . . . followed . . . healed . . . ordered not to make him manifest") and omitting everything that could be considered as superfluous. Even though Jesus knows about the Pharisees' plot against him, he refuses to mount an active resistance against them.

16. *not to make him manifest*: Taken over from Mark 3:11, Jesus' injunction to silence in Matthew bypasses the reactions of the unclean spirits ("you are the Son of God") and is directed toward the many who followed him and those who were

healed. Matthew found a rationale for Jesus' behavior in the Servant Song of Isa 42:1-4 (=Matt 12:18-21).

17. *might be fulfilled*: Given the introduction in Matt 12:15-16, in which Jesus refuses to confront the Pharisees directly and commands that he not be made manifest, the precise point of the fulfillment of Isa 42:1-4 appears in the phrase "he will not wrangle or cry aloud" (Matt 12:19). The quotation is introduced by Matthew's usual formula for fulfillment quotations.

18. *my servant*: The Hebrew of Isa 42:1 (*'abdî*) could be translated *ho doulos mou*. But Matthew follows the Septuagint (*ho pais mou*), which at least introduces the ambiguity that he might be referring to Jesus as both Servant and Son.

whom I have chosen: After a beginning that corresponds to the Hebrew text of Isa 42:1 ("Behold my servant"), the rest of the verse departs from both the Hebrew and the Greek. The wording ("whom I have chosen, my beloved one with whom my soul is well pleased") is much like that of the heavenly voice at Jesus' baptism (Matt 3:17) and transfiguration (17:5).

19. *wrangle*: Both the Hebrew and the Greek suggest "cry out." The verb *erisei* ("wrangle") is best understood as Matthew's adaptation of the biblical text in order to apply it more directly to Jesus' refusal to contend publicly with the Pharisees (Matt 12:15). Likewise, "in the streets" makes more vivid the words for "outside" in Hebrew (*bĕhûṣ*) and Greek (*exō*).

20. *He will not break a bruised reed*: Though not the same as the Septuagint, the Greek of Matt 12:20ab can be recognized as a translation from the Hebrew. The emphasis of the Servant Song in Isa 42:1-4 is the meekness and gentleness of the Servant, not his suffering. So too is the thrust of its application in Matt 12:18-21.

until he brings justice to victory: The final phrase in Matt 12:20 cannot be readily derived from Isa 42:3c in either the Hebrew ("he will faithfully bring forth justice") or the Greek. There has been a join with Isa 42:4b ("until he has established justice upon the earth") with the omission of Isa 42:4a. There also seems to have been some influence from Hab 1:4 with regard to "for victory/forever."

21. *the Gentiles will hope*: Matthew agrees with the Septuagint. The Hebrew has "and the coastlands wait for his law." The Matthean text thus includes the idea of the Gentiles sharing in the vocation of God's meek and gentle Servant.

Interpretation

The Markan summary of Jesus' healings by the Sea of Galilee (Mark 3:7-12) has been greatly abbreviated by Matthew (Matt 12:15-16) and turned into the occasion for a fulfillment quotation (Matt 12:17-21 = Isa 42:1-14). In a context that focuses on the rejection of Jesus (Matt 12:1-4, 22-50) Matt 12:15-21 serves as a reminder concerning the real identity of Jesus as God's Servant/Son, much as Matt 11:25-30 linked Jesus to the wisdom of God.

The quotation about the meek and gentle Servant of God (Isa 42:1-4) explains why Jesus withdrew from the synagogue of the Pharisees (see Matt 12:9) and why he deliberately avoided making his true identity public: That is how God's meek and gentle Servant operates. From this perspective the most important part of the quotation comes in Matt 12:19 (''he will not wrangle or cry aloud''). Nevertheless, other elements in Matthew's free adaptation of the biblical text (his version does not fully agree with any other ancient version) also add to the evangelist's picture of Jesus.

Jesus is God's Servant and Son, for the Greek term *pais* is ambiguous, an ambiguity probably deliberately exploited by Matthew who elsewhere gives much attention to Jesus as the Son of God. The remainder of Matt 12:18a (''whom I have chosen, my beloved one with whom my soul is well pleased'') recalls the heavenly voice at Jesus' baptism (see Matt 3:17) and points forward to the heavenly voice at the transfiguration (see Matt 17:5). The quotation also serves to identify Jesus as the bearer of the Holy Spirit (''I will put my spirit upon him''), perhaps in contrast to those who control ''their synagogue'' (12:9). Finally, two elements in the quotation suggest that Jesus has significance for Gentiles: ''he will announce judgment to the Gentiles'' (12:18); ''in his name the Gentiles will hope'' (12:21).

For members of the Matthean community, Matt 12:15-21 would have underscored Jesus' power as a healer already made clear in chapters 8–9 and in 12:9-14. It would also have added to their picture of the identity of Jesus according to the characteristics mentioned in the preceding paragraph. In the polemical context of chapter 12 (and of chs. 11–14 as a whole) this text may also have been taken as a criticism of the Pharisees and ''their synagogue,'' for their failure to recognize Jesus as the Servant of God and the bearer of the Holy Spirit.

In actualizing this text it is important not to assimilate the Servant song (Isa 42:1-4) quoted here to the other Servant songs, especially Isa 52:13–53:12 with its clear emphasis on the Servant's suffering. In Matt 12:15-21 the focus is the meekness and gentleness of the Servant, along with the other Christological themes: Servant/Son, the one approved by God, the bearer of the Holy Spirit, and Jesus' significance for the Gentiles.

For Reference and Further Study

Doyle, B. R. ''A Concern of the Evangelist: Pharisees in Matthew 12.'' *Australian Biblical Review* 34 (1986) 17–34.

Neyrey, J. H. ''The Thematic Use of Isaiah 42:1-4 in Matthew 12.'' *Bib* 63 (1982) 457–73.

28. *The Source of Jesus' Power* (12:22-37)

22. Then a blind and mute demoniac was brought to him, and he healed him so that the mute spoke and saw. 23. And all the crowds were amazed and said: "Is not this the Son of David?" 24. But the Pharisees heard this and said: "This man does not cast out demons except in Beelzebul, prince of demons."

25. Knowing their thoughts he said to them: "Every kingdom divided against itself is left desolate, and every city or household divided against itself will not stand. 26. And if Satan casts out Satan, he is divided against himself. How therefore will his kingdom stand? 27. And if I cast out demons in Beezebul, in whom do your own sons cast them out? Therefore they will be your judges. 28. But if I cast out demons in the spirit of God, then the kingdom of God has arrived among you. 29. Or how can anyone enter the house of a strong man and seize his goods unless he first bind the strong man? And then he will seize his household. 30. Whoever is not with me is against me, and whoever does not gather with me scatters.

31. "Therefore I say to you, every sin and blasphemy will be forgiven human beings, but blasphemy against the Spirit will not be forgiven. 32. And whoever says a word against the Son of Man, it will be forgiven him. But whoever speaks against the Holy Spirit, it will not be forgiven him—neither in this age nor in the age to come.

33. "Either make the tree good and its fruit good, or make the tree bad and its fruit bad. For from the fruit the tree is known. 34. Brood of vipers, how can you being evil say good things? For from the abundance of the heart the mouth speaks. 35. The good person brings forth good things from a good treasury, and the evil person brings forth evil things from an evil treasury. 36. But I say to you that every idle word that people speak, they will give account about it in the day of judgment. 37. For by your words you will be justified, and by your words you will be condemned."

Notes

22. *blind and mute*: In Matt 9:32 and Luke 11:14 the man is only "mute." The demonic possession results in his blindness and muteness; it is not a third condition. The result of Jesus' healing him is that he both speaks and sees, that is, both conditions are healed.

23. *Is not this the Son of David?*: The crowds connect the miraculous healing with Jesus' identity as David's Son, perhaps on the basis of Isa 29:18 ("In that day . . . the eyes of the blind shall see") and 35:5-6 ("Then the eyes of the blind shall be opened . . . the tongue of the dumb sing for joy"). The point of connection between healing and the Son of David may be the figure of Solomon, the son of David (see Matt 9:27; 15:22; 20:30-31).

24. *the Pharisees heard*: There is a contrast between the blind and mute demoniac and the Pharisees, who seem to hear but in fact do not correctly perceive what

happens around them (see Matt 12:2). The crowds correctly infer from the healing that Jesus is the Son of David, whereas the Pharisees incorrectly conclude that Jesus heals by means of demonic power.

Beelzebul: The manuscripts contain three forms of the name: Beelzebul, Beelzebub, and Beezebul. Its meaning is even more complicated. "Baal-zebub" (2 Kgs 1:2, 6), the Philistine god of Ekron, is already a pun intended to ridicule that god as "lord of flies." The first element in the name ("Ba'al") clearly means "lord." The second element ("zebul") has been interpreted to mean "prince," "heavenly region," "dung," or "enmity." In the NT (Matt 12:24; Mark 3:22; Luke 11:16) he is called the "prince of demons," thus suggesting that the etymology was no longer important and that Beelzebul was identified with Satan (see Matt 4:1-11).

25. *every kingdom divided against itself*: The point of this consideration and those that follow rests on an apocalyptic division between the kingdom of God and the kingdom of Satan. The two are taken to be mutually exclusive. Jesus' exorcisms (see Matt 12:22-24) are blows against the kingdom of Satan and therefore cannot be understood as done by the power of Satan.

every city or household: Like "kingdom," both terms refer to a domain or sphere of power. By way of synonymous parallelism the point made in the part of the saying about the kingdom is reinforced by its application to a city or a household.

26. *Satan*: The use of Satan as a proper name here (see Matt 4:1-11) indicates an identification with "Beelzebul, prince of demons" (Matt 12:24). The saying also expresses Jesus' basic defense against his foes: If Satan was acting through Jesus, he would be destroying his own kingdom and thus acting at cross-purposes with it.

27. *your own sons*: The expression refers to Jewish exorcists, some of whom were Pharisees (Tob 8:1-5; Acts 19:13-16). The thrust of Jesus' argument is to place his own exorcisms alongside theirs, and to challenge his opponents to interpret the origin of these exorcisms. If the acts of other Jewish exorcists come from the Holy Spirit, why not those of Jesus too?

28. *in the Spirit of God*: Luke 11:20 reads "in the finger of God." Given Luke's special interest in the Holy Spirit, one can assume that Q had "in the finger of God" and Matthew was responsible for the change. The Q version alluded to Exod 8:19 ("This is the finger of God"); see also Deut 9:10; Ps 8:3. Matthew has avoided an anthropomorphism regarding God and clarified the meaning by his change. He has also recalled the assertion made in Matt 12:18 on the basis of Isa 42:1 ("I will place my spirit upon him"). The basic meaning of Q remains: Jesus casts out demons by God's power.

the kingdom of God has arrived among you: Instead of the usual Matthean "kingdom of heaven," the phrase of Q ("kingdom of God") is retained. The verb *ephthasen* ("has arrived") is much bolder than *ēngiken* (see Matt 3:2; 4:17), suggesting the presence of God's kingdom through the exorcisms of Jesus; see 1 Thess 2:16 ("God's wrath has come upon them").

29. *a strong man*: In its present context the parable concerns Jesus and Satan ("the strong man"). For the idea of binding Satan and thus neutralizing his power,

see Rev 20:2-3. The point is that Jesus has already bound up Satan, and his exorcisms should be understood as signs of the victory over Satan.

30. *Whoever is not with me*: The logical connection of this saying with the preceding is loose. The idea seems to be that in the struggle in which Jesus is a major figure neutrality is impossible. One must be on one side or the other. It is clear which side Jesus is on. Matt 12:30 is a challenge to the audience to declare which side they are on. They are on someone's side, whether they admit it or not. According to J. L. Houlden (*Theology* 82 [1979] 251–59) the Matthean version of the saying reflects a Church anxious to define and delimit itself in relation to enemies and unwanted friends, sensitive about the principle of orthodoxy, and keen to assert the credentials of Jesus and his true followers.

31. *blasphemy against the Spirit*: The Greek term ''blasphemy'' means to injure the reputation of someone. In the OT (see Lev 24:16) it pertains to the name of Yahweh. This charge is brought against Jesus by the scribe (Matt 9:3) and the high priest (26:65). Here it is said that the only unforgivable blasphemy is that against the Holy Spirit. In the present context this refers to ascribing the source of Jesus' power to demons rather than the Holy Spirit.

32. *The Son of Man*: The ''Son of Man'' title appears in three major contexts in the Gospels: generic, passion predictions, or future figure. In what sense is it meant here? The first sense seems most likely, that is, it concerns blasphemy against Jesus as a representative figure for humankind. Even this blasphemy can be forgiven. But blasphemy against the Spirit (attributing Jesus' power to demons) will not be forgiven.

neither in this age nor in the age to come: Matthew uses the apocalyptic two-age schema (see Luke 12:10) to indicate that blasphemy against the Holy Spirit will never be forgiven.

33. *make the tree good*: The point of the saying is that the quality of a person is shown by actions. The fruit of Jesus' actions—especially his healings and exorcisms—is good. Therefore his person must be good (''from the fruit the tree is known''). The reference to the bad fruit and the bad tree prepares for the denunciation in the next verse. For a use of the same analogy see Matt 7:16-20.

34. *brood of vipers*: The same epithet is used by John the Baptist against the Pharisees and Sadducees (Matt 3:7) and by Jesus against the scribes and Pharisees (Matt 23:33). The following saying is based on the principle that words reflect the quality of the person. It is used to attack the Pharisees (see 12:24) as ''being evil.''

35. *from a good treasury*: Luke tries to make the saying more specific by his phrase ''from the good treasury to the heart'' (see Luke 6:45). The meaning is the same as the tree-fruit analogy in Matt 12:33; that is, the relation between deeds and the doer. Jesus' good deeds proceed from his good ''treasury.''

36. *idle word*: The phrase is a paradoxical description of the Pharisees' objections to Jesus. The term *argos* means literally ''without work, without effect'' (see Matt 20:3, 6). It is coupled with ''word'' (*rēma*), which in some OT contexts applied to God has a powerful effect (''my word . . . shall accomplish that which I purpose,'' Isa 55:12).

37. *you will be justified*: The person changes from second plural (see Matt 12:34) to second singular, perhaps indicating the use in Matt 12:37 of material from another source. The last-judgment saying underlines the critical importance of words as a criterion for judgment.

INTERPRETATION

Departing from his usual practice of compressing his sources, Matthew in 12:22-37 has blended material from Q and Mark to present a lengthy response by Jesus to his critics' accusations about the source of his power to heal and expel demons. The setting for the reply (Matt 12:22-24) is the healing of a demoniac unable to see or to speak (=Luke 11:14-15; Matt 9:32-34). The doublet in Matt 9:32-34 suggests that Matthew may deliberately be reusing material here. The major change in comparison with the parallel versions comes in the crowd's question: "Is not this the Son of David?" (Matt 12:23).

The first part of Jesus' reply (Matt 12:25-30) answers the question about the source of Jesus' power with reference to sayings about the kingdom divided against itself. There is no doubt about Jesus' power as an exorcist. The debate concerns the source of his power. While some of Matt 12:25-30 closely parallels Mark 3:22-27, the even closer and apparently independent parallels with Luke 11:14-15, 17-23 suggest that Matthew's primary source was Q. The second part (Matt 12:31-37) seems to combine material from Mark 3:28-30 and Q (Luke 12:10; 6:43-45). The result is a long reflection on the Holy Spirit as the source of Jesus' power.

The literary form of the reflection is a speech, though a somewhat choppy one. The combination of various sources (which were themselves already composites) gives the impression of rapid movement, with the individual elements not making exactly the same points. The thrust of the first part of Jesus' reply (Matt 12:25-30) is that Satan could not be the source of Jesus' power, since Jesus' exorcisms are blows against Satan's kingdom. A sharp division is assumed between Satan's kingdom and God's kingdom. Since Jesus' exorcisms cannot be attributed to Satan's kingdom, therefore they must proceed from God's power, which is identified as the Holy Spirit.

The thrust of the second part (Matt 12:31-37) is that mistaking the source of Jesus' power constitutes blasphemy against the Holy Spirit, the only unforgivable sin (12:31-32). This idea yields to reflections on the relation between the deeds/words and the quality of a person (12:33-37), which not only establish the goodness of Jesus but also serve to make insinuations about the bad character of his opponents. In the polemical context of Matthew 11–14 the two parts of Jesus' reply establish him as squarely on the side of God in the struggle against Satan and suggest that his opponents may be on the wrong side.

The background of this debate is to be found in texts about Jewish exorcists, Solomon, and Jesus the magician. Acts 19:13-20 tells the strange story of the seven sons of Sceva, a Jewish high priest, who are classed among "some of the itinerant Jewish exorcists" at Ephesus. The demon claims to know Jesus and Paul but not the sons of Sceva, and puts them to rout. There was also a tendency to classify some of Israel's great heroes from the past as exorcists. Thus in *Genesis Apocryphon* 20:16-30 Abraham serves as an exorcist for the Pharaoh, and in *Prayer of Nabonidus* Daniel is an exorcist for the Babylonian king.

In the face of Jesus' exorcism of the blind and mute demoniac the amazed crowd asks: "Is not this the Son of David?" (Matt 12:23). The association of Solomon, the son of David, with magic and demons becomes a major theme in portrayals of Solomon in NT times. For a full presentation of the evidence, see D. C. Duling, "Solomon, Exorcism, and the Son of David," *HTR* 68 (1975) 235–52, in which he traces the trajectory of Solomon as exorcist from the biblical references to his wisdom (see 1 Kgs 4:29-34 and the OT Wisdom books) through intertestamental references to his power over demons (see 11QPs Ap[a]; *Bib. Ant.* 60; Josephus *Ant.* 8:45-49; *Testament of Solomon*) to later Jewish references to the use of Solomon's ring in binding demons (see *b. Gitt.* 68a and incantation bowls). Typical is David's warning to the evil spirits that "after a time one born from my loins (= Solomon) will rule over you" (*Bib. Ant.* 60:3). This background related to Solomon as exorcist highlights the distinctively Matthean response of the crowd: "Is not this the son of David?" Matthew may well be alluding to such ideas about the Son of David and deliberately placing Jesus in line with them.

The major point at issue in the debate between the Pharisees and Jesus in Matt 12:22-37 is the source of Jesus' power as an exorcist. Even the opponents admit Jesus' powers, but they quarrel about its origin. For a full treatment of evidence pertaining to Jesus as exorcising magical powers, see M. Smith, *Jesus the Magician* (San Francisco: Harper & Row, 1978). The debate about the source of Jesus' miraculous power lived on in the later rabbinic evaluation of Jesus: "He practiced sorcery and beguiled and led Israel astray." What is at issue in that quotation is not the power of Jesus but rather the meaning of his miracles.

The question of the meaning of Jesus' miracles was surely alive in Matthew's community as it confronted other Jewish groups after A.D. 70. Matthew's collection of Q and Markan sayings appears in response to a division of opinion regarding this issue: Are Jesus' exorcisms signs that he is the Son of David (as the crowd supposes), or have they been done through Beelzebul's power (as the Pharisees charge)? The fact that Jesus' reply confronts the charge of the Pharisees (Matt 12:24) suggests that the charge had special significance for the Matthean community as it sought to clarify its own identity vis-à-vis the Pharisees and their successors.

The essence of Jesus' reply, of course, is that the Holy Spirit was the source of his power as an exorcist. It was a logical absurdity to think otherwise, according to Matt 12:25-30, and a sign of bad faith on the Pharisees' part, according to Matt 12:31-37.

Yet the source of Jesus' power is not the whole story of the meaning of his miracles. The exorcisms emerge as signs of the presence of God's kingdom: "But if I cast out demons in the Spirit of God, then the kingdom of God has arrived among you" (Matt 12:28). This explicit emphasis on the presence of God's kingdom is rare in the Synoptic tradition (see also Matt 11:12/Luke 16:16; Luke 17:21). Perhaps the clearest of the "present" or "realized" eschatological sayings in the Gospels, Matt 12:28 reminds us that Jesus' miracles were intended neither as spectacular displays nor as proofs of his divinity but rather as anticipations of the fullness of God's kingdom among us.

The miracles of Jesus pose problems for both the excessively credulous and the excessively skeptical among us. Those who preach and teach about Jesus' miracles need to help people today to appreciate the inclusive and flexible approach of the Bible toward "signs and wonders" as opposed to the Enlightenment idea of miracle as the suspension of the laws of nature. They must also follow the lead of Matt 12:28 in emphasizing Jesus' miracles as signs that in his ministry God's kingdom was present and that the meaning of his miracles resides in their function as indicators of the kingdom's presence.

29. *The Sign of Jonah* (12:38-42)

38. Then some of the scribes and Pharisees said to him: "Teacher, we wish to see a sign from you." 39. But he answered and said to them: "An evil and adulterous generation seeks a sign, and no sign will be given it except the sign of Jonah the prophet. 40. For just as Jonah was in the belly of the sea-monster three days and three nights, so will the Son of Man be in the heart of the earth three days and three nights. 41. The men of Nineveh will arise in judgment with this generation and condemn it. For they repented at Jonah's preaching, and behold more than Jonah is here. 42. The queen of the south will arise in judgment with this generation and condemn it. For she came from the ends of the earth to hear Solomon's wisdom, and behold more than Solomon is here."

Notes

38. *scribes and Pharisees*: Mention of the Pharisees aligns this passage with other controversies in Matthew 12 (see 12:2, 9, 24). Other versions have somewhat differ-

ent formulas: "the Pharisees and Sadducees" (Matt 16:1), "the Pharisees" (Mark 8:11), and "others" (Luke 11:16).

a sign: Here "sign" could not simply mean miracle, since Jesus had already supplied many of them (as in Matt 12:22). It must refer to some assurance or authentication that Jesus is truly from God. Thus the debate about the source of Jesus' power (see Matt 12:25-37) is resumed. According to 1 Cor 1:22 "Jews demand signs."

39. *evil and adulterous generation*: The term "adulterous" is used as a metaphor to describe infidelity with respect to God. The assumption is that God's relationship to his people is like that of a marriage. The charge implied by the epithet is that this generation has been unfaithful. The best known use of the metaphor is Hosea 1–3; see also Isa 57:3; Jer 3:9; 9:2; Ezek 16:38.

except the sign of Jonah: According to Mark 8:12 no sign at all will be given. According to Luke 11:30 the sign of Jonah is Jesus' preaching of repentance to the marginalized, as Jonah preached it to the pagan people of Nineveh. Matt 12:40 with its reference to Jesus' death and resurrection gives a very different approach to the sign of Jonah.

40. *in the belly of the sea-monster three days and three nights*: The description of Jonah is taken from Jon 1:17 (=2:1 in Hebrew). The three days and nights schema does not fit Jesus exactly since his resurrection occurred on the third day, after two nights in the tomb. Nevertheless, the point of comparison is clearly return to life after apparent/real death.

41. *men of Nineveh*: The Q version of the sign of Jonah is rejoined, with repentance serving as the point of comparison. The scene is the last judgment. The pagan Ninevites who repented at Jonah's preaching will condemn Jews of Jesus' generation for their failure to repent in response to Jesus' preaching. They repented, even though they were pagans and had a lesser preacher (Jonah).

42. *queen of the south*: The story of the visit of the Queen of Sheba (=Saba in southwest Arabia) to Solomon is told in 1 Kgs 10:1-13. Whereas she came a great distance to hear the wisdom of Solomon, Jews of Jesus' own generation failed to respond to his preaching to them.

INTERPRETATION

Comparison of Mark 8:11-12 and Matt 12:38-42/Luke 11:16, 29-32 indicates that there were two versions of the "sign" controversy—one in which Jesus refuses to give any sign at all (Mark), and the other in which the only sign given is that of Jonah (Q). The Markan "no sign" version can be explained either as the more primitive version or as a part of the Markan "secrecy" motif. The problem encountered in the Q "sign of Jonah" version concerns the nature of the sign and its message with respect to Jesus.

The Q version in Luke 11:16, 29-32 gives the impression of being a composite consisting of the narrative framework (11:16), the sign of Jonah saying and its explanation (11:29-30), and the two comparisons of "this generation" with the biblical examples of the queen of the south and the men of Nineveh (11:31-32). The latter two units were probably joined by their references to "this generation" and to the Jonah story.

The Q version expressed in Luke has been reshaped by Matthew in two major ways. He has smoothed out the order by placing all the Jonah material together (Matt 12:39-41) and leaving the "queen of the south" to the end (12:42). He has also given the "sign of Jonah" a different interpretation by inserting the death-resurrection comparison in Matt 12:40. Whereas in Q and Luke the sign of Jonah is the preaching of repentance to an unlikely audience (Gentiles in Jonah's case, the "marginal" in Jesus' case), in Matthew the sign of Jonah is first and foremost life out of death after three days. Whether Matt 12:40 was traditional or created by Matthew, it affords a different angle on the Jonah-Jesus relationship.

In its Matthean form the "sign of Jonah" text contains a scene in which Jesus is questioned by scribes and Pharisees (12:38) along with Jesus' response (12:39-42). In light of earlier references to Pharisees in Matthew 12 (see vv. 2, 9, 24) the atmosphere is one of controversy with the implication that Jesus includes his questioners in "the evil and adulterous generation."

The Jewish background is to be found primarily in the Book of Jonah. In Matthew Jonah has a double sign-value. First he provides a type of Jesus' death and resurrection by his being swallowed by the great fish and then being deposited alive on the dry land (1:17; 2:10). Even though Jonah does not really die and his stay in the fish's belly is three days and three nights, the major point of similarity is a kind of death and resurrection experienced by both Jonah and Jesus. This comparison is Matthew's particular contribution to the Jonah-Jesus typology.

The other sign-value of Jonah for understanding Jesus concerns the preaching of repentance. Jonah, the reluctant prophet, tries to avoid God's commission to preach repentance to Nineveh by going in the opposite direction to Tarshish (=Spain, perhaps). The reason for Jonah's flight was that he knew that God would be gracious and merciful to Israel's enemies (see Jonah 4:2). Despite Jonah's unwillingness, he eventually does preach repentance to the people of Nineveh and their repentance preserves them from destruction (see Jonah 3:1-10). In this context the sign of Jonah is that pagans repent at the preaching of a Jewish prophet. In Q and Luke this sign of Jonah was the repentance of the marginal (tax collectors, prostitutes, etc.) at Jesus' preaching. While retaining this element of the Jonah-Jesus typology, Matthew has added the death-resurrection dimension by his inclusion of Matt 12:40.

The secondary biblical background of Matt 12:38-42 is the story of the visit of the queen of Sheba (=Saba in Arabia) to Solomon (see 1 Kgs 10:1-13). She comes a great distance to test for herself Solomon's reputation for wisdom. The point of similarity between Solomon and Jesus according to Matt 10:42 is their wisdom. The differences, however, are more important: Jesus' wisdom is greater than Solomon's was, and the queen approved Solomon's wisdom after having travelled a long distance whereas the scribes and Pharisees reject Jesus' wisdom right in their own land.

The Matthean version of the "sign of Jonah" controversy (Matt 12:38-42) was part of a defense of Jesus and an explanation why his message was not universally accepted by his fellow Jews. On the one hand, it aligns Jesus with the biblical figures Jonah and Solomon, only to insist that he is greater than both. It finds in those biblical characters precedents for Jesus' death and resurrection, his preaching of repentance, and his wisdom. On the other hand, it contrasts the positive responses to Jonah and Solomon with the negative responses to Jesus on the part of the scribes and Pharisees. Those negative responses are judged amazing and even incredible because "more than Jonah/Solomon is here." The text provided several important messages for a Jewish-Christian community concerned with explaining its conviction that Jesus was the "fullness" of Judaism and its experience of large-scale rejection by other Jews.

Modern audiences instinctively identify the sign of Jonah with Jesus' death and resurrection on the basis of Matt 12:40. Such readers need exposure to the complexity of the debate about the "sign" and the ambiguity of the Jonah typology, especially the Lukan idea of Jesus' preaching to the marginal people of his time. Likewise the emphasis on Jonah ought not to preclude attention to the wisdom of Jesus alluded to by Matt 12:42. This rich text can be developed by preachers and teachers in a variety of ways.

30. *This Evil Generation; the Family of Jesus* (12:43-50)

43. "When an unclean spirit goes forth from a person, it travels through waterless places seeking rest, and it does not find it. 44. Then it says: 'I will go back to my house from which I came forth.' And it goes and finds it unoccupied and swept clean and put in order. 45. Then it goes and brings with itself seven other spirits worse than itself, and it enters and dwells there. And the last state of that person is worse than the first. And so it will be for this evil generation."

46. While he was still speaking to the crowds, his mother and brothers were standing outside, seeking to speak to him. 47. Someone said to him: "Your mother and your brothers are standing outside, seeking to speak to you." 48. He answered and said to the one speaking to him: "Who is my mother, and who are my brothers?" 49. And he stretched out his hand to his disciples and said: "Behold my mother and my brothers. 50. For who-

ever does the will of my Father in heaven, he is my brother and sister and mother."

Notes

43. *an unclean spirit*: The whole speech of Jesus in Matt 12:25-42 has been occasioned by the exorcism of a demon in Matt 12:22. The idea that the wilderness ("waterless places") was the abode of demons appears in Isa 34:14-15; Lev 16:10. Jesus was tested by the devil in the wilderness (see Matt 4:1-11).

44. *unoccupied*: Only Matthew adds this qualifier to the following two qualifiers. Its presence provides a preliminary image to "swept clean and put in order," suggesting that the emptiness of the house calls out for the arrival of a new tenant.

45. *the last state*: The eight devils now occupying the house will be harder to expel than the one demon was previously. So the situation has become much worse.

    for this evil generation: The concluding sentence, found only in Matthew, applies the story to the generation of Jesus. It suggests that the exorcisms done by Jesus were only an interlude and promises that worse things will happen. The Lukan context (Luke 11:23-26) uses the story in an individual context (see Luke 11:23), not in the historical context indicated by Matthew.

46. *his mother and brothers*: The term "brothers" (*adelphoi*) has been interpreted in several ways: the blood brothers of Jesus born of Mary and Joseph; the half-brothers of Jesus, the children of Joseph's prior marriage; or the cousins of Jesus based on the fact that "brother" can cover a wide range of relationships. It is doubtful that Matthew knew the tradition about the perpetual virginity of Mary (see Matt 1:25).

47. *Someone said*: Some important ancient manuscripts omit the entire verse. The best argument for its inclusion is verse 48, which demands something like verse 47; its omission could be explained by its similarity in wording to verse 46. An argument against its inclusion is Matthew's tendency to omit whatever does not move the story along. But Matt 12:47 merely repeats what has already been said in 12:46.

49. *his disciples*: By his words and actions Jesus redefines membership in his family. He also defines discipleship as doing the will of his heavenly Father (see Matt 12:50). By omitting Mark 3:20-21 Matthew avoids the suggestion that Jesus' family ("those around him") thought that he was mad. In Matthew the family functions more as a literary foil than as a solid opposition to Jesus.

Interpretation

From the perspective of sources and literary forms the last two texts in Matthew 12—the story about the return of the evil spirit (12:43-45) and the statement about the true family of Jesus (12:46-50)—have little in common. The first text (12:43-45) is a parable-like narrative based almost entirely on

Q (see Luke 11:24-26). Matthew's distinctive contribution comes in the application contained in the final sentence: "And so it will be for this evil generation." This comment takes the parable out of its mysterious realm and offers an interpretation, or at least an application: The exorcisms done by Jesus provide only a temporary respite from demon possession; an even worse period is in store for "this evil generation." At the same time, Matthew's comment expresses an alienation, or even separation, on Jesus' part from "this evil generation" (see Matt 12:39).

The second text (Matt 12:46-50) is a pronouncement by Jesus about his true family; it is based on Mark 3:31-35. As in Mark, it expresses an alienation, or even separation, on Jesus' part from his own family. When placed beside Matt 12:43-45 as the climax of a section devoted to the rejection of Jesus (Matthew 11–12) and leading into an exploration of the reasons for Jesus' rejection (Matt 13:1-52), the statement about Jesus' true family (Matt 12:46-50) takes on a pivotal significance. Matthew has joined the two texts on the basis of their content. Both concern Jesus' alienation and separation—from "this evil generation" and from his earthly family.

The biblical background for these texts is the theme of the people of God; see D. J. Harrington, *God's People in Christ: New Testament Perspectives on the Church and Judaism* (Philadelphia: Fortress, 1980). The basic shape of God's relation to Israel remains the same throughout its history: It is the result of God's gracious offer of election, is communal in nature, and takes the form of a covenant between God and Israel. But in post-exilic times there was a tendency to narrow down who in Israel really continues this special relationship with God. Only those who avoid marriages with non-Jews, or observe circumcision or Sabbath regulations, or belong to the right group count with respect to this special relationship. The destruction of the Jerusalem Temple and of Jerusalem in A.D. 70 made this relationship even more problematic, for the major unifying religious institution—the Temple—no longer existed. And so a major matter of debate in Jesus' time was the identity of the people of God. It was an even more controversial issue in the time when Matthew wrote his Gospel.

The message of Matt 12:43-50 to Matthew's community as it tried to define itself vis-à-vis other Jewish groups after A.D. 70 would have been something like the following: The exorcisms performed by Jesus were only an interlude or temporary victory; this "evil generation" will see an even worse infestation of demons (Matt 12:43-45). The true family of Jesus (= the Church as the people of God) is made up of those who do God's will (Matt 12:46-50). Here there may also be a criticism of a Christian group that took its leadership from Jesus' family. Matt 12:43-50 distinguishes the community of Jesus from "this evil generation" and the blood relatives of Jesus. It reduces membership in the community of Jesus to one simple requirement: doing the will of God.

The idea of the Church as the family of Jesus joined together by its dedication to doing God's will remains a powerful theme. It must, however, remain faithful to the premise that God's will has been expressed in the Scriptures and in the example of Jesus. It must also face the fact that in families there are often problems, crises, and conflicts. The Church as the family of Jesus should not be allowed to degenerate into vagueness or romanticism.

31. *The Parable of the Sower* (13:1-23)

1. On that day Jesus went out of the house and sat by the sea. 2. And great crowds gathered about him so that he got into a boat and sat down, and all the crowd stood on the shore. 3. And he told them many things in parables, saying: "Behold, the sower went out to sow. 4. And while he was sowing, some (seeds) fell upon the path, and the birds came and ate them up. 5. Some fell upon the rocky ground where they did not have much soil, and immediately they sprouted up because they did not have depth of soil. 6. But when the sun rose they were burned, and because they had no root they withered away. 7. Some fell upon the thorns, and the thorns grew up and choked them. 8. Some fell upon the good soil and brought forth fruit—some a hundred, some sixty, some thirty. 9. Whoever has ears, should listen."

10. And the disciples approached him and said: "Why do you speak to them in parables?" 11. He answered and said to them: "Because to you it has been granted to know the mysteries of the kingdom of heaven, but to those it has not been granted. 12. For whoever has, it will be given to him, and he will get a great abundance. Whoever does not have, even what he has will be taken from him. 13. Therefore I speak to them in parables, because seeing they do not see and hearing they do not hear nor understand. 14. And with them is fulfilled the prophecy of Isaiah that says: 'You shall indeed hear and not understand, and you shall indeed see and not perceive, 15. for the heart of this people has become fat and they are hard of hearing and they have closed their eyes, lest they see with their eyes and hear with their ears and understand with their heart and turn, and I shall heal them.' 16. But blessed are the eyes because they see, and your ears because they hear. 17. For Amen I say to you that many prophets and righteous ones desired to see what you see and have not seen it and to hear what you hear and have not heard it.

18. "Hear then the parable of the sower. 19. When anyone hears the word of the kingdom and does not understand, the evil one comes and seizes what was sown in his heart—this is what was sown upon the path. 20. That which was sown on the rocky ground—this is the one who hears the word and immediately receives it with joy. 21. Yet he does not have

root in himself but lasts only for a while, and when there is tribulation or persecution on account of the word immediately he stumbles. 22. That which is sown in the thorns—this is the one who hears the word, but the care of this age and the deceitfulness of wealth choke the word, and it proves unfruitful. 23. That which is sown in the good soil—this is the one who hears the word and understands it, who bears fruit and yields in one case a hundred, in another sixty, in another thirty."

Notes

1. *on that day*: Matthew modifies Mark 4:1 ("And again he began to teach by the sea") in several ways: "On that day" connects Matt 13:1-52 with the preceding chapter and makes the text into a "day of parables." "Out of the house" follows on Jesus' being in the house in Matt 12:46-50. In sitting by the sea Jesus adopts the customary posture of the teacher who is the center of the crowd's attention.

2. *he got into a boat*: This picturesque scene is taken over from Mark 4:1. We are to imagine that so great was the crowd's interest in Jesus that the only way in which Jesus could be seen and heard was to speak from a boat off the shore of the Sea of Galilee. The audience for the "day of parables" is the "crowd." The thrust of many parables will be how members of the crowd respond to the preaching of Jesus.

3. *in parables*: Jesus' characteristic mode of teaching the crowd is through "parables," a term with several meanings in Semitic languages, ranging from "story" to "riddle." Reasons why Jesus adopted this style of teaching are presented in Matt 13:10-17 and 13:34-35. By adding biblical quotations (Isa 6:9-10; Ps 78:2) to the Markan source, Matthew suggests that it was God's will as expressed in Scripture.

   the sower: Despite the traditional title of the parable as "the sower" (see Matt 13:18), the real focus is the seeds and their yields. More important than the fate of the *four* different plantings is the contrast between the three unsuccessful plantings and the fourth superabundantly successful one.

4. *some (seeds) fell upon the path*: The sower sows on some unpromising soils: the path where people walk (13:4), the rocky ground without depth of soil (13:5), and among the thorns (13:7). Is the farmer foolish to sow in such places? Or is the sower's prodigality and generosity emphasized? Jeremias (*Parables*, 11-12) insists that the sower simply follows good Palestinian farming practices according to which sowing precedes plowing. In other words, the sower intended to come back and plow the seeds into the soil. This initially attractive explanation does not correspond well to what really happens in the parable. Rather than trying to defend the verisimilitude of the parable, it is better to take the peculiar actions of the sower as part of the "unusual" dimension of the story.

5. *the rocky ground*: Many parts of Palestine have a thin layer of topsoil covering limestone. The description of what happens to the seeds sown in such soil shows a knowledge of the land and farming. But as in the preceding and following

cases there is no indication that the sower plans to come back and plow or do anything else. Once the seed is sown it is on its own.

7. *thorns*: The term is probably generic, referring to various kinds of brambles, thistles, nettles, etc. Such bushes might be used to mark off the boundaries of a farmer's field and to keep animals from intruding. The image may be that of a farmer casting seed near the edge of his property.

8. *good soil*: The assumption is that all the seeds are good. The problem is the soil in which the seeds have been sown. In contrast to the first three soils (the path, the rocky ground, the thorns) the good soil yields an amazingly rich harvest.

   some a hundred: Such a yield is highly unusual, and is part of the extravagance of the parable. Matthew has reversed Mark's ascending order (''thirtyfold and sixtyfold and a hundredfold'') to emphasize the unusual yield. He has also omitted the peculiar use in Mark 4:8 of the numeral ''one'' to serve as the equivalent of the English expression ''—fold.''

9. *Whoever has ears*: The same expression was used in Matt 11:15 to call attention to a significant but somewhat obscure teaching. Here the audience is presumably to grasp the message that the response to the seed (= the word of the kingdom; see Matt 13:19) is mixed. But the result arising from the positive response will be abundant beyond all imagining.

10. *the disciples*: The awkward expression in Mark 4:10 (''those about him with the Twelve'') has been sharpened and simplified. Also Matthew has them ask a direct question instead of the implied question in Mark 4:10 (''asked him concerning the parables''). Thus there is a clear line between the disciples of Jesus and the others.

11. *to you it has been granted*: We are probably to assume a ''divine passive'' construction here. In other words, the unexpressed subject is God (''God has granted . . .''). Typical of Jewish style, the construction also preserves an air of ''mystery'' while dealing with a mysterious process. Nevertheless, the subject would have been clear to Matthew's readers.

    the mysteries of the kingdom of heaven: The use of ''heaven'' as a substitute for ''God'' is typical of Matthew's style. The same practice appears in 1 Maccabees and stems from Jewish reverence for the divine name. The ''mysteries'' is to be taken in its apocalyptic sense as in Daniel 2—the purposes of God with respect to his kingdom. There may also be a parallel with Rom 11:25 where the term refers to Jewish rejection of Jesus.

12. *For whoever has*: In its other uses (Matt 25:29; Mark 4:25; Luke 8:18) the saying is a warning against resting on one's spiritual privileges. Here Matthew has inserted it to increase the valuation of the disciples' privileges and the loss experienced by those outside: Those to whom God has granted knowledge will get even more, whereas the others will lose even what little they have.

13. *Therefore I speak*: The sentence refers back to what precedes—the division between those to whom the mysteries have been revealed and those to whom they have not been revealed. Jesus' speaking in parables is presented as related to that division and even preserving it. The division is traced back to God's own

decree by the allusion to (Matt 13:13) and full quotation of (Matt 13:14-15) Isa 6:9-10.

because seeing they do not see: The introductory conjunction *hoti* ("because") instead of Mark's *hina* ("in order that") is often interpreted as ascribing fault to those who do not see and removing the perverse idea that Jesus deliberately taught obscurely. But Matthew does not differ too radically from Mark here; both divided Jesus' audience into two groups—insiders and outsiders. Matthew omits the last part of Mark 4:12 ("lest they should turn again, and be forgiven").

14. *with them is fulfilled*: The introduction to the biblical quotation differs from the other formula quotations, though the key word "fulfilled" is present. The quotation of Isa 6:9-10 follows the Septuagint exactly (see Acts 28:26-27). The quotation clarifies the allusion in Matt 13:13 (see Mark 4:12) by giving the full text.

You shall indeed hear: The quotation of Isa 6:9-10 places the negative reaction to Jesus' teaching in line with the response promised by God to Isaiah, thus explaining the rejection as in accord with God's will. The Isaiah passage is the classic source of the "hardening" motif (see Rom 11:25). The repentance motif omitted from Mark 4:12 is picked up at the end of Isa 6:10.

16. *blessed are the eyes*: The saying in Matt 13:16-17 appears in Luke 10:23-24 where it follows the Father-Son saying used in Matt 11:25-27. Its use here provides the reverse of Isa 6:9-10 by describing the blessedness of those who have been granted the privilege of knowing the mysteries of God's kingdom. Matthew seems to have added the phrase "and your ears because they hear."

17. *prophets and righteous ones*: Not only are the disciples blessed in comparison with other Jews but even in comparison with the great Jewish heroes of the past. The Lukan parallel (Luke 10:24) reads "prophets and kings." Given Matthew's fondness for the "righteousness" vocabulary and his insistence on the "better righteousness" (Matt 5:20), the change can be attributed to him.

18. *the parable of the sower*: This expression is the source of the traditional title for the parable. Nevertheless the focus of attention is not the sower. The title derives from the opening sentence of the parable ("Behold, the sower went out to sow"), and is not expressive of its full content or its proper interpretation.

19. *the word of the kingdom*: This way of referring to Jesus' message is unusual for the Gospels. It prepares for the subsequent references to "the Word" in Matt 13:20, 22, 23 as a technical term for the "gospel"—a usage common in Acts and the Epistles but found only in redactional material in Mark (1:45; 2:2; 4:33; 8:32; 16:20) and Luke (1:2).

the evil one: Found only here and in 13:38 in Matthew, this way of referring to the devil is more common in the Johannine corpus (see John 17:15; 1 John 2:13-14; 3:12; 5:18-19). In the parallel texts Mark 4:15 reads "the Satan" and Luke 8:12 "the devil." The "heart" takes in both the intellectual and emotional dimensions. There may be an allusion to the Jewish teaching on the "evil inclination" in which the evil takes part in the struggle; see G. H. Cohen Stuart, *The Struggle in Man between Good and Evil. An Inquiry into the Origin of the Rabbinic Concept of Yeṣer Hara'* (Kampen: Kok, 1984).

21. *root*: The term "root" is used as a metaphor for internal stability (see Col 2:7; Eph 3:17). Much of the vocabulary in this section—"sow" in the sense of "preach," "lasts only for a while," "deceitfulness," "wealth," etc.—is unusual for the Gospels but typical of the Epistles. This phenomenon suggests that the interpretation of the parable reflects the experiences of the early Church and must be ascribed to it (see Jeremias, *Parables*, 77–78).

22. *this age*: The Greek word *aiōn* can refer to time ("this age") or place ("this world"). In fact the Greek here has no demonstrative adjective ("this"), though it can and should be supplied (see Matt 13:39). Underlying the expression is the Jewish eschatological division between "this age/world" and "the age/world to come."

Interpretation

Matt 13:1-52 features seven (or eight) parables. Taking over some material from Mark 4:1-34, Matthew has enlarged and supplemented his source, making it into the third major discourse of Jesus. As the third of Jesus' five discourses and occurring in the middle of the Gospel, the "day of the parables" assumes pivotal significance. With this discourse the audience for Jesus' teaching shifts from the crowds and the disciples to basically the disciples.

The major theme in Matthew's presentation of Jesus' parables is the mystery of the rejection and acceptance of Jesus' word of the kingdom. Thus he is confronting what was surely a reality both during Jesus' own public ministry and within Matthew's experience toward the end of the first century A.D. For Matthew the parables helped to illumine what was a painful reality for Jewish Christians: Not all Jews accepted the Christian claims about Jesus.

Thus the situation facing Matthew and his community was similar to that treated by Paul in Romans 9—11. There Paul sought to solve the problem of Jewish rejection and Gentile acceptance of the gospel by the image of the olive tree. The remnant (Jewish Christians such as Paul) constituted the principle of continuity. Gentile Christians have been grafted onto the olive tree, while non-Christian Jews have been cut off from it. That this mystery is in accord with God's will is "proved" by many quotations from the Scriptures.

Matthew's problem was the same as Paul's—the mystery of varied reactions to the gospel and how to deal with them. It is unlikely that Matthew was entering directly into conversation with Paul on the matter. At any rate, he shows no knowledge of Paul's adventurous solution to the mystery: "a hardening has come upon part of Israel, until the full number of the Gentiles come in, and so all Israel will be saved" (Rom 11:25-26). Although Matthew does exploit the "hardening" motif (see Matt 13:10-17), he has no interest in a fixed number of Gentiles or the final (eschatological?) salvation of all Israel. He writes some thirty years after Paul and in a different place from Paul. The problem of the mixed reception of the gospel remains a real one. Matthew's solution is more limited than Paul's was. It focuses on the past and present, not the future.

In this reading of Matthew 13 the parables concern relations between Jewish Christians (with their Gentile-Christian associates) and other Jews, between those who accept Jesus' "word of the kingdom" and those who do not. This is not the usual approach to the text today. In light of redaction-critical study of Matthew it has become common to view these parables as confronting the "mixed" character of Christians within the Matthean community; that is, the presence of evil in the community. An even more common line of interpretation is to view them as concerned with the Church over against Israel. Our approach is different. The Matthean community views itself as part of Israel, indeed the "best" part. It must explain to itself and to anyone else who may be interested why some Jews accept the gospel and some do not.

Thus the problem facing Matthew was an inner-Jewish situation, not unlike the problem that Jesus himself encountered in his preaching. The difference, of course, arises from the cross and resurrection, from the exalted claims made by Christians about them and the scandal that they constituted for other Jews.

The primary literary form in which this problem is handled is the parable. The most helpful definition of a parable is the one by C. H. Dodd: "a metaphor or simile drawn from nature or common life, arresting the hearer by its vividness or strangeness, and leaving the mind in sufficient doubt of its precise application to tease it into active thought" (p. 5). Various aspects of this definition are confirmed throughout Matt 13:1-52.

The subject matter of the parables is the kingdom of heaven. Every parable but the parable of the sower in Matt 13:1-52 begins with the phrase: "The kingdom of heaven is like . . ." (see 13:24, 31, 33, 44, 45, 47, [52?]). And there is no doubt that the parable of the sower concerns responses to the kingdom of heaven.

The outline for the parables is somewhat unclear. Jesus first addresses the crowds (13:2), instructs the disciples (13:10-23), and addresses "them" (13:24, 31). Then Matthew explains why Jesus always addressed the crowds in parables (13:34-35). Many interpreters assume that the whole first part (13:3-33), except 13:10-23, was meant for the crowds. They find great significance in 13:36 ("he left the crowds and came into the house") as marking off the second part in which the disciples alone are addressed (13:37-52).

Without accepting or rejecting this two-part division, we have divided the translation and comments along other lines: the parable of the sower and its interpretation (Matt 13:1-23), and more parables and interpretations

(13:24-52). This procedure allows us to look at one large unit and related material, and then at several smaller units as constituting a large unit.

The first part of Matthew's "day of parables" (Matt 13:1-23) follows Mark 4:1-20 quite closely. The general structure is the same: the setting (Matt 13:1-3a = Mark 4:1-2), the parable of the sower (Matt 13:3b-9 = Mark 4:3-9), the reason for speaking in parables (Matt 13:10-17 = Mark 4:10-12), and the interpretation of the parable (Matt 13:18-23 = Mark 4:13-20). Whereas Matthew basically reproduces the Markan texts of the parable and its interpretation, he has expanded the setting somewhat and added greatly to the reason for speaking in parables. This overview indicates that what especially concerned Matthew was Jesus' reason for speaking in parables and the contrasting reactions to his parables.

The scene (Matt 13:1-3a) is taken over from Mark and embellished to connect the narrative with what now preceded it. Since Jesus was in a house in Matt 12:46-50, he must now go forth from the house. The picturesque scene of Jesus seated in a boat off the shore and the crowd standing on the shore is taken over from Mark. Matthew's reader would be expected to envision some point along the western shore of the Sea of Galilee. The scene provides an appropriate setting for the final parable in the series—the parable of the fishing net (Matt 13:47-50).

The so-called parable of the sower (Matt 13:3b-9) really focuses on the seeds and their respective yields. The sower merely initiates the action. If we assume that this parable goes back to Jesus (as most interpreters do), it would have been especially appropriate for an audience made up largely of Galilean farmers. Even nonfarmers in an agricultural society would have had some familiarity with seeds and harvests. There is every reason to assume that Matthew's readers also knew something about such matters and could easily relate to them.

There is a longstanding debate about the sower's farming practices. His most eloquent defender was Joachim Jeremias (in *Parables*, 11-12), who insisted that "what appears to the western mind as bad farming is simply customary usage under Palestinian conditions." The basic point is that in Palestine sowing preceded plowing, and so we can assume that the sower intended to come back and plow the seeds into the soil. But the text does not even hint at such a procedure and says nothing about the sower's return. The sower's prodigality is best interpreted as part of the "unusual" character of the story that helps to catch the hearer's attention and to build up tension and suspense.

That the parable of the sower concerns something beyond agriculture is suggested by two texts in 4 Ezra, a Palestinian Jewish writing composed around A.D. 100 that reflects on the theological implications of the destruction of Jerusalem and its Temple in A.D. 70. In this work roughly contemporary with Matthew's Gospel the seed-harvest metaphor is prominent: "For just as the farmer sows many seeds upon the ground and plants a multitude of seedlings, and yet not all that have been sown will come up in due season, and not all that were planted will take root; so all those who have been sown in the world will not be saved" (4 Ezra 8:41). In 4 Ezra 9:31 the seed is equated with the Law ("I sow my Law in you"), and a distinction is made between the eternal character of the seed (the Law) and the perishable character of those who receive the Law but sin (9:32-37). In the Christian context of the Gospels the seed is Jesus' "word of the kingdom," but there is a concern in both the Jewish apocalyptic and early Christian traditions for explaining why not all the plantlings reach an abundant harvest and why only some will do so.

Matthew's most extensive rewriting and adaptation appears in the section about the reason for Jesus' speaking in parables (Matt 13:10-17). He has simplified and clarified the setting, added a saying (Matt 13:12) from Mark 4:25, given the full Septuagint text of Isa 6:9-10, and included a Q saying found also in Luke 10:23-24. The effect of all these editorial modifications and additions is to heighten the contrast between those who have received Jesus' "word of the kingdom" and those who have not.

The theological presupposition of Matt 13:10-17 (and Mark 4:10-12) is the "hardening" motif found in Isa 6:9-10. The allusion to this text in Mark 4:12 is taken over in Matt 13:13, and then the full text is provided in Matt 13:14-15. The biblical context is God's commissioning of Isaiah the prophet. At the end of Isaiah's vision of God's majesty the prophet is sent forth with the paradoxical mission of increasing the obduracy of those to whom he proclaims God's will. The prophet is to continue until destruction and exile occur and only a "stump" (Isa 6:13) or remnant remains. The text would have been an effective tool for early Christians in their efforts to relate Jesus to major biblical figures (here the prophet Isaiah) and to explain why not all Jews accepted the message of Jesus. It also appears in Acts 28:26-27 and John 12:40, and is alluded to in Romans 9–11. Without explaining precisely why the message of Isaiah (and of Jesus) is rejected, the quotation describes the phenomenon of "hardening" on the people's part and presents it as in accord with the Scripture and therefore God's will.

The reasons for the people's "hardening" are spelled out in the interpretation given in the so-called "allegorical" interpretation (Matt 13:18-23) taken over from Mark 4:13-20. The vocabulary is more typical of the Epistles than of the Gospels. The situations described in it probably reflect the failures of some early Christians. It is often taken as a kind of "examination of conscience" or sermon outline based on the parable of the sower. Even the most learned and persistent champion of the authentic words of Jesus attributed this text to the early Church. Thus Joachim Jeremias confessed: "I have long held out against the conclusion that this interpretation must be ascribed to the primitive church; but on linguistic grounds alone it is unavoidable" (*Parables*, 77).

Even though the vocabulary and content of the interpretation suggest an origin in the early Church, such an origin does not necessarily determine Matthew's use of the text. Matthew's major interest was to explain why some Jews refused Jesus' "word of the kingdom." He used the interpretation as a list of reasons why his fellow Jews did not accept and act upon Jesus' preaching: the evil one's activity (Matt 13:19), personal shallowness (13:20-21), and worldly concerns and desire for wealth (13:22). He contrasted them with the ideal disciple who "hears the word and understands" (13:23). Whereas the original interpretation may well have circulated to explain problems within the Christian community after Jesus' death and resurrection, Matthew set it back into Jesus' earthly ministry and used it to illumine the mysterious situation in which some Jews accepted and some Jews rejected the preaching of Jesus.

Matthew took over the parable of the sower, the reason for Jesus' speaking in parables, and the interpretation of the parables from Mark. This material would have been especially appealing to a Jewish-Christian evangelist trying to explain to his largely Jewish-Christian community the mixed reception accorded by Jews to Jesus' preaching. The problem of the gospel's mixed reception was already present in the parable itself, which can be attributed with some confidence to the earthly Jesus. The parable contrasted those who acted upon Jesus' word and those who did not. The additional material reflects further grappling with this difficult and painful matter.

For the Matthean community as it tried to define its identity vis-à-vis other Jews, each part of Matt 13:1-23 carried a slightly different message. Jesus' parable of the sower (13:3b-9) contrasted the three kinds of seeds and soils that do not flourish and the good soil in which a marvelous harvest emerges. The ideal disciple "brings forth fruit" (13:8) in a quantity beyond all imagining, whereas the others fail to produce anything of lasting value. The Matthean community would naturally identify itself with the last seed and soil, and their Jewish rivals or perhaps other Jews in general who had some exposure to Jesus' preaching with the other seeds and soils.

The "insider" status of the Matthean community is strengthened by the sayings about Jesus' use of parables (13:10-17). The spiritual insight of the Matthean Christians is a gift from God that is progressively enriched (13:11-12); they have been blessed beyond the prophets and just ones of old (13:16-17). On the other hand, the obduracy of the "outsiders" is in accord with God's will as expressed in Isa 6:9-10 (13:13-15).

The interpretation of the parable (13:18-23) supplies some concrete reasons for the obduracy of the outsiders: the evil one's activity, personal shallowness, and worldly concerns and the desire for wealth. It also adds to the ideal of the insiders: they hear the word and understand (13:23). It gave the Matthean community at least some insight into what is admittedly a mystery—the mystery of election and rejection. Although the vocabulary of the interpretation reflects the experience within the Church, Matthew's community most likely took it first as a way of explaining their relations with other Jews and only secondarily as referring to problems within the Church.

The "insider"-"outsider" approach to Matt 13:1-23 makes the parable of the sower and related material into a "sectarian" piece that builds up the identity of the "insiders" often at the expense of the "outsiders." Those who seek to actualize such texts in preaching and teaching must recognize the dangers of "sectarian" thinking and make them clear to their audiences. They should stress the positive identity of the Matthean Christians as those who bear fruit, who hear Jesus' word and understand. They need to explain that the "insider"-"outsider" conflict here is a quarrel largely among Jews.

The texts also invite reflection on the mystery of election—a major doctrine for both Jews and Christians—and its reverse—the mystery of rejecting God's word. They also give an insight into the complicated process of tradition that was involved in the making of our Gospels: the parable of Jesus, the early Church's interpretation of it, efforts to deal with the mystery of election/rejection, and the evangelist's framing of the various materials and use of it in the setting of his community.

For Reference and Further Study

Dodd, C. H. *The Parables of the Kingdom.* New York: Scribner's, 1961.

Donahue, J. R. *The Gospel in Parable.* Philadelphia: Fortress, 1988.

Gerhardsson, B. "The Seven Parables in Matthew xiii." *NTS* 19 (1972) 16–37.

Gnilka, J. *Die Verstockung Israels. Isaias 6, 9-10 in der Theologie der Synoptiker.* Munich: Kösel, 1961.

Jeremias, J. *The Parables of Jesus.* New York: Scribner's, 1963.

Kingsbury, J. D. *The Parables of Jesus in Matthew 13. A Study in Redaction-Criticism.* Richmond: John Knox, 1969.

32. *Other Parables* (13:24-52)

24. He set before them another parable, saying: "The kingdom of heaven is like a man who sowed good seed in his field. 25. But while people were sleeping his enemy came and sowed weeds among the wheat and went away. 26. When the stalk sprouted and bore fruit, then the weeds appeared also. 27. The servants of the householder came and said to him: "Sir, did you not sow good seed in your field? How then does it have weeds?" 28. He said to them: "An enemy has done this." The servants said to him: "Do you wish that we go and gather them up?" 29. He said: "No, lest in gathering up the weeds you uproot the wheat along with them. 30. Let them both grow together until the harvest; and at harvest-time I will say to the harvesters: 'Gather the weeds first and tie them in bundles to burn them, but the wheat gather into my barn.' "

31. He set before them another parable, saying: "The kingdom of heaven is like a mustard seed that a man takes and sows in his field. 32. It is smaller than all seeds; but when it grows, it is greater than all garden plants and becomes a tree, so that the birds of the heavens come and nest in its branches."

33. He spoke another parable to them: "The kingdom of heaven is like leaven that a woman takes and hides in three measures of flour until the whole has been leavened."

34. Jesus spoke all these things in parables to the crowds, and he said nothing to them without a parable, 35. in order that what was said through the prophet might be fulfilled: "I will open my mouth in parables, I will utter things hidden from the foundation (of the world)."

36. Then he left the crowds and came into the house. And his disciples came to him and said: "Explain to us the parable of the weeds of the field." 37. He answered and said: "The one who sowed the good seed is the Son of Man. 38. The field is the world. The good seed—these are the sons of the kingdom. The weeds are the sons of the evil one. 39. The enemy who sowed them is the devil. The harvest is the close of the age. The harvesters are angels. 40. Just as the weeds are gathered and burned in the fire, so will it be at the close of the age. 41. The Son of Man will send his angels, and they will gather from his kingdom all the causes of sin and those doing lawless deeds 42. and they will cast them into the furnace of fire. There will be weeping and gnashing of teeth. 43. Then the righteous will shine like the sun in the kingdom of their Father. Whoever has ears should listen.

44. "The kingdom of heaven is like a treasure hidden in the field that a man finds and hides, and out of his joy he goes and sells whatever he has and buys that field. 45. Again the kingdom of heaven is like a merchant seeking fine pearls. 46. On finding one precious pearl he goes and sells everything that he has and buys it.

47. "Again the kingdom of heaven is like a dragnet cast into the sea and taking in every kind (of fish), 48. which, when it has been filled, they pull up on the shore, and they sit down and gather the good ones into contain-

ers and throw out the bad ones. 49. So it will be at the close of the age. The angels will go forth and separate out the evil ones from the midst of the righteous ones, 50. and cast them into the furnace of fire. There will be weeping and gnashing of teeth.

51. "Have you understood all these things?" They said to him: "Yes." 52. He said to them: "Therefore every scribe who has become a disciple for the kingdom of heaven is like a householder who brings out of his treasury new things and old things."

Notes

24. *before them*: Who is the audience? After insisting on the public character of Jesus' teaching at the outset (see Matt 13:1-3a), the bulk of Jesus' instruction up to this point (13:10-23) has been private teaching of the disciples. From a narrative perspective "them" would seem to refer to Jesus' disciples. But Matt 13:34 ("Jesus spoke all these things in parables to the crowds") implies that the audience of Matt 13:24-33 is the crowds.

    is like a man who: The kingdom is like the whole picture drawn in Matt 13:24b-30, not simply the man. As in Matt 13:3b-9 the seed and the process of growth are used to illustrate the nature of God's kingdom. The typically Matthean "kingdom of heaven" is used to refer to the "kingdom of God."

25. *while people were sleeping*: Since a similar motif appears in the parable of the seed growing by itself (Mark 4:26-29), this parable is often explained as the development of or substitute for the Markan parable. At any rate the parables give contrasting pictures of the present until the fullness of the kingdom: trouble-free growth (Mark 4:26-29), and a mixture of good and bad (Matt 13:24-30).

    weeds: The Greek *zizanion* refers to a noxious weed that in its early stages closely resembles wheat and cannot be readily distinguished from it. The Hebrew term is *zûn*, and the Aramaic *zûna*, which the rabbis associated with the root *znh* ("to commit fornication") and explained as the product of sexual excesses in the plant world before the Flood (Lachs, 224).

28. *an enemy has done this*: The phrase blames the presence of evil ones on the "evil one" (see Matt 13:19). It is hard not to make identifications when reading the story: the householder is Jesus, the servants are his followers, the evil ones are their opponents, the evil one is Satan, etc. The disciples want to know how to react to the presence of the evil ones before the close of the age. For the full-scale interpretation see Matt 13:36-43.

30. *Let them both grow together*: The householder's response is one of tolerance in the present. The disciples' acting on their own to separate the good and the bad runs the risk of rooting out the good along with the bad (13:29). The task of judging between good and bad is left to the householder at the harvest and his harvesters.

    until the harvest: For the harvest as an OT metaphor for the last judgment, see Joel 3:13; Hos 6:11; Jer 51:33, etc. See also Rev 14:15-16 as well as 4 Ezra 4:28-29 and 2 Baruch 70:2. In the allegorical explanation (Matt 13:36-43) we are told that "the harvest is the close of the age" (13:40).

to burn them: The bundled weeds would normally be used for fuel and thus destroyed. The good wheat, by way of contrast, could be used in a variety of productive ways.

31. *set before them*: Compared with the narrative frameworks in Mark 4:30 and Luke 13:18, Matthew's framework is simple. It seems likely that Matthew had access to two versions of the parable of the mustard seed (the one in Mark 4:31-32 and the Q version [=Luke 13:19]), and that he used features from both.

    mustard seed: While it is an exaggeration to call the mustard seed the smallest of all seeds, the point of the parable is the small size of the seed in relation to the mature plant. See also Matt 17:20 where the small mustard seed is used to describe the power of faith to move a mountain. Matthew derived the smallest/greatest contrast from Mark 4:31-32; it is not in Luke 13:19 (=Q).

32. *becomes a tree*: This phrase comes from Q; it is absent in Mark 4:32. Its presence prepares for the OT allusion to God's kingdom as a tree in whose branches the birds nest. A mustard bush/tree could reach a height of from eight to twelve feet. Mark 4:32 has the birds nesting beneath the shade of the mustard bush.

    nest: The OT texts most pertinent to the images in Matt 13:32 are Ezek 17:22-24, 31; Ps 104:12; and Dan 4:10-12, 20-27. There may be an allusion to the ingathering of the Gentiles (see *Joseph and Aseneth* 15:7), though this motif is not emphasized here. What is important is the now familiar contrast between the small beginnings of the kingdom and its huge result.

33. *is like leaven*: Leaven is a fermenting agent (like yeast) added to a batch of dough and causing it to rise and expand. Here it is assumed to be a positive life-giving force (not as in Matt 16:6 and 1 Cor 5:6-8).

    three measures of flour: According to Jeremias (*Parables*, 147) this amount would be something like fifty pounds of flour and the bread baked from this amount would provide a meal for more than a hundred persons. As in the parable of the mustard seed there is a contrast between the small amount of leaven and the huge result.

34. *to the crowds*: The phrase makes clear that the crowds were part of the audience for the parables. After the first parable (13:3b-9) this has not been made explicit, and one could imagine that the disciples were the only members of the audience. Matthew omits the idea of Jesus giving the disciples private instruction ("privately to his own disciples he explained everything," Mark 4:34), perhaps because he had already made similar points in Matt 13:10-17 (see Matt 13:36).

35. *through the prophet*: This fulfillment quotation is from Ps 78 (77 LXX):2, suggesting that for Matthew "prophet" was a flexible term. The first half of the quotation conforms exactly to the Septuagint, whereas the second half is an independent translation in which the key word is "hidden." The quotation suggests that the obscurity of Jesus' parables is in accord with God's will as expressed in the Scriptures (see Matt 13:10-17).

    from the foundation (of the world): The phrase "of the world" is not part of Ps

78:2, nor do all the manuscripts of Matt 13:35 have it. But many manuscripts do have it, the context cries out for it, and it is present in Matt 25:34.

36. *Explain to us the parable of the weeds*: The idea of private instruction mentioned in Mark 4:34 is illustrated by means of an allegorical explanation (Matt 13:37-39) and a short apocalypse (13:40-43). On the basis of thirty-seven linguistic features Jeremias (*Parables*, 82-84) declared that it is impossible to avoid the conclusion that the interpretation is the work of Matthew himself.

37. *Son of Man*: The allegorical explanation is a kind of lexicon of seven terms and their equivalents. Most of the identifications arise quite naturally from the parable. The identification of the sower as the Son of Man sets up the apocalyptic scenario in 13:40-43. In both the lexicon and the apocalypse the themes of tolerance in the present and patient waiting are ignored. The same dynamic occurs in 13:49-50.

38. *the sons of the kingdom*: These hear the word and understand it (Matt 13:23), in contrast to the sons of the evil one. In Matt 8:12 "sons of the kingdom" refers to those Jews who will be excluded from the banquet in the kingdom. Here, however, the phrases appear in a positive context to describe the ideal response to Jesus' preaching.

39. *the harvest is the close of the age*: For the background to this image, see the note on Matt 13:30. What follows in 13:40-43 is a picture of the eschatological harvest.

41. *The Son of Man will send his angels*: The only other NT references to the angels of the Son of Man are Matt 16:27 and 24:31. The idea of the kingdom of the Son of Man ("from his kingdom") is unique. Contra Jeremias (*Parables*, 82), there is no reason to identify the kingdom of the Son of Man with the Church or to envision a sharp distinction between the kingdom of the Son of Man and the kingdom of heaven/God.

they will gather: The gathering takes place for the purpose of destruction. In the verb "gather" (*syllegō*) there is probably an allusion to Zeph 1:3. This probability is strengthened by the Hebrew text of Zeph 1:3, which contains the obscure phrase "the stumbling blocks with the wicked," which underlies Matthew's "all the causes of sin and those doing lawless deeds."

42. *cast them into the furnace of fire*: The phrase is taken from Dan 3:6, 11, 15, 20. Yet the OT context is not as directly apocalyptic as the Matthean context is.

weeping and gnashing of teeth: The same expression appears in Matt 8:12; 13:50; 22:13; 24:51; and 25:30, where it occurs in the apocalyptic context.

43. *the righteous will shine*: The reward of the righteous reminds one of Dan 12:3: "And those who are wise shall shine like the brightness of the firmament; and those who turn many to righteousness, like the stars forever and ever." There may be a connection between the "wise" of Daniel and the Matthean disciple who "hears the word and understands."

in the kingdom of their Father: See the note on Matt 13:41. The idea here seems to be that the Son of Man delivers the kingdom to the Father at the close of the age (see Matt 25:34; 1 Cor 15:24).

44. *like a treasure hidden in the field*: Again the kingdom is compared to the whole picture that follows. The two parables (the treasure and the pearl) probably circulated as a pair. They were included in Matthew's "day of parables" on the catchword basis of the term "field" in the first parable. Political conditions in Palestine and the continuing threat of invasion made the burial of one's valuables a common way of protecting them. The implication here seems to be that the present owner had no knowledge of what was hidden in the field. The rabbis debated precisely this point—whether the buyer of the field is entitled to any treasure found in it (Lachs, 229). The parable assumes that he was.

buys that field: The emphasis of this parable (and that of the pearl) is on the great value of what is found (=the kingdom) and the single-minded response that it should elicit. Note the qualification "out of his joy." The emphasis is on the great value of what is discovered, not on what is given up or on the struggle.

45. *like a merchant seeking fine pearls*: The qualification "seeking fine pearls" introduces a different dynamic from the parable of the treasure. The precious material there was a surprise, whereas here it is the result of a deliberate search. In other respects the emphasis is the same: the great value of what is found (=the kingdom), and the single-minded response that it should elicit.

46. *one precious pearl*: Jeremias (*Parables*, 199-200) suggests that the expression is an Aramaism that should be translated "a specially valuable pearl." The association of pearls with other precious stones in Rev 17:4; 18:12, 16; 21:21 indicates their status in the Greco-Roman world.

47. *like a dragnet cast into the sea*: The fish-net is a "seine-net," which is either dragged between two boats, or is laid out by a single boat and drawn to land with long ropes (Jeremias, *Parables*, 225). The dynamic of this parable is the same as that of the wheat and the weeds (Matt 13:24-30); they form a pair.

48. *when it has been filled*: Just as the wheat and weeds must come to ripeness, so the net must be filled before a separating judgment can take place. The term "filled" is related to the "full number" assigned to the Gentiles in Rom 11:25. But here there is no Jew-Gentile distinction. Rather it is righteous versus wicked (or those who hear Jesus' word and those who do not).

the bad ones: The term *sapra* refers to (1) inedible sea-creatures and (2) unclean fish (see Lev 11:10-12) not having fins and scales. As in the parable of the wheat and weeds, the time of separation comes when a certain fullness has been reached. The "bad ones" are thrown out, not thrown back into the sea.

49. *So it will be at the close of the age*: The explanation is similar to that of the wheat and weeds (see Matt 13:36-43); it too probably comes from Matthew himself. The idea of the angels performing the separation appears in Matt 13:41 also. In both cases their role was probably determined by the plural harvesters and fishermen in the parables.

50. *the furnace of fire*: This phrase and what follows ("weeping and gnashing of teeth") appeared also in Matt 13:42. Again the ideas of tolerance and patient waiting implied in the parable proper have given way to themes of judgment and punishment.

51. *understood*: Here "all these things" refers to Jesus' teachings about the kingdom as they are expressed in the parables. They include the presence of the kingdom, its small beginnings, the varied responses to it, its extraordinary fullness in the future, and the judgment that will finally occur.

52. *every scribe who has become a disciple*: The expression is sometimes taken as a self-portrait of the evangelist. Originally charged with drawing up legal documents, scribes developed skill in legal matters and the interpretation of the Torah. The verb *mathēteutheis* ("who has become a disciple," or "has been trained") even sounds like the name "Matthew." Whether it alludes to Matthew or not, the more general application is to the Matthean Christian who treasures the old (the Jewish heritage) and the new (what has happened in and through Jesus).

like a householder: The comparison is with the householder who brings out of his treasury new things and old things. Both new and old are valued; the new does not make the old useless.

Interpretation

The rest of Matthew's "day of parables" combines material from Mark, Matthew's special tradition, and Matthew himself: the parable of the wheat and weeds (13:24-30), the parable of the mustard seed (13:31-32), the parable of the leaven (13:33), the reason for Jesus' use of parables (13:34-35), an explanation of the parable of the wheat and weeds (13:36-43), the parables of the hidden treasure (13:44), and the pearl (13:45-46), the parable of the dragnet (13:47-50), and the parable of the householder (13:51-52). Matthew used Mark for 13:31-32, 34-35. He probably composed the two explanations (13:36-43, 49-50) by himself. The remainder (13:24-30, 33, 44-48) is most likely attributable to M, the special tradition(s) found only in Matthew.

The parable of the wheat and weeds (13:24-30) follows upon the parable of the sower. The setting is agricultural, and the subject is the mixed reception accorded Jesus' word of the kingdom. The problem faced in the parable is the fact that some Jews accept and others reject the gospel. The issue before the Christians is, How do we react to this reality? The parable, which surely has allegorical features (though not as many as Matt 13:36-43 supplies), counsels patience and tolerance in the present. The assumption behind this counsel is the confidence that at the final judgment there will be a separation between the just and the unjust along with appropriate rewards and punishments.

The same dynamic underlies the parable of the dragnet (13:47-50). Though not the elaborate story that Matt 13:24-30 is, the problem is the same: how to deal with the mixed response accorded the gospel. And the solution is also the same: patience and tolerance until the final judgment, when God will set matters straight.

The parables, which are so close as to constitute a pair, reflect an approach common in Jewish apocalyptic writings. A good example is the ''instruction'' on the two spirits in the Qumran *Manual of Discipline* (1QS cols. 3–4). That text divides humankind into two segments: The ''sons of light'' who follow the Prince of Light and do the deeds of light, and the ''sons of darkness'' who follow the ''Angel of Darkness'' and do the deeds of darkness. These two groups walk in their two ways until the final end. But God ''has set an end for the existence of perversity; and at the time of visitation he will destroy it forever. Then truth shall arise in the world forever'' (1QS 4:18-19). The same point is made later: ''For God has allotted these spirits in equal parts until the final end, the time of renewal'' (1QS 4:25).

The two parables and the Qumran text try to deal with what their writers reckoned as misguided and even morally reprehensible behavior. The particular problem facing both groups is how are the ''insiders'' to react. The solution is to leave judgment to God in the end-time. For the present the proper response is patience and tolerance born from the conviction that in the end God will make all things right.

The other four parables (13:31-32, 33, 44, 45-46) come in pairs. All concern the kingdom of heaven but not the particular problem of the mixed response to Jesus' preaching about the kingdom. Rather they provide information about the nature of the Kingdom and how one should respond to it.

At this point the basic significance of these disparate materials in Matt 13:24-52 is clear. The general topic is the kingdom of God. The particular problem is the mystery of the rejection and acceptance of Jesus' word of the kingdom. The two traditional parables—the wheat and the weeds, and the dragnet—put forth a message of trust in God's final judgment in the future and patient tolerance in the present. If it is correct to attribute the explanations of those parables (13:36-43, 49-50) to Matthew himself, then it seems that his special interest was the future judgment. Nevertheless, he was sufficiently concerned also with the theme of patient tolerance that he included the two parables.

The two pairs of parables in Matt 13:31-33 and 13:44-46 highlight the contrast between small beginnings and great results as well as the inestimable value of the kingdom. They serve to make rejection of Jesus' message and the presence of the kingdom in his ministry all the more mysterious. The quotation of Ps 78 (77):2 added to the saying about Jesus' use of parables in teaching the crowds asserts that this style of teaching—and its resultant incomprehension—was in accord with God's will.

If we are correct that Matt 13:1-52 concerns the same basic problem as Romans 9–11 does, it appears that Matthew has focused on only part of the problem and given reasons for Jewish rejection of the gospel. He has also advised Christians on how to deal with their fellow Jews who reject the gospel.

The message of patient tolerance and leaving to God the settling of scores is timely today also. For a world in which so many conflicts occur on the basis of religion, race, ethnic identity, and so forth, this is sound advice. As Christians and Jews try to work toward a more positive and trusting relationship, Matthew's message is at least a first, minimal step on the way to recovering the fuller and more adequate approach outlined by Paul in Romans 11. And, of course, readers of all generations need to be reminded of the wondrous promise and surpassing value of the kingdom of God that are sketched so neatly in the little parables in pairs.

33. *Rejection by His Own* (13:53-58)

53. And when Jesus finished these parables, he went away from there. 54.
And coming into his hometown he taught them in their synagogue, so that
they were amazed and said: "Where did this fellow get this wisdom and
mighty works? 55. Is not this the son of the craftsman? Is not his mother
called Mary and his brothers James and Joseph and Simon and Judas? 56.
And are not all his sisters among us? Where then did this fellow get all
this?" 57. And they took offense at him. But Jesus said to them: "A prophet
is not without honor except in his hometown and in his own household."
58. And he did not do many mighty works there on account of their unbelief.

Notes

53. *Jesus finished these parables*: The Matthean transition gives the impression that the parables and related matter in Matt 13:1-52 were delivered as a single speech. The term "finished" (*teleō*) appears at the end of other Matthean discourses (7:28; 11:1; 19:1; 26:1) and serves as a sign that a major speech has concluded and now Jesus moves on to other activities.

54. *hometown*: The Greek term *patris* is ambiguous. It can mean "fatherland, homeland" in the broad sense or "hometown, one's own part of the country" in the narrow sense. Here the narrow sense is meant. The rest of the story assumes it, since it is obviously the place where Jesus' family lives (see Luke 4:16) and where he is known to his neighbors. Efforts to interpret *patris* as Israel in general go much too far.

in their synagogue: Mark 6:2 simply reads "in the synagogue." In Matthew "their synagogue" is used to describe the synagogues controlled by the Jewish opponents of the Christian community. Here it is not quite so clear, since "their" could merely refer to the people of Nazareth. Even so, their hostile reaction to Jesus and his teaching places them on the side of the opponents of Jesus and his followers.

they were amazed: The initial reaction is surprise—at least neutral and perhaps even positive. At the end their negative attitude ("they took offense at him") is assigned to their unbelief. The longer version in Luke 4:16-30 gives much more attention to the shifts in the crowd's reactions.

this wisdom and mighty works: The phrase summarizes Jesus' activities as a teacher and healer. Unlike Luke 4:16-30 which serves as Jesus' inaugural discourse, in Matthew there has been ample material illustrating the wisdom and mighty works of Jesus. The crowd wants to know the origin ("from where?") of Jesus' power: Is it from God or the devil?

55. *the son of the craftsman*: The usual translation of *tektōn* is "carpenter," one who works with wood. That may be too narrow a translation, and a more general term like "craftsman" or "builder" may be preferable. Note that Mark 6:3 reads: "Is not this the craftsman?" Matthew modifies it to "son of the craftsman," because to him and his readers Jesus was much more than a craftsman.

Is not his mother called Mary: The reference to Jesus in Mark 6:3 as "son of Mary" is unusual or perhaps even insulting, since a son would normally be named with reference to his father ("son of Joseph"). It is unlikely that Mark wanted to indicate that Joseph was dead or that he was alluding to Jesus' virginal conception. Matthew has modified the unusual or insulting reference.

his brothers: From antiquity this term has been interpreted in three different ways: Jesus' siblings, the children of Mary and Joseph (Helvidius); Joseph's children by an earlier marriage, therefore the step brothers (and sisters) of Jesus (Epiphanius); or relatives such as cousins (Jerome). It is not clear that Matthew knew the tradition of the perpetual virginity of Mary (see Matt 1:25). For a full discussion see *Mary in the New Testament*, 65-72.

Joseph: In the other three names (James, Simon, Judas) Matt 13:55 agrees with Mark 6:3. But most manuscripts of Mark 6:3 read "Justus" where Matt 13:55 has "Joseph."

56. *Where then . . .* : Matthew has the crowd begin and end with the same question about the origin of Jesus' teaching and mighty works (cf. Mark 6:3).

57. *they took offense at him*: The verb derives from the stem *skandal-*, which refers to a stumbling block. In other words, the people took offense at Jesus and so turned their anger and opposition against him.

a prophet is not without honor: Jesus' comment on the situation has the ring of a popular proverb and is entirely appropriate to the situation. Between "hometown" and "household" Mark 6:4 has "and among his relatives."

58. *he did not do many mighty works there*: It is usually said that Matthew softens Mark 6:5 ("he could not do any mighty work there") which seems to make Jesus' ability to heal dependent upon the faith of the people. That may be so. Yet Matt 13:58 can simply be taken as an economical version of the long and awkward sentence in Mark 6:5. Both agree that Jesus did do *some* mighty works there.

Interpretation

The rejection of Jesus in the synagogue of his hometown occurs immediately after the "day of parables" in which the major theme is the rejection of Jesus and his message. Between the Markan parables-discourse (Mark 4:1-34) and the rejection at Nazareth (Mark 6:1-6) there is a series of Jesus' mighty deeds in which he shows his power over the storm (Mark 4:35-41), demons (5:1-20), and sickness and death (5:21-43). Matthew has already used this material in chapters 8–9, and so in his narrative the "day of parables" is followed immediately by the rejection at Nazareth. Thus the rejection of Jesus mentioned in the parables is made concrete and "comes home."

Moreover, the "day of parables" was preceded in Matt 12:46-50 (as in Mark 3:31-35) with the contrast between the natural family of Jesus ("his mother and his brothers") and his "real," spiritual family ("whoever does the will of my Father in heaven"). Thus in Matthew's outline the day of parables with its theme of the rejection of Jesus' preaching is sandwiched in between texts that deal with Jesus' family and neighbors.

Matthew follows Mark's text fairly closely. Most of his changes are editorial rather than substantive. In both Gospels the reader has already been given abundant examples of Jesus' teaching and mighty deeds. A very different situation pertains in Luke 4:16-30, where the incident in Nazareth takes place at the very beginning of Jesus' public ministry. In general, Matthew's version is shorter and clearer than Mark's is. Matthew's most distinctive change is the expression "their synagogue" (Matt 13:54) in place of "the synagogue" (Mark 6:2).

Given the presence of Jesus' family and their neighbors as well as the use of the term *patris* ("hometown"), the reader would assume that the incident takes place in Nazareth (see Matt 2:23). The synagogue was a place of gathering or assembly where Jews could hear the Scriptures, pray, and listen to teaching and exhortations. The Greek word *synagōgē* means "gathering" and can refer both to the assembly of people and to the place where they assemble. The archaeological evidence for Jewish synagogues in Palestine is abundant from the third century A.D. onward; see L. T. Levine (ed.), *Ancient Synagogues Revealed* (Detroit: Wayne State University, 1982). But the origin of the synagogues is shrouded in mystery, and the first century A.D. is a shadowy period in the history of the synagogue. With regard to Matt 13:53-58 it is difficult to be certain how Matthew's readers would have imagined the scene. Did they think of an "assembly of people" or a "building?" The problem is that we do not know how formal and fixed an institution the synagogue was in the first century, and how closely it was associated with a building. At any rate, there was no obstacle to someone like Jesus teaching in the synagogue (see also Luke 4:16-30 for more hints about the order of the synagogue service).

The episode takes place in the cultural context of village life. Even if Matthew's readers lived in a big city like Antioch, they would have known the dynamics of village life in the ancient Near East. While not a tiny village, Nazareth was hardly a major city either (see John 1:46). People knew one another and kept track of family lines. They measured themselves in relation to one another, not as autonomous individuals in the modern West; see B. J. Malina, "The Individual and the Community—Personality in the Social World of Early Christianity," *BTB* 9 (1979) 126–38.

Because the people of Nazareth knew about Jesus' family and presumably knew him personally from the past, they assumed that they knew all there was to know. They cannot understand that the source of his wisdom and mighty deeds is God.

To readers conversant with synagogues and village life the story of Jesus' rejection at Nazareth would have been easily understandable. Matthew's readers, however, would have been especially sensitive to his change of Mark's text to read "in their synagogue." The expression has already occurred in Matt 4:23; 9:35; 10:17; 12:9; see also the "synagogues of the hypocrites" (6:2, 5; 23:6, 34). It refers to the Jewish communities led and controlled by the opponents of the Matthean community. Matthew's use of "their synagogue" suggests that there is a kinship between the people of Nazareth who rejected Jesus and those Jews who reject him in Matthew's day.

The placing of this episode immediately after the "day of parables" without the intervening "mighty deeds" of Mark 4:35–5:41 has the effect of making concrete and personal the opposition to Jesus reflected upon in Matt 13:1-52. It also raises the question about who constitutes the true family of Jesus (see Matt 12:46-50). The Matthean community, of course, viewed itself as the true family of Jesus in contrast with the people of Nazareth and perhaps even members of Jesus' own family.

One approach to actualizing this text is to present it as an example of the "prejudice of familiarity." Because the people of Jesus' hometown assumed that they already knew all there was to know about Jesus, they dismissed him. In fact, their knowledge was superficial and insignificant in comparison with what Matthew has told us about him. But Jesus' neighbors use their past knowledge of Jesus to categorize him and dismiss him. While twentieth-century Western readers may not share the experience of village life, they do meet the prejudice of familiarity in their offices, schools, churches, and families. "Where did this fellow get all this?" is not a reaction peculiar to the first century in Palestine.

For Reference and Further Study

Van Segbroeck, F. "Jésus rejeté par sa patrie (Mt 13, 54-58)." *Bib* 49 (1968) 167–98.

34. *The Death of John the Baptist* (14:1-12)

1. In that time Herod the tetrarch heard about the fame of Jesus. 2. And he said to his servants: "This is John the Baptist. He has been raised from the dead, and therefore the powers are at work in him." 3. For Herod had seized John, bound him, and put him in prison on account of Herodias the wife of Philip his brother. 4. For John said to him: "It is not lawful for you to have her." 5. And he wished to kill him but was afraid of the crowd, because they held him as a prophet. 6. But when it was Herod's birthday the daughter of Herodias danced in their midst and pleased Herod, 7. so that he swore with an oath to give to her whatever she might ask. 8. Prompted by her mother, she said: "Give to me here upon a platter the head of John the Baptist." 9. The king became sad but on account of the oaths and the guests he commanded it to be given. 10. And he sent and had John beheaded in prison. 11. And his head was brought upon the platter and given to the girl, and she brought it to her mother. 12. And his disciples came forward and took the corpse and buried him, and they went and told Jesus.

Notes

1. *tetrarch*: In place of Mark's designation of Herod Antipas as "king," Matthew provides the more correct "tetrarch." After Herod the Great's death in 4 B.C. his kingdom had been divided among his sons, with Herod Antipas receiving control over Galilee and Perea. The word "tetrarch" means "ruler of a fourth" or "one of four rulers" (see Luke 3:1). A tetrarch was lower than an ethnarch ("ruler of a nation"), which in turn was lower than a king. Note, however, Matt 14:9 where Matthew joins Mark 6:26 in referring to Herod Antipas as a king.

2. *he said to his servants*: There is some ambiguity in the manuscripts of Mark 6:14 whether the proper reading is "he said" or "they said." Most textual critics prefer "they said" because of what follows in Mark 6:15. For Matthew, however, it was clear that here "Herod" is the speaker.

   the powers are at work in him: The "powers" allude to miraculous happenings. The mighty deeds done by Jesus are attributed to supernatural powers at work in John the Baptist "living again." Herod's reasoning is not inconsistent with John 10:41 ("John did no sign"), since it is based on new powers granted to John after his resurrection from the dead. Matthew omits other popular speculations about Jesus (Elijah, the prophet) found in Mark 6:15 (and Luke 9:8), though he does use the list in Matt 16:13-14.

3. *in prison*: According to Josephus, John the Baptist was imprisoned at Machaerus, located at the northeast corner of the Dead Sea near the Judean wilderness. The court of Herod was located at Tiberias in Galilee. It is not clear precisely where the reader is to imagine the events of Matthew 14:3-12 to have taken place. For a defense of Machaerus as the place in the light of recent excavations, see F. Manns, "Marc 6, 21-29 à la lumière des dernières fouilles du Machéronte," *SBFLA* 31 (1981) 287–90.

Herodias: Matthew follows Mark in erroneously describing Herodias as the wife of Philip. In fact she was first married to a paternal half-uncle named Herod whom she abandoned to marry Herod Antipas, another half-uncle (see Josephus, *Ant.* 18:136).

4. *it is not lawful*: The law in question is Lev 18:16: "You shall not uncover the nakedness of your brother's wife; she is your brother's nakedness" (see Lev 20:21). In his work of abbreviation Matthew left out mention of Herodias' resentment of John's claims and thus decreases the dramatic impact. He makes Herod Antipas into the main opponent and renders the actions of Herodias and Salome somewhat mysterious.

5. *they held him as a prophet*: Matthew's description of Herod's estimation of John is shorter and less complicated than Mark's from a literary perspective. It is also somewhat closer to Josephus' account from a historical perspective. In the process the portrayal of Herodias as a Jezebel figure (see 1 Kings 21) is softened.

6. *it was Herod's birthday*: Mark 6:21 gives a guest-list ("his courtiers and officers and the leading men of Galilee") that suggests that the banquet took place in Tiberias rather than Machaerus. Matthew's omission of this list may have been due simply to his editorial technique of omitting extraneous details. It is possible, however, that he sought to avoid the impression that Tiberias was the place of the banquet.

   the daughter of Herodias danced: According to Josephus her name was Salome. She was the daughter of Herodias and Herod. She later married her uncle Herod Philip the tetrarch. That a Herodian princess should perform a dance in the setting of Herod's birthday party seems odd (see Esther 1, where Queen Vashti refuses such a display). Given the morals of the Herod family, however, it is not impossible.

7. *to give her whatever she might ask*: Mark 6:23 ("up to half my kingdom") is a clear allusion to Esth 5:3 and the promise of the Persian king Ahasaerus to Esther ("It shall be given you, even to the half of my kingdom"). Matthew either was not sensitive to the allusion or deliberately sought to suppress it.

8. *upon a platter the head of John*: The Greek term *pinax* originally referred to a board or plank. It later came to mean a wide, flat dish. In the Markan account where John's death is more the result of Herodias' scheming, the request made by Salome constitutes a gruesome climax. In Matthew the dramatic effect is not so clear.

9. *the king became sad*: Herod is portrayed as torn between his public promise and the horrible request. His reputation is more important than the killing of John. The OT model of one who made a foolish vow is Jephthah (see Judg 11:29-40). Herod's oaths and the presence of the guests lead him forward into even greater depravity. Note that Matthew follows Mark 6:26 in referring to Herod as a king.

10. *had John beheaded in prison*: The implication is that John was imprisoned not far from where the birthday party was taking place.

11. *the girl*: The Greek word *korasion* appears also in Matt 9:24-25, where it describes the twelve-year-old daughter of Jairus. Salome, who was born in A.D. 10, would

have been at least eighteen or nineteen during this incident. The idea of passing around John's head adds to the reader's revulsion.

12. *took the corpse*: The action by John's disciples points forward to what will happen to the corpse of Jesus (see Matt 27:57-61), thus suggesting that the parallelism between John and Jesus extends even to their deaths. Only Matthew adds that John's disciples informed Jesus about what had taken place.

Interpretation

Following the rejection of Jesus in his hometown comes an account of Herod Antipas, who ruled over the territory in which Jesus' hometown was situated and over the entire area in which Jesus carried out his Galilean ministry. In this account Herod expresses the opinion that Jesus was really John the Baptist come back to life. There is no way of knowing how widespread this opinion was. That there were similarities between John and Jesus has already been emphasized in Matt 3:1–4:17. But no other source goes so far as Mark 6:14 (= Matt 14:2) in equating the two and making Jesus into the reincarnation of John.

Herod's speculation about the relationship between John and Jesus leads to a flashback (Matt 14:3-12) about how John died. In 4:12 Matthew had told us that John had been arrested and Jesus had been informed about it. Now he tells us with the help of his Markan source how John came to die. In doing so he continues the theme of the rejection of Jesus by his own—first by his neighbors in Nazareth (Matt 13:53-58) and now by the political ruler of his home area.

Matthew's story of John's death follows Mark 6:14-29. A glance at a Gospel synopsis shows that Matthew has shortened and simplified his Markan source—typical ways in which Matthew acted as an editor. The most notable change comes in Matthew's tendency to shift the attention to Herod Antipas and to put on him more of the blame for John's death (see Matt 14:3-10).

There is another ancient narrative about John's death—in Josephus' *Antiquities* 18:118-119. Josephus had already described John as a good man who exhorted Jews to lead righteous lives and to join in baptism. The apocalyptic dimension of John's preaching is completely omitted by Josephus. Nevertheless, according to Josephus, Herod Antipas became alarmed at John's popularity and feared that his movement might result in some form of sedition: "Herod decided therefore that it would be much better to strike first and be rid of him before his work led to an uprising, than to wait for an upheaval, get involved in a difficult situation, and see his mistake." And so, according to Josephus, Herod had John brought in chains to Machaerus and put to death in that stronghold.

There are some clear differences between Josephus and Mark regarding the death of John the Baptist. Whereas in Josephus it occurs at Machaerus (a fortress-place across the Jordan, in the southern part of Herod's Perean territory), one might assume from the guest-list in Mark 6:21 ("his courtiers and officers and the leading men of Galilee") that it took place in Tiberias where Herod Antipas had his court. For Josephus, John was perceived by Herod as a political threat who had to be eliminated. But for Mark, John's death came as the result of John's criticism of the marriage between Herod Antipas and Herodias that constituted incest according to Lev 18:16; 20:21 in the sense of marrying the wife of one's own brother. Also the Markan account seems to have gotten the relationships within the Herod family a bit confused. Herodias had been married to Herod, not Philip; Salome married Philip.

Mark's mistake about the marriage relationship may give us a clue about the roots of his story. It is a popular tale, even a piece of gossip or scandal. It is told in a very artistic way, making Herodias into an archetypal villain, Herod Antipas into a weak fool, and Salome into a mindless temptress. It may well have a factual basis. Nevertheless, there are clear affinities with the OT stories of Jezebel (1 Kings 21) and the book of Esther (the banquet scene, the dancing girl, the king's promise of "up to half my kingdom"). On the contrary, Josephus' story is far less vivid in artistry and far more political in its concern. John is presented as another threat to the political stability of Palestine. Herod had him executed as such, though in Josephus' estimate he was wrong to do so and was punished for it.

Matthew repeats Mark's story, though in an abbreviated and simplified form. It is worth noting that Matthew plays down the role of Herodias and lessens the OT reminiscence of Jezebel and Esther. Herod Antipas becomes a more prominent agent (see Matt 14:3-5) from the start, not simply a willing dupe of the women's plot. Is it possible that Matthew too knew a story about John's death like the one incorporated into Josephus' *Antiquities* and tried to join it together with Mark's story?

As in Mark 6:14-29, a major theme in Matthew's story of John's death is its function as a preview of Jesus' death. Both are rejected by political rulers and executed without cause and without legal formality being observed. The task of burying each is left to their followers. As John went, so Jesus will go. For early Christians facing opposition the example given by John and Jesus would have been powerful.

As we have seen, Matthew heightens the role of Herod Antipas in John's death. Whether he did so because he knew the story that Josephus knew or for some other reason, the effect is to emphasize the rejection of Jesus by his own. First it was the people of Nazareth (13:53-58). Here it is the ruler of Galilee who has John executed and thinks of Jesus along the same lines. Herod Antipas had official status. The rejection of John and Jesus by him was significant for Matthew's community as they tried to sort out where they stood with respect to Jewish and Gentile rulers.

The contrasting characters in the story give a clue toward its actualization. The fearless prophet John who proclaims God's will without concern for the consequences stands over against Herod Antipas, Herodias, and Salome—an unattractive, even despicable bunch. Taken as an opposing pair, they make concrete the contrast between good and evil sketched in some of the parables of chapter 13.

The fate of the faithful prophet is another theme appropriate for actualization. The line of faithful prophets neither began with John nor does it end with Jesus. Rather it reaches back to the great figures of the Hebrew Bible and forward to the courageous martyrs of the Jewish and Christian traditions. The dynamics of this theme—personal courage, fidelity to principles, opposition from evil people, tragic death—are available in Matt 14:1-12.

For Reference and Further Study

Cope, L. "The Death of John the Baptist in the Gospel of Matthew; or, the Case of the Confusing Conjunction." *CBQ* 38 (1976) 515–19.

Murphy-O'Connor, J. "The Structure of Matthew XIV–XVII." *RB* 82 (1975) 360–84.

35. *The Feeding of the Five Thousand* (14:13-21)

13. On hearing this Jesus went away from there in a boat to a deserted place
by himself. But the crowds heard and followed him by foot from the cities.
14. On coming forth he saw a great crowd and took pity on them and healed
their sick. 15. When it was evening the disciples approached him, saying:
"The place is deserted, and the hour has already passed. Dismiss the crowds
in order that they may go away into the villages and buy food for themselves." 16. But Jesus said to them: "They have no need to go away. You
give them something to eat." 17. But they said to him: "We do not have
anything here except five loaves and two fish." 18. But he said: "Bring them
here to me." 19. And he commanded the crowds to recline upon the grass,
took the five loaves and two fish, looked up to heaven and blessed, and
broke, and gave to his disciples the loaves; and the disciples (gave) to the
crowds. 20. And all ate and were satisfied. And they took what was left
over of the fragments, twelve baskets full. 21. And about five thousand men
apart from women and children were eating.

Notes

13. *hearing this*: In Matthew's narrative what Jesus heard was the report of John's death (14:12), though the sequence is awkward since the story of John's death was a flashback. Since Matthew had already used the sending forth of the twelve in chapter 10, he could not use the apostles' return (see Mark 6:30-31) at this point.

a deserted place: The Greek word for "deserted" is *erēmos,* which is related to the term for "desert." The reader is not supposed to imagine a real desert here since the place is obviously by the Sea of Galilee. Nevertheless, the presence of *erēmos* brings with it the allusion to ancient Israel's wandering in the wilderness and God's feeding Israel with the manna.

the crowds heard and followed him: Matthew omits the note in Mark 6:33 that the crowds on foot got to the deserted place before Jesus did. The omission is best understood as part of Matthew's editorial policy of avoiding extraneous details.

14. *took pity on them*: Matthew omits the reason for Jesus' pity according to Mark 6:34: "for they were like sheep not having a shepherd" (see Num 27:17; 1 Kgs 22:17; Ezek 34:5-6).

healed their sick: The statement about Jesus' healing activity takes the place of the expression in Mark 6:34: "and he began to teach them many things." It implies that the crowds stayed around more for Jesus' healing activity than for his teaching.

15. *the hour has already passed*: The "hour" is the time for dinner. That the "deserted place" is not a desert is indicated by the presence of towns round about in which the people could buy food. The traditional location of the multiplication is the region of et-Tabgha.

16. *They have no need to go away*: Matthew adds this brief comment by Jesus as a way of shortening and clarifying the exchange in Mark 6:37-38. Jesus makes the disciples understand right from the start that he is not thinking about having the crowds go away and get food in the surrounding villages. Instead the disciples are to give them food.

17. *five loaves and two fish*: There is no clear symbolic significance associated with the numbers five and two. The reason for the fish has always been a puzzle for those who search for symbolism. It has been interpreted as proof that fish were used in early Christian Eucharists, as related to the quails on which Israel was fed in the wilderness (Num 11:31; Wis 19:12), or as part of the messianic banquet (4 Ezra 6:52; 2 Bar 29:4).

18. *Bring them here to me*: This command by Jesus (not in Mark 6:38) establishes the dynamics of the Matthean episode in which Jesus gives orders and the disciples carry them out.

19. *to recline upon the grass*: Matthew simplifies the colorful and complicated description in Mark 6:39-40. Since reclining referred to the position for eating, the idea is that Jesus ordered the crowds to get ready to eat.

looked up to heaven and blessed: Jesus performs the role of the father at a typical Jewish meal. The blessing would have been the traditional Jewish blessing before meals: "Blessed are You, O Lord our God, king of the universe, who brings forth bread from the earth." The blessing is followed by the breaking of the bread and the distribution of the pieces. The language here points forward to the Last Supper (Matt 26:26).

the loaves: Note that unlike in Mark 6:41 there is no mention of the distribution of fish, despite the fact that they were just mentioned. The distribution by the disciples is sometimes explained as part of the Eucharistic anticipation in the story. Matthew makes explicit the disciples' share in giving out the bread.

20. *all ate and were satisfied*: There may be an allusion here to Deut 8:10 ("you shall eat and be full, and you shall bless the Lord your God"), though the word for "satisfied" is not the same in Matt/Mark and the Septuagint.

twelve baskets: The Greek word *kōphinos* refers to large heavy baskets, made of wicker. Juvenal (*Satires* 3.14; 6.542) used the term in Latin to refer to the baskets in which Jews carried food. The number "twelve" is generally accorded symbolic significance associated with the twelve tribes of Israel.

21. *apart from women and children*: By adding this phrase to Mark 6:44 Matthew enlarges the numbers of people affected by the multiplication, thus making it even more spectacular.

Interpretation

Matthew's account of Jesus feeding the five thousand is paralleled in the other three Gospels (see Mark 6:35-44; Luke 9:12-17; John 6:1-15). The story of Jesus feeding four thousand people appears in Matt 15:32-39 and Mark 8:1-10. The first feeding story in Matthew is clearly based on Mark 6:35-44 as its source. Matthew has abbreviated and simplified the Markan account. His chief contribution has been to upgrade the image of Jesus' disciples. Whereas in Mark the disciples misunderstand much of what takes place and need explanations at every point, in Matthew they show more understanding and function more clearly and positively as assistants to Jesus. They understand but are lacking in faith.

The first multiplication of loaves and fish in Matthew is occasioned by the enthusiasm of the crowds following Jesus and his ministering to them (Matt 14:13-14). Because the crowds are in an isolated place and without food, the disciples suggest that Jesus send them away to buy food in the nearby villages. Jesus refuses their suggestion and orders the disciples to feed the crowds. When they protest that they have only five loaves and two fish, Jesus nevertheless proceeds to feed the crowds by means of the five loaves and two fish, with the disciples serving as distributors. The amazing result is that all ate and were satisfied, and there was even a huge amount of leftovers.

In Matthew's order of events the first feeding follows the flashback about the death of John the Baptist, which also took place in the context of a banquet. The juxtaposition of Herod's banquet and Jesus' banquet is powerful. At Herod's banquet there is pride and arrogance, scheming, and even murder. It takes place at a royal court. At Jesus' banquet there is healing, trust, and sharing. It takes place in a "deserted" place—an *erēmos* like the wilderness in which ancient Israel was fed with manna.

The biblical model for Jesus feeding the five thousand appears in 2 Kings 4:42-44. The prophet Elisha orders his servant to set twenty loaves of barley and some fresh ears of grain before a hundred men. The servant resists at first but then follows the prophet's order. The crowd is fed, and there is even some left over:

> A man came from Ba'al-shal'ishah, bringing the man of God bread of the first fruits, twenty loaves of barley, and fresh ears of grain in his sack. And Elisha said, "Give to the men, that they may eat." But his servant said, "How am I to set this before a hundred men?" So he repeated, "Give them to the men, that they may eat, for thus says the Lord, 'They shall eat and have some left.' " So he set it before them. And they ate, and had some left, according to the word of the Lord.

There are some obvious parallels between 2 Kgs 4:42-44 and Matt 14:13-21: the small amount of food available, the skepticism and protests of the servant and Jesus' disciples, the successful feeding of a large crowd, and the surprising amount of food left over. The numbers in the Matthean account, of course, are much larger than those of the OT text, indicating a certain superiority on Jesus' part.

While the Matthean account points backward to the Elisha story, it also is worded in such a way as to point forward to Jesus' Last Supper and to the Christian celebration of the Eucharist. This motif is clearest in Matt 14:19: ". . . took the five loaves and two fish, looked up to heaven and blessed, and broke, and gave to his disciples the loaves." On the one hand, this wording prepares the reader for Matt 26:26: "Jesus took bread and blessed and broke it and gave it to his disciples . . ." On the other hand, the Matthean Christians were most likely familiar with the content of Matt 26:26 from their Eucharistic celebrations and were therefore sensitive to the Eucharistic dimension of the multiplication story.

The forward thrust of the Matthean multiplication account does not stop with the Last Supper and the Eucharist. Rather it points beyond to the kingdom of God pictured in Jewish and Christian piety as a banquet. A familiar OT example of this motif is Isa 25:6: "On this mountain the Lord of hosts will make for all peoples a feast of fat things, a feast of wine on the lees, of fat things full of marrow, of wine on the lees well refined." The motif seems to have been the presupposition on which the ritual meals of the Qumran community were based (see 1 QS 6:4-5; 1QS^{a} 2:17-22); those meals were understood to be anticipations of the heavenly banquet in God's kingdom.

The banquet saying in Matt 8:11-12 (''many will come from east and west and sit at table with Abraham, Isaac, and Jacob in the kingdom of heaven'') and the banquet parable in Matt 22:1-10 (''The kingdom of heaven may be compared to a king who gave a marriage feast for his son . . .'') are obvious Matthean examples of this motif.

The historical basis of the multiplication of the loaves and fish has long been a topic of controversy. On the one hand, it appears in all four Gospels and twice in two of them (Matthew and Mark), thus passing the test of multiple attestation. On the other hand, the accounts contain some elements that carry symbolic significance: the setting in the wilderness, the pattern set by Elisha in 2 Kgs 4:42-44, the assimilation of the language to that of the Last Supper and the Eucharist, and the number (twelve) of baskets containing the leftovers. Was there an event behind the symbolic narrative, and what was its nature?

Rationalistic explanations seem embarrassingly shallow. One such explanation suggests that Jesus urged the crowd to share among themselves the food that individuals had brought along. Then this ''miracle'' of sharing was interpreted as a miraculous action performed by Jesus. On the other hand, taking the accounts as a perfect reproduction of what actually took place can lead the reader to miss the rich symbolism present in the texts. This is probably a case in which we will never be absolutely certain about the event behind the text, and it is fruitless to spend too much time and effort in worrying about it.

The attentive reader of Matthew's Gospel might be impressed by two peculiar features in Matt 14:13-21: the narrative link with Herod's banquet, and the effort to improve the image of Jesus' disciples. By contrasting it to Herod Antipas' banquet with its immoral actions leading up to the death of John the Baptist, the banquet over which Jesus presides in the wilderness emerges all the more splendidly. By giving Jesus' disciples a more positive role in the story and having them obey Jesus' commands, Matthew has continued his conscious program of upgrading the picture of the twelve that he found in his Markan source.

Nevertheless, the central theme of Matt 14:13-21 is the banquet over which Jesus presides. By following Mark's lead, Matthew is careful to place the wilderness banquet in line with the Last Supper and the Church's Eucharist. The way in which the story is told also relates it to God's feeding of Israel in the wilderness (*erēmos*) and to Elisha's miraculous feeding of one hundred men. Other developments of the banquet theme in Matthew (8:11-12; 22:1-10) take the reader beyond the confines of past and present experience to the banquet that celebrates the fullness of God's kingdom.

The banquet theme supplies the principal motif for actualization. The multiplication story provides a way of linking the human experience of sharing a meal with the biblical background and the future hopes of God's people. This linkage provides a theological depth for grasping the many aspects of the mystery of the Eucharist.

For Reference and Further Study

Fowler, R. M. *Loaves and Fishes. The Function of the Feeding Stories in the Gospel of Mark.* SBLDS 54. Chico, Calif.: Scholars Press, 1981.
Held, H. J. *Tradition and Interpretation in Matthew,* 181–84.
van Cangh, J.-M. *La multiplication des pains et l'Eucharistie.* LD 86. Paris: Cerf, 1975.

36. *Walking on the Water* (14:22-36)

22. And immediately he forced the disciples to enter the boat and precede him to the other side, while he dismissed the crowds. 23. And after he dismissed the crowds, he went up to the hill-country by himself to pray. Since it was evening he was alone there. 24. But the boat was already many stadia away from the land, being harassed by the waves, for the wind was against it. 25. In the fourth watch of the night he came to them, walking upon the sea. 26. When the disciples saw him walking upon the sea, they were disturbed and said: "It is a ghost." And they shouted out from fear. 27. Immediately Jesus spoke to them, saying: "Take courage. It is I. Fear not!" 28. Peter answered him and said: "Lord, if it is you, command me to come to you upon the waters." 29. He said: "Come!" And Peter got down from the boat and walked about upon the waters and came to Jesus. 30. But on seeing the strong wind he became afraid, and when he began to sink he shouted out, saying: "Lord, save me!" 31. Jesus immediately stretched out his hand and took hold of him, and said to him: "O you of little faith, why did you doubt?" 32. And when they got into the boat the wind subsided. 33. Those in the boat paid homage to him, saying: "Truly you are the Son of God."

34. And when they had crossed over they came to land at Gennesaret. 35. And the men of that place recognized him and sent round to all that area, and they brought to him all those who were faring badly. 36. And they begged him that only they might touch the fringe of his garment. And whoever touched it were made well.

Notes

22. *forced*: Matthew follows Mark in developing a highly emotional mood around Jesus and the disciples, with Jesus fully in command. He omits the Markan desti-

nation ("to Bethsaida"), at the northeast of the Sea of Galilee, probably because they end up in Gennesaret at the northwest side, below Capernaum (see Matt 14:34).

23. *hill-country*: The Greek word *oros* can also be translated as "mountain." It is doubtful that it has a symbolic significance here (unlike Matt 5:1); "hill-country" is more appropriate to the terrain in the area around the Sea of Galilee.

to pray: Matthew makes little of Jesus at prayer in comparison with the other evangelists. Apart from his instructions about prayer in Matt 6:5-15 this is the first reference to Jesus at prayer. Only in the Gethsemane pericope do we get a glimpse into the content of Jesus' prayer and his relationship with the Father (see Matt 26:36-46).

24. *many stadia away from the land*: A *stadion* was about 200 yards long. The Sea of Galilee was nearly four and a half miles wide. According to Mark 6:47 they were "in the middle of the sea," though that need not be taken literally. The narrative emphasizes the wide separation between Jesus and the disciples.

being harassed: In Matt 14:24 the participle, which carries the idea of torture or torment, modifies the boat, whereas in Mark 6:48 it goes with the disciples. Both texts trace the situation to the "contrary" wind.

25. *the fourth watch*: The fourth and last watch of the night occurred between 3:00 and 6:00 A.M. The time of the epiphany indicates how long the disciples had been struggling and Jesus had been praying. Some commentators see a connection with God's intervention against the Egyptians according to Exod 14:20 ("in the morning watch").

walking upon the sea: The phrase is repeated in Matt 14:26, adding to the emphasis on the fact that Jesus does something unusual, something that only God does. Matthew omits the mysterious but important sentence in Mark 6:48: "He wanted to pass by them" (see H. Fleddermann, *CBQ* 45 [1983] 389–95).

26. *ghost*: An OT example of a ghost is the spirit of Samuel raised from the dead by the witch of En-dor (see 1 Samuel 28).

27. *"It is I"*: The expression has a rich background in Isa 41:4 and 43:10 where it functions as a divine name (see also Exod 3:14; Deut 32:39). It appears alongside "fear not" in Isaiah 43 several times. The use of such language identifies Jesus as the one who reveals the God of Israel and is uniquely related to that God.

28. *Peter*: As at other decisive points in Matthew's narrative (see 15:15; 16:16; 17:4; 18:21; 19:27; 26:33, 35), Peter serves as spokesman for the Twelve by responding to the statement of Jesus.

upon the waters: Here and in the following verse the term *hydata* ("waters") is used instead of *thalassa* ("sea") which had been used up to this point. Peter is portrayed as having perceived the import of Jesus' self-designation "I am he." He too wants to do what God alone does.

30. *"Lord, save me!"*: The disciples had made a similar plea in the stilling of the storm (see Matt 8:25). The OT background for their cry is found in Psalm 69 (especially vv. 1-2, 14-15)—the cry of those in danger of drowning.

31. *you of little faith*: Jesus addresses Peter with the characteristic expression used in Matthew to describe the Twelve. Their faith is neither perfect nor absent; it is "little" (see Matt 6:30; 8:26; 16:8; 17:20). Peter's initial success and subsequent failure provide the model of the "little faith" of the Matthean disciples.

 why did you doubt: The same word for "doubt" (*distazō*) appears in the climactic scene in Matt 28:16-20 in which some of the eleven disciples are said to have "doubted" the presence of the risen Lord.

32. *the wind subsided*: At this point Jesus has rejoined the disciples (see 14:22) after having manifested something of his true nature. Peter (see 14:29) has also returned to the safety of the boat. The image of the storm being stilled probably echoes Pss 89:10-11; 107:29; Job 26:11-12; and Jonah 1:11-12, 15.

33. *paid homage*: The same verb *proskyneō* ("do homage, worship") appears in Matt 2:2, 8, 11; 8:2; 9:18; 15:25; 20:20; 28:9, 17. Matthew's disciples go on to confess that Jesus is the Son of God (see Matt 3:17; 16:16; 17:5; 27:54), whereas according to Mark 6:52 their heart was hardened and they failed to understand.

34. *Gennesaret*: This site is usually located on the western shore of the Sea of Galilee, south of Capernaum. By omitting the original destination of Bethsaida in Matt 14:22 Matthew has avoided the impression of a wayward journey that failed to reach its goal.

35. *the men of that place*: The enthusiastic reception accorded to Jesus by the people of Gennesaret contrasts sharply with the reception given him by the Pharisees and scribes from Jerusalem in chapter 15.

36. *touch the fringe of his garments*: Matthew has abbreviated Mark 6:55-56 substantially but left the most vivid detail—the plan of the woman with the flow of blood (Mark 5:25-34; Matt 9:20-22) to touch the fringe of Jesus' garment. The "fringe" probably refers to the tassels worn by pious Jews as a reminder to keep God's commandments (see Num 15:38-40; Deut 22:12).

 were made well: The Greek term derived from *sōzō* can also mean "save." The summary in Matt 14:34-36 has the effect of bringing back to the reader's attention the idea of Jesus as healer.

INTERPRETATION

The Matthean account of Jesus walking on the waters follows Mark 6:45-52 to a large extent in wording and in emphasis. Both focus on the manifestation of Jesus ("It is I") as one who does what God does, thus suggesting a divine identity for him. The chief departure made by Matthew comes in the portrayal of the disciples. Matthew has inserted the episode about Peter walking on the waters (14:28-31). Moreover, the Matthean disciples correctly deduce from the epiphany that Jesus is the Son of God (14:33), unlike the Markan disciples whose hearts remain hardened (Mark 6:52).

As was the case with the stilling of the storm (Matt 8:23-27) there is a rich biblical background to the story of Jesus walking on the waters. For the ideas of distress at sea and God calming the rough waters, Psalm 107:23-32 provides a particularly graphic description:

> Some went down to the sea in ships, doing business on the great waters;
> they saw the deeds of the Lord, his wondrous works in the deep,
> For he commanded, and raised the stormy wind, which lifted up the waves of the sea.
> They mounted up to heaven, they went down to the depths;
> their courage melted away in their evil plight;
> they reeled and staggered like drunken men, and were at their wits' end.
> Then they cried to the Lord in their trouble, and he delivered them from their distress;
> he made the storm be still, and the waves of the sea were hushed.
> Then they were glad because they had quiet, and he brought them to their desired haven.
> Let them thank the Lord for his steadfast love, for his wonderful works to the sons of men!
> Let them extol him in the congregation of the people,
> and praise him in the assembly of the elders.

A similar description appears in Jonah 1.

This present episode goes beyond the stilling of the storm by inserting the picture of Jesus walking upon the sea. Just as in stilling the storm Jesus does what God does (see Ps 107:29), so in walking upon the waters he does what God does: "who alone stretched out the heavens and trampled the waves of the sea" (Job 9:8). In many cases the motif of God walking upon the waters appears in connection with the exodus from Egypt and the crossing of the sea (see Exod 14:13-31; Ps 77:20; Isa 43:16; 51:10; Hab 3:15). Thus the episode carries an implicit claim about the divinity of Jesus.

The most obvious contribution by Matthew to the episode is the insertion of the story of Peter walking on the waters (14:28-31). Though the story may have been part of a special Peter tradition available to Matthew, there are indications that Matthew himself has written the present account (see the Matthean words *thalassa, katapontizein,* and *distazō*). The Peter story also has a rich biblical background with respect to a person in danger of drowning and the divine rescue of such a person. In Ps 69:2 the speaker recounts his experience of almost drowning ("I have come into deep waters, and the flood sweeps over me"). In such a situation the speaker cries out: "Save me, O God!" (v. 1) and "Let not the flood sweep over me" (v. 15). For another example of a psalm about rescue from the danger of drowning, see Jonah 2. Again, in rescuing the drowning Peter, Jesus does what the Bible customarily attributes to God: "Stretch forth thy hand from on high, rescue me and deliver me from the many waters'' (Ps 144:7; see also Pss 18:16; 107:28, 30). So the implicit claim of the main story has been bolstered by the addition of a second story.

The images of drowning and rescue are prominent in the Qumran *Thanksgiving Hymns*. They are used mainly as ways of talking about the proper attitude during persecution—acknowledgment of the dangers and trust in God during persecution (see 1QH 3:6, 12-18; 6:22-25; 7:4-5). *Testament of Naphtali* 6:1-10 provides an elaborate picture of the ''ship of Jacob'' faring badly in a storm. When the storm ceased, the ship reached the land and was at peace: ''Then Jacob, our father, approached, and we all rejoiced with one accord'' (6:10). These texts suggest that in NT times the imagery of storm and rescue at sea was known and used.

Recognition of such image-patterns in the Bible and other Jewish writings raises the question of the historical basis of what is narrated in Matt 14:22-36. The rationalist explanation that Jesus was merely on shore and the disciples were not far out is hardly worth mentioning. On the other hand, a full-blown symbolic interpretation that identifies the boat as the Church, the mountain as equivalent of Sinai the sacred mountain, and so forth seems to evacuate the Matthean account of all concreteness. As in the account of the multiplication of the loaves and fish, it is difficult to know precisely where to draw the line between symbolism and history.

The heart of Matt 14:22-36 is an epiphany; that is, the manifestation of Jesus as doing what God does (walking on the sea and rescuing those in danger of drowning) and identifying himself in the way God speaks of himself (''I am he''). Peter as representative of the Twelve tries to share in Jesus' power and does so for a while—as long as his faith remains strong. When the ''littleness'' of his faith shows through, he needs to be rescued from drowning by Jesus. Surrounding the major episodes are two geographical scenes—one that explains how Jesus and the disciples got separated (14:22-23), and a summary of Jesus' healing activities at Gennesaret (14:34-36).

The primary message of Matt 14:22-36 for the Matthean community concerned the identity of Jesus, who does what God does and speaks as God does in the Bible. The epiphany of Jesus' identity to the disciples paralleled early Christian realizations and claims about him.

The new element in the Matthean account is the portrayal of Peter and the other disciples. As happens throughout the second half of Matthew's Gospel, Peter emerges as the spokesman for the Twelve and representative of their strengths and weaknesses. The disciples appear in a more positive light than they do in Mark. Yet they are far from being perfect. They are characterized as having a ''little faith.'' The picture of Peter in Matt 14:28-31 is the most memorable representation of the ''little faith'' attributed to the disciples. What Peter does is the enactment of ''little faith.'' Nevertheless,

Peter joins the other disciples in correctly identifying Jesus as the "Son of God." For all their weaknesses they come to understand who Jesus really is.

The major theme for actualization that emerges from this text is identity—that of Jesus and of the disciples. The rich biblical background of the account needs emphasis among those who seek only the spectacular. The picture of Peter is a consolation to all Christians who recognize that they like him as yet have only a "little faith." The epiphany of Jesus and his power to save those in distress provide the basis for courage in the face of the recognition of "little faith."

For Reference and Further Study

Heil, J. P. *Jesus Walking on the Sea. Meaning and Gospel Functions of Matt 14:22-33, Mark 6:45-52 and John 6:15b-21.* Rome: Biblical Institute Press, 1981.

Kratz, R. "Der Seewandel des Petrus (Mt 14, 28-31)." *Bibel und Leben* 15 (1974) 86–101.

37. *Debate about Tradition* (15:1-20)

1. Then Pharisees and scribes from Jerusalem approached Jesus, saying:
2. "Why do your disciples transgress the tradition of the elders? For they
do not wash their hands when they eat bread." 3. But he answered and
said to them: "And why do you transgress the commandment of God
through your tradition? 4. For God said: 'Honor father and mother' and
'Let whoever speaks evil of father and mother surely die.' 5. But you say:
'Whoever may say to father or mother: "Whatever you might gain from
me is a gift," 6. shall not honor his father or his mother.' And you have
made void the word of God through your tradition. 7. Hypocrites, well did
Isaiah prophesy about you, saying: 8. 'This people honors me with lips,
but their heart is far away from me. 9. They honor me in vain, teaching
as doctrines the commandments of human beings.' "

10. And he called the crowd and said to them: "Hear and understand.
11. What goes into the mouth does not defile the person, but what comes
out of the mouth—this defiles a person." 12. Then the disciples approached
and said to him: "Did you know that the Pharisees were offended when
they heard this statement?" 13. But he answered and said: "Every plant
that my heavenly father has not planted will be rooted out. 14. Let them
be. They are blind leaders of the blind. If a blind person leads a blind person, both will fall into a pit." 15. Peter answered and said to him: "Explain
the parable to us." 16. But he said: "Are you still without understanding?
17. Do you not know that everything that goes into the mouth moves into
the stomach and passes out into the latrine? 18. What come out from the

mouth come forth from the heart—these defile the person. 19. For from the heart come forth evil thoughts, murders, adulteries, fornications, thieveries, false witnesses, blasphemies. 20. These are what defile the person. Eating with unwashed hands does not defile the person."

Notes

1. *Pharisees and scribes from Jerusalem:* Since what follows seems to have been a lively issue in Pharisaism, the presence of Pharisees is significant. Not all Pharisees were scribes, nor were all scribes Pharisees (see Mark 2:16; Acts 23:9). The statement that they came "from Jerusalem" gives an official character to the delegation and suggests that the controversy takes place in Galilee (as 14:34-36 also indicates).

2. *tradition of the elders:* The expression refers to the body of laws and customs that supplement or arise out of the Torah. This tradition is traced back to Moses on Sinai (*m. 'Abot* 1:1) and reached written codification in the Mishnah around A.D. 200. The Pharisees were the great proponents of this tradition, whereas the Sadducees rejected it entirely.

   they do not wash their hands: The issue is not personal hygiene. Rather, it is a matter of ritual purification to remove defilement caused by contact with unclean things. Matthew has softened the blunt and embarrassing charges that the disciples eat with defiled hands (see Mark 7:2, 5). He also omits Mark's explanation of Jewish customs in Mark 7:3-4, presumably because his readers know about them and perhaps because he took exception to Mark's comment that all Jews did these things.

3. *why do you transgress:* Instead of answering the question put to him, Jesus responds with a question put to the opponents. The thrust of Jesus' question is that by so focusing on their tradition they neglect the divine commands expressed in the Torah. The *korban* illustration (15:4-6) has nothing to do with ritual purity. But it does show how the tradition has been allowed to take precedence over the Torah.

4. *God said:* This expression prepares for the contrasting expression in 15:5: "But you say." What God says is a combination of Exod 20:12/Deut 5:16 ("Honor father and mother") and Exod 21:17/Lev 20:9 ("Whoever speaks evil"). In the Jewish context the commandment about honoring one's parents is directed to adults and involves caring for and supporting elderly parents, not simply having a good opinion of them.

5. *a gift:* Matthew has omitted the technical Hebrew/Aramaic term *korban*, presumably because his readers did not need such help. The charge is that the custom of declaring something sacred and a gift to God has become a device for depriving parents of what they should rightfully expect from their children, thus turning out to be a means of voiding the commandment from God to honor one's parents.

6. *shall not honor:* Matthew makes the Pharisaic teaching into a counterversion of the biblical commandment.

7. *Hypocrites:* The term originally described an actor who performed behind a mask and thus came to refer to someone who pretended to be someone or something that he was not. There was a large theatre where such "hypocrites" performed in Sepphoris, near Nazareth, and so the term may well have been current in first-century Palestine. It is a very common charge in Matthew 23 and elsewhere (Matt 6:2, 5, 16; 7:5; 22:18; 24:51).

8. *'This people honors me . . .'* The quotation of Isa 29:13 in Matt 15:8-9 is much closer to the Septuagint than to the Hebrew text. The chief departure from the Septuagint comes in the final clause ("teaching commandments of human beings and doctrines"). The charge is that the Pharisees and scribes by substituting human traditions for God's commandments are far from God and do not worship him properly. They pay only "lip service" (Col 2:22). Matthew has changed the order in Mark by placing the *korban* illustration first (Matt 15:4-6 = Mark 7:10-13) and the quotation from Isaiah second (Matt 15:7-9 = Mark 7:6-7). He has omitted the sweeping conclusion drawn in Mark 7:8 ("Leaving behind the commandment of God you hold fast to the tradition of human beings").

10. *the crowd:* The crowd was not mentioned in Matt 15:1, though its presence was assumed as spectators to the dispute. They function now as the audience for the general statement delivered in Matt 15:11.

11. *What goes into the mouth:* The general statement is based on a distinction between ritual defilement and moral defilement. It gives precedence to moral matters over ritual matters. Matthew omits the comment in Mark 7:19 ("making all things clean"). Matthew probably did not agree with Mark that Jesus had abolished the Jewish food laws; this was a matter of great debate in early Christianity (see Gal 2:11-14; Rom 14:19-20; Col 2:20-23; Acts 10:14-15; etc.)

12. *the Pharisees were offended:* By his insertion of Matt 15:12-15 Matthew makes the controversy into a debate between Jesus and the Pharisees, thus avoiding the sweeping conclusions drawn by Mark about the abolition of the food laws. The "scandal" root underlies the verb translated "were offended."

13. *every plant:* The idea of the righteous community as a plant derives from Isa 60:21 ("the shoot of my planting"). It was applied by the Qumran community to itself (1QS 8:5; 11:8; CD 1:7) and by other Jews to their communities (Jub 1:16; 7:34; 21:24; 1 Enoch 10:16; 84:6; 93:2; Psalms of Solomon 14:3). From Matt 15:13 it appears that the Pharisees also used this image for themselves. Its appropriateness is contested on the grounds that God has not planted this plant, which will finally be rooted out.

14. *Let them be:* The patient tolerance recommended in Matt 13:24-30, 36-43, 47-50 is here applied to the Pharisees. The plant imagery used here fits nicely with the seed parables, confirming our interpretation that Matthew 13 is evidence for the Matthean community's effort to articulate its own identity vis-à-vis other Jewish groups.

leaders of the blind: Again there seems to be a play on a title being used by a rival Jewish group. In Rom 2:19 it is assumed to be positive: "if you are sure that you are a guide to the blind, a light to those in darkness . . ." In Luke 6:39 it is not directed against the Pharisees. Rather it is a parable addressed to followers of Jesus.

15. *Peter:* Acting again as spokesman for the group, Peter asks for an explanation of "the parable." The term refers back to Matt 15:11 which is taken to be an enigmatic saying or mashal. The dynamic of parables for the crowd and explanations for the disciples is prominent in Matt 13:1-52.

17. *everything that goes into the mouth:* The verse explains and expands upon the first part of Jesus' saying in Matt 15:11. It is based on the Hebrew idea of the heart as the place of human understanding and feeling (see 15:18), which is contrasted here to the stomach and bowels. The distinction between ritual and moral purity is rare in Judaism, which tends to think in terms of the whole person.

19. *evil thoughts:* Matthew has reduced Mark's catalogue of vices from thirteen to seven. His selection may have had some connection to the Ten Commandments ("murders, adulteries, fornications, thieveries, false witnesses"). For other lists of vices see Gal 5:19-21; Rom 1:29-31; 1 Pet 4:3; and 1 QS 4:9-11.

20. *Eating with unwashed hands:* With this final statement Matthew returns the debate to its starting point in Matt 15:2 and avoids the sweeping conclusion drawn by Mark. It is for Matthew a matter of the tradition of the elders, not the abolition of the Jewish food laws.

INTERPRETATION

In his account of Jesus' debate about the "tradition of the elders" (Matt 15:1-20) Matthew has taken over most of Mark 7:1-23 but reshaped the episode into something quite different from what it was in the source. Whereas Mark 7:1-23 concerns the biblical laws of purity, Matt 15:1-20 deals with the tradition of the elders.

The thrust of Mark's account comes in his parenthetical comment "making all foods clean" (Mark 7:19), which draws the radical conclusion that Jesus abrogated the OT laws regarding unclean foods. If Jesus himself had been so clear and direct on this matter, there probably would not have occurred the many debates among early Christians on whether Gentiles were obligated to observe the Jewish food laws. At any rate, Matthew resisted this radical conclusion and omitted Mark's parenthetical comment.

What is at stake in Matt 15:1-20 is the "tradition of the elders." A major element in the Pharisaic movement was the idea of a tradition alongside the Torah. This tradition made concrete more general teachings in the Torah or covered matters not treated in the Torah. The tradition was alleged to be very ancient, traceable back even to Moses on Sinai (see *m. 'Abot* 1:1).

It was rejected by the Sadducees as an innovation. But it was probably a necessary innovation if Judaism was to adapt to its new place in the Greco-Roman world and to avoid being perceived as an antique.

The Pharisees were the major proponents of the tradition of the elders. They supported this tradition not only as a way of updating and concretizing the Torah but also as a means of encouraging holiness among themselves and among Jews in general. Two of their efforts along these lines—handwashing before meals, and the practice of *korban*—are the matters for debate in Matt 15:1-20.

The rule about washing one's hands before eating is difficult to find in the Torah. The best starting point appears to be Lev 15:11: "Any one whom he that has the discharge touches without having rinsed his hands in water shall wash his clothes, and bathe himself in water, and be unclean until the evening." This text implies that rinsing one's hands removes uncleanness. The cleanliness under discussion here is not so much a matter of physical hygiene as it is ritual cleanliness; that is, what qualifies one for or disqualifies one from participating in the life of the people, especially the cultic life associated with the Jerusalem Temple. The earliest and clearest witness about the Pharisaic practice of washing hands before eating appears in Mark 7:1-5 (see also John 2:6; *m. Yad.* 1:1; *m. Hag.* 2:5). This practice was not necessarily a mainstream Pharisaic custom, still less a universal Jewish custom (despite Mark 7:3). Rather it was a superogatory ("above and beyond the call of duty") activity championed by a group within Pharisaism that was especially concerned to observe the Bible's program of levitical holiness and to avoid ritual uncleanness. If this conclusion is correct, then Jesus is being asked why his disciples (and presumably he himself) do not take up this superogatory practice. Jesus then is commenting on a controversy within Pharisaism.

Instead of dealing directly with the handwashing controversy, Jesus turns to another controversial issue within Pharisaism—the *korban*—in order to show that too much attention to the tradition of the elders can lead to neglect of the commandments in the Torah. The *korban* was the practice by which something could be declared "sacred" and a gift to God, and thereby exempted from the claims of others. A good example of this practice is provided by an Aramaic inscription on an ossuary found at Jebel Hallet eṭ-Ṭuri southeast of Jerusalem: "Everything that a man will find to his profit in this ossuary (is) an offering (*qrbn*) to God from the one within it." The late first-century B.C. text is a warning to tomb robbers that whatever of value is in the ossuary has been dedicated to God and is not intended for profane use.

The case described in Mark 7:11-12 (Matt 15:5-6) concerns some property or possession owned by a son. When the son declares it "*korban*," he is able to avoid the claims of his parents upon it. The charge attributed to Jesus is that the *korban* practice is being used as a way of getting around one's obligations to support one's parents as they are set forth in the Torah. Therefore the tradition of the elders is being used at cross-purposes to the Torah, not as a clarification or supplement.

As we have seen, Mark found in these debates the grounds for Jesus abrogating the Jewish food laws (''making all foods clean''). Matthew has revised Mark 7:1-23 to make Jesus criticize the tradition of the elders without going so far as to have him criticize the Torah. Matthew has omitted Mark's explanation of Jewish ritual washings (Mark 7:2-4) and his comment about Jesus making all foods clean (7:19). He has reordered the material so as to place the *korban* issue (Matt 15:4-6) before the quotation from Isa 29:13 (Matt 15:7-9). He has inserted a direct attack on the Pharisees (Matt 15:12-14) and concluded by declaring that eating with unwashed hands does not defile a man (Matt 15:20). The effect of these editorial changes is to narrow the debate to the validity of the Pharisaic tradition on two matters—washing hands before eating, and the *korban*. On both matters Jesus opposes the Pharisaic tradition without touching the commandments in the Torah.

Matthew's reworking of Mark 7:1-23 tells a great deal about the concerns of his community and their approach to Jesus. By narrowing Mark's account to a debate about the tradition of the elders, Matthew has avoided a conflict between Jesus and the Torah and has backed away from the radical conclusion (''making all foods clean'') proposed by Mark.

At the same time he has used the text to illumine the relation between the Matthean community and their Jewish rivals, here represented by the Pharisees and scribes from Jerusalem. On two controversial issues in Pharisaic circles—handwashing before eating, and the *korban*—he appeals to the example of Jesus, who apparently saw no reason why his disciples should observe the superogatory practice of washing hands before eating, and who rejected the consequences of the *korban* practice when it allowed one to get around the Torah.

Moreover, the debate also provided Matthew the opportunity to insert a sharp criticism of the Pharisees (15:12-14). To their probable self-description as the ''plant'' he has Jesus deny that the heavenly Father has planted this plant and to warn that it will be rooted out. He also has Jesus apply the Q saying (see Luke 6:39) in a negative sense to the Pharisees as ''blind leaders of the blind.'' So Matthew's version of Jesus' debate with the Pharisees and scribes from Jerusalem provided his community with Jesus' own position on these matters and enabled them to arrive at the proper attitudes toward the Pharisees and their tradition of the elders.

In presenting this text in preaching or teaching it is important to respect the distinctiveness of Matthew's version. Whereas Mark found warrant for Jesus' abrogation of the Jewish food laws (Mark 7:19) in his saying in Mark 7:15 (''there is nothing outside a person by coming into him can defile him, but the things coming out of a person are what defile the person''), Matthew backed away from such a far-reaching conclusion. This is another case of diverse perspectives within the NT itself.

It is important also to respect the historical situation of Matthew's editing. His largely Jewish-Christian community found itself in competition with other Jewish groups, especially those represented by the Pharisees and scribes in the text. It was largely a "family" quarrel among Jews, and it was very emotional as Matt 15:12-14 indicates. It is vital to place such texts in their historical setting, lest they be viewed as battles between Christianity and Judaism and read as examples of or incitements to anti-Semitism.

For Reference and Further Study

Barth, G. *Tradition and Interpretation in Matthew,* 86–90.

Booth, R. P. *Jesus and the Laws of Purity. Tradition History and Legal History in Mark 7.* JSNT Sup 13. Sheffield: JSOT Press, 1986.

Fitzmyer, J. A. "The Aramaic *qorban* Inscription from Jebel Hallet eṭ-Ṭuri and Mk 7:11/Mt 15:5." *JBL* 78 (1959) 60-65; also in *Essays on the Semitic Background of the New Testament* (London: Chapman, 1971; Missoula: Scholars Press, 1974) 93–100.

38. *The Canaanite Woman* (15:21-28)

21. And Jesus went forth from there and withdrew to the region of Tyre
and Sidon. 22. And behold a Canaanite woman came forth from those
regions and shouted out, saying: "Have mercy on me, Lord, Son of David;
my daughter is cruelly tormented by a demon." 23. But he did not answer
her a word. And his disciples approached him and asked him, saying: "Dismiss her, for she is shouting out after us." 24. But he answered and said:
"I have been sent only to the lost sheep of the house of Israel." 25. But
she came and did homage to him, saying: "Lord, help me." 26. But he
answered and said: "It is not good to take the children's bread and throw
it to the dogs." 27. But she said: "Yes, Lord. For even the dogs eat from
the crumbs that fall from their master's table." 28. Then Jesus answered
and said to her: "O woman, great is your faith. Let it be done to you as
you wish." And her daughter was healed from that hour.

Notes

21. *to the region of Tyre and Sidon:* The reason for Jesus' departure is not made explicit: Was it because of opposition to his teaching in 15:1-20, or the demands of the crowd at Gennesaret (14:34-36), or the desire for some solitude (14:13-14)?

Tyre and Sidon were on the Mediterranean coast; they traditionally designated the pagan region northwest of Jewish territory (see Matt 11:22). Did Jesus enter that region, or merely go in its direction?

22. *a Canaanite woman came forth from those regions:* Unlike Mark 7:26 ("a Greek, a Syrophoenician by birth"), Matthew calls her a "Canaanite," the ancient designation of the pagan inhabitants of the area. Matthew also omits the "secrecy" motif in Mark 7:24. It is possible to envision the Matthean episode as having taken place on Jewish soil, with the pagan woman coming forth from her own land to meet Jesus who was traveling in the direction of Tyre and Sidon. This scenario involves translating *eis* in Matt 15:21 as "to" or "toward," not "into," and subordinating the prepositional phrase "from those regions" (15:22) to the participle "came forth." The scenario would be consistent with Jesus' directive to his disciples to confine their mission to the lost sheep of Israel (see Matt 10:5-6).

    Lord, Son of David: Matthew has transformed into direct discourse what is narrated in Mark 7:25. For the motif of the healing Son of David, see D. C. Duling, "Solomon, Exorcism, and the Son of David," *HTR* 68 (1975) 235–52. It is not clear whether the daughter is with the woman or at home. According to Mark 7:30 she was at home.

23. *"Dismiss her":* The disciples' advice is ambiguous. It could mean that Jesus should comply with the woman's request and get rid of her in that way. Or it could mean that Jesus should simply get rid of her to avoid the trouble that she was causing. In view of the apparent non sequitur between 15:23 and 24, Lachs (248) suggests that the object of "dismiss" was originally the demon or that "her" be applied to the daughter suffering from the demon.

24. *to the lost sheep of the house of Israel:* This saying is unique to Matthew (cf. Mark 7:25). But it has parallels in Matt 9:36; 10:6; 18:12. The initial part ("I was sent") has connections with the Johannine-sending Christology. It is not clear whether the "lost sheep" refers to the lost within Israel, or to all Israel considered as lost.

25. *did homage to him:* Matthew shortens and specifies Mark 7:25 ("she fell at his feet") by using a term that he used frequently to express the proper attitude of people toward Jesus.

26. *and throw it to the dogs:* Matthew's omission of Mark 7:25a ("let the children be fed first") is puzzling, since it would seem to express Matthew's own approach to Jewish-Gentile relations. The assumption of the saying taken over by Matthew is that "children" represents Israel and "dogs" represents Gentiles. The harshness of the saying is softened somewhat by the use of the diminutive *kynarion* ("puppy") and by the assumption in 15:27 that these are "house-dogs." Be that as it may, Jesus clearly affirms the traditional Jewish approach to salvation history—to the Jews first.

27. *the dogs eat from the crumbs:* The implication of the woman's clever reply is that the dogs indeed are fed and satisfied. Behind her saying is the idea that Gentiles as well as Jews are fed by God. This incident would naturally have been important in the Matthean community, given its emphasis on the Jewish roots of Jesus and the mission to the Gentiles.

28. *great is your faith:* Matthew makes explicit a motif not mentioned by Mark, thus turning the whole incident into another instance of "praying faith." Whereas for Mark the girl was at home and this was a healing at a distance, in Matthew the healing may be assumed to have occurred in the presence of Jesus and the mother.

Interpretation

In Matthew's account of Jesus healing the Canaanite woman's daughter we have an example of the evangelist's literary approach to the Markan miracle stories and confront an issue of particular importance to the Matthean community—the relative positions of Jews and Gentiles in God's plan of salvation.

Matthew has reshaped Mark's account in several ways. While technically a healing story, Mark 7:24-30 features the conversation between the Syro-Phoenician woman and Jesus. Building on this fact, Matthew expands greatly the conversational element so that the woman addresses Jesus three times (vv. 22, 25, 27) and Jesus answers her twice (vv. 24, 28). Moreover, the disciples address Jesus once, and he replies to them (vv. 23-24). The Matthean version is clearly a dialogue, with the girl's sickness and healing providing the situation.

The theme of prayer is also heightened by Matthew. The mother addresses Jesus as Lord (vv. 22, 25, 27) and Son of David (v. 22). By recasting narrative portions of Mark 7:24-30 into dialogues, Matthew has reshaped the woman's role into that of a petitioner. Jesus' final comment in v. 28 ("great is your faith") suggests that the reason for his willingness to heal the daughter stems from his recognition of the mother's great faith. Thus Matthew portrays the mother as another model of praying faith.

It is also possible that Matthew has deliberately changed elements of the Markan scenario. He has Jesus withdrawing to the region of Tyre and Sidon. But it is not certain that Jesus actually arrived in pagan territory since the preposition *eis* could be taken as "toward" or "in the direction of" (v. 21). The Canaanite woman "comes forth" from those regions, perhaps to meet Jesus on Jewish soil. While it is grammatically possible to assume the same scenario as in Mark 7:24-30, another reading is possible—one that would conform Jesus' missionary practice to what is set forth for his disciples in Matt 10:5 ("Go nowhere among the Gentiles").

Another possible change in the Markan scenario comes with regard to where the daughter is. In Mark 7:24-30 she remains at home (7:30) and is healed at a distance. If we had only Matthew's account, we might imagine her as accompanying the mother and as healed in her mother's presence (see Matt 15:22, 28).

The editorial care that Matthew expended on Mark 7:24-30 can be explained in part by the theological theme that the story quite naturally raised—Jews and Gentiles in God's plan of salvation. Matthew highlights this theme from the start by referring to the woman as a "Canaanite" (15:22). At the very center of the text he places a saying that represents Jesus' position on the scope of his earthly mission: "I have been sent only to the lost sheep of the house of Israel" (v. 24). Nevertheless, the Matthean Jesus is prodded by his Gentile conversation-partner to admit some place for Gentiles too in God's plan of salvation.

The pre-exilic vision of the Gentiles streaming to the Temple Mount at Jerusalem in procession (see Isa 2:2-4) was taken up and developed in the post-exilic parts of the canonical book of Isaiah (chaps. 40–66). A sample of pertinent texts from Second Isaiah will suffice at this point: The vocation of Israel is to be "a light to the nations" (Isa 42:6; 49:6); God issues an invitation to all the ends of the earth to turn to him, be saved, and worship him (45:22-23); the Law of God and his justice will go forth as "a light to the peoples" (51:4-5); God will bring foreigners to his holy mountain so that they may join in the worship there (56:7); and the nations shall come to Israel's light, who is God (60:2).

The universalism of Second and Third Isaiah was not the only post-exilic position regarding the place of the Gentiles in God's plan. The books of Ezra (especially chaps. 9–10) and Nehemiah (see 10:30; 13:23-31) took a more negative position, particularly with regard to intermarriage, toward Jewish involvement with Gentiles.

The apparent contradiction between universalism and exclusivism can be clarified, if not resolved, by calling to mind the nature of Jewish universalism. Gentiles approach the God of Israel through Israel. This process is displayed beautifully in Zech 8:20-23, which develops the picture drawn previously in Isa 2:2-4. The peoples of the earth come to seek the Lord of hosts in Jerusalem. Then in a magnificent word-picture the prophet says: "In those days ten men from the nations of every tongue shall take hold of the robe of the Jew, saying, 'Let us go with you, for we have heard that God is with you' " (Zech 8:23). This kind of dynamic is played out in Matthew's version of the conversation between Jesus and the Canaanite woman.

In his revision of Mark 7:24-30, Matthew has turned the episode into a conversation and portrayed the Canaanite woman as a model of "praying faith." What made the story of the Canaanite woman especially significant for the Matthean community was her identity as a Gentile.

Relations between Jews and Gentiles were a very sensitive topic for the Matthean community. Though the majority of the community seems to have been Jewish by birth, some were Gentiles by birth. The conversation between Jesus and the Canaanite woman in Matt 15:21-28 would have functioned as a model or at least a causal explanation why Jews and Gentiles could exist together in the same Christian community.

On the one hand, the Matthean episode preserves the salvation-historical precedence of Israel in accord with the biblical and later Jewish tradition. The God of Israel is approached by Gentiles through Jesus the Jew. Matthew may even have limited Jesus' activity to Jewish soil by having the Gentile woman come to him. If so, Jesus follows the rule laid down for his disciples (''Go nowhere among the Gentiles'') in Matt 10:5.

On the other hand, there is a place for Gentiles at the banquet of God's kingdom (see the treatment of Matt 14:13-21), a fact that the Canaanite woman recalls by her play on Jesus' saying about the children (Israel) and the dogs (Gentiles). Her request is honored finally on the basis of her faith in Jesus' power—the criterion by which Gentiles become part of the Christian community.

In a time and place (today, in the West) where an ''easy'' universalism is fashionable and claims about the divine election of peoples and persons are regarded with suspicion or even revulsion, it is important to help others grasp the biblical doctrine of the chosen people. If one wishes to be true to the biblical witness, it is necessary to present clearly what the Scriptures say about the chosenness of Israel and how Christians share in it through Jesus. The God of Jesus is the God of Israel. Gentiles call upon and experience this God through Jesus as representative of the Jewish people. The roots of Christianity are Jewish. Gentile Christians have been grafted onto the olive tree (see Rom 11:17, 24).

For Reference and Further Study

Held, H. J. *Tradition and Interpretation in Matthew,* 197–200.

Légasse, S. ''L'épisode de la Cananéenne d'après Mt 15,21-28.'' *BLE* 73 (1972) 21–40.

Neyrey, J. H. ''Decision Making in the Early Church. The Case of the Canaanite Woman (Mt 15:21-28).'' *ScEs* 33 (1981) 373–78.

Woschitz, K. M. ''Erzählter Glaube. Die Geschichte von starken Glauben als Geschichte Gottes mit Juden und Heiden (Mt 15, 21-28 par).'' *ZTK* 107 (1985) 319–32.

39. *Healings* (15:29-31)

29. And Jesus passed over from there and came by the Sea of Galilee, and he went up the mountain and sat there. 30. And there approached him great crowds, having with them maimed, blind, lame, mute, and many others; and they put them by his feet, and he healed them, 31. so that the crowd was amazed at seeing the mute speaking, the maimed healthy, and the lame walking, and the blind seeing. And they glorified the God of Israel.

Notes

29. *Jesus passed over from there:* Matthew has rewritten Mark 7:31 so thoroughly that only the Sea of Galilee remains of the four place names. He may have done so to avoid the roundabout itinerary of Mark 7:31. Perhaps more important still was Matthew's desire to avoid the impression that Jesus was in Tyre, Sidon, and the Decapolis—all Gentile territories.

30. *great crowds:* Matthew expands the healing of the deaf man with the speech impediment (Mark 7:32-37) into a general healing of all kinds of afflictions. Perhaps he did so because of the almost magical character of the healing ritual, with its use of spittle, Aramaic formulas, and command to secrecy. At any rate, all the traces of the Markan story have been omitted.

mute: The Greek word *kōphos* carries the double sense of "deaf" and "dumb," i.e., incapable of speaking.

31. *the mute speaking:* The list corresponds to the classes of people listed in Matt 15:30, but the order is different. The response of glorifying the God of Israel could suggest that those doing the glorifying were Gentiles, not Jews. If they were Jews, one would expect "they glorified God."

Interpretation

Matthew has transformed the exotic story of Jesus healing the man who was deaf and with a speech impediment (Mark 7:31-37) into a general healing session for various afflictions. The transformation can be explained from several angles: Matthew liked to double (=expand) healings (see Matt 20:29-34; Mark 10:46-52); he may have been put off by the magical procedure in Mark 7:31-37; or he may have been disappointed by omission of the theme of faith or of an explicit theological element of Christology or discipleship.

The Markan account with its rare term *mogilalos* ("speaking with difficulty") contains an allusion to the Septuagint of Isa 35:5-6. Matthew's treatment of this allusion is puzzling. On the one hand, he passed up the opportunity to point out another fulfillment quotation ("all this took place in order to fulfill . . .''). On the other hand, his expansion of the incident seems to have been guided by the kinds of illnesses listed in Isa 35:5-6: ''Then the eyes of the *blind* shall be opened, and the ears of the *deaf* (=mute) shall hear. Then the *lame* will leap like a hart. . . . '' There is no ''maimed'' in the OT quotation, nor does Matthew use *mogilalos*.

Besides turning Mark's exotic tale into a general healing, Matthew has set a different scene. By way of introduction he has omitted the names of Gentile places (Tyre, Sidon, the Decapolis) and situated the general healing by the Sea of Galilee, in Jewish territory. Thus he remains consistent with the principle expressed in Matt 15:24 (''I was sent only to the lost sheep of the house of Israel'').

At the end of the story (''they glorified the God of Israel'') Matthew may, however, be suggesting that the recipients of these healings may have been Gentiles. Otherwise, the terminology is a bit odd. If this is so, the message to the Matthean community would be similar to that of Matt 15:21-28. If not, then the text is just another summary about the remarkable healing powers of Jesus.

Whether those doing it were Jews or Gentiles, glorifying God emerges as the appropriate response to the healing power of Jesus.

For Reference and Further Study

Held, H. J. *Tradition and Interpretation in Matthew,* 207–11.

40. *Feeding of the Four Thousand* (15:32-39)

32. Jesus called together his disciples and said: ''I have pity on the crowd, because they have already been with me for three days and they do not have anything to eat. And I do not wish to send them away fasting, lest they faint on the way.'' 33. And the disciples said to him: ''Where are we to get so much bread in the wilderness so as to satisfy such a large crowd?'' 34. And Jesus said to them: ''How many loaves of bread do you have?'' They said: ''Seven, and a few small fish.'' 35. And he ordered the crowd to sit down on the ground, 36. and he took the seven loaves and the fish, and giving thanks he broke and gave to the disciples, the disciples then to the crowds. 37. And all ate and were satisfied. And they took away what remained of the fragments, seven baskets full. 38. And four thousand men apart from women and children were eating. 39. And after dismissing the crowds, he entered the boat and came into the region of Magadan.

Notes

32. *for three days:* The first feeding story (Matt 14:13-21) seems to have taken place in a single day. Matthew has basically retained what is found in Mark 8:1-3 but has deleted some unnecessary material (8:1a; 8:3b). Unlike in Matt 14:14 he has retained Mark's reason why Jesus had pity on the crowds.

33. *so much bread in the wilderness:* The combination of "wilderness" and "bread" calls to mind the OT manna motif. There is no mention of fish here. Despite the previous multiplication (Matt 14:13-21) the disciples show surprise, as if they were going through the procedure for the first time.

34. *seven, and a few small fish:* The number "seven" is often given a symbolic value, as a reference to the Gentiles (the seventy nations of the world, the seven "deacons" of Acts 6:1-7, etc.). Matthew has taken the mention of fish from Mark 8:7 and combined it with the bread, so that there is only one action.

36. *giving thanks:* Whereas in Matt 14:19/Mark 6:41 Jesus "blessed," here and in Mark 8:6 he gives thanks (*eucharistēsas*). Again (and more explicitly) Jesus' action anticipates the Church's celebrations of the Eucharist. Matthew omits Jesus' blessing of the fish and their distribution (Mark 8:7) by mentioning the fish in 15:34 and omitting them in 15:36, probably to heighten assimilation to the Eucharist.

37. *seven baskets:* Instead of the term *kōphinos* Matt 15:37/Mark 8:8 uses *spyris*. Some see a contrast between "Jewish baskets" and "Gentile baskets." Again many interpreters find a symbolic significance in the number seven (= Gentiles), in contrast to the number twelve in Matt 14:20/Mark 6:43 (= Jews, the twelve tribes).

38. *apart from women and children:* As in Matt 14:21 this qualification expands the number of the crowd and adds to the magnitude of the miracle.

39. *the region of Magadan:* Mark 8:10 reads Dalmanutha. Nothing certain is known about either Magadan or Dalmanutha. Some manuscripts of Matthew read "Magdala(n)," based on the Semitic root for "tower." On the western shore of the Sea of Galilee, Magdala (modern Tarichaeae) is between Capernaum to the north and Tiberias to the south.

Interpretation

As in Mark 8:1-10 Matthew presents a second multiplication of loaves and fishes. The Jewish background and theological significance of the second feeding miracle are basically the same as those of the first, and so the material gathered in the exposition of Matt 14:13-21 need not be repeated here.

Despite the many similarities between the two multiplications there are some obvious differences between the feeding of the five thousand (14:13-21) and the four thousand (15:32-39). In the latter the crowd has been with Jesus for three days; the disciples know what food is available; and seven baskets of fragments are left over. Many interpreters discern elements that pertain to Gentiles: the number of loaves (seven) and the baskets of leftovers (seven), the Greek word for "basket" (*spyris*), etc. Just as Jesus fed a Jewish crowd in 14:13-21, so here he feeds a Gentile crowd. The Gentile dimension is probably more certain for Mark than for Matthew. If it is present in Matthew, there is no indication that the feeding takes place on Gentile soil.

Although Matthew has taken over Mark's account almost totally, he has made some editorial modifications that give a clue to his understanding of the episode. As in the first episode Matthew heightens the role of the disciples. In their response to Jesus they assume that it is their responsibility to supply food for the crowds (15:33). They know right away how much food is available (15:34). They serve as distributors of the food ("the disciples then to the crowds," 15:36).

Another distinctive Matthean motif is the treatment of the fish. Mark has two separate distributions—one for bread, the other for fish. Matthew has only the distribution of the bread. He mentions "a few small fish" (15:34) and says that Jesus took the fish along with the loaves (15:36). But then the fish drop out of the account altogether. Matthew's treatment of the fish is generally explained as a further heightening of the Eucharistic dimension already present in all the multiplication accounts. Since fish were not used in most (any?) Eucharistic celebrations, the gradual suppression of their mention in the account corresponds to the increasing emphasis on the Eucharistic aspect of the story.

The basic significance of the feeding of the four thousand for Matthew's community remains the same as that of the feeding of the five thousand. The special accents of the second feeding have already been mentioned. The role of the disciples as intermediaries between Jesus and the crowd is expanded, thus contributing to Matthew's generally more favorable presentation of the disciples. The assimilation of the feeding to the Church's celebration of the Eucharist is also heightened by Matthew. And there may be a continuation of Jesus' ministry to non-Jews (see Matt 15:21-28, 29-31), though most likely still in Jewish territory.

The themes for actualization flow from Matthew's special interests: the role of ministers in the Church, the richness of the Eucharist, and the significance of Jesus for Gentiles. Of course, the themes common to the two feedings can also be developed: the manna in the wilderness, the Elisha-Jesus typology, God's provision of food for his people, anticipation of the Last Supper, pledge of the messianic banquet, etc.

For Reference and Further Study

Held, H. J. *Tradition and Interpretation in Matthew,* 185–87.

41. *A Controversy and a Conversation* (16:1-12)

1. And the Pharisees and Sadducees approached, and to test him they asked him to show to them a sign from heaven. 2. But he answered and said to them: "When it is evening you say 'fair weather, for the sky is red.' 3. And in the morning 'today a storm, for the sky is red and threatening.' You know how to discern the appearance of the sky, but the signs of the times you cannot. 4. An evil and adulterous generation seeks a sign, and no sign will be given to it except the sign of Jonah." And he left them and went away.

5. When the disciples came to the other side, they had forgotten to bring bread. 6. But Jesus said to them: "Watch out and beware of the leaven of the Pharisees and Sadducees." 7. They discussed among themselves, saying: "We did not bring bread." 8. Jesus knew this and said: "Why are you discussing among yourselves, men of little faith, that you do not have bread? 9. Do you not yet understand, nor do you not remember the five loaves for the five thousand and how many baskets you took away? 10. Nor the seven loaves for the four thousand and how many hampers you took away? 11. How do you not understand that I did not speak to you about bread? Beware of the leaven of the Pharisees and Sadducees." 12. Then they understood that he said to beware not of the leaven for bread but of the teaching of the Pharisees and Sadducees.

Notes

1. *the Pharisees and Sadducees:* It is unusual that these rival groups should be linked to form a united front against Jesus. But they do so on four occasions in Matt 16:1-12 (vv. 1, 6, 11, 12); otherwise they are joined only in Matt 3:7. The fact that their action is described as a "test" of Jesus (*peirazontes*) indicates their ill will toward Jesus and perhaps even a connection with Satan the tempter (4:1-11).

   sign from heaven: The qualification "from heaven" is a way of saying "from God." The opponents expect that Jesus will be unable to produce such a spectacular public display and thus be exposed as a fraud and lose all public support. For the phenomenon of "sign prophets" in first-century Judaism see the discussion below.

2. *when it is evening:* The digression about the "signs of the weather" in Matt 16:2-3 is omitted in several important manuscripts. It may have been omitted to conform to local weather conditions. Or it may have been added on the basis of Luke 12:54-56 or a similar source. If it came from Matthew, the point is clear: You know how to read the signs of the weather but not the signs of the times.

4. *evil and adulterous generation:* See the notes on Matt 12:39. The adjective "adulterous" refers to the people's infidelity with respect to God. Here in contrast to Matt 12:38-42 the "sign of Jonah" is given no interpretation. In both 12:39 and 16:4 Matthew departed from the Markan Jesus' steadfast refusal to give any sign (see Mark 8:13), probably on the basis of the Q version of the episode (see Luke 11:29).

5. *they had forgotten:* Matthew omits the extraneous and confusing note in Mark 8:14: "and they had only one loaf with them in the boat." Whereas in Mark the dialogue takes place in the boat, in Matthew it occurs on the shore, on "the other side" of the Sea of Galilee. What precise geographical spot is meant is unclear.

6. *the leaven of the Pharisees and Sadducees:* Matthew substitutes "Sadducees" for Mark's mysterious "Herod," thus retaining the "united front" of 16:1. "Leaven" refers to something with an inner vitality. In this context it describes an evil influence that spreads like an infection. In rabbinic literature "leaven" was used as a metaphor for sin or corruption (Lachs, 253-54). Here it describes teaching to be avoided.

8. *men of little faith:* Matthew inserts into Jesus' interrogation of the disciples his characteristic designation of them as "men of little faith" (*oligopistoi*) as in Matt 6:30; 8:26; 14:31. By reducing the barrage of questions in Mark 8:17-20 to two reminders about the feedings of the five thousand (16:9 = 14:17-21) and the four thousand (16:10 = 15:34-38) instead of seven separate questions, Matthew has softened the harsh criticism of the disciples that is typical of Mark.

11. *leaven:* The identification between "leaven" and "teaching" may reflect an Aramaic word-play: *ḥămîrā'* ("leaven") and *'amîrā'* ("teaching, word"). See A. Negoita and C. Daniel, "L'enigme du levain," *NovT* 9 (1967) 306–14.

12. *the teaching of the Pharisees and Sadducees:* Matthew has added to Mark 8:14-21 a conclusion that makes clear that the leaven under discussion is the teaching of Jesus' opponents. Whereas in Mark the focus of attention is the incomprehension of the disciples, in Matthew it is the "leaven" (=teaching) of the Pharisees and Sadducees.

Interpretation

Matthew's source in 16:1-12 was Mark 8:11-21. There are two incidents: Jesus' controversy with the Pharisees and Sadducees about a sign from heaven (16:1-4 = Mark 8:11-13), and Jesus' conversation with his disciples about the "leaven" (teaching) of the Pharisees and Sadducees (16:5-12 = Mark 8:14-21). By his editing Matthew has imposed a unity on the two episodes and changed the focus of the second episode from Jesus' disciples to his opponents.

In both episodes according to Matthew the opponents are the Pharisees and Sadducees (16:1, 6, 11, 12). The first episode is Matthew's version of Mark 8:11-13, whereas Matt 12:38-42 was Matthew's version of the Q text. Matthew, however, retained the "sign of Jonah," from Q instead of the "no sign" of Mark 8:12. If the digression about the weather came from the evangelist and was not a later scribal gloss, then we must credit Matthew with a play on "signs" of the weather and of the times.

The second episode (16:5-12) is Matthew's version of Mark 8:14-21. By his subtle editing Matthew has changed the conversation from a devastating demonstration of Jesus' disciples' failure to understand him into a criticism of the Pharisees and Sadducees. Their seeking a sign from heaven becomes an instance of the corrupting effect of their teaching. As in the first episode, the target of Jesus' remarks is the Pharisees and Sadducees (16:6, 11, 12). Matthew deliberately tones down the harshness of Jesus' questioning of the disciples, passes off their obtuseness as a symptom of their "little faith," and uses their misunderstanding as the occasion for clarifying Jesus' teaching (as in the Fourth Gospel). By adding the concluding explanation (16:11-12) in which first Jesus and then Matthew make the point that Jesus was really talking about the evil effects of his opponents' teaching, Matthew has completed the transformation of the Markan account. It is no longer a criticism of Jesus' disciples. Rather it is now an attack on Jesus' Jewish opponents.

According to Matt 16:1 the Pharisees and Sadducees "tested" or "tempted" Jesus by asking him to show them a "sign from heaven." It may be that the first readers of Matthew's Gospel understood such a request in terms of the "sign prophets" that were part of the scene in first-century Palestine. In contrast to classical prophets who delivered oracles from God, sign prophets led movements and performed actions of deliverance as agents of God according to patterns set by Moses, Joshua, and other biblical figures. See R. A. Horsley, " 'Like One of the Prophets of Old': Two Types of Popular Prophets at the Time of Jesus," *CBQ* 47 (1985) 435–63. Thus Jesus' opponents may have been asking him to do a sign that would mark Israel's political (as well as spiritual) deliverance. If he failed, Jesus would be exposed as a fraud. If he succeeded, all to the good.

One such "sign prophet" was Theudas, who in A.D. 45 or 46, according to Josephus (*Ant.* 20:97-98; see Acts 5:36), "persuaded the majority of the masses to take up their possessions and to follow him to the Jordan River. He stated that he was a prophet and that at his command the river would be parted and would provide them an easy passage." The Roman procurator Cuspius Fadus quickly put down the movement and had Theudas and many of his followers executed. Josephus calls Theudas a *goēs*, meaning "magician, wizard, impostor," and says that he "deceived" many by his talk. His judgment, of course, came after the failure of Theudas to produce a "sign from heaven."

The Sadducees were no longer a force in Matthew's day. By making the Pharisees and Sadducees into a united front against Jesus, Matthew wished to make a statement first about Jesus' day and only secondarily a comment on his own day. Nevertheless, the two groups symbolized the Jewish religious leadership making common cause against Jesus. The application to Matthew's day was easy enough.

The opponents' search for a sign is classed as an exercise in temptation (16:1). They are more sensitive to the weather than to the signs of the times (16:2-3). They will get no sign except the sign of Jonah (16:4). Their seeking a sign is an example of their evil and harmful teaching (16:6, 11-12). Matthew has turned Mark's critique of Jesus' disciples into a polemic against the Jewish opponents of Jesus (and of his own community).

Religious obtuseness takes many forms, and it is certainly not limited to the Pharisees and Sadducees. Preachers and educators might use Matt 16:1-12 as a challenge to "religious" people today to examine their own failings and to stand under the criticisms levelled against Jesus' opponents.

42. *Promise to Peter; First Passion Prediction* (16:13-28)

13. When Jesus came into the area of Caesarea Philippi, he asked his disciples, saying: "Who do people say that the Son of Man is?" 14. They said: "Some John the Baptist, others Elijah, others Jeremiah, or one of the prophets." 15. He said to them: "Who do you say that I am?" 16. Simon Peter answered and said: "You are the Messiah, the Son of the living God." 17. Jesus answered and said to him: "Blessed are you, Simon Bar-Jonah, for flesh and blood have not revealed this to you but your Father who is in heaven. 18. And I say to you that you are Peter, and upon this rock I will build my church, and the gates of Hades will not prevail over it. 19. I will give to you the keys of the kingdom of heaven; and whatever you bind on earth will be bound in heaven, and whatever you loose on earth will be loosed in heaven." 20. Then he ordered the disciples that they should tell no one that he was the Messiah.

21. From then Jesus the Messiah began to show his disciples that he had to go off to Jerusalem and suffer much from the elders and chief priests and scribes, and be put to death, and on the third day be raised up. 22. And Peter took hold of him and began to rebuke him, saying: "God forbid, Lord! This will not be so for you." 23. But he turned to Peter and said: "Get behind me, Satan. You are a stumbling block to me because you think the things not of God but of men."

24. Then Jesus said to his disciples: "If anyone wishes to come after me, let him deny himself and take up his cross and follow me. 25. For whoever wishes to save his life will lose it. But whoever loses his life for my sake will find it. 26. For what does it profit a man if he gains the whole world but forfeits his life? Or what will a man give in exchange for his life? 27. For the Son of Man is to come in the glory of his Father with his angels, and then he will repay to each according to his activity. 28. Amen I say to you: 'There are some of those standing here who will not taste death until they see the Son of Man coming in his kingdom.'"

NOTES

13. *Caesarea Philippi:* Located on the southern slope of Mount Hermon at one of the sources of the Jordan River, the site in antiquity was known as a shrine to the god Pan. The Roman emperor Augustus gave the city to Herod the Great. When Herod's son Philip rebuilt the city, he changed its name from Panion to Caesarea Philippi (after the emperor and himself).

    that the Son of Man is: Mark 8:27 and Luke 9:18 read "that I am." Here Matthew uses "Son of Man" as a way of talking about Jesus. It functions as a title connected with the many other instances of "Son of Man" in the Gospel, not as a generic term or simply as a personal pronoun.

14. *Jeremiah:* In Matt 14:1 the list in Mark 6:15 was omitted. Here the list is taken over from Mark 8:28, with the addition of Jeremiah. For speculation about John's return from the dead see Matt 14:1. The return of Elijah is based on his having been taken up into heaven (2 Kgs 2:11); for his expected return see Mal 3:1, 23. The "prophet" may be some unidentified figure or perhaps the "prophet like Moses" promised in Deut 18:15. The addition of Jeremiah to the list is consistent with Matthew's general interest in Jeremiah as a figure of Jesus. Jeremiah is named in three texts (Matt 2:17; 16:14; 27:9), and there are several allusions to the book of Jeremiah (Matt 7:15-23; 11:28-30; 23:37-39). There are also Jeremiah motifs in Jesus' Temple discourse: the sending of the prophets, the murder of the prophets, and the prophetic judgment against the Temple (see Jeremiah 7; 26; Matt 23:29–24:2).

16. *the Messiah, the Son of the living God:* For the term "Messiah/Christ" see the interpretation of Matt 11:1-19. Although the evangelist has already used the title for Jesus (see 1:1, 16-18; 11:2), this is the first time that one of Jesus' disciples uses it of him. For the expression "the living God" see Ps 42:2; 84:2; Hos 1:10; etc. It becomes even more common in the NT (Matt 26:63; Acts 14:15; Rom 9:26; etc.). The "Son of the living God" title "corrects" any false impressions related to "Messiah."

17. *Blessed are you:* For the "beatitude" form see Matt 5:3-12. The blessing confirms Peter's insight about Jesus as a divine revelation. Peter is the only individual disciple named as a recipient of Jesus' blessing. Compare Mark 8:29-30 where Jesus passes from Peter's confession of him as the Messiah to a command to silence and a reprimand.

    Simon Bar-Jonah: The word *bar* is Aramaic for "son." If Simon's father were named Jonah after the prophet, it would be very unusual. Most interpreters suppose that he was named Yohanan (=John). The interpretation as *biryôn* ("revolutionary, anarchist") is unlikely. For Peter's father's name as John, see John 1:42 and 21:15.

    flesh and blood: The expression refers to the whole human being in weakness and limitation (see 1 Cor 15:50; Gal 1:16), in contrast to the heavenly Father.

18. *Peter . . . rock:* In Matt 10:2 Simon is said to have been called "Peter." In Greek there is a play on the name *Petros* and the word *petra* ("rock"). In Aramaic the play is more perfect on *kephā'*. Peter/Cephas may not have been a proper name

but rather a nickname, which perhaps had some connection with Peter's personal characteristics ("Rocky").

church: Here and 18:17 are the only occurrences of *ekklēsia* in Matthew. The use of this term may have been part of the attempt to distinguish the Church from "their synagogues" (4:23; 9:35; 10:17; 12:9; 13:54; 23:34). The Dead Sea community referred to itself as the "assembly of God" (*qĕhal 'el*) in 1 QM 4:10. There is no reason why Jesus could not have applied a similar term to his followers.

gates of Hades: Hades was a Greek god whose name means "the unseen one." The Greek word was used to translate Hebrew terms for the underworld or Sheol. In Acts 2:27, 31 it refers to the abode of the dead; for the gates of Sheol see Isa 38:10. The idea in Matt 16:18 is that death and other powers opposed to God will not triumph over the Church (=assembly) of Jesus' disciples.

19. *the keys of the kingdom of heaven:* For the kingdom as a place to be entered, see Matt 7:21. According to Matt 23:13 the scribes and Pharisees shut the kingdom of heaven. For the installation of the gate-keeper Eliakim over the royal household see Isa 22:15-25. Peter's role in the kingdom is like that of the steward Eliakim in the king's palace.

bind . . . loose: The expression can be interpreted in several ways: laying down rules and making exemptions, imposing and lifting excommunications, forgiving and not forgiving sins, or performing exorcisms. See 18:18 where the power to bind and loose is given to the community. The idea is that God will ratify and stand behind what Peter (and the others) enact.

20. *that he was the Messiah:* Matthew rejoins Mark 8:30 with the command to silence. But instead of "about him" he gives a fuller expression "that he was the Messiah." This device resumes Matt 16:16 (=Mark 8:29). It also points forward to Matt 16:21-28 in which the disciples must learn what the messiahship of Jesus means.

21. *From then:* The same expression appears in Matt 4:17. Many interpreters see this expression in 4:17 and 16:21 as marking important points in Matthew's outline of Jesus' story and as determining the structure of the Gospel. It is one among several structural principles in the Gospel, and what follows in 16:21-28 ought not to be cut off from what precedes in 16:13-20.

he had to go off to Jerusalem: Matthew omits "Son of Man" (but see 16:13) and gives Jerusalem as the goal of Jesus' journey. Note that among Jesus' enemies the Pharisees are not mentioned. Matthew (like Luke 9:22) prefers "on the third day" to the less precise "after three days" in Mark 9:31. For the third day as marking a decisive turning point, see Hos 6:2; Jonah 1:17; 2:10.

22. *"God forbid, Lord!":* The Greek exclamation could be translated: "(May God) be gracious to you, Lord!" Only Matthew gives the direct address of Peter to Jesus; Mark 8:32 merely reports that Peter began to rebuke Jesus.

23. *a stumbling block to me:* Matthew adds the idea of Peter as a *skandalon* (see 13:41; 18:7). There may be a play on Peter as the rock (16:18). Those who deny Jesus' passion and death are on the side of Satan (see 4:10). By addressing Peter as

"Satan" Jesus indicates that his false interpretation of Jesus' messiahship is a temptation. For Satan in the OT see Job 1–2 and Zech 3:1-2.

24. *to his disciples:* By omitting the reference to the crowd in Mark 8:34 Matthew removes the instructions that follow from the public realm and restricts them to the disciples.

take up his cross: Matthew already used the material in 16:24-25 (Mark 8:34-35) in 10:38-39. See the notes there on the image of the cross and the meaning of *psychē* ("life"). Here the sayings link the passion of Jesus (16:21) to the sufferings of Jesus' followers.

26. *gains the whole world:* The phrase refers to having access to the richness and abundance of creation. Yet this is not the same as finding one's life (*psychē*), which is more valuable than all worldly goods and obtained only with reference to Jesus' passion and death.

27. *he will repay to each:* To the apocalyptic scene in Mark 8:38, Matthew has added the idea of judgment according to one's deeds (see Ps 62:13; Prov 24:12). The idea is also prominent in Paul's letters (see Rom 14:12; 1 Cor 4:5; 2 Cor 5:10). This practical Christianity with its emphasis on action was dear to Matthew's heart.

28. *the Son of Man coming:* Mark 9:1 and Luke 9:27 talk about "the kingdom of God coming." For the kingdom of the Son of Man see Matt 13:42 and 20:21. The promise raises the same problems and holds out the same hope as Matt 10:22-23. The most obvious referent of the promise is the fullness of God's kingdom. But coming before the transfiguration (17:1-8), the saying may refer to that event as a preview or anticipation of God's kingdom.

INTERPRETATION

In Matt 16:13-28 the evangelist follows and adapts Mark 8:27–9:1 with the obvious exception of the addition to Peter's confession in 16:16b-19. In following Mark, Matthew takes over the pattern of identification of Jesus (Mark 8:27-30 = Matt 16:13-20), passion prediction (Mark 8:31-33 = Matt 16:21-23), and instruction on discipleship (Mark 8:34–9:1 = Matt 16:24-28).

Most of Matthew's changes in his Markan source are minor editorial touches. The most striking include the addition of Jeremiah to the list of popular guesses about Jesus' identity (16:14), the specification "that he was the Messiah" (16:20), the direct speech of Peter (16:22) and Jesus' calling him a stumbling block (16:23), the promise about judgment according to deeds (16:27), and the idea of the Son of Man coming in his kingdom (16:28).

The major change is the expansion of Peter's confession in 16:16b-19. This material has no parallel in Mark or in any other Gospel source. By inserting it into his Markan source Matthew has altered the flow of the story. Whereas in Mark Peter's confession is rejected or at least corrected, in Matthew it serves as the basis for Jesus' blessing of Peter. The focus on Peter as the one who gets involved when problems emerge is typically Matthean (see Matt 15:15; 17:24-27; 18:21-22). In this text Peter is praised as the recipient of a divine revelation (16:17), called the foundation of the Church (16:18), and given special authority (16:19).

The very Semitic character of the language in Matt 16:16b-19 ("Simon Bar-Jona," "flesh and blood," the Peter-rock pun, etc.) suggests that the piece originally circulated in Aramaic or at least in a highly Semitized Greek. We are most likely dealing with a pre-Matthean tradition that Matthew inserted into the text.

From where did the tradition come? Some argue that it came directly from the earthly Jesus. This view is based on the Semitic speech and the fact of Peter's special role among the twelve. Others argue that the tradition arose in the Church at Antioch where Peter was looked upon as the founding apostle of the Church there. Thus the story would reflect an attempt at establishing Peter's authority by tracing it back to Jesus' time. Still others suggest that it arose in the story of a resurrection appearance to Peter. According to 1 Cor 15:5 the risen Jesus appeared to Cephas/Peter. Since Matthew has no such account (cf. Luke 24:34; John 21:15-17), perhaps he retrojected the appearance story into the career of the earthly Jesus.

None of these three explanations about the origin of the material in Matt 16:16b-19 can be proved with certainty. Neither can anyone of them be dismissed. What is striking is the continuing interest in Peter. If Peter died around A.D. 60 and Matthew wrote around A.D. 85, why did Matthew and his community retain their special interest in Peter some twenty-five years after his death?

Most of the motifs in Matt 16:16b-19 have already been treated or are explained sufficiently in the notes. But three motifs deserve comment because they may escape notice: Caesarea Philippi as a place of divine revelation, the rock-foundation of the Church, and the keys of the kingdom.

Caesarea Philippi is located north of the Sea of Galilee, in the territory of Dan, not far from Mount Hermon. There according to Matt 16:13 (following Mark 8:27) Peter correctly identified Jesus as "the Messiah, the Son of the living God" (16:16b). Jesus in turn praised Peter because God (not "flesh and blood") had revealed this mystery to him. In 1 Enoch 12–16 the divine mysteries of heaven are revealed to Enoch in the same area: "And I went and sat down upon the waters of Dan—in Dan which is on the southwest of Hermon—and I read their memorial prayers until I fell asleep. And behold a dream came to me and visions fell upon me" (1 Enoch 13:7-8). Some interpreters also locate the visionary ascent of Levi to the heavenly temple in the same area (see T. Levi 2–7). The Aramaic version of T. Levi reads: "I lay down and I settled at (the waters of Dan) . . . Then I was shown visions." For a full treatment of this motif, see G. W. E. Nickelsburg, "Enoch,

Levi, and Peter: Recipients of Revelation in Upper Galilee," *JBL* 100 (1981) 575–600.

The motif of Peter as "rock" probably had something to do with his character ("Rocky"). The nickname preceded his role (see Matt 10:2) of serving as foundation for the Church. But the use of the image of rock as foundation for the community can be traced back to Isa 51:1-2: "Look to the rock from which you were hewn, and to the quarry from which you were digged. Look to Abraham your father and to Sarah who bore you." Another important text pertaining to this theme is Ps 118:22: "The stone which the builders rejected has become the head of the corner."

There is no doubt that in the NT the capstone or keystone described in Ps 118:22 is Christ (see Matt 21:42; Mark 12:10; Luke 20:17; Acts 4:11; 1 Pet 2:4, 7-8). But there is some variation as to who is the foundation of the Church. According to 1 Cor 3:11 "no other foundation can anyone lay than that which is laid, which is Jesus Christ." On the other hand, according to Eph 2:20 the household of God is "built upon the foundation of the apostles and prophets, Christ Jesus himself being the cornerstone" (see 2 Tim 2:19). In Matt 16:18 the rock on which the Church is built is Peter. For the Qumran community as a strong building on rock see 1QH 6:24-28: "my soul went down to the gates of death . . . it is Thou who will set the foundation upon rock . . . in order to build a stout building."

The motif of the keys is rooted in Isaiah's prophecy to Shebna that he would be replaced as chief steward over the royal household by Eliakim: "I will place on his shoulder the key of the house of David; he shall open, and none shall shut; and he shall shut, and none shall open" (Isa 22:22). Just as Eliakim is to have command over entry and exit in the royal palace, so Peter has charge over entry and exit in the kingdom of heaven. Peter appears as the prime minister and major-domo of the kingdom proclaimed by Jesus.

It is hard to be sure about the role of Peter in the Matthean community's controversy in the late first century. It is significant that twenty-five years after his death Peter retained at least a historical importance. Beyond that is speculative. But within the community Peter may have functioned as the founding apostle or patron saint. Perhaps the leaders traced their spiritual pedigree back through Peter much as the rabbis did through their teachers.

The reference to the Christian community as the *ekklēsia* ("Church") in Matt 16:18 may be an earlier example of the differentiation by title. Whereas Jewish Christians adopted the Greek title *ekklēsia* for their communities, other Jews took the term *synagōgē* for theirs. This tension can already be felt in Matthew's references to "their synagogues" and the "synagogues of the hypocrites."

Matt 16:21-28 contains the first of the passion predictions (see 17:22-23; 20:17-19) and links the sufferings of the disciples to Jesus' sufferings. To both insiders and outsiders the passion predictions had the effect of claiming that Jesus knew what awaited him (and his followers) and that he embraced his sufferings and was even in control of the events around him. That Jesus had an intimation of the fate that awaited him in Jerusalem is historically plausible, given the political climate of Palestine regarding "sign prophets" and other popular leaders. That he foretold the events in the precise language of the Gospel passion predictions is less plausible, especially in light of the disciples' failure to respond appropriately during the passion itself. Note that the Pharisees are not listed among the opponents of Jesus in 16:21.

The promise to Peter in Matt 16:17-19 is foundational for any treatment of the Petrine office or papacy. Analysis of this text indicates that it is based on a pre-Matthean tradition and that Peter held an interest for Jewish Christians around A.D. 85 or 90. The text attributes to Peter a certain preeminence and even primacy among the twelve apostles. The quarrel among Christians through the centuries revolves around two further questions: Has Peter's primacy been handed on to successors? Has this primacy been carried on by the bishops of Rome? Catholics answer these questions in the affirmative, whereas other Christians do not.

Another aspect in actualizing Matt 16:13-28 is the connection between the messiahship of Jesus and suffering—his own and those of his followers. By his refusal to accept this connection Peter the "rock" turns into the "stumbling block" (*skandalon*) (see 16:18, 23).

For Reference and Further Study

Bigane, J. E. *Faith, Christ, or Peter: Matthew 16:18 in Sixteenth Century Roman Catholic Exegesis.* Washington, D.C.: University Press of America, 1981.

Brown, R. E. and others. *Peter in the New Testament.* New York–Toronto: Paulist, 1973; Minneapolis: Augsburg.

Burgess, J. A. *A History of the Exegesis of Matthew 16:17-19 from 1781 to 1965.* Ann Arbor, Mich.: Edwards Bros., 1976.

Caragounis, C. C. *Peter and the Rock.* Berlin–New York: de Gruyter, 1990.

Cullmann, O. *Peter: Disciple, Apostle, Martyr. A Historical and Theological Study.* Philadelphia: Westminster, 1962.

Kingsbury, J. D. "The Figure of Peter in Matthew's Gospel As a Theological Problem." *JBL* 98 (1979) 67–83.

Luz, U. "The Primacy Text (Mt. 16:18)." *Princeton Seminary Bulletin* 12 (1991) 41–55.

Wilcox, M. "Peter and the Rock: A Fresh Look at Matthew XVI, 17–19." *NTS* 22 (1975) 73–88.

43. *The Transfiguration and Elijah* (17:1-13)

1. And after six days Jesus took along Peter and James and John his brother, and brought them up to a high mountain apart. 2. And he was transfigured before them, and his face shone like the sun and his garments became white like the light. 3. And behold there appeared to them Moses and Elijah, conversing with him. 4. Peter answered and said to Jesus: "Lord, it is good that we be here. If you wish, I will make here three booths—one for you and one for Moses and one for Elijah." 5. While he was still speaking, behold a bright cloud overshadowed them, and behold a voice from the cloud was saying: "This is my beloved Son with whom I am well pleased. Listen to him." 6. When the disciples heard, they fell on their faces and became very much afraid. 7. And Jesus approached and touched them and said: "Arise and do not fear." 8. When they lifted up their eyes, they saw no one except Jesus only.

9. And as they were coming down from the mountain, Jesus commanded them, saying: "Tell no one the vision until the Son of Man has been raised from the dead." 10. And his disciples asked him, saying: "Why do the scribes say that Elijah must come first?" 11. He answered and said: "Elijah comes, and he will restore all things. 12. I say to you that Elijah has already come, and they did not know him, but they did to him what they wished. So also the Son of Man must suffer at their hands." 13. Then the disciples understood that he spoke to them about John the Baptist.

Notes

1. *after six days*: Some find in this time indicator an allusion to the Sinai revelation (Exod 24:16) or the day of the resurrection or the feast of Tabernacles (six days after the Day of Atonement).

   Peter, James, and John: The three form an inner circle among the twelve (see 26:37). They were among the first disciples whom Jesus called (see 4:18-22). Matthew omits the word *monas* ("alone") in Mark 9:2, because it was unnecessary. He does note that John was the brother of James.

   high mountain: Mountains are the usual sites for revelations and theophanies (see Matt 5:1; 28:16). The transfiguration has been traditionally located on Mount Tabor. In light of the traditions surrounding it as a place of revelation, Mount Hermon is also a good candidate.

2. *he was transfigured*: The Greek term *metemorphōthē* indicates that the form of Jesus was changed. What is described does not conform to the Greek idea of metamorphosis or the idea of interior transformation elsewhere in the NT (see Rom 12:2; 2 Cor 3:18). Rather the disciples receive a preview of glory that will belong to Jesus in the eschaton and the fullness of God's kingdom.

his face shone: Matthew adds the note about Jesus' shining face and omits the idea of the fuller getting clothes white (see Mark 9:3). For the righteous shining like the sun in God's kingdom see Matt 13:43. For the brilliance of Moses' face when he came down from Sinai see Exod 34:29.

3. *Moses and Elijah*: Matthew has changed the peculiar order in Mark 9:4 (''Elijah with Moses''), thus suggesting that the two represent the Law and the Prophets (see Matt 5:17; 7:12; 11:13; 22:40). There may also be a reference to their having been taken up into heaven (Deut 34:6; 2 Kgs 2:11) or their expected roles in the coming kingdom (Deut 18:15, 18; Mal 3:23-24).

4. *Lord*: Instead of ''Rabbi'' Peter calls Jesus ''Lord'' or ''Master'' (*kyrie*), part of Matthew's deliberate avoidance of applying Rabbi to Jesus (see 23:8). Peter is also more deferential in Matthew (''if you wish'') and volunteers to build the tents by himself (''I will make''). With the tents there may be a reference to the feast of Tabernacles (see Lev 23:39-43). Peter wishes to prolong this anticipation of the end-time. Matthew omits the editorial comment in Mark 9:6 (''For he did not know what to say, for they were exceedingly afraid'').

5. *bright cloud*: For the cloud as a vehicle for God's presence see Exod 16:10; 19:9; 24:15-16; 33:9. For the verb ''overshadow'' see Exod 40:35. See also 2 Macc 2:8: ''the glory of the Lord will be seen in the cloud.''

   a voice: The message of the voice is the same as that at the baptism of Jesus in Matt 3:17. It combines allusions to the Messiah (''my Son,'' see Ps 2:7), the ''beloved'' (Isaac; see Gen 22:2), and God's Servant (Isa 42:1; 44:2). The Matthean addition ''Listen to him'' may allude to the prophet like Moses in Deut 18:15 (''him you shall heed'').

6. *When the disciples heard*: Matthew moved the ''fear'' to follow the voice (see Mark 9:6) and describes the disciples' reaction in terms used with regard to apocalyptic visions in Dan 8:17-18; 10:7-9.

8. *no one except Jesus only*: The experience ends abruptly. Before the eternal glory of Jesus can begin to take its permanent form, he must make his way to the Cross in Jerusalem.

9. *tell no one the vision*: By inserting the word ''vision'' (*horama*) Matthew indicates his own interpretation of the transfiguration. Matthew omits the disciples' puzzlement about the meaning of ''to be raised from the dead'' (see Mark 9:10).

10. *Elijah must come first*: According to Mal 3:23-24 (=4:5-6) the return of Elijah will precede the coming of the Day of the Lord. But whether Elijah was to be the forerunner of the Messiah is not so clear; see the note on Matt 11:14 for the recent debate on this matter.

12. *they did not know him*: Matthew's addition to Mark 9:13 reflects his interest in faith and understanding. His omission of ''as it is written of him'' can be traced to the absence of such a text in the OT.

13. *about John the Baptist*: Matthew's editorial addition forestalls any doubt or confusion regarding the identity of the Elijah figure. See Matt 11:14: ''And if you are willing to accept it, he is Elijah who is to come.''

Interpretation

Matthew's source for the transfiguration and the conversation about Elijah (17:1-13) was Mark 9:2-13. His changes are generally minor. The most notable are the following: Peter's address to Jesus as "Lord" instead of "Rabbi" (17:4), the lengthy description of the disciples' reaction (17:6-7), the characterization of the experience as a "vision" (17:9), the omission of Mark's suggestions about the fulfillment of Scripture (17:11, 12), and the comment that the Elijah figure was John the Baptist (17:13). Other Matthean editorial contributions are discussed in the notes.

By his editing (especially in 17:6-7) Matthew has given the transfiguration story a neater structure. After introducing the scene in 17:1 (when?, who?, where?), he presents a visual episode (17:2-3) and Peter's reaction (17:4) and then an auditory episode (17:5) and the disciples' response (17:6-7), and closes off the story (17:8). The connection with the conversation about Elijah (already in Mark) links the anticipation of Jesus' glorification in the transfiguration to the passion and to the coming of God's kingdom (associated with Elijah).

The precise genre of the transfiguration story is elusive. Attempts at interpreting it as a resurrection appearance fail at every point. Matthew calls it a "vision" (*horama*) in 17:9. The content (a preview of Jesus' eschatological glorification) and some of the literary features (especially the disciples' reaction in 17:6-7) suggest that it be called an apocalyptic vision.

The transfiguration account (17:1-8) blends features from the Sinai theophany (Exodus 24) and the apocalyptic visions of the book of Daniel. The Sinai features include the high mountain, the time "after six days," the shining face of Jesus (see Exod 34:29), the figure of Moses, and the bright cloud. There may also be some connection with Moses and his three companions (Aaron, Nadab, and Abihu).

The apocalyptic features come first of all from the content: the anticipation of Jesus' future glory. In an apocalyptic vision the seer (Daniel, Enoch, etc.) is granted a vision of what goes on in the heavens or what will happen in the future. So as they make their way up to Jerusalem, Jesus' disciples are granted a vision of who he really is and what he will be in God's kingdom. Matthew went out of his way to emphasize this dimension of the transfiguration by assimilating the disciples' reaction in 17:6-7 to those of Daniel in Dan 8:17-18; 10:7-9 and by labelling the event as a "vision" (17:9).

The figure of Elijah links the two episodes. By straightening out the order to read "Moses and Elijah" instead of Mark's "Elijah with Moses" Matthew made the two figures to be representatives of the Law (Moses) and the Prophets (Elijah). These two biblical figures also carried apocalyptic significance, since there was mystery surrounding their passing and speculations about their future roles. Thus they would be appropriate conversation partners for Jesus in an apocalyptic vision giving a preview of his glory.

Speculation about Elijah's role in the coming of God's kingdom was expressed in Mal 4:5 (=3:23 in Hebrew): "Behold, I will send you Elijah the prophet before the great and terrible day of the Lord comes." Matthew agrees with other early Christians that this prophecy had been fulfilled by John the Baptist whose dress and lifestyle were those of Elijah (see Matt 3:4).

In the debate with non-Christian Jews the transfiguration establishes the link between Jesus on the one hand and Moses and Elijah on the other. In the Matthean context the story becomes part of Matthew's program of showing how Jesus came to fulfill the Law and the Prophets (see Matt 5:17). Perfect harmony exists among these three figures.

The conversation about Elijah concerns the correct interpretation of Mal 4:5 (=3:23). The context ("Why do the scribes say . . . ?") suggests that the text had become a topic of debate. The Christian interpretation was that the Elijah figure prophesied by Malachi was John the Baptist. This approach to biblical prophecy parallels that of the Qumran community which understood biblical prophecies to be "mysteries" that were resolved in the life and history of their own community.

Besides these two main points there are some "sideways" glances at the Jewish opponents of the Matthean community. Peter does not address Jesus as "Rabbi," which apparently was an important title among the opponents (see Matt 23:8). In fact, that is how Judas addresses Jesus when he betrays him (see 26:25). Also, Matthew cleans up Mark's loose talk about the suffering Son of Man and the fulfillment of Scripture. Since there are no such texts, Matthew omits Mark's suggestions that there are, thus avoiding possible criticisms that Christians do not know the Hebrew Scriptures.

The transfiguration poses challenges and opportunities for teachers and preachers. The chief problem is that of genre. If one takes it as a strictly factual report, one can miss the rich symbolism. If one focuses on the symbolism, the text can dissolve into an allegory. Matthew's characterization of it as a "vision" is helpful, and the recognition of its links with apocalyptic visions is also important. In the context of Jesus' final journey up to Jerusalem the transfiguration balances off the passion predictions and the calls to follow Jesus in his sufferings. It provides a preview of the glory of the resurrection.

The conversation about Elijah/John the Baptist indicates the decisive moment that salvation history has reached. The suffering of the Son of Man is integrated into the scenario of apocalyptic events.

For Reference and Further Study

Carlston, C.E. "Transfiguration and Resurrection." *JBL* 80 (1961) 223–40.
Moiser, J. "Moses and Elijah." *ExpTim* 96 (1985) 216–17.
Pedersen, S. "Die Proklamation Jesu als des eschatologischen Offenbarungsträgers (Mt xvii 1–13)." *NovT* 17 (1975) 241–64.

44. *The Disciples' Little Faith* (17:14-20)

14. And when they came to the crowd, a man approached him and knelt before him, 15. and said: "Lord, have mercy on my son for he is moonstruck and suffers terribly. For he falls sometimes into fire and sometimes into water. 16. And I brought him to your disciples, and they could not heal him." 17. Jesus answered and said: "O faithless and perverse generation, how long will I be with you? How long will I put up with you? Bring him here to me." 18. And Jesus commanded him, and the demon went forth from him, and the boy was healed from that hour. 19. Then the disciples approached Jesus privately and said: "Why could we not cast this out?" 20. But he said to them: "Because of your little faith. Amen I say to you, if you have faith like a mustard seed and say to this mountain: 'Move from here to there,' it will move; and nothing will be impossible to you."

Notes

14. *knelt*: Matthew summarizes the long introduction in Mark 9:14-16 by using one of his favorite words for coming near Jesus (*prosēlthen*) and by having the man kneel (*gonypetōn*) before Jesus, thus highlighting the prayerful attitude displayed by the man in the presence of Jesus.

15. *Lord, have mercy*: The man's address to Jesus is turned into a prayer. Compare Mark 9:17: "Teacher, I brought my son. . . . "

    moonstruck: The Greek verb is derived from the word for moon *selēnē/selēniazetai*. The Latin word *luna* is the origin of "lunatic." In other words, the boy's condition is related to the phases of the moon. From what was believed in ancient medicine and from the symptoms of frequent falls, the boy's condition is usually held to be epilepsy. See Matt 4:24.

16. *they could not heal him*: In this part of the Gospel, Matthew emphasizes the failures of the disciples (see Matt 14:15-17, 26, 30-31; 15:16, 23; 16:5, 22; 17:4, 10) with respect to understanding and faith. In 2 Kgs 4:31 Gehazi tries unsuccessfully to revive a child. His master Elisha later succeeds in restoring the boy to life.

17. *faithless and perverse generation*: The Matthean Jesus speaks the language attributed to Moses in Deut 32:5: "they are a perverse and crooked generation." For

the language of the questions "how long?" see Num 14:27; Ps 6:4; 13:1-2; 35:17; etc. Matthew omits the encounter between Jesus and the boy's father in Mark 9:20-25.

18. *the demon went forth*: The assumption of the story is that the epilepsy was caused by a demon. Thus the healing of the boy is at root an exorcism. For Jesus' exorcisms as blows against Satan and his kingdom, see Matt 12:24-32. The healing is immediate and complete.

20. *your little faith*: For the characterization of the disciples as *oligopistoi* ("men of little faith") see Matt 6:30; 8:26; 14:31; 16:8. Their "little faith" contrasts with the "unbelief" shown in the synagogue at Nazareth (13:58) and the perfect trust in God's power displayed by Jesus.

    faith like a mustard seed: The parable in Matt 13:31-32 had already described the mustard seed as "the smallest of all seeds" and contrasted it with the marvelous growth that one can expect from it. The ability to move mountains belonged to God (see Isa 40:4; 49:11; 54:10) and quickly became part of various apocalyptic scenarios.

21. Some manuscripts have the following: "But this kind never comes out except by prayer and fasting." It may have been inserted from Mark 9:29. It is possible that Matthew deliberately omitted it and a later scribe reinstated it. Even in Mark it is mysterious in content.

Interpretation

Matthew has taken the long and colorful account of Jesus healing a possessed boy in Mark 9:14-29 and shifted the focus from the faith of the boy's father to the "little faith" of Jesus' disciples. As was his custom in editing Mark's miracle stories, Matthew omitted what struck him as unnecessary details: the varied audience (Mark 9:14-16), the conversation about the boy's condition between Jesus and the father (Mark 9:20-24), and the graphic description of the healing (Mark 9:26). The father appears as an exemplar of faith in Jesus by his posture ("approached him and knelt") and his address ("Lord, have mercy") in Matt 17:14-15. But he is quickly moved off the stage, so that the story becomes an encounter between Jesus and his disciples.

The Matthean version really concerns the disciples' little faith (*oligopistia*). Their inability to heal the boy is traced to their "little faith" (17:20), and thus Jesus' lament in 17:17 ("O faithless and perverse generation") is directed toward the disciples rather than to the father, the crowds, or the whole people. The judgment about their little faith in 17:20 provides the occasion for Matthew to use a Q-saying (see Luke 17:6) about the power of even a "little faith," though there is some tension between the negative and positive meanings given to "little faith" in the two parts of the verse.

Matthew's shift of focus to the disciples was dictated by the context. From 16:5 the disciples have been in the spotlight along with Jesus—in the conversation about the loaves (16:5-12), in Peter's confession of faith and the subsequent instruction (16:13-28), and the transfiguration (17:1-13). After 17:14-20 come a passion prediction and an incident involving Peter (17:22-27). All this builds up to the lengthy instruction directed to the disciples in Matthew 18. In this block where every incident features the disciples, Matthew determined to make Mark's healing of the "epileptic" boy with its focus on the father's faith into a lesson about the "little faith" displayed by Jesus' disciples. He balanced off their "little faith" with a promise of what even a "little faith" can accomplish (17:20b).

Even though Mark's account of the boy's condition is graphic, it is not as clear as Matthew's is: "he is moonstruck and suffers terribly. For he falls sometimes into fire and sometimes into water." The term "moonstruck" reflects the Greek *selēniazetai*, which connects the condition with the phases of the moon (*selēnē*) or even the moon goddess "Selene." Thus Matthew reflects ancient ideas about epilepsy. The word "epilepsy" derives from the Greek verb for "seize" (*epilambanō*), an obvious reference to the seizures suffered by epileptics. In the Jewish apocalyptic milieu of the Gospels these seizures were attributed to demons, who were ultimately under the control of the chief demon Satan. The mention of "fire" and "water" may have some connection with the primal elements of the universe. For ancient views about epilepsy (and other seizures) as the "sacred disease" see the treatise attributed to Hippocrates in LCL 2.127-83 in which the author argues against popular conceptions and advises treatment by natural means: "It is not, in my opinion, any more divine or sacred than other diseases." The Gospel account assumes the popular perception, not the medical approach.

Matthew's primary reason for shifting the focus to the disciples was literary context; now practically everything in chapters 16–18 deals with the disciples. Nevertheless, even this rather unenthusiastic portrait of Jesus' disciples in 17:14-20 figured in the controversy with non-Christian Jewish leaders. The defection of the disciples, the betrayal by Judas, and the denial by Peter were solid parts of the Christian tradition. Matthew never denied these embarrassing facts. But he does tone down the negative and even hostile picture of the Twelve in Mark, which was based largely on literary grounds (the disciples as foils for Jesus). By adding episodes about Peter and by toning down the unflattering picture of the disciples drawn in the second half of Mark, Matthew balances things off and produces a more acceptable image. Even though opponents of the Matthean community could point to the failures of Jesus' first followers, Matthew placed before them and (more importantly) his own community a picture of earnest but fallible people whose attitude before Jesus' resurrection was a "little faith."

Teachers and preachers today must be quick to point out the (false) assumptions surrounding epilepsy in antiquity. While it is perfectly understandable that the evangelists would share those assumptions and could discuss epilepsy only in that way, the Gospel texts should not be used to propagate ideas about epilepsy as "lunacy" and "demonic possession."

Matthew's attention to the disciples' "little faith" opens up a rich topic. The weakness of Jesus' first companions has been a source of encouragement for fallible Christians through the centuries. And the reminder of what even a little faith can achieve (17:20) is a great consolation. By turning another Markan miracle story into an example of "praying faith" (17:14-15) Matthew has also instructed us on the proper attitude toward Jesus in prayer.

45. *Second Passion Prediction; Temple Tax* (17:22-27)

22. As they were gathering in Galilee, Jesus said to them: "The Son of Man is to be handed over into the hands of men, 23. and they will kill him, and on the third day he will be raised up." And they became very sad.

24. When they came into Capernaum, those collecting the half-shekel approached Peter and said: "Does your teacher pay the half-shekel?" 25. He said, "Yes." And as he was coming into the house, Jesus spoke first to him: "What do you think, Simon? From whom do the kings of the earth take tariffs or head-taxes? From their own sons or from others?" 26. When he said "From others," Jesus said to him: "Then the sons are free. 27. But in order that we may not scandalize them, go to the sea, cast a hook, and take the first fish that comes up, and on opening its mouth you will find a shekel. Take that and give it to them for me and you."

Notes

22. *gathering in Galilee*: This is the first place-reference since Caesarea Philippi in 16:13. It could be taken as suggesting that the intervening events occurred outside Galilee, but this interpretation is unlikely. The verb *systrephomenōn* is also somewhat ambiguous. Matthew omits the secret motif in Mark 9:30: "and he did not wish that anyone know."

23. *they became very sad*: Matthew takes over the passion prediction from Mark 9:31 with very minor changes. But he alters the disciples' reaction; see Mark 9:32: "But they did not understand the saying, and they were afraid to ask." The Matthean disciples understand and react appropriately (if not perfectly) in keeping with Jesus' teaching.

24. *Capernaum*: Matthew may have taken the place-name from Mark 9:33. But since Peter lived in Capernaum (see 8:14) and there was a tax office there (see 9:9),

the story may have had some connection with Capernaum in the pre-Matthean tradition.

half-shekel: The Greek word *didrachma* means a "double-drachma" or a "two drachma piece." It was roughly equal to a half-shekel among the Jews. For information about the annual Temple tax among the Jews see below.

25. *kings of the earth*: The expression alludes to Ps 2:2: "the kings of the earth." It refers to rulers in general but probably would have been taken to refer particularly to the Romans and their collaborators in the land of Israel. There is a comparison implied with the King of the Universe.

tariffs or head-taxes: The term *telos* describes indirect taxes or customs duties (see Matt 9:9). The word *kēnsos* can mean "poll tax" or "head tax." It is hard to know with what precision these two terms are used here. They are most likely a general expression for all indirect and direct taxes.

26. *the sons are free*: Those of the household of kings or rulers do not pay taxes. Other people pay taxes to them. As Son of God Jesus had no obligation to pay tax for the support of the Jerusalem Temple since it was his Father's house (see Luke 2:49).

27. *a shekel*: The Greek *statēr* equals four drachmas, enough to pay the Temple tax for both Jesus and Peter. In rabbinic literature there is a parallel story about a pearl found in a fish (see *b. Šabb.* 119a).

Interpretation

In 17:22-23 Matthew made his own the second Markan passion prediction (Mark 9:30-32) in which the Son of Man's betrayal, execution, and resurrection are foretold. Matthew's major editorial contribution here was the framework in which the prediction has been placed: the gathering in Galilee (17:22a), and the disciples' response of sadness (17:23b).

The Temple-tax episode appears to have come from Matthew's special tradition (M). By reason of its content it most likely originated while the Temple was still standing, that is, before A.D. 70. It consists of brief narrative comments that give coherence to conversations between the tax collectors and Peter (vv. 24b-25a), and between Jesus and Peter (vv. 25c-27). It is still another story in Matthew in which Peter assumes the role as spokesman for Jesus' disciples (see 14:28-33; 15:15; 16:16-19; 18:21-22).

The tax at issue in Matt 17:24-27 is usually understood to be the tax levied on every Jew to help pay for the Jerusalem Temple and its upkeep: "We also lay upon ourselves the obligation to charge ourselves yearly with the third part of the shekel for the service of the house of our God" (Neh 10:32). The amount was later raised to a half-shekel in the light of Exod 30:11-16: "half a shekel as an offering to the Lord." Even outside the land of Israel this obligation was taken seriously and endowed with spiritual hopes. Philo claims that "the donors bring them [their contributions] cheerfully and gladly, expecting that payment will give them release from slavery or healing of diseases and the enjoyment of liberty fully secured and also complete preservation from danger" (*Special Laws* 1:77). Likewise the Jews of Babylonia organized a system for collecting and safeguarding the Temple tax (Josephus, *Ant.* 18:312). After the destruction of the Jerusalem Temple in A.D. 70 the Romans kept the tax but diverted the half-shekel (*fiscus iudaicus*) to pay for the temple of Jupiter Capitolinus in Rome (Josephus, *War* 7:218).

Matt 17:24-27 makes the most sense when one assumes that the Temple tax was at issue. The logic of the story revolves around the confession of Jesus as the Son of God. Since the Jerusalem Temple is the house of God, the Son of God (and those who are sons through him; see Rom 8:14, 16, 19, 21) is not obligated to pay for the upkeep of his Father's house. Thus the story carries an implicit Christology about Jesus' divine sonship and extends his privileges to his followers. The logic is the rabbinic *qal wĕḥômer* ("from the light [case] to the heavy"): If the children of the kings of the earth do not pay taxes toward the upkeep of the royal buildings, certainly the Son of God need not pay the Temple tax.

Yet "in order that we may not scandalize them" (17:27) Jesus devises a miraculous way in which he and Peter pay the Temple tax. Whom might they scandalize? The most obvious and dangerous subject of Christian scandal would be the Roman officials. But probably even more on Matthew's mind here were his fellow Jews. What would happen if Jesus' followers refused to pay the Temple tax? They would cease to be considered Jews. And that was something that neither Jesus nor Matthew wanted. Nevertheless, the Jewish Christians considered payment of the Temple tax a theological anomaly in view of their faith in Jesus as Son of God. So the episode in Matt 17:24-27 gave them a theological rationale for why they had no obligation to pay the tax as well as a prudential strategy ("that we may not scandalize them") for paying the tax. With diversion of the tax after A.D. 70 to a pagan temple it became even more important that Jewish Christians have a position on this matter. The episode in Matt 17:24-27 allowed them to hold on to their theological claims about Jesus, to retain their standing as Jews, and to keep out of trouble with the Romans.

Matthew's major contribution to the second passion prediction concerned the disciples' reaction: "they became very sad." Matthew deliberately suppressed Mark's comment that the disciples failed to understand. The Matthean response of sadness is an entirely fitting emotion with respect to Jesus' passion.

The episode in Matt 17:24-27 fits in with the general early Christian attitude toward taxes and the state (see Matt 22:15-22; Rom 13:1-7; 1 Pet 2:13-17; Titus 3:1. Compare Revelation for another approach). But how Christians today relate to the state need not be dictated by these texts, since the total situation has to be taken into account. Closer to Matthew's heart here was balancing his identities both as a Jew and a follower of Jesus. He retained his faith in Jesus as the Son of God and his identity as a Jew by paying the Temple tax. This episode allowed Jewish Christians such as Matthew to be Jewish and Christian.

For Reference and Further Study

Cassidy, R. J. "Matthew 17:24-27—A Word on Civil Taxes." *CBQ* 41 (1979) 571–80.

Homeau, H. A. "On Fishing for Staters: Matthew 17:27." *ExpTim* 85 (1974) 340–42.

Légasse, S. "Jésus et l'impôt du Temple (Matthieu 17, 24–27)." *SciEsp* 24 (1972) 361–77.

Thompson, W. G. *Matthew's Advice to a Divided Community. Mt. 17, 22-18, 35.* AB 44. Rome: Biblical Institute Press, 1970.

46. *Care for the "Little Ones"* (18:1-14)

1. In that time the disciples approached Jesus and said: "Who is greatest in the kingdom of heaven?" 2. And summoning a child, he placed him in the midst of them, 3. and said: "Amen I say to you, unless you turn and become like children, you shall not enter the kingdom of heaven. 4. Whoever will humble himself like this child, this one is the greatest in the kingdom of heaven.

5. "And who receives one such child in my name, receives me. 6. But whoever causes to sin one of these little ones who believe in me, it is better for him that a millstone be hung about his neck and he be drowned in the depth of the sea. 7. Woe to the world because of scandals. For it is necessary that scandals come, but woe to the man through whom the scandal comes. 8. If your hand or your foot causes you to sin, cut it off and cast it from you. It is better for you to enter into life maimed or lame than having two hands or two feet to be cast into the eternal fire. 9. And if your eye causes you to sin, pluck it out and cast it from you. It is better for you to enter life with one eye than having two eyes to be cast into the gehenna of fire.

10. "See that you do not despise one of these little ones. For I say to you that their angels in heaven always behold the face of my Father in heaven. 12. What do you think? If a man has a hundred sheep and one of them wanders off, will he not leave the ninety-nine on the hills and go and seek out the lost one? 13. And if he happens to find it, Amen I say to you that he will rejoice over it more than over the ninety-nine that did not wander off. 14. So it is not the will of your Father in heaven that one of these little ones be lost."

Notes

1. *the disciples approached Jesus*: Matthew changes what had been a heated dispute in Mark 9:33-34 among the disciples into a question put to Jesus by the disciples. By adding "in the kingdom of heaven" he transforms their query into a more spiritual concern than preeminence among the disciples. The unit is rounded off in 18:4 by the same expression: "the greatest in the kingdom of heaven."

2. *child*: The term *paidion* refers to children under the age of twelve. Since such children had no social status or political significance, Jesus' symbolic action in placing the child in the disciples' midst was an appropriate way to undercut their speculations about status in the kingdom.

4. *humble himself*: Verses 3-4 are the negative and positive formulations of the basic point. The humility praised here has a strong social-status component: Only by becoming a "nobody" and disregarding social status can one expect to become great in God's kingdom. See Matt 5:3 where the kingdom is promised to the poor in spirit.

5. *one such child*: If *paidion* refers to a real child as in 18:2, the verse goes with 18:1-4 and describes a welcoming attitude toward children. But if the verse goes with 18:6-9, *paidion* is used as a metaphor and functions as a synonym for "little one" in 18:6.

   receives me: For the idea of receiving Christ by receiving those who belong to him, see Matt 10:40 and 25:31-46. For Christ's enduring presence in the community see 28:20. The expression "in my name" is the equivalent of "because of me" or "because I commanded it."

6. *causes to sin*: The verb *skandalizō* and its noun *skandalon* appear six times in Matt 18:6-9. A "scandal" is a trap or stumbling block upon the way. In a religious or moral context it refers to temptation to sin or encitement to apostasy. For Matthew's particular concern about scandal, see Matt 5:29-30; 11:6; 15:12; 16:23; 17:27; 24:10; 26:31-32.

   these little ones: The qualifying phrase "who believe in me" makes clear that the term is used metaphorically to describe members of the community. For treating the "little ones" in an appropriate way, see Matt 10:42; 25:40, 45.

   mill-stone: The Greek is *mylos onikos* ("a donkey mill"), that is, a large mill worked by a donkey. Matthew stresses the fate of the agent of scandal by having him drowned in "the depth" of the sea. So the one with a huge stone around his neck sinks to the deepest part of the sea.

7. *it is necessary that scandals come*: Matthew adds this comment. Even though scandals must come, the agent of scandal must bear the responsibility. For the necessity of scandals see Matt 24:10; for the principle as applied to Judas, see Matt 26:24.

8. *your hand or your foot*: Matt 18:8-9 is a simplified version of Mark 9:43-48; it omits the mysterious quotation of Isa 66:24 in 9:48: "their worm does not die, and the fire is not quenched." In the context of Matthew 18 the body-parts may be

metaphorical references to those who cause scandal in the community and the need to excommunicate them (see 1 Cor 5:1-5).

eternal fire: Mark 9:43 has "unquenchable fire." The parallel expression in Matt 18:9 is "gehenna of fire": for other occurrences of "gehenna," see Matt 5:22, 29, 30; 10:28; 23:15, 33. The term "Gehenna" referred originally to the Valley of Hinnom located west and south of Jerusalem along the Kidron Valley. In the NT it designates the place or state of the final punishment of the wicked.

10. *these little ones*: The metaphorical use of *mikroi* is continued from 18:6. Their guardian angels (see Acts 12:15) are said to have unrestricted access to the divine presence. Therefore these particularly precious people are not to be despised.

11. Some manuscripts add: "For the Son of Man came to seek and save the lost." The same sentence appears in Luke 19:10. It was probably inserted in Matt 18:11 to serve as a bridge between 18:10 and 18:12-14.

12. *one of them wanders off*: In Ezekiel 34 the shepherds of Israel are criticized: "the strayed you have not brought back" (34:6). God promises to serve as the shepherd: "I will seek the lost, and I will bring back the strayed" (34:15-16). For the verb "wander off" or "go astray" (*planaō*) see Matt 24:4, 5, 11, 24.

13. *if he happens to find it*: The parallel in Luke 15:5 reads: "when he has found it." Matthew gives a subtle reminder that the search is not always successful. Joy over the finding of the lost sheep need not imply lack of concern for those who never strayed (see Luke 15:25-32).

14. *the will of your Father*: The reading "my Father" reflects the influence of "my Father" in 18:10. The Greek literally says "the will before your Father," which is a kind of "targumism" to avoid direct speech about God (see *Targum Isaiah* 53:6, 10). Matthew's application identifies the shepherd as God (see Ezek 34:15).

Interpretation

The fourth major discourse in the Gospel (18:1-35) breaks into two parts; the first part (18:1-14) deals with the "little ones," and the second part (18:15-35) concerns the brother who sins. Each part ends with a parable—the lost sheep (18:12-14), and the king and his servant (18:21-35).

The movement of the first part (18:1-14) is attached first to the word for "child" (*paidion*) in 18:2-5 and then to "little ones" (*mikroi*) in 18:6, 10, 14. The realistic use of the term "child" in 18:2 soon yields to metaphorical applications as the text proceeds. A major problem in interpreting Matt 18:1-14 is determining the extent to which it should be taken as a literary and theological unity. Even though the material arose independently and the same words carry different meanings, it is possible to read the text as a unified instruction on life within the community.

The audience for the fourth discourse is Jesus' disciples (18:1). The first unit (18:2-4) is Jesus' response to their question about greatness in the kingdom of heaven. In editing Mark 9:33-36, Matthew has improved the disciples' image again by having them question Jesus directly rather than having him intervene in their quarrel. Also the issue is no longer greatness among Jesus' disciples but rather greatness in the kingdom of heaven. And Jesus' symbolic action with the child is given an explicit interpretation in 18:3-4 (cf. Mark 9:36).

In the second unit (18:5-9; see Mark 9:37, 42-50) the focus shifts from the child as symbol to the "little ones" who can be led into sin. The keyword is "scandal." In 18:7 Matthew has added a comment on the necessity of scandals and the responsibility of those through whom scandals come. Given the community context of 18:8-9, the references to parts of the body (hand, foot, eye) probably are to be taken as metaphors for those who cause scandal.

Matthew's adaptation of the Q-parable of the lost sheep (Luke 15:4-7) reflects the experience of the community. He distinguishes between "wandering off" (18:12-13) and "perishing" or "being lost" (18:14). The shepherd searches out the "strays" to prevent them from perishing. That the search was not always successful is suggested by the Matthean qualification in 18:13 ("if he happens to find it").

The Essene community at Qumran provides some enlightening parallels for interpreting Jesus' discourse in Matthew 18. The disciples' question about greatness in the kingdom of heaven (18:1) is appropriate for a community in which social status was taken seriously. The Qumran community was highly structured; at ceremonies (1QS 2:19-25) and assemblies (6:8-13) a hierarchical order of priests, Levites, and the "many" was strictly observed: "And no man shall go down from the place he must occupy, nor raise himself above the place to which his lot assigns him" (1QS 2:23). The appendix to the *Community Rule* (1QSa) suggests that the hierarchical order observed at the community's meals was understood to be an anticipation or prefigurement of what would happen with the coming of God's kingdom.

Thus the disciples' question about greatness in God's kingdom fits into first-century Judaism. Jesus' response about becoming like a "child" challenges cultural assumptions about social status. The child is not so much a symbol of sinlessness or dependence here but rather an example of a social "nobody." The child had no status and no social importance. Jesus challenges his followers not to think in terms of social hierarchies. The "humility" that he recommends involves putting aside such considerations and being willing to become a social "nobody."

The depiction of a city or a community in terms of a human body was common in the first century. See H. Conzelmann, *1 Corinthians* (Philadelphia: Fortress, 1975) 211 for the references to classical sources. In 1 Corinthians 12–14 Paul used the image of the body to correct abuses within the Christian community at Corinth. Thus it is not impossible that in the community context of Matthew 18 the sayings about body-parts (18:8-9) carried a community interpretation.

The Qumran *Manual of Discipline* 2:11b-17 envisions the possibility of expelling a member who "has left before him whatever causes him to fall into iniquity and to turn away from God." The sentence passed on such a one who has fallen takes the form of a curse: "May God set him apart for evil, and may he be cut off from the midst of the sons of light, because he has turned away from God on account of his idols and of that which causes him to stumble into sin!"

Matthew's adaptations of Mark 9:33-37, 42-50 and Q (=Luke 15:4-7) suggest that in chapter 18 his basic concern was life *within* the Christian community. Thus he addresses the problems of status-seeking, scandal, and straying members. He shows particular interest in those whom he calls the "little ones" (see 10:42), probably people of undistinguished status and modest personal gifts whose pastoral care Matthew viewed as especially important.

Although the focus of attention in Matt 18:1-14 is community life, there may also be a "side-glance" outside. The text may contrast the lack of concern for social status within Jesus' community and the fondness for status and honorific titles in the early rabbinic community (see Matt 23:5-12). And it outlines processes for dealing with those who need to be cut off and with the strays who need to be reconciled. Since such processes were used by the Essene and early rabbinic communities, it was only natural that the Matthean Christians should have their own procedures and that their rules might help to define their community identity for both insiders and outsiders.

Since Matt 18:1-14 concerns life within the community, the potential for actualization is very rich. The passage calls into question our ideas about social status and personal importance—both in God's kingdom and in our lives on earth. It admits the reality of sin within the Church, while outlining procedures for dealing with those who cause others to sin. It displays pastoral zeal especially for the marginal ("little ones") and the "strays," according to the example of God the Shepherd. It is both sobering and encouraging to recognize that the Church of the first century had the same problems that Christians today face.

For Reference and Further Study

Addley, W. P. "Matthew 18 and the Church as the Body of Christ." *Biblical Theology* 26 (1976) 12–18.

Légasse, S. *Jésus et l'enfant.* Paris: Gabalda, 1969.

Schweizer, E. "Matthew's View of the Church in His 18th Chapter." *Australian Biblical Review* 21 (1973) 7–14.

47. *The Brother Who Sins* (18:15-35)

15. "If your brother sins [against you], go, reprove him between you and him alone. If he listens to you, you have gained your brother. 16. If he does not listen, take with you one or two others in order that every word may be confirmed by the mouth of two or three witnesses. 17. If he refuses to listen to them, tell the church. And if he refuses to listen to the church, let him be to you like a Gentile and a tax collector. 18. Amen I say to you, whatever you bind on earth will be bound in heaven, and whatever you loose on earth will be loosed in heaven.

19. "Again I say to you that if two of you agree about any case on earth that they might ask, it will be done for them by my Father in heaven. 20. For wherever two or three are gathered in my name, there I am in the midst of them."

21. Then Peter approached and said to him: "Lord, how often shall my brother sin against me and I forgive him? As many as seven times?" 22. Jesus said to him: "I do not say to you 'as many as seven times,' but 'as many as seventy times seven times.'

23. "Therefore the kingdom of God may be compared to a king who wished to settle accounts with his servants. 24. When he began to settle, there was brought before him a man who owed ten thousand talents. 25. Since he did not have the money to pay him back, the master ordered that he and the wife and children and all that he had be sold and he be paid back. 26. The servant fell down, paid him homage, and said: 'Be patient with me, and I will pay everything back to you.' 27. The master had pity on that servant and released him and forgave him the loan. 28. But that servant went out and found one of his fellow servants who owed him a hundred denarii, and he took hold of him and choked him, saying: 'Pay back whatever you owe.' 29. His fellow servant fell down and called upon him, saying: 'Be patient with me, and I will pay you back.' 30. But he was not willing. He went and threw him into prison until he should pay back what was owed. 31. When his fellow servants saw what happened, they became very sad and went and informed their master all that had happened. 32. Then his master summoned him and said to him: 'Wicked servant, I forgave you all that debt, when you begged me. 33. Should you also not have had mercy on your fellow servant as I had mercy on you?' 34. And his master grew angry and handed him over to the torturers until he might pay back everything owed to him. 35. So also my heavenly Father will do to you, unless each of you forgive his brother from your hearts."

Notes

15. [*against you*]: This phrase is absent from many important manuscripts. It was probably a scribal addition under the influence of Matt 18:21. Thus in the original Matthean text the offense was unspecified but most likely had implications for the entire community as the three-step process implies.

reprove him: The first step in the process of correction is based on Lev 19:17: "You shall not hate your brother in your heart, but you shall reason with your neighbor, lest you bear sin because of him." The verb *elegxon* suggests the influence of the Septuagint text of Lev 19:17 (*elegmō elegxeis*).

16. *one or two others*: The second step is based on Deut 19:15: "only on the evidence of two witnesses, or of three witnesses, shall a charge be sustained." The biblical procedure presupposes a criminal offense, not a problem within a community. To what do the one or two witness? Is it the offense committed by the erring member, or is it his unwillingness to repent?

17. *church*: See Matt 16:18 for the only other use of *ekklēsia* in the Gospels. The local congregation is meant, whether in formal assembly for meeting or through its board of elders. The term *ekklēsia* distinguishes the Christian community from "their synagogues."

    like a Gentile and a tax collector: The expression presupposes a largely Jewish-Christian milieu (see Matt 5:46-47; 6:7) in which such people are looked down upon. Nevertheless, earlier in the Gospel such persons have shown great faith in Jesus (8:1-11; 9:9-13; 11:19; 15:21-28). The sentence sounds like a decree of excommunication. For shunning erring Christians, see 1 Cor 5:1-5; 2 Thess 3:6-15; 2 John 10.

18. *whatever you bind*: The power to bind and loose, previously bestowed on Peter in 16:19, is now given to the disciples at large. Taken in context with 18:15-17, that power would seem to concern either the imposing (and lifting) of decrees of excommunication or the forgiving (and not forgiving) of sins.

19. *about any case*: The Greek word *pragma* ("case") continues the juridical context established in 18:15-18. The ideas of agreement, common prayer, and Christ's presence are here in the service of exercising the power to bind and loose in the case of the brother who sins.

20. *wherever two or three are gathered*: The context continues to be judicial, not directly liturgical. In rabbinic writings the context is usually study of the Torah: "if two sit together and words of the Law pass between them, the divine presence abides between them" (*m. 'Abot* 3:2).

21. *how often . . . against me*: Peter again serves as spokesman for the group (see 17:24). Here unlike 18:15 the sin is a personal offense against a community member ("against me") such as lying, slander, etc. Peter obviously imagines that he was being very generous in his willingness to forgive up to seven times.

22. *seventy times seven times*: The number *hebdomēkontakis hepta* can be translated also as seventy-seven times. Whether it be 77 or 490 times, the point is that there can be no limits to the willingness to forgive. The numbers allude to Gen 4:24: "If Cain is avenged sevenfold, truly Lamech seventy-sevenfold."

23. *Therefore*: Yet the parable illustrates not the quantity of forgiveness (how often?) but the quality by giving the reason for "no limits": If God places no limits, humans cannot place a limit. On the other hand, those who place limits on forgiving others will have limits placed on their forgiveness by God.

servants: Despite the term *douloi* ("slaves") these are high officials in the king's bureaucracy (see 18:28, 31).

24. *ten thousand talents*: A "talent" was a very high measure of money, worth between six thousand and ten thousand denarii when one denarius was a day's pay (20:2). So ten thousand talents is an astronomical sum (like a billion dollars for us), a debt so large that the servant could never repay it (see 18:26).

25. *wife and children*: Although some biblical texts assume that children could be sold into slavery to make up their father's debts (2 Kgs 4:1; Isa 50:1; Neh 5:5), this was not the practice in Jesus' time. Under no circumstances in Jewish law could the wife be taken. We are to assume that the king was understood to be a Gentile. Since the proceeds from the sale could not repay the debt, the king's action must have been intended as punishment.

27. *loan*: The only NT occurrence of *daneion* transforms the "debt" into a "loan." In response to the servant's plea for patience (18:26) the master not only remits the debt but also shows amazing sensitivity and generosity by calling it euphemistically a "loan."

28. *a hundred denarii*: Compared to the debt of ten thousand talents this was a piddling sum (100 days' wages) that could easily be paid back if the servant showed patience. His treatment of the fellow servant contrasts sharply with that shown to him by the king.

33. *as I had mercy on you*: The wicked servant learned nothing from the mercy displayed to him. For the connection between our willingness to forgive others and God's willingness to forgive us see Matt 6:14-15. In fact, the parable is the dramatization of that principle.

35. *So also my heavenly Father will do*: The threat of punishment against those who refuse to forgive others has been made in 18:34 ("his master grew angry and handed him over to the torturers"). Thus Matthew underscores the reality of punishment for sin. Torture was not allowed under Jewish law but was widespread in antiquity.

Interpretation

The material parallel to Matt 18:15-35 occurs in Luke 17:3 (correcting a brother) and 17:4 (forgiving a brother seven times). These parallels indicate that Matthew took over the two basic ideas from Q and expanded them greatly with traditional materials. The keyword that holds the material together is "brother." The first part concerns correcting the brother who sins (18:15-20), and the second part deals with how often a brother may be forgiven (18:21-35).

The three-step procedure for reconciling a brother in 18:15-17 (one-on-one, with one or two further witnesses, the Church) probably reflects the practice of the Matthean community. In this context the sayings about binding and loosing (18:18) and two or three gathered in Jesus' name should be interpreted in the framework of reconciliation within the community (18:19-20).

Peter's question about the limits of forgiveness ("as many as seven times?") is given a response that renders the question absurd (18:21-22). The parable of the unforgiving servant (18:23-34) explains why. After setting the situation (18:23), the parable narrates encounters between the king and his servant (18:24-27), that servant and his fellow servant (18:28-30), and the king and his servant again (18:31-34). The final verse (18:35) underlines the lesson to be drawn from the parable. The parable presumes Jewish concepts about God's mercy and justice. God is willing to show mercy to sinners, but they must be prepared to show mercy to other people. To those who refuse to be merciful God will show strict justice.

The three-step procedure for reconciling a brother who sins (18:15-17) was practiced also among the Qumran Essenes: "They shall reprove each other in truth and humility and loving charity towards the other" (1QS 5:24-25). The brother who sins against another brother "shall be reproved on the very same day . . . Also let no cause be brought before the Many, by one man against another, unless reproof has been made before witnesses" (1QS 5:26–6:2; see CD 9:2-3). Though rooted in Scripture (see Lev 19:17; Deut 19:15), the Qumran and Matthean communities developed their own procedures for dealing with cases within the community. The goal of such procedures was twofold: to make the sinner objectify and "own" his sin at every stage, and to recall the sinner to full community by recognizing and repenting of his sin. Whether the Matthean Christians picked up the three-step procedure from the Essenes or the two groups developed it independently cannot be determined.

As in the section about the "little ones" (18:1-14), so the material about the "brother who sins" (18:15-35) is directed primarily toward members of the Matthean community—their attitudes and their behavior. The text outlines a process to be used in bringing back to full communion a member who sins (18:15-17). The sayings about binding and loosing (18:18) and the two or three gathered in Jesus' name (18:19-20)—whatever their original context may have been and whatever their applications have been through the centuries—provided a theological foundation for community decisions: God stands behind them, and Jesus abides within the community gathered in his name. The parable about the unjust servant (18:23-35) reveals the foolishness of placing any limits upon forgiveness within the community.

The parallel between Matt 18:15-17 and *Manual of Discipline* 5:25–6:1 shows that the problem of the brother who sins and how to deal with him was a concern for Jews in the first century. Though we cannot be certain, it is probable that those who controlled "their synagogues" developed similar procedures. In the parable of the unforgiving servant (18:23-35) the divine attributes of justice and mercy so emphasized in rabbinic Judaism are placed in relation: If you want mercy from God, be merciful to others. If you exact justice from others, expect the same from God (see Matt 6:14-15).

The implications of Matt 18:15-35 for life within the Church today are great. The text outlines a clear procedure designed to help the sinner recognize the sin and return to the community. It roots reconciliation and forgiveness of sins in God's mercy, and thus reveals the foolishness of those who try to set limits on their willingness to forgive others.

For Reference and Further Study

Deidun, T. "The Parable of the Unmerciful Servant (Mt 18:23-35)." *BTB* (1976) 203–24.

García Martínez, F. "La represión fraterna en Qumrán y Mt 18, 15-17." *Filologia Neotestamentaria* 2 (1989) 23–40.

Lona, H. E. " 'In meinem Namen versammelt.' Mt 18,20 und liturgisches Handeln." *Archiv für Liturgiewissenschaft* 27 (1985) 373–404.

Pfitzner, V. C. "Purified Community—Purified Sinner. Expulsion from the community according to Matthew 18:15-18 and 1 Corinthians 5:1-5." *Australian Biblical Review* 30 (1982) 34–55.

Scott, B. B. "The King's Accounting. Matthew 18:23-34." *JBL* 104 (1985) 429–42.

Sievers, J. " 'Where Two or Three . . .': The Rabbinic Concept of Shekhinah and Matthew 18:20." *SIDIC* 17 (1984) 4–10.

48. *Marriage and Divorce, Celibacy, Children* (19:1-15)

1. And when Jesus finished these words, he went away from Galilee and came into the region of Judea across the Jordan. 2. And large crowds followed him, and he healed them there.

3. And Pharisees came up to him and tested him, saying: "Is it lawful for a man to divorce his wife for any cause?" 4. He answered and said: "Have you not read that he who created them from the beginning made them male and female? 5. And he said: 'On account of this a man shall leave father and mother, and be joined to his wife, and the two shall become one flesh?' 6. As a result they are no longer two but one flesh. What God has joined together, let not man separate." 7. They said to him: "Why did Moses command to give a writ of separation and to divorce?" 8. He

said to them: "On account of your hardness of heart Moses allowed you to divorce your wives. But from the beginning it was not so. 9. I say to you that whoever divorces his wife except for sexual irregularity and marries another commits adultery."

10. The disciples said to him: "If this is the case of a man with his wife, it is better not to marry." 11. He said to them: "Not all can accept this teaching but those to whom it is given. 12. For there are eunuchs who were born such from the mother's womb, and there are eunuchs who have been made eunuchs by men, and there are eunuchs who have made themselves such on account of the kingdom of heaven. Whoever can accept it, let him accept it."

13. Then children were brought to him that he might lay hands on them and pray. But the disciples rebuked them. 14. Jesus said: "Let the children come to me and do not hinder them. For to such belongs the kingdom of heaven." 15. And he laid hands on them and went away from there.

Notes

1. *when Jesus finished*: Jesus' fourth major discourse ends as the others do with the verb "finish" (*teleō*); see 7:28; 11:1; 13:53; 26:1. At this point Jesus moves his ministry from Galilee to Judea. By traveling through Perea across the Jordan Jesus avoids Samaria on his way up to Jerusalem (cf. Luke 9:52).

2. *large crowds followed*: Matthew made several changes in Mark 10:1b: adding "large," using "followed" (the usual word for discipleship), and stating that Jesus healed the crowds (rather than teaching them).

3. *for any cause*: By adding this phrase to Mark 10:2 Matthew moved the Pharisees' question from one about the legality of divorce to one about the grounds for divorce. The Matthean issue becomes, For what reason may a man divorce his wife? For the debate within Judaism see the discussion below.

4. *he who created them*: The positive element in Jesus' teaching involves God's will in creation. This is established by joining two quotations from Genesis 1–2: God made them "male and female" (Gen 1:27), and willed that they become "one flesh" (Gen 2:24). Matthew's quotation of Gen 2:24 includes the phrase "and be joined to his wife," which strengthens the idea of indissolubility.

6. *let not man separate*: The "man" here is the husband, not some third party like a judge. In Judaism marriage was a contract, which could be broken by the male partner. Such a case is envisioned in Deut 24:1. For the formulas used in a bill of divorce see the discussion below.

7. *Moses command*: The Pharisees take Deut 24:1 as a positive commandment, whereas Jesus in 19:8 understood it as merely a concession because of people's "hardness of heart." He contrasts this concession with God's original will for men and women expressed in the creation story.

9. *apart from sexual irregularity*: See the notes on Matt 5:32. The term *porneia* may refer to (1) sexual misconduct on the woman's part or (2) marriage within the

degrees of kinship forbidden by Lev 18:6-18. Matthew omits Mark 10:12, in which the wife is depicted as initiating the divorce procedure—something at least very unusual within Judaism. Mark 10:12 is often explained as an adaptation to Roman law.

10. *it is better not to marry*: The disciples' comment seems inappropriate, as if the attraction of marriage depended on easy divorce. It really serves the literary purpose of introducing the "eunuch saying" in 19:12.

11. *this teaching*: Does "this teaching" refer back to the disciples' comment in 19:10 ("it is better not to marry")? Or does it refer to Jesus' teaching on marriage and divorce in 19:3-9? The former seems more likely. There is a longstanding debate about the subject of the "eunuch saying": Is it celibacy, or is it remarriage after the death or divorce of the spouse?

12. *on account of the kingdom of heaven*: The third member of the "eunuch saying" supplies the proper motivation for celibacy—dedication to the kingdom of heaven. For negative attitudes toward the practice of castration in the OT, see Deut 23:1; Lev 22:24. The unusual character of this teaching is underscored by the concluding comment: "Whoever can accept it . . ."

13. *that he might lay hands on them and pray*: Matthew makes the enigmatic statement in Mark 10:13 ("that he might touch them") into the ritual imparting of a blessing by a famous teacher. The youth of the children is expressed by the passive verb ("were brought"). Why the disciples were annoyed is not clear.

14. *do not hinder them*: Any connection with the early Christian debate about infant baptism (see Acts 8:36; 10:47; 11:17) is unlikely at Matthew's level. As was his custom, Matthew omits the reference to Jesus' emotions in Mark 10:14 ("he was indignant").

    to such belongs the kingdom: As in Matt 18:3 the child is presented as a model. In this case the idea is that the child receives the kingdom for what it is—a gift. A child has no social claim on the kingdom, nor can the child claim it on the basis of achievements. In later Judaism the child's religious duties begin only at twelve or thirteen, with the so-called Bar Mitzvah.

Interpretation

With chapter 19 Matthew rejoins Mark's narrative, which will serve as his basic source for the remainder of the Gospel. Mark 10:1-16 recounts the start of Jesus' ministry in Judea. After finishing off the fourth major discourse and setting the scene for Jesus' teaching (19:1-2=Mark 10:1), Matthew reshaped Jesus' teaching on marriage and divorce (Mark 10:2-12) to make its argument more coherent and place it more firmly in the context of Judaism (19:3-9). By adding "for any cause" in 19:3 and reserving the possibility of an exception in 19:9 ("except for sexual irregularity") Matthew has made Jesus a party in the first-century Jewish debate about the proper grounds for divorce (see below). He also restructured the argument so that the positive argument about God's will for men and women from the creation comes first and the concession made by Moses comes second. The Matthean account follows the neat order of question (19:3, 7) and answer (19:4-6, 8-9). The case of a wife initiating divorce—more common in Roman law than in Jewish law—is omitted entirely (see Mark 10:12).

Between Mark 10:12 and 10:13 Matthew has inserted the "eunuch saying" (19:10-12), which recommends celibacy undertaken "on account of the kingdom of heaven" as an alternative to marriage. The saying insists that such celibacy is a gift and is not for everyone.

With the blessing of the children (19:13-15) Matthew rejoins Mark (10:13-16) but makes the event a more formal ceremony in which the teacher imparts a blessing to the children. The climax of the account is the representation of the young children as exemplars for how to receive God's kingdom.

Divorce is alluded to in the Hebrew Bible only indirectly. Deut 24:1-4 refers to the practice in ruling on the case of a second marriage to the same woman after she had been married to someone else. The case is introduced as follows: "When a man takes a wife and marries her, if then she finds no favor in his eyes because he has found some indecency in her, and he writes her a bill of divorce and puts it in her hand and sends her out of the house . . ." (24:1). The text makes clear that it is the husband's prerogative to initiate the divorce and that the divorce consists in the husband presenting the wife with a document (whereby she is free to marry someone else) and sending her away.

The problem comes with the reason for divorce ("because he has found some indecency"). The Hebrew is *'erwat dabar*. The precise interpretation of *'erwat dabar* was a matter of controversy in the first century. According to *m. Giṭṭin* 9:10 the School of Shammai reversed the order of the words to read *debar 'erwāh* ("something shameful"), which they interpreted as sexual misconduct. The two exceptive clauses in Matt 5:32 (*logos porneias*) and 19:9 (*epi porneia*) seem to take a stand with the school of Shammai against the more liberal views of the School of Hillel (even if the wife spoils a dish for him) and Rabbi Aqiba (even if he found another more beautiful than she is). Jesus' own teaching on divorce seems to have been even stricter (no divorce at all), perhaps in agreement with the Qumran Essenes (see CD 4:19–5:2; 11QTemple, though the interpretation of these texts remains controverted). For a full treatment of the NT marriage and divorce texts, see B. Vawter, "Divorce and the New Testament," *CBQ* 39 (1977) 528–42.

The literary genre in which the Matthean Jesus establishes his position on marriage and divorce is a scriptural debate. The assumption of the argument is that Gen 1:27 and 2:24 expressed God's original will for the human race and that the indirect description of divorce in Deut 24:1 was only a temporary concession.

The practice of celibacy was unusual in ancient Judaism. Later rabbinic statements are very strong on this matter: "Rabbi Eliezer said: 'Any Jew who does not have a wife is not a man' " (*b. Yebam.* 63a). But in the first century the Essenes and the Therapeutae, members of Jewish sects who lived a "monastic" life, were celibate. Likewise, John the Baptist, Jesus, and Paul do not seem to have married. The rabbinic emphasis on the duty of marriage need not be read back so as to cover all forms of first century Judaism. What is most important about Matt 19:10-12 is the motivation proposed for voluntary celibacy: "on account of the kingdom of heaven."

The blessing of the children (19:13-15) is loosely connected to the preceding material by subject matter. The connection between the imposition of hands and imparting a blessing is as old as Gen 48:14-15: "Israel stretched out his right hand . . . and he blessed Joseph . . ." That a teacher like Jesus should be asked to impart a blessing on children was not unusual. What was unusual in the Greco-Roman world was Jesus' willingness to take children seriously as persons and to propose them as models for human behavior, especially in receiving the kingdom of God.

In the context of the late first-century Jewish debate Matt 19:1-15 provided Jesus' positions on some controversial issues: marriage and the grounds for divorce, celibacy, and children. Matthew took great pains to situate these teachings in a Jewish context. Nevertheless, he also wished to highlight the distinctive views of Jesus on these matters: Monogamy was God's will from the beginning, and divorce is only a concession; celibacy undertaken "on account of the kingdom of heaven" is a praiseworthy state, though not meant for all; children are real persons and embody the attitude that all should have toward God's kingdom.

The issues of marriage and divorce, celibacy, and the status of children remain controversial today. Sometimes the debated aspects distract attention from the more basic teachings of Jesus on these matters. The ideal of marriage as a lifelong commitment in which two people become one remains a magnificent (if often elusive) ideal. The idea of a celibate life consecrated to the kingdom of heaven is a striking challenge to the values of modern Western societies. The respect for children and their ability to symbolize the proper approach to God's kingdom seems particularly important in view of recent revelations about child abuse.

In each of these issues the Matthean Jesus speaks from within Judaism and takes a position that at least was not foreign to some Jews in the first century. In these debates we find ourselves at the point before Jewish and Christian positions hardened into opposing viewpoints and opposing religions: easy divorce versus no divorce (in theory), marriage as duty versus celibacy as a superior state, and no religious obligations for children under twelve versus children as blessed and as exemplars of receiving God's kingdom.

For Reference and Further Study

Moloney, F. J. "Matthew 19,3-12 and Celibacy." *JSNT* 2 (1979) 42–60.
Quesnell, Q. " 'Made Themselves Eunuchs for the Kingdom of Heaven.' " *CBQ* 30 (1968) 335–58.
Sand, A. *Reich Gottes und Eheverzicht im Evangelium nach Matthäus.* Stuttgart: Katholisches Bibelwerk, 1983.

49. *The Dangers of Wealth* (19:16-30)

16. And behold one came up to him and said: "Teacher, what good thing shall I do that I might have eternal life?" 17. He said to him: "Why do you ask me about what is good? One is the good one. But if you wish to enter into life, keep the commandments." 18. He said to him: "Which ones?" Jesus said: "You shall not murder. You shall not commit adultery. You shall not steal. You shall not bear false witness. 19. Honor father and mother. And you shall love your neighbor as yourself." 20. The young man said to him: "I have kept all these. What am I still lacking?" 21. Jesus said to him: "If you wish to be perfect, go sell your possessions and give to the poor, and you will have treasure in heaven, and come follow me." 22. When the young man heard this word, he went away sad. For he had many possessions.

23. Jesus said to his disciples: "Amen I say to you that a rich man will enter the kingdom of heaven with difficulty. 24. Again I say to you that it is easier for a camel to enter through the eye of a needle than for a rich man to enter into the kingdom of God." 25. When the disciples heard this they were very surprised and said: "Then who can be saved?" 26. Jesus looked up and said to them: "With human beings this is impossible, but with God all things are possible."

27. Then Peter answered and said to him: "Behold we have left everything and followed you. What then shall be ours?" 28. Jesus said to them: "Amen I say to you that you who have followed me—in the new age when the Son of Man will sit upon his throne of glory, you yourselves will sit upon twelve thrones, judging the twelve tribes of Israel. 29. And everyone who has left houses or brothers or sisters or father or mother or children or fields on account of my name will receive a hundredfold and will inherit eternal life. 30. But many first will be last, and last first."

Notes

16. *what good thing*: Matthew simplifies the appearance of the questioner (see Mark 10:17), revealing only at the end that he was wealthy (19:22). He also avoids

the strange banter in Mark 10:17-18 by transferring the adjective "good" to "thing" instead of Mark 10:17 ("Good teacher, what shall I do?").

18. *Which ones?*: The list that follows is taken from the second part of the Decalogue (Exod 20:12-17; Deut 5:16-21). Matthew omits the intrusive "do not defraud" in Mark 10:19. He adds the command to love one's neighbor (Lev 19:18; see Gal 5:14; Jas 2:8). Keeping these qualifies one to enter the kingdom and enjoy eternal life in it.

20. *young man*: Only Matthew (see also 9:22) identifies the questioner as a young man (*neaniskos*); cf. Mark 10:20, 22; Luke 18:21, 23. Matthew omits the reference to Jesus' emotions in Mark 10:21 ("Jesus looking upon him loved him").

21. *If you wish to be perfect*: Only Matthew prefaces Jesus' challenge with the conditional clause. For an earlier challenge to be perfect, see Matt 5:48. Giving up possessions is not incumbent on all, nor is it presented as absolutely necessary for the man to enter eternal life. But in his case possessions seem to be the obstacle in his following the path of full discipleship.

22. *he had many possessions*: The young man's possessions probably included property and the benefits resulting from it. Jesus invited him to a life of discipleship, which meant traveling from place to place to proclaim the coming of God's kingdom. His reaction in refusing the call leads to a series of sayings on wealth as an obstacle to discipleship and even entering the kingdom.

23. *with difficulty*: Now the topic under discussion is not the call to discipleship but entering the kingdom (see 19:16-19). Even that is very difficult for a rich man; see the discussion below about the dangers of wealth. Matthew omits the disciples' amazement at Jesus' teaching in Mark 10:24 and Jesus' repetition of the saying.

24. *a camel . . . through the eye of a needle*: The hyperbole suggests that it is impossible for a rich man to enter the kingdom. Rabbinic literature uses the figure of an elephant passing through a needle's eye to describe something that is impossible (see *b. Ber.* 55b). The manuscript reading *kamilon* ("rope") instead of *kamēlon* ("camel") tries to soften the hyperbole. There is no basis to the idea that in ancient Jerusalem there was a gate called the "Needle" or one that was so narrow that a camel could barely squeeze through.

25. *who can be saved?*: According to Deut 28:1-14 and other texts wealth and related blessings were a consequence of obeying the voice of the Lord. If wealthy people cannot enter eternal life, how can anyone else do so? Jesus' response in 19:26 emphasizes that salvation is finally a gift from God, not a human achievement.

28. *in the new age*: In response to Peter's question about the reward for those who follow Jesus (19:27), Jesus promises a share in the Son of Man's glory. The Greek term *palingenesia* ("rebirth") has a rich background in Greco-Roman philosophy. But here it is used to describe the new age/world to be ushered in by the full coming of God's kingdom.

the twelve tribes of Israel: For the Son of Man enthroned in glory see Daniel 7, and Matt 25:31-46. See also 1 Enoch 45:3; 51:3; 55:4; 61:8; 62:2. The twelve disciples share in Jesus' glory and his task as judge. There is no reason to interpret the twelve tribes of Israel as a symbol for the Church. Matthew meant Israel.

29. *father or mother*: Matthew reversed the order of the list in Mark 10:29-30 ("mother or father"). He also omitted some key Markan phrases: "and on account of the gospel"; "now in this age . . . and in the age to come"; and "with persecutions." Matthew does not rule out the hundredfold in this age, but shows more interest in the age to come.

30. *and last first*: In the context of Matt 19:16-29 the saying alludes to the "great reversal" that underlies the teaching about wealth and poverty. In the context of what follows (20:1-16) the saying brackets (19:30; 20:16) the story of workers who are paid in the reverse order of their hiring.

INTERPRETATION

The three sub-units in Matt 19:16-30 follow Mark 10:17-31: Jesus' encounter with the rich young man (19:16-22 = Mark 10:17-22), his instruction on the dangers of wealth (19:23-26 = Mark 10:23-27), and his promise in answer to Peter's question (19:27-30 = Mark 10:28-30). In the first sub-unit (19:16-22) Matthew introduces the command to love one's neighbor as oneself (19:19), thus providing a new theological basis for the rich young man's giving away of his many possessions. Also by inserting the condition "If you wish to be perfect" (19:21), Matthew seems to leave room for two grades of religious observance: keeping the commandments (19:16-20), and following Jesus as a full-fledged disciple (19:21-22). The young man refuses to take the step into the second grade. Nevertheless, Jesus indicates that if he keeps the commandments he will "enter into life" (19:17).

Apart from omitting the disciples' puzzlement at Jesus' teaching (19:23; see Mark 10:24) Matthew's second sub-unit follows Mark 10:23-27 closely. But in Matt 19:27-30 the evangelist inserts the picture of the "new age" when the Son of Man will sit in glory along with the twelve apostles to judge the twelve tribes of Israel (19:28). Thus Matthew places the primary and most spectacular reward for discipleship in the age/world to come, and he ties it in with the destiny of all Israel. The symbolism of the twelve tribes of Israel was undoubtedly present in the institution of the twelve apostles. The group gathered around Jesus represents Israel (but not the new Israel!). Their eschatological function will be to preside at the judgment of all Israel. For the judgment of the Gentiles see Matt 25:31-46.

In dealing with Matt 19:16-30 it is customary to point to the Jewish assumption of wealth as a blessing from God upon the righteous (see Deut 28:1-14) and to contrast that with the Christian ideal of renunciation of material goods for the sake of the kingdom. But such comparisons are misleading.

It is clear that the Qumran Essenes practiced voluntary renunciation of their material goods on entering the community. According to *Manual of Discipline* 1:11-13, "all the volunteers that cling to his truth shall bring all their understanding and powers and possessions into the Community of God to purify . . . all their possessions according to His righteous Counsel." For other references to the practice of voluntary poverty in the sect see 1 QS 6:19, 22; 9:8-9, 22. The theological context for the Qumran community's lifestyle was preparation for the full coming of God's kingdom.

Also, warnings about the dangers of wealth were familiar from the biblical tradition. In his picture of the day of wrath Ezekiel calls attention to the inability of silver and gold to deliver those for whom "it was the stumbling block of their iniquity" (Ezek 7:19). The wisdom tradition counsels balance and moderation: "Better is a little with the fear of the Lord than great treasure and trouble with it" (Prov 15:16); "give me neither poverty nor riches . . . lest I be full and deny thee, and say, 'Who is the Lord?' " (Prov 30:8-9). Perhaps the most eloquent warning about the dangers of wealth appears in Sirach 31:5-7:

> He who loves gold will not be justified.
>   and he who pursues money will be led astray by it.
> Many have come to ruin because of gold,
>   and their destruction has met them face to face.
> It is a stumbling block to those who are devoted to it.
>   and every fool will be taken captive by it.

With these teachings about the dangers of wealth Matthew places Jesus in the prophetic and wisdom traditions. The renunciation of material goods was not entirely foreign to first-century Judaism, as the Qumran *Manual of Discipline* shows. Nevertheless, the early Christians lived a different lifestyle from that of the Essenes. They did not cultivate the monastic form of life that the Qumran community did. They were more concerned with proclaiming the coming kingdom than simply waiting for it. It is possible that Matthew's addition to the list of commandments in 19:19 ("And you shall love your neighbor as yourself") adds to the renunciation of material goods proposed to the rich young man a note of social concern. By giving away his possessions to the poor and following Jesus, the young man would deprive himself of the opportunity to practice almsgiving in the future. The insertion of the love-command in 19:19 could soften that deprivation by an appeal to the "golden rule" (see Matt 7:12).

In the context of the Matthean community's conflict with other Jewish groups the most important claim appears in Matt 19:28: "in the new age when the Son of Man will sit upon his throne of glory, you yourselves will sit upon twelve thrones, judging the twelve tribes of Israel." The saying promises to the twelve apostles a decisive eschatological role vis-à-vis Israel. There is no need to identify the twelve tribes with the Church or to talk about the "new Israel." The twelve remain within Israel and exercise their function as judges for the twelve tribes. The point is that at the eschaton Jesus and his disciples will be revealed as the most important persons among the Jewish people. Though such claims appeared fantastic to the opponents, for the Matthean Christians they offered hope in the dark days of the late first century.

The most obvious matters for actualization in Matt 19:16-30 are the challenges to renunciation of goods and to recognition of the dangers of wealth. If such teachings were difficult in first-century Palestine, they are far more so in the affluent West of the late twentieth century! Most people in our society find such teachings to be utterly foreign and impracticable. Nevertheless, they remain major themes in the Gospels.

In Matt 19:16-22 there seems to be a distinction between keeping the commandments and full discipleship. Nevertheless, keeping the commandments is assumed to be sufficient to "have eternal life" and "to enter into life" (19:16-17). In Christian history this distinction has been used as the basis for a division between ordinary Christians and those who practice the "evangelical counsels" (poverty, chastity, and obedience) in monastic or other religious communities. Modern commentators are quick to deny that such a distinction exists in Matt 19:16-22 so as to indicate two levels of Christian life.

But the rich young man was not a Christian! He was a Jew. When he asked about having eternal life, the answer he got from Jesus was "Keep the commandments." If he does so, he will enter into life (19:17). This text seems to envision the possibility of salvation for Jews apart from the route of Christian discipleship (to which the rich young man is nevertheless invited, if he wishes to be perfect).

For Reference and Further Study

Burnett, F. W. "*Palingenesia* in Matt. 19, 28: A Window to the Matthean Community." *JSNT* 17 (1983) 60–72.

Derrett, J. D. M. "Palingenesia (Matthew 19.28)." *JSNT* 20 (1984) 51–58.

Theissen, G. " 'Wir haben alles verlassen.' " *NovT* 19 (1977) 161–96.

50. *The Parable of the Good Employer* (20:1-16)

1. "For the kingdom of heaven is like a householder who went out early in the morning to hire workers for his vineyard. 2. After he agreed with the workers for a denarius a day, he sent them into his vineyard. 3. And when he went out about the third hour, he saw others standing in the marketplace without work, 4. and he said to them: 'You go into the vineyard too, and whatever is just I will give to you.' 5. They went forth. Again he went out about the sixth and ninth hour, and he did the same. 6. About the eleventh hour he went out and found others standing around, and said to them: 'Why have you stood here all day without work?' 7. They said to him: 'Because no one hired us.' He said to them: 'You go into the vineyard too.' 8. When it was evening, the master of the vineyard said to his steward: 'Call the workers and give them pay, beginning from the last up to the first.' 9. Those who came around the eleventh hour received a denarius. 10. And those who came first thought that they would receive more. And they also received one denarius. 11. When they received it they murmured against the householder, 12. saying: 'These last ones worked one hour, and you made them equal to us who have borne the burden of the day and the heat.' 13. He answered one of them and said: 'Friend, I did you no injustice. Did you not agree with me for a denarius? 14. Take what is yours and go. I choose to give to this last one as to you. 15. Is it not allowed to me to do what I wish with my own? Or is your eye evil because I am good?' 16. So the last will be first, and the first last."

Notes

1. *vineyard*: For the vineyard as a symbol for Israel, see the discussion below. Note that the householder rather than the steward (see 20:8) goes out to do the hiring. The introductory phrase "the kingdom of heaven is like . . ." suggests that the kingdom is like the entire parable that follows, not just the householder.

2. *a denarius a day*: The agreed price is apparently the average day's wage for such a worker. See Tobit 5:15. These workers are day-laborers, whereas in the vineyard parable in Matt 21:33-46 the workers seem to have steady employment. At harvest-time it would be especially appropriate to hire day-laborers. This fact may hint at an eschatological element to Matt 20:1-16.

3. *about the third hour*: Even though the Jewish day began at sunset, the hours were counted from sunrise. The third hour would be about 9 A.M., the sixth and the ninth hours (Matt 20:5) noon and 3 P.M., and the eleventh hour (20:6) 5 P.M.

4. *whatever is just*: After the first group was hired, the householder specified no sum. His claim to pay whatever is just prepares for the grumbling of the first group (20:12) and the master's response "I did you no injustice" (20:13). The workers hired after dawn did not expect the daily wage of a full denarius.

7. *Because no one hired us*: The response of the last group is puzzling. Why did the householder not hire a full complement of workers? Why did he need more workers so late in the day? Was it because the work was so pressing or because the first workers did not work efficiently? These questions, while interesting, fail to take the story on its own terms.

8. *When it was evening*: It was customary that a day-laborer be paid the very evening of his work: "The wages of a hired servant shall not remain with you all night until the morning" (Lev 19:13). The surprises are that payment begins with those hired last and that all the workers receive the same wages.

10. *those who came first*: Because they are paid last they become spectators through the entire process. They naturally expected to receive more (even though they agreed to a denarius) and grumbled against the householder when their expectations were disappointed. After all, they had worked twelve hours (not one), and they had experienced the severe heat.

13. *Friend, I did you no injustice*: The laborers had omitted any honorific address in their words to the householder in 20:12. He addresses them as "friend" (*hetaire*); see 22:12; 26:50. In all three cases the person is in the wrong. He is not cheating the workers since they had agreed to the wage of a denarius for the day's work.

15. *is your eye evil*: For the "evil eye" see Matt 6:23. Here the image is used to describe envy, jealousy, and lack of generosity. The first workers begrudge the master's generosity.

16. *the last will be first*: The same saying appeared in Matt 19:30, thus providing a framework for the parable. The framework is appropriate only to the order of payment (20:8). All the workers are rewarded with the same pay.

Interpretation

Peculiar to Matthew, this parable appears as an illustration of the saying in Matt 19:30 (=Mark 10:31) about the last being first and the first being last. That saying is repeated in Matt 20:16, and the Markan source (10:32-34) is taken up again at 20:17. Nevertheless, the connection between the saying and the parable is somewhat weak, since the only point really in common comes with the order of payment in 20:8. The order of payment, while necessary to the dramatic presentation (otherwise how would the first workers hired know what the others received?), is not the core of the parable.

The parable contains two major parts: the hiring of the workers (20:1-7), and the paying of the workers (20:8-15). In the first part (20:1-7) the householder (*oikodespotēs*) goes out to the marketplace to hire day-laborers for his vineyard. He meets with and hires four (or five) different groups throughout the day: at dawn (20:1-2), at the third hour (20:3-4), at the sixth and ninth hours (20:5), and at the eleventh hour (20:6-7). The second part (20:8-15) takes place at the vineyard. At the accounting the owner is called "lord" or "master" (*kyrios*). This part consists of the payment (20:8-10), the protest by the first workers hired (20:11-12), and the response by the owner (20:13-15). The owner's defense of his generous action joins direct statements and rhetorical questions.

The traditional title of the parable is "the workers in the vineyard." But the laborers are really only foils for the central character who is the householder/master. Therefore some argue that a better title is "the good employer" since he is the main character from start to finish. A recent variation designed to take account of the master's unusual payment practice is the "affirmative action employer."

Underlying the parable is the identification of the employer as God. But as is the case with most parables, that identification should not be pressed too hard. Efforts to identify the steward (20:8) as Jesus go too far in the direction of allegory. Likewise, the latecomers correspond to the tax collectors and sinners who turned their lives around in response to Jesus. The ones hired first are those who have been religiously observant all along, like the scribes and Pharisees. But again these identifications ought not to be pushed too far or made more precise.

The key to interpreting the parable is the image of the vineyard as a symbol for Israel, the same symbolism that underlies the vineyard parable in Matt 21:33-46. The most explicit source of the symbolism is Isa 5:1-7: "My beloved had a vineyard . . . the vineyard of the Lord of hosts is the house of Israel." The same vineyard = Israel symbolism appears in Jer 12:10: "Many shepherds have destroyed my vineyard."

Joined with the vineyard symbolism is the idea of the last judgment as a harvest (see Matt 13:39). The fact that the householder needs more and more workers indicates that harvest-time is near. In the evening, at the end of the day, there is a settling of accounts and the distribution of rewards. The one who oversees the accounting is the lord/master (*kyrios*) of the vineyard.

With its vineyard and harvest symbolism the parable of "the good employer" concerns the last judgment and should be so interpreted. The issue treated in the parable is why the latecomers receive the same reward as those who came earlier to work. The answer is that the kingdom is God's gift to give and we must not begrudge God his generosity.

The parable of the good employer defends Jesus' special concern for the marginal in Jewish society ("a friend of tax collectors and sinners," according to Matt 11:19). A recurring complaint against his ministry was his association with disreputable people, an association that he never denied: "I came not to call the righteous, but sinners" (Matt 9:13). This parable, like the prodigal son (Luke 15:11-32), defends this association by appealing to the generosity of God. Just as it is possible to entitle Luke 15:11-32 the "prodigal father," so one can call Matt 20:1-15 the "prodigal employer."

There is a balance between God's justice and God's mercy. Those who were hired first receive a just reward, one to which they had already agreed (20:1-2). The fact that the latecomers received the same reward can be credited to God's mercy (20:13-15).

The criticisms about those with whom Jesus associated continued after his death. Their prominence in the Gospels indicates that such objections became part of the debate between Jewish Christians and their rivals. Parables such as the good employer gave the Matthean community a means of defending Jesus against these charges and a rationale for welcoming "tax collectors and sinners" (see Matt 9:9-13) into their own company.

The parable offers a rich doctrine of God: the relation between divine justice and mercy, God's generosity toward "the last," and the sureness of reward (and punishment) at the last judgment. It helps to ground the Church's ministry to the marginal in society, especially those who are spiritually on the edge.

Reliance on God's generosity ought not to blind us to the need for the pastoral care of those who bear "the burden of the day and the heat" (20:12). Their reaction needs to be taken seriously. They must be led to acknowledge the justice of God, to appreciate the generosity of God toward sinners, and to enter into the joy of repentance (see Luke 15:25-32).

For Reference and Further Study

Barré, M. L. "The Workers in the Vineyard." *Bible Today* 24 (1986) 173–80.

Culbertson, P. "Reclaiming the Matthean Vineyard Parables." *Encounter* 49 (1988) 257–83.

Derrett, J. D. M. "Workers in the Vineyard: A Parable of Jesus." *JJS* 25 (1974) 64–91.

Manns, F. "L'arrière-plan socio-économique de la Parabole des ouvriers de la onzième heure et ses limites." *Antonianum* 55 (1980) 258–68.

51. *The Cup of Suffering* (20:17-28)

17. And as Jesus was going up to Jerusalem, he took the Twelve aside and on the way said to them: 18. "Behold we are going up to Jerusalem, and the Son of Man will be handed over to the chief priests and scribes, and they will condemn him to death, 19. and deliver him to the Gentiles to be mocked and scourged and crucified, and on the third day he will be raised."

20. Then the mother of the sons of Zebedee with her sons approached him, did him homage, and asked something from him. 21. He said to her: "What do you wish?" She said to him: "Command that these two sons of mine sit one at your right and one at your left in your kingdom." 22. Jesus answered and said: "You do not know what you are asking. Can you drink the cup that I am going to drink?" They said to him: "We can." 23. He said to them: "You will drink my cup, but to sit at my right and my left is not mine to give but it is for those for whom it has been prepared by my Father." 24. When the ten heard, they were indignant about the two brothers. 25. But Jesus called them and said: "You know that the rulers of the Gentiles lord it over them and the great ones exercise authority over them. 26. It shall not be so among you. But whoever wishes to be great among you shall be your servant, 27. and whoever wishes to be first among you shall be your slave. 28. Likewise the Son of Man did not come to be served but to serve and to give his life as a ransom for many."

Notes

17. *As Jesus was going up*: Matthew has rewritten Mark 10:32 to present Jesus as fully in charge and to soften the negative portrait of the disciples ("they were amazed . . . afraid"). There are several minor textual problems connected with Matthew's text: "was about to go up"; "the twelve disciples"; "on the way."

18. *we are going up*: In comparison with Matt 16:21; 17:22-23 the third passion prediction is more detailed: It foretells the handing over of Jesus to the chief priests (26:57) and his condemnation by them (26:66); the handing over to the Romans (27:2); the mocking, scourging, and crucifixion (27:26-30; 27:32-44); and the resurrection (28:1-10).

19. *crucified*: Matthew specifies the mode of Jesus' death as crucifixion, whereas Mark 10:34 says "they will kill (him)." Crucifixion was a Roman penalty. Jews administered the death penalty by stoning, burning, beheading, and strangling (*m. Sanh.* 7:1). Once more Matthew changes "after three days" to "on the third day" (see Matt 16:21; 17:23).

20. *the mother*: In Mark 10:35 James and John approached Jesus directly with the request. Since the request shows a deep misunderstanding of Jesus' teaching, the change seems to have been part of Matthew's program of protecting and improving the image of Jesus' disciples. The device is dropped in 20:22 where Jesus addresses the sons of Zebedee directly.

21. *one at your right and one at your left*: The mother's request picks up on the picture sketched in Matt 19:28. At table and in other formal situations the most important person was in the center, the next most important at his right, and the third most important at the left. Matthew says "in your kingdom" rather than "in your glory" (Mark 10:37). Both expressions refer to life in God's kingdom.

22. *the cup*: For the background to the cup of suffering and death see the discussion below. Matthew omits the references to "baptism" (drowning as a mode of death) in Mark 10:38, 39, probably because they might be misunderstood in view of the use of "baptism" as the way of describing Christian initiation (see Matt 28:19).

    we can: The mother has disappeared. The two disciples' confident reply is ironic in light of the cowardice that they and the other disciples show during the passion (see 26:56).

23. *you will drink my cup*: The primary reference here is to the suffering that the disciples will share. For the martyrdom of James see Acts 12:2. Various legends surround the death of John, but precise information about his death is hard to come by (see John 21:23).

    not mine to give: Matthew (cf. Mark 10:40) assigns this prerogative to the Father. Since the saying implies the subordination of Jesus to God the Father, it was used by the Arians in early Christological debates. It remains unclear for whom these places are prepared.

24. *they were indignant*: The disciples' indignation probably stems from jealousy rather than the correct understanding of Jesus' teaching. By omitting "and" (Mark 10:42) at the start of the next verse Matthew tied even closer the teaching about service to the disciples' misunderstanding.

25. *the rulers of the Gentiles*: The mode of leadership among the Gentiles is described in very strong terms: *katakyrieuousin* ("lord it over") and *katexousiazousin* ("exercise authority"). The prefix *kata-* implies domination *over* another; the roots to which they are attached appear in the common NT words for "Lord" (*kyrios*) and "power" (*exousia*).

26. *your servant*: The terms used to describe the Christian ideal of servant-leadership are humble words: *diakonos* ("one who waits on tables") and *doulos* ("slave"). These terms contrast with the "power" words used to describe leadership among the Gentiles in 20:25.

27. *your slave*: Mark 10:44 has "slave of all." Matthew has brought the second expression into line with the first ("your servant").

28. *as a ransom for many*: The word *lytron* ("ransom") describes the deliverance of a captive by means of a purchase. The expression "for many" alludes to the Servant figure in Isa 53:11-12. To "give one's life" means to endure martyrdom (see 1 Macc 2:50; 6:44). The Son of Man's service in giving his life effects more than the rulers of the Gentiles could ever achieve.

INTERPRETATION

Jesus and his disciples near the end of their journey up to Jerusalem. That journey began with Peter's confession at Caesarea Philippi (Matt 16:13-20) and ends with Jesus' entrance into Jerusalem in Matt 21:1. For the entire journey narrative and even for the idea of a final journey Matthew has followed Mark 8:27–10:52.

In Matt 20:17-28 the source is Mark 10:32-45. Matthew has taken over the pattern or outline that was so important to Mark: passion prediction (20:17-19), misunderstanding by the disciples (20:20-24), and corrective teaching about following Jesus (20:25-28). This same Markan outline was adopted for the first two passion predictions (16:21-28; and 17:22-23; 18:1-4).

The minor editorial changes introduced by Matthew are treated in the notes. The major modification concerns the image of the disciple. By way of introduction (20:17) Matthew omits the references to the amazement and fear of the disciples (see Mark 10:32). He has Jesus take charge of the journey and cuts down the description of his followers. Matthew also "improves" the image of the disciples by having the mother of Zebedee's sons make the request on their behalf. That the first followers of Jesus (see 4:18-22) should have so thoroughly misunderstood Jesus' teaching was probably as hard for Matthew to accept as it is for us. And so he took the step of blaming their mother for the request for prominent places in the kingdom. He dropped this substitution by 20:22 where Jesus enters direct conversation with Zebedee's sons. Matthew's vindication of the disciples and the improvement of their image are not complete. But the kind of changes that he made in 20:17-28 shows that Mark's negative portrayal of them caused problems for Matthew.

In response to the disciples' request Jesus asks: "Can you drink the cup that I am going to drink?" Matthew's omission of the potentially confusing references to the "baptism" of suffering (see Mark 10:38, 39) gives even more prominence to the image of the cup.

Whereas the disciples imagine that Jesus refers to the joy of the messianic banquet in the kingdom of heaven, he is really talking about his suffering and death—a fate in which the disciples themselves will share (20:23). In so doing Jesus calls on the biblical image of the "cup" of suffering. That image was especially prominent among the prophets to describe the destruction of Jerusalem and the exile of its leaders in the early sixth century B.C.: "Take from my hand this cup of the wine of wrath" (Jer 25:15); "if those who did not deserve to drink the cup must drink it" (Jer 49:12); "Babylon was a golden cup in the Lord's hand, making all the earth drunken" (Jer 51:7); "to you also the cup shall pass" (Lam 4:21); "you shall drink your sister's cup . . . a cup of horror and desolation" (Ezek 23:32-33); "you who have drunk at the hand of the Lord the cup of his wrath" (Isa 51:17).

So the image of the "cup" of Israel's suffering is used to symbolize the sufferings of Jesus. The image reappears in the accounts of Jesus' Last Supper (26:27) and his prayer in Gethsemane (26:39, 42). Thus the image of the cup connects Jesus' passion with the tradition of Israel's suffering in the past. Jesus stands firmly within the tradition of Israel, not outside it or over against it. The "cup" also provides an important dimension to the appreciation of the Eucharist: Sharing the "cup" of Jesus involves sharing in his passion and death and in Israel's tradition of suffering.

The message of Matt 20:17-28 for the Matthean community was twofold: Jesus foretold the shameful events that befell him, and leadership in Jesus' community means service to others. The first part of the message answered the critics of the Christian movement by claiming that Jesus the Son of God was very much in control of his own destiny and willingly gave up his life as a "ransom for many" (20:28). The part about becoming the "servant" (*diakonos*) and "slave" (*doulos*) of others not only provided a challenge to those within the Matthean community but also may have carried a criticism of Jewish communities that were cultivating honorific titles such as "rabbi," "father," and "master" (23:10).

The misunderstanding and confusion surrounding the third passion prediction reminds us how hard it is to understand and accept any suffering and especially the suffering of Jesus. The challenge to act upon the ideal of servant leadership remains difficult. There is always a temptation to turn even humble words like *diakonos* and *doulos* into honorific titles, despite their most basic meanings. Finally the "cup" image has great potential for actualization. With the "cup" image Matthew ties Jesus' sufferings to Israel's sufferings in its defeat and exile. The Eucharistic "cup" ties the Lord's Supper to Jesus' passion and to Israel's past.

52. *The Healing Son of David* (20:29-34)

29. And as they went forth from Jericho a large crowd followed him. 30. And behold two blind men were sitting by the road. When they heard that Jesus was passing by, they shouted out, saying: "Lord, have mercy on us, Son of David." 31. The crowd rebuked them that they should be silent. But they shouted even more, saying: "Lord, have mercy on us, Son of David." 32. Jesus stopped and called them and said: "What do you wish that I should do?" 33. And they said to him: "Lord, that our eyes may be opened." 34. Jesus took pity on them and touched their eyes, and immediately they saw again and followed him.

Notes

29. *from Jericho*: Matthew smoothes out the awkward sequence in Mark 10:46 whereby they come to Jericho and then go out of it. Jericho is five miles west of the Jordan, and fifteen miles northeast of Jerusalem. We are probably to imagine the scene at a settlement near the ancient site, not at the winter palace complex built by Herod the Great.

30. *two blind men*: Mark 10:46 has one blind "beggar" named Bartimaeus, the son of Timaeus. See also Matt 8:28 where there are two demoniacs (cf. Mark 5:2) and Matt 9:27 where there are two blind men. Why Matthew had a fondness for such doublings has received no satisfactory explanation. In this case the doubling may have been influenced by the omission of Mark 8:22-26.

    Jesus was passing by: Some commentators find in the verb *paragei* ("pass by") an allusion to God's "passing through" the land of Egypt on the first Passover (see Exod 12:11-12). The same term appears in Matt 9:27. Other coincidences in vocabulary include "touch" (9:29; 20:34) and "follow" (9:27; 20:30).

    Lord: Here and in 20:31 Matthew prefaces the prayer of the two blind men with "Lord" (see Matt 8:25 for another example of praying faith). Since Matthew eliminates the explicit references to faith in the story (see Mark 10:52; Matt 9:28-29), he must have considered the two requests enough to include the element of faith.

33. *that our eyes may be opened*: For giving sight to the blind as the sign of the day of the Lord see: "In that day . . . the eyes of the blind shall see" (Isa 29:18); "Then the eyes of the blind shall be opened" (35:5).

34. *Jesus took pity*: Matthew supplies the emotional term *splagchnistheis* (cf. Mark 10:52; Matt 9:29). As in Matt 9:29 Jesus touches the eyes of the blind men. Matthew omits the references to faith in Mark 10:52 and Matt 9:29.

    followed him: According to Mark 10:52 Bartimaeus followed Jesus "on the way," that is, up to Jerusalem. But Mark never mentions Bartimaeus again. Perhaps Matthew plays down the impression that the two men became Jesus' disciples by omitting "on the way."

Interpretation

The healing of the two blind men in Matt 20:29-34 is clearly based on the Bartimaeus story in Mark 10:46-52, a story that Matthew already used even more freely in Matt 9:27-31. In adapting the Markan account in 20:29-34 Matthew has eliminated some details: the coming to and going out of Jericho, the name Bartimaeus and the description of him as a "beggar," the complicated process whereby the blind man approaches Jesus (Mark 10:49-50), the explicit emphasis on faith, and the idea that Bartimaeus followed Jesus "on the way" (of discipleship). In Mark Bartimaeus is the first one to address Jesus publicly as "Son of David." Furthermore, Mark uses the healing of blind men (Mark 8:22-26; 10:46-52) to bracket the central section of his Gospel, whereas Matthew omits the first of those stories. Matthew clearly does not attribute the same pivotal importance that Mark did to the Bartimaeus story. Matthew presents it as an example of the healing power of the Son of David and his mercy ("have mercy on us" in 20:30, 31; "Jesus took pity," in 20:34).

Another element that emerges from Matthew's editing is an emphasis on conversation. Even though the term "faith" is absent, the theme is stressed nonetheless by means of the literary structure of the text. After the scene is set and the characters are introduced (20:29-30a), the blind men shout out "Lord, have mercy on us, Son of David" and the crowd quiets them (20:30b-31a), they shout out the same prayer again and Jesus summons them (20:31b-32a), and Jesus asks them what they want and they tell him that they want to have their eyes opened (20:32b-33). Thus the central section takes the form of a conversation or dialogue of faith in three movements. The story ends with a display of power and mercy by the Son of David.

The two blind men address Jesus as "Son of David": "Lord, have mercy on us, Son of David" (20:30, 31). Matthew presents the Son of David as a healer. He heals two blind men in 9:27-31, a blind and mute demoniac in 12:22-24, the daughter of the Canaanite woman in 15:21-28, and two blind men in 20:29-34. In each case Jesus performs his healing actions precisely as the "Son of David." This title is thus prominent in Jesus' ministry of healing every disease and infirmity (see 4:23; 9:35; 10:1; etc.).

The most famous "Son of David" was Solomon. It is possible that a Solomon-Christology is in the background of Matthew's portrait of Jesus as the "therapeutic Son of David." The root of this tradition was the biblical description of Solomon as "wiser than all other men" (1 Kgs 4:31). In intertestamental literature there are references to Solomon's dominion over demons (Josephus, *Ant.* 8:45-49; *Bib. Ant.* 60; 11Q Ps Ap[a]; *Testament of Solomon*). The ring of Solomon had power to bind demons according to *b. Gitt.* 68a and the incantation bowls. For a full study of this motif see D. C. Duling, "Solomon, Exorcism, and the Son of David," *HTR* 68 (1975) 235–52. Matthew has moved beyond concentration on the Son of David as an exorcist and portrayed Jesus the Son of David as one who heals many kinds of diseases and infirmities. So when the two blind men call on Jesus as the "Son of David," they bring up associations with the Solomon tradition and ask Jesus to heal their blindness.

What kind of Son of David was Jesus? From the genealogy of Jesus in Matt 1:1-17 it is clear that Son of David was an important title for Matthew and his community. But establishing genealogical descent does not exhaust Jesus' identity as the Son of David. Jesus does what Solomon (according to contemporary sources) did. He not only casts out demons but also heals every disease and infirmity. His healing ministry is directed especially to those on the margin of Jewish society: the blind, the possessed, and the Gentiles. With his concept of Jesus as the therapeutic Son of David, Matthew explained to other Jews why Jesus could associate and minister to such persons and still retain his dignity and importance as the Son of David.

The healing of the two blind men in Matt 20:29-34 is another example of "praying faith" at work. The powerful Son of David shows mercy to those in need. He waits only for us to show faith by articulating our trust in his power and in his mercy. Thus the Matthean version of the Bartimaeus story can serve as a lesson in the dynamics and efficacy of prayer.

For Reference and Further Study

Duling, D. C. "The Therapeutic Son of David: An Element in Matthew's Christological Apologetic." *NTS* 24 (1978) 392–410.

Kingsbury, J. D. "The Title 'Son of David' in Matthew's Gospel." *JBL* 95 (1976) 591–602.

Loader, W. R. G. "Son of David, Blindness, Possession, and Duality in Matthew." *CBQ* 44 (1982) 570–85.

53. *Jesus' Entrance into Jerusalem and Its Temple* (21:1-17)

1. And when they drew near to Jerusalem and came to Bethphage, to the Mount of Olives, then Jesus sent two disciples, 2. saying to them: "Go into the village opposite you, and immediately you will find an ass tied and a colt with it. Untie them and bring them to me. 3. And if anyone says anything to you, say that 'the master has need of them,' and he will send them immediately." 4. This took place in order that what was said through the prophet might be fulfilled: 5. "Tell the daughter of Zion, 'Behold your king comes to you, meek and seated upon an ass and upon a colt, the foal of a beast of burden.' " 6. The disciples went and did as Jesus ordered them. 7. They brought the ass and the foal, and put garments on them; and he sat upon them. 8. Most of the crowd spread their own garments on the road; others cut branches from the trees and spread them on the road. 9. The crowds that went before him and those that followed shouted out, saying: "Hosanna to the Son of David. Blessed is he who comes in the name of the Lord. Hosanna in the highest." 10. And when he entered Jerusalem, the whole city shook, saying: "Who is this?" 11. The crowds said: "This is the prophet Jesus who is from Nazareth of Galilee."

12. And Jesus entered the temple area and drove out all those who were selling and buying in the temple area, and he overturned the tables of the moneychangers and the benches of those selling doves. 13. And he said

to them: "It is written: 'My house shall be called a house of prayer, but you have made it a den of bandits.' "

14. And blind and lame people approached him in the temple area, and he healed them. 15. When the chief priests and the scribes saw the wonders that he did and the children shouting in the temple area and saying: "Hosanna to the Son of David," they became indignant, 16. and said to him: "Do you hear what these are saying?" But Jesus said to them: "Yes. Have you never read that 'Out of the mouth of infants and sucklings you have brought perfect praise?' " 17. And leaving them he went out of the city to Bethany, and he lodged there.

Notes

1. *Bethphage*: The name means "house of figs"; it was a small village east of Jerusalem. The Mount of Olives runs parallel to the eastern side of Jerusalem. According to Zech 14:4 a great eschatological battle would take place there. See Josephus (*Ant.* 20:167-72) for the story of a messianic pretender who claimed to be able to bring down Jerusalem's walls while standing on the Mount of Olives.
2. *an ass tied and a colt with it*: Mark 11:2 has a "colt tied." The doubling of the animals may be due to Matthew's literal reading of the parallelism in Zech 9:9 ("riding on an ass, on a colt the foal of an ass"). The term *polos* ("colt") could refer to a young horse but here it must mean a young donkey in light of Zech 9:9.
3. *'the master has need of it'*: It is not clear that Jesus' instructions reflect an arrangement that he had made beforehand with the owner or indicate a supernatural foreknowledge. Likewise, the term *kyrios* is ambiguous. It can mean "master" or "teacher" but to early Christian readers it meant "Lord."
4. *might be fulfilled*: Matthew makes explicit the OT quotation behind Mark 11:10. The first part ("Tell the daughter of Zion") is from Isa 62:11. The second part is Zech 9:9 ("Behold your king comes . . ."). Matthew thus presents Jesus' entrance into Jerusalem as the fulfillment of OT prophecy.
5. *meek and seated upon an ass*: Matthew omits from Zech 9:9 "righteous and victorious is he," thus leaving the emphasis on Jesus as the "meek" or humble king. The "and" between the ass and the colt led Matthew to imagine that there were two animals (see 21:2).
6. *as Jesus ordered them*: Matthew omits Mark 11:4b-6 in which the disciples carry out Jesus' orders. The omission highlights the fulfillment of Scripture and plays down the idea of Jesus' foreknowledge (or his prior arrangement).
7. *he sat upon them*: It is not clear whether "them" refers to the garments or to the animals, though ultimately both are meant.
8. *branches*: The ceremonial use of palm branches was more appropriate to the feasts of Tabernacles and Hanukkah than to Passover (see Lev 23:39-43; 1 Macc 13:51; 2 Macc 10:7).

9. *Hosanna*: The Greek transliteration of the Hebrew *hôšî'â-nā'* means literally "save, please" but here functions as a greeting of homage rather than a plea for help. The rest of the greeting comes from Ps 118:26. Matthew omitted the second part of the greeting in Mark 11:10 ("Blessed is the coming kingdom of our Father David").

10. *the whole city shook*: The verb "shook" is *eseisthē*, a strong word used to describe the effects of an earthquake. By adding 21:10-11 Matthew enlarges the impact that Jesus' entrance made.

11. *the prophet*: The people of Jerusalem refer to Jesus' reputation that has preceded him. As yet they have no experience of him. To Matthew's readers there may have been an allusion to the prophet like Moses (see Deut 18:15, 18).

12. *the Temple area*: The term *hieron* refers here to the whole Temple enclosure rather than the holy of holies. Those "selling and buying" were dealing in sacrificial victims and other cultic necessities in the Court of the Gentiles. The money-changers gave out Jewish or Tyrian coins in exchange for Greek or Roman money (see Exod 30:11-16). Those selling doves provided sacrifices for women, lepers, and others (Lev 12:6-8; 14:22; 15:14, 29).

13. *house of prayer*: The quotation is from Isa 56:7. But Matthew omits "for all the nations (= Gentiles)," probably because such a claim made no sense to him after A.D. 70. The phrase "den of bandits" comes from Jer 7:11.

14. *blind and lame*: According to 2 Sam 5:8 "the blind and the lame shall not come into the house (of the Lord)." Their presence in the Temple area is already unusual. And Matthew's additional account of their healing (21:14-16) contributes to the messianic excitement (see Isa 35:5-6). Note the connection in 21:15 with the healings and Jesus as the Son of David.

16. *"Out of the mouth . . ."*: Jesus quotes Ps 8:3 to explain why the children were singing the praises of the Son of David.

17. *Bethany*: This village about two miles east of Jerusalem became Jesus' base of operation during Passover time.

Interpretation

For his accounts of Jesus' entrance into Jerusalem and its Temple (21:1-17) Matthew followed Mark 11:1-11, omitting what he perceived to be the unnecessary repetition in Mark 11:4b-6 when the disciples carry out Jesus' instructions. By his additions (21:4-5, 10-11, 14-16) and restructuring (21:12-13) Matthew turned his Markan source into two episodes—Jesus' entrance into the city of Jerusalem (21:1-11), and his entrance into the Temple area (21:12-17)—and highlighted the motif of the fulfillment of Scripture.

In the first episode (21:1-11) Matthew makes explicit what was only implicit in Mark: Jesus' mode of entrance as the "meek and humble king" fulfills Zech 9:9. The crowd greets Jesus with Ps 118:26: "Blessed is he who comes in the name of the Lord'' (21:9). The ''shaken'' city wonders about the ''prophet'' (see Deut 18:15, 18).

The second episode (21:12-17) concerns Jesus' activities in the Temple area. Matthew goes directly into what Mark (see 11:15-17) placed on the ''second day'' of Jesus' stay in Jerusalem: the so-called cleansing of the Temple. The justification for this action is the combination of Isa 56:7 and Jer 7:11. The response by the children to Jesus' healing the blind and the lame in the Temple area is presented as the fulfillment of Ps 8:3. Matthew rejoins the Markan account by having Jesus lodge in Bethany (21:17=Mark 11:11b). In both episodes Matthew's major theme is the fulfillment of Scripture.

Jesus' entrance into Jerusalem (21:1-11) takes place from the East, by way of the Mount of Olives. According to Zech 14:4 on the ''day of the Lord'' (understood in Jesus' time as the eschaton) important events are to take place there: ''On that day his [the Lord's] feet shall stand on the Mount of Olives which lies before Jerusalem on the east.'' The king who enters Jerusalem in Zech 9:9 is most likely the Lord himself as the divine warrior: ''Lo, your king comes to you; triumphant and victorious is he, humble and riding on an ass, on a colt the foal of an ass.'' In Matt 21:5 Zech 9:9 is applied to Jesus. By the omission of ''triumphant and victorious is he'' Matthew brings out even more effectively the theme of Jesus the humble king.

In imagining Jesus' entrance into the Temple area (21:12-17) one should think of a large area with the holy of holies at its center. The commercial activity surrounding it was both necessary and natural in light of the sacrificial system that was the heart of the Temple area. Jesus' action is best seen as a symbolic action in keeping with the prophets' symbolic actions. John 2:14-22 places it at the beginning of Jesus' public ministry and interprets it as a foreshadowing of Jesus' resurrection. In the Temple area Jesus continues his ministry as the ''therapeutic Son of David'' by healing people who really should not have been there. Thus Jesus does what was expected of the Messiah according to *Psalms of Solomon* 17:30: ''And he will purge Jerusalem and make it holy as it was even from the beginning.'' Jesus probably intended his action to symbolize the restored and perfected worship that would accompany the fullness of God's kingdom. But his disruption of commercial activity in the Temple area probably won him no friends in Jerusalem, since the city's economy depended in large part on pilgrims who spent money in Jerusalem during the great religious festivals.

According to Matthew's (and Mark's) chronology these episodes were Jesus' first encounter with Jerusalem and the Temple. Following Mark, Matthew imbues them with eschatological significance (Zech 9:9; 14:4; ''the whole city shook''). For Matthew and his rivals the Temple was a thing of the past. Nevertheless, Matthew portrays Jesus as the ''Lord'' of the city and of the Temple area. By his symbolic action Jesus indicates that something was wrong with the order of worship in his own day and thus foreshadows its destruction in A.D. 70. Furthermore, everything that Jesus does in entering the city and its Temple fulfills the Scriptures. As he takes possession of the city and its Temple Jesus plays the biblical role of the meek and humble king.

With Jesus' entrance into Jerusalem we enter passion week. At the very start we are introduced to some of Matthew's characteristic perspectives on Jesus' passion: Jesus is in control of events; everything takes place according to the Scriptures; and even though he suffers, he maintains his identity as Lord and Son of David.

For Reference and Further Study

Hiers, R. H. "Purification of the Temple: Preparation for the Kingdom of God." *JBL* 90 (1971) 82–90.

Watty, W. W. "Jesus and the Temple—Cleansing or Cursing?" *ExpTim* 93 (1982) 235–39.

54. *The Fig Tree* (21:18-22)

18. In the morning as he was returning to the city he grew hungry. 19. And seeing a fig tree by the road he came to it and found nothing on it except leaves. And he said to it: "May there no longer be fruit from you forever!" And the fig tree withered up immediately. 20. And when the disciples saw it, they were amazed and said: "How did the fig tree wither up immediately?" 21. Jesus answered and said to them: "Amen I say to you, if you have faith and do not doubt, you will do not only what was done with the fig tree but if you say to this mountain: 'Be taken up and cast into the sea,' it will be. 22. And everything that you ask in prayer with faith you will receive."

Notes

18. *In the morning*: Matthew (unlike Mark) placed the cleansing of the Temple shortly after Jesus' arrival in Jerusalem. Matthew also breaks up the "sandwich" effect of Mark 11:12-21 in which the cleansing of the Temple comes between the two parts of the fig tree episode.

19. *nothing on it except leaves*: Matthew omits the comment in Mark 11:13 ("it was not the season for figs"), thus making Jesus' conduct appear more rational. For the fig tree parable see Luke 13:6-9. Some interpreters argue that the parable grew into this incident in which Jesus makes the fig tree wither.

withered up immediately: Mark's sandwich technique leaves some space between Jesus' condemnation of the fig tree and its withering up (see Mark 11:14, 20). Matthew stresses the idea of its "immediate" drying up (see 21:19, 20).

20. *the disciples*: In Mark 11:21 the spokesman for the disciples is Peter. It is unusual that Matthew, who likes to present Peter as the spokesman for the disciples, should pass up such an opportunity here.

21. *if you have faith*: Matthew follows Mark 11:22-25 in turning the fig tree story into a lesson on the power of prayer (see Matt 17:20). He makes the connection tighter by his mention of the fig tree ("what was done with the fig tree"). The reference to the need for faith is repeated in 17:22 ("in prayer with faith").

Interpretation

The cursing of the fig tree (Matt 21:18-22) is unusual in the Synoptic tradition: In it Jesus destroys property (see Matt 8:28-34) and seems to behave irrationally. Moreover it is the only miracle that occurs in the environs of Jerusalem. Some interpreters explain it as originally a symbolic action. Others view it as the development of the fig tree parable in Luke 13:6-9. Both Mark and Matthew understood it as an event (a display of power on Jesus' part), which served as the occasion for teachings on the power of prayer.

Matthew has dissolved the intricate structure of Mark 11:12-21 by placing the cleansing of the Temple on the first day of Jesus' arrival in Jerusalem. He emphasizes that the fig tree withered up "immediately" and links the instruction on prayer to the fig tree theme.

The fig tree was (and is) a familiar sight in Palestine. It is a large shade tree with palm-shaped leaves (see Gen 3:7). It bears sweet pear-shaped fruit more than once a year. It is often associated with the grapevine as a symbol of peace and prosperity (1 Kgs 4:25).

There was a symbolic dimension to the fig tree episode; it was not just a display of (destructive) power. It is probably to be read in light of Jer 8:13: "When I would gather them, says the Lord, there are no grapes on the vine, nor figs on the fig tree." If "them" refers to the people of Israel, the context makes clear that the barrenness of the people was due to the bad leadership of the scribes, wise men, prophets, and priests (see Jer 8:4-12). Another use of fig tree imagery appears in Hos 9:10, 16: "Like the first fruit on the fig tree in its first season I saw your fathers . . . Ephraim is stricken, their root is dried up, they shall bear no fruit." Here the withering of Ephraim is punishment for its disobedience to God.

The proximity of the cleansing of the Temple and the withering of the fig tree suggest that both episodes carried a symbolic significance for Matthew's first readers, and that the significance concerned Israel. But Matthew does not deny the place of Israel in salvation history and even contends that in his brand of Jewish Christianity that preeminence is carried on.

Matthew's major contention concerned leadership in the people of God. The cleansing of the Temple raised questions about the Temple leadership that allowed the Temple to degenerate into a "den of bandits." If Jer 8:13 (and its context) can serve as a guide to the fig tree episode, then again the thrust of this Matthean text is a criticism of the leadership which led Israel into its disobedience, a leadership continued by the leaders of "their synagogues."

The lesson that Matthew (and Mark) drew from the strange episode of the fig tree was the power of prayer. Though the lesson seems artificial and tacked on, it is nonetheless the lesson that the evangelists found.

Modern commentators often find in the cleansing of the Temple and the fig tree story the rejection of Israel as a whole. It is as if Jesus stood over against and outside of Israel. But that stance does not fit with Matthew's vision or with what we know of Jesus. Matthew's quarrel was with the leadership of "their synagogues"; Jesus' problems came from Israel's leaders. There is no warrant for generalizing these symbolic actions to take in all Israel.

For Reference and Further Study

Giesen, H. "Der verdorrte Feigenbaum—Eine symbolische Aussage?" *BZ* 20 (1976) 95–111.

Münderlein, G. "Die Verfluchung des Feigenbaumes." *NTS* 10 (1963) 89–104.

Telford, W. R. *The Barren Temple and the Withered Tree*. Sheffield: JSOT, 1980.

55. *Jesus and John* (21:23-32)

23. And when he came into the temple area, the chief priests and the elders of the people approached him, saying: "By what authority do you do these things? And who gave you this power?" 24. Jesus answered and said to them: "I too will ask you a question, which if you tell me, I also will say by what power I do these things. 25. John's baptism—where was it from? From heaven or from human beings?" They discussed among themselves, saying: "If we say 'from heaven,' he will say to us: 'Why did you not believe in him?' 26. But if we say 'from human beings,' we are afraid of the crowd. For all hold John to be a prophet." 27. And they answered and said to Jesus: "We do not know." He said to them: "Neither will I tell you by what authority I do these things."

28. "What do you think? A man had two sons. He approached the first one and said: 'Son, go today, work in the vineyard.' 29. He answered and said: 'I will not.' But later he changed his mind and went off. 30. He approached the other and said the same thing. But he answered and said: 'I will, sir.' And he did not go off. 31. Which of the two did the father's will?" They said: "The first." Jesus said to them: "Amen I say to you that the tax collectors and the prostitutes will enter the kingdom of God ahead of you. 32. For John came to you in the way of righteousness and you did not believe him. But the tax collectors and prostitutes believed him. When you saw it, you did not repent afterward to believe him."

Notes

23. *By what authority*: The chief priests and elders will be the prime Jewish opponents of Jesus during the passion. They hope to force Jesus into a public admission that his power comes directly from God, thus opening him up to a charge of blasphemy (see 26:65). The expression "these things" refers to his entrance into Jerusalem and cleansing of the Temple.

24. *I too will ask*: The counterquestion is found often in rabbinic writings. It is frequently a way to avoid answering a question. In this case it reduces Jesus' opponents to silence while making clear the divine origin of Jesus' teaching and action.

25. *From heaven or from human beings*: The word "heaven" is Matthew's typical substitution for "God." If the opponents admit that John's baptism was from God, they must explain why they had not said that publicly. If they say it was purely human, then they must defend themselves against those who admired and followed John.

27. *"We do not know"*: Those who set a trap for Jesus have now fallen into a trap. The assumption of the account is that the power of both John and Jesus comes from God. The opponents have been reduced to silence.

28. *in the vineyard*: For the symbolism of the vineyard see Matt 20:1-16 and 21:33-46. The application of the parable of the two sons to John the Baptist links it to what precedes (21:23-27), and the vineyard theme joins it to what follows (21:33-46).

29. *"I will not"*: Other manuscripts have different orders: (1) The first son says "yes" but does nothing. The second son says "no" but repents. The latter does the father's will. (2) The first son says "no" but repents. The second son says "yes" but does nothing. The *latter* does the father's will!

31. *the tax collectors and the prostitutes*: These two classes of people were regarded as immoral because tax collectors cheated and prostitutes committed sexual sins. They were also prime examples of Jews who worked closely with the occupying Roman forces. Tax collectors took money from Jews for an alien power, and prostitutes sold their services often to Roman soldiers.

enter the kingdom: For the biblical background and meaning of this idiom, see J. Marcus, "Entering into the Kingly Power of God," *JBL* 107 (1988) 663–75.

32. *you did not believe him*: The final verse applies the parable to the chief priests and elders (21:23). They are contrasted with despicable members of Jewish society and come out the worse in the comparison.

Interpretation

With the debate about John's authority (21:23-27) Matthew presents the first of five controversies between Jesus and his opponents in Jerusalem (see also 22:15-46). The series of debates is interrupted by three parables (21:28–22:14).

The first controversy (21:23-27) follows Mark 11:27-33. Jesus' partners in debate are the chief priests and elders. Their effort to engineer Jesus into a public blasphemy is thwarted by his counterquestion about the source of John's baptism. Recognizing that they are on the horns of a dilemma ("from heaven or from human beings?"), they are reduced to silence and are exposed as insincere.

The criticism of the chief priests and elders is continued by means of the first of the three parables (21:28-32). The application of the parable to the reception accorded John the Baptist (21:31b-32) links the two units. Again the opponents are forced into an admission in which they condemn themselves. They are revealed as less responsive to God's prophets John and Jesus than the dregs of Jewish society have been.

The background of these two texts (21:23-27, 28-32) is the popular enthusiasm that John the Baptist aroused. Josephus (see *Ant.* 18:118) describes it as follows: "When others too joined the crowds about him, because they were aroused to the highest degree by his sermons, Herod became alarmed. Eloquence that had so great an effect on mankind might lead to some form of sedition, for it looked as if they would be guided by John in everything that they did."

The chief priests and elders constituted the Jewish leadership in Jerusalem, with the Temple as its symbolic center. They worked alongside the Roman officials and Herod Antipas to maintain the peace and security of the people. John's movement posed for them not only a religious threat (because it was not Temple centered) but also a political threat (because it promised to get out of hand). Therefore they would have been slow to approve John's baptism as coming "from heaven" (because it would harm their relations with the Romans and Herod Antipas). On the other hand, they could hardly dismiss it in public as a purely human invention (because it was apparently so popular with Jews).

The five controversies and three parables in Matt 21:23–22:46 offer comments on the opponents of Jesus, especially those who claimed political and/or religious leadership. In the first controversy (21:23-27) and the first parable (21:28-32) the chief priests and elders are criticized. Those Jews who worked with the Romans to preserve the status quo were afraid to render a public judgment on John the Baptist. Even the tax collectors and sinners—groups especially despised for collaborating with the Romans—were more admirable than the chief priests and elders. The Jewish leaders are compared to the son who said "yes" to the father but failed to carry through by practicing their principles.

These units emphasize the heavenly origin of the ministry of both John and Jesus and the effect that they had on some surprising (marginal) people. They also move forward Matthew's systematic critique of the Jewish leaders of Jesus' (and his own) day. Note that the target is not the Jewish people as a whole but rather their leaders.

For Reference and Further Study

Gibson, J. "Hoi Telōnai kai hai Pornai." *JTS* 32 (1981) 429–33.

Ogawa, A. "Parables de l'Israël véritable? Reconsidération critique de Mt. xxi 28-xxii 14." *NovT* 21 (1979) 121–49.

Richards, W. L. "Another Look at the Parable of the Two Sons." *Biblical Research* 23 (1978) 5–14.

56. *The Parable of the Vineyard* (21:33-46)

33. "Hear another parable. There was a householder who planted a vineyard and set a hedge around it and dug a winepress in it and built a tower and let it out to tenant farmers and went off to another country. 34. When the season for fruit drew near, he sent his servants to the tenant farmers to get his fruit. 35. And the tenant farmers took hold of his servants—one they beat, one they killed, one they stoned. 36. Again he sent other servants, more than the first, and they did the same to them. 37. Finally he sent to them his own son, saying: 'They will respect my son.' 38. But when the tenant farmers saw the son, they said among themselves: 'This is the heir. Come let us kill him and have his inheritance.' 39. And they took hold of him and cast him outside the vineyard and killed him. 40. When the owner of the vineyard comes, what will he do to those tenant farmers?" 41. They said to him: "He will put those wicked fellows to a miserable death and will give over the vineyard to other tenant farmers who will give to him the fruits in their proper times."

42. Jesus said to them: "Have you never read in the Scriptures: 'The stone that the builders rejected, this has become the head of the corner. This was the Lord's doing, and it is marvelous in our eyes?' 43. Therefore

I say to you that the kingdom of God will be taken away from them and given to a nation bearing fruit." 45. When the chief priests and the Pharisees heard his parables, they knew that he spoke about them. 46. And they sought to arrest him but feared the crowds, since they held him as a prophet.

Notes

33. *another parable*: To take account of the parable of the two sons (21:28-32) Matthew has modified the introduction to the parable of the vineyard in Mark 12:1. He also identified the owner as a householder (see 13:27, 52; 20:1, 11).

    vineyard: For the economic and biblical background of the description of the vineyard see below. The hedge was intended to keep animals away; the winepress was used for crushing the grapes and making the wine; and the tower was both a watchpost and a shelter for those who tended the vineyard.

34. *servants*: Mark 12:2-5 has three servants sent individually and then many others. It is pointless to try to identify them as Moses, Joshua, David, and so forth. Matthew simplifies the story by having the master send two batches of servants (21:34, 36). He describes the bad treatment they received (beating, killing, stoning) only once.

37. *his own son*: Matthew omits the adjective "beloved" (*agapētos*) from Mark 12:6 (see Luke 20:13). The expression "when the season for fruit drew near" (21:34) and the adverb "finally" (21:37) may give the story an eschatological dimension.

38. *have his inheritance*: The idea is that the father would be still alive even though the son is dead. Therefore the tenant farmers' action would be illegal and irregular. Recognition of this problem may lay behind Matthew's change of Mark 12:7 ("the inheritance will be ours") to ("let us . . . have his inheritance").

39. *cast him outside the vineyard and kill him*: According to Mark 12:8 they first killed the son and then cast him outside. Matthew's change was motivated by Jesus' own death outside the walls of Jerusalem (27:33). See also Heb 13:12: "Jesus suffered outside the gate."

41. *miserable death*: Matthew interpreted the fate of the tenant farmers in connection with the destruction of Jerusalem in A.D. 70 and so heightens Mark 12:19. He also forces Jesus' questioners (the chief priests and Pharisees according to 21:45) to answer his question and thus to foretell their own destiny.

    to other tenant farmers: These are presumably the leaders of the Jewish-Christian community. They are not the same as "all Israel" (which is the vineyard). There is no reason here to assume that the "others" are Gentiles and that the handing over of leadership involves the rejection of Israel.

42. *Have you never read*: This form of a question is used elsewhere by Matthew in conflicts with opponents (12:3, 5; 19:4; 21:16; 22:31). The formula emphasizes that correct reading of the Scriptures takes place in the Jewish-Christian community.

the stone that the builders rejected: The quotation of Psalm 118:22-23 is from the Septuagint. The rejected stone (Jesus) has become the cornerstone (which keeps the walls of the building together) or the capstone (which holds up an arch or a gateway). The "rejected stone" quotation is applied to Jesus in Acts 4:11 and 1 Pet 2:7 (see also Rom 9:33; 1 Pet 2:6, 8). There may be a play on *'eben* ("stone") and *ben* ("son").

43. *given to a nation bearing fruit*: The term *ethnos* can mean a "group of people." In 21:45 the chief priests and Pharisees perceive the sentence as applying to them. As in 21:41 it is not necessary to take it as applying to Gentiles or to the Church as a "third race."

44. Many manuscripts include the following sentence: "And he who falls on this stone will be broken to pieces; but when it falls on any one, it will crush him." Its presence is usually explained as an interpolation from Luke 20:18. It would fit better directly after Matt 21:42.

45. *the chief priests and the Pharisees*: Mark does not specify the audience. By doing so Matthew applies the parable to the chief priests and Pharisees and suggests that it contributed to their determination to arrest Jesus. The crowds thought of Jesus as they thought of John the Baptist (see Matt 21:26).

Interpretation

In 21:33-46 Matthew has taken over the parable of the vineyard from Mark 12:1-12. That parable relates the harsh treatment given to Jesus and the harsh treatment given to God's earlier messengers. There are some clear allegorical features: the vineyard is Israel; the tenant farmers are Israel's leaders; the householder is God; the earlier messengers are the prophets; and the son is Jesus. The other elements in the story (the hedge, the winepress, etc.) have no obvious allegorical significance. There are problems in tracing the parable back to Jesus himself: the use of the Greek Bible (21:33, 42), the allegorism, the foreknowledge of Jesus' death (21:38), and the reference to Jerusalem's destruction (21:41). It is possible that something like this parable originated with Jesus and was developed and expanded within the early Church until it was taken over by Mark.

Matthew gave the parable a suitable introduction (21:33a), simplified the sending of the earlier messengers (21:34, 36), explained the tenant farmers' plan to seize the inheritance (21:38), adapted the son's death to Jesus' death (21:39), and turned the end of the parable into a conversation (21:41-46). The conversation partners are identified as the chief priests and the Pharisees (21:45). Thus the parable becomes part of the controversy theme that dominates chapters 21–23. The opponents are forced to draw their own conclusion about their fate (21:41). The Matthean ideal of "bearing fruit" (3:8,

10; 7:16-20; 12:33; 13:8; 21:19) is introduced (21:41, 43). And there is talk of a transfer of authority from one group to another (21:41, 43).

Readers in late first-century Palestine or Syria would have been familiar with the economic system presupposed in the parable of the vineyard. Absentee land owners let out their farms and vineyards to sharecroppers who worked the land in exchange for a fee or a percentage. The bulk of the profits belonged to the land owner, who at the appropriate times sent his agents to collect what was owed him. The tenant farmers' plan to inherit the vineyard (21:38) was an illegal and ultimately foolish action, as long as the owner remained alive. Matthew suggests that this plan was a desperate folly by his change in 21:38 ("let us . . . have his inheritance").

Besides these economic realities the readers would also have been familiar with the portrayal of Israel as a vineyard in Isa 5:1-7. The influence of this passage is made clear in the first sentence of the parable: "My beloved had a vineyard on a very fertile hill. He digged it and cleared it of stones, and planted it with choice vines; he built a watch tower in the midst of it, and hewed out a wine vat in it" (Isa 5:1-2=Matt 21:33). Lest there be any doubt, Isaiah tells us that "the vineyard of the Lord of hosts is the house of Israel" (Isa 5:7). Despite all the efforts God expended on the vineyard, "it yielded wild grapes" (Isa 5:2) and therefore God determined to destroy it.

The parable of the vineyard (and especially its Matthean applications in 21:41, 43) is often taken as evidence for Christian replacement or supersession of Israel as the people of God. But is that an accurate reading of the text?

Isa 5:1-7 makes no mention of tenant farmers. They are introduced in the Gospel parable. In Isa 5:1-7 the vineyard itself is to be destroyed (see 5:5-6). In Matt 21:40-41 the tenant farmers are put to death and the vineyard is handed over to others. In the present Matthean context the parable of the vineyard functions as a controversy that shows how and why Jesus' opponents sought to have him killed. In the framework that Matthew has constructed for the parable (21:45-46) the chief priests and Pharisees perceive that the parable applies to them. All these lines of evidence indicate that the parable concerns the *leadership* of Israel. Matthew contends that the tenant farmers, not the vineyard, must be replaced. In this light it seems unwise to take *ethnos* in 21:43 ("the kingdom of God will be . . . given to a nation bearing fruit") as a reference to the Gentile Church or even the Church understood as a "third race" beside Jews and Gentiles. It should be understood in its most basic sense as a "group of people," in this case the leaders of the Jewish Christian community.

The basic theological thrust of the parable of the vineyard is to place the suffering and death of Jesus in line with the mistreatment of God's messengers throughout the centuries. But since this text is so important in Jewish-Christian dialogue, it should be read carefully with an eye to the context of Matt 21:41, 43. The context—a dispute with Israel's leaders—should control the interpretation of *ethnos* and supersessionist claims should be avoided.

For Reference and Further Study

Hubaut, M. ''La parabole des vignerons homicides: son authenticité, sa visée première.'' *RTL* 6 (1975) 51–61.

Kingsbury, J. D. ''The Parable of the Wicked Husbandmen and the Secret of Jesus' Divine Sonship in Matthew: Some Literary-Critical Observations.'' *JBL* 105 (1986) 643–55.

Lowe, M. ''From the Parable of the Vineyard to a Pre-Synoptic Source.'' *NTS* 28 (1982) 257–63.

Snodgrass, K. *The Parable of the Wicked Tenants.* Tübingen: Mohr-Siebeck, 1983.

57. *The Parable of the Wedding Feast* (22:1-14)

1. And Jesus answered again and spoke to them in parables, saying: 2. ''The kingdom of heaven may be compared to a king who gave a wedding feast for his son. 3. And he sent his servants to summon those who had been invited to the wedding feast, but they were not willing to come. 4. Again he sent other servants, saying: 'Tell those who have been invited: ''Behold I have prepared my meal; my oxen and fatted calves have been slaughtered, and all are ready. Come to the wedding feast.'' ' 5. But they paid no attention and went off, one to his own farm, one to his own business. 6. The rest, however, seized his servants, insulted them, and killed them. 7. But the king grew angry, sent his armies, destroyed those murderers, and burned down their city. 8. Then he said to his servants: 'The wedding feast is ready, but those who were invited are not worthy. 9. Go therefore to the thoroughfares, and invite to the wedding feast whomever you find.' 10. And those servants went out to the streets, gathered all whom they found, evil and good alike. And the wedding hall was filled with guests. 11. When the king came in to look at the guests, he saw there a man not wearing a wedding garment. 12. And he said to him: 'Friend, how did you come in here, not having a wedding garment?' But he was silent. 13. Then the king said to the waiters: 'Tie him up hand and foot, and cast him into the darkness outside. There will be weeping and gnashing of teeth there. 14. For many are called, but few are chosen.' ''

Notes

1. *to them*: The audience for this parable is the same as that for the preceding one—the chief priests and Pharisees (see 21:45).

2. *wedding feast*: The occasion in Matt 22:1-14 is a royal wedding feast for the king's son. In Luke 14:15-24 the occasion is simply a great supper. In 22:4 it is called *ariston*, which refers to the noon meal or to a meal in general. The wedding festivities would be expected to continue over several days.

3. *sent his servants*: The language of the parable, especially in the sending of the servants (see 22:4) and the bad treatment they received, is similar to that of the preceding parable. In Luke 14:15-24 the invited guests make excuses but do not use force against the messengers as in Matt 22:6.

   to summon those who had been invited: This story (and Luke 14:16-17) seems to assume that there were two invitations, one sometime beforehand and the other when the banquet was ready (as in 22:4, "I have prepared my meal").

7. *burned down their city*: Matt 22:7 is a very graphic description of how the king punished those who mistreated his emissaries. No such statement appears in Luke 14:15-24. The Matthean statement is usually taken as a description after the fact of what happened to Jerusalem in A.D. 70.

9. *thoroughfares*: The term *diexodos* is sometimes taken to mean "street-crossing," but it more likely refers to the place where the street goes through the city boundary and out into open country. The servants have to make a real effort to find the new guests by going out to the countryside.

10. *evil and good alike*: The phrase prepares for 22:11-13 in which mere admission to the kingdom is not enough to guarantee staying in it. In the first part of the parable it serves as an acknowledgment of the mixed nature of those who are called by Jesus to God's kingdom (see Matt 13:1-52).

11. *not wearing a wedding garment*: The king's inspection of the hall and the guests constitutes a judgment scene. The absence of the wedding garment carries some symbolic significance; what it is, however, is difficult to know. A prior problem is how someone unexpectedly invited to the banquet was to be wearing clothes suitable for the wedding banquet.

12. *Friend*: For the use of *hetaire* ("friend") in a context where the questioner knows the answer or is putting the other person on the spot, see Matt 20:13; 26:50.

13. *darkness outside*: For the same punishment see Matt 8:12; 25:30. For "weeping and gnashing of teeth" see Matt 8:12; 13:42, 50; 24:51; 25:30.

14. *Many are called*: The general saying is used to illustrate both parts of the parable: Many are invited to the banquet of the kingdom (22:1-10), but only a few pass the scrutiny of the judgment (22:11-13). For similar ideas see 4 Ezra 8:3: "Many have been created, but few will be saved"; 4 Ezra 9:16: "There are more who perish than those who will be saved"; see also 2 Bar 44:15.

Interpretation

With the parable of the wedding feast (22:1-14), Matthew again interrupts the Markan sequence that he has followed from the end of chapter 18. The parable is the third in a series of three parables (21:28-32; 21:33-46;

22:1-14). After it Matthew resumes the Markan sequence with four more controversies (22:15-46).

The parable of the great supper in Luke 14:15-21 is similar in several respects to Matt 22:1-14. The kingdom of God is compared to a banquet to which many refuse the invitation and so the host has to bring in unlikely guests so as to get a full banquet hall. The similarity suggests that such a parable appeared in Q. But the differences are so great that either Matthew used a variant version or he has been especially creative in his adaptation.

The parable of the wedding feast has two parts: the invitations (22:1-10), and the ejection (22:11-13). The final saying (22:14) sums up the whole parable. Some explain the problem of how the guest in the second part was supposed to show up in a wedding garment on such short notice by arguing that the two parts were originally independent parables.

The first part (22:1-10) tells about invitations rejected (22:3-6) and accepted (22:8-10). In return for the violence done to his messengers the king sends his armies to destroy his enemies and their city (22:7). The vocabulary and dynamic are similar to the parable of the vineyard (21:33-46) and may have been influenced by it. The second part (22:11-13) has no Lukan parallel. It may once have been a separate parable, but the language of 22:13 ("darkness outside . . . weeping and gnashing of teeth") is characteristically Matthean.

In Jewish and early Christian writings, the kingdom of God is often compared to a banquet. Jesus' meals with tax collectors and sinners and especially his Last Supper with his disciples symbolized what life in God's kingdom will be like. And so the use of the royal wedding banquet to teach about the kingdom of heaven (22:2) is part of a rich tradition.

The distinctive motif of Matt 22:1-14 is invitation. Some accept the king's invitation but others do not. In the background of the parable or at least in the minds of Matthew's Jewish-Christian readers may have been the invitation to Lady Wisdom's banquet in Proverbs 9. Throughout Proverbs 1–9 the sharp division between the wise and the foolish is symbolized by the personal figures Lady Wisdom and Dame Folly. The contrast reaches a climax in chapter 9 where the banquets of the two figures are compared. Behind the motif is the idea that at a banquet wisdom can be shared (as in the term "symposium").

Lady Wisdom readies her banquet and issues invitations: "She has slaughtered her beasts, she has mixed her wine, she has also set her table. She has sent out her maids to call from the highest places in town" (Prov 9:2-3). Her summons is to "walk in the way of insight" (Prov 9:6). By way of contrast Dame Folly acts like a prostitute (see Prov 9:13-18), sitting at the door of her house and calling to the passers-by.

In the Matthean parable, of course, only the king issues invitations and the emphasis is on rejection and acceptance of the invitation to the banquet.

It makes the further point that it is not enough to show up at the banquet; one must be prepared to enter into the banquet as a full participant.

For Matthew the parable of the wedding feast helped to explain the mixed reception of the gospel within Israel (as in chapter 13). God through his servants, through Jesus, and through Jesus' disciples issued the invitation. Those to whom it was most appropriate—the Jewish leaders—not only refused it but some even did violence to the messengers. Therefore the invitation was offered to people out on the highways, and they accepted. This group may have represented the marginal people within Israel ("tax collectors and sinners") who accepted Jesus' message. Or it may even explain the presence of Gentiles within the Jewish Christian community (see Rom 11:12, "their failure means riches for the Gentiles"). Whatever the symbolic significance of the wedding garment was, the parable ends with the warning that admission into God's banquet is no guarantee of staying there.

In response to bad treatment given his messengers "the king grew angry, sent his armies, destroyed those murderers, and burned down their city" (22:7). This sentence is usually interpreted as a description of the Roman destruction of Jerusalem in A.D. 70 and as an indication that Matthew's Gospel was composed in the late first century. The idea of the Roman armies as instruments of God's wrath would present no problem for Jews familiar with the biblical idea of foreign armies (Assyrians, Babylonians, Persians) as serving Yahweh's purposes. If Matt 22:7 does describe the events of A.D. 70, then one can see Matthew's interpretation of the destruction of Jerusalem: God brought it about because some in Israel rejected the invitation to God's kingdom (the gospel) and mistreated his messengers (especially Jesus). Since the parable was directed to the chief priests and Pharisees (21:45), the ones really responsible for Jerusalem's fall were its alleged spiritual leaders.

The parable of the wedding feast is an outline of salvation history from a Christian perspective. It explains the fall of Jerusalem and the inclusion of marginal people in God's kingdom. But it also provides a warning that mere admission is not enough; an appropriate response is needed. Care must be taken lest Matt 22:7 be made an indictment of the whole Jewish people and part of the "wandering Jew" myth, that is, that Jews are condemned to wander the earth without a homeland because they killed Christ. The target of the parable was (some) "chief priests and Pharisees" (21:45).

For Reference and Further Study

Lemcio, E. E. "The Parables of the Great Supper and the Wedding Feast: History, Redaction and Canon." *Horizons in Biblical Theology* 8 (1986) 1–26.

Manns, F. "Une tradition rabbinique reinterprétée dans l'évangile de Mt 22,1-10 et en Rm 11, 30-32." *Antonianum* 63 (1988) 416–26.

Meyer, B. F. "Many (=All) are Called, but Few (=Not All) are Chosen." *NTS* 36 (1990) 89-97.
Palmer, H. "Just Married, Cannot Come." *NovT* 18 (1976) 241–57.
Radl, W. "Zur Struktur der eschatologischen Gleichnisse Jesu." *TTZ* 92 (1983) 122–33.

58. *Taxes to Caesar* (22:15-22)

15. Then the Pharisees went and took counsel how they might entrap him
in speech. 16. And they sent to him their disciples along with the Herodians, saying: "Teacher, we know that you are true and teach the way of
God in truth; and you care for no one, nor do you regard anyone's position. 17. So tell us what you think: Is it lawful to pay tax to Caesar, or not?"
18. Aware of their malice, Jesus said: "Why are you testing me, hypocrites?
19. Show me the coin of the tax." They brought to him a denarius. 20. And
he said to them: "Whose image is it, and whose inscription?" 21. They
said to him: "Caesar's." Then he said to them: "Give back Caesar's things
to Caesar and God's things to God." 22. When they heard it they were
amazed. And they left him and went away.

Notes

15. *the Pharisees went*: Matthew makes the Pharisees into the ones who initiate the plot to trap Jesus (cf. Mark 12:13, where Pharisees are sent). For the expression "take counsel" see Matt 12:14; 27:1, 7; 28:12. The verb *pagideuō* ("set a snare or trap") appears only here in the NT. The effect of Matthew's introduction is to emphasize the wickedness of the questioners, who happen to be Pharisees.

16. *Herodians*: These were supporters of the dynasty begun by Herod the Great. In Jesus' day they would be supporters of Herod Antipas, whose seat of power was Galilee. Their presence in a story set in Judea is somewhat strange. Since Herod Antipas retained his power through Roman sufferance, the Herodians would be expected to support paying the tax.

    the way of God: The opponents' attempt at gaining Jesus' benevolence is so overstated as to gain the opposite effect. Matthew rearranged the statements in Mark 12:14 to make clear the two points: why Jesus can be called "true," and his well-known frankness (without respect for persons).

17. *Is it lawful*: The questioners want to know whether it is acceptable in the eyes of God to pay the poll tax (*kēnsos*) to the Romans. For the history and nature of the tax see the discussion below.

18. *malice*: As part of his tendency to criticize the Pharisees even more than Mark did, Matthew transfers the charge of "hypocrisy" to an address "hypocrites" and sums up their activity as malice. He retains from Mark 12:15 the idea that the Pharisees were "testing" Jesus.

19. *the coin of the tax*: The poll tax (*kēnsos/census*) had to be paid in Roman coinage. For the nature of the coin and the inscription on it, see the discussion below.

21. *Caesar's things to Caesar*: Since the tax was paid in Roman coinage and therefore the coins belonged to the emperor, paying the poll tax was simply a matter of giving back to the emperor what was his already. By adding "God's things to God" Jesus turns the incident into a challenge to be as careful about one's obligations to God as one is about one's obligations to Caesar.

22. *they were amazed*: Their amazement is usually explained with reference to the fact that Jesus avoided giving too much offense to various Jewish groups. But they may have been even more amazed at his skill in transposing the discussion to talk about God instead of Caesar.

Interpretation

In the remainder of chapter 22 Matthew rejoins Mark 12:13-37 for four more controversies: taxes to Caesar (22:15-22), resurrection (22:23-33), the greatest commandment (22:34-40), and David's son (22:41-46). They complete the series begun with the question about John's authority (21:23-27), and interrupted by three parables (21:28–22:14).

While following Mark 12:13-17 in the essential wording and story-line, Matthew has sharpened the opposition between Jesus and the Pharisees. The effort to trap Jesus is initiated by the Pharisees (22:15), who send some of their disciples along with the Herodians to question Jesus. Their guile and ill will toward Jesus is heightened by having Jesus know their "malice" and address them as "hypocrites." When they find themselves bested in the debate, they slink away (22:22b).

The episode takes the form of a conversation in which the opponents think that they have maneuvered Jesus into an embarrassing position. By his response Jesus manages to move the conversation to a higher level and to give a reasonable but relatively inoffensive answer to the original question.

The tax under debate was the *kēnsos* ("poll tax" or "head tax," *census* in Latin). The payment of such a tax was a prerequisite for living peacefully as a subject of the Roman empire and exercising the rights associated with that status. With the imposition of direct Roman rule in A.D. 6 over the province of Judea a poll tax was exacted from men, women, and slaves from age twelve or fourteen to sixty-five. This tax was to be paid in Roman currency. The Gospel accounts (Matt 22:19 parr.) indicate that the tax amounted to a denarius, a full day's pay for a laborer (see Matt 20:2). In Jesus' day the most widely circulated denarius bore the image of the emperor Tiberius and the Latin inscription *Tiberius Caesar Divi Augusti Filius Augustus Pontifex Maximus* ("Tiberius Caesar, august son of the divine Augustus, high priest"). Tiberius reigned as Roman emperor between A.D. 14 and 37.

The existence of the "head tax" and the mode of its payment were sources of political discontent among Jews. The Pharisees managed to coexist with the Romans, and their position on paying the tax was probably about the same as that of Jesus. The Herodians presumably supported the tax since they remained in power only with the support of the Romans. Ardent nationalists opposed the tax and sometimes made it the occasion of rebellion.

In the Matthean account the Pharisees take the offensive against Jesus. Their aim seems to be to get him to make a public statement on the matter. If Jesus opposes paying the tax, he gets in trouble with the Roman officials. If Jesus agrees with paying the tax, he loses face with the ardent nationalists. In fact, Jesus recommends that the tax be paid on the grounds that it is the emperor's coinage to begin with. That technicality allows him to avoid the broader question of cooperation with or resistance to the Roman government. At the same time he manages to turn the answer into a spiritual challenge to be diligent about "God's things." That early Christians paid taxes to the Romans is indicated by Rom 13:1-7; 1 Pet 2:13-17; and Matt 17:24-27. With 22:15-22 Matthew furthered his negative portrait of the Pharisees and also established Jesus' position vis-à-vis the Roman empire—a position of limited cooperation.

Throughout Christian history there has been a tendency to use this text as the basis for a doctrine of "Church and state," often with the conclusion that they are separate spheres and sometimes with the consequence that obedience to the state in its sphere is practically absolute. But this text and others like it (Rom 13:1-7; 1 Pet 2:13-17; and Matt 17:24-27) should not be pressed into a metaphysics or a political philosophy. For a very negative view of the Roman empire see Revelation 17–18. Matthew was more interested in Jesus' skill in getting out of his opponents' trap and in his challenge to pay as much (and more) attention to "God's things" as to "Caesar's things."

For Reference and Further Study

Giblin, C. H. "'The Things of God' in the Question Concerning Tribute to Caesar (Lk 20:25; Mk 12:17; Mt 22:21)." *CBQ* 33 (1971) 510–27.

59. *Resurrection* (22:23-33)

23. On that day Sadducees who say that there is no resurrection approached him. And they asked him, 24. saying: "Teacher, Moses said: 'If anyone dies without having children, his brother shall marry his wife and raise up children for his brother.' 25. There were seven brothers among us. And the first married and died, and not having children he left his wife to his brother. 26. Likewise also the second and the third up to the seventh. 27. Finally the wife of all of them died. 28. In the resurrection to which of the seven will she be the wife? For all had her." 29. Jesus answered and said to them: "You err because you do not know the Scriptures or the power of God. 30. For in the resurrection they neither marry nor are given in marriage but are like angels in heaven. 31. About the resurrection of the dead have you not read what was said to you by God, saying: 32. 'I am the God of Abraham and the God of Isaac and the God of Jacob.' He is not God of the dead but the living." 33. When the crowds heard it, they were astonished at his teaching.

Notes

23. *Sadducees*: The opponents in the preceding texts were the chief priests (21:23; 21:45), elders (21:33), and Pharisees (21:45; 22:15). This episode shows how yet another group manifests hostility toward Jesus. For the Sadducees' views on resurrection see the discussion below.

24. *Moses said*: Matthew has "said" instead of "wrote for us" in Mark 12:19. What follows is a version of the statute about levirate marriage in Deut 25:5-10. The Latin *levir* is the "husband's brother." According to this statute the husband's brother had the right to marry the widow. See the case of Ruth as an example. The verb "marry" (*epigambreusei*) is taken from Gen 38:8.

25. *seven brothers*: Taking Deut 25:5-10 as its starting point, the case of the seven brothers and the one wife is intended to reduce to absurdity the belief in resurrection and to prove the incompatibility of that belief with the Pentateuch. Since all seven had her as a wife, whose wife will she be? There may be an allusion to Sarah, the daughter of Raguel, who outlived seven husbands (Tobit 3:8; 6:14).

29. *the Scriptures or the power of God*: Jesus takes these in reverse order by showing that the Sadducees do not understand the meaning of resurrection (22:30) or the meaning of the Pentateuch (22:31-32).

30. *like angels in heaven*: For resurrected life as angelic see 2 Bar 51:10: "For they will live in the heights of that world and they will be like the angels and be equal to the stars." See also 1 Enoch 104:4; *b. Ber.* 17a; 1 Cor 15:35-50. Since resurrected life will be very different from earthly life, the Sadducees' example really does not have the force to overturn belief in resurrection.

31. *have you not read*: Matthew simplifies the Markan introduction by omitting "in the book of Moses about the bush." Instead he uses his usual "have you not read?" (see Matt 12:3; 12:5; 19:4; 21:16; 21:42).

32. *the God of Abraham*: Since Exod 3:6, 15-16 are from the Pentateuch, the Sadducees must take their evidence seriously. The biblical verses are taken to mean that God continues a personal relationship with Israel's ancestors and therefore they must still be alive. This makes part of the Pentateuch into a witness for belief in resurrection.

33. *the crowds*: Matthew has added this verse to remind the reader of the distinction between the Jewish leaders and the Jewish crowds. Whereas the leaders continue in hostility, the crowds at least are amazed at Jesus' ability to outwit his opponents.

Interpretation

The last three Jerusalem controversies concern the interpretation of Scripture. At each point Jesus emerges as the correct and authoritative interpreter. Although these texts have been taken over from Mark, they fit perfectly with Matthew's overall theology and prepare for the harsh criticisms of the scribes and Pharisees in chapter 23.

In the debate about resurrection (Matt 22:23-33; Mark 12:18-27) the Sadducees use Deut 25:5-10 (the law about levirate marriage) to bolster their contention that belief in resurrection is not only absent from but even incompatible with the Pentateuch. The Sadducees first cite the text and then give an extreme example based on it (22:24-28). Jesus' answer (22:29-32) first shows that the Sadducees do not understand the meaning of resurrected life and then contends that the Pentateuch itself (Exod 3:6, 15-16) contains evidence for belief in resurrection. Thus the "controversy" is really a debate about the interpretation of Scripture.

Matthew's chief innovation is the addition of the sentence about the crowd's astonishment (22:33). This has the effect of continuing the distinction between the Jewish leaders (who are outwitted by Jesus) and the ordinary people (who still showed interest in him).

The background to the debate in Matt 22:23-33 is supplied by Josephus in *Ant*. 18:16: "The Sadducees hold that the soul perishes along with the body. They own no observances of any sort apart from the laws; in fact, they reckon it a virtue to dispute with the teachers of the path of wisdom that they pursue." Their objection to belief in resurrection arose at least in part from the fact that the biblical texts that served as the basis for that belief (Isa 25:8; 26:19; Ps 73:24-25; Dan 12:1-3) were not in the Torah (the first five books of the Bible, that is, the Pentateuch).

The Pharisees championed belief in resurrection (see Acts 23:8; Josephus, *Ant*. 18:14), and Jesus shared their belief. In Matt 22:23-33 he engages the Sadducees in a scriptural debate. He negates their "reduction to absurdity" on the basis of Deut 25:5-10 by a daring reading of Exod 3:6, 15-16.

If God identifies himself to Moses as the God of Abraham, Isaac, and Jacob, those patriarchs must have been still alive in Moses' time. But since it was well known that all three had died, their life must be resurrected life. Thus the disputatious Sadducees are shown that belief in resurrection is found in the Torah. Though by modern standards this use of Scripture seems artificial, it was consistent with Jewish methods of interpretation in Jesus' day.

In Matthew's day the Sadducees had ceased to be an important force in Jewish life. Their inclusion in Matt 22:23-33 shows that Jewish leaders from all sides opposed Jesus and that he proved himself their superior in debate. The text also indicates areas of agreement between Jesus and the Pharisees, especially on the issue of resurrection. Moreover, it presents Jesus as an interpreter of Scripture, able to match wits with the best of them and to triumph over them in debate. Finally, it emphasizes in 22:33 the continuing interest shown by the crowds (unlike their leaders) in Jesus.

Matt 22:23-33 continues the theme of Jesus as the authoritative interpreter of Scripture. It also points forward to his own resurrection (see Matt 28:1-10). Jesus' defense of the Pharisaic position on resurrection here is significant for those concerned with Christian-Jewish relations. Though it is wrong to call Jesus a Pharisee, he clearly had much in common with the Pharisees and showed great interest in their agenda even when rejecting it.

For Reference and Further Study

Cohn-Sherbok, D. M. "Jesus' Defence of the Resurrection of the Dead." *JSNT* 11 (1981) 64–73.

60. *The Great Commandment* (22:34-40)

34. When the Pharisees heard that he silenced the Sadducees, they gathered together. 35. And one of them [a lawyer] asked him in order to test him: 36. "Teacher, which is the great commandment in the Law?" 37. He said to him: " 'You shall love the Lord your God with your whole heart and with your whole soul and with your whole mind.' 38. This is the great and first commandment. 39. The second is like it. 'You shall love your neighbor as yourself.' 40. On these two commandments hang the whole Law and the Prophets."

Notes

34. *the Pharisees*: In Mark 12:28 Jesus is approached by a friendly scribe; in Luke 10:25 the questioner is a lawyer. Matthew turns the episode into a debate with

the Pharisees. In the description of their "gathering" there may be an allusion to Ps 2:2 ("and the rulers gather together against the Lord and his anointed"). There may also be a reference to the synagogue in the verb *synagō* ("gather").

35. [*a lawyer*]: The textual evidence for the word is not overwhelming. Matthew does not use it elsewhere, and it may have been inserted from Luke 10:25. The idea that he was "testing" Jesus (*peirazōn*) and the address as "teacher" seem to come from Luke 10:25 (or better, the Q source behind both Matt 22:35 and Luke 10:25).

36. *the great commandment*: The Greek text has no article "the." The expression can be understood as a superlative ("greatest"). Later rabbis counted up 613 commandments in the Torah—248 positive ("you shall") and 365 negative ("you shall not").

37. *You shall love the Lord*: Jesus' answer takes the form of a quotation of Deut 6:5. This was recited several times a day by pious Jews as part of the Shema. At the end the word *dianoia* appears in place of the Septuagint's *dynamis* ("power"). One is to love God with heart, soul, and "mind."

39. *the second is like it*: Mark 12:31 has simply: "The second is this." Matthew wants to suggest that the command to love one's neighbor stands on the same level as Deut 6:5. Love of God and love of neighbor are not identified but they are of equal gravity.

you shall love your neighbor as yourself: The second commandment is a quotation of Lev 19:18. In the OT context "neighbor" means fellow Israelite. For other NT uses of Lev 19:18 see Rom 13:9; Gal 5:14; Jas 2:8. There is no hint in the Bible of the modern psychological emphasis on the need for self-esteem and the idea that one must love oneself before loving others.

40. *hang*: The Greek word *krematai* ("hang") depends on the Hebrew verb *tālâ*. The image is that of a large mass suspended by means of two ropes or hairs.

Interpretation

The second scriptural debate concerns the "great commandment" (22:34-40). Matthew has turned Mark's friendly discussion between Jesus and an earnest scribe (Mark 12:28-34) into a confrontation with the Pharisees. The confrontational tone may have been suggested by the Q version (see Luke 10:25-28), but making the Pharisees into the opponents of Jesus here was Matthew's distinctive move. The Pharisees would have been pleased by Jesus' answer to the Sadducees about resurrection (22:23-33). But now they find themselves drawn into debate with Jesus.

The core of Jesus' answer to the Pharisees' query is taken over from Mark 12:30-31: the combination of the commandments to love God (Deut 6:5) and neighbor (Lev 19:18). To it Matthew adds two points: the neighbor-commandment is on the same level as the God-commandment (22:39a); by these two great commandments all the other teachings in the Torah are supported (22:40).

The presence of 613 precepts in the Torah presented a problem for those who took them to be the revelation of God's will for Israel. How could anyone keep track of all these precepts? Are some more important than others? This problem was handled in several ways. A distinction was drawn between "heavy" or serious commandments like honoring one's parents (Deut 5:16) and "light" commandments like the law of the bird's nest (Deut 22:6-7). Both were to be taken seriously, and the reward for observing both was the same (see the note on Matt 5:19). Another strategy was for prominent teachers to provide a summary statement of the Torah (see the discussion connected with Matt 7:12). So in *b. Šabb.* 31a Hillel says: "What is hateful to you do not to your neighbor; that is the whole Torah, while the rest is commentary on it; go and learn it."

Jesus' summary statement is perfectly traditional and orthodox. It combines two positive commandments in the Torah: "You shall love the Lord your God (Deut 6:5) . . . your neighbor as yourself" (Lev 19:18). If there is any originality in Jesus' answer, it lies in the combination of these two commandments.

Did Jesus' summary mean that his followers could disregard the other 611 precepts of the Torah? At least Matthew did not take it that way. His claim that on these two commandments "hang the whole Law and the Prophets" (22:40) assumes that the whole Law remains in force (at least in theory). Jesus' love-commandment goes to the root of things and provides a coherent principle for appreciating and observing the other commandments.

With the destruction of the Jerusalem Temple in A.D. 70 and the loss of Jewish political control in the land of Israel, the Torah became even more significant in Jewish life than ever before. The author of 2 Baruch said it well: "Zion has been taken away from us, and we have nothing now apart from the Mighty One and his Law" (85:3). In 22:34-40 Matthew presents the Christian perspective on the Torah in the form of Jesus' summary statement. It was something to which Jewish Christians could point as expressing their position. The fact that Matthew went out of his way to place Jesus' summary in the context of a hostile debate with the Pharisees indicates that it was used in exactly that way.

The so-called "love-commandment" is often used to distinguish Jews and Christians: Jews have the Law, and Christians have love. Would Matthew have agreed? I doubt it. Matthew saw the love-commandment as giving meaning and direction to the whole Torah. Other early Christian theologians and the tradition of the Church have gone beyond Matthew on this point. Nevertheless, his voice within the canon of Scripture should be respected and not made to say something foreign to his theological outlook. He understood the commandment(s) to love God and neighbor as providing a coherent perspective for observing the Torah.

For Reference and Further Study

Fuller, R. H., ed. *Essays on the Love Commandment.* Philadelphia: Fortress, 1978.

Furnish, V. P. *The Love Command in the New Testament.* Nashville–New York: Abingdon, 1972.

Hultgren, A. J. "The Double Commandment of Love in Mt 22:34-40. Its Sources and Composition." *CBQ* 36 (1974) 373–378.

Perkins, P. *Love Commands in the New Testament.* New York–Ramsey, N.J.: Paulist, 1982.

61. *David's Son or Lord?* (22:41-46)

41. When the Pharisees gathered together, Jesus asked them, 42. saying: "What do you think about the Messiah? Whose son is he?" They said to him: "David's." 43. He said to them: "How is it that David in the Spirit calls him 'Lord,' saying: 44. 'The Lord said to my Lord: "Sit at my right hand until I put your enemies beneath your feet?"' 45. If David calls him 'Lord,' how is he his son?" 46. And no one could answer him a word, nor did anyone dare to ask him anything any longer from that time onward.

Notes

41. *the Pharisees*: Whereas Mark 12:35 does not specify the audience, Matthew says that they were Pharisees. The use of the verb "gather together" (*synagō*) here and in 22:34 may tie these Pharisees to the leaders of "their synagogues" (see Ps 2:2).

42. *David's*: For the Messiah as David's son see Jer 23:5 ("I will raise up for David a righteous branch") and Isa 11:1, 10 ("a shoot from the stump of Jesse . . . the root of Jesse"). See also *Psalms of Solomon* 17:21: "raise up for them their king, the Son of David, to rule over your servant Israel."

43. *David in the Spirit*: The formula reflects Jewish beliefs about the origin of Scripture: David spoke in a "spirit of prophecy," that is, under God's inspiration. The text does not assume the level of theological development regarding the Spirit found even in Paul's letters. That David spoke in Ps 110:1 is essential to the argument.

44. *The Lord said to my Lord*: For a full treatment of Ps 110:1 see below. The argument hinges on the word "Lord." In the Hebrew text Yahweh speaks to "my Lord" (the king). In Greek the same word *kyrios* is used for both Yahweh and the king.

45. *how is he his son?*: If David is the speaker in Ps 110:1 and the second "Lord" is some superior to David, Son of David is not an adequate representation of who is being talked about. That person must be Son of God.

46. *nor did anyone dare*: Matthew has transferred and expanded Mark 12:34b ("after that no one dared to ask him any question").

Interpretation

The third in the series of scriptural debates concerns the correct interpretation of Ps 110:1. Though based on Mark 12:35-37, this final controversy is even more significant for Matthew by reason of his emphasis on Jesus' fulfillment of Scripture and as a lead-in to chapter 23. In the debate Jesus establishes that "Son of David" does not exhaust the identity of the Messiah.

Matthew's chief contribution here is the framework for the debate. Whereas in Mark 12:35 Jesus is in the Temple area and asks an unspecified audience "How do the scribes say that the Messiah is Son of David?," in Matt 22:41 the Pharisees gather and Jesus interrogates them: "What do you think about the Messiah? Whose son is he?" Also, Matthew provides an ending for the series of five controversies and three parables: Jesus has effectively silenced all his enemies (22:46).

The last scriptural debate concerns the proper interpretation of Psalm 110:1. The text quoted in Matt 22:44 is basically the Greek Septuagint; the only difference involves substituting "beneath" (*hypokatō*) for "footstool" (*hypopodion*). The debate hinges on David as the speaker of the Psalm. The original setting of the psalm was the rite of crowning a new king at which God promises him special honor and protection. So in Ps 110:1 David talks about Yahweh (*kyrios*) speaking to "my lord" (the new king, also translated *kyrios*). If David calls the new king (here understood to be the future Messiah) "lord" (*kyrios*), the figure about whom he speaks must be more than David's son.

Psalm 110:1 was very popular in early Christian circles. It was commonly used to ground the exaltation/ascension of Jesus to God's "right hand" (see Acts 2:34-35; 1 Cor 15:25; Heb 1:3; 8:1; 10:12; Mark 16:19). Here, however, it makes a point about the identity of the Messiah: The usual conviction that the Messiah is David's Son does not go far enough. Playing on the title *kyrios* ("master, lord") for Jesus as a teacher, the text suggests an identity between Jesus' lordship and Yahweh's. It contends that Jesus is Messiah, Son of David, Lord, and Son of God.

In this final and climactic debate Jesus bests the Pharisees at the interpretation of Scripture, thus establishing himself as the authoritative interpreter. The incident also supplies a "biblical basis" for the Christological titles applied to Jesus by the early Christians. Of course, the opponents of the Matthean community would not have been impressed by the exegesis of Ps 110:1 or the Christological claims tied to it. But the text would have supplied biblical confirmation for Christians who already held that Jesus was the key to interpreting Israel's Scriptures and that Jesus is Lord.

Most readers today find the argument in Matt 21:41-46 hard to follow. And when they come to understand it, the logic seems artificial and strained. Nevertheless, this little text contains some very important Christological titles and faith-claims about Jesus. If the major difference between Jews and Christians today concerns their opinions about Jesus, then this text and its claims deserve particular attention.

For Reference and Further Study

Hay, D. M. *Glory at the Right Hand. Psalm 110 in Early Christianity.* Nashville—New York: Abingdon, 1973.

Neugebauer, F. "Die Davidssohnfrage (Mark xii. 35-7 parr.) und der Menschensohn." *NTS* 21 (1974) 81–108.

62. *Good Deeds and Prestige* (23:1-12)

1. Then Jesus spoke to the crowds and his disciples, 2. saying: "The scribes and the Pharisees sit on Moses' seat. 3. So everything that they might tell you, do it and observe it; but do not act according to their works. For they preach and do not practice. 4. They bind heavy burdens and put them on people's shoulders, but they themselves are not willing to move them by their own finger. 5. All their deeds they do to be seen by people. They widen out their phylacteries and enlarge their fringes. 6. They love the first place at banquets and the first seats in the synagogues 7. and greetings in the marketplaces and being called 'Rabbi' by people. 8. But you—do not be called 'Rabbi,' for you have one teacher. All of you are brothers. 9. Do not call yourselves 'Father' on earth, for you have one heavenly Father. 10. Do not be called 'Masters,' for your own Master is the Christ. 11. The greatest among you shall be your servant. 12. Whoever will exalt himself will be humbled, and whoever will humble himself will be exalted."

Notes

1. *to the crowds and his disciples*: As the discourse progresses, Jesus seems to be talking to his disciples and the Matthean community leaders: "But you—do not be called

'Rabbi' '' (v. 8). While he criticizes the opponents of the Matthean community, he also offers advice to Christians on how to behave in an appropriate way.

2. *scribes and Pharisees*: The day-to-day governance of the Jewish community is attributed to these two groups. Though the historical situation was more complex, Matthew symbolizes Jewish official opposition to Jesus by these groups. Note that there is no mention of the ''chief priests and elders,'' who exercised leadership before A.D. 70 in Jerusalem, and are the primary opponents of Jesus in the passion narratives.

   sit: The Greek verb is aorist, which usually refers to a past action. It may be a Semitism in which the perfect is used for the present. Or it may refer to the period in which the scribes and Pharisees consolidated their power. Or it may be looking back at the pre-destruction period when the scribes and Pharisees had some power and influence. The first option is more probable.

   Moses' seat: Since E. L. Sukenik claimed to have found such a seat at the front of the synagogues at Hammath-Tiberias and Chorazin, this expression has been taken literally. However, the archaeological evidence is slim and late. In Jesus' and Matthew's day, most synagogues were probably not structures dedicated to a single purpose. Thus ''Moses' seat'' is best understood as a common metaphor for the teaching and ruling authority of the scribes and Pharisees in the Jewish community. It later took shape in architecture.

3. *do it and observe it*: This startling acknowledgment of scribal and Pharisaic authority (see Matt 5:20-48; 16:11-12) can be explained three ways: (1) In the narrative, Jesus simply acknowledges the de facto community leaders. (2) The saying may come from early Jewish-Christian circles whose teaching Matthew wishes to incorporate and qualify. (3) Matthew acknowledges the de facto power of the dominant Jewish community and then proceeds to criticize and attack it in the rest of the chapter.

   They preach and do not practice: Matthew introduces his main theme and criticism of the Jewish community leadership, hypocrisy. In fact, Second Temple Jewish literature and later rabbinic literature emphasize the necessity for matching teaching with behavior (*Lev. Rab.* 35:7). Hypocrisy is a charge leveled frequently against the established authorities by sects and protest groups.

4. *They bind heavy burdens*: Jewish law and custom are criticized as being too difficult to live. In contrast, Matthew claims that Jesus' burden is light (11:30). This criticism is then linked to a criticism of the community leaders for not easing the burdens. It is likely that the ''burdens'' refer to the Pharisaic/rabbinic application of priestly purity laws to everyday life and to their stress on tithing and Sabbath observance. The Pharisaic program for the reform of Jewish life differed from that of Jesus and the Matthean community.

5. *phylacteries*: Several biblical passages speak of a sign, memorial, and frontlets between the eyes and on the arm (Exod 13:1-16; Deut 6:4-9; 11:13-22). Rabbinic practice was to inscribe these passages on parchment, enclose them in leather boxes, and strap them to the forehead and arm during morning prayer. The boxes are called phylacteries. This passage is the earliest use of that term, which can also refer to amulets. Hence Matthew's use of the term may be polemical. The

discovery of leather phylacteries at Qumran makes it probable that "phylacteries" here refers to the same religious article. Rabbinic tradition usually refers to them as *tefillin*. The Qumran phylacteries had slightly different texts. See J. H. Tigay, "On the Term Phylacteries (Matt 23:5)," *HTR* 72 (1979) 45–53.

fringes: In accordance with the biblical command (Num 15:38-39; Deut 22:12) Jews wore tassels on the corners of their outer garments. For Jesus' practice, see Matt 9:20; 14:36.

6. *first place*: The Greek term *protoklisia* ("first place for reclining") refers to the place of honor at a dinner, beside the host. The "first seats" in the synagogue refers to the best or most desirable places. In both cases the scribes and Pharisees are accused of excessive interest in status and show.

7. *Rabbi*: Literally, "My Lord." Rabbi was an honorific title in general use in the first century. That seems to be the sense in this verse. However, in 23:8 "Rabbi" is understood as a designation of a teacher. This technical usage of the title came into vogue after the destruction of the Temple when it was used for the emerging "rabbinic" sages. Matthew's usage probably mirrors the usage of the title by the Jewish community for its teachers. In Matthew only Judas calls Jesus "Rabbi" (26:25, 49), thus reflecting its pejorative connotation and its usage by disciples for their teachers. For similar late first-century usage, see John 1:38; 3:26. See H. Shanks, "Is the Title 'Rabbi' Anachronistic in the Gospels?" *JQR* 53 (1962–63) 337–45.

9. *Father*: The Aramaic title "Abba," Father, was used for elders and also for the revered dead. See the rabbinic tractate *'Abot* ("Sayings of the Fathers"). Matthew associates the title with God alone. See R. S. Barbour, "Uncomfortable Words: VIII. Status and Titles," *ExpTim* 82 (1971) 137–42.

10. *Masters*: The Greek word is used for a guide and a teacher. Perhaps it equals Hebrew *moreh*. This verse has the same meaning as verse 8. The reference to "the Christ" shows that it is an early Church saying, or at least reflects the confession of the early Church in its present form. For the saying in 23:11, see its earlier use in 20:26.

12. *Whoever will exalt himself*: Similar sayings appear in Ezek 21:31; Prov 29:23; Job 22:29; Isa 3:17; 10:33. The NT with its strong eschatological message tends to modify the dynamic of those OT texts.

Interpretation

Though Matthew 23 is an uninterrupted discourse by Jesus to the crowds and disciples (23:1), it is not usually counted as one of the five sermons because it does not end with the formula, "And when Jesus had finished all these sayings . . . ," and because it is mainly a polemic rather than a compendium of teaching on an important subject. The attack on the Pharisees and scribes takes place in the area of the Temple, the central institution of

Judaism. It is preceded by a series of disputes in chapters 21–22, which lead to increased hostility ("Then the Pharisees went and took counsel how to entrap him in his talk . . ." [22:15]) and to an end to the disputes ("From that day no one dared to ask him any more questions" [22:46]). It is followed by the prediction that the Temple will be destroyed (24:2) and warnings concerning the end of the world. Thus chapter 23 summarizes the previous conflict between Jesus and his opponents, and prepares for the arrest and death of Jesus which follow in chapter 26.

Matthew has taken a brief Markan denunciation of the scribes (Mark 12:38-40) and expanded it into a major polemic against the scribes and Pharisees, using Q material preserved also in Luke 11:37-52. His arrangement of these earlier sources, introduction of new material, and virulent tone bespeak lively clashes between his community and the leadership of the Jewish community in his city. Mark ended Jesus' "Jerusalem ministry" with a warning against the scribes who desired prestige and honor and yet devoured widows' houses and with the contrasting story of the widow giving to the Temple out of her poverty (12:38-44). Q, as reflected in Luke, had three woes addressed to the Pharisees and three addressed to the scribes. Q and Luke took care to separate the Pharisees' interest in tithes and synagogues from the scribes' (and lawyers') roles concerning public decision making, leadership, and instruction. Luke locates the denunciation of the Pharisees and scribes during Jesus' journey to Jerusalem and associates it with the continuing hostility of Jesus' opponents (11:53-54) and instruction to the disciples concerning hypocrisy and confessing Jesus.

The object of Jesus' criticisms in chapter 23 is "the scribes and the Pharisees" (23:2; see also 23:13, 15, 23, 27, 29). For a full synthesis and interpretation of the biblical and other evidence about them, see Anthony J. Saldarini, *Pharisees, Scribes and Sadducees in Palestinian Society: A Sociological Approach* (Wilmington: Michael Glazier, 1988).

The term "scribe" applied originally and primarily to one who exercised the occupation of copying documents and contracts for government officials and others with authority. Those who knew how to read and write at this professional level had also to be familiar with the content about which they wrote. By the time of the book of Sirach (about 200 B.C.) the scribes involved themselves in affairs of government and functioned as intellectuals. In Matthew and other NT writings, however, scribes appear both as a learned class and as part of the Jewish leadership arrayed against Jesus and the other early Christians. The scribes probably contributed certain elements to the early rabbinic movement: stress on study, knowledge of the Torah, and learned argument.

The Pharisees formed a religious movement, mainly in Palestine, from the second century B.C. to the first century A.D. They were distinguished from the Sadducees by their beliefs in free will, the survival of the soul after death, and rewards and punishments after death. Besides the Torah they relied upon the other books of Scripture and on an oral tradition to supplement and adapt the Torah. The Pharisees (probably based on the Hebrew *pĕrûšîm* for "separated ones") had elements of both a political movement (as seen in their political influence at various points in Jewish history) and a philosophical-religious school analogous to various Greco-Roman schools. Before A.D. 70 their special concerns included ritual purity, tithing, and Sabbath observance. In Matthew's Gospel they appear as the chief rivals of Jesus and his disciples. Their impact on the early rabbinic movement is suggested by the vehemence with which Matthew opposed them, the agenda that emerged among the rabbis, and the rabbinic efforts to affirm a continuity with the Pharisees and their most prominent teachers. Josephus' generally positive portrait of them may reflect not only his own positive experience among them but also his desire to encourage the Romans to look favorably on the Pharisees in the late first century as the most appropriate vehicle for restoring and renewing the Jewish people.

Matthew uses the scribes and Pharisees as negative examples to define true Christian leadership. He also denounces them in order to legitimate the authority of the new Christian community against the more established authorities in the Jewish communities. The powers and status of the Jewish authorities are graphically portrayed in 23:4-7: They impose burdens, wear special insignia, claim privileged positions, and seek public honor. Against this common Near Eastern tendency toward social hierarchy Matthew forbids the use of titles and the exercise of highly authoritative roles (23:8-12). The honorific title "Rabbi," used increasingly for the teachers of emerging rabbinic Judaism in the post-destruction period, is to be avoided because only Jesus is teacher and all his followers are brethren. In addition, the Matthean community wishes to distinguish itself sharply from the Jewish community with whom they are in conflict. The common Semitic title for an elder, Abba ("Father"), is to be reserved for God, and the title "Master" for the Christ. The members of the community are to be "servants" to one another.

This resistance to hierarchically structured roles and emphasis on equality is typical of sects in the first generation. All the members have begun a new life together and are to participate fully and equally in the emerging community. The Matthean community, emerging from the shadow of the larger, established, and dominant Jewish community, is a new sect which defines itself by differing from the traditional mode of community organization. The elders of established families and officials appointed by the government usually oversaw the application of community laws and customs, adjudicated disputes, and maintained public order. The members of Matthew's community have broken from their network of family and friends, and begun a new, nontraditional community. Matthew's attack on the Jewish authorities tends to weaken their legitimacy for the Matthean community and establish the authority of the community's own leaders.

Matthew's model of egalitarian communal leadership has been largely ignored by Church communities, except at the inception of various reform movements. Though the title "Rabbi" ceased to be used among Christians, probably because it became a central title within Judaism, the traditional Semitic title "Father" gained wide usage, as did a number of other honorific titles reflecting the power or status of their holders. The struggle between the sociological necessity for institutionalization and the mandate for community fellowship affected the Matthean community as it does many Christian communities today.

For Reference and Further Study

Garland, D. E. *The Intention of Matthew 23.* Leiden: Brill, 1979.

Hoet, R. *"Omnes autem vos fratres estis." Etude du concept ecclésiologique des "frères" selon Mt 23,8-12.* Rome: Gregorian University Press, 1982.

Viviano, B. T. "Social World and Community Leadership: The Case of Matthew 23.1-12, 34." *JSNT* 39 (1990) 3-21.

Zimmermann, A. F. *Die urchristlichen Lehrer.* 2nd ed. Tübingen: Mohr-Siebeck, 1988.

63. *The Woes against the Scribes and Pharisees* (23:13-31)

13. "Woe to you, scribes and Pharisees, hypocrites, because you shut up the kingdom of heaven before people. For you yourselves do not come in, nor do you allow those coming in to enter.

15. "Woe to you, scribes and Pharisees, hypocrites, because you travel the sea and the dry land to make one proselyte, and when he becomes one, you make him twice as much a son of Gehenna as you are.

16. "Woe to you, blind guides who say: 'Whoever swears by the temple,
it is nothing. But whoever swears by the gold of the temple is bound.' 17.
Blind fools, for which is greater—the gold or the temple that makes holy
the gold? 18. And furthermore—'Whoever swears by the altar, it is nothing. But whoever swears by the gold upon it is bound.' 19. You blind ones,
for which is greater—the gift or the altar that makes holy the gift? 20. Whoever swears by the altar swears by it and by everything upon it. 21. And
whoever swears by the temple swears by it and by him who inhabits it.
22. And whoever swears by heaven swears by the throne of God and by
him who sits upon it. 23. Woe to you, scribes and Pharisees, hypocrites,
because you tithe mint and dill and cummin, and you have neglected the
weightier matters of the Law—judgment and mercy and faith. 24. These
you should have done without neglecting those. Blind guides, you strain

out the gnat and swallow the camel. 25. Woe to you, scribes and Pharisees, hypocrites, because you purify the outside of the cup and the plate, but inside they are full of robbery and self-indulgence. 26. Blind Pharisee, purify first the inside of the cup in order that its outside also may be pure. 27. Woe to you, scribes and Pharisees, hypocrites, because you are like whitewashed tombs, which appear beautiful on the outside, but on the inside they are full of the bones of the dead and all impurity. 28. So also you appear on the outside as righteous to people, but on the inside you are full of hypocrisy and lawlessness. 29. Woe to you, scribes and Pharisees, hypocrites, because you build the tombs of prophets and decorate the tombs of the righteous, 30. and you say: 'If we lived in the days of our fathers, we would not have participated in the blood of the prophets.' 31. Thus you bear witness against yourselves that you are the sons of those who murdered the prophets."

Notes

13. *hypocrites*: For earlier uses of this term applied to the opponents of Jesus, see Matt 6:2, 5, 16; 7:5; 15:7; 22:18. It appears in this section six times (23:13, 15, 23, 25, 27, 29).

    you shut up the kingdom: The charge assumes that the scribes and Pharisees have an authoritative position (see 23:2-3). By hindering the spread of the gospel of Jesus they close themselves and others out of the kingdom.

14. Some manuscripts add: "Woe to you, scribes and Pharisees, hypocrites, for you devour widows' houses and for a pretense you make long prayers; therefore you will receive the greater condemnation." This is generally seen as an interpolation from Mark 12:40 (or Luke 20:47). It is absent from the best and earliest manuscripts. Those that have it place it either before or after 23:13.

15. *to make one proselyte*: The word *prosēlytos* means "one who has come over" (from paganism to Judaism). There are indications of Jewish missionary activity after A.D. 70 (see Justin's *Dialogue with Trypho* 121–122). The second part of the "woe" probably refers to the great zeal shown by converts to any religion or cause.

16. *Blind guides*: Only here is the introduction to the "woes" varied. The epithet follows from the description of convert-making in 23:15.

    swears by the Temple: What follows in 23:16-22 reflects efforts to retain the system of oaths while avoiding too easy and familiar use of the divine name. It presupposes a system of casuistry by which one swore not by God or God's name but by sacred things; even within those substitutes a casuistry developed (see Matt 5:34-35).

22. *swears by the throne of God*: Jesus cuts through the casuistry to argue that any real oath demands the intention to appeal to God. A similar position is taken in the Mishnah: "All substitute words for vows are as the vows" (*m. Ned.* 1:1).

23. *tithe*: To tithe is to set aside one-tenth of the produce. In the Bible tithes were placed on grain, wine, oil, and flocks (Deut 14:23). There was a tendency to make

tithing apply to all produce: "All that which is a food, and is watched over, and its growth is from the soil is liable to tithes" (*m. Ma'aser.* 1:1). Jesus criticizes this extension so as to include even spices while neglecting what he regarded as more important matters. Nevertheless he counsels compliance with the tithing.

24. *swallow the camel*: The camel was an unclean animal (Lev 11:4; Deut 14:7) and therefore could not be eaten by Jews. The hyperbole thus takes on a further irony that those who claim to be most observant are missing the really important matters. There may be a play on the words for "cummin" and "camel."

25. *you purify the outside*: The fifth woe may allude to the early rabbinic controversy about the purity of cups; see J. Neusner, " 'First Cleanse the Inside': The 'Halakhic' Background of a Controversy-Saying," *NTS* 22 (1976) 486-95. Jesus turns it into a moral exhortation on the importance of interior purity.

27. *like whitewashed tombs*: The usual explanation is that tombs were whitewashed as a warning so that one could avoid ritual defilement by contact with the dead. Jesus uses this practice to contrast exterior and interior purity. For another explanation see S. T. Lachs, "On Matthew 23:27-28," *HTR* 68 (1975) 385–88.

29. *you build the tombs of prophets*: The usual explanation is that in Jesus' time there was a large-scale project to build monuments to the heroes of Israel's past; see J. Jeremias, *Heiligengräber in Jesu Umwelt* (Göttingen: Vandenhoeck & Ruprecht, 1958). Jesus finds a continuity, not a distancing, in the behavior of those who build the tombs.

INTERPRETATION

The seven "woes" against the scribes and Pharisees (23:13-31) are Matthew's version of Q material found in Luke 11:37-52. In Luke there are four woes against the Pharisees (on the cups, tithing spices, best seats in synagogues and public greetings, tombs) and three against the "lawyers" (on loading others with burdens, building tombs for the prophets, taking away the key of knowledge). Matthew has repackaged this material into a full-scale denunciation of the "scribes and Pharisees." These were probably taken to represent the leaders of the Jewish groups that stood as Matthew's rivals. The fundamental charge laid against them is hypocrisy—a gap between appearance and reality, between saying and doing, caused by a misplaced hierarchy of values and excessive emphasis on external matters to neglect of the interior.

The woes against the scribes and Pharisees serve as the equivalent to the Beatitudes that introduce the Sermon on the Mount (5:3-12). The parallel is so striking that chapter 23 is sometimes taken as the introduction to the fifth and final discourse. There is, however, a shift of audience and tone at the start of chapter 24.

In adopting the "woe" form for Jesus' criticisms, Matthew followed the biblical tradition of public denunciations found frequently in the prophets

Amos (5:18-20; 6:1-7) and Isaiah (5:8-10, 11-14, 18-19, 20, 21, 22-24; 10:1-3; 28:1-4; 29:1-4, 15; 30:1-3; 31:1-4; see also Mic 2:1-4). These prophetic denunciations begin with "woe" addressed usually to people with power and/or influence. Then comes a description of their evil action along with an announcement of a judgment against them. The goal of these denunciations is to highlight evil actions or patterns, and to warn the people at large not to follow those who do them. This biblical literary form was well suited for Jesus' climactic denunciation of the scribes and Pharisees.

With the seven "woes" Matthew focused on points of conflict between the Jewish Christians and the more powerful early rabbinic movement. He accused the opponents of hindering the spread of the gospel (23:13) and raising up enemies against it (23:15), of engaging in foolish casuistry regarding oaths (23:16-22), of having misplaced priorities (23:23-24), of pursuing external things at the expense of internal matters (23:25-26, 27-28), and of kinship with those who murdered the prophets of old (23:29-31). By having Jesus use the familiar form of prophetic denunciation ("woe . . . "), Matthew provides his own community and other Jews of his day with a sharp warning against following the leadership of the "scribes and Pharisees." Matthew has been building up to this passage through the entire Gospel. With it he expresses the full critique of his Jewish opponents.

Some further points should be borne in mind when reading this text. The criticisms are levelled against those with power and/or influence as in the prophetic denunciations, not against the whole people of Israel. The aberrations denounced by Jesus were also denounced by other Jewish teachers in the rabbinic tradition. The goal of the denunciations is to highlight the error, to preserve others from it, and perhaps to bring back those who err to the way of righteousness. The Matthean Jesus speaks as a prophet sent to Israel, not as an opponent of Israel. And even in the midst of his denunciations he expresses respect for the minutiae of the Torah: "These you should have done without neglecting those" (23:23).

The prophetic warnings of Jesus in Matt 23:13-31 can serve as a checklist for all who exercise leadership in church or synagogue. Excessive casuistry, misplaced priorities, overemphasis on externals, etc., are found in every religious denomination.

With regard to Christian-Jewish relations, Matt 23:13-31 is a very sensitive text. Anti-Semites have used it as a quarry for their caricatures of Jews and Judaism. That is why it is so important to attend to the Matthean context—the limited group being addressed and criticized, the literary form used, and the goal of the prophetic denunciation. Matthew's target was the leadership of a specific group, not all Israel.

64. *Final Warning* (23:32-39)

32. "And you, fill up the measure of your fathers. 33. You serpents, brood of vipers, how will you flee from the judgment of Gehenna? 34. Therefore behold I send to you prophets and sages and scribes. Some of them you will kill and crucify, and some of them you will scourge in your synagogues and you will pursue from city to city, 35. so that there may come upon you all the righteous blood poured out upon the earth from the blood of Abel the righteous until the blood of Zechariah the son of Barachiah, whom you murdered between the temple and the altar. 36. Amen I say to you, all these will come upon this generation. 37. Jerusalem, Jerusalem, you who kill the prophets and stone those sent to it, how often did I wish to gather together your children, as a bird gathers her fledglings under her wings, and you were not willing! 38. Behold your house is forsaken to you and desolate. 39. For I say to you, you will not see me from now until you say: 'Blessed is he who comes in the name of the Lord.' "

Notes

32. *the measure of your fathers*: The saying implies that there is a measure or quota of evil that must be filled before the end will come. It alludes back to the preceding saying that places the scribes and Pharisees in line with those who killed the prophets. The tone is ironic: You might as well fill that quota so we all can face the judgment.

33. *serpents, brood of vipers*: Jesus addresses the scribes and Pharisees as John the Baptist did in Matt 3:7. The idea is that when the quota of evil is filled and the judgment comes the scribes and Pharisees will come and have to face their fitting punishment.

34. *I send you prophets*: The emphasis is not on the sending but rather on the reception. The messengers seem to be Christian missionaries active between Jesus' death and the writing of the Gospel. The reference to crucifixion (a Roman punishment) takes what happened to Jesus as exemplary. The "your synagogues" distances the Christians from their Jewish rivals.

35. *Zechariah*: The three possibilities are (1) the OT prophet Zechariah son of Barachiah, (2) Zechariah son of Jehoiada in 2 Chr 24:20-22, and (3) Zechariah son of Bareis (Josephus, *War* 4:334-44). For the author of Q it was option 2. For Matthew and his community it was probably option 3, though all three seemed to have gotten mixed together.

36. *this generation*: For other warnings to "this generation" see Matt 11:16; 12:39, 41; 16:4; 17:17; 24:34. The threat appears to be the destruction of Jerusalem, already a reality when Matthew wrote. The destruction is taken as a punishment for persecuting the prophets of old and the Christian missionaries.

37. *as a bird gathers her fledglings*: For the image applied to God see Ps 36:7: "The children of men take refuge in the shadow of thy wings." See also Ps 17:8; 57:1; 61:4; Deut 32:11; Ruth 2:12.

38. *your house*: Does *oikos* ("house") refer to Jerusalem or the Temple (or both)? From Matthew's perspective the saying referred to the destruction of Jerusalem and its Temple. But what did it mean in Q (see Luke 13:35), which was put together before the Temple's destruction?

39. *until you say*: The quotation of Ps 118:26 already appears in Matt 21:9; therefore the subject is not Jesus' entry into Jerusalem. It must be his return as Son of Man (a major topic in chapters 24–25). The preposition *heōs* ("until") seems to have a conditional sense: Only if and when Jerusalem recites Ps 118:26, will the Son of Man come.

Interpretation

The third part of the discourse against the scribes and Pharisees (23:32-39) begins with an ironic challenge ("fill up the measure of your fathers") in 23:32 and a warning that they will not escape eternal punishment in 23:33—another piece of irony since the Pharisees insisted on rewards and punishments after death. The second section (23:34-36) presents an indictment against the scribes and Pharisees for mistreating the Christian missionaries and a threat that vengeance will be exacted for the bloodshed. The third section (23:37-39) repeats the indictment-threat pattern. In both cases Matthew has taken the material from Q (see Luke 11:49-51; 13:34-35). At a few points the meaning may have changed in the new context. For example, Matthew's readers probably took the reference to Zechariah son of Barachiah (23:35) as meaning the Zechariah who was murdered in the Temple area by two Zealots in A.D. 67 (Josephus, *War* 4:334-44). They also would have taken the description of the forsaken and desolate "house" (23:38) as a reference to the destruction of the Jerusalem Temple. What these verses meant in Q is hard to know if they were read before A.D. 65 or so.

The final part of Matthew 23 continues the rhetoric of prophetic speech. The two examples of indictment-threat reflect an OT form found in 2 Kings 1:3-4. When Ahaziah the king of Israel inquires of Baal-zebub the god of Ekron whether he will recover, Elijah is told to say to the kings' messengers: "Is it because there is no god in Israel that you are going to inquire of Baal-zebub, the god of Ekron?" The indictment or complaint is that by inquiring of Baal-zebub (not yet connected with Satan) Ahaziah effectively denies the power of Yahweh. Next comes the threat: "You shall not come down from the bed to which you have gone, but you shall surely die."

A similar pattern or outline underlies Matt 23:34-36 and 23:37-39. First there is an indictment or complaint (23:34, 37) and then a threat of disaster

(23:35, 38). The final sentence in each unit is part of the threat. But taken together, they tend to offset one another. The first (23:36) promises vengeance on "this generation" (understood by Matthew's community as the destruction of Jerusalem in A.D. 70), whereas the second (23:39) appears to delay the Son of Man's coming and make it conditional upon Jerusalem's willingness to say "Blessed is he who comes in the name of the Lord."

The literary setting of 23:32-36 leads one to assume that it is directed to the scribes and Pharisees. In 23:37-39 the audience shifts to Jerusalem personified and addressed. Jesus addresses his audience both as a prophet and as Wisdom sent from God.

For the Matthean community this passage answered the complaints raised by the apocalyptists after A.D. 70: "You have destroyed your people and have preserved your enemies" (4 Ezra 3:30); "You (Babylon) are happy and Zion has been destroyed" (2 Baruch 11:2). Matthew suggests that Jerusalem's destruction is the result of the mistreatment of Jesus and his emissaries as well as of the prophets of old. Because of this "your house is forsaken to you and desolate" (23:38).

In reading 23:32-39 it is important to attend to the audience addressed and the rhetoric used. The audience is not all Israel; it is part of Israel. It is possible to expand the audience for homiletic purposes to refer to the human race in general or even the Church. But that homiletic application must be recognized for what it is. The rhetoric is that of a Jewish prophet speaking to and within his people, not outside his people.

For Reference and Further Study

Allison, D. C. "Matt. 23:39 = Luke 13:35b as a Conditional Prophecy." *JSNT* 18 (1983) 75–84.

Ross, J. M. "Which Zachariah?" *Irish Biblical Studies* 9 (1987) 70–73.

65. *The Beginning of the Birthpangs* (24:1-14)

1. And Jesus went out of the temple and was going away, and his disciples approached him to show to him the buildings of the temple. 2. He answered and said to them: "You see all these, do you not? Amen I say to you, there will not be left here a stone upon a stone that will not be thrown down."

3. As he was sitting on the Mount of Olives the disciples approached him privately, saying: "Tell us when these things will happen and what will be the sign of your presence and of the end of the age?" 4. Jesus answered and said to them: "See lest anyone lead you astray. 5. For many will come in my name, saying 'I am the Messiah' and will lead many astray. 6. You will hear about wars and rumors of wars. See that you are not frightened. For it is necessary that such happen, but it is not yet the end. 7. For nation will rise against nation, and kingdom against kingdom, and there will be famines and earthquakes in various places. 8. All these are the beginning of the birthpangs.

9. "Then they will hand you over to tribulation and they will put you to death, and you will be hated by all the Gentiles on account of my name. 10. And then many will stumble and hand over one another and hate one another. 11. And many false prophets will arise and deceive many. 12. And because wickedness is multiplied the love of many will grow cold. 13. But whoever endures to the end, this one will be saved. 14. And this gospel of the kingdom will be proclaimed in all the world as a witness to all the Gentiles, and then the end will come."

Notes

1. *Jesus went out of the temple*: The word "temple" refers to the temple area, not to one building like the holy of holies. According to the Matthean narrative Jesus entered the temple area at Matt 21:23. And so the various controversies and the denunciation of the scribes and Pharisees all have been set in the temple area. By omitting the passage about the widow's offering (Mark 12:41-44; Luke 21:1-4) and substituting the woes upon Jerusalem (Matt 23:37-39) Matthew has linked Jerusalem's destruction and the end-time.

   to show to him the buildings: In Mark 13:1 one of Jesus' disciples says to him: "Look how many stones and buildings there are!" Matthew has the disciples as a group approach (*prosēlthon*) Jesus and turns the direct statement into a description. Their comment concerns the magnificent rebuilding projects undertaken by Herod the Great (see John 2:20).

2. *stone upon a stone*: Jesus' saying points to the destruction of Herod's Temple. It comes back in the account of his trial before the Sanhedrin (Matt 26:61) and while he is on the cross (Matt 27:40). It can be taken as a prophetic warning in the tradition of Jeremiah (see Jer 7:14; 9:11). Or it can be seen as already having been fulfilled for Matthew and his community in the Roman destruction of Jerusalem in A.D. 70 (see also Luke 19:41-44).

3. *Mount of Olives*: The Mount of Olives is an appropriate place for Jesus' eschatological discourse in light of Zech 14:4: "On that day (=the day of the Lord) his (=the Lord's) feet shall stand in the Mount of Olives which lies before Jerusalem on the east; and the Mount of Olives shall be split in two . . ."

   the disciples: Mark 13:3 limits the audience to an inner circle of four: Peter, James, John, and Andrew (see Mark 1:16-20; Matt 4:18-22), the first four disciples called by Jesus.

   of your presence and of the end of the age: These expressions, which are peculiar to Matthew, make more concrete the vague remark in Mark 13:4 ("when these things are to be accomplished"). The reference to "your" (=Jesus') *parousia* ("presence, coming, arrival") prepares the reader to identify Jesus and the Son of Man whose parousia is described in 24:27, 37, 39. The "end" (*synteleia*) alludes to the two ages/worlds pattern common in Jewish apocalypticism which distinguished this age/world from the one to come.

5. *saying 'I am the Messiah'*: According to Mark 13:6 such deceivers say "I am (he)." Matthew's change may suggest that "in my name" means the name of the Messiah/Christ rather than Jesus. If so, then the saying would allude to a more common and understandable phenomenon in Israel's history than those who claimed to be Jesus. For such figures in the first century see Josephus, *Ant.* 17:271-285 and Acts 5:35-39. The claim "I am the Messiah" would have been the equivalent of claiming royal power and thus carried political-revolutionary implications.

7. *nation will rise*: Matt 24:6-7 agrees with Mark 13:7-8 in denying that wars, famines, and earthquakes constitute the end (*telos*). For wars as a sign of the Messiah's coming, see 4 Ezra 13:31-32: "And they shall plan to make war against one another, city against city, place against place . . . then my son will be revealed." For famines and earthquakes among the "twelve calamities" see 2 Bar 27:6-7.

8. *the beginning of the birthpangs*: The terrors and torments preceding the coming of the messianic age are compared to the onset of labor pains that a woman endures in giving birth.

9. *you will be hated by all the Gentiles*: Matthew already used Mark 13:9-13 in the missionary discourse in Matt 10:17-22. Here he has composed a new version on the basis of Mark 13:9-13. In this sentence he has identified the "all" as Gentiles (*ethnē*). The persecution envisioned in Matt 24:9 is from outside the community and probably referred to both Jews and Gentiles as persecutors.

10. *hand over one another*: The scene shifts from trouble coming from outside the community to trouble within the community. The descriptions of those who stumble and hand over one another and hate one another allude to sad experiences undergone by the community. The inspiration for the language came from Mark 13:12 (=Matt 10:21), which is an apocalyptic commonplace about division within the family.

11. *many false prophets*: For an earlier reference to problems within the community regarding prophets, see Matt 7:21-23 ("Lord, Lord, did we not prophesy in your name . . . ?"). The inspiration here was Mark 13:6, which refers to deceivers who claim "I am (he)".

12. *the love of many will grow cold*: Although the idea of charity within the community cannot be excluded, the reference to wickedness (*anomia*) multiplying suggests that *agapē* ("love") referred primarily to fidelity to the divine rule enjoined by Jesus. The extinction of love is the equivalent of apostasy. See S. Légasse, "Le refroidissement de l'amour avant la fin (Mt 24, 12)," *SNTU* 8 ('83) 91–102.

13. *whoever endures*: Matt 24:13 has been taken verbatim from Mark 13:13b. But the intervening Matthean material in Matt 24:10-12 relates perseverance not only to persecution from the outside (Mark 13:13a; Matt 24:9) but also to dissension within the community.

14. *gospel of the kingdom*: The "good news" refers to God's plan made manifest in the life and teaching of Jesus (see Matt 26:13). By placing this saying significantly later than Mark 13:10 in the sequence Matthew has effectively introduced a delay in the parousia and close of the age.

    to all the Gentiles: If Matthew wants to encourage his community to participate in the Gentile mission, he gives them here the powerful motive that, when the gospel has been preached to all nations, then the end will come (see Rom 11:25-26).

Interpretation

The beginning of Jesus's apocalyptic discourse according to Matthew (24:1-8) follows the text of Mark 13:1-8 quite closely. The second part (Matt 24:9-14) is an adaptation of Mark 13:9-13, which Matthew had already used in Matt 10:17-25.

Matthew's changes in the first part (24:1-8) reflect his familiar editorial practices: He omits (presumably as unnecessary) information about the location of the Mount of Olives as "opposite the Temple" (Mark 13:3) and the list of the four disciples who constituted the "inner circle" (Mark 13:3). He adds important precisions to Mark's vague "when these things are all to be accomplished" (Mark 13:4) by tying them to the *parousia* ("presence") of Jesus and the "end of the age" (Matt 24:3). Likewise in Matt 24:5 Matthew turns the ambiguous "I am (he)" of Mark 13:6 into "I am the Messiah."

In the second part (24:9-14) Matthew is freer in his approach to Mark. Having already used Mark 13:9-13 in the mission discourse (Matt 10:17-22), he reuses some material here (Matt 24:9, 13). But he has also added a piece in Matt 24:10-12, which implies friction within the Christian community, the appearance of false prophets, and the rise of "lawlessness" (*anomia*). Thus Matthew makes room on the apocalyptic timetable for problems to develop within the Christian community. His second major change comes in Matt 24:14, which clearly takes its inspiration from Mark 13:10 ("the gospel must first be preached to all nations"). By placing it after the internal dissensions sketched in Matt 24:10-12 Matthew has effectively put off the parousia and the end of the age while placing in context the troubles within the community. By his additions to various phrases ("gospel of the kingdom," "in all the world," "and then the end will come") and by his characteristic use of *ethnē* to mean "Gentiles" Matthew has provided a wide framework like that proposed by Paul in Rom 11:25-26: "a hardening has come upon part of Israel, until the full number of Gentiles come in, and so all Israel will be saved." The Gentile mission must be carried out in its fullness before the end will come.

The "end" refers to the end of the present age/world and the arrival of God's kingdom in its fullness. In Jewish apocalyptic literature there are several lists of signs that precede the "end": 1 Enoch 99:4-7; Jubilees 23; Sibylline Oracles 3:796-808; 4 Ezra 4:51–5:13; 8:63–9:6; and 2 Baruch 25–27. Typical of this kind of listing is 4 Ezra, a Jewish apocalypse composed in the late first century A.D. to try to explain how God could have allowed the Jerusalem Temple to be destroyed and to consider what God may still have in store for Israel.

A good parallel to Matt 24:5-7 is provided by 4 Ezra 9:3-4: "there shall appear in the world earthquakes, tumult of peoples, intrigues of nations, wavering of leaders, confusion of princes." The moral and spiritual confusion within the community that is sketched in Matt 24:9-14 is paralleled in 4 Ezra 5:1-2, 9-10: "those who dwell on earth shall be seized with great terror, and the way of truth shall be hidden, and the land shall be barren of faith. And unrighteousness shall be increased beyond what you yourself see, and beyond what you heard formerly . . . and all friends shall conquer one another; then shall reason hide itself, and wisdom shall withdraw into its chamber, and it shall be sought by many but shall not be found, and unrighteousness and unrestraint shall increase on earth."

Another such scenario, this one directly related to the coming of the Messiah, appears in *m. Soṭah* 9:15: "With the advent of (literally, on the heels of) the Messiah presumptuousness shall increase and produce shall soar in cost; the vine shall yield its fruit but the wine will be costly; and the heathens shall be converted to heresy and there shall be no rebuke. The house of meeting shall become one for adultery. And Galilee shall be devastated and Galban shall become desolate; and the people of the border shall wander from town to town, and none will show them compassion. And the wisdom of the scribes shall be decadent, and those who fear sin shall be loathsome; and truth shall be absent. The young shall put the elders to shame, and elders shall rise up before little ones."

Thus Matthew agreed with both apocalyptic and rabbinic Jews that the "end" and/or the coming of the Messiah would be accompanied by natural calamities, wars, and moral and spiritual confusion. His counsel was patience ("whoever endures to the end, this one will be saved"), based on the recognition that this is only the "beginning of the birthpangs" (24:8). For Matthew (and other Christians) the close of this age/world would be marked by the parousia of Jesus the Son of Man. Before that the good news of the kingdom "had to be preached in all the world to all the Gentiles" (24:14). And before that there would be division and confusion even within the community.

Matt 24:1-14 is a Christian adaptation of Jewish traditions about the signs preceding the end. It leaves time for problems to develop within the community and for a world-wide mission. The goal or end of these happenings is the parousia of Jesus.

This Christian scenario placed Matthew in dialogue (and probably conflict) with those Jews outside the Christian circle, for it contradicted their alternative scenarios. It also spoke directly to Christian fear and confusion about the "end." Without denying the "birthpangs" tradition, Matthew offered a message of patience and hope by making the parousia of Jesus the goal of these "sufferings" and by lengthening the timetable until the Gentile mission could be carried out in its fullness. He also helped Christians to deal with problems within their own community (defections, delations, hatreds, false prophets, *anomia*) by placing them within the outline of things that must happen.

The mission to "all the nations" and hope for Jesus' parousia ("second coming") have long been part of Christian theology. Placing these traditions in their Jewish context enables readers today to see how early Christian theologians like Matthew operated and to appreciate better the message of hope that emerges from Matt 24:1-14. God is guiding human history toward its goal, despite the problems and sufferings of the present time. That goal is the parousia and the end of this age/world.

For Reference and Further Study

Agbanou, V. K. *Le discours eschatologique de Matthieu 24-25: Tradition et rédaction.* Paris: Gabalda, 1983.

Burnett, F. W. *The Testimony of Jesus-Sophia. A Redaction-Critical Study of the Eschatological Discourse in Matthew.* Washington, D.C.: University of America Press, 1981.

Thompson, W. G. "An Historical Perspective in the Gospel of Matthew." *JBL* 93 (1974) 243–62.

66. *The Coming of the Son of Man* (24:15-31)

15. "So when you see the abomination that makes desolate spoken of by Daniel the prophet standing in the holy place (let the reader understand), 16. then let those who are in Judea flee into the mountains; 17. let whoever is on the roof not come down to take things from his house, 18. and whoever is in the field not turn back to take his cloak. 19. Woe to those who are pregnant and nursing in those days. 20. Pray that your flight not be in winter or on the Sabbath. 21. For then there will be a great tribulation, the like of which there has not been from the beginning of the world until now, and never will be. 22. And if those days were not shortened, all flesh would not be saved. But on account of the chosen ones those days will be shortened.

23. "Then if anyone says to you: 'Behold here is the Messiah, or here,' do not believe it. 24. For false messiahs and false prophets will arise, and they will show great signs and wonders, so as to deceive, if possible, even the chosen ones. 25. Behold, I have told you beforehand. 26. So if they say to you: 'Behold he is in the wilderness,' do not go out. 'Behold he is in the inner rooms,' do not believe it. 27. For as lightning goes forth from the east and shines as far as the west, so shall the coming of the Son of Man be. 28. Wherever the corpse may be, there the eagles will be gathered.

29. "Immediately after the tribulation of those days the sun will be darkened, and the moon will not give its light, and the stars will fall from the heaven, and the powers of the heavens will be shaken. 30. And then the sign of the Son of Man will appear in the heaven, and then all the tribes of the earth will mourn, and they will see the Son of Man coming upon the clouds of the heaven with power and much glory. 31. And he will send his angels with the great trumpet, and they will gather his chosen ones from the four winds from one end of heaven to the other."

Notes

15. *the abomination that makes desolate*: The Greek phrase *to bdelygma tou erēmōseōs* ("the abomination of desolation") is based on the Hebrew expression in Dan 9:27; 11:31; 12:11 (*hašîqqûṣ mĕšômēm*), which in turn was a parody on the name of the deity whose worship was set up in the Jerusalem Temple in 167 B.C. under the Seleucid king Antiochus IV Epiphanes. The deity was the Semitic "Lord of Heaven," which in Hebrew was *ba'al šāmayîm*. For *ba'al* ("lord") the substitution was *šîqqûṣ* ("abomination"). The word *mĕšômēm* ("that which makes desolate") was a pun on the word for "heavens" (*šāmayîm*).

spoken of by Daniel the prophet: Matthew adds to Mark 13:14 an indication of where in the Bible the phrase appears, lest there be any confusion among his readers. He also adds "in the holy place" (=the Jerusalem Temple) to specify Mark's vague "where it ought not to be."

(let the reader understand): Matthew preserves the parenthetical comment in Mark 13:14. The parenthesis is often interpreted as a reference to the threat by the emperor Caligula in A.D. 40 to set up a statue of himself in the Jerusalem Temple. In other words, the reader is directed to find an analogy between what transpired under Antiochus IV Epiphanes in the second century B.C. and under Caligula in A.D. 40. Luke 21:20 interprets the "abomination" as the Roman attack on Jerusalem in A.D. 70 ("when you see Jerusalem surrounded by armies, then know that its desolation has come near").

17. *whoever is on the roof*: Roofs of houses were usually flat and used for various purposes: sitting in the evening, eating, celebrating, drying fruits and vegetables, etc. The description suggests an outside access stairway. The point of the warning is to move as quickly as possible without allowing oneself to be distracted.

18. *his cloak*: The Greek term *himation* refers to the outer garment or long coat. Someone working in a field might discard it while engaged in strenuous activity. The image is that the cloak has been left to the side in the field. The warning is not to go back to fetch it.

19. *those who are pregnant and nursing*: Since such persons would find travel difficult, the sudden appearance of the "abomination" and the need to flee quickly would be especially onerous on them.

20. *on the Sabbath*: Matthew has added this qualification to Mark 13:18 ("in winter"). It indicates that for Matthew and his community Sabbath observance remained a live issue. In winter travel in Palestine was difficult because of the rain and its filling the wadis. On the Sabbath a Jew was not allowed to take long journeys, and so would face a "crisis of conscience" if this were to happen on the Sabbath. See G. N. Stanton, " 'Pray that your flight may not be in winter or on a Sabbath' (Matthew 24.20)." *JSNT* 37 (1989) 17–30.

21. *great tribulation*: The Greek term *thlipsis* ("affliction, tribulation") in Mark 13:19 is qualified by Matthew as "great." The following phrases ("the like of which . . .") are clearly dependent on the Greek of Dan 12:1, which introduces the victory of the righteous and the resurrection of the dead at the end-time.

22. *those days will be shortened*: Matthew prefers the "divine passive" construction to Mark 13:20 ("the Lord shortened . . . be shortened"). But the primary actor is clearly God. The motif of God's shortening the days before the fullness of the kingdom appears in *Bib. Ant.* 19:13 ("I will command the years and order the times, and they will be shortened") as well as 2 Bar 83:1 ("For the Most High will surely hasten his times, and he will certainly cause his periods to arrive"). In neither case is there a reference to the "chosen ones" as the reason why God will shorten the times.

the chosen ones: The "chosen ones" or the "elect" is a term applied frequently in the OT to the Israelites and in the NT to the Christians. God is the one who has chosen or elected. His choice is based not on accomplishments or natural superiority of the chosen ones. The choice places the chosen ones to live in accord with God's purposes (see Deut 7:6-11).

24. *false messiahs and false prophets*: The prediction refers back to Matt 24:5, which also envisions the rise of false messiahs (see Josephus, *Ant.* 17:271-285; Acts 5:35-39). As Josephus shows, such characters were part of Jewish history throughout the first century A.D. Matthew underlines their fiendish purpose: "so as to deceive, if possible, even the chosen ones."

26. *in the wilderness . . . in the inner rooms*: The point of these distinctively Matthean warnings is to indicate that the coming of the Son of Man will not be a hidden event. There will be no need to search him out. As Matt 24:27 shows, his coming will be as clear and public as the lightning flashing across the sky.

28. *the eagles will be gathered*: One would expect "vultures" rather than "eagles." Perhaps the Hebrew term for "eagle" (*nešer*) should be translated as "vulture." Both Aristotle (*Hist. An.* 9:32) and Pliny (*Hist. Nat.* 10:3) classed the vulture among the eagles. The point of the proverb in this context is to stress the clear and public nature of the coming of the Son of Man.

29. *the sun will be darkened*: The list of cosmic signs is a way of saying that all creation will signal the coming of the Son of Man. The words that make up the list echo certain OT texts: Isa 13:10; Ezek 32:7; Amos 8:9; Joel 2:10, 31; 3:15; Isa 34:4; Hag 2:6, 21. However, nowhere in the OT are these cosmic signs associated with the coming of the Son of Man.

30. *the sign of the Son of Man*: The *sēmeion* of the Son of Man and the trumpet accompanying the angels (24:31, "with the great trumpet") add to the motif of the gathering of the scattered people of God. For the *sēmeion* as "banner" or "standard" in such a context see Isa 11:12; 49:22; for the trumpet in this context see Isa 27:13. For full discussion see T. F. Glasson, "The Ensign of the Son of Man (Matt. XXIV, 30)," *JTS* 15 (1964) 299–300.

all the tribes of the earth will mourn: The motif of the tribes mourning may allude to Zech 12:10-12. If that be the source, then careful readers may have been aware of a reference to Jesus' death as viewed in light of Zech 12:10 ("they will look upon him whom they have pierced," see John 19:37; Rev 1:7).

they will see the Son of Man: The description is taken from Dan 7:13, though here it is clear that for Matthew the Son of Man is Jesus, not "the one in human form."

31. *they will gather his chosen ones*: God's gathering the elect is described in Deut 30:4; Isa 11:11, 16; 27:12; Ezek 39:27; and other OT and Jewish texts. But nowhere in the OT does the Son of Man perform this role (see Mark 13:27). Perhaps that is why Matthew has the angels carry out this task ("they will gather"). For a similar task carried out by angels see Matt 13:49-50.

Interpretation

As Matthew continues the scenario of events leading to the coming of the Son of Man, he treats the "abomination of desolation" and the "great tribulation" (24:15-22 = Mark 13:14-20), the warning about false prophets (24:23-28 = Mark 13:21-23), and the coming of the Son of Man (24:29-31

= Mark 13:24-27). In these pericopes Matthew followed his Markan sources, apart from adding a few supplements along the way.

In the first pericope (24:15-22) Matthew directs the reader to information about the "abomination" in the Book of Daniel and notes that it was "in the holy place" (24:15). To the wish that the flight not take place in winter he added the hope that it not occur on the Sabbath—presumably because it would constitute a crisis of conscience (24:20). The tribulation is qualified as "great" in 24:21. While the "shortening" of the days for the sake of the elect is clearly the work of God, Matthew prefers the "divine passive" construction in 24:22, in keeping with his Jewish reverence in talking about God.

To the Markan version of the second pericope (24:23-28) he has added a series of sayings (24:26-28) that emphasize the clear and public character of the Son of Man's coming. It will not be hidden (24:26) but rather clear as lightning in the sky (24:27) and unmistakable (24:28). To the Markan picture of the Son of Man's coming (24:29-31) he has added a few motifs: the "sign" of the Son of Man, the mourning of the tribes, and the trumpet. Also he has the angels (not the Son of Man) gather the chosen ones.

Most of the images and phrases in Matt 24:15-31 come from the Hebrew Bible, though they appear here in an apocalyptic context that is more developed than what one finds in the Hebrew Bible. The only "pure" apocalypse in the Hebrew Bible is the Book of Daniel, and it is not surprising therefore to find that Daniel is the major biblical influence on the Synoptic apocalypse. By adding the phrase "spoken of by Daniel the prophet" in 24:15 Matthew has deliberately underlined this influence.

The "abomination that makes desolate" is first found in Dan 9:27; 11:31; 12:11. It derives from the cult of Ba'al Shamin ("the Lord of the heavens") that Antiochus IV Epiphanes set up in the Jerusalem Temple. The expression is a word-play or pun in which *šîqqûṣ* ("abomination") substitutes for "Ba'al" and *mĕšômēm* ("makes desolate") substitutes for "heavens." The term described not a statue or image but rather some kind of sacred stone erected on the altar of burnt offerings in the Jerusalem Temple. Though sometimes portrayed as a form of Greek religion, in fact Antiochus' program seems to have been an attempt to assimilate Jewish religion to the widespread Semitic worship of the "Lord of the heavens."

In Matthew's time the "abomination that makes desolate" had lost its specificity in connection with Antiochus IV Epiphanes and his desecration of the Jerusalem Temple in the second century B.C. In the history of the expression's tradition it may have been applied to the emperor Caligula's attempt to have a statue of himself set up in the Jerusalem Temple in A.D. 40 (see Josephus, *Ant.* 18:261; Philo, *De Legatione* 188, 207-208; Tacitus, *Histories* 5.9). In other words the Caligula incident may have been interpreted as a repetition of the Antiochus episode. From Matthew's perspective, however, the new incident is still future. Unlike Luke 21:20 Matthew resists identifying the "abomination" with the destruction of Jerusalem in A.D. 70. And first the good news of the kingdom must be preached to all the world (24:14).

In Matt 24:21 reference is made to "a great tribulation, the like of which there has not been from the beginning of the world until now, and never will be." This motif also is rooted in the Book of Daniel. After a long and detailed survey of history in Daniel 11 that goes up to the time of Antiochus IV Epiphanes (175-164 B.C.), the vision given to Daniel reaches its climax when "Michael the great prince who has charge of your people" shall arise (Dan 12:1). Then there shall be "a time of trouble such as never has been since there was a nation till that time." The way in which the "great tribulation" is described is clearly designed to evoke connections with the apocalyptic scene in Dan 12:1-3.

The references to God shortening the days for the sake of the elect in Matt 24:22 presuppose the existence of an apocalyptic timetable. And again the only place in the Hebrew Bible where such timetables are given is the Book of Daniel. The question there is how long before the "new order" decreed by Antiochus is destroyed and things in the Temple and in Jerusalem are as they should be. In fact the Book of Daniel provides several answers: "a time, two times, and a half a time" (Dan 7:25); 2,300 evenings and mornings = 1,150 days (8:13); three and a half years (9:27); "a time, two times, and a half a time" (12:7); 1,290 days (12:11); and 1,334 days (12:12). The claim of Matt 24:22 is that God will shorten his timetable for the sake of the elect.

The major motif in Matt 24:15-31, for which all else is preparation, is the coming of the Son of Man. Throughout the Gospel the "Son of Man" title appears in various contexts: the passion predictions, sayings on other topics, etc. But here the context is clearly supplied by the Book of Daniel. In Daniel 7 the "Ancient of Days" hands over dominion and glory and kingdom to "one like a Son of Man" (7:13-14). The ceremony takes place in the heavenly court, and the "one like a Son of Man" comes with the clouds of heaven. The expression "one like a Son of Man" suggests someone or something other than a human being. The most common interpretations are the collective (Israel as a people) and the angelic (Michael as leader of the heavenly and earthly hosts). In Matt 25:30 the Son of Man is identified as Jesus. And the way in which his "second coming" is described deliberately evokes Dan 7:13-14: "they will see the Son of Man coming upon the clouds of the heaven with power and much glory."

The Book of Daniel provided the key images and vocabulary for Christian apocalypticism as it did for other forms of Jewish apocalypticism. The challenge facing early Christians like Matthew was to find a place for Jesus within the framework of apocalypticism. Perhaps it was Jesus' own use of the "Son of Man" title in nonapocalyptic contexts that led to his identification with the mysterious figure of Dan 7:13-14. At any rate Jewish-Christian apocalyptists made it their starting point and shaped the other elements in the tradition ("the abomination that makes desolate," the "great tribulation," calculations of the time left) around Jesus' coming as Son of Man.

While Matthew shared the apocalyptic vocabulary with other Christians and Jews, there is one addition in Matt 24:20 that is important for understanding the peculiar character of his situation and his Gospel. To the hope that the flight not be in the winter Matthew added the phrase "nor on the Sabbath." This addition indicates that for him Sabbath observance remained important, and he feared the crisis of conscience that might develop for pious Jews forced to travel on the Sabbath.

The thrust of Matt 24:15-31 is hope for the coming Son of Man. Careful examination of the text shows the extent to which apocalyptic (and especially the Book of Daniel) was the "mother of Christian theology." It also shows that despite its many borrowings from other apocalyptic writings the Synoptic apocalypse is essentially focused on the person of Jesus as the Son of Man.

67. *Parables of Watchfulness* (24:32-51)

32. "From the fig tree learn the lesson: As soon as its branch becomes tender and it puts forth leaves, you know that the harvest is near. 33. So also you, when you see all these things, you know that he is near at the gates. 34. Amen I say to you that this generation will not pass away until all these things happen. 35. Heaven and earth will pass away, but my words will not pass away. 36. But about that day and hour no one knows, neither the angels of heaven nor the Son, but the Father alone.

37. "For as the days of Noah were, so the coming of the Son of Man will be. 38. For as in those days before the flood they were eating and drinking, marrying and being given in marriage, until the day when Noah entered the ark, 39. and they did not know it until the flood came and took them all away, so the coming of the Son of Man will be. 40. Then two men will be in the field. One is taken away, and one is left. 41. Two women will be grinding at the mill. One is taken, and one is left. 42. Watch, therefore, because you do not know in what day your Lord is coming. 43. That you know—if the householder knew in what watch the thief was coming, he would watch and not allow his house to be broken into. 44. And so you be prepared because the Son of Man is coming at a time you do not expect.

45. "Who then is the faithful and wise servant whom the master placed over his household to give to them food at the proper time? 46. Blessed is that servant whom, when his master comes, he will find him doing so. 47. Amen I say to you that he will set him over all his goods. 48. But if that evil servant says in his heart: 'My master is delayed,' 49. and he begins to beat his fellow servants, and eats and drinks with drunkards, 50. the

master of that servant will come on the day on which he does not expect him and in the hour he does not know, 51. and he will cut him in pieces, and will put him with the hypocrites. There will be weeping and gnashing of teeth there."

Notes

32. *the lesson*: The Greek word *parabolē* is used to mean "lesson" or the "meaning of the illustration" connected with the fig tree.

it puts forth leaves: Unlike most trees in Palestine, the fig tree sheds its leaves in winter. Its budding and producing leaves in spring are the signs that summer is not far off.

33. *he is near*: The "he" who is near is the Son of Man (see Matt 24:30). The events that must precede his coming ("all these things") must happen before his coming. When they have happened, know that he is near at the gates.

34. *this generation*: The phrase "all these things" would most obviously refer to the events leading up to the coming of the Son of Man, though some interpreters connect it with Jesus' death and resurrection. The warning would therefore tie in the Son of Man's coming to the generation close to Jesus, though some interpreters understand *genea* as "race" or "people" (=Israel). At any rate the warning about the closeness of the Son of Man's coming is balanced by Matt 24:36.

35. *my words will not pass away*: Jesus' solemn saying is reminiscent of Isa 40:8: "The grass withers, the flower fades; but the word of the Lord will stand forever." It also alludes back to his statement in Matt 5:18: "till heaven and earth pass away, not an iota, not a dot, will pass from the Law until all is accomplished." Thus Jesus echoes about himself what is said first about the word of Yahweh and then about the Torah. See also Isa 51:6.

36. *no one knows*: The denial that anyone (including the angels and even the Son) knows the exact time balances off what had already been said in 24:34 about "this generation." Many manuscripts omit "nor the Son." But the best manuscripts contain it, and the syntax of the sentence ("neither the angels . . . but the Father alone") demands it. Its omission is easily explained as arising from the doctrinal difficulty that it presented.

37. *as the days of Noah were*: The point of comparison between the days of Noah and the coming of the Son of Man is the unexpectedness of the crisis. There is no reference to the wickedness that prevailed before the flood nor any baptismal typology as in 1 Pet 3:20-21. So unexpected was the flood that people did not recognize it until it had already come upon them. This theme is not emphasized in Genesis 6. Matthew omits the Q material about Lot and his wife in Luke 17:28-29, 31-32.

40. *one is taken away*: The verb *paralambanetai* has eschatological overtones. The point of the "two men in the field" and the "two women at the mill" comparisons is the division that will be caused (or better, be clear) at the Son of Man's com-

ing. Two people who are doing the same tasks and therefore look the same—one will become part of God's kingdom, and the other will be left behind, when the Son of Man comes. The Lukan version has two men in the same bed and two women grinding together (Luke 17:34-35).

42. *Watch*: In view of the unexpectedness and the decisiveness of the Son of Man's coming illustrated in the two comparisons, the proper attitude is watchfulness or vigilance. Since the precise time of the Lord's coming is not known (see also 24:36), the only fitting attitude is constant vigilance (since it could happen at any time).

43. *he would watch*: The comparison of an expected event to a thief breaking in appears in 1 Thess 5:2; 2 Pet 3:10; Rev 3:3; 16:15. But here the thief's arrival is expected and the time is known. If the householder knew exactly when the thief was coming, he would make the necessary preparations against the thief. Comparison with Luke 12:39-40 shows that Matthew added "he would watch," thus stressing the theme of constant watchfulness.

44. *so you be prepared*: Since the coming of the Son of Man remains mysterious ("at a time you do not expect"), one is to be on guard constantly, treating every moment as if it was the moment of the Son of Man's coming.

45. *the faithful and wise servant*: The characteristics of the first servant are expressed in the adjectives *pistos* and *phronimos*. For *pistos* as the ideal characteristic of a Christian leader, see 1 Cor 4:1-2, 17; Col 1:7; Eph 6:21; and Titus 1:9. The idea is more "reliable, trustworthy" than "believing." The question here is which of the two servants described in the parable is the reliable and prudent one?

46. *Blessed is that servant*: The master's return is a surprise; no one knew when he was coming. If the master finds the servant doing what he is charged to do—presiding over the distribution of food in the household—the master will declare that reliable servant "blessed" or "happy," and increase his responsibilities by placing him over the administration of the whole household.

48. *that evil servant*: Despite the claim of J. Jeremias (*Parables*, 55) that "the parable speaks of one, not of two servants," there seems to be a second servant in Matthew's version. Matthew has added the qualification "evil" (*kakos*), thus differentiating the second servant from the first one.

    My master is delayed: This provides the second servant with an excuse to abuse his fellow servants and to behave badly. It has become customary to interpret this reflection on the second servant's part as a reference to the delay of the parousia and to focus on the internal problems of the Christian community. But it may be possible to take it as embracing the Jewish community (including Jewish Christians).

49. *his fellow servants*: Instead of Luke 12:45 ("servants and maidservants") Matthew includes a reminder that the steward is a "fellow servant" (*syndoulos*) of those whom he abuses.

50. *on the day on which he does not expect him*: This expression (see also Luke 12:46) ties the parable into the warning that introduced it: "be prepared because the

Son of Man is coming at a time you do not expect'' (24:44), thus giving us the perspective that Matthew places upon it.

51. *he will cut him in pieces*: This literal translation suggests the punishment of dismemberment. But how then could he be put with the hypocrites? Some suggest a metaphorical sense that would describe separation from the community or excommunication as in the Qumran *Manual of Discipline* (1QS 1:10-11; 2:16-17; 6:24-25; 7:1-2, 16; 8:21-23).

the hypocrites: Whereas Luke 12:46 reads ''the faithless'' (*apistoi*), Matthew uses the term ''hypocrites,'' one of his favorite words, one usually applied to the scribes and Pharisees (see Matt 23:15, 23, 25, 27, 29).

weeping and gnashing of teeth: This sentence appears elsewhere as a conclusion in Matt 8:12; 13:42, 50; and 22:13. Since it does not appear in Luke 12:46, it must have been Matthew's characteristic addition to the Q version. It refers to the finality of the final condemnation and the sadness surrounding it.

Interpretation

This section of Matthew's eschatological discourse contains the end of Mark's version (Mark 13:28-37) as well as assorted Q material. Besides the full-scale parable in Matt 24:45-51 it presents several small parables: the fig tree (24:32), the days of Noah (24:37-39), the two men in the field and the two women at the mill (24:40-41), and the householder and the thief (24:43). All these disparate materials are placed in the context of Jesus' warning ''be prepared'' (24:44). Since the time of the Son of Man's coming remains unknown, the proper attitude is constant watchfulness.

At the beginning of the section (24:32-36) Matthew follows Mark 13:28-32 with only a few changes (*heōs an* for *mechris hou* in 24:34, the addition of *monos* in 24:36). But by modifying Mark 13:33-37 he has destroyed the chiastic structure: A—parable (Mark 13:28-29), B—saying about the time of the end (13:30), C—saying about Jesus authority (13:31), B¹—saying about the time (13:32), A¹—parable (13:33-37). Thus Mark balanced the saying about ''this generation'' (13:30) with the affirmation that only the Father knows the precise time (13:32). The parable about the signs of the end time (13:28-29) is balanced by one about constant vigilance (13:33-37). The statement about the authority of Jesus' words constitutes the center of the interlocking structure. Though Matthew has departed from this neat parallelism at the end, the effect is to ''overload'' the part about constant vigilance (Mark 13:33-37 = Matt 24:37-51) and thus to increase its prominence as a theme.

The theme of constant vigilance in view of uncertainty regarding the time of the Son of Man's coming is expanded by Matthew with material taken mainly from Q: the parable of the days of Noah (Matt 24:37-39 = Luke 17:26-27), the twin parable about two men in the field and two women at the mill (Matt 24:40-41 = Luke 17:34-35), the parable about the householder and the thief (Matt 24:43-44 = Luke 12:39-40), and the parable of the two servants (Matt 24:45-51 = Luke 12:41-46). The exhortation to watchfulness (Matt 24:42) is taken over from Mark 13:35, and the whole of Matt 24:37-51 can be seen as an expanded version of Mark 13:33-37. Whereas the point of Mark's neatly balanced structure was to suggest an evenhandedness between the signs taking place in "this generation" and uncertainty about the time of the Son of Man's coming, Matthew has shifted the structure toward the theme of constant watchfulness in the face of uncertainty regarding the time of the Son of Man's coming.

Prominent in early Jewish-Christian scenarios regarding the kingdom of God was the coming of the Son of Man, who was of course identified as Jesus. Thus Matthew refers several times to the parousia of this Son of Man (see Matt 24:3, 27, 37, 39). Whether the Son of Man figured in other Jewish apocalyptic scenarios is a matter of debate, which need not concern us here. Another feature of apocalyptic scenarios was the attempt to achieve clarity regarding the precise time of the end. This tradition of calculating the times began (or at least had an early example) in the Book of Daniel. As we saw with reference to the time during which the worship set up in the Jerusalem Temple by Antiochus IV Epiphanes would prevail, the Book of Daniel offered several timetables: a "time, two times, and a half a time" (Dan 7:25); 2,300 evenings and mornings = 1,150 days (8:13); three and a half years (9:27); "a time, two times, and a half a time" (12:7); 1,290 days (12:11); and 1,334 days (12:12). These calculations add up to about three and a half years, but there is clearly an attempt to lengthen out the time probably to deal with unfulfilled prophecy. Given the apocalyptic context of Daniel with its hopes for a new age and the fullness of God's kingdom, it is not surprising that there should develop in Jewish apocalyptic circles a fascination with calculating the apocalyptic timetables.

It is also not surprising that a strong skepticism should arise in response to the failure of such calculations. An example of such skepticism is expressed in 2 Pet 3:3-4: ". . . scoffers will come in the last days with scoffing, following their own passions and saying: 'Where is the promise of his coming (parousia)? For ever since the fathers fell asleep, all things have continued as they were from the beginning of creation.' " Though from a somewhat later time than Matthew, 2 Peter reflects a taunt posed by outsiders to Christians in the early second century A.D. and probably also in the late first century. This taunt probably shattered the confidence of Christians too, who began to doubt that "all these things" would take place in "this generation" (see Matt 24:34). So the situation behind the parables of watchfulness in Matt 24:32-51 was very likely the Christian connection between the parousia of the Son of Man and the end-time, the Jewish and Christian concern with calculating the time before the end, and the embarrassment caused by the nonappearance of the Son of Man.

It has become customary among modern scholars to interpret material like Matt 24:32-51 as referring to problems within the Matthean community. In the face of uncertainty and confusion among Christians about the coming of the Son of Man, Matthew urged confidence in the eventual appearance of the Son of Man and constant watchfulness in the meantime. But without changing the fundamental message of the material, it may be preferable to read Matt 24:32-51 first of all in the framework of the quarrel between the Matthean community and the Jewish group(s) that opposed it. After all, the scoffers of 2 Pet 3:3-4 seem to have been outside the Christian community too.

The position of Matthew's Jewish opponents would go something as follows: "You Christians have inserted into the apocalyptic scenario the coming of your Son of Man. When is he going to come? You say in 'this generation.' Well, where is he? In fact, we are skeptical about the whole business of apocalyptic scenarios and timetables, to say nothing about the Son of Man." Such may well have been the position of "formative Judaism" after the debacle of the Jewish revolt of A.D. 66 to 70 and in response not only to Christians but also to the apocalyptic revisionists who produced 4 Ezra and 2 Baruch.

The Matthean response is heard most clearly in what the evangelist has added to his Markan source. While preserving some of the balance between clear signs and imminent parousia (Matt 24:32-34) on the one hand and uncertainty about the time (Matt 24:36) on the other, Matthew has tipped the balance toward the theme of the uncertain time and the appropriate stance of constant watchfulness by adding the Q material in Matt 24:37-51.

Matthew's response to his Jewish opponents would run something like this: No one knows the precise time of the Son of Man's coming. Nevertheless, we believe that his coming is certain (see Matt 24:35) on the authority of the Son of Man himself. His coming will be unexpected, as was the flood in the days of Noah (24:37-39). It will, moreover, separate people in judgment (24:40-41). The Christian position is this: "Watch, therefore, because you do not know in what day your Lord is coming" (24:42). That watchfulness is illustrated by the parables of the householder and the thief (24:43-44) and of the two servants (24:45-51). According to the second of those parables success or failure in constant watchfulness is the criterion by which people will be judged when the Son of Man comes.

Matthew's twin emphasis on the uncertainty about when the Son of Man will come and the attitude of constant watchfulness in the meantime has shaped mainline Christian theology through the centuries. Careful analysis of Matt 24:32-51 shows how he developed this approach out of even earlier traditions. In the encounter with (nonapocalyptic) Judaism after A.D. 70 one can also see how Christianity became a major vehicle for the survival of apocalypticism. This Christian apocalypticism, however, is not given to speculations and timetables. While retaining a strong faith in God's direction of history and a hope that it will mean the vindication of the just, Matthew made them into a framework for Christian action in the present. Thus he brought about union between eschatology and ethics. Christians should always act as if the coming of the Son of Man were near.

68. *The Parable of the Ten Maidens* (25:1-13)

1. "Then the kingdom of heaven may be compared to ten maidens who took their lamps and went out to meet the bridegroom. 2. Five of them were foolish, and five wise. 3. For the foolish ones, in taking the lamps, did not take oil with them. 4. But the wise ones took oil in flasks with their lamps. 5. As the bridegroom was delayed, all of them grew drowsy and slept. 6. But at midnight a shout went up: 'Behold the bridegroom. Go out to meet him!' 7. Then all those maidens arose and trimmed their lamps. 8. The foolish ones said to the wise: 'Give us some of your oil because our lamps are going out.' 9. The wise ones answered and said: 'Perhaps there will not be enough for us and for you. Go instead to the dealers, and buy for yourselves.' 10. When they went away to buy the bridegroom came, and those who were ready went in with him into the marriage feast, and the door was closed. 11. Later the other maidens came and said: 'Lord, lord, open to us.' 12. But he answered and said: 'Amen, I say to you, I do not know you.' 13. Watch therefore, because you do not know the day or the hour.' "

Notes

1. *ten maidens*: The Greek word for "maiden" here is *parthenos*, the same term applied to Mary in Matt 1:23. It could be translated "virgins," though the issue of virginity is irrelevant to the story. The rendering "bridesmaids" is not quite accurate since they are at the household of the groom. The comparison ("the kingdom of heaven may be compared to") is with the whole story that follows, not simply with the maidens.

   their lamps: Jeremias (*Parables*, 174) says that *lampades* refers to "candles protected by a shade." But why would the maidens need oil for such devices? They must rather have been some kind of oil-fed lamps.

   to meet the bridegroom: The setting of the parable is the return of the groom from the house of the bride's father. He would be taking the bride from her father's house into his own house (or that of his father). The maidens are to welcome bride and groom into the household. Some manuscripts add "and the bride," probably in light of the customary way of conducting a wedding.

3. *the foolish ones*: This group is judged "foolish" (*morai*) because they failed to foresee the possibility that the bridegroom might be delayed and so they neglected

to take along an extra supply of oil. The bridegroom's delay (see 25:6) gives them a chance to do something but they fail to take their opportunity.

4. *in flasks*: The wise (*phronimoi*) took along an extra supply of oil in *aggeia*, small jugs with handles. The assumption is that all ten maidens go a fairly long distance down the road to meet the bridegroom with his bride.

5. *the bridegroom was delayed*: At the bride's house the bridegroom had to complete the negotiations with the bride's father. A dispute regarding the terms would not have been unrealistic, and this could have been the implied cause of his late return home. The verb for "delay" (*chronizō*) is the same as the one used in Matt 24:48 with reference to the delay of the master of the household.

7. *trimmed their lamps*: Awakened from sleep by news of the bridegroom's appearance, the ten maidens ready their lamps. Jeremias (*Parables*, 175) explains the verb *ekosmēsan* as follows: "they snuff the lamps, removing the burnt wick, and fill them with oil, so that they may burn brightly again."

9. *Perhaps*: Some manuscripts have a more direct and harsher response: "No, there will not be enough for us and for you." At any rate the dilemma facing the wise maidens is that, if they share their oil, both groups will end up without enough oil.

   buy for yourselves: That the oil dealers would be open at midnight is unlikely. But the details in a story like this should not be pressed too strictly. And it is just possible that some shops where oil could be bought remained open; see A. W. Argyle, "Wedding Customs at the Time of Jesus," *ExpTim* 86 (1975) 214–15.

10. *the marriage feast*: The plural of *gamos* ("marriage") is used to describe the wedding celebration (*gamoi*), as was customary in Greek. See also Matt 22:1-14. For the idea of a group refused admission to a marriage feast because they were not properly prepared, see Matt 22:11-14.

11. *"Lord, Lord, open to us:"* See Matt 7:21-22 for others who say "Lord, Lord" but fail to enter the kingdom of heaven.

12. *I do not know you*: The formula is the equivalent of "I will have nothing to do with you" (Jeremias, *Parables*, 175). Peter uses the same formula in Matt 26:74 with reference to Jesus. The bridegroom's statement would be easier to accept if the maidens had come from the bride's household. The "foolish" maidens find themselves rejected by both the "wise" maidens and the bridegroom.

13. *Watch*: Though well suited to Matthew's context (see Matt 24:32-51), the concluding exhortation is not entirely appropriate since all the maidens fell asleep. The foolishness of some consisted in their failure to foresee and provide for their needs.

Interpretation

Like Matt 24:45-51, so the parable of the ten maidens (Matt 25:1-13) illustrates the saying in 24:42: "Watch therefore because you do not know in what day your Lord comes." It too contrasts characters—this time wise and foolish maidens—in an effort to show the need for constant watchfulness in the face of the coming Son of Man.

There is a longstanding debate about the extent to which the parable of the ten maidens should be interpreted as an allegory. Since for many interpreters allegory implies creation by the early Church, a decision about this matter has importance for the way one looks at the history of the text. The allegorical interpretation understands the parable as an allegory of the parousia of Christ, the heavenly bridegroom (Jeremias, *Parables*, 51-53). According to the allegorical approach the bridegroom is Christ, the ten maidens are the Christian community waiting for Christ, the delay of the bridegroom is the postponement of the parousia, his sudden coming is the unexpected arrival of the parousia, the rejection of the foolish maidens is the last judgment, and perhaps the foolish virgins represent Israel and the wise ones the Gentiles.

That the parable of the ten maidens has some allegorical features must be admitted. But that it is a full-fledged allegory in which each detail has another significance is unlikely. Of the items listed in the preceding paragraph the Jewish-Gentile division has no basis in the text. Nevertheless the story clearly operates at two levels: that of an unusual event at a wedding feast, and that of the parousia of the Son of Man.

The features of the wedding feast are basically true to the customs of first-century Palestine insofar as we can know them. For a lengthy discussion of first-century Jewish marriage practices, see the discussion with reference to Matt 1:18-25. The scene of the parable is the groom's house. Ten maidens await his return from the bride's house to which the groom has gone to determine and sign the marriage contract with the bride's father, and to bring the bride to his own house (or that of his father). The ten maidens seem to be attached to the groom's household, though his statement to the foolish maidens ("I do not know you") suggests a link with the bride's household. Since negotiations about the terms of the marriage contract could get involved, perhaps the groom's delay should not be considered unusual. At any rate, his return after dark is assumed since all the maidens took lamps along with them. At his return with his bride, the wedding feast could begin at his own household. So there is nothing out of the ordinary in the story with respect to first-century Jewish wedding customs.

The unusual elements concern the ten maidens. They go forth (it seems) from the groom's house. Some take along extra oil for their lamps, but others do not. Because the groom is delayed, all go to sleep. On being awakened by the announcement that the groom is coming, the foolish maidens realize that they do not have enough oil and go off to buy some. While they are away, the groom arrives and goes with the wedding party to the marriage feast. The foolish maidens find themselves locked out. The moral of the story is "Watch therefore, because you do not know the day or the hour" (25:13).

A central figure in the story is the bridegroom. Once it is admitted that the parable is more than an interesting story about an unusual wedding, the question arises, Who is the bridegroom? The Hebrew Bible witnesses to a tradition of identifying God as the bridegroom of Israel. For example, Isa 54:5 ("your Maker is your husband, the Lord of hosts is his name"), Jer 31:32 ("I was their husband, says the Lord"), Hosea 2:16 ("in that day, says the Lord, you will call me, 'My husband,' "), etc. In the New Testament, however, Jesus appears as the bridegroom: "Can the wedding guests mourn as long as the bridegroom is with them? The days will come when the bridegroom is taken away from them, and then they will fast" (Matt 9:15). The tradition of Christ the bridegroom appears also in John 3:29; 2 Cor 11:2; Eph 5:21-33; Rev 21:2, 9; 22:17.

If the parable of the ten maidens goes back to Jesus, it is possible that he was talking about God as the bridegroom and that he referred to the imminent but unpredictable coming of God's kingdom. But in the Matthean context the bridegroom must be the Son of Man, who is identified as Jesus. From Matt 24:29 onward the main topic has been the coming of the Son of Man and the attitude of constant watchfulness one should display until he comes. There is, of course, Christological significance in the fact that a title applied to God in the Hebrew Bible is applied to Jesus in the New Testament.

The bridegroom of the parable is the Son of Man. The ten maidens become positive and negative models on how to act in view of the Son of Man's delayed arrival. The wise maidens are ever vigilant and prepared for his unexpected arrival. The foolish ones are not ready. The allegorical interpretation according to which the wise are Gentiles and the foolish are Jews has no basis whatever in the text and may be dismissed right away. The more common approach is to identify the ten maidens with members of the Christian community. The point of the parable is to provide positive and negative models about behavior in the face of the Son of Man's coming.

Neither interpretation does justice to the situation of Matthew's community. The problem facing them was how they related to other Jews, especially those who refused to follow the Christian way of Judaism. If we identify Matthew's opponents as representatives of early "formative Judaism," Matthew may well have been criticizing their disinterest in apocalyptic. Perhaps as a reaction against the fanaticism that issued in the destruction of the Jerusalem Temple in A.D. 70 those Jews, whose movement later developed into rabbinism, for the most part avoided apocalyptic speculations. They probably viewed the continuing Christian interest in apocalypticism as unhealthy and dangerous. On the other hand, Christians like Matthew viewed their opponents' disinterest in and antipathy toward apocalypticism as foolish and shortsighted. Such people will not exhibit the constant watchfulness demanded by the coming of the Son of Man. In the Matthean context then the parable of the ten maidens is another comment on the relation between the Matthean community (with its attitude of constant watchfulness in light of the uncertain coming of the Son of Man) and their Jewish opponents (with their suspicion about apocalyptic and their disinterest in talk about the Son of Man's coming).

Interpreting the parable of the ten maidens on the level of the Matthean community's experience highlights the longstanding split between Christians and Jews over apocalyptic. There have been (and are) apocalyptic Jews and nonapocalyptic Christians. But on the whole Christians have kept alive the tradition of apocalyptic and Jews have been suspicious of it (mainly because of the unfortunate consequences that have befallen Jews who dabbled in it). Attention to this parable shows two contrasting attitudes toward the coming Son of Man. Matthew warned his opponents to be on watch always and to take seriously the early Christian conviction about the parousia.

For Reference and Further Study

Feuillet, A. "Les epousailles messianiques et les références au Cantique des cantiques dans les évangiles synoptiques." *Revue Thomiste* 84 (1984) 399–424.

Puig i Tarrech, A. *La parabole des dix vierges (Mt 25, 1-13)*. AB 102. Rome: Biblical Institute Press, 1984.

69. *The Parable of the Talents* (25:14-30)

14. "For (it will be) like a man away on a journey. He summoned his servants and handed over to them his property. 15. And he gave to one five talents, to another two, and to another one, each according to his own capability. And he went away on a journey. 16. The one who received the five talents went right away and did business with them and gained another five. 17. Likewise the one with two gained another two. 18. But the one who received the one went away, dug up the ground, and hid his master's money. 19. After a long time the master of those servants came and settled accounts with them. 20. And the one who received the five talents came forward and presented another five talents, saying: 'Sir, you handed over to me five talents. Look, I have gained another five talents.' 21. His master said to him: 'Well done, good and faithful servant; you were faithful over a few things, I will set you over many. Enter into the joy of your master.' 22. The one with two talents came forward and said: 'Sir, you handed over to me two talents. Look, I have gained another two talents.' 23. His master

said to him: 'Well done, good and faithful servant; you were faithful over a few things; I will set you over many. Enter into the joy of your master.'
24. And he who had received the one talent came forward and said: 'Sir, I knew that you are a hard man, reaping where you did not sow, and gathering where you have not scattered. 25. And being afraid I went away and hid your talent in the ground. Look, you have what is yours.' 26. His master answered and said to him: 'You wicked and lazy servant, you knew that I reap where I did not sow, and I gather where I did not scatter. 27.
You should have invested my money with the moneychangers; and when I came, I would have gotten back what is mine with interest. 28. So take away the talent from him and give it to the one having ten talents. 29. For to everyone who has it will be given, and he will have an abundance. But the one who does not have—even what he has will be taken away from him. 30. And throw that useless servant into the darkness outside. There will be weeping and gnashing of teeth there.' "

Notes

14. *(it will be) like a man*: The introduction to the parable is unusually short; perhaps the more elaborate introduction in Matt 25:1 was understood to do double duty. There is no reason to allegorize the initial details by seeing in the man "away on a journey" a reference to Jesus' ascension or in "his property" a reference to the gift of the Spirit.

15. *five talents*: It is difficult to be precise about the amount constituted by a talent or its modern equivalent. One commentator describes it as "the wage of an ordinary worker for fifteen years." At any rate, the point is not the precise amount but rather that it was a large sum (like a "million dollars" or a "huge amount" in modern speech).

    according to his own capability: The master calibrated the amount according to ability to each servant. This motif coupled with the use of "talent" in the story line led to the use of the term "talent" to describe one's natural ability to do something.

18. *dug up the ground and hid his master's money*: Whereas the first two servants invested their talents, the third servant buried his one talent. According to Jeremias (*Parables*, 61), burying money was regarded as the best security against theft. Whoever buried money was freed from liability, whereas whoever tied up entrusted money in a cloth was responsible for its loss (see Luke 19:20).

19. *after a long time*: The phrase continues the "delay" motif found in the preceding parables (see Matt 24:48; 25:5). It, plus the reference to the "master" (*kyrios*) and the settling of accounts, makes the parable into a story about the last judgment.

21. *Enter into the joy of your master*: Whereas the master's comment up to that point implied that successful handling of responsibility would merit even greater responsibility, his final directive suggests the positive verdict passed at the final judgment. See the same comments directed to the second servant in Matt 25:23.

24. *you are a hard man*: This qualification is omitted in the master's description of himself in Matt 25:26. There he admits to the truth of harvesting only where he did not sow and reaping only where he had not scattered (seed).

25. *being afraid*: The servant says his failure to act was because of fear, whereas in Matt 25:26 the master calls him "wicked and lazy." There are differences in perceptions between the two characters.

27. *moneychangers*: The word *trapezitēs* derives from the term for table (*trapeza*). Moneychangers operated from tables set up near the city gate or the Temple. If the reference is specifically to moneychangers, then the master envisions the interest that they charged for their transactions. If it is a more generic reference to bankers, then he would have been talking about the interest accruing from their transactions.

29. *it will be given*: The saying is probably to be taken as a "divine" passive; i.e., God will give . . . God will take away. The point seems to be: "The rich get richer, and the poor get poorer." While loosely connected with the parable, the saying does not exhaust its main point, which is responsible activity in the face of the Son of Man's coming.

30. *the darkness outside*: This expression alludes to condemnation at the last judgment, and so is the opposite of "Enter into the joy of your master" (Matt 25:21, 23).

weeping and gnashing of teeth: The same expression was used in Matt 8:12; 13:42, 50; 22:13; and 24:51. It describes the frustration of those excluded from the master's joy.

Interpretation

The parable of the talents (Matt 25:14-30) is the third in a series of parables dealing with the proper attitude to and behavior in the face of the coming Son of Man. It recommends responsible activity in this situation. Its emphasis is on positive action as opposed to fearful and/or lazy inactivity. There are obvious parallels with the parable of the pounds in Luke 19:11-27, though the precise relationship remains a controverted matter. The focus of our exposition will be the Matthean version in its Matthean context.

The Matthean context is the parousia of the Son of Man. Matthew gives special attention to the Markan theme of constant watchfulness because no one knows when the Son of Man is coming (Mark 13:35). This theme is developed by the parables of the two servants (24:45-51), the ten maidens (25:1-13), and the talents (25:14-30). All three parables contribute to the picture of what constitutes responsible behavior in preparation for the coming of the Son of Man.

Whatever the history of the development of the parable of the talents may have been, its present form in Matt 25:14-30 contains some "allegorical" features. Jeremias (*Parables*, 59) finds in the Lukan parable of the pounds allusions to Herod Archelaus and his struggle for power in the early first century A.D. Such allusions are much harder to find in the Matthean version, which comes third in a series of three parables about the master of a house being absent for a time and returning unexpectedly to demand an accounting or to make a judgment. The master is "away on a journey" (25:14, 15). Then "after a long time" (25:19) he returns and settles accounts. Those who have acted positively and responsibly are summoned to enter into their master's joy (25:21, 23), while the one who failed to act out of fear or laziness is condemned to darkness outside (25:30). This parable leads into the judgment scene in Matt 25:31-46 in which the Son of Man acts as judge for "all the Gentiles." Thus the Matthean parable of the talents clearly concerns the coming of the Son of Man and how one should behave in anticipation of it. Its message is positive action instead of fearful or lazy inaction.

The phenomenon of the absentee master entrusting property to stewards was apparently familiar to first-century Jews, including the Matthean Christians (see Matt 21:33-41). In the parable the first motive of the master in entrusting his property to his servants is to determine which were capable of assuming even more responsibility. But this testing yields to a second motive: determining which should share his joy. This movement is an indication in the parable that the story is not merely about everyday experience. It is about God's kingdom and the Son of Man's parousia.

The Matthean parable of the talents is usually taken as an exhortation directed to Christians, who should work diligently in the present and avoid laziness and fear in the face of the Son of Man's coming. That there were problems along these lines is indicated by Paul's letters to the Thessalonians. This tradition has continued to the present in the form of the title "parable of the talents," with the accompanying exhortations about using one's talents and the loss of any eschatological perspective.

Students of the parables who trace this parable back to Jesus usually find a different audience and the criticism of a group within Judaism (or of the Jewish people as a whole). But given Matthew's own setting, why could not this have been the background for the Matthean version of the parable also? The third servant who fails to do anything with his one talent except to preserve it by burying it away—could he not be Matthew's symbol for the movement within Judaism after A.D. 70 that sought to preserve the Jewish patrimony by building a "hedge" or "fence" around the Torah (see *m. 'Abot* 1:1)? This approach to the parable sees it as part of Matthew's attack on his Jewish opponents for their failure to preserve the proper apocalyptic spirit. At the same time it serves as an apology or defense for the Matthean community by helping them to put into perspective their opponents' program: It amounts to burying the treasures of Judaism, whereas the Christian program (with its missionary activity) makes that treasure all the more fruitful and will bring about a share in the eternal joy of the Son of Man.

If (as I maintain) the next text (Matt 25:31-46) concerns Gentile treatment of Christian missionaries, there is a smooth transition from Matt 25:14-30. In the Matthean setting then the parable of the talents contrasted the enterprising and successful Jewish-Christian missionaries (the first two servants) and the fearful and/or lazy Jewish movement that we call "formative Judaism" (the third servant). All this, of course, is viewed from the Jewish-Christian perspective and (as is the case with all apologetics) was intended primarily for internal consumption by the Matthean community. The parable of the talents enabled the Matthean Christians to locate themselves and their opponents.

The usual moralizing approach to Matt 25:14-30 ("use your talents to the best of your ability") does not take into account the eschatological horizon that is essential to the parable. The return of the master and the accounting are essential aspects of the story, and they should not be omitted in teaching and preaching. The interpretation suggested here—part of the polemic involved in the struggle between Matthean Christianity and formative Judaism—has to be handled carefully lest it occasion anti-Semitism and negative attitudes toward Judaism. This line of exposition, however, does give a sharp insight into the roots of the parting between Christians and Jews in the late first century A.D. It conveys a sense of what Matthean Christians thought about other Jews as they faced the common crisis of reconstructing Judaism now that Jerusalem and its Temple lay in ruins.

For Reference and Further Study

Puig i Tarrech, A. "La parabole des talents (Mt 25, 14-30) ou des mines (Lc 19, 11-28)." *Revista Catalana Teologia* 10 (1985) 269–317.

70. *The Judgment* (25:31-46)

31. "When the Son of Man comes in his glory and all his angels with him, then he will sit upon his glorious throne. 32. And all the Gentiles will be gathered before him, and he will separate them one from another, as the shepherd separates sheep from goats, 33. and he will place the sheep at his right, the goats at the left. 34. Then the king will say to those on his right: 'Come, you blessed of my Father, inherit the kingdom prepared for you from the beginning of the world. 35. For I was hungry and you gave me to eat, I was thirsty and you gave me drink, I was a stranger and you took me in, 36. naked and you clothed me, I was sick and you visited me, I was in prison and you came to me.' 37. Then the righteous will answer and say: 'Lord, when did we see you hungry and we gave you nourish-

ment, or thirsty and we gave you drink? 38. When did we see you a stranger and we took you in, or naked and we clothed you? 39. When did we see you sick or in prison and we came to you?' 40. The king will answer and say to them: 'Amen I say to you, as long as you did it for one of these least brothers of mine, you did it for me.' 41. Then he will say to those at the left: 'Go away from me, you accursed, into the everlasting fire prepared for the devil and his angels. 42. For I was hungry, and you did not give me to eat, I was thirsty and you did not give me drink, 43. I was a stranger and you did not take me in, naked and you did not clothe me, sick and in prison and you did not visit me.' 44. Then these too will answer and say: 'Lord, when did we see you hungry or thirsty or a stranger or naked or sick or in prison, and we did not minister to you?' 45. Then he will answer them and say: 'Amen I say to you, as long as you did not do it for one of these least, you did not do it for me.' 46. And these will go away into everlasting punishment, but the righteous into everlasting life."

Notes

31. *Son of Man*: The background is Dan 7:13-14 where the Ancient of Days hands on power and glory to the "one like a Son of Man." Here the Son of Man is assumed to exercise the power of judge at the final judgment. There is an emphasis on his glory ("in his glory . . . upon his glorious throne").

32. *all the Gentiles will be gathered*: The verb is in the divine passive; that is, God (or the Son of Man and his angels) will do the gathering. The Greek phrase *panta ta ethnē* is usually translated as "all the nations" (including Israel). But elsewhere in Matthew (see 4:15; 6:32; 10:5, 18; 12:18, 21; 20:19, 25; 21:43; 24:7, 9, 14; 28:19) *ethnē* and *panta ta ethnē* refer to nations other than Israel; that is, the Gentiles.

    sheep from goats: According to Jeremias (*Parables*, 206) mixed flocks are customary in Palestine. In the evening the shepherd separates the sheep from the goats since the goats need to be kept warm at night (because the cold harms them) whereas the sheep prefer open air at night. Since the sheep are more valuable, they are given better treatment in the parable (see vv. 33-34). See also J. M. Court, "Right and Left: the Implications for Matthew 25.31-46," *NTS* 31 (1985) 223–33.

34. *the king*: Here and in verse 40 the glorious Son of Man presiding in judgment is called "the king." This title continues the motif of Jesus' kingship that began in the infancy narrative (see 1:1, 20; 2:2, 13-14) and will be further exploited with irony in the passion narrative (see 27:11, 29, 37, 42). Here we see Jesus as king in full glory—with no need for irony or hiddenness.

    blessed of my Father: Some commentators use this phrase to argue that the Father, not the Son of Man, is the real judge. The idea is that the Son of Man only ratifies what the Father had already determined. But more likely is the reverse: The Son of Man judges, and the righteous are then qualified to enter into eternal joy of the Father's kingdom.

    from the beginning of the world: For the figure of Wisdom having been created from the beginning of the world, see Prov 8:22-31. Later such a beginning was attributed to the Torah and to other important things (for such a list see *m. 'Abot* 5:6).

35. *you took me in*: Jeremias (*Parables*, 207) describes *synagō* here as "translation Greek" based on Aramaic *kĕnas*, which means (1) to gather and (2) to show hospitality.

36. *I was in prison*: This item does not appear in Jewish lists of good works (apart from this one), mainly since imprisonment was rare among Jews (because they did not build jails). The text may even assume "house arrest."

37. *the righteous*: These are at the right hand of the Son of Man and are symbolized by the sheep. The triple "when?" of their question (vv. 37, 38, 39) indicates that they cannot understand how they could have done such acts of mercy to the Son of Man.

40. *for one of these least brothers of mine*: In several earlier Matthean texts the "least brothers" seem to be Christians (see Matt 10:40-42; 18:6, 14). If they are Christians here (either missionaries or disciples = Christians), the claim is that the Son of Man identifies himself with such Christians and that Gentiles (*ta ethnē*) will be judged "righteous" or "accursed" on the basis of their acts of mercy toward them.

41. *the everlasting fire*: The adjective *aiōnion* here and in verse 46 ("everlasting punishment" . . . "everlasting life") pertains to the age/world to come. The assumption behind the experience is the Jewish apocalyptic schema of "this age/world" and "the age/world to come."

    prepared: Some manuscripts read "which my Father prepared." The short reading is favored by the external evidence and what was said before in Matt 25:34. In either case the meaning is the same, since it is a "divine passive" construction (God prepared it).

45. *one of these least*: See the discussion on Matt 25:40. The term *elachistos* ("least") is the superlative of *mikros* ("little one"), a term used several times early by Matthew to refer to members of Jesus' following (see Matt 10:42; 11:11; 18:6, 10, 14). Gentiles are said to have had contact with the Son of Man through his disciples (see Matt 10:40-42).

Interpretation

There is a longstanding debate about the literary form of Matt 25:31-46: Is it a parable or not? The answer, of course, depends on how one defines "parable." Rather than go deeply into what is finally a dispute about definition, it is sufficient to say that Matt 25:31-46 is first and foremost a judgment scene. At this judgment the Son of Man presides, rewarding some and condemning others.

The structure of the judgment scene is simple but dramatic. After introducing (25:31-33) the judge and those being judged ("all the Gentiles"), the story has the judge/king address the "blessed" and explain why they have been invited to share the king's blessedness (25:34-36). When these ask for a clarification (25:37-39), the king explains that in doing acts of mercy for "one of these least brothers of mine" they did it for him (25:40). The same sequence is followed for the "accursed": the sentence and the reason for it (25:41-43), the request for a clarification (25:44), and the king's explanation (25:45). The final verse (25:46) summarizes the judgment process: The wicked go to everlasting punishment and the righteous to everlasting life.

The judgment scene in Matt 25:31-46 comes after three parables about preparing for the coming of the Son of Man. In each case everyone knows that the master/bridegroom will come eventually no matter how long he may be delayed. In the meantime what is demanded is constant watchfulness. In this test the wicked servant, the foolish maidens, and the fearful/lazy steward fail. But the faithful servant, the wise maidens, and the enterprising stewards succeed. Everyone should have known what to do. Some did it, and others did not. If these parables can be traced back to Jesus, their audience was Jewish—with some division made between Jews who were prepared for the Son of Man's coming and Jews who were not prepared. In our interpretation of the Matthean forms of the parables we have argued that they addressed Jewish Christians and other Jews—providing a warning to be on watch constantly.

The usual interpretation of Matt 25:31-46 takes it as a judgment scene in which *panta ta ethnē* (25:32) involves all humanity ("all the nations") and "these least brothers of mine" (25:40; see 25:45) includes all people in distress of some kind. The interpretation incorporated in our translation and defended in the notes takes *panta ta ethnē* as "all the Gentiles" and "these least brothers of mine" as Christians, either missionaries or ordinary Christians. This interpretation is based on what *ethnē* ("nations, Gentiles") and *adelphoi* ("brothers") mean elsewhere in Matthew's Gospel. If in their Matthean context they mean "Gentiles" and "disciples of Jesus" respectively, there is good reason to assume that this was their meaning in Matt 25:31-46.

If these translations are accepted, then a different interpretation emerges. Those being judged are Gentiles. The issue at the judgment scene is: By what criterion are Gentiles to be declared just or condemned by the Son of Man? The answer is: By their deeds of mercy done to the disciples of Jesus (missionaries or ordinary Christians), because such deeds have been done to the Son of Man. The basis for this criterion is the identification between Jesus and his disciples: "Whoever receives you receives me, and whoever receives me receives him who sent me" (Matt 10:40).

According to our interpretation, Matt 25:31-46 concerns the judgment of the Gentiles by the Son of Man. A separate judgment for Gentiles is consistent with Matt 19:28: "When the Son of Man shall sit on his glorious throne, you who have followed me will also sit on twelve thrones, judging the twelve tribes of Israel.'' Whereas the twelve apostles have a special role in the judgment of Israel, no such role is attributed to them in the judgment of the Gentiles. That is the task of the Son of Man.

The idea of separate judgments for Jews and Gentiles appears elsewhere in the New Testament. The most familiar text is Rom 2:9-10: ''There will be tribulation and distress for every human being who does evil, the Jew first and also the Greek (= Gentile), but glory and honor and peace for everyone who does good, the Jew first and also the Greek.'' Other allusions to this motif occur in 1 Cor 6:2-3 (''the saints will judge the world'') and 1 Pet 4:17 (''For the time has come for judgment to begin with the household of God; and if it begins with us, what will be the end of those who do not obey the gospel of God?'').

The early Christian expectation of separate judgments for Jews and Gentiles had its basis in Jewish tradition. Having roots in Ezekiel 39 (''all the nations shall see my judgment,'' v. 21) and Joel 3, the theme of separate judgments appears frequently in apocalyptic and other Jewish writings: 1 Enoch 91:14 (''in the ninth week the righteous judgment shall be revealed to the whole world''), Psalms of Solomon 17:29 (''he [= the Messiah] will judge peoples and nations in the wisdom of his righteousness''), 4 Ezra 13:33-49 (''he, my Son, will reprove the assembled nations for their ungodliness''), 2 Baruch 72 (''he [my Anointed One] will call all nations, and some of them he will spare, and others he will kill''), and *Testament of Benjamin* 10:8-9 (''the Lord first judges Israel for the wrong she has committed and then he shall do the same for all the nations'').

These texts establish the existence of the idea of separate judgments for Jews and Gentiles. In several cases the judge is the Messiah. Even more important for our interpretation of Matt 25:31-46, however, is the reference in 2 Baruch 72:4-6 to the criterion to be used in judging the Gentiles: ''Every nation which has not known Israel and which has not trodden down the seed of Jacob will live . . . All those, now, who have ruled over you or have known you, will be delivered up to the sword.'' The standard by which the Gentiles are to be judged is their treatment of Israel.

These Jewish ideas about the judgment of the Gentiles—a separate judgment, by the Messiah, on the basis of their treatment of Israel—provide the background for Matt 25:31-46. What is new or different here is the identification between the Son of Man and ''these least brothers of mine'' (25:40, 45), and this as a mode of Emmanuel's presence (see 28:20).

The Matthean version of the judgment of the Gentiles (25:31-46) departs from the usual emphasis on the relationship between Matthean Christians and other Jews. It acknowledges the presence of non-Jews who were not Christians and tries to explain how and why such persons can be part of God's kingdom. How? By acts of mercy to Christians. Why? Because such acts are done to the Son of Man/King (see Matt 10:40-42).

This interpretation is sometimes rejected because it leaves Matt 25:31-46 with little relevance for contemporary ethics or homiletics. My response is that the usual or traditional interpretation deals with the wrong problem: the value of good works for the poor and needy at the final judgment. The right problem is: By what criterion can non-Jews and non-Christians enter God's kingdom? The value of good works is treated in many biblical texts. Matt 25:31-46 is one of the very few texts that deals with the salvation of Gentiles. That makes it a precious resource for dealing with what is a major theological issue in the late twentieth century.

With regard to the "good works" tradition, homilists can easily make the transition from Gentiles to Christians: If good works to Christians are so important for non-Christians (and non-Jews) to perform, how much more are they to be expected from Christians (and Jews)! If Gentiles are rewarded for good deeds done to strangers and needy people, so also Christians (and Jews) will be rewarded for such actions.

For Reference and Further Study

Brandenburger, E. *Das Recht des Weltenrichters. Untersuchung zu Matthäus 25,31-46.* SBS 99. Stuttgart: Katholisches Bibelwerk, 1980.

Catchpole, D. R. "The Poor on Earth and the Son of Man in Heaven. A Reappraisal of Matthew XXV. 31–46." *BJRULM* 61 (1979) 355-97.

Christian, P. *Jesus und seine geringsten Brüder. Mt 25,31-46 redaktionsgeschichtlich untersucht.* Leipzig: St. Benno, 1975.

Cope, L. "Matthew XXV 31-46. 'The Sheep and the Goats' Reinterpreted." *NovT* 11 (1969) 32–44.

Donahue, J. R. "The 'Parable' of the Sheep and the Goats: A Challenge to Christian Ethics." *TS* 47 (1986) 3-31.

Gray, S. W. *The Least of My Brothers: Matthew 25:31-46. A History of Interpretation.* SBLDS 114. Atlanta: Scholars, 1989.

Pikaza, X. "Salvación y condena del Hijo del Hombre (Trasfondo Veterotestamentario y Judío de Mt 25, 34.41.46)." *Salmanticensis* 27 (1980) 419–38.

Via, D. O. "Ethical Responsibility and Human Wholeness in Matthew 25:31-46." *HTR* 80 (1987) 79–100.

Weren, W. J. C. *De broeders van de Mensenzoon. Mt 25,31-46 als toegang tot de eschatologie van Matteüs.* Amsterdam: Ton Bolland, 1979.

71. *The Plot to Kill Jesus* (26:1-16)

1. And when Jesus finished all those words, he said to his disciples: 2. "You know that after two days it is the Passover, and the Son of Man will be handed over to be crucified." 3. Then the chief priests and elders of the people assembled at the courtyard of the high priest who was called Caiaphas. 4. And they planned how they might seize Jesus by cunning and kill him. 5. But they said: "Not during the feast, lest there be a riot among the people."

6. When Jesus was in Bethany in the house of Simon the leper, 7. a woman approached him, having an alabaster flask of precious ointment, and she poured it on his head as he reclined at table. 8. On seeing this the disciples became indignant and said: "Why this waste? 9. For this could have been sold for much and given to the poor." 10. Jesus knew this and said to them: "Why do you bother the woman? For she has done a beautiful deed for me. 11. For you always have the poor with you, but you do not always have me. 12. In pouring this ointment upon my body she has prepared me for burial. 13. Amen I say to you, wherever this gospel will be preached in the whole world, what she has done will also be spoken of in memory of her."

14. Then one of the Twelve, who was called Judas Iscariot, went to the chief priests 15. and said: "What are you willing to give me that I should hand him over to you?" They determined on thirty pieces of silver for him. 16. And from then on he sought an opportune time to hand him over.

Notes

1. *Jesus finished*: For the fifth and last time a major speech of Jesus' ends with the verb *teleō* (see Matt 7:28; 11:1; 13:53; 19:1). The adjective "all" ("all these words") indicates that the five major speeches have come to a close. The phrase may also allude to Deut 32:45 ("when Moses had finished speaking all these words").

2. *the Passover*: What is told by the narrator in Mark 14:1 and Luke 22:1 is placed directly on Jesus' lips by Matthew. There is no reference to the feast of unleavened bread, as in the other Gospels, which was the old spring agricultural festival that had been combined with the celebration of Israel's release from bondage in Egypt in the Passover.

   the Son of Man will be handed over: Only this passion prediction connects Jesus' death to Passover; see Matt 16:21; 17:22-23; 20:18-19. Even before the plot of the high priests and elders with Judas is set in motion, Jesus knows the fate that awaits him this Passover. The verb "will be handed over" carries with it the idea of conformity with God's plan and Jesus' fidelity to his destiny.

3. *the chief priests and elders*: In contrast with the body of the Gospel where the scribes and Pharisees constitute the principal opponents of Jesus, in the passion narrative the chief priests and elders assume the Jewish direction of events that lead

to Jesus' death. Only after Jesus' death (Matt 27:62) do the Pharisees reappear along with the chief priests to secure a guard for Jesus' tomb.

courtyard: The Greek term *aulē* means courtyard; that is, space, near a house or other buildings, enclosed but open to the sky. It can also mean "palace, house, farm" by extension. The courtyard of the high priest is also the place in which Peter denies Jesus (see Matt 26:69).

Caiaphas: He held the office of high priest from A.D. 18 to 36, having succeeded his father-in-law Annas. He is assumed to have been the high priest during the passion of Jesus (see also John 11:49-52; 18:14). Luke 3:2 and Acts 4:6 assume that Annas still played a major role in the functioning of the high priesthood.

5. *Not during the feast*: Passover was a pilgrimage feast when many Jews came up to Jerusalem. These pilgrimages were frequently occasions for civil unrest, as Josephus' *War* shows, in the first century A.D. The officials probably wanted to arrest Jesus *before* the beginning of the Passover festival. However, the Markan chronology, followed by Matthew, places the arrest *during* the festival—which is unlikely on historical grounds. Another way to interpret "not during the feast" is to assume that the officials wanted to wait until *after* the feast to arrest Jesus but Judas' treachery made it possible for them to do so earlier.

6. *in Bethany*: Bethany was a village about two miles east of Jerusalem. According to Matt 21:17 Jesus was lodging there during the Passover festival. Matthew follows Mark 14:3 in assigning the incident to the house of Simon the leper (perhaps someone healed by Jesus), whereas John 12:1-2 assigns it to the house of Lazarus, Mary, and Martha.

7. *an alabaster flask of precious ointment*: Alabaster is a translucent gypsum that could be carved into the shape of a flask for storing perfume. The long, narrow neck could be snapped off to allow for pouring. Matthew simplifies the description in Mark 14:3 ("of pure nard, very costly") and omits the estimate of its value in Mark 14:5 ("more than three hundred denarii"). Matthew uses his typical word (*prosēlthen*) for those who approach Jesus.

   she poured it on his head: Some interpreters find in the woman's action an allusion to the coronation ritual of the king in ancient Israel (see 1 Sam 16:12-13; 1 Kgs 1:39), thus symbolizing her confession that Jesus is the Messiah. In fact it is difficult to be certain about the woman's motives and intentions beyond her desire to pay respect to Jesus.

8. *the disciples became indignant*: Only Matthew singles out the disciples as the indignant party; the other evangelists have "some" (Mark 14:4), "the Pharisee" (Luke 7:39), and Judas (John 12:4). Matthew's specification can be explained on literary grounds (the logic of the scene) or on theological grounds (the story had a particular message for the Matthean community, whose wealth made it unduly concerned with money).

10. *a beautiful deed*: The beauty of the woman's deed resides in its timeliness. The exchange between the disciples and Jesus is not a criticism of almsgiving. Rather opportunities for almsgiving are always present but the death of Jesus is a onetime occurrence. It is to the woman's credit that she recognizes the moment of Jesus, whereas the disciples do not.

12. *she has prepared me for burial*: Jesus interprets her action as the anointing connected with burial. Since Matthew understood her action as the equivalent of the anointing for burial, he omits mention of anointing as the reason for the woman to go to the tomb on Easter Sunday (see Mark 16:1 "so that they might go and anoint him," cf. Matt 28:1).

13. *this gospel*: The reference is more likely to the "good news" about Jesus rather than to Matthew's Gospel in particular.

    in memory of her: The woman is not named in the story. There is no reason to identify her as Mary Magdalene, an identification that results from the joining of Luke 7:36-50 and 8:1-3. In John 12:1-8 the woman is identified as Mary of Bethany. Neither Matthew nor Mark provides a clue about her name.

14. *Judas Iscariot*: That Jesus was betrayed by one of his own disciples is not the kind of thing that early Christians would invent. The name "Iscariot" probably means "man of Kerioth" (see Josh 15:25); more unlikely is Iscariot a form of the Latin *sicarius* ("dagger man," a term for Jewish terrorists in the first century A.D.).

15. *"What are you willing to give me?"*: Judas' question to the chief priests suggests that his motive in betraying Jesus was greed. Here Matthew is more precise than Mark 14:10 or Luke 22:4 in ascribing to him a motive for what remains a puzzling action. All attempts at explaining why Judas did what he did remain speculations.

    thirty pieces of silver: Only Matthew gives an exact sum (see Mark 14:11; Luke 22:5), which is the value placed on a slave in Exod 21:32. In Zech 11:12 thirty pieces of silver is the wage of the shepherd, who casts them back into the treasury (see Zech 11:13). The allusion to Zech 11:12-13 prepares for the story of Judas' death in Matt 27:3-10.

16. *from then on he sought an opportune time*: In Matt 4:17 and 16:21 the phrase *apo tote* ("from then on") marks an important transition in the story of Jesus. The word *eukairia* ("an opportune time") carries the irony that what is an opportune time for the plot of Judas and the chief priests is an even more opportune time for all humankind in light of the significance of Jesus' death at Passover.

Interpretation

The plot to kill Jesus emerges from three scenes in Matt 26:1-16: Jesus' resolve to celebrate Passover in Jerusalem and the Jewish officials' resolve to put him to death (26:1-5), the anointing of Jesus for burial by an unnamed woman (26:6-13), and Judas' offer to betray Jesus for thirty pieces of silver (26:14-16). In these three episodes Matthew follows Mark 14:1-11 as his source but modifies it in characteristic ways: fondness for direct discourse (Matt 26:2), omission of unnecessary details (26:7, 9), and the heightening of biblical resonances (26:15). Even more than in Mark, everything proceeds according to the divine plan (especially as this is revealed in Scripture) and Jesus is in control of the course of events. Thus the narrative introducing the Matthean passion account is a kind of overture, making us sensitive to the characteristic literary and theological concerns of the evangelist throughout his presentation of Jesus' passion and death.

A major feature in the plot to kill Jesus is irony. In the three episodes some characters (chief priests and elders, the disciples, Judas) act in apparently rational ways. But the reader knows the realities behind the appearances that make their actions tragic and perverse. This use of irony presupposes a familiarity with Jewish (and early Christian) institutions.

The plot to kill Jesus (Matt 26:1-5) is set at Passover time—the annual spring celebration of Israel's liberation from slavery in Egypt. The Son of Man, who is King of the Jews, will be crucified at the Jewish festival of freedom. The leaders—the chief priests and elders of the people, not the scribes and Pharisees—plan how to avoid any public disturbance during Passover, lest they give offense to their Roman overlords. Those who should be celebrating freedom make plans to preserve their servitude by killing the one who can give them true freedom.

In the anointing episode (Matt 26:6-13) a Jewish institution with many meanings—joy and luxury, strength, divine approval, consecration—is interpreted as preparation for Jesus' burial. The woman's insight about Jesus and her love for him stand in sharp contrast to the attitudes of the chief priests and elders in the preceding episode and to the attitude of Judas in what follows. She is also contrasted with Jesus' own disciples who see her action as a waste of good money that could be given to the poor. Only Jesus sees the timeliness of her action as preparation for his burial.

When Judas offers to betray Jesus for thirty pieces of silver (Matt 26:14-16), the price matches the value placed on a slave gored by an ox (Exod 21:32). Judas, who had been one of the Twelve and exposed to Jesus' teaching and healing activities, betrays him for money, whereas the unnamed woman has just lavished upon Jesus' head an alabaster jar of expensive ointment.

From these many ironies associated with institutions and characters Jesus emerges as knowing what is happening and why it must happen. And the reader of Matthew's passion account is able to share Jesus' privileged perspective on the events of the passion.

The Matthean community was probably familiar with the story of Jesus' passion—if not from Mark's Gospel, at least from oral tradition. The apologetic problem facing them (and all early Christians) was how to explain Jesus' death at the hands of a Roman official (Pilate) by a Roman mode of execution (crucifixion). The passion story lays the responsibility for the plot that ended in Jesus' death with the chief priests and elders on one hand and Judas on the other. It does not—probably because it could not—avoid the embarrassing participation by one of Jesus' own disciples. It must also explain why the Jewish rites of burial were omitted in Jesus' case; in fact, they had already been carried out in the anointing of Jesus by the unnamed woman. Matthew's special contributions were two: the clear statement by

Jesus that he knows his fate (26:2), and the suggestion that Judas' betrayal of Jesus took place according to the Scriptures (26:15).

The mystery of Judas' treachery will continue to fascinate people as long as the Gospels are read. It is hard for most people to make sense out of what he did. Yet the action of the unnamed woman is in the long run more important as a positive model of Christian faith. Nothing is said about her sinfulness (see Luke 7:36-50). Rather she is simply a model of enthusiastic love for Jesus. Her devotion leads her to do precisely the right thing at the right time. While the officials and Judas search for an "opportune time" (26:16) to hand Jesus over, she found the opportune time to anoint Jesus for burial.

For Reference and Further Study

Brown, R. E. "The Passion according to Matthew." *Worship* 58 (1984) 98–107.

Senior, D. P. *The Passion Narrative according to Matthew. A Redactional Study.* BETL 39. Gembloux: Duculot, 1975.

________. *The Passion of Jesus in the Gospel of Matthew.* Wilmington, Del.: Glazier, 1985.

72. *Jesus' Last Passover* (26:17-35)

17. On the first day of Unleavened Bread the disciples approached Jesus and said: "Where do you wish that we should prepare for you to eat the Passover?" 18. He said: "Go into the city to a certain one and say to him: 'The teacher says: "My time is near. With you I am to keep the Passover with my disciples." ' " 19. And the disciples did as Jesus ordered them, and they prepared the Passover. 20. When it was evening he reclined with the Twelve.

21. And as they were eating he said: "Amen I say to you that one of you will hand me over." 22. And being very sad each one began to say to him: "It is not I, is it, Lord?" 23. He answered and said: "One who dips the hand with me in the bowl, this one will hand me over. 24. The Son of Man goes as it is written about him. But woe to that man through whom the Son of Man is handed over. It were better for him if that man had not been born." 25. Judas who was handing him over answered and said: "It is not I, is it, Rabbi?" He said to him: "You have said it."

26. As they were eating Jesus took bread and blessed and broke and gave to his disciples and said: "Take, eat. This is my body." 27. And he took the cup and gave thanks and gave it to them, saying: "Drink from it, all of you. 28. For this is my blood of the covenant which is poured out for many for the forgiveness of sins. 29. I say to you, I will not drink from

now on from this product of the vine until that day when I drink it with you anew in the kingdom of my Father."

30. And they sang hymns and went out to the Mount of Olives. 31. Then Jesus said to them: "All of you will be scandalized at me in this very night. For it is written, 'I will strike the shepherd, and the sheep of the flock will be scattered.' 32. But after I have been raised up I will go before you into Galilee." 33. But Peter answered and said to him: "Even if all will be scandalized at you, I will never be scandalized." 34. Jesus said to him: "Amen I say to you that in this very night before the cock crows you will deny me three times." 35. Peter said to him: "Even if I must die with you, I will not deny you." And so all the disciples said.

Notes

17. *On the first day of Unleavened Bread*: An alternate name for Passover (see Mark 14:1), Unleavened Bread refers to the Jewish practice of eating only bread without leaven during the eight days of the Passover festival. Matthew follows Mark 14:12 in using "the first day" to refer to the daytime before the evening on which Passover/Unleavened Bread began.

18. *to a certain one*: Matthew simplifies the complicated procedure outlined in Mark 14:13-14, which suggests prophetic knowledge on Jesus' part. Matthew's emphasis is more on Jesus' taking charge of the situation and willingly meeting his fate.

    My time is near: While Judas and the Jewish officials seek an "opportune time" (*eukairia*) to seize Jesus (see Matt 26:16), Jesus announces that his "time" (*kairos*) is near. The *kairos* of Jesus refers to his death and resurrection, which have eschatological dimensions.

    I am to keep: The use of the present tense of the verb (*poiō*) adds to the sense of destiny/fate that is already so strong throughout the passion story. The idea that Jesus is to keep the Passover with his disciples highlights a bond that will often appear fragile during the passion.

19. *as Jesus ordered them*: This distinctively Matthean comment continues the theme of Jesus taking charge of events during the passion. The impression given is that the events of the passion have been carefully orchestrated by Jesus even though they lead to his death.

20. *he reclined*: Individual couches, which were lower and smaller than beds, were used for festive banquets and for the reception of honored guests. Jews took over this custom from the Greeks. The reclining couches could be used either for Passover or for a special meal in anticipation of Passover.

21. *one of you will hand me over*: Based on Mark 14:18, this statement by Jesus indicates his knowledge about the plot against his life and contributes to the theme of his taking charge of events.

22. *It is not I, is it, Lord?*: The construction in which the disciples' question is expressed demands a negative response. They address him as "Lord," a promi-

nent Matthean title for Jesus; there is no title at all in Mark 14:19. In Matt 26:25 Judas asks the same question with the title "Rabbi."

23. *One who dips the hand*: The practice of sharing food from common bowls was part of the Passover ritual. Thus the betrayer violates not only the bond between those who eat together but also the bond among those who celebrate Passover as a household. See Ps 41:9: "Even my bosom friend in whom I trusted, who ate of my bread, has lifted his heel against me."

24. *as it is written about him*: There is no specific OT reference to the suffering and death of the Son of Man. The fulfillment is tied to the person of Jesus taken as a whole, not to one title for him. The verse simply expresses the early Christian conviction that Jesus' suffering and death took place "according to the Scriptures."

    woe to that man: While affirming that Jesus' death was according to the Scriptures, the second part of the saying also imputes responsibility to Judas for his betrayal of Jesus. Judas is not a pawn or a puppet in the carrying out of the divine plan.

25. *It is not I, is it, Rabbi?*: Judas uses the same question-form (expecting a negative answer) as the other disciples did in Matt 26:22. However, he uses the title "Rabbi" instead of Lord. Likewise in betraying Jesus, Judas will also hail him as Rabbi (Matt 26:49). The use of the title "Rabbi" has already been criticized in Matt 23:7-8 ("you are not to be called Rabbi").

    you have said it: Jesus uses the same expression in response to the high priest (Matt 26:64) and to Pilate (27:11), in both cases to confirm a truth spoken by the questioner. Whereas Judas' question expects a negative answer, it gets a positive one.

26. *As they were eating*: The use of the same introductory formula as in Matt 26:21 suggests that 26:21-25 and 26:26-29 (=Mark 14:18-21 and 14:22-25) may have been separate pericopes in the tradition.

    blessed: Jesus performs the actions that would have been familiar at Jewish Sabbath and holiday meals. His "blessing" is not so much a consecration as it is a blessing/thanksgiving: "Blessed are you, Lord our God, king of the universe, who brings forth bread from the earth . . ." In the blessing over the wine God is addressed as "creator of the fruit of the vine."

    take, eat: Sharing in Jesus' bread means sharing in his death ("this is my body"). Thus Jesus gives new meaning to actions customary at Jewish meals—sharing the loaf of bread and the cup of wine. Matthew's additional imperative "eat" is usually interpreted as part of a tendency to conform the account to the liturgical practice of the churches.

27. *he took the cup*: There is no interval of time between Jesus' actions with the bread and with the cup; at a Passover meal in the strict sense such an interval would be expected (see 1 Cor 11:25: "In the same way also the cup, after supper, saying . . .").

    Drink from it, all of you: What Mark 14:23 expresses in narrative form ("and all drank from it"), Matthew expresses as a command from Jesus. This charge, which introduces a symmetry between the bread and the cup, perhaps reflects the "liturgical" formula current in the Matthean community, and contributes to the theme of Jesus taking control of events in the passion.

28. *my blood of the covenant*: As with the bread in Matt 26:26, Jesus uses the cup to invite his disciples to share in his fate. The "blood of the covenant" refers to Exod 24:8 where Moses seals God's covenant with Israel by sprinkling the people with an animal's blood. The phrase "poured out for many" alludes to Isa 53:12, which describes the effects of the suffering of God's Servant.

for the forgiveness of sins: This phrase is Matthew's distinctive contribution to the NT Last Supper accounts of the Eucharist. Building on insights in the fourth Servant song (Isa 52:13–53:12), the phrase climaxes Matthew's special emphasis on Jesus' power to forgive sins (see Matt 1:21; 5:23-24; 6:12, 14, 15; 9:6; 18:21-35).

29. *I will not drink*: Jesus' promise suggests that his Last Supper anticipates the banquet in God's kingdom that will express complete fellowship with God. Two brief additions by Matthew add some new dimensions to Mark 26:29: "from now on" sharpens the saying's role as a passion prediction, and "with you" heightens his communal relationship with the disciples.

30. *they sang hymns*: The Passover meal traditionally concluded with Psalms 113–118, the so-called great Hallel, which proclaim God's power to redeem and his faithfulness in leading Israel to freedom. There is no way to be certain that Jesus and his disciples sang these precise psalms, especially if the Last Supper anticipated Passover. But they at least would have been appropriate for the season and as a context for Jesus' death.

Mount of Olives: The high hill east of Jerusalem is a fairly good place for growing olives in the poor land around Jerusalem. At a pilgrimage feast like Passover the Mount of Olives would have served as a campsite for the large crowds unable to find lodging. Jesus had lodged in Bethany (see Mt 21:17) but went to the Mount of Olives after the Last Supper.

31. *scandalized at me in this very night*: Matthew adds to Mark 14:27 the specification "at me in this very night," thus making Jesus' statement more concrete and continuing the motif of Jesus being in control of events. The idea is that Jesus will become for them a stumbling block. The idea has already appeared in Matt 11:6; 13:57; 15:12.

I will strike the shepherd: The OT quotation is taken from Zech 13:7 and carries on the Matthean fulfillment theme. Both the Hebrew and Greek texts read "Strike the shepherd. . . ." The Markan/Matthean "I will strike" suggests that God does the striking, continuing the idea of the divine plan.

32. *I will go before you into Galilee*: Jesus promises a return to where he gathered his disciples and exercised his public ministry. Unlike Mark where there are no (extant) appearances of the risen Jesus in Galilee, Matt 26:32 points forward to the climactic appearance of Jesus to the eleven disciples on the mountain in Galilee (Matt 28:16-20).

33. *I will never be scandalized*: Peter's denial that he would ever be scandalized by Jesus prepares for his threefold rejection of Jesus in Matt 26:69-75. His contradic-

tion of Jesus' passion prediction echoes his earlier contradiction of the first passion prediction (see Matt 16:21-23).

34. *before the cock crows*: The time of the cock's crowing would be very early in the morning (midnight to 3:00 A.M.). The prediction of Jesus corresponds to the triple denial by Peter in Matt 26:69-75.

INTERPRETATION

Matthew's account of Jesus' last Passover (Matt 26:17-35) follows Mark 14:12-31 very closely. It consists of four episodes: the preparations (26:17-20), Jesus' prediction of his betrayal (26:21-25), the Last Supper (26:26-29), and Jesus' prediction of abandonment by his disciples (26:30-35). What links the four episodes together is Passover: preparation for it, celebration of it, and its aftermath. The Passover meal is the occasion at which the plot against Jesus (26:1-16) can be carried out (26:36–27:66).

The few changes introduced by Matthew into his Markan source reflect his editorial practices and special interests. In the account of preparations for Passover (26:17-20) Matthew simplifies the detailed and complicated procedure by which the disciples come to recognize the one at whose house they will celebrate the feast. At several points throughout the entire Passover narrative Jesus shows himself to be in control of events, at times by knowing beforehand what awaits him (26:19, 23, 25, 26-29, 31-35) and at other times by giving orders (26:18-19, 26-27). The minor changes introduced by Matthew in the Eucharistic words of institution (26:26-29)—"eat . . . drink from it, all of you . . . for the forgiveness of sins"—may reflect the evangelist's experience of liturgy in his own community. The passages about Judas (26:21-25) and Peter (26:30-35) carry forward Matthew's special interests in these two disciples of Jesus.

The setting for the four episodes in Matt 26:17-35 is Passover. For a full discussion of this feast, see A. J. Saldarini, *Jesus and Passover* (New York-Ramsey, N.J.: Paulist, 1984). The word "Passover" derives from Exod 12:13: "When I see the blood, I will pass over you, and no plague shall fall upon you to destroy you, when I smite the land of Egypt." The festival celebrates Israel's liberation under Moses' leadership from slavery in Egypt. It is possible that the elements of Passover were connected with the rituals of herdsmen and farmers. But the earliest accounts (Exodus 12–13) integrate those elements carefully into the story of Israel's miraculous escape from Egypt.

The essential features of the Passover celebration include the eating of the roasted lamb, the sprinkling of blood upon the entry to the house, the avoidance of leaven and the eating of unleavened bread only, and the consecration of the first born. In Jesus' time Passover was one of the pilgrimage feasts (Exod 23:14-17; 34:18-26). The goal of the pilgrimage in Jesus' day was the Jerusalem Temple: "Three times a year all your males shall appear before the Lord your God at the place which he will choose: at the feast of unleavened bread (=Passover), at the feast of weeks, and at the feast of booths" (Deut 16:16). Within this pilgrimage framework the Jerusalem Temple became the center of the Passover celebration. While compliance with the pilgrimage regulation was far from perfect, Passover surely was a time in which the population of Jerusalem swelled, with pilgrims perhaps outnumbering regular inhabitants two to one. The festival began at sundown, on the fifteenth of Nisan; according to Jewish reckoning the day began at sundown. On the afternoon of the fourteenth of Nisan, lambs were ritually slaughtered in the Temple and then brought to the households where they would be eaten.

The Gospels portray the last days of Jesus against the background of the Passover pilgrimage. Jesus and his disciples go up to Jerusalem to celebrate the Passover there. Their preparations for the Last Supper reflect the problems facing all the pilgrims—getting a place in which to eat the meal and making the arrangements. The large crowds of pilgrims coming to Jerusalem made Passover and the other pilgrimage festivals (Pentecost and Tabernacles) tense and potentially explosive times. With Jews from all over Israel and from abroad converging on Jerusalem, with the theme of liberation from slavery being especially prominent at Passover, the possibility of an uprising was always present. And that is why the Roman governor Pontius Pilate came to Jerusalem before Jesus' last Passover—to supervise the crowds and to put down immediately the beginning of any popular uprising.

Was Jesus' Last Supper an official Passover meal? The Gospels are divided on this matter. According to John, Jesus was executed on the afternoon before the first day of Passover—when the lambs were being sacrificed in the Jerusalem Temple (see John 19:31, 42). Everything had to be completed before the Passover celebration began (see John 18:28). According to Mark (who is followed on this point by Matthew and Luke), Jesus ate the Passover meal with his disciples and then was arrested, tried, and executed during the Passover festival. On historical grounds, however, it is highly unlikely that Jewish officials would have done what Mark attributes to them during the Passover. Thus John's chronology is more likely.

In the Johannine framework the Last Supper took place before the beginning of Passover and thus was an anticipation of the Passover meal. What makes the Markan Last Supper a Passover meal is Mark 14:12-16 (=Matt 26:17-20), which talks about Jesus' arrangements for the Passover: "on the first day of Unleavened Bread, when they sacrifice the Passover" (14:12). This passage probably reflects the early Christian tendency to draw the Last Supper even closer than it originally was to Passover. As the Markan-Matthean account proceeds, however, there is no mention of the Passover lamb or any other peculiar features associated with Passover. Apart from

Mark 14:12-16 (Matt 26:17-20) one would assume that Jesus' Last Supper was a regular meal with the overtones of the Passover season—something like holding a Christmas party on December 24. This schema is consistent with the plan of the high priests and elders to avoid arresting Jesus *during* the feast; they do so beforehand.

Whatever the precise nature of the Last Supper, the background for it was Passover. An essential element of Passover was the meal shared by the household. This central Passover institution becomes the vehicle for Jesus' climactic meal with his disciples—a meal that recalled the many meals throughout his public ministry, that expressed the bond existing between Jesus and his own, and that pointed forward to the future meal of God's kingdom. This meal also expressed the covenantal relationship between God and Israel (see Exod 24:3-11) that had its roots in the experience of the first Passover. The Passover theme of liberation from slavery finds an echo in Matthew's addition to the words over the cup "for the forgiveness of sins" (Matt 26:28).

The story of Jesus' last Passover (or more correctly, his anticipation of it) would have been especially meaningful to Matthew's community. The Jewish Christians in it would have been very sensitive to the themes and rituals of Passover. They may well have continued to celebrate it. But they faced—as all Jews did after the destruction of the Jerusalem Temple in A.D. 70—a serious problem: How to celebrate Passover now that pilgrimage to Jerusalem and slaughter of lambs in the Temple were no longer possible? The rabbis responded to this problem by transforming the domestic, sacrificial meal described in the Bible into a nonsacrificial seder meal; see B. M. Bokser, "Was the Last Supper a Passover Seder?" *Bible Review* 3/2 (1987) 24-33. The Matthean (and other) Christians found in Jesus' Last Passover/Supper a fresh and distinctive way to resolve the difficulty posed by the new circumstances of the late first century A.D. They tied Jesus' final meal ever more closely to the Jewish Passover (see Mark 14:12-16; Matt 14:17-20) and found in Jesus' death and resurrection a way to express the great themes of Passover. The Matthean additions in Matt 26:26-29 ("eat . . . drink from it, all of you . . . for the forgiveness of sins") probably reflect the process by which the repetition of Jesus' Last Supper developed into the central ritual of the Christian community and enabled Christians to celebrate Passover at any time and in any place.

What has already been said about Passover and the Eucharist provides abundant material for actualization. Another important theme for preaching and teaching is supplied by the contrast in characters: The treacherous Judas and the tragically overconfident Peter are carefully measured against Jesus, the model of fidelity, who accepts his fate even though he knows many of its details beforehand.

73. *The Arrest of Jesus* (26:36-56)

36. Then Jesus came with them to the place called Gethsemane, and he said to the disciples: "Stay here while I go over there and pray." 37. And taking along Peter and the two sons of Zebedee, he began to be sad and to be distressed. 38. Then he said to them: "My soul is sorrowful unto death. Remain here and keep watch with me." 39. And he went forward a little and fell upon his face in prayer and said: "My father, if it is possible, let this cup pass away from me. But not as I wish, but as you do." 40. And he came to the disciples and found them sleeping, and he said to Peter: "Could you not keep watch for one hour with me? 41. Keep watch and pray lest you enter into temptation. The spirit is willing, but the flesh is weak." 42. Going away again a second time he prayed, saying: "My father, if this cannot pass away unless I drink it, let your will be done." 43. And again he went and found them sleeping, for their eyes were heavy with sleep. 44. And he left them again and went away and prayed a third time, saying the same words again. 45. Then he came to the disciples and said to them: "Sleep on and rest. Behold the hour has drawn near, and the Son of Man is being handed over into the hands of sinners. 46. Arise, let us go. Behold he who hands me over has drawn near."

47. And while he was still speaking, behold Judas, one of the Twelve, came. And with him was a large crowd with swords and clubs from the chief priests and elders of the people. 48. The one handing him over gave to them a signal, saying: "The one whom I kiss is he. Seize him." 49. And he went right up to Jesus and said: "Hello, Rabbi!" And he kissed him. 50. Jesus said to him: "Friend, why are you here?" Then they came up to Jesus and placed their hands upon Jesus and seized him. 51. And behold one of those with Jesus stretched out his hand and drew his sword and struck the servant of the chief priest and took off his ear. 52. Then Jesus said to him: "Put back your sword into its place. For all those who take the sword will perish by the sword. 53. Or do you think that I cannot call upon my father, and he would provide me with more than twelve legions of angels? 54. But how then would the Scriptures be fulfilled that so it must be?" 55. In that very hour Jesus said to the crowds: "Have you come with swords and clubs to arrest me as if for a revolutionary? Every day I sat teaching in the temple, and you did not seize me. 56. But all this has taken place in order that the Scriptures of the prophets may be fulfilled." Then all the disciples left him and fled.

Notes

36. *Jesus came with them*: Mark 14:32 reads "they came." Matthew's expression highlights Jesus and his direction of events in the passion.

Gethsemane: The name means "oil press." Matthew and Mark imply that it was on or near the Mount of Olives. Luke 22:39 simply reads "the Mount of Olives," and John 18:1 locates it "across the brook Kedron where there was a garden."

37. *the two sons of Zebedee*: Mark 14:33 names them as James and John, who along with Peter formed a kind of inner circle among the Twelve. Along with Andrew they were first to be called by Jesus (Matt 4:18-22). They were also witnesses to the transfiguration (see 17:1-8). Like Peter (Matt 16:21-23), they had to be instructed about the cross (Matt 20:20-28).

to be sad and to be distressed: For Mark's more vivid *ekthambeisthai* Matthew substitutes the generic *lypeisthai* ("be sad"). He preserves the unusual verb *adēmonein* ("be distressed"), which appears elsewhere in the NT only at Phil 2:26.

38. *My soul is sorrowful unto death*: The first part of the sentence alludes to Psalms 42:6; 43:5 with its combination of *perilypos* and *psychē*. The qualification "unto death" emphasizes the seriousness of the situation that Jesus finds himself in. In the second part of the verse Matthew's addition "with me" underlines the personal bond between Jesus and his disciples.

39. *fell upon his face in prayer*: Mark 14:35 reads "he fell upon the ground and prayed." Matthew was probably thinking of the Hebrew verb used to describe "prostration" (*hištaḥăwâ*) either before God or some important person. His change heightens the atmosphere of prayer already prominent in the text.

My father: There are many similarities between the Lord's Prayer (Matt 6:9-13) and Jesus' prayer at Gethsemane. These have been explained in various ways: Jesus alludes to his own prayer; the evangelists shaped Jesus' prayer in the garden to conform to the Lord's Prayer; or Jesus taught his disciples the Lord's Prayer on the Mount of Olives. Whatever explanation is accepted, there is a close connection with the Lord's Prayer.

this cup: In the OT the "cup" image can refer to a person's lot or fate (see Jer 49:12; Ezek 23:31-34). In Matt 20:20-28 the image had already appeared in connection with Jesus' suffering and death ("Can you drink the cup that I am to drink?"). The use of the image here indicates that Jesus had to school himself to accept the suffering that awaited him. His resolution ("But not as I wish, but as you do") echoes the Lord's Prayer ("Thy will be done on earth").

41. *lest you enter into temptation*: The reason why the disciples should keep watch with Jesus evokes another part of the Lord's Prayer ("lead us not into temptation"). In both cases the word *peirasmos* alludes to the final, decisive test that accompanies the coming of God's kingdom (see Rev 3:10).

the spirit is willing: The Markan saying sounds like a proverb. It does not contrast spirit and flesh as distinct principles so much as it suggests that these two aspects are at war within the individual. It is an especially appropriate description of the disciples in Matthew who are marked by "little faith" and show a mixed profile of strength and weakness, insight and spiritual blindness.

42. *if this cannot pass away*: The wording of Jesus' second prayer is not given in Mark 14:39. In fact, Matthew's wording of it is based on Mark 14:35 ("he prayed that, if possible, the hour might pass away from him"). By placing the prayer directly on Jesus' lips Matthew has given content to Jesus' second prayer and focused more attention on him. He has also added some precisions to the prayer ("if this cannot pass away . . . let your will be done") that highlight Jesus' acceptance of his imminent sufferings in the spirit of the Lord's Prayer ("Thy will be done").

43. *heavy with sleep*: Matthew omits mention of the disciples' confusion ("and they did not know what to answer him," Mark 14:40), in keeping with his more favorable portrayal of Jesus' disciples.

44. *prayed a third time*: What is only implicit in Mark 14:41 is made explicit by Matthew, in order to shift the focus from the disciples to Jesus. The content of Jesus' third prayer is said to be the same as that of his second prayer.

45. *Sleep on and rest*: When so translated, Jesus' words expressed resignation at the weakness and failure of his disciples. It is often taken as a question ("Are you still sleeping and resting?"), which seems to express surprise and indignation.

Behold the hour has drawn near: Here *hōra* ("hour") is used something like it is used in the Fourth Gospel—to describe the time of Jesus' passion and death as the decisive moment in salvation history. The verb *engiken* ("has drawn near") appears also in Matt 26:46 to describe the approach of Judas that will set these events in motion. Again Jesus knows the fate that awaits him and appears to be in control of the whole situation.

46. *he who hands me over*: Of course, in the story line this is Judas. But the assumption is that everything takes place in accordance with God's will ("the Son of Man is being handed over").

47. *a large crowd*: The loose term "crowd" (*ochlos*) does not carry the organized military connotation of *speira* ("band of soldiers") in John 18:3. Nevertheless, Mark and Matthew probably envisioned a delegation from the Temple police under the authority of the chief priests and elders. Matthew qualifies Mark 14:43 ("a crowd") with the adjective "large" (*polys*).

48. *a signal*: The customary romantic picture of Jesus in Gethsemane has him at prayer in splendid isolation. But during the Passover pilgrimage the Mount of Olives would have been crowded with pilgrims. To prevent confusion and even rioting, Judas and the officials had to have a pre-arranged signal in order to arrest the right man as quickly and smoothly as possible.

49. *"Hello, Rabbi!" And he kissed him*: Matthew expands the simpler salutation in Mark 14:45 ("Rabbi") with "Hello" or "Hail" (*Chaire*). Only Judas addresses Jesus as "Rabbi" in Matthew (see Matt 26:25); it is a negative term for Matthew, probably because it was being used by the opponents of his community (see Matt 23:7-8). The greeting and kiss were primarily signs of respect, and only secondarily signs of friendship.

50. *"Friend, why are you here?"*: Despite his foreknowledge of Judas' intention (see Matt 26:45-46), Jesus addresses him as "friend." Jesus' question is difficult to translate. Some translators take it as a statement, supplying an imperative ("Friend, do that for which you are here"). This approach is more consistent with the theme of Jesus' foreknowledge. Matthew has added Jesus' question to Mark 14:45.

51. *one of those with Jesus*: According to Mark 14:47 "one of the bystanders" cuts off the ear of the chief priest's servant. He seems to be only one of the crowd (not a disciple), and his action is part of the chaos accompanying the arrest of Jesus. But in John 18:10 Simon Peter does the deed. In Luke 22:51 Jesus restores

the ear of the servant. Matthew assumes that the perpetrator is a disciple of Jesus and makes no mention of a healing.

52. *Then Jesus said*: Matthew uses the incident in Mark 14:47 as the occasion for some special teaching by Jesus on how and why he is being arrested.

all those who take the sword: A similar saying appears in Rev 13:10: "If anyone slays with the sword, with the sword must he be slain." Matthew presents Jesus as faithful to his own principles of nonviolence (Matt 5:38-42) and love of enemies (5:43-48).

53. *more than twelve legions of angels*: The idea of the angelic hosts fighting on the side of the righteous in the eschatological battle is prominent in Jewish apocalyptic works, especially in the Qumran *War Scroll*: "for the angels of holiness shall accompany their armies" (1 QM 7:6). Jesus refused to turn his death into that kind of cosmic conflict, though the assumption is that he could have done so.

54. *the Scriptures be fulfilled*: From what is said in Matt 26:56 the "Scriptures" must refer to Zech 13:7 ("I will strike the shepherd, and the sheep of the flock will be scattered," see Matt 26:31).

55. *revolutionary*: The Greek term *lēstēs* can describe a "robber, bandit" or a "revolutionary." In fact, it probably combines the two ideas in the form of a "social bandit" of which "Robin Hood" would be a type. In English "bandit" seems nonpolitical and "revolutionary" completely political. Since Jesus was executed as "King of the Jews," there must have been some political overtone to the officials' perception of him.

every day: But for Matthew, who follows Mark's chronology, Jesus has only taught for a few days in Jerusalem. He taught in the "Temple area," not in the more sacred parts of the Temple.

Interpretation

The arrest of Jesus takes place in the garden of Gethsemane. The account consists of two episodes: Jesus' prayer and the disciples' weakness (Matt 26:36-46), and the seizure of Jesus (Matt 26:47-56). In these episodes, as elsewhere in the passion narrative, Matthew follows Mark 14:32-42 and 14:43-52 closely.

In the first episode, however, Matthew places more emphasis on Jesus. In Mark 14:32-42 there is a double focus (Jesus and his disciples), with the contrast between the two a very important theme. Without losing the double focus or the contrast, Matthew heightens the role of Jesus. Jesus directs the activities of the group (26:36). He prays three times, and we learn the content of all three prayers (26:39, 41, 44). His posture is one of respect before his heavenly Father (26:39). The echoes of the Lord's Prayer already present in Mark 14:32-42 become even stronger (26:39, 41, 42).

In the second episode Matthew uses the incident about the ear of the chief priest's servant as the occasion for Jesus to explain why he (and his heavenly Father) allow the arrest to happen at all. Whereas in Mark 14:47 it is not clear whether the perpetrator is one of Jesus' circle, in Matt 26:51 he is clearly "with Jesus." Then Jesus shows himself faithful to his own peaceful principles (26:52), admits that he could get heavenly helpers (26:53), and explains that the arrest and other events of the passion take place according to the Scriptures (26:54). Matthew omits the mysterious incident of the flight of the young man (Mark 14:51-52), which is probably intended as a concrete illustration of the flight of the disciples (14:50 = Matt 26:56).

At the moment of Jesus' arrest he asks: "Have you come with swords and clubs to arrest me as if for a revolutionary?" (Matt 26:55 = Mark 14:48). The word translated as "revolutionary" here is *lēstēs*. Although its basic meaning is "robber" or "bandit," its use by Josephus (see *Ant.* 20:160-172) suggests that, when the New Testament was being written, it may also have carried a social-political connotation. The translation "revolutionary" is probably too strong, but at least it warns the reader not to pass over the term too quickly.

The people whom Josephus calls *lēstēs* were not simply thieves. They seem to have been more like modern terrorists. According to Josephus, Palestine in the late fifties of the first century A.D. was infested by brigands and impostors. Writing from the perspective of the failure of the Jewish revolt against Rome in A.D. 66-73 and with a bias toward his Roman patrons, Josephus shows little sympathy for these "brigands and impostors." Nevertheless, even from the skewed descriptions given by Josephus, it is clear that there was a political dimension to the activities of such persons.

The "brigands" were the equivalent of modern political terrorists, who were willing to carry out assassinations even in the Temple area: "they slew some because they were private enemies, and others because they were paid to do so by someone else" (*Ant.* 20:165). The "impostors" (the word *goēs* can also mean "magicians") relied more on public demonstrations to win a popular following. In the same context (*Ant.* 20:167-172) Josephus speaks first about "impostors and deceivers" who led a crowd out into the desert on the promise that they would see "signs and wonders" done in accord with God's providence. Then he tells about an Egyptian prophet who urged a crowd to go to the Mount of Olives where they might view the walls of Jerusalem fall down at his command and might join him in entering the city and taking control of it. For full treatment of revolutionary movements in first-century Palestine, see R. A. Horsley and J. S. Hanson, *Bandits, Prophets, and Messiahs: Popular Movements at the Time of Jesus* (Minneapolis: Winston-Seabury, 1985), and Horsley, *Jesus and the Spiral of Violence: Popular Jewish Resistance in Roman Palestine* (San Francisco: Harper & Row, 1987).

The incidents related by Josephus took place after Jesus' death (A.D. 30) and before the composition of Matthew's Gospel (A.D. 85-90). Nevertheless they at least give an impression of the intense political atmosphere that permeated first-century Palestine. Some of Jesus' opponents would have classified him as a *lēstēs* ("brigand") and/or a *goēs* ("magician").

The thrust of Matthew's account of Jesus' arrest would have been to show that Jesus was neither a brigand nor a magician. The customary portrayal of Jesus' prayer in Gethsemane is one of quiet isolation. But that is not the picture that first-century Jewish Christians would have had. Familiar with pilgrimages to Jerusalem—the crowds and the chaos, the political demonstrations and uprisings, Matthew's readers would have imagined anything but quiet isolation. Their vision of the scene on the Mount of Olives, with crowds of pilgrims camping out, would have been consistent with the precautions taken by Judas and the officials. They knew the need for a signal and the possibility of a riot erupting. Within this framework, Matt 26:36-56 tries to show that Jesus was neither a brigand nor a magician.

The first episode (26:36-46) emphasizes that Jesus allowed himself to be arrested because he perceived it as part of God's will for him according to the Scriptures. The easy way out would have been for Jesus to have returned to Bethany (see Matt 21:17) and thus avoided arrest. But giving himself to prayer and schooling himself to accept God's will, Jesus remains in Gethsemane and makes his arrest possible. The second episode (Matt 26:47-56) directly rebuts the charges that Jesus was a *lēstēs* ("brigand") or a *goēs* ("impostor/magician"). Jesus rebukes his disciple for using his sword and states that he is no *lēstēs* (26:51-52, 55). By refusing to call upon his Father's twelve legions of angels (26:53) Jesus avoids doing what a *goēs* might promise. Thus the Matthean account of Jesus' arrest argues that Jesus was faithful to the will of his Father as expressed in the Scriptures, and that he was certainly not a brigand or an impostor/magician. In this way Matthew may well have been countering assessments of Jesus that were being offered by the opponents of the Matthean community.

The two episodes that constitute the arrest of Jesus have fascinated generations of Christians. Usually bringing to the text strong presuppositions about the divinity of Jesus, such readers have puzzled over Jesus' need to pray as he does in the Gospel texts. The scene constructed by such readers is one of quiet isolation, late at night. The betrayal by Judas, usually viewed as a treacherous failure in friendship, is equally puzzling. The emphasis of these interpreters is psychological, individualistic, and romantic.

Yet when Jesus' arrest is set in its historical-political context of first-century Palestine, a different picture emerges. Jesus is arrested as if he were a "brigand" and/or an "impostor/magician." He was not. Jesus recognized the injustice of the charges against him. Nevertheless he did not run away—because he was convinced that these events were taking place "according to the Scriptures." The "political" reading of these texts does not drive out the more spiritual, traditional approach. But it does give any reading of these texts a sounder and more intelligible horizon. The passion of Jesus was woven into the fabric of social conditions and events in first-century Palestine.

For Reference and Further Study

Stanley, D. M. *Jesus in Gethsemane.* New York–Ramsey, N.J.: Paulist, 1980.

74. *The Jewish "Trial" and Peter's Denial* (26:57-75)

57. Those who had arrested Jesus led him away to Caiaphas the chief priest,
where the scribes and the elders were gathered. 58. But Peter followed him
from afar to the courtyard of the chief priest, and he entered and sat with
the servants to see the end. 59. The chief priests and the whole Sanhedrin
sought false witness against Jesus in order to put him to death, 60. and
they did not find it, though many false witnesses came forward. At last
two came forward 61. and said: "This man said: 'I can destroy the temple
of God and in three days build it up.' " 62. And the chief priest arose and
said to him: "Don't you answer? Why do these bear witness against you?"
63. Jesus was silent. And the chief priest said to him: "I adjure by the living God that you tell us if you are the Messiah, the Son of God." 64. Jesus
said to him: "You have said it. But I say to you, hereafter you will see the
Son of Man seated at the right hand of the Power and coming upon the
clouds of heaven." 65. Then the chief priest tore his garments and said:
"He has blasphemed. What further need do we have of witnesses? See,
now you have heard the blasphemy. 66. What do you think ought to be
done?" They answered and said: "He is deserving of death." 67. Then they
spat in his face and struck him, and some slapped him, 68. saying: "Prophesy to us, Messiah, who is it who struck you?" 69. But Peter was sitting
outside in the courtyard. And a maidservant approached him, saying: "You
also were with Jesus the Galilean." 70. He denied it before all, saying: "I
do not know what you are saying." 71. Another maidservant saw him going
out into the gateway, and she said to those there: "This one was with Jesus
the Nazarene." 72. And again he denied with an oath: "I do not know the
man." 73. After a little while the bystanders approached and said to Peter:
"Surely you too are one of them, for even your speech reveals you." 74.
Then he began to curse and swear: "I do not know the man." And immediately a cock crowed. 75. And Peter remembered the word that Jesus
said: "Before the cock crows you will deny me three times." And he went
outside and wept bitterly.

Notes

57. *to Caiaphas*: For the house of Caiaphas as the place of plotting against Jesus and for information about Caiaphas, see the note on Matt 26:3-5. While some kind of hearing involving Jesus most likely took place at the house of Caiaphas, that an official trial involving the whole Sanhedrin occurred during the first night of Passover is very unlikely on all counts.

58. *to see the end*: In place of Mark 14:54 ("and he was warming himself by the fire") Matthew states why Peter came ("to see the end"). The change is consistent with Matthew's tendency to cut out what he perceived to be extraneous details.

59. *false witness*: Matthew uses the term *pseudomartyria* ("false witness") instead of *martyria* ("witness") in Mark 14:55. He got the idea from Mark 14:56 ("many bore false witness against him").

60. *two came forward*: For a death sentence the testimony of two witnesses was needed: "On the evidence of two witnesses or of three witnesses he that is to die shall be put to death; a person shall not be put to death on the evidence of one witness" (Deut 17:6). The "Susanna" story in the Greek version of Daniel illustrates how this rule could be used to protect the innocent and to bring to light false witnesses.

61. *I can destroy the Temple of God*: Matthew softens Mark 14:58 ("I will destroy this Temple"). He also omits the distinction between "made by hands" and "not made by hands" (=by God). For three days as a period in which a decisive change occurs, see Hos 6:2. The charge against Jesus is rooted in his cleansing of the Temple (Matt 21:12-13) and his saying about "not one stone left upon another" (Matt 24:2).

62. *Don't you answer?*: The silence of Jesus evokes the posture of the Servant in Second Isaiah: "He was oppressed, and he was afflicted, yet he opened not his mouth . . . like a sheep that before its shearers is dumb, so he opened not his mouth" (Isa 53:7).

63. *the Messiah, the Son of God*: The chief priest uses an oath-formula to force Jesus to make a confession (see Matt 5:33-37; 23:16-22). The two titles that he uses have been especially prominent throughout Matthew, so that his use of them constitutes an example of irony. Whereas for Caiaphas Jesus was not the Messiah or Son of God, the reader of the Gospel has by now been convinced that he is. Also, Caiaphas uses the titles in a narrow, traditional sense whereas the reader of the Gospel understands them in a deeper, more comprehensive sense. In Caiaphas's eyes Jesus was another one of those brigands/impostors described by Josephus.

64. *Son of Man*: The picture of the Son of Man is taken from Dan 7:13-14: "with the clouds of heaven there came one like a son of man . . . to him was given dominion." The reference to the "right hand" of God evokes Ps 110:1: "The Lord said to my lord: 'Sit at my right hand . . .' " Thus Jesus' many references to himself as Son of Man and the allusions to him as Lord reach a climax at the hearing before the Sanhedrin.

the Power: Jesus avoids using the name of God and so employs a substitute, thus giving no cause for the charge of blasphemy levelled by the chief priest.

65. *He has blasphemed*: The technical meaning of blasphemy involves the misuse of the divine name, and the punishment for it is death by stoning: "He who blasphemes the name of the Lord shall be put to death; all the congregation shall stone him" (Lev 24:16). According to *m. Sanh.* 7:5 "the blasphemer is not guilty until he pronounces the name." In such a case the judges were expected to stand and rend their garments. Thus "blasphemy" is used loosely in this context.

66. *deserving of death*: But Jesus had not committed blasphemy in the technical sense of misusing the divine name. Thus the suggestion is that the verdict against him was unjust. Nevertheless the verdict of the Sanhedrin is not the final legal procedure. There is also a hearing in the morning (Matt 27:1-2) and the meeting with Pilate (27:11-31).

67. *they spat in his face*: The logic of Matthew's account demands that it was the members of the Sanhedrin who were responsible for the abuse visited upon Jesus. Mark 14:65 ("some") is ambiguous, and Luke 22:63 ("the men who were holding Jesus") suggests that it was those who had arrested Jesus.

68. *Prophesy to us, Messiah*: According to *Psalms of Solomon* 17:37 the Messiah is to be "powerful in the holy spirit and wise in the counsel of understanding with strength and righteousness" (see Isa 11:2). Matthew adds the address "Messiah" to the command of the abusers, thus reminding the reader of the irony involved in the mocking of Jesus.

69. *You also were with Jesus*: Having finished the story of Jesus' trial before the Sanhedrin, Matthew picks up again the story of Peter (see Matt 26:58) in order to contrast Jesus' heroic fidelity and Peter's cowardice. In the earlier episodes of Matthew 26 being "with Jesus" is a major theme (see 26:18, 29, 36, 38, 40). Peter's denial of it here is thus made all the more heinous.

70. *before all*: By adding "before all" to Mark 14:68 Matthew makes what could be understood as a person-to-person denial into a public action on Peter's part.

71. *gateway*: In place of the rare Markan term *proaulion* ("forecourt, gateway") Matthew uses the more common term *pylōn*. Peter's denials are marked also by movement from the courtyard (26:69) to the gateway (26:71) and outside (26:75).

72. *with an oath*: Matthew heightens the negative character of Peter's second denial of Jesus by adding that he did so with an oath—in direct contradiction to Jesus' own teaching (see Matt 5:33-37).

73. *even your speech reveals you*: Mark 14:70 has the bystanders identify Peter as a Galilean ("You too are a Galilean"). Matthew's change explains how they knew that—from his speech. Whether one can isolate a Galilean dialect of Aramaic in the first century is debatable. Nevertheless that there were local peculiarities of speech is quite likely.

74. *he began to curse and swear*: As in Matt 26:72 Peter's denial is made worse by his use of oaths (see Matt 5:33-37; 23:16-22).

75. *before the cock crows*: Thus Jesus' prediction in Matt 26:34 is fulfilled. In both cases Matthew simplifies Mark's expression "before a cock crows twice."

INTERPRETATION

As is the case throughout the passion narrative Matthew follows Mark 14:53-72 closely, even to the point of reproducing the "sandwich" effect in joining the "trial" of Jesus before the Jewish officials (Matt 26:57, 59-68) and Peter's denial of Jesus (26:58, 69-75). This technique highlights the contrast between the fidelity of Jesus and the cowardice of Peter.

As the narrative proceeds, Matthew's major contribution is to make explicit what is already present in Mark: Peter came "to see the end" of Jesus (26:58); the officials sought "false witnesses" (26:59); Jesus *could* have destroyed the temple (26:61); the officials mocked Jesus (26:67-68); Peter's denial of Jesus involved oaths (26:70, 72); and Peter's speech marked him as a Galilean (26:73).

Both Matthew and Mark present these episodes as the "Jewish trial" of Jesus. They locate it at the house of the high priest and place it on the first day of Passover—a few hours after the beginning of the feast at sundown, at a time when Jewish officials would normally have been eating the Passover meal with family and friends.

On the historical level there are problems with this scenario. The house of the high priest was a very unlikely setting for a meeting of the "whole Sanhedrin." Moreover, there is some confusion over what the "whole Sanhedrin" was. Was it a religious or a political body? Was it functioning as a "supreme court?" Or was it simply an investigatory committee, or an *ad hoc* committee charged with carrying out a specific task? See E. Rivkin, "Beth Din, Boulé, Sanhedrin: A Tragedy of Errors," *HUCA* 46 (1975) 181–99. Apart from the place and nature of the Sanhedrin there is doubt whether this kind of meeting of major Jewish officials ("the chief priests and the whole Sanhedrin," 26:59) would have occurred on the first night of Passover.

In this case the sequence of events in the Fourth Gospel is more plausible. According to John, Jesus was arrested and executed before Passover began (see John 13:1; 19:31, 42). There the major legal formality is the trial before Pilate (18:28–19:22), and the event at the chief priest's house (Annas, the father-in-law of Caiaphas) is an investigatory hearing prior to Jesus' being sent off to Pilate for trial. On the historical level the Johannine scenario—a preliminary investigation (on a small scale) held at the chief priest's house on the evening before the day on which Passover began—is more likely than the Synoptic scenario. The Synoptic version is most likely the combination of two tendencies in early Christianity: the tendency to bring out the Passover aspect of the Last Supper by making it a Passover meal, and the tendency to shift blame for Jesus' death from the Roman governor Pilate to the Jewish religious and political leaders. Thus Mark (followed by Matthew and Luke) or his source has transformed a preliminary hearing held at the chief priest's house on the night before the first day of Passover into a full-scale trial before the Sanhedrin on the first day of Passover.

Two charges are raised against Jesus: He threatened to destroy the Temple (Mark 14:58 = Matt 26:61), and he made claims that amounted to blasphemy (Mark 14:62 = Matt 26:63). Matthew's version of the first charge says that Jesus alleged: "I can destroy the Temple of God and in three days build it up." Matthew has omitted the "made by hands"/"not made by hands" contrast in Mark 14:58 and modified Jesus' claim from "I will destroy" to "I can destroy." There may well have been something to this charge. It fits with Jesus' prophetic action in "cleansing" the Temple (Matt 21:12-13; Mark 11:15-17; Luke 19:45-46; John 2:13-16). It also fits with Jesus' statement about the Temple's destruction ("there will not be left here one stone upon another, that will not be thrown down," Matt 24:2; Mark 13:2; Luke 21:6). It is not the kind of saying that early Christians might invent and place on Jesus' lips, for at least after A.D. 70 the Jerusalem Temple had been destroyed by the Romans and no new Temple had been erected. In fact, early Christians were somewhat embarrassed by it as its various versions show: "I can destroy . . ." (Matt 26:61); "he spoke of the temple of his body" (John 2:21); "we have heard him say that this Jesus of Nazareth will destroy this place, and will change the customs which Moses delivered to us" (Acts 6:14). On the other hand, there is little or no Jewish evidence for the combination of the destruction and restoration of the Temple in a single saying.

So there is very likely something to the first charge raised against Jesus: that he would destroy the Temple and in three days rebuild it. In the context of Jesus' preaching of God's kingdom such a statement may have contrasted the worship of God in this age (at the Jerusalem Temple) and in the age to come (when God's kingdom comes). The period of "three days" alludes to the change or decisive turn of events (see Hosea 6:2). Here Jesus may have been speaking in God's name or as God's agent. Such talk would have threatened the chief priests and elders of the people, for they took charge of and controlled the Jerusalem Temple. Even the common folk of the area would have been alarmed, because the rebuilding and upkeep of the Jerusalem Temple constituted the major industry of the city. Talk about destroying the Temple was incendiary, and may have contributed to gaining local support for executing Jesus.

Matthew's version of the second charge appears in the chief priest's order to Jesus to state whether he is "the Messiah, the Son of God" (Matt 26:63). Here Matthew has changed Mark's "of the Blessed One" to "of God." Son of God could be taken as a synonym for "Messiah" (see Ps 2:7, "He said to me, 'You are my son' "), though surely it meant more to Jewish Christians than it did to other Jews. As a charge on the lips of the chief priest "Messiah" would have referred to the class of troublemakers described by Josephus as "brigands and impostors," that is, false messiahs: Judas who had ambition for royal rank (*Ant.* 17:278-284), Simon who was proclaimed king (*Ant.* 17:273-277), and Athronges who had the temerity to aspire to the kingship (*Ant.* 17:278-284). Josephus summarizes the situation as follows: "And so Judea was filled with brigandage. Anyone might make himself king as the head of a band of rebels whom he fell in with, and then would press on to the destruction of the community, causing trouble to few Romans and then only to a small degree but bringing the greatest slaughter upon their own people" (*Ant.* 17:285). Thus Jesus was probably viewed as one in a series of political-religious messianic pretenders in first-century Palestine. The Roman equivalent of "Messiah" (the "anointed one," especially the king) would have been "the King of the Jews," the very title that figures so prominently in Jesus' condemnation and execution by the Romans (see Matt 27:11, 29, 37).

According to Matt 26:57-75 (and Mark 14:53-72) there were two charges against Jesus: He threatened to destroy the Jerusalem Temple, and he claimed to be the Messiah. When set in the historical context of Jesus' time one can understand how serious such charges were. But Matthew wrote from the perspective of the late first century A.D., after the Temple had been destroyed, and out of the conviction that Jesus was indeed the Messiah, and more than that, the Son of God in a sense that surpassed Jewish messianic hopes. According to Matthew, Jesus only claimed that he *could* destroy the Temple. While the claim that he was the Messiah was true, it was true in a sense different from the meaning assumed by his opponents. Therefore from Matthew's perspective the Jewish "trial" and condemnation of Jesus were a sham based upon "false witness" (Matt 26:59). The irony was, of course, that at a deeper level the charges were true: Jesus could have destroyed the Jerusalem Temple, and he was the Messiah, the Son of God. The "sham" character of the trial reaches its climax when the judges themselves join in the physical abuse of Jesus (26:67-68).

Besides explaining how Jesus got condemned to death, Matthew also followed Mark in contrasting the fidelity of Jesus and the cowardice of Peter. There is no doubt that Peter denied Jesus during the passion. It is certainly not the kind of thing that early Christians would have invented, and yet it is found in all four Gospels (Matt 26:69-75; Mark 14:66-72; Luke 22:56-62; John 18:25-27). The "sandwich" technique used in the Markan and Matthean accounts highlights the character of Jesus at the expense of Peter. Jesus is the model to be imitated, and Peter the model to be avoided. Nevertheless, for the Matthean community (and for all Christian communities past and present) Peter also serves as a model for sinners—a reminder that forgiveness and rehabilitation are always possible for even the worst of sinners.

In teaching about the Jewish "trial" of Jesus it is important to be clear about the differences between the Johannine and Synoptic versions, and to recognize the historical improbabilities connected with the Synoptic scenario. The two charges against Jesus must also be carefully examined with an eye toward what they meant in Jesus' time and how Christians would have interpreted and understood them. And the negative and positive dimensions of Peter's denial of Jesus deserve equal attention, along with Jesus' own example of fidelity and honesty.

For Reference and Further Study

Blinzler, J. *The Trial of Jesus.* Westminster, Md.: Newman, 1959.

Brandon, S. G. F. *The Trial of Jesus of Nazareth.* New York: Stein & Day, 1968.

Gerhardsson, B. "Confession and Denial before Men: Observations on Matt. 26:57–27:2." *JSNT* 13 (1981) 46–66.

Rivkin, E. *What Crucified Jesus?* Nashville: Abingdon, 1984.

Sloyan, G. S. *Jesus on Trial. The Development of the Passion Narratives and Their Historical and Ecumenical Implications.* Philadelphia: Fortress, 1973.

Wilson, W. R. *The Execution of Jesus. A Judicial, Literary and Historical Investigation.* New York: Scribner's, 1970.

Winter, P. *On the Trial of Jesus.* Berlin: de Gruyter, 1961.

75. *The Condemnation of Jesus and Judas' Death* (27:1-10)

1. When it was early morning all the chief priests and the elders of the people took counsel against Jesus to put him to death, 2. and they bound him and led him away and handed him over to Pilate the governor.

3. Then when Judas the one who handed him over saw that he had been condemned, he changed his mind and returned the thirty silver pieces to the chief priests and elders, 4. saying: "I have sinned, by handing over innocent blood." But they said: "What is that to us? You see to it." 5. And he threw the silver pieces into the temple and withdrew. And he went out and hanged himself. 6. The chief priests took the silver pieces and said: "It is not allowed to put these in the temple-treasury, since it is the price of blood." 7. On taking counsel they bought with them the field of a potter as a burial-place for foreigners. 8. Therefore that field has been called "field of blood" until this day. 9. Then what was said through Jeremiah the prophet was fulfilled: "And they took thirty silver pieces, the price of the one for whom the price was set, on whom they had set a price from the sons of Israel, 10. and they gave them for the potter's field, as the Lord directed me."

Notes

1. *took counsel*: The same expression is used with reference to a decision in Matt 12:14; 22:15; 27:7; 28:12. It is not clear that the chief priests and elders had made

a firm decision about Jesus in their evening session. Matt 26:66 states that they said that Jesus deserved death, whereas Mark 14:64 observes that "all condemned him." At any rate, their morning session according to Matthew constituted official action.

2. *to Pilate*: Thus the Jewish officials fulfill Jesus' passion prediction in Matt 20:18-19: "The Son of Man will be delivered to the chief priests and scribes, and they will condemn him to death, and deliver him to the Gentiles . . .". Pontius Pilate was the Roman governor of Judea from A.D. 26 to 36. Though his residence was at Caesarea Maritima, he would have been in Jerusalem during Passover to keep the peace among the pilgrims.

3. *he changed his mind*: Matthew avoids the usual term for "repentance" (*metanoia*), thus placing Judas' action in a category different from Peter's in Matt 26:75. Judas determines to return the thirty silver pieces given to him by the chief priests in Matt 26:14-16.

4. *innocent blood*: The expression refers to the "blood of an innocent person," in this case the blood of Jesus. Related expressions appear in Matt 23:35 ("just blood poured out on the ground") and 27:24 ("I am innocent of the blood of this man"). Judas fell under the curse of Deut 27:25: "Cursed be he who takes a bribe to slay an innocent person."

5. *he threw the silver pieces into the Temple*: Thus Judas tries to return the money to its source (see 26:14-16). The assumption is that the chief priests had returned to the Temple area. Judas' suicide by hanging is reminiscent of the fate of Ahithophel according to 2 Sam 17:23. According to Acts 1:18 Judas fell headlong (from a roof?) and burst open.

6. *the price of blood*: Even the chief priests recognize that the money given to Judas was "blood money." Though they refuse to accept it into the Temple treasury (*korbanan*, see Mark 7:11), they nevertheless had given it to Judas and now freely touch it.

7. *the field of a potter*: Presumably the field had belonged to a potter. Some interpreters find a play on the Hebrew words for "treasury" (*'ôṣer*) and "potter" (*yôṣer*) in Zech 11:13. There is probably also an allusion to Jeremiah 18–19, which is full of "potter" images.

8. *field of blood*: Acts 1:19 provides a transliteration of the Aramaic equivalent "Akeldama" (="field of blood"). The idea is that, since it was bought with "blood money," it remains a field of blood. The qualification "until this day" suggests that Matthew's readers could see the place for themselves.

9. *Jeremiah*: In fact the following quotation is taken from the book of Zechariah. The reference to Jeremiah may come from a connection drawn with Jer 19:11 ("Men shall bury in Topheth because there will be no place else to bury") and the potter's earthen flask.

   And they took: The quotation in Matt 27:9-10 is loosely based on Zech 11:13: "Then the Lord said to me, 'Cast it (=my wages of thirty shekels of silver) into the treasury'—the lordly price at which I was paid off by them. So I took the thirty shekels of silver and cast them into the treasury in the house of the Lord." In the Hebrew manuscripts the word "potter" (*yôṣer*) appears in place of "treasury" (*'ôṣer*).

Interpretation

Matt 27:1-2 follows Mark 15:1 in narrating a second Jewish legal proceeding. Since Matthew did not state explicitly that Jesus had been officially condemned (see Matt 26:66; Mark 14:64), it was all the more necessary for him to include the morning proceeding at which the chief priests and elders handed over Jesus to Pilate.

The next episode—the death of Judas (Matt 27:3-10)—has no parallel in any Gospel. The other NT account of Judas' death appears in Acts 1:18-19 where it is told by way of flashback to explain how the circle of the Twelve came to be reconstituted. The Matthean and Lukan accounts of Judas' death have two basic points in common: Judas died a violent death, and he was connected with the "field of blood." But there are striking differences: According to Matthew, Judas committed suicide; the "field of blood" was so named because the priests purchased it with the thirty silver pieces that they had paid Judas to betray Jesus; and the field was known as the potter's field. According to Acts 1:18-19 Judas himself bought the field; it was called the "field of blood" because Judas died his violent (probably accidental) death there. Neither story can be readily derived from the other; they are better viewed as independent versions of the basic narrative relating Judas' death and linking him with the "field of blood."

In the Matthean context the story of Judas' death confirms Jesus' warning in Matt 26:24: "Woe to that man by whom the Son of Man is betrayed." It also provides a foil to Peter in Matt 26:69-75: Whereas Peter repented and was restored to right relationship with God, Judas merely changed his mind but could not bring himself to repent. The passage also carries on and adds to the "fulfillment of Scriptures" theme so prominent in the Gospel.

The concluding Scripture quotation is basic to understand the Matthean version of Judas' death. Wrongly ascribed to Jeremiah, the quotation in Matt 27:9-10 is most obviously from Zech 11:13. Nevertheless there are elements of Jer 18:2-3 and 32:7-9 in the text. The text as it now stands draws together several threads from the narrative: the thirty silver pieces, the purchase of the field by the priests, and the idea of a potter's field. In the background of the account is a word-play based on the Hebrew terms for "treasury" (*'ôṣer*) and "potter" (*yôṣer*), terms that are confused in the textual tradition of Zech 11:13. The money that Judas tried to return to the temple-treasury (*'ôṣer*) was used to purchase the field of a potter (*yôṣer*).

Matthew's chief interests in the story of Judas' death involved the fulfillment of Scripture and the shameful behavior of the chief priests. That Judas betrayed Jesus and met a violent death needed explanation not only for Jewish Christians but also for those outside the Matthean community. The explanation most satisfying to Matthew was that these events took place in accord with the Scriptures. He was also adding to his negative portrayal of the chief priests: They recognized that their thirty silver pieces was blood money. Still they paid off Judas with it, and disposed of the money in buying the potter's field. Yet they too acted in fulfillment of the Scriptures.

The character of Judas has fascinated and mystified generations of Christians. His fate according to Matt 27:3-10 is usually taken as the model of death by suicide. But the other motifs in the Matthean account and the very different story told by Acts 1:18-19 indicate that matters were a good deal more complicated than the popular perception allows.

For Reference and Further Study

Senior, D. "The Fate of the Betrayer. A Redactional Study of Matthew XXVII,3-10." *ETL* 48 (1972) 372–426.

__________. "A Case Study in Matthean Creativity. Matthew 27:3-10." *BR* 19 (1974) 23–36.

van Unnik, W. C. "The Death of Judas in Saint Matthew's Gospel," *ATR* suppl. 3 (1974) 44–57.

76. *The Condemnation of Jesus* (27:11-26)

11. Jesus stood before the governor. And the governor asked him, saying: "Are you the king of the Jews?" Jesus said: "You say so." 12. And when he was accused by the chief priests and elders, he answered nothing. 13. Then Pilate said to him: "Do you not hear how many things they charge against you?" 14. And he did not answer him with regard to even one charge, so that the governor was much amazed.

15. At the feast the governor was accustomed to release one prisoner to the crowd, whomever they wished. 16. They then held a notorious prisoner called Barabbas. 17. When they had gathered, Pilate said to them: "Whom do you wish that I should release to you—Barabbas or Jesus called the Messiah?" 18. For he knew that they handed him over out of envy. 19. While he was sitting upon the judgment seat, his wife sent to him, saying: "Have nothing to do with that just man. For I have suffered much today in a dream on account of him." 20. But the chief priests and the elders

persuaded the crowds to ask for Barabbas and to destroy Jesus. 21. The governor answered and said to them: "Which of the two shall I release to you?" They said: "Barabbas." 22. Pilate said to them: "What shall I do with Jesus called the Messiah?" All said: "Let him be crucified!" 23. But he said, "What evil has he done?" But they shouted all the more, saying: "Let him be crucified!"

24. When Pilate saw that he gained nothing but the uproar was becoming greater, he took water and washed his hands before the crowd, saying: "I am innocent of the blood of this man. You see to him." 25. And all the people answered and said: "His blood be upon us and upon our children." 26. Then he released Barabbas to them. After he had Jesus scourged, he handed him over to be crucified.

Notes

11. *before the governor*: After the excursus on Judas' death, Matthew brings back the narrative to the ongoing trial of Jesus and rejoins the account begun in 27:1-2. Matthew calls Pilate by his title *hēgemōn* ("governor"). Pilate was the "prefect" of Judea from A.D. 26 to 36. Since capital cases were reserved to the Romans (see John 18:31), the Jewish officials had to work through Pilate in order to get Jesus executed.

    the king of the Jews: This title is the "secular" translation of "Messiah." To a Roman official like Pilate it would have meant political danger connected with popular Jewish uprisings. Jesus is executed in connection with the application of this title to him (see Matt 27:29, 37).

    "You say so": As elsewhere in the passion narrative (see Matt 26:25, 64), such a response seems to be an affirmation. But the affirmation is couched in irony, for Pilate and the Jewish officials understand the term differently from Jesus, Matthew, and the readers.

12. *he answered nothing*: By refusing to dignify the charges with a response, Jesus acts as God's Servant: "He will not cry or lift up his voice, or make it heard in the streets" (Isa 42:2; see Matt 12:19); "like a sheep that before its shearers is dumb, so he opened not his mouth" (Isa 53:7).

14. *the governor was much amazed*: Perhaps Matthew's readers were reminded of the fourth Servant song: "so shall he startle many nations; kings shall shut their mouths because of him" (Isa 52:15).

15. *accustomed to release*: The only ancient evidence for this "custom" of an annual release of a prisoner at Passover comes from the Gospels (see Matt 27:15; Mark 15:6; John 18:39). It may have been an occasional practice that some understood to be an annual custom. Or the practice may simply not have been noted in the sources that have survived to our day.

16. *a notorious prisoner called Barabbas*: In some manuscripts the prisoner is called "Jesus Barabbas" here and in Matt 27:17. The name "Barabbas" should probably be interpreted "son of Abba (=father)." His first name "Jesus" may have

been suppressed in the transmission of the text because as Origen said "in the whole range of the Scriptures we know that no one who is a sinner [is called] Jesus." (see *TCGNT*, 67-68). According to Mark 15:7 Barabbas was a revolutionary and a murderer: "And among the rebels in prison, who had committed murder in the insurrection, there was a man called Barabbas." Matthew omits this description, perhaps to avoid giving the impression that Pilate classed Jesus in the same category as Barabbas.

17. *Whom do you wish?*: Mark 15:9 reads: "Do you wish that I should release to you the King of the Jews?" Matthew sharpens Pilate's question in order to make it into a dramatic choice between the notorious (Jesus) Barabbas or Jesus the Messiah, thus focusing attention on the chief priests, elders, and the crowd.

18. *envy*: The chief priests were responsible for handing Jesus over to Pilate (see Matt 27:2, 12). The claim is that they resented Jesus' increasing influence over the people and so acted out of envy.

19. *judgment seat*: The word *bēma* refers to the tribunal or judicial bench or platform from which an official decision was made. John 19:13 locates Pilate's *bēma* "at a place called The Pavement, and in Hebrew, Gabbatha." The traditional location is the Fortress Antonia on the Via Dolorosa in Jerusalem. But now it seems more likely that Pilate lodged in Herod's palace where the citadel is today.

    his wife sent to him: The episode involving Pilate's wife is found only in Matthew, and its themes are particularly Matthean. Jesus is called a "just" man (*dikaios*) as in Matt 1:19; 3:15; 5:6; etc. Divine messages are communicated by means of dreams as in Matt 1:20; 2:12, 13, 19-20. The Gentile woman's insight contrasts with the spiritual obtuseness of the chief priests and elders in Matt 27:20.

20. *to destroy Jesus*: Matthew adds this phrase to Mark 15:11 as part of his ongoing emphasis on the choice placed before the chief priests, elders, and crowds. The release of Barabbas will have as its consequence the destruction of Jesus. Matthew also elaborates Mark's description of what the chief priests did ("stirred up the crowd") by having them persuade the crowds to ask for Barabbas.

21. *Which of the two*: Again Matthew adds to Mark 15:12 a direct question put by Pilate to the crowds (demanding that they make a choice) and a clear response by them (Barabbas).

22. *Let him be crucified*: Under the persuasion of the chief priests and elders the crowds pass sentence on Jesus. Whereas Mark 15:13, 14 uses the imperative (*staurōson*), Matt 27:22, 23 uses the subjunctive (*staurōthētō*) perhaps to capture the "official" role that the crowds play in passing sentence on Jesus. They repeat the sentence even after Pilate has reminded them that Jesus had done no wrong.

24. *took water and washed his hands*: Pilate's action follows Jewish rather than Roman custom. The most important OT texts are Deut 21:6-9; Ps 26:6-10; and Isa 1:15-16. The action would have been understood by Jews as a protestation of innocence: "Our hands did not shed this blood, neither did our eyes see it shed" (Deut 21:7).

25. *all the people*: Whereas previously in the narrative Matthew referred to the *ochloi* ("crowds"), here he changes the designation to *pas ho laos* ("all the people").

The word *laos* carries a collective sense and refers to Israel as a whole (see Matt 1:21; 2:4, 6; 4:16, 23; etc.).

His blood be upon us and upon our children: The crowd accepts the responsibility for Jesus' death with a well-known biblical formula (see Lev 20:9-16; Josh 2:19-20; 2 Sam 1:16; 14:9; Jer 51:35). The phrase "upon our children" may limit the responsibility to one generation—that of the destruction of the Jerusalem Temple A.D. 70 and Matthew's Jewish opponents.

26. *he handed him over to be crucified*: Pilate accepts the people's decision and releases Barabbas to them. The purpose of the scourging was to weaken Jesus for the crucifixion. Sometimes scourging was used as a punishment by itself (see Matt 10:17; Acts 5:40; 22:19; 2 Cor 11:24-25). Originally a Roman punishment, the preceding NT texts indicate that it was used also by Jews. Pilate then continues the "handing over" of Jesus.

Interpretation

Matthew's account of Jesus' trial before Pilate (Matt 27:11-26) follows Mark 15:1-15 in its essentials. In doing so it nearly disguises the fact that Pontius Pilate, the Roman prefect of Judea, was legally responsible for Jesus' death by crucifixion. It is doubtful whether Jews could carry out the death penalty (see John 18:31). Moreover, crucifixion was a Roman punishment. If Jesus had been executed for blasphemy (see Mark 14:64), the proper punishment was death by stoning (see Lev 24:16). Though the Jewish leaders were very likely involved in the process, the main legal formalities surrounding Jesus' death were carried out by the Romans under Pilate.

Matthew, however, followed Mark's lead in presenting the hearing at the chief priest's house (Matt 26:57-68; Mark 14:53-65) as the real trial, and the real trial before Pilate (Matt 27:11-26; Mark 15:1-15) as a confirmatory hearing. After the Roman triumph over the Jews in the first Jewish revolt (A.D. 66-73) it was natural that Matthew and other early Christians would stress Jewish participation and pass over whatever fault might attach to Rome. A similar tendency marks the writings of the Jewish historian Josephus, who wrote about the first Jewish revolt in the late first century A.D. under the patronage of the Roman emperors. Josephus blames the revolt on the leaders of the various Jewish factions and generally presents the Romans in a favorable light. Furthermore, Matthew seems to have discerned a connection between the chief priests and elders (along with the crowds that they persuaded) in Jesus' day, and the Jewish rivals of the Christian movement in the late first century.

The changes that Matthew introduced into Mark 15:1-15 were guided by a desire to make the idea of decision or choice on the part of the Jewish leaders and crowds even clearer. They are given a choice for or against Jesus, and they make their choice against Jesus.

The two major Matthean additions develop the theme of choice. In response to her dream Pilate's wife warns her husband to "have nothing to do with that just man" (Matt 27:19). Her warning precedes the description of the efforts by the chief priests and elders to persuade the crowd to ask for Barabbas and to have Jesus killed (27:20). In the second major addition (Matt 27:24-25) Pilate makes a public show of his noninvolvement in the death of Jesus, and "all the people" take upon themselves the responsibility for Jesus' death. In both cases Romans declare Jesus to be innocent, but Jews push on and demand his execution.

Most of the minor changes also reflect the motif of deliberate choice on the Jewish side, with Pilate merely raising questions and acceding to the crowd's demands: "Whom do you wish . . . ?" (Matt 27:17); "Which of the two shall I release . . . ?" (27:21). According to Matt 27:20 their choice was between asking for Barabbas and destroying Jesus. Their response is phrased in the language of a legal decision: "Let him be crucified!" (27:22, 23). So Matthew's overriding concern in editing his Markan source for the trial before Pilate was to give even more emphasis than Mark did to the deliberate choice against Jesus by the Jewish leaders and the crowds under their influence.

The Markan-Matthean portrayal of Pilate as just but weak contrasts with the assessments of him by other first-century Jewish writers. Pilate served as "prefect" or governor of Judea from A.D. 26 to 36. After Herod Archelaus (one of the sons of Herod the Great) was deposed in A.D. 6, the affairs of Judea were directed by a Roman governor. Pilate held the position for a long time, probably not so much because of his efficiency, but more because the emperor Tiberius was notoriously slow in making new appointments.

During his governorship Pilate clashed repeatedly with his Jewish subjects. Pilate brought into Jerusalem the standards of a military unit that bore the image of the emperor (see Josephus, *War* 2:169-74; *Ant.* 18:55-59). He took money from the Temple treasury to build an aqueduct for Jerusalem (*War* 2:175-77; *Ant.* 18:60-62). He brought into Jerusalem shields dedicated to Tiberius (Philo, *Legatio ad Gaium* 299-305). He brutally put down a disturbance among the Samaritans (*Ant.* 18:85-90) and is said to have mixed the blood of certain Galileans with their sacrifices (Luke 13:1).

Josephus reports Pilate's deeds, without spending much time on evaluating his character. Philo, however, is not so circumspect. In describing the bringing into Jerusalem of the shields dedicated to Tiberius, Philo states that Pilate did this not so much to honor Tiberius as to annoy the multitude (*Legatio ad Gaium* 299). He goes on to say that Pilate was "naturally inflexible, a blend of self-will and relentlessness" (301). According to Philo, Pilate only backed down on this matter "for he feared that if they actually sent an embassy [to the emperor Tiberius] they would also expose the rest of his conduct as governor by stating in full the briberies, the insults, the robberies, the outrages and wanton injuries, the executions without trial constantly repeated, the ceaseless and supremely grievous cruelty'' (302).

The Gospels' account of Pilate as just but weak should not be dismissed solely on the strength of Philo's evaluation of his character. One must allow for Philo's ideological concerns as well as those of the evangelists. And it is true that in some of the incidents involving Pilate—the standards and the shields—he backed off when Jewish pressure became too great. Could not the threat of riot in Jerusalem during Passover have led him to back off in the case of Barabbas and Jesus?

However a historian might divide up the contributions of the Jewish leaders and Pilate toward Jesus' death (there must have been some collaboration), the focus of Matthew's attention was the Jewish leaders and the crowds under their sway. The Matthean account of the Pilate trial reaches its climax when ''all the people'' accept the responsibility for Jesus' execution: ''His blood be upon us and upon our children'' (Matt 27:25). This text has often been used to base the idea of a divine curse upon the Jewish people, condemning them to wandering and persecution, for having put to death the Son of God. This idea (of inherited Jewish guilt for deicide) has been rejected by most Christians today, and officially so in the Second Vatican Council's *Nostra aetate* 4.

Yet the question remains, What are we to make out of ''His blood be upon us and upon our children'' (Matt 27:25)? A now standard approach to the text is to limit the responsibility to the small group of Jews who might have made up the crowds at Passover time in A.D. 30. At most the trial of Jesus would have attracted a relatively small number of people. The vast majority of inhabitants and pilgrims would not have noticed what was going on with regard to Jesus. But this approach does not really fit Matthew.

Throughout the passion narrative Matthew has used the term *ochlos* to refer to the crowd. But in Matt 27:25 he switches to *pas ho laos* (''all the people''). Elsewhere in his Gospel, Matthew uses *laos* to refer to the Jewish people taken as a collectivity. Matthew meant more than the small group of Jews who gathered around Pilate's judgment seat at Passover time in A.D. 30. That group fulfilled a representative function vis-à-vis Jesus and the Christian community.

Given Matthew's concern for Christian identity within Judaism, it seems likely that for him ''all the people'' represented the Jewish opponents of the Church. The problem is that of Romans 9–11 and Matthew 13: Why have not all (indeed most) Jews accepted the gospel? But Matthew is dealing with this problem in light of the destruction of the Jerusalem Temple. In this framework ''upon our children'' should be taken seriously as a reference to the next generation—the children of those Jews responsible (at least in part) for Jesus' death. The ''hardening'' that has come on part of Israel (see Rom 11:25-26) led to the events of A.D. 70, according to Matthew, who apparently saw a link between those Jews who had a hand in Jesus' condemnation and those Jews who were rivals of his own community after A.D. 70.

Matthew 27:11-26 (and especially 27:25) is a major text in the history and present reality of Christian-Jewish relations. Teachers and preachers have a serious obligation to work through this text with care and objectivity. They must give attention to the conflicting portraits of Pilate in the Gospels and other Jewish sources. They must help others to see Matthew's special interest in the Jewish leaders and crowds and his comparative lack of interest in Pilate. Above all it is necessary to read Matt 27:25 ("His blood be upon us and upon our children") in its Matthean setting, not as applying to all Jews at all times or to just the small percentage of Jews in Jerusalem who involved themselves in Jesus' trial before Pilate. The Matthean setting involves both the time of Jesus and the time after A.D. 70, and it is rooted in an inner-Jewish quarrel.

For Reference and Further Study

Fitzmyer, J. A. "Anti-Semitism and the Cry of 'All the People' (Mt 27:25)." *TS* 26 (1965) 667–71.

Kampling, R. *Das Blut Christi und die Juden. Mt 27, 25 bei den lateinischsprachigen christlichen Autoren bis zu Leo dem Grossen.* NTAb 16. Münster: Aschendorff, 1984.

Kosmala, H. " 'His Blood on Us and Our Children' (The Background of Mat. 27,24-25)." *ASTI* 7 (1968–69) 94–126.

Maccoby, H. Z. "Jesus and Barabbas." *NTS* 16 (1969) 55–60.

Mora, V. *Le refus d'Israël. Matthieu 27, 25.* LD 124. Paris: Cerf, 1986.

77. *The Crucifixion of Jesus* (27:27-44)

27. Then the soldiers of the governor took Jesus into the praetorium, and they gathered to him the whole cohort. 28. And they stripped him and put a scarlet cloak around him. 29. And after plaiting a crown of thorns they put it on his head and a reed in his right hand. And they genuflected before him and mocked him, saying: "Hail, King of the Jews!" 30. And they spat upon him and took the reed and struck him on his head. 31. And when they had mocked him, they stripped off the cloak and clothed him with his garments and led him away to crucify him. 32. And they went out and found a Cyrenean man, Simon by name, and they forced him to carry his cross.

33. And they came to the place called Golgotha, which is called "place of the skull." 34. And they gave to him to drink wine mixed with gall. And after tasting it he did not want to drink it. 35. And when they crucified

him, they divided his garments by casting lots. 36. And they sat down and kept watch over him there. 37. And over his head they placed the charge against him, which was written: "This is Jesus, the King of the Jews."

38. Then two revolutionaries were crucified with him, one at his right and one at his left. 39. The passers-by derided him, shaking their heads, 40. and saying: "You who destroy the temple and in three days build it, save yourself, if you are the Son of God, and come down from the cross." 41. Likewise the chief priests with the scribes and elders mocked and said: 42. "He saved others; he cannot save himself. He is the King of Israel; let him come down now from the cross, and we will believe in him. 43. He has trusted in God; let him deliver him now if he wishes him. For he said that 'I am the Son of God.' " 44. And the revolutionaries crucified along with him insulted him in the same way.

Notes

27. *praetorium*: Originally the Latin designation for the praetor's tent in a camp, the term came also to designate the official residence of the Roman governor. In the case of Pilate the praetorium described the place at which he stayed in Jerusalem—either at Herod's palace at the western edge of the city or at the fortress Antonia north of the Temple area.

the whole cohort: A "cohort" (*speira*) consisted of 600 men and constituted the tenth part of a legion. Given the large number of men, its use in the scene of Jesus' mockery must have been simply to designate a group of soldiers. The mockery is carried out by the "soldiers of the governor" according to Matthew. Mark 15:16a merely says "the soldiers," and Luke 23:11-12 indicates that it was done by the soldiers of Herod Antipas.

28. *a scarlet cloak*: According to Mark 15:17 the soldiers clothed Jesus in purple, the color associated with royalty and the rich (because of the complex process by which the dye was made). But where did the soldiers get a purple cloak? Matthew changes the color to "scarlet," which was the color of the cloaks customarily worn by Roman soldiers. These soldiers would not have been ethnic Romans but rather Syrians or other locals in Roman employ.

29. *a crown of thorns*: The thorns from which the crown was made have been variously identified as paliurus, thorny burnet, or Christ-thorn. The reason for the crown was more mockery than inflicting pain. The crown may have been intended as a play on images of Roman emperors (on coins, etc.) who bore radiant crowns.

and a reed in his right hand: Matthew probably developed this picture from Mark 15:19 ("they struck him on the head with a reed") and thus built up the mock game played by the soldiers. He has also reordered the sequence of events (kneeling, acclaiming, spitting, striking) to improve on Mark's confused order (acclaiming, striking, spitting, kneeling).

"Hail, King of the Jews": The soldiers use the term of the official charge against Jesus (see Matt 27:37). As is the case throughout the passion story the irony is

that Jesus really is "King of the Jews," that is, the Messiah, even though the soldiers fail to perceive this and use the term in mockery. Their greeting plays on the traditional greeting given to the Roman emperor, "Hail, Caesar."

32. *a Cyrenean man, Simon by name*: Cyrene is present-day Libya. Simon may have been a pilgrim to Jerusalem for Passover. Or he may have already taken up residence in the land of Israel. Matthew omits (as unnecessary details?) the notes in Mark 15:21 that Simon came from the countryside and was the father of Alexander and Rufus (perhaps known in the Markan community).

they forced him to carry his cross: It was customary for the condemned prisoner to carry his own crossbeam. Perhaps because Jesus had become too weak, the Roman soldiers "impressed into public service" (*ēggareusan*) Simon of Cyrene. See Matt 5:41 ("whoever forces you to go one mile") for the same custom.

33. *Golgotha*: The Latin translation is *calvaria*, hence our word "Calvary." The term "skull" may refer either to its function as a place of execution or to its physical shape (a hill like a skull). In view of Jewish and Roman execution procedures, it must have been outside the city walls (see John 19:20; Heb 13:12; Matt 21:39).

34. *wine mixed with gall*: Mark 15:23 has "wine drugged with myrrh," which refers to the practice of offering the condemned person a narcotic to ease the pain (see *b. Sanh.* 43a). Matthew's change to "wine mixed with gall" probably is based on Ps 69:21 ("they gave me poison for food, and for my thirst they gave me vinegar to drink"). Perhaps Matthew envisioned an offer of poison by which Jesus could avoid the pain entirely.

35. *when they crucified him*: Matthew goes beyond Mark 15:24 in not dwelling on the physical sufferings involved in crucifixion by describing the crucifixion in a subordinate clause.

they divided his garments: The condemned man's clothes became the property of the executioners. Matthew and other early Christians found in this practice the fulfillment of Ps 22:18 ("they divide my garments among them, and for my raiment they cast lots").

36. *kept watch over him there*: Matthew introduces this note, probably as part of his theme that there was a watch on Jesus from the start of his crucifixion to his burial (see Matt 27:36, 39-44, 47, 54, 55-56, 61, 62-66) and therefore there could be no truth to the story that the disciples stole his body (28:11-15).

37. *King of the Jews*: All the evangelists agree that this was the official charge on which Jesus was executed. According to John 19:20 it was written in three languages: Hebrew (=Aramaic), Latin, and Greek. It surely was based on the Roman perception of Jesus as a potential political rebel. From the Christian perspective the "charge" was ironically correct but with a meaning different from the one intended by Pilate.

38. *revolutionaries*: The translation of *lēstai* probably goes too far, but the traditional rendering "thieves" does not go far enough in bringing out the probably "political" dimension connected with the term. Their presence with Jesus brings to fulfillment what was said about the Servant: "he was numbered with the transgressors" (Isa 53:12).

39. *the passers-by derided him*: The verb here is *eblasphēmoun*, which suggests that "blasphemy" in Matt 26:65 was not used in its technical sense either. By "shaking their heads" the passers-by fulfill Ps 22:7: "All who see me mock at me, they make mouths at me, they wag their heads."

40. *if you are the Son of God*: Matthew's addition to Mark 15:30 is reminiscent of the testing story (see Matt 4:1-11, especially vv. 3, 6). The passers-by bring up the first charge in Jesus' Jewish trial (Matt 26:61)—about destroying the Temple. In Matthew's perspective the destruction of the Jerusalem Temple in A.D. 70 was caused by the death of Jesus (see Matt 21:41, 43).

43. *He has trusted in God*: To the mockery of the chief priests and scribes in Mark 15:31-32, Matthew has added Matt 27:43 which alludes to Ps 22:8: "He committed his cause to the Lord; let him deliver him." There is probably also reference to the figure of the "suffering righteous one" of Wisdom 2, especially 2:18: "for if the righteous man is God's son, he will help him and will deliver him from the hand of his adversaries."

44. *insulted him in the same way*: Mark and Matthew know nothing about the "good thief" of Luke 23:39-43. The reviling by those crucified along with Jesus may allude to Ps 69:9: "the insults of those who insult them have fallen on me."

Interpretation

Matthew's account of Jesus' crucifixion (27:27-44) consists of three scenes: the mockery of Jesus as "King of the Jews" (Matt 27:27-32), the crucifixion (27:33-37), and the derision of Jesus (27:38-44). For these scenes Matthew followed Mark 15:16-32, which itself was already the product of sophisticated theological reflection.

The Markan (or more likely, pre-Markan) theological reflection on Jesus' crucifixion focused on the irony of his condemnation as "King of the Jews" and the fulfillment of the Scriptures. In the mockery-scene (27:27-32) the soldiers put Jesus through a mock ritual in which they dress Jesus as a clown-king and salute him as they would salute the emperor. Though the mockery involved physical abuse, its major thrust was the personal abuse and insults visited upon Jesus. Besides marking some minor changes ("scarlet" instead of "purple" cloak) and omissions ("inside the courtyard" in Mark 15:16 and "coming from the countryside, the father of Alexander and Rufus" in Mark 15:20), Matthew has expanded and given a more logical order to the events that constituted the mockery in Matt 27:29. Nevertheless, the basic thrust of the Markan and Matthean accounts is the same: Jesus who is mocked as King of the Jews really is the Messiah (=King of the Jews), and so the soldiers unwittingly speak the truth in deed and word.

The crucifixion scene (Matt 27:33-37 = Mark 15:22-26) continues the irony. The charge on which Jesus is crucified, the charge set upon his cross, is that he is "King of the Jews" (27:37). To Romans like Pilate this means "Jewish revolutionary,'' and to Jews like the chief priests and elders it refers to false claims made about Jesus by his followers and the general populace. But to Christian readers of the Gospels the title expresses a truth beyond that which the opponents of Jesus could have imagined.

A second theme in the crucifixion scene is the fulfillment of Scripture. The two major quarries for fulfillment texts were Psalms 22 and 69. The division of Jesus' garments in Matt 27:35 echoes what is said in Ps 22:18, and the potion offered Jesus in Matt 27:34 is reminiscent of Ps 69:21. In fact, the most important change introduced by Matthew (''wine mixed with gall'') stems from his desire to bring out more clearly the allusion to Ps 69:21. Matthew also begins his theme about the guard watching over Jesus' body from his crucifixion to his resurrection (''they sat down and kept watch over him there'').

In the derision (Matt 27:38-44 = Mark 15:27-32) the passers-by bring up the charge that Jesus would destroy the Temple, and the chief priests along with the scribes and elders raise the charge that Jesus claimed to be King of Israel. From Matthew's perspective there is ironic truth in their statements. The destruction of the Jerusalem Temple in A.D. 70 was a consequence of the rejection of Jesus (see Matt 21:41, 43), and Jesus really was the King of Israel from the start (see Matt 2:1-12). The theme of the fulfillment of Scripture continues as the passers-by ''shake their heads'' at Jesus (Matt 27:39 = Ps 22:7) and Jesus is insulted by those crucified along with him (Matt 27:44 = Ps 69:9; Isa 53:12). Matthew enriches the fulfillment theme in Matt 27:43 by adding an allusion to the figure of the ''suffering righteous one'' (Ps 22:8; Wis 2:18, 20). Moreover, he has underlined Jesus' identity as the Son of God by two further additions: ''if you are the Son of God'' (27:40), and ''he said that 'I am the Son of God' '' (27:43).

On the whole, Matthew follows and adds to the two major themes in Mark's account of Jesus' crucifixion: the ironical confessions of Jesus as King of the Jews, and the fulfillment of Scripture. The account as it came to Matthew was already the product of sophisticated theological reflection. It took for granted an appreciation of Jesus' physical sufferings and tried to suggest an interpretation of them.

The ancient evidence concerning crucifixion is gathered in M. Hengel's *Crucifixion: In the ancient world and the folly of the message of the cross* (Philadelphia: Fortress, 1977). Crucifixion as a penalty was quite widespread in antiquity. It was inflicted by the Romans above all on the lower classes, that is, slaves, violent criminals, and political rebels. The chief reason for its use seems to have been its effect as a deterrent, since it was carried out publicly. Among Jews it carried the additional stigma of a curse: ''for a hanged man is accursed by God'' (Deut 21:23).

Excavations at Giv'at ha-Mivtar, north of Jerusalem, in the late 1960s, uncovered the remains of a man between twenty-four and twenty-eight years of age. Study of his foot and leg bones have indicated that he had been crucified and how the punishment was carried out: "the feet were joined almost parallel, both transfixed by the same nail at the heels, with the legs adjacent; the knees were doubled, the right one overlapping the left; the trunk was contorted; the upper limbs were stretched out, each stabbed by a nail in the forearm. A 'sedecula' ("small seat") was used on the cross. The feet were hacked from the legs at the time of removal from the cross" (see N. Haas, "Anthropological Observations on the Skeletal Remains from Giv'at ha-Mivtar," *IEJ* 20 [1970] 38–59). There was, however, no one way in which crucifixion was carried out, and there is even debate about this case.

Recognition of basic facts about crucifixion—its use on rebels and slaves, the curse attached to it by Deut 21:23, the intense physical suffering, its public character and function as a deterrent, the casual disposal of the corpse—leads one to appreciate the scandal posed by the early Christian proclamation of the gospel ("the word of the cross," according to 1 Cor 1:18). That the reconciliation of the cosmos should be tied to the death of Jesus on the cross was difficult to accept, to say the least.

In this context it is easy to say why Matthew and other early Christians concentrated on the ironical truth that Jesus was King of the Jews and on how his crucifixion fulfilled the Scriptures. The physical pain connected with crucifixion could be taken as known by his readers. What needed explanation is how this could have happened at all to the hero of the Christian community. The answer is that all took place according to God's will as expressed in the Scriptures; throughout it all Jesus remained King of the Jews.

For centuries Christians have concentrated on the physical sufferings of the crucified Jesus. The importance of this emphasis cannot be denied. But Matthew and the other NT writers suggest that concern with the meaning of Jesus' crucifixion is also important. Two important elements in interpreting Jesus' death are his identity as King of the Jews and his submission to God's will as expressed in the Scriptures.

For Reference and Further Study

Fitzmyer, J. A. "Crucifixion in Ancient Palestine, Qumran Literature, and the New Testament." *CBQ* 40 (1978) 493–513.

78. *The Death of Jesus* (27:45-56)

45. From the sixth hour there was darkness over the whole land until the ninth hour. 46. About the ninth hour Jesus cried out in a loud voice, saying: "Eli, Eli, lema sabachthani? That is, My God, my God, why have you abandoned me?" 47. Some of those standing there heard and said: "This one is calling Elijah." 48. And one of them ran immediately and took a sponge, filled it with sour wine, and put it on a reed, and gave him to drink. 49. But the rest said: "Let him alone! Let us see if Elijah comes to save him." 50. Jesus again cried out in a loud voice and gave up his spirit.

51. And behold the curtain of the temple was divided from top to bottom in two, and the earth was shaken, and the rocks were split. 52. And the tombs were opened, and many bodies of saints who had fallen asleep were raised. 53. And they came out of the tombs after his resurrection and entered into the holy city and appeared to many. 54. But the centurion and those with him guarding Jesus saw the earthquake and what happened, and they were much afraid, saying: "Truly this one is the Son of God."

55. There were many women there looking on from afar, who had followed Jesus from Galilee, ministering to him. 56. Among them were Mary Magdalene, and Mary the mother of James and Joseph, and the mother of the sons of Zebedee.

Notes

45. *darkness*: The darkness lasted from the sixth hour (noon) until the ninth hour (3:00 P.M.). Whether Matthew understood it to extend over the Jerusalem area or the whole land of Israel or over the whole world is not clear. The portent stands in line with Amos 8:9 (" 'And on that day,' says the Lord God, 'I will make the sun go down at noon and darken the earth in broad daylight' ") and Exod 10:22 ("there was thick darkness in all the land of Egypt").

46. *Eli, Eli*: In a mixture of Hebrew and Aramaic Jesus shouts out the opening of Psalm 22—the psalm of the righteous sufferer. Then the narrator supplies a Greek translation. While not downplaying the mental and emotional sufferings of Jesus, it is necessary to read the whole psalm and to recognize the profession of trust in God's power that forms its climax (see Ps 22:22-31).

47. *is calling Elijah*: The similarity between "My God" ("Eli") and Elijah leads to confusion about whom Jesus is calling. Elijah was believed to have been taken up into heaven (2 Kings 2). During life he served as defender of the defenseless, and after his assumption was thought to function as helper of those in desperate need.

48. *took a sponge, filled it with sour wine*: The term *oxos* ("sour wine, vinegar") refers to a cheap wine used by the lower classes. Its use in this context probably alludes to the second part of Ps 69:21: "and for my thirst they gave me vinegar to drink" (see Matt 27:34 = Ps 69:21a). Whether Matthew understood this ac-

tion as compassionate or insulting is difficult to know. He was probably more interested in its role in fulfilling Scripture.

49. *if Elijah comes to save him*: Instead of "to take him down" in Mark 15:36, Matthew substitutes the participle of *sōzō* ("to save")—a term that is prominent throughout the Gospel in reference to Jesus' mission from Matt 1:21 onward ("he will save his people from their sins") and throughout Psalm 22 (see vv. 5, 8, 21). Some important manuscripts add: "And another took a spear and pierced his side, and out came water and blood." The sentence is most likely an intrusion from John 19:34, though in the Matthean sequence it occurs before Jesus' death (cf. John 19:30). For a defense of the Matthean variant as authentic, see S. Pennells, "The Spear Thrust (Mt 27:49b, *v.l.* / Jn 19:34)," *JSNT* 19 (1983) 99–115.

50. *again cried out*: Matthew's change of Mark 15:37 ("uttered a loud cry") suggests that Jesus once more recited Psalm 22. This is confirmed by the use of "cry," which is prominent in Psalm 22 (see vv. 2, 5, 24) as the stance of the suffering righteous one.

    gave up his spirit: The Greek word for "spirit" is *pneuma*. An idiomatic English translation would be "gave up the ghost." There is no direct reference to the Holy Spirit here. Jesus returns to his heavenly Father the gift of life that is symbolized in the life-breath (*pneuma*).

51. *the curtain of the Temple*: Matthew follows Mark 15:38 for the first of the portents accompanying Jesus' death. The Temple curtain under consideration was probably the inner curtain in front of the holy of holies (see Exod 26:31-35; 40:21). The precise significance of the rending of the Temple veil was debated by Christian writers in the second and third centuries (see M. de Jonge, "Matthew 27:51 in Early Christian Exegesis," *HTR* 79 [1986] 67–79). There may not be a single meaning to it. Modern commentators usually see it as a comment on the end of the old way of worshipping God or even of the Old Covenant. Matthew may have viewed it as the first stage in the destruction of the Jerusalem Temple, which from his perspective was a past event.

    the earth was shaken: The earthquake serves as the prelude to the resurrection of the dead. In describing the destruction of the Jerusalem Temple in A.D. 70 Josephus (*War* 6) mentions several cosmic portents: a star and a comet over the city, a bright light at 3 A.M. at Passover, a cow giving birth to a lamb, and the spontaneous opening of the east gate of the inner sanctuary.

52. *many bodies of saints . . . were raised*: What may have been an existing apocalyptic fragment based on Ezekiel 37 has been inserted by Matthew to underline the decisive significance of Jesus' death as the event that makes possible the resurrection of others. For a similar idea, see 1 Corinthians 15. These resurrections anticipate the fullness that accompanies the end-time.

53. *after his resurrection*: Matthew has inserted into the scenario based on Ezekiel 37 a qualifier ("after his resurrection") that confuses the sequence of events that he narrates. The qualifier is really a theological correction that ties the resurrection of the saints to that of Jesus (not simply to his death).

54. *the centurion*: Matthew expands Mark 15:39 in two ways: by having the centurion accompanied by those "guarding Jesus" (see Matt 27:36), and by making the confession into a response to the cosmic portents that accompanied Jesus' death. The result of the changes is to make the confession ("Truly this one is the Son of God") into a chorus. There may also be thus an allusion to Ps 22:27-28 ("all the families of the nations").

55. *many women*: Matthew adds the adjective "many" to Mark 15:40. He also explains how these women know Jesus; they had been part of his movement from Galilee. The point of this explanation is that they had known Jesus beforehand, witnessed his death and burial, and went to the correct tomb on Easter Sunday morning.

56. *Mary Magdalene*: She is the principle of continuity par excellence and is acknowledged as such by all four Gospels (as well as the apocryphal Gospels). In Matthew she and the "other Mary" witness Jesus' death (27:56), his place of burial (27:61), and the empty tomb (28:1).

    Mary the mother of James and Joseph: According to Matt 13:55 Jesus had "brothers" named James and Joseph (and Simon and Judas). Could the "other Mary" be the mother of Jesus? According to Mark 15:40 this Mary was "the mother of James the younger and of Joses."

    the mother of the sons of Zebedee: The last woman on the list in Mark 15:41 is named Salome. Matthew identifies her as the mother of the sons of Zebedee, whom he inserted previously in Matt 20:20-21 (cf. Mark 10:35). She is not mentioned again in the narratives that follow (cf. Mark 16:1).

INTERPRETATION

Matthew's story of Jesus' death is told in three scenes: Jesus' death on the cross (27:45-50), the portents accompanying his death (27:51-54), and the women as witnesses (27:55-56). The major addition to Mark 15:33-41 comes in Matt 27:51b-53, a description of portents featuring the resurrection of the saints in Jerusalem. The description is based on Ezekiel 37:1-14, and it most likely existed in a slightly simpler form before Matthew used it. Matthew wanted to show that Jesus' death marks a turning point in human history because it makes possible the resurrection of other human beings (see 1 Cor 15:20-23). The surprising feature in the apocalyptic scenario is that it anticipates Jesus' own resurrection. The phrase "after his resurrection" in Matt 27:53 suggests that Matthew himself or an early corrector caught the problem. The addition of the apocalyptic scenario in Matt 27:51b-53 in turn serves as the occasion for Matthew to associate the guards with the centurion and to make their confession of Jesus as "Son of God" into a collective event, a kind of chorus.

Matthew has also introduced some minor changes. The bystanders at the cross wonder whether Elijah will come to "save" Jesus (27:49) instead of "to take him down" (Mark 15:36). The dying Jesus "cries out again"—with the verb "cry out" and the adverb "again" (27:50) pointing to a repetition of Jesus' recitation of Psalm 22 (see 27:46). In the list of women witnesses Matthew agrees with Mark 15:40 on Mary Magdalene but differs on the other two: Mary, the mother of James and Joseph (Jesus' own mother?), and the mother of the sons of Zebedee (see Matt 20:20-21).

Once more the focus of Matthew's (and Mark's) attention is not the physical sufferings of Jesus. These are taken for granted and serve as the occasion for interpreting the significance of Jesus' death. The following summary of medical evidence is based on W. D. Edwards, W. J. Gabel, and F. E. Hosmer, "On the Physical Death of Jesus Christ," *Journal of the American Medical Association* 255 (1986) 1455–63:

> Jesus had suffered great emotional stress as evidenced by hematidrosis, abandonment by his disciples, and a physical beating after the first Jewish trial. The severe scourging, with its intense pain and appreciable blood loss, most probably left Jesus in a preshock state. The most prominent causes of death by crucifixion were hypovolemic shock and exhaustion asphyxia. Other possible contributing factors included dehydration, stress-induced arrhythmias, and congestive heart failure with the rapid accumulation of pericardial and perhaps pleural effusions. Crucifracture, if performed, led to an asphyxic death within minutes. It remains unsettled whether Jesus died of cardiac rupture or of cardiorespiratory failure.

See also the critique of this article by D. E. Smith, "An Autopsy of an Autopsy. Biblical Illiteracy Among Medical Doctors," *Westar Magazine* 1 (1987) 14–15.

Matthew, however, describes the death of Jesus simply and with eloquent understatement: Jesus "gave up his spirit" (27:50b). He (following Mark and other early Christians) was more concerned with the meaning of Jesus' death as "according to the Scriptures."

The darkness at noon (27:45) probably alludes to Amos 8:9, and the sponge filled with sour wine completes the reference to Ps 69:21 begun in 27:34. But the main text is Psalm 22. The words of Jesus on the cross ("My God, my God, why have you abandoned me?") quote from the beginning of that psalm in which a righteous sufferer laments his sufferings but places his fate in God's power. Like other biblical lament psalms it is a frank recognition of suffering coupled with an affirmation of trust. It is dangerous to draw conclusions about Jesus' psychology or emotional state from Psalm 22. The early Christians were more interested in portraying him as the suffering righteous one and his death as "according to the Scriptures."

Matthew seems to have taken over and expanded the resonances of Psalm 22 in the Markan account of Jesus' death. In describing Elijah's function as "saving" (27:49) and Jesus' last act as "crying out" (27:50) Matthew uses two words that are very prominent in Psalm 22. He also implies that Jesus recited Psalm 22 "again" at the moment of his death (27:50). The chorus formed by the centurion and the guards (27:54) may allude to Psalm 22:27, since those confessing Jesus as "Son of God" are assumed to be Gentiles: "All the ends of the earth shall remember and turn to the Lord; and all the families of the nations shall worship before him."

The biblical inspiration for the portents surrounding Jesus' death (Matt 27:51b-53) is Ezekiel 37:1-14—Ezekiel's vision of the dry bones returning to life. In the apocalyptic fragment used by Matthew what Ezekiel presents as visionary becomes a reality. The key verses (Ezek 37:11-14) connect the resurrection of the dead with the restoration of Israel in its land:

> Then he said to me, "Son of man, these bones are the whole house of Israel. Behold, they say, 'Our bones are dried up, and our hope is lost; we are clean cut off.' Therefore prophesy, and say to them, 'Thus says the Lord God: Behold, I will open your graves, and raise you from your graves, O my people; and I will bring you home into the land of Israel. And you shall know that I am the Lord, when I open your graves, and raise you from your graves, O my people. And I will put my Spirit within you, and you shall live, and I will place you in your own land; then you shall know that I, the Lord, have spoken, and I have done it, says the Lord.'"

Thus the death and resurrection of Jesus anticipate the restoration of the saints in the land of Israel.

By now the meaning of Jesus' death for the Matthean community should be clear: It took place according to the Scriptures and (along with his own resurrection) anticipated the general resurrection of the righteous (see Dan 12:1-3). These Matthean emphases served to counter the charges from Jews and Gentiles alike that Jesus died a criminal's death in shame and that the movement initiated by him should have ended then and there. Matthew's answer to these charges is that what to some eyes was the execution of a rebel was in fact willed by God in accord with the Scriptures and that his death holds a central place in God's plan of salvation.

Again Matthew's interests differ from those of people today. We naturally focus on the physical sufferings of Jesus and the historical details surrounding them. We gravitate toward speculation on Jesus' emotional state at his death: Did he really feel abandoned by God? While our questions are important too, we need to recognize that ours is not the only approach to Jesus' death. Matthew shows us another way—a focus on the meaning of Jesus' death. His approach is also typically Matthean. He grounds Jesus' death in Jewish tradition by appealing especially to biblical phrases and themes. His concern is to show that Jesus' death occurred according to the Scriptures.

For Reference and Further Study

Aguirre, R. *Exégesis de Mateo, 27,51b-53. Para una teología de la muerte de Jesús en el Evangelio de Mateo.* Vitoria: Editorial EST, 1980.

_________. "El Reino de Dios y la muerte de Jesús en el evangelio de Mateo." *Estudios Eclesiasticos* 54 (1979) 363–82.

de Jonge, M. "Matthew 27:51 in Early Christian Exegesis." *HTR* 79 (1986) 67–79.

Hill, D. "Matthew 27:51–53 in the Theology of the Evangelist." *Irish Biblical Studies* 7 (1985) 76–87.

Senior, D. "The Death of Jesus and the Resurrection of the Holy Ones (Mt 27:51–53)." *CBQ* 38 (1976) 312–29.

79. *The Burial of Jesus* (27:57-66)

57. When it was evening there came a rich man from Arimathea, whose name was Joseph, who himself had been a disciple to Jesus. 58. This one approached Pilate and requested the body of Jesus. Then Pilate ordered it to be given over. 59. And Joseph took the body and wrapped it in a clean linen cloth, 60. and placed it in his new tomb that he had cut in the rock; and after rolling a large stone into the entrance of the tomb, he went away. 61. Mary Magdalene and the other Mary were sitting there opposite the tomb.

62. On the next day, which was after the Preparation, the chief priests and the Pharisees gathered before Pilate, 63. saying: "We remember that that deceiver while still alive said: 'After three days I will be raised.' 64. Order that the tomb be secured until the third day, lest his disciples come and steal him and say to the people 'He has been raised from the dead,' and the last deception will be worse than the first." 65. Pilate said to them: "You have a guard. Go, secure it as you know how." 66. They went and secured the tomb by sealing the stone along with a guard.

Notes

57. *a rich man from Arimathea*: Matthew omits the complicated chronological information in Mark 15:42 ("since it was the day of Preparation, that is, the day before the Sabbath"), though he does give a simplified version in Matt 27:62. Only Matthew calls Joseph "rich" (*plousios*), probably a deduction from his owning a tomb near Jerusalem, though there may be some connection with Isa 53:9: "and they made his grave with wicked men but his body lay with a rich man"; see W. B. Barrick, "The Rich Man from Arimathea (Matt 27:57-60) and 1Q Isa[a]," *JBL* 96 (1977) 235–39. Arimathea is variously identified as Hebrew Ramathaim, Ramoth, or Ramah.

who himself had been a disciple: Mark 15:43 describes Joseph as "a respected member of the council, who was also himself looking for the kingdom of God." Matthew's changes avoid the impression that Joseph was a party to the condemnation of Jesus by the Sanhedrin (see Mark 14:64, "all condemned him") and interpret the vague "looking for the kingdom" as membership among the followers of Jesus.

58. *requested the body of Jesus*: Matthew omits the complicated interchange between Pilate and the centurion in Mark 15:44-45a. The haste with which Jesus' burial was carried out probably had some connection with Deut 21:23: "His body shall not remain all night upon the tree, but you shall bury him the same day."

59. *clean linen cloth*: The Greek word is *sindōn*, which is sometimes translated "shroud" and identified as the Shroud of Turin. According to John 19:40 (see 20:6) Jesus was wrapped in linen cloths (*othonia*).

60. *tomb . . . cut in the rock*: Jerusalem is encircled by soft limestone rock out of which caves can be quarried or exist naturally. The area outside the walls of Jerusalem has been described as a gigantic cemetery. Joseph is said to have had a tomb cut out of the rock and allowed Jesus to use it. The large stone rolled in front of the entrance would serve to keep tomb robbers away.

61. *were sitting there opposite the tomb*: The same women who saw Jesus die—Mary Magdalene and the other Mary—also saw where he was buried. They could not have gotten the wrong tomb on Easter (see Matt 28:1).

62. *the next day, which was after the Preparation*: The word *paraskeuē* ("preparation") refers to the day before the feast of the Sabbath. The phrase as a whole refers to the Sabbath itself in a roundabout way. Perhaps Matthew was eager to use the rare word *paraskeuē* from Mark 15:42.

the chief priests and the Pharisees: The Pharisees reappear after being off the scene during the passion narrative. That they would have joined the chief priests on the Sabbath for such an embassy to Pilate is unlikely from a historical perspective.

63. *'After three days I will be raised'*: The opponents bring back the claims made by Jesus in Matt 16:21; 17:9; 17:23; 20:19 and point forward to the angel's proclamation in 28:6.

64. *the last deception*: The opponents' fear that Jesus' disciples would steal his body prepares for the story devised by the chief priests and guards in Matt 28:11-15. The "last deception" would be that Jesus was raised from the dead. It is difficult to be more precise about the "first" deception than to say that it refers to popular enthusiasm for Jesus as a leader ("King of the Jews").

65. *You have a guard*: The Greek term *koustodia* derives from the Latin *custodia* and refers to a guard of soldiers. Pilate's directive is ambiguous. Is he telling them to deploy their own Temple police? Or is he putting a guard at their disposal ("take a guard")? For the outcome see Matt 28:11-15. At any rate, the guard is under the direct control of the chief priests.

Interpretation

Matthew's account of Jesus' burial contains two segments: the placing of Jesus' body in the tomb (27:57-61) and the setting of a guard of soldiers over the tomb (27:62-66). The first episode is taken from Mark 15:42-47, and the second episode is without parallel in the Gospels. Both episodes provide evidence that Jesus was really dead, and that friends and foes alike knew where he was buried.

Matt 27:57-61 presents a somewhat different picture of Joseph of Arimathea from what appears in Mark 15:42-47. Whereas Mark could be taken to imply that Joseph as a member of the Sanhedrin took part in the condemnation of Jesus and saw to Jesus' burial only out of general motives ("looking for the kingdom of God"), Matthew insists that he had been a disciple of Jesus and makes no mention of his being a member of the council (*bouleutēs*). He also describes Joseph as "rich."

Other differences between Mark 15:42-47 and Matt 27:57-61 are attributable to Matthew's tendency to simplify Mark's account. Thus he omits the complicated reference to the day in Mark 15:42 ("since it was the day of Preparation, that is, the day before the Sabbath") and the account of the conversation between Pilate and the centurion about Jesus' death (Mark 15:44-45a). Matthew adds a few adjectives. Besides calling Joseph "rich" (Matt 27:57) he notes that the linen cloth was "clean" (27:59), that the tomb was "new" (27:60), and that the stone was "large" (27:60).

Despite the differences between Matt 27:57-61 and Mark 15:42-47 the basic thrust is the same. Both texts confirm that Jesus was really dead and that the women—Mary Magdalene and the "other Mary"—saw where Jesus was buried.

The same basic points are made also in the episode about setting the guard (Matt 27:62-66). Matthew may have composed this piece on his own as a defense against rumors that the disciples had stolen Jesus' body. Or he may have had access to a "Jerusalem source" for events connected with the passion (see Matt 27:3-10; 27:19; 27:51b-53; 27:62-66; 28:11-15). In either case the presuppositions of the second episode are that both Pilate and the Jewish leaders agree that Jesus was really dead, and that they knew where he was buried. The story about the guard is meant to give the lie to the rumor that Jesus' body had been stolen (see Matt 28:11-15). Thus the death of Jesus and the place of his tomb have been confirmed first by his friends and then by his foes.

From the NT and Jewish sources it is possible to gain some knowledge about the procedures surrounding Jesus' burial. The body of the deceased was washed (see Acts 9:37), anointed with oil and various spices (see Mark 16:1; Luke 24:1; John 12:7; 19:39), and wrapped in a shroud or linen cloths (Matt 27:59; Mark 15:46; Luke 23:53; John 19:40). The tomb in which Jesus was buried was the property of Joseph of Arimathea, part of the cemetery complex that surrounded Jerusalem. According to Matt 27:60 (see Mark 15:46; Luke 23:53; John 19:41) the tomb had been cut out of the limestone recently and Jesus was the first person to have been buried there.

The tomb was really a cave and was designed for multiple burials. After the corpse had been prepared for burial, it would have been laid out on one of the niches (*kôkîm*) or "bunk-like" platforms cut out of the sides of the cave. In Jesus' day the practice of secondary burial was in use. That is, the corpse would remain laid out on the niche for one year, and then the bones would be gathered (*ossilegium*) and placed in a stone "bone-box" (ossuary). On the box the name or names of the deceased might be inscribed. Thus a tomb might be used for entire families over several generations. For full treatments of Jewish burial practices see S. Safrai in *The Jewish People in the First Century* (Philadelphia: Fortress, 1976) 2.773-87; and E. M. Meyers, *Jewish Ossuaries: Reburial and Rebirth* (BibOr 24; Rome: Biblical Institute Press, 1971).

Given the circumstances of Jesus' death and the time constraints of Passover and the Sabbath, the burial of Jesus took place in great haste. At the same time, there was nothing particularly unusual about Jesus' burial. The owner of the tomb was known. The tomb had been sealed with a "large" stone—probably a large, round, flat (donut-like) stone fitted into a groove in front of the entrance to the tomb. And women followers of Jesus knew exactly where the tomb was. According to Matthew, so did the chief priests and Pharisees, and they set a guard of soldiers over it.

The Matthean account of Jesus' burial, especially the addition in Matt 27:62-66, indicates a controversy between Christians and their opponents. The opponents apparently claimed that Jesus' disciples had stolen his body (see Matt 28:11-15). Note that no one was arguing that the tomb was not empty. All agreed that the tomb was empty. The issue was how did it get empty. Matthew carefully established that Jesus was really dead, that the place of his burial was known to both friends and foes, and that there was a guard on the tomb under the direction of the chief priests and Pharisees. Thus he prepares for the Christian explanation of the empty tomb: Jesus was raised from the dead.

The story of Jesus' burial is a necessary presupposition for the resurrection. Belief in his resurrection cannot be established simply by establishing that the tomb was empty. Familiarity with Jewish burial customs in the first-century at least allows modern readers to get an accurate picture of the events being described. From the perspective of spirituality what shines forth from this text is the faithful witness of Mary Magdalene and the "other Mary." When everyone else had deserted the cause of Jesus, they remained with him until the very end.

For Reference and Further Study

Craig, W. L. "The Guard at the Tomb." *NTS* 30 (1984) 273–81.

80. *The Empty Tomb* (28:1-15)

1. After the Sabbath, at dawn on the first day of the week, Mary Magdalene and the other Mary came to see the tomb. 2. And behold there was a great earthquake. For an angel of the Lord descended from heaven and came and rolled away the stone and sat upon it. 3. His appearance was like lightning, and his clothing was as white as snow. 4. Out of fear of him the guards were shaken, and they became like dead men. 5. The angel answered and said to the women: "Do not be afraid. For I know that you seek Jesus who has been crucified. 6. He is not here. For he has been raised, as he said. Go, see the place where he was laid out. 7. And go quickly and say to his disciples: 'He has been raised from the dead; and behold he goes before you to Galilee—there you will see him.' Behold I have told you." 8. And they went away quickly from the tomb with fear and great joy, and they ran to tell his disciples. 9. And behold Jesus met them and said: "Greetings!" They came up and took hold of his feet and did homage to him. 10. Then Jesus said to them: "Do not be afraid. Go, tell your brothers that they should go off to Galilee, and there they will see me."

11. While they were going, some of the guard came into the city and told the chief priests all that had happened. 12. And when they gathered with the elders and took counsel, they gave sufficient silver pieces to the soldiers, 13. saying: "Say that his disciples came by night and stole him while we were asleep. 14. And if this is heard by the governor, we will persuade him and keep you free from care." 15. These took the money and did as they were instructed. And this story has been spread among Jews until this day.

Notes

1. *After the Sabbath*: The adverb *opse* is used as a preposition to mean "after." The adverb means "late"—so late that it becomes "after." Matthew notes that the women's visit took place "at dawn" (*epiphōskousę*); the other evangelists say "very early" (Mark 16:2); "at early dawn" (Luke 24:1); and "early" (John 20:1).

   the other Mary: Mary Magdalene and the "other Mary" remain the principles of continuity throughout the passion. These two women who saw Jesus die (Matt 27:56) and saw him buried (27:61) discovered his tomb empty on Easter Sunday morning (28:1). Matthew omits "anointing" as the reason for their going to the tomb (see Mark 16:1), perhaps because in his account Jesus had already been anointed for burial (see Matt 26:12). According to T. R. W. Longstaff, "The Women at the Tomb: Matthew 28:1 Re-examined," *NTS* 27 (1981) 277–82, it was a Jewish custom to watch the tomb of a loved one until the third day after death to ensure that premature burial had not taken place (see *Semaḥot* 8:1).

2. *a great earthquake*: Matthew uses the word *seismos* ("earthquake") not only in the stilling of the storm (8:24) but also in apocalyptic contexts—the eschatological discourse (24:7) and the resurrection of the saints (27:54). Here it underscores the resurrection of Jesus as an apocalyptic event.

   an angel of the Lord: Just as angels were prominent in the infancy narratives in communicating and clarifying God's will, so the angel here explains what happened and what the women are to do. Matthew uses the "angel" to identify the mysterious "young man" (*neaniskos*) of Mark 16:5 and to explain how the stone got rolled away from the entrance to the tomb (see Mark 16:3, "Who will roll away the stone . . . ?").

3. *his appearance*: In comparison with Mark 16:5 ("dressed in a white robe") Matthew gives a heightened picture of the angel's appearance. Yet the angel seems a bit less glorious than the transfigured Christ ("his face shone like the sun, and his garments became white as light") according to Matt 17:2.

4. *the guards*: Matthew continues the idea of a band of soldiers assigned to keep watch over Jesus' tomb lest his body be stolen (see Matt 27:62-66; 28:11-15). The verb "were shaken" (*eseisthēsan*) derives from the same root as "earthquake" (*seismos*) in Matt 28:2. The figure of the angel and the *seismos* explain how the guards could be overcome and powerless to keep Jesus' body under guard.

5. *the angel answered*: One of the reasons that led Matthew to identify the "young man" of Mark 16:5 as an angel was his role as the interpreter of the scene. The "angelic interpreter" is a common figure in apocalyptic writings from the Book of Zechariah onward.

6. *He is not here. For he has been raised, as he said*: Matthew has added "as he said" (see Mark 16:6), thus linking resurrection to the three passion predictions (see Matt 16:21-23; 17:22-23; 20:18-19). The explanation ("he has been raised") does not follow directly from the fact that the tomb was found empty. Rather it is the interpretation or explanation given to the empty tomb.

7. *say to his disciples*: Given Matthew's particular interest in Peter, it is surprising that he omits the explicit mention of Peter in Mark 16:7 ("say to his disciples and to Peter"). Matthew adds to the proclamation "he has been raised from the dead."

   to Galilee—there you will see him: The sentence reminds the reader of Jesus' promise in Matt 26:32 that after he was raised up, he would go before his disciples to Galilee. In Luke 24 and John 20 the appearances of the risen Jesus take place in the area of Jerusalem. In Matt 28:16-20 and John 21 he appears in Galilee. The text of Mark 16 breaks off at verse 8; Mark 16:9-20 is a later addition.

   I have told you: Mark 16:7 reads "as he told you," which Matthew has already used in Matt 28:6. The change here may be intended to refute the charge that the disciples had staged the whole sequence of events.

8. *with fear and great joy*: Whereas in Mark 16:8 fear reduces the women to silence, in Matt 28:8 their joy leads them to proclaim to the disciples what they had seen.

9. *Jesus met them*: The appearance of Jesus to the women sounds like a compressed version of John 20:11-18. The distinctive Matthean terms "they came up (=approached) . . . did homage to him" suggest the correct stance toward the risen Lord (see Matt 28:16-20) and indicate that Matthew has shaped the story for his own purposes, especially to emphasize worship as the proper attitude toward Jesus (see Matt 2:1-12).

10. *they should go off to Galilee*: There is a striking similarity between the messages of the angel and of the risen Jesus. So much so that they seem to be doublets (two versions of the same story). The repetition serves the function of placing even more emphasis on the climactic appearance in Galilee (Matt 28:16-20).

11. *some of the guard*: The use of the Latin loanword *koustodia* links Matt 28:11-15 to 27:62-66. That the guards report to the chief priests follows from Matt 27:65 where Pilate says "You have a guard." But it does not solve the problem whether the soldiers are the Temple police under the chief priest's command or Roman soldiers under Pilate's command.

12. *took counsel*: The plan of the high priests and elders, who have been the chief antagonists of Jesus since the beginning of the passion story, is called a *symboulion* (see Matt 12:14; 22:15; 27:7). According to Matthew they bribed the guards to say that Jesus' disciples stole his body.

14. *we will persuade him*: The chief priests and elders are confident that Pilate too would wish to avoid any popular enthusiasm and possible uprising connected with the empty tomb.

15. *until this day*: The expression suggests that a substantial amount of time has intervened between the event and the time of the writer. It also indicates that the rumor still circulates and needs a refutation from the Christian side.

Interpretation

Though clearly based on Mark 16:1-8, Matthew's account of the empty tomb of Jesus (28:1-15) is a reworked and expanded version. The first part (28:1-8) is a reworking in which Matthew seems most concerned to tidy up the Markan narrative. Matthew is careful to name the same two women as the principles of continuity regarding Jesus' death, burial, and empty tomb (Matt 27:55, 61; 28:1) in contrast to the inconsistent lists in Mark (15:40, 47; 16:1). He does not say that the women went to the tomb to anoint Jesus' body as Mark 16:1 does, since it had already been anointed by the unnamed woman (Matt 26:12; Mark 14:8). The mysterious "young man" of Mark 16:5 is identified as an angel in Matt 28:2, 5. The Markan mystery of how the stone had been rolled away (16:3-4) is cleared up by attributing this act to the angel (Matt 28:2). The apocalyptic character of Jesus' resurrection is underlined by references to the *seismos* (28:2, 4) and by the figure of the angelic interpreter (28:5-7). The strange silence attributed to the women by Mark 16:8 is turned into a joyful proclamation to the disciples in Matt 28:8. On the whole, Matthew shows more freedom in dealing with the empty tomb than with the passion narrative. His reworking of Mark 16:1-8 is a rather radical revision.

The second part (Matt 28:9-15) has no parallel in Mark. It consists of two sections: the appearance of the risen Jesus (28:9-10), and the plot between the chief priests and the guards (28:11-15). If Matt 28:9-10 is a compression of the appearance to Mary Magdalene in John 20:11-18, Matthew has edited it with particular emphasis on the women's response to the risen Jesus: They approach (*proselthousai*) and worship (*prosekynēsan*) him (Matt 28:9). Then the risen Jesus delivers to the women the same message that the angel had previously delivered at the tomb. This double stress on Galilee as the place in which the disciples will see Jesus serves to prepare for the climactic appearance in Matt 28:16-20.

The second section (Matt 28:11-15) takes up the story of the guard at the tomb. How the guard came to be was described in Matt 27:62-66. Matthew has already explained that at the appearance of the angel at the tomb the guards were overwhelmed by the *seismos* and fainted out of fear (Matt 28:4). This section explains why the guards did not corroborate the testimony of Mary Magdalene and the other Mary: They were bribed by the chief priests and elders to say that Jesus' disciples stole his body.

According to Matt 28:6 the angel announced to the women: "He is not here. For he has been raised." There is no NT account of Jesus' resurrection; there are only stories of the empty tomb and appearances of the risen Jesus. Yet from the Christian perspective the resurrection of Jesus is the presupposition not only of these stories but of the entire New Testament: "If Christ has not been raised, then our preaching is in vain and your faith is in vain" (1 Cor 15:14).

Resurrection refers to a rising from death to life. It is not the same as resuscitation or reanimation. It assumes that the person has died and has been dead for a period of time, and when resurrected, will not die again. Among Jews of Jesus' time resurrection was expected to occur at the end of human history as part of the coming of God's kingdom. Then the just would be restored to full life—body and soul; and the wicked would either be restored for eternal punishment or annihilated. Resurrection was understood as eschatological and corporate. The kind of immortality related to resurrection is not a consequence of human nature (as in the Greek doctrine of the immortality of the soul) but rather a gift from God.

Except in a few late texts (Dan 12:1-3; 2 Maccabees 7) it is difficult to find an OT basis for the Jewish belief in resurrection. There are, of course, texts that speak about the restoration of Israel (see Ezek 37:1-14; Hos 6:1-2; 13:14) and of individuals (Gen 5:21-24; 1 Kgs 17:17-24; 2 Kgs 2:1-13; 4:20-37; Isa 53:10; Ps 16:10). There are phrases in Isaiah that move toward a doctrine of resurrection: "He will swallow up death forever" (25:8); "Thy dead shall live, their bodies shall rise. O dwellers in the dust, awake and sing for joy!" (26:19). The clearest affirmation of Jewish faith in resurrection comes in Dan 12:2: "And many of those who sleep in the dust of the earth shall awake, some to everlasting life, and some to shame and everlasting contempt." Even in NT times, however, not all Jews accepted resurrection as an article of faith. Whereas the Pharisees championed it, the Sadducees rejected it (see Acts 23:6-8; Matt 22:23; Mark 12:18; Luke 20:27).

The early Christians followed the Pharisees regarding belief in the resurrection of the dead, with one notable difference. According to Christian faith Jesus has anticipated the eschatological resurrection that will accompany God's kingdom in its fullness. Or to put it another way, the resurrection of Jesus is a sign that God's kingdom has already broken into human history.

When early Christians proclaimed that Jesus "has been raised," they generally used the passive voice as a way of indicating that it was the Father's action in Christ: God raised up Jesus. For evidence they appealed first of all to the appearances of the risen Jesus to his disciples and other believers: "he appeared to Cephas, then to the Twelve. Then he appeared to more than five hundred brethren at one time, most of whom are still alive, though some have fallen asleep. Then he appeared to James, then to all the apostles. Last of all, as to one untimely born, he appeared also to me" (1 Cor 15:5-8). The Gospels (Matthew 28; Luke 24; John 20–21; Mark 16:9-20) provide still other appearances of the risen Jesus. These appearances all are experienced by those who already knew or believed in Jesus. Care is taken to insist that these experiences were not dreams, visions, hallucinations, etc. Jesus is not a ghost; he eats and drinks, though his risen body has certain superhuman properties (see John 20:19).

The other type of account connected with the resurrection of Jesus is the empty tomb story. The angel's announcement in Matt 28:6 expresses the nature of such accounts: "He is not here. For he has been raised." The emptiness of the tomb demands an explanation. Several explanations are possible: The women got the wrong tomb; the disciples stole the body; Jesus revived from only apparent death and wandered off on his own; or Jesus was raised from the dead.

Matthew narrows down the explanation to two options: Either the disciples stole Jesus' body (as his Jewish opponents maintained), or Jesus had been raised from the dead. In his narrative of Jesus on the cross Matthew gathered testimony that Jesus was really dead (see Matt 27:54, 57-66) and that Mary Magdalene and the "other Mary" knew where he was buried (see Matt 27:55-56, 61; 28:1). Matthew notes that the rumor about the disciples having stolen Jesus' body "has been spread among Jews until this day'' (28:15). The phrase suggests that this explanation remained current among the Jewish opponents of the Matthean community. The references to the guard set over Jesus' tomb (Matt 27:62-66; 28:4, 11-15) are clearly designed to combat their explanation. According to those texts the chief priests had guards at Jesus' tomb, the guards fainted at the earthquake and angelic appearance, and then the two groups concocted the story about the stealing of Jesus' body. Thus Matthew tries to show how the story arose and why it should not be believed. The only remaining option is the angel's explanation that Jesus had been raised.

The polemical context indicated by Matt 28:15 helps to explain why Matthew felt the need to tidy up Mark's account of the empty tomb. Using data already in Mark 16:1-8, Matthew revised the story to make it more consistent and more convincing. Whatever the origin of the curious doublet whereby the angel and the risen Jesus give the same message to the women (see Matt 28:7-10), the effect is to highlight Galilee as the place for the climactic appearance in 28:16-20. If Matthew and his opponents were located in Galilee, this emphasis on Galilee would add to the readers' interest—just as mentions of one's hometown usually increase interest in a book or motion picture today.

The Matthean account of the empty tomb, with its strong note of controversy, provides an important lesson for readers today. The empty tomb is the necessary presupposition for Christian belief in Jesus' resurrection. By itself it does not prove Jesus' resurrection, for the emptiness of the tomb can be explained in several ways. Christians must also appeal to the appearance stories and to the growth and development of the Church as additional supports for their belief.

The controversy surrounding the empty tomb ought not to obscure the startling content of the early Christian proclamation about Jesus: ''He has been raised'' (Matt 28:6). An event reserved for the end of human history has happened in the midst of human history. In the special case of Jesus God has shown his eschatological power by raising Jesus. To this extent at least the kingdom of God is among us.

81. *The Great Commission* (28:16-20)

16. The eleven disciples came into Galilee to the mountain to which Jesus had directed them. 17. And on seeing him they paid him homage, but some hesitated. 18. And Jesus approached and spoke to them, saying: "All power in heaven and on earth has been given to me. 19. Go, make disciples of all the Gentiles, baptizing them in the name of the Father and of the Son and of the Holy Spirit, 20. teaching them to observe all that I have commanded you. And behold I am with you all days until the end of the age."

Notes

16. *eleven disciples*: The circle of the Twelve who accompanied Jesus has been depleted by the defection and suicide of Judas (see Matt 27:3-10). Matthew says nothing about restoring the number to twelve as in Acts 1:12-26.

    into Galilee to the mountain: The disciples' movement takes place in accord with Jesus' prophecy in Matt 26:32 and the double announcement by the angel and Jesus in Matt 28:7, 10. Speculation about which mountain it was is pointless. No direct connection is made with the mount of transfiguration (Matt 17:1). In fact up to this point no mention was made of a mountain in connection with the appearance.

17. *on seeing him they paid him homage*: The emphasis is less on the fact of the appearance ("on seeing him") and more on the proper response of worship or homage (see Matt 2:2, 8, 11; 4:9-10; 8:2; etc.).

    but some hesitated: The Greek verb *distazō* can be translated "hesitate" or "doubt." There is a longstanding grammatical debate about whether all of the eleven disciples both paid Jesus homage and doubted, or some paid homage and others doubted. From a grammatical perspective it would appear that some worshipped Jesus and others doubted him; see P. W. van der Horst, "Once More: The Translation of *hoi de* in Matthew 28:17," *JSNT* 27 (1986) 27–30. Why they hesitated or doubted is not clear. Perhaps it was at the possibility of such an experience or at the appropriateness of "worshipping" Jesus.

18. *Jesus approached*: Whereas in Matthew others usually approach Jesus, here he approaches (*proselthōn*) the eleven disciples.

    all power in heaven and on earth: With this claim the risen Jesus accepts what is said about the "one like a Son of Man" in Dan 7:14: "And to him was given dominion and glory and kingdom, that all peoples, nations, and languages should serve him. . . . "

19. *make disciples of all the Gentiles*: In Jesus' final command Matthew's favorite term *mathētēs* ("disciple") is made into a verb ("make disciples"). Does the phrase *panta ta ethnē* refer to the Gentiles (non-Jews) or does it include Israel also ("the nations")? Several lines of argument point to it as referring to Gentiles only: the use of Greek *ethnē* and Hebrew *gôyîm* at the time, the uses of *ethnos/ethnē* elsewhere in Matthew, the use of *panta ta ethnē* to refer to Gentiles (Matt 24:9,

14; 25:32), the theology that the gospel be preached to Jews first (Matt 10:5), and patristic interpretations. See D. R. A. Hare and D. J. Harrington, " 'Make Disciples of All the Gentiles' (Mt 28:19)," *CBQ* 37 (1975) 359–69. For a rebuttal see J. P. Meier, "Nations or Gentiles in Matthew 28:19?" *CBQ* 39 (1977) 94–102.

baptizing them: There has been no preparation for mention of baptism up to this point. The Trinitarian formula accompanying Jesus' command adds to the suspicion that the risen Jesus' language has been shaped in light of the experience of the early Church, in this case by a baptismal formula (see *Didache* 7:1-3).

20. *teaching*: The disciples are commanded to carry on what was a major task of the earthly Jesus in the Gospel. The content of their teaching ("all that I have commanded you") and what is expected of them ("to observe") treats the teaching of Jesus as authoritative.

I am with you: Jesus' promise serves as an inclusion with the name "Emmanuel" ("God with us") in Matt 1:22-23. See also Jesus' self-revelation while walking on the water ("it is I") in 14:23 and his promise to be present where two or three are gathered in his name (see Matt 18:20). In Matthew the risen Jesus fulfills the functions attributed elsewhere in the New Testament to the Holy Spirit.

until the end of the age: The promise assumes the division between "this age (world)/the age (world) to come," which is familiar from Jewish apocalyptic writings. It envisions an abiding presence of the risen Lord among Christians.

INTERPRETATION

The climactic appearance of the risen Jesus to the eleven disciples in Galilee (Matt 28:16-20) is found only in Matthew's Gospel. It consists of the appearance proper (28:16-18a) and the declaration by Jesus (28:18b-20). The declaration may be divided into three segments: the self-revelation of Jesus' power and authority (18b), the mission-charge to the disciples (19-20a), and the promise to be present and to help (20b). A detailed analysis of vocabulary and style indicates that in all likelihood Matthew himself composed the passage; see J. D. Kingsbury, "The Composition and Christology of Matt 28:16-20," *JBL* 93 (1974) 573–84.

A major scholarly concern in studying Matt 28:16-20 has been the search for a biblical prototype of Jesus' great commission. The language of Dan 7:14 (especially in the Septuagint) makes it a likely inspiration for the segment about Jesus' power and authority (18b) as well as the references to the *ethnē* ("all peoples, nations, and languages should serve him") and to the presence of the risen Lord for "all days" ("his dominion is an everlasting dominion, which shall not pass away, and his kingdom one that shall not be destroyed"). With this scene of the "one like a Son of Man" receiving power from the "Ancient of Days" the various uses of the "Son of Man" title throughout the Gospel—generic, death and resurrection, apocalyptic figure—come together in one climactic scene and reach their fullness in the risen Jesus.

Not all the elements in Matt 28:18b-20 are explained by reference to Dan 7:14. And so various scholars have pointed to other possible prototypes: the theophany in Exodus 19–20, the priestly blessing in Num 6:22-27, the prophetic commissions, and the royal decree of Cyrus in 2 Chr 36:23. Other scholars have attempted to get behind the Matthean text and to reconstruct the source or sources at the evangelist's disposal. While there is some value in such endeavors, the more important matter is to determine what the text as it stands may have meant for the Matthean community.

It is possible to view Matt 28:16-20 as a summary of the whole Gospel. Jesus whose story has been told throughout the Gospel appears as the risen Lord who is worthy to be approached in an attitude of homage or worship. The teacher par excellence commissions his disciples to carry on his teaching mission. The Son of Man affirms that all authority has been given to him. The Son of God directs that the Gentiles be baptized in his name. And "Emmanuel" (see Matt 1:22-23) promises to be with his followers until the end of the present age. Thus many of the major Christological motifs developed in the course of the Gospel return at a mature level in Matt 28:16-20.

The theme of discipleship also reaches maturity in the climactic appearance. The inner circle of Jesus' disciples who previously were characterized as showing "little faith" react appropriately (but with some diffidence) to the risen Lord. And they receive their commission to make disciples, baptize, and teach as well as the promise of Jesus' helping presence (the Matthean equivalence of the Holy Spirit). Thus the theme of discipleship so prominent throughout the Gospel comes to a certain ripeness in Matt 28:16-20.

If the disciples are commissioned to make disciples of "all the Gentiles," the great commission may well have also carried a very concrete message to the Matthean community. It would have had the function of urging a largely Jewish-Christian group to seek new members not so much from their fellow Jews as from non-Jews. The gospel, which was preached first to Jews (see Matt 10:5), is now to be opened up to non-Jews. Therefore the great commission may mark the beginning of a new chapter in the history of the Matthean community. At the same time it might carry the implication that all the Jews who could be expected to come to faith in Jesus had already done so. The mission field changes from other Jews to Gentiles. The Church and the synagogue in Matthew's area are thus on the way to definitive separation.

As a summary of the entire Gospel, Matt 28:16-20 brings out its most important themes: The Father has given Jesus supreme and universal authority. The disciples are to share their discipleship not only with their fellow Jews but also with non-Jews. The spirit of the risen Jesus will guide and protect the Church until God's kingdom comes in its fullness.

For Reference and Further Study

Barth, G. *Tradition and Interpretation,* 131–37.

Friedrich, G. "Die formale Struktur von Mt 28, 18-20." *ZTK* 80 (1983) 137–83.

Hubbard, B. J. *The Matthean Redaction of a Primitive Apostolic Commissioning: An Exegesis of Matthew 28:16-20.* SBLDS 19. Missoula: Scholars, 1974.

Kingsbury, J. D. "The Composition and Christology of Matt 28:16-20." *JBL* 93 (1974) 573–84.

Lange, J. *Das Erscheinen des Auferstandenen im Evangelium nach Matthäus. Eine traditions- und redaktiongeschichtliche Untersuchung zu Mt 28, 16-20.* Würzburg: Echter, 1973.

Malina, B. J. "The Literary Structure and Form of Matt. XXVIII. 16-20." *NTS* 17 (1970) 87–103.

Schaberg, J. *The Father, the Son and the Holy Spirit. The Triadic Phrase in Matthew 28:19b.* SBLDS 61. Chico: Scholars, 1982.

Zumstein, J. "Matthieu 28:16-20." *RTP* 22 (1972) 14–33.

INDEXES

1. *PRINCIPAL ANCIENT PARALLELS*

1. Old Testament

Genesis
1:2 62
1:27 273
2:24 273
4:17-26 31
4:24 269
6:1-4 79–80
19 141
22:10 63
28:12 63
48:14-15 276

Exodus
1–2 47
3:6 313
3:15-16 313
7–8 48
10:22 399
12:13 369
20:8-11 175
20:12 229
20:13 86
20:14 87
20:16 88
21:17 229
21:32 364
22:26-27 89
23:12 175
24 255
24:3-11 371
24:8 368
30:11-16 261, 294
34:21 172, 175

Leviticus
13–14 112–13
15:11 232
18:6-18 92, 274
18:16 215
19:2 90
19:12 88
19:13 283
19:17 103, 269
19:18 89, 105, 315–16
20:9 229
24:5-9 172
24:16 380

Numbers
24:17 42, 48–49, 137

Deuteronomy
5:6 229
5:12-15 175
5:17 86
5:18 87
5:20 88
6–8 68–70
6:5 315–16
6:13 67
6:16 67, 69
7:6-9 68
8:2 69
8:3 66
8:5 68
8:10 220
14:1 89
15:9 101
16:16 370
17:6 379
19:15 269
21:7 389
21:15-17 101
21:23 397–98, 405
22:6-7 81
22:23-27 34, 37
23:25 172
24:1 87, 273
25:1-3 145
25:5-10 312–13
27:25 385
31:12 108
32:5 257
32:45 109, 361

Judges
13:5, 7 46

1 Samuel
21:1-6 172, 174

2 Samuel
5:2 43
5:8 294

1 Kings
10:1-13 188–190
19:20 119
21 217
22:17 137

2 Kings
1:3-4 329
1:8 51, 53
2–6 133–34
4:31 257
4:42-44 221
13:2 38

Isaiah
1:9-10 165
2:2-4 237
2:2-5 80
5:1-7 284, 304
6:9-10 196, 200
7:14 35-36, 40
8:23–9:1 71, 74
11:1 46
14 165
22:22 251
23:1-12 165
25:6 221
29:13 230
29:18 182
35:5-6 159, 182, 239–40
40–66 237
40:3 51, 54
40:6-8 102
40:8 342
42:1-4 180–81
42:2 388
51:1-2 251
52:15 388
53:4 115, 117
53:7 379, 388
53:11-12 287
53:12 368, 395
54:5 350
56:7 294
60:2 44
60:21 230
61:2-3 79
62:11 293
65:4 120
65:24 95
66:1 88

Jeremiah
7:11 294
8:4-12 297
8:13 297–98
12:10 284
15:7 59
16:16 72
19:11 385
31:15-17 44–45
31:32 350

Ezekiel
7:19 280
28 165
34:5 187
34:6 265
34:15-16 265
37:1-14 400–01, 403
38:19 120

Hosea
2:16 350
6:2 379, 382
6:6 126, 129, 172
9:10, 16 297
11:1 44

Amos
8:9 399

Micah
5:1(2) 43
7:6 145, 147

Zechariah
8:20-23 237
9:9 293, 295
11:13 385–86
12:10-12 338
13:7 137, 368, 375
14:4 293, 295, 332

Malachi
4:5 256

Psalms
1 82
2:2 315
2:7 382
8:3 294
22 399–403
22:1 399
22:7 396
22:8 396
22:18 395
22:27-28 401
24:3-4 79
36:7 329
37:11 79
41:9 367
69 224, 226–27
69:9 396
69:21 395, 399–400
72:10 44
74:13-14 123
78:2 205–06, 209
89:10-12 123
91 67
107:5-9 79
107:23-30 123
107:23-32 226
107:29 120
110:1 317–19, 379
118:22 251
118:22-23 303
118:26 294, 329

Job
9:8 226

Proverbs
9:1-18 307
14:21 79
15:16 280
17:5 79
27:1 102
30:8-9 280

Ruth
4:18-22 28, 31–32

Esther
5:3 215, 217

Daniel
7:13-14 340–41, 379
7:14 414–16
12:2 412
12:3 206

Ezra
9–10 237

Nehemiah
10:30 237
10:32 261
13:23-31 237

1 Chronicles
2–3 28–29, 31–32
29:11-12 95

2 Chronicles
18:16 137
36:16 80

Sirach
31:5-7 280
51:1-12 169
51:23-30 170
51:26 168

Tobit
4:15 105

Wisdom
2:18 396

2. Early Jewish Writings

2 Baruch
11:2 330
27:6-7 332
29:4 123
51:10 312
72 359
72:4-6 359
83:1 337
85:3 316

Biblical Antiquities
1–10 31
9:9-15 47-48
9:10 38
19:13 337
60:3 186

1 Enoch
91, 93 95
91:14 359

4 Ezra
3:30 330
5:1-2, 9-10 334
7:77 101
8:3 306
8:41 200
9:3-4 334
9:16 306
9:31-37 200
13:31-32 332
13:33-49 359

Jubilees
4:7-33 31
8:5-9 31

Psalms of Solomon
17–18 159–60
17:30 295
17:37 380

Testament of Benjamin
10:8-9 359

Testament of Moses
10 95

Testament of Naphtali
6:1-10 227

3. Dead Sea Scrolls

Damascus Document
4:19–5:2 275
9:2-3 271
11:13-14 173, 176–77

Genesis Apocryphon
20:16-30 186
20:28-29 131

Manual of Discipline
1:10 89
1:11-13 280
2:11-17 267
2:23 266
3–4 110, 124, 209
3:8-9 60
5:24–6:2 271
9:21 89

Thanksgiving Hymns
6:24-28 251

War Scroll
4:10 248
7:6 375

4. Josephus and Philo

Antiquities
2:205-37 48
17:271-85 332, 338, 383–84

18:16 313
18:116-19 52, 155, 161
18:118 300
18:118-19 216
18:312 262
20:97-98 245
20:160-72 293, 376

Jewish War
4:334-44 329
7:43 9
7:218 262

Legation to Gaius
299–305 391–92

Life of Moses
1:276 49

Special Laws
1:77 262

5. Rabbinic Writings

a. *Mishnah*

'Abot
1:1 86, 229, 231, 354
1:4-15 138
1:13 140
2:1 81
2:8 138
3:2 269
5:6 357

Berakot
3:1 119
5:5 151, 153

Gittin
9:10 92, 275

Ketubot
4:4 132

Ma'aśerot
1:1 326

Nedarim
1:1 325

Šabbat
7:2 172

Sanhedrin
3:12 88
7:1 286
7:5 380

Soṭa
1:5 35
1:7 103
9:15 334

Yoma
8:6 173

b. *Tosefta*

Pe'a
4:18 101

c. *Babylonian Talmud*

'Arakin
16b 103

Berakot
29a 140
34b 114, 116–17
55b 278
58b 145

'Erubin
43a-b 161

Gittin
68a 291

Šabbat
31a 105, 316
119a 261

Semaḥot
8:1 409

Yebamot
63a 276

d. *Other Writings*

Canticles Rabba
2:14 144–45

Exodus Rabba
1 103

Targum Neofiti of Genesis
22:10 63
28:12 63

6. New Testament

Mark
1:2-6 52
1:7-8 59
1:9-11 62–63
1:14-20 73
1:29-34 116
1:40-45 115
2:1-12 123
2:13-22 127
2:23–3:6 174–75
3:7-12 180–81
3:13-19 137
3:22-30 185
4:1-20 199
4:21-34 208
4:35-41 122
5:1-20 122
5:21-43 133
6:1-6 212
6:7-13 141
6:14-29 216

6:35-44 220
6:45-52 225
7:1-23 231–32
7:24-30 236–37
7:31-37 239–40
8:1-10 241–42
8:11-21 244–45
8:27–9:1 249–50
9:2-13 255–56
9:14-29 258–59
9:30-32 261
9:33-50 266
10:1-12 274–75
10:17-31 279
10:32-45 288
10:46-52 290–91
11:1-11 294–95
11:12-14 297
11:15-17 295
11:18-21 297
11:27-33 300
12:1-12 303-04
12:13-17 310
12:18-27 313
12:28-34 315
12:35-37 318
13:1-13 333–34
13:14-27 338–39
13:28-37 344
14:1-11 363–64
14:12-31 369
14:32-52 375–76
14:53-72 381–82
15:1-15 386, 390–91
15:16-32 396–97
15:33-41 401–02
15:42-47 406
16:1-8 410–11

Luke
1–2 53
3:7-9 56
3:16-17 59
3:23-38 30, 32–33
4:1-13 68–69
6:20-23 82
7:1-10 115–16
7:18-35 158–59
10:7 140
10:13-15 164
10:21-22 168
11:2-4 97–98
11:24-26 192
11:29-30 189
11:37-52 322, 326–27, 329
13:34-35 329
14:15-21 307
15:4-7 266
17:26-27 344–45
17:34-35 343
19:11-27 353–54

John
1:6-9 54
1:19-23 54
7:42 43
9:2 124
19:13 389
19:34 400

Acts
1:18-19 385–86
5:35-39 332, 338
18:24-28 54
19:1-7 54
19:13-20 186

Romans
2:9-10 359
5–8 124
9–11 197–98, 209–10
11:17, 24 238
11:25-26 333–34

1 Corinthians
3:11 251
6:2-3 359
9:14 140
11:25 367
12–14 266
15:14 411

2 Corinthians
11:7 140

Ephesians
2:20 251

James
4:11-12 103

1 Peter
4:17 359

2 Peter
3:3-4 345

Revelation
13:10 375

7. Early Christian Writings

Didache
7:3 415
8:1 126, 128
8:3 98–99
9:5 103
11–13 142, 153
12 140
14:1 178

Ignatius, Magnesians
9:1 178

2. *SUBJECTS*

Abomination of Desolation, 336–39
Announcement of Birth, 38
Anthropology, 150–51, 153
Anti-Semitism, 20–22
Apocalyptic, 255, 339–41
Apostleship, 153

Banquet, 220–23, 242, 307–08
Baptism, 60, 63–65
Barabbas, 388–89
Beatitudes, 78, 82–83
Bridegroom, 349–51
Burial, 406–07

Caesarea Philippi, 250–51
Capernaum, 71
Celibacy, 276
Children, 266
Christology, 18
Church, 251
Community, 266–67, 270–72
Crucifixion, 397–98, 401–03
Cup, 288–89, 373
Cynics, 142

Daniel, 339–41
Day of the Lord, 56
Disciples, 19
Divorce, 87–88, 91–92, 273, 275
Dreams, 37–38

Eighteen Benedictions, 98–99
Elijah, 161, 254–56
Elisha, 133–34, 221
Epilepsy, 259
Even Bohan, 4
Exorcism, 186–87

Fasting, 128
Fig tree, 297
Fishing, 72
Flock (of Israel), 137
Food Laws, 232–33
Fourth Ezra, 12–13, 108
Fulfillment Quotations, 17, 38–39

Galilee, 73–74
Genealogies, 30–33
Gentiles, 49, 71, 117, 414–16
Golden Rule, 105–06

Hanina ben Dosa, 114, 116–17
Hardening, 200–01
Herod Antipas, 214–18
Herod Archaelaus, 45
Herod the Great, 41–42
Hippocrates, 259

Illegitimacy, 39
Irony, 364

Jebel Hallet eṭ-Ṭuri Inscription, 232
Jeremiah, 247
Jewish Piety, 96–97
John the Baptist, 52–55, 158–62, 216–18, 300
Jonah, 188–89
Josephus, 10–12, 52–53, 390–91

Kaddish, 95
King of the Jews, 388, 396–98
Kingdom, 18–19, 51, 57–58, 72, 79
Korban, 232–33

Last Judgment, 280–81, 357–60
Leprosy, 112
"Little Faith," 258–60

Magi, 42, 48–49
Marriage, 36, 349–51
Messiah, 159–60, 247
Miracles, 187
Missionaries, 142–44
Moses, 46–49

Nazareth, 45

Ossuary, 407

Papias, 3–4
Parables, 198–99
Parousia, 333–35, 345–47, 353–55
Passover, 369–71
People of God, 19, 192–93
Persecution, 146–48
Peter, 226–28, 250–52, 383
Pharisees, 15–16, 56–58, 322
Pilate, 385, 388–93
Plan of Salvation, 237–38
Prayer Before Meals, 220, 367
Prayer of Nabonidus, 186
Prophet, 329–30
Proselyte Baptism, 60

Queen of Sheba, 188–90
Qumran Community, 50–51, 54, 60, 89, 221, 230, 248, 256, 266, 271, 280, 344

Rabbinic Movement, 14–15
Reception of the Gospel, 197–202, 208–09
Resurrection, 313–14, 410–13
Retribution, 110
Revolutionaries, 376–78, 382–83
Ritual Purity, 59–60, 232–33

Sabbath, 174–79
Sadducees, 56–58
Scribes, 322
Second Baruch, 13, 108
Sending Christology, 154
Sermon on the Mount, 76–77
Servant of God, 180–81
Sign Prophets, 245–46
Signs of the End, 334
Sinners, 128
Solomon, 186, 291
Son of Abraham, 31–32
Son of David, 31–32, 291–92, 295, 317–19
Son of God, 66, 68–70
Son of Man, 147–48
Storm at Sea, 123, 226–27
Synagogue, 212–13
Synoptic Problem, 6–7
Syria, 73

Targums, 63–64
Taxes, 127–28, 261–62, 310–11
Temple, 295, 382–83
Testing, 66, 68–70
Thanksgiving Hymns, 166, 169, 227
Theudas, 245
Tiberius, 310
Toledot Yeshu, 39
Torah, 17–18, 83–84, 90–92, 316
Tradition, 231–34
Treatise of Shem, 42
Trial of Jesus, 381–84, 390–93
Twelve Tribes, 138

Unrepentant Cities, 165–66

Vineyard, 284, 304

Wisdom, 169–70
Woes, 326–27
Women, 32

3. *AUTHORS*

Addley, W. P., 267
Agbanou, V. K., 335
Aguirre, R., 404
Aland, K., 3, 7
Allen, W. C., 22
Allison, D. C., 23, 106, 154, 157, 330
Annen, F., 125
Argyle, A. W., 348

Bacchiocchi, S., 170
Bacon, B. W., 23
Banks, R., 84
Barbour, R. S., 321
Barré, M., 79, 285
Barrick, W. B., 404
Barth, G., 23, 179, 234, 417
Bartnicki, R., 144, 149
Bauer, D. R., 23
Bauman, C., 77
Beare, F. W., 22, 139
Betz, H. D., 77, 111
Betz, O., 61
Bigane, J. E., 252
Black, D. A., 78, 86
Black, M., 154
Blinzler, J., 384
Bokser, B. M., 371
Bonnard, P., 22
Booth, R. P., 234
Bornkamm, G., 23, 125
Brandenburger, E., 360
Brandon, S. G. F., 384
Brooks, S. H., 7, 23
Brown, R. E., 28, 40, 50, 252, 365
Brown, S., 139
Burgess, J. A., 252
Burnett, F. W., 281, 335

Cameron, P. S., 157
Campbell, K. M., 81
Caragounis, C. C., 252
Carlston, C. E., 257
Carmignac, J., 99
Casey, M., 125
Cassidy, R. J., 263
Catchpole, D. R., 360
Christian, P., 360
Cohen, M., 179
Cohen Stuart, G. H., 196
Cohn-Sherbok, D. M., 179, 314
Comber, J. A., 166
Conrad, E. W., 40
Conzelmann, H., 266
Cook, M. J., 20
Cope, L., 23, 218, 360
Court, J. M., 356
Craig, W. L., 408
Crawford, B., 149
Culbertson, P., 285
Cullmann, O., 252

Daniel, C., 244
Davies, S. L., 51
Davies, W. D., 23, 40, 48, 50
Deidun, T., 272
de Jonge, M., 400, 404
Derrett, J. D. M., 131, 281, 285
Deutsch, C., 170, 171
de Vaux, R., 36
Didier, M., 23
Dodd, C. H., 198, 202
Donahue, J. R., 130, 202, 360
Dorneich, M., 99
Doyle, B. R., 181
Duling, D. C., 132, 186, 235, 291, 292

Dunn, J. D. G., 59, 65
Dupont, J., 68, 70, 84

Edwards, W. D., 402

Faierstein, M., 157
Feldman, L. H., 55
Fenton, J. C., 23
Feuillet, A., 351
Filson, F. V., 23
Fitzmyer, J. A., 40, 88, 92, 157, 234, 393, 398
Fleddermann, H., 224
Flusser, D., 106
Fowler, R. M., 223
France, R. T., 23, 44, 50
Frankemölle, H., 23
Frerichs, W. S., 159
Freyne, S., 74
Friedlander, G., 77
Friedrich, G., 417
Fuller, R. H., 317
Furnish, V. P., 317

Gabel, W. J., 402
García Martínez, F., 272
Garland, D. E., 324
Gerhardsson, B., 23, 68, 70, 202, 384
Giblin, C. H., 311
Gibson, J., 301
Giesen, H., 298
Glasson, T. F., 338
Gnilka, J., 3, 23, 61, 202
Gnuse, R., 50
Grassi, J. A., 139
Gray, S. W., 360
Green, W. S., 159
Guelich, R. A., 77, 85
Gundry, R. H., 23

Haas, N., 398
Hamerton-Kelly, R., 85
Hanson, J. S., 376
Hare, D. R. A., 24, 147, 415
Harner, P. B., 99
Harrington, D. J., 192, 415
Hay, D. M., 319
Heater, H., 28
Heil, J. P., 228
Held, H. J., 23, 223, 238, 240, 242
Hengel, M., 125
Hicks, J. M., 179
Hiers, R. H., 296
Hill, D., 23, 111, 130, 404
Hoet, R., 324
Holmes, M. W., 80
Homeau, H. A., 263
Hooker, M. D., 144
Horsley, R. A., 92, 245, 376
Hosmer, F. E., 402
Houlden, J. L., 184
Howard, G., 4, 24
Howell, D. B., 24
Hubaut, M., 305
Hubbard, B. J., 417
Hultgren, A. J., 317
Hummel, R., 24
Hutter, M., 135

Jeremias, J., 194, 197, 199, 200, 202, 205, 206, 207, 326, 343, 347, 348, 349, 352, 353, 356, 357
Johnson, M. D., 33

Kampling, R., 393
Keck, L. E., 65
Kee, A., 130
Keener, C. S., 86
Kiley, M., 130
Kilpatrick, G. D., 24
Kingsbury, J. D., 24, 118, 202, 252, 292, 305, 415, 417
Kissinger, W. S., 77
Kloppenborg, J. S., 171
Kosch, D., 157
Kosmala, H., 393
Krämer, M., 111
Kratz, R., 228
Krieger, K. S., 73, 75
Kunzi, M., 149

Lachs, S. T., 24, 88, 91, 102, 109, 141, 204, 207, 235, 244, 326
Lagrange, M.-J., 23

Lambrecht, J., 77, 93
Lange, J., 24, 417
Lapide, P., 77
Légasse, S., 238, 263, 267, 333
Lemcio, E. E., 308
LeMoyne, J., 58
Lentzen-Deis, F., 63, 65
Levine, A.-J., 24
Levine, E., 179
Levine, L. T., 212
Limbeck, M., 23
Loader, W. G., 292
Lohfink, G., 61, 73, 75, 78, 93
Lohmeyer, E., 23
Lona, H. E., 272
Longstaff, T. R. W., 409
López Fernández, E., 171
Lowe, M., 305
Luz, U., 23, 75, 85, 252

Maccoby, H. Z., 393
MacLaurin, E. C. B., 149
Maher, M., 171
Malina, B. J., 213, 417
Mangan, C., 99
Manns, F., 214, 285, 308
Marcus, J., 299
Marshall, I. H., 154
Mattill, A. J., 111
Maxwell-Stuart, G., 106
McCarthy, D. J., 68
McConnell, R. S., 24
McDermott, J. M., 149
McEleney, N. M., 94
McNeile, A. H., 23
Meier, J. P., 23, 24, 55, 415
Menahem, R., 58
Meyer, B. F., 309
Meyers, E. M., 74, 407
Miguens, M., 40
Minear, P. T., 88, 93
Mitton, C. L., 156
Moiser, J., 257
Moloney, F. J., 277
Mora, V., 21, 393
Morosco, R. E., 139
Münderlein, H., 298
Murphy-O'Connor, J., 218

Negoita, A., 244
Neugebauer, F., 319
Neusner, J., 15, 24, 58, 61, 159, 326
Neyrey, J. H., 181, 238
Nickelsburg, G. W. E., 250, 251

Ogawa, A., 301
Olsthoorn, M. F., 106
Orsatti, M., 33
Orton, D. E., 24
Overman, J. A., 24

Palmer, H., 309
Patte, D., 23
Pedersen, S., 257
Pennells, S., 400
Perkins, P., 317
Perlewitz, M., 24
Perrin, N., 158
Pfitzner, V. C., 272
Pikaza, X., 360
Plummer, A., 23
Przybylski, B., 24, 70
Puig i Tarrech, A., 351, 355

Quesnell, Q., 277
Quinn, J. D., 28

Radl, W., 309
Richards, W. L., 301
Rivkin, E., 58, 381, 384
Robbins, V. K., 135
Rosenberg, R., 42
Ross, J. M., 75, 330

Sabourin, L., 23, 149
Safrai, S., 36, 106, 407
Saldarini, A. J., 15, 58, 322, 369
Sand, A., 23, 24, 277
Sandmel, S., 20, 21
Schaberg, J., 39, 40, 417
Schechter, S., 56
Schenk, W., 24
Schmahl, G., 50

Schweizer, E., 23, 267
Scobie, C. H. H., 55
Scott, B. B., 272
Senior, D. P., 24, 365, 387, 404
Shanks, H., 321
Shehadeh, L. R., 73
Shuler, P. L., 24
Sigal, P., 24
Sievers, J., 272
Sloyan, G. S., 384
Smith, D. E., 402
Smith, M., 186
Smith, R. H., 23
Snodgrass, K., 305
Soares-Prabhu, G. M., 40, 75
Stanley, D. M., 378
Stanton, G. N., 24, 171, 337
Stendahl, K., 24, 40
Strange, J. F., 74
Strecker, G., 25, 77
Suggs, J. M., 25, 158
Sukenik, E. L., 320

Tatum, W. B., 33
Telford, W. R., 298
Theissen, G., 119, 142, 156, 281
Thomas, J., 61
Thompson, W. G., 118, 263, 335
Thysman, R., 25
Tigay, J. H., 321
Trilling, W., 25

van Boxel, P. S., 93
van Cangh, J.-M., 223
van der Horst, P. W., 414
Van Segbroeck, F., 213
van Tilborg, S., 25
van Unnik, W. C., 387
Vawter, B., 275
Verseput, D. S., 162
Via, D. O., 360
Viviano, B. T., 72, 324
von Lips, H., 103

Waetjen, H. C., 33
Wagner, G., 25
Walker, R., 25
Watty, W. W., 296
Weaver, D. J., 139
Wegner, U., 118
Weren, W. J. C., 360
Wilcox, M., 252
Wilkins, M. J., 25
Wilson, R. R., 30, 33
Wilson, W. R., 384
Wink, W., 55
Winter, P., 384
Witherington, B., 93
Woschitz, K. M., 238
Wuellner, W., 72

Yeivin, Z., 163

Zakowitch, Y., 28
Zeller, D., 118
Zimmermann, A. F., 324
Zumstein, J., 25, 417